The Family Experience

The Family Experience
A Reader in Cultural Diversity

Third Edition

Mark Hutter
Rowan University

Allyn and Bacon
Boston • London • Toronto • Sydney • Tokyo • Singapore

Series Editor: *Sarah L. Kelbaugh*
Editor in Chief, Social Sciences: *Karen Hanson*
Editorial Assistant: *Jennifer DiDomenico*
Marketing Manager: *Brooke Stoner*
Editorial Production Service: *Chestnut Hill Enterprises, Inc.*
Manufacturing Buyer: *Julie McNeill*
Cover Administrator: *Jennifer Hart*

Copyright © 2000, 1997 by Allyn & Bacon
A Pearson Education Company
160 Gould Street
Needham Heights, MA 02494

Internet: www.abacon.com

Between the time Website information is gathered and published, some sites may have closed. Also, the transcription of URLs can result in typographical errors. The publisher would appreciate notification where these occur so that they may be corrected in subsequent editions.

Library of Congress Cataloging-in-Publication Data

The family experience : a reader in cultural diversity / edited, and
  with introductions by Mark Hutter. — 3rd ed.
     p.   cm.
  Includes bibliographical references.
  ISBN 0-205-30547-4
  1. Family—United States Cross-cultural studies. 2. Sex—United
States Cross-cultural studies. 3. Intergenerational relations—
United States Cross-cultural studies. 4. Problem families—United
States Cross-cultural studies. I. Hutter, Mark.
HQ535.F342   1999
306.85—dc21   99-26253
                                                   CIP

Printed in the United States of America

10 9 8 7 6 5 4 3 2 1   04 03 02 01 00 99

To the memory
of my parents
and in-laws

Contents

       Coontz explodes myths regarding the family of the past and demonstrates how it has always been vulnerable to social and economic change.

       The author summarizes the nature of immigrant family life during the period 1876–1925. Instead of viewing this period as socially disorganized, the author maintains that insufficient attention has been given to the interactional patterns developing among the immigrant groups in American cities.

       The link between African and African American families is examined within the historical and socioeconomic context of the American experience.

A leading conservative proponent of traditional family roles and values makes the argument that accelerated changes in the family during the last twenty-five years have led to family decline.

This influential study examines Italian American women's "kin-work" activities such as visiting, keeping in touch with kin through letter-writing, card-sending, and telephoning as well as organizing kinship gatherings. Kin work is seen as crucial in sustaining a sense of family that extends beyond the nuclear one.

This article examines how Mexican American women transformed traditional networks based on the family, religion, and culture to political assets to improve the quality of their community life.

The economic behavior of recent Vietnamese immigrants to the United States is examined within the context of their family structure and how these families have adapted to circumstances in a new land.

The authors examine factors that account for the differential prevalence of a rape culture at college fraternities. The structure of campus life and

Preface

In the earlier editions of this book, I referred to the great debate in higher education regarding the nature and quality of the college curriculum and what, if any, place "outsiders"—women, people of color, and ethnic groups—should have in it. This debate continues. In many ways it is a continuation of the major redirection of historical study that began about thirty-five years ago. The "new social history" stressed day-to-day experiences of ordinary people. It sensitized us to the importance of studying women, the poor, working people, and racial and ethnic minorities in order to have a better understanding of our past. No longer would history be restricted to the study of great men and of epochal events that emphasized the powerful and neglected the rest of us.

For the last twenty years, colleges and universities have become concerned with the integration of issues regarding gender, race, class, and ethnicity. Often the resolution of this concern is to try to achieve a balance between the traditional core curriculum, which emphasized white, male-dominated Western culture, and the more recent diversified curriculum that reflects global concerns, the study of non-Western cultures, and the inclusion of women, minorities, and persons of color.

Sociology formally recognizes the importance of internationalizing the curriculum and integrating issues of gender, race, class, and ethnicity. What sociology has actually attained, however, is the "ghettoization" of that curriculum. In terms of internationalization, sociology has developed separate and distinct courses under the general rubric "Comparative Sociology"; more specifically courses with such titles as "Sociology of the Middle East," or "Sociology of India." Regarding gender, race, class, and ethnicity, we often find separate and distinct courses with such titles as Gender Roles, Sociology of Women, Ethnic Studies, and African-American Studies. For the introductory sociology course, a welcome change has been the recent introduction of a number of books and course syllabi reflecting this new sensitivity for curriculum integration. However, for most first- and second-year sociology courses, including the sociology of the family, they continue to devote their attention to what often proves to be white middle-class concerns. When cross-cultural and multicultural materials are introduced into institutional courses such as the family, they are often perceived as upper-level courses.

The undergraduate sociology of the family course has begun to incorporate a greater awareness of gender. Matters of ethnicity, race, and class are now being given greater recognition, but for the most part, they are separated from the curriculum and are either not discussed or relegated to peripheral study topics. The result is that a major characteristic of the American family—its class and cultural diversity—is omitted from discussion.

The third edition of this anthology continues to provide the student with materials integrating gender, class, race, and ethnicity into the sociology of the family curriculum. In this edition, fourteen readings are new, reflecting current concerns that include family and community involvements, kinship interaction patterns, teenage pregnancy, homeless families, family violence, generational relationships, and gender roles and economic matters. Many of the readings reflect a social-policy orientation to looking at family continuity and change. Taken together, this book reveals both historical trends and unique variations that widen our understanding of the diversity of the family. The readings inform and increase understanding of the patterns and dynamics of the American family.

The selected readings reflect my continued concern for materials that get at the "guts" of the family experience. They are biased toward an ethnographic, qualitative orientation. A conscious attempt has been made to avoid using articles that are overly quantitative and "number crunching." The goal is to provide the reader with scholarly materials that are interesting and free of unnecessary jargon.

The organizational structure follows the standard format of sociology of family courses. Each part of the book contains an introductory essay that outlines the major issues and concerns to be discussed. For each reading, a brief overview is provided to orient the reader and highlight its sociological significance. The goal is an anthology that can be used with or without an accompanying textbook in sociology of the family courses.

Acknowledgments

Rowan University (formerly Glassboro State College and Rowan College of New Jersey) and its students, faculty, and administration have fostered the viewpoint expressed in this book. Their emphasis on the integration of gender, ethnicity, race, and class into the curriculum and their openness to interdisciplinary studies has enriched my worldview. Administrative and teaching involvement in Rowan University's Honors Program has been especially rewarding. Over the years, I have benefitted from participation in a number of National Institute of the Humanities Summer Institutes and Seminars, and I am most appreciative of the directors and fellow participants for sharing their perspectives with me. Also, and most important, through professional activities with Alpha Kappa Delta, the International Sociology Honors Society, and the Society for the Study of Symbolic Interaction, I have been able to extend my understanding of curriculum matters and pedagogical concerns.

The sociology editor at Allyn and Bacon, Sarah Kelbaugh, her staff, and the production editor at Chestnut Hill Enterprieses provided the support necessary to ensure the completion of this edition. Much thanks is expressed to past reviewers as well as to the reviewers of this edition: Norma Gaines-Hanks, University of Delaware; Elisabeth O. Burgess, Georgia State University; Carmenza Gallo, Queens College of the City University of New York; Lynda Dickson, University of Colorado at Colorado Springs; and Arlene Dallalfar, Lesley College.

The authors and publishers of these articles are thankfully acknowledged for granting permission to reprint their works. My wife, Lorraine, and my children, Daniel and Elizabeth, have made my life emotionally and intellectually meaningful. My parents and my parents-in-law taught me to value and understand the immigrant-ethnic family experience, and, by so doing, they enriched my life.

General Introduction

The average man—or woman—of fifty years or more ago had the greatest respect for the institution called the family, and wished to learn nothing about it. According to the Victorian ideology, all husbands and wives lived together in perfect amity; all children loved the parents to whom they were indebted for the gift of life; and if these things were not true, they should be, and even if one knew that these things were not true, he ought not to mention it. Everything that concerned the life of men and women and their children was shrouded, like a dark deed, from the light.

Today all that is changed. Gone is the concealment of the way in which life begins, gone the irrational sanctity of the home. The pathos which once protected the family from discussion clings to it no more. Now we do not want to be ignorant about the family; we want to learn as much about it as we can and to understand it as completely as possible. We are engaged in the process of reconstructing our family institutions through criticism and discussion (Waller 1938, p. 13).

Willard Waller was one of the most prominent American family sociologists of the mid-twentieth century. These words, written more than sixty years ago in his seminal work, *The Family: A Dynamic Interpretation,* are reflective of his gadfly status in American sociology. His contemporaries did not agree with his critical—some would say scathing—look at the middle-class American family. Most had a much more sanguine view of the American family system that reflected their own middle-class biases. They saw harmony and concord, not tension and discord. Their perspective was shared by the popular media, which typified the American family as exclusively Caucasian, affluent, and residing in suburban and rural areas in peaceful harmony.

Indeed, American sociology was so uncritical of the family that it failed to foresee the revolution that swept across the United States beginning in the early 1960s and continues to the present. Social protest movements called for equality and civil rights for all those "forgotten" in affluent America. These movements, led by "outsiders"—people of color, ethnic groups, feminists, and gays—ushered in a wave of new thought in the study of the family that stressed the diversity of the American experience. These outsiders led American sociology to at last follow the call made by Willard Waller to engage "in the process of reconstructing our family institutions through criticism and discussion."

New conceptual frameworks allowed us to "see" family phenomena formerly hidden from view. We began to understand patterns and dynamics of family violence that we once did not even know existed. Further, new family structures—including dual-career families, single-parent families, and families reconstituted by divorce and remarriage—increases in the rates of desertion and divorce, teenage pregnancy, abortion, singlehood, voluntary childlessness, and the feminization of poverty underwent sociological scrutiny and analysis.

The nature of marriage, family, and kinship systems in American society has undergone a new examination. Conventional assumptions about the necessity of maintaining kinship relations and the role of the nuclear family in today's world are being questioned: What are the proper gender roles for women and men? Is parenthood an inevitable and desirable consequence of maturation? A new, more permissive sexual morality led to the reexamination of previously held beliefs and attitudes regarding premarital and extramarital sexual relations, out-of-wedlock pregnancies, and abortions.

Family structures have fluctuated considerably in the last thirty years. More couples than ever before have voluntarily chosen to have fewer children. Many have voluntarily chosen childlessness. Still others have reconsidered that decision and opted to have children in later years. Divorce rates that were accelerating in the 1970s have leveled off and stabilized but remain at a higher rate than ever before in U.S. history.

New family patterns have emerged. That cohabitation has, for many, become an American way of life comments not only on premarital or nonmarital relationships but has implication for marital relationships as well. For those who eventually marry, the full implication of cohabitation as a facilitator for, or a hindrance to, marital adjustment and happiness is still unknown. Singlehood is accepted by many. Media discussion of the "marriage squeeze" raises questions on whether singlehood is a voluntary permanent option, or a state caused principally by the relatively low number of eligible men for "career" women. Regardless, singlehood involves a different series of life commitments than marriage and family.

Women have been particularly affected by and have affected family life. The number of single-parent families headed by women has been steadily growing. Much of this increase was caused by the rising divorce rate, but another major factor was the rising illegitimacy rate, especially among poor teenage females. These trends have led to the feminization of poverty. Women's labor force participation has been constantly rising in the last fifty years. Further, a significant number of working wives have children, especially young children. Because mothers are generally the primary caretakers, women have had to juggle their career aspirations and family responsibilities. This has led to the demand for increased day-care facilities and to talk of a "mommy-track" career ladder depending on the ages of children and the husband's occupational and familial career patterns.

The legitimacy of abortion has become the crystallizing issue in reaction to changes in family behavior. Passions ignite over the issue. A polarization has developed between "pro-choice" and "pro-life" advocates that has as its fundamental basis the nature of family values and individual options. Homosexuality is yet another area that has become a debating ground for issues regarding changes in the family. The debate on the acceptability of homosexuality as a legitimate alternative family lifestyle has been exacerbated by the deadly disease AIDS. Fear of AIDS has been used to incite the expression of homophobia and the rejection of gay rights.

The controversy surrounding sexuality, marriage, and the family has entered the world of politics and public policy more than ever before. Laws regarding abortion and homosexuality are continually argued, challenged, and changed. Laws regarding illegitimacy, and regulations regarding welfare for single-parent households, are being written, argued, rewritten, and reargued. Politics continues to intrude on the government's responsibility to provide public support for child-care facilities. Arguments and counterarguments continue on this issue between traditionalists, who seek to preserve "natural" family values, and proponents of individual options in a family system more amicable to family diversity. The divorce revolution brought about by no-fault legislation has had the unintended consequence of dramatically improving the economic situation of divorcing husbands/fathers while at the same time leading to the povertization of wives/mothers and children. Economic discrimination of women justified by a traditional belief in women's "natural" role in the family and the inappropriateness of their participating in the workplace still exists. Although increased attention has recently been given to parallel concerns regarding men's roles, this has not generated nearly the same attention and controversy as women's commitments and options.

As a result of all these changes, debates, and controversies, there has been great discussion about the future of the family. A widespread view declares that the family is a dying institution and expresses much concern about the implications for the "American way of life." A counter view holds that the "family" itself is not dying, but rather that one form of the family is declining and being replaced by new types of families that are supportive of individuals of both sexes and of all ages. These new family forms will usher in emancipatory and egalitarian transformations in sexual relations that include, but are not limited to, marital and family relations.

To understand the contemporary status of the American family, and to be able to predict its future, is vital. Unfortunately, American sociology has only recently recognized the importance of studying the historical and cultural diversity of family systems. In the last fifteen years, American sociology has increasingly realized that comparative and multicultural analysis can frequently help in understanding things that are so near to us they are difficult to see. Ignoring such diversity, in fact, distorts analysis of the American family; diversity in American families is the very essence of the American family.

The aim here is to develop understanding of the causes, conditions, consequences, and implications of American family diversity for individual, family, and society. This book looks at the diversity of the family experience through time. A multicultural approach is the best way to answer questions about family processes and structures and their relationship to other societal institutions. The family is a prime reflector of the major societal changes experienced in the twentieth century. The study of the family experience allows us to see the impact of broader patterns of societal change on individuals and their everyday lives. The rapid economic, political, and social changes characteristic of present times make such a comparative perspective crucial.

Reference

Waller, Willard. 1938. *The Family: A Dynamic Interpretation.* New York: Dryden.

Part I

Multicultural Perspectives

In this the last decade of the twentieth century, we can look back at more than two centuries of continual economic, religious, political, and social upheavals throughout the world. Massive modifications and breakdowns of social structures and cultural values have been associated with social and individual crises in which everyday experiences could no longer be taken for granted. Conventional assumptions regarding gender role relationships, marriage, and the family have been under scrutiny and challenge. The sociological perspective is vital to understand these social forces that have affected people's lives.

Throughout history, the family has been the social institution that has stood at the very center of society. For most people, the family is the most important group to which they belong throughout their lives. The family provides intimate and enduring relationships and acts as a mediator between its members and the larger society. It transmits the traditional ways of a culture to each new generation. It is the primary socializing agent and a continuing force in shaping people's lives. Through the family women and men satisfy most of their interpersonal, emotional, and sexual needs. Children are raised in families, providing a tangible link among past, present, and future generations. The family provides the setting in which individuals are socialized and motivated for integration into occupational, religious, political, and social positions that ensure the continuation of societal institutions and structures.

These prefatory remarks suggest why the family is vital to the society and to the individual. It should, therefore, be apparent that changes in the family will have serious ramifications for a given society and its people. Sociology as a discipline developed in the early nineteenth century as a response to the major changes that occurred first in Western Europe and the United States and then rapidly spread through the rest of the world as a consequence of Western colonization. The sociological perspective on marriage and the family was to view it in terms of the social forces that affect people's lives.

Prior to the nineteenth century, Western thought generally held to a biblical belief in the origins of the family stemming from God's creation of the world, including Adam and Eve. Although there was a recognition of relatively minor familial changes over time, the biblical family form and its underlying patriarchal ideological precepts were seen as continuing intact into the nineteenth century. Western thought clung to uniformity throughout the world in terms of family structures, processes, and underlying familial beliefs and values. These governed the behavior of men, women, and children in families.

This belief in the worldwide uniformity of the family underwent severe challenge and was finally discarded as a result of a number of important factors. Western societies were industrializing and urbanizing at a rapid rate, destroying the old societal class systems as a new social class structure developed. Individual rights, duties, and obligations were redefined, and the relationships of the individual to the family and the family to the larger community were reworked. Western colonial expansionism and imperialism fostered a new economic system that had global implications for all cultures. Contacts were being made with people whose systems of family life were markedly different from each other. The recognition of worldwide family diversity led to the overthrow of the belief that there was a single family form. What was needed was an alternative theoretical perspective to reevaluate the origins of the family. This alternative perspective took the form of evolutionary theory.

The theory of evolutionary change developed by Charles Darwin in his *Origin of Species* in 1859 was the culmination of an intellectual revolution begun much earlier that promoted the idea of progressive development. As the theory of evolution became the dominant form in explaining biological principles, social scientists of the nineteenth century developed belief that there was a link between biological and cultural evolution. These social scientists were called Social Darwinists. Their basic tenet was that since biological evolution proceeded through a series of stages (from the simple to the complex), the same process would hold for cultures.

Henry Sumner Maine, Lewis Henry Morgan, J. J. Bachofen, and Herbert Spencer were among those who applied evolutionary theories to the study of the human family. Social Darwinists seemingly dealt with such nonimmediate concerns as the origins and historical development of the family, yet their theories had social and political implications. Social Darwinism provided "scientific" legitimation for Western colonization and exploitation of "primitive" peoples through the erroneous belief that Western culture represented "civilization" and non-Western cultures, particularly among nonliterate, low-technology societies, represented a primeval state of savagery or barbarity. And through its advocacy of evolutionary progress, Social Darwinism provided laissez-faire guidelines that supported neglect of the poorer classes of American and Western European societies. It also had implications for the roles of men and women in nineteenth-century family systems. By arguing for a patriarchal evolutionary theory of male supremacy and dominance over females, Social Darwinists gave implicit support to the Victorian notions of male supremacy and female dependency.

An important rebuttal to Social Darwinism that in part also developed out of evolutionary theory was made by Friedrich Engels ([1884]1972) in *The Origins of the Family, Private Property, and the State.* Concerns for gender role egalitarianism, as opposed to patriarchy and male sexual dominance, achieved their fullest evolutionary theory expression in this work. Engels' evolutionary theory saw economic factors as the primary determinants of social change and linked particular technological forms with particular family forms. Echoing Lewis Henry Morgan, Engels depicted the stage of savagery as one with no economic inequalities and no private ownership of property. The family form was group marriage based on matriarchy. During the stage of barbarism, men gained economic control over the means of production. In civilization, the last stage, women became subjugated to the male-dominated economic system and monogamy. This stage, in Engels' view, rather than representing the apex of marital and familial forms, represented the victory of private property over common ownership and group marriage. Engels speculated that the coming of socialist revolution would usher in a new evolutionary stage marked by gender equality and by common ownership of property.

Engels' main achievement was in defining the family as an economic unit. This has become a major focus in much of the subsequent historical research on the family and is of great theoretical importance in the sociology of the family. But, insofar as Engels' Marxist view constituted a branch of evolutionary thought, it was subject to many of the same objections (see below) raised against other evolutionary theories.

By the end of the nineteenth century, the popularity of Social Darwinism was rapidly declining. Contributing to the decline were the methodological weaknesses of the approach (data obtained by nontrained, impressionistic, and biased travelers and missionaries) and growing rejection of both its explicit value assumptions on the superiority of Western family forms and its belief in unilinear evolutionary development of the family. More importantly, the shift in the focus of the sociology of the family was at least in part precipitated by the sweeping changes in U.S. and European societies during the nineteenth century. There was a dramatic increase of awareness to such conditions as poverty, child labor, desertions, prostitution, illegitimacy, and abuse of women and children. Social scientists were appalled by the excesses of industrial urban society and the calamitous changes in the family system.

The Industrial Revolution dramatically changed the nature of economic and social life. The factory system developed, and with its development there was a transformation from home industries in rural areas to factories. Rural people were lured by the greater economic opportunities that the city promised. The domestic economy of the preindustrial family disappeared. The rural- and village-based family system no longer served as a productive unit. The domestic economy had enabled the family to combine economic activities with the supervision and training of its children; the development of the factory system led to a major change in the the division of labor in family roles.

Patriarchal authority was weakened with urbanization. Previously, in rural and village settings, fathers reigned supreme; they were knowledgeable in economic skills and were able to train their children. The great diversity of city life rendered this socialization function relatively useless. The rapid change of industrial technology and the innumerable forms of work necessitated a more formal institutional setting—the school—to help raise the children. Laws came into existence to regulate the amount of time children were allowed to work and their work conditions. Laws also required that children attend school. These legal changes reflected the change in the family situation of the urban setting; families were no longer available or able to watch constantly over their children.

The separation of work from the home had important implications for family members. Increasingly, men became the sole provider for the family and the women and children developed a life centered around the family, the home, and the school. Their contacts with the outside world diminished, and they were removed from community involvements. The family's withdrawal from the community was characterized by its hostile attitude toward the surrounding city. The city was thought of as a sprawling and planless development bereft of meaningful community and neighborhood relationships. The tremendous movement of a large population into the industrial centers provided little opportunity for the family to form deep or lasting ties with neighbors. Instead, the family viewed neighbors with suspicion and wariness. Exaggerated beliefs developed on the prevalence of urban poverty, crime, and disorganization.

Social scientists began to see the decline in the importance of kinship and community involvements and the changes in the makeup of the nuclear family as more important areas of investigation than the study of the evolutionary transformations of the family. Their research and theories focused on the causal connections relating family change to the larger industrial and urban developments occurring in the last two centuries. Much attention has also been given to theoretical analyses of the effects these changes have had on the individual, on women, men, and children, on the family, on kinship structures, and on the larger community and the society.

For almost 200 years sociologists have wrestled with these concerns. The readings in the first part of this book focus on the relationship between societal change and the family. By necessity, this examination must be informed by the desire to understand these changes in the context of immigration and ethnic family experiences in the United States.

Chapter One opens with Stephanie Coontz's (Reading 1) social historical examination of the family in the United States. With a broad historical brush stroke, Coontz compares the contemporary family to the realities and myths of the family in the past. She is particularly sensitive to the diversity of the American family both in terms of structure and ethnicity. Of particular interest is her examination of the 1950s, which is seen as a benchmark era for the "traditional" norms of the two-parent family with husband as "breadwinner" and wife as "breadbaker." This is the family depicted on such television shows as "Father Knows Best" and "Ozzie and Harriet." Coontz observes that the 1950s was the most atypical decade in the history of American marriage and family life. To understand marriage and family life we must examine it in its historical and economic context. By so doing, not only will we get a better grasp of that family type but also such analysis is invaluable in understanding today's marriage and family patterns. We should not be misled by our myths of the past and the "way we never were" in trying to understand the present.

In the late nineteenth and early twentieth centuries there was mass immigration to the United States largely in response to the massive industrial growth of American cities. In Reading 2, "Immigrant Families in the City," by Mark Hutter, the editor of this anthology, there is an examination of the urban ways of life of some of these immigrant family groups.

Immigrants from these areas concentrated in the industrial cities of the Northeast and the Midwest, where job opportunities were plentiful and chances of success were greatest. The ultimate success of an immigrant group depended in large part on its ability to re-establish a normal pattern of family life in the United States. However, popular as well as sociological opinion saw the emerging immigrant ghettos as settings of social disorganiza-tion, with alienation, anomie, social isolation, juvenile delinquency, crime, mental illness, suicide, child abuse, separation, and divorce as inherent characteristics of urban life. The social reform movement that developed during this time period saw family disorganization as pervasive and as a consequence arising from governmental nonsupervision of industrial and urban institutions. In Reading 2, the nature of the social organizational patterns that were developing among these immigrant groups is examined.

The history of the African American family in the United States reflects to a large degree many of the historical turning points and changes experienced by the American family of European origin. However, the African American family experience also has unique characteristics that stem from its African origins as well as from the extraordinary historical experience it has had in the United States. The study of the African American family's historical experience has been influenced by a discussion on the relative importance of the African cultural heritage on African American family organization. Niara Sudarkasa (Reading 3) provides an overview of African family and Black American family structure as it developed in the political and economic context of U.S. history. The cultural and historical importance placed on the extended consanguineal kinship relationship over the importance of the marital or conjugal relationship is seen to distinguish the African American family from the American family of European origin.

The concluding reading in this chapter (Reading 4), by David Popenoe, is concerned with a contemporary issue that has dominated much public debate. For many, the decline or "breakdown of the family" is seen as a primary factor for the rise of a host of social ills including the extensive use of drugs, startling increases in teenage pregnancies, family vio-lence and child neglect, the decline in educational standards, and the overall decline in soci-etal morality and ethics. The debate is closely linked with "decline of community" and "self-centered" or "self-development" arguments. This perspective argues that close-knit bonds of moral reciprocity have declined and have been replaced in its stead with a vocab-ulary of individualism. As a consequence, the middle class finds itself without a language of commitment in which to create its moral discourse (Bellah et al., 1985).

Robert Bellah and his associates (1985) emphasize that one theme has been of central concern to sociologists since the nineteenth century: the debate about individualism versus social commitment and individual rights versus civic responsibility. America's moral dilemma is seen to revolve around the conflict between the desire for fierce individualism on the one hand and the need for community and commitment on the other. Bellah and his colleagues find that the failure of contemporary Americans is in their weakening of motivational commitments to collective purposes of families, communities, and the nation. The unchecked growth of individualism, "inside the family as well as outside it," is the cause of the society's general decline (Bellah et al., 1985:90). An all-powerful market economy is seen to have fostered individualism and achieved its first manifestation in the family by allowing its members to freely choose love matches. More recently, individualism appears in the form of the quest for personal growth that is not necessarily associated with commitment and emotional bonds. As a consequence, the security of lasting relationships and of stable marriages is in jeopardy as individuals seek self-knowledge and self-realization. The meaning of one's life is no longer seen to be anchored or derived from one's relationships with one's parents or children.

David Popenoe (Reading 4) builds on Bellah's assessment of the decline of American character by seeing its counterpart in the decline of the American family. Popenoe concludes by suggesting the forms that social policy should take to restore the traditional family.

The counter-argument to the conservative position is that the changes in the American family that have occurred in the last thirty years do not represent a decline of the family but rather the opportunity for the empowerment of women. The decline is not of the family, but rather of a particular form of family life based on traditional nineteenth-century notions of father as the good provider and mother as the moral guardian of the home. Critics of the conservative viewpoint believe that increased attention to underlying family processes, particularly in terms of how the family deals with new stresses, reaches out for assistance, adopts new roles, alters patterns of courtship and sexuality, and satisfactorily adapts to social change, is needed. Also, the difficulties for family members associated with family change must be investigated to better understand them and deal with them. This, in their view, is more constructive than bemoaning the loss of traditional gender roles in the family.

The readings in Chapter Two, "The Family, Kinship, and the Community," focus on the relationship of the nuclear family to both the extended family and the larger community. Family historians have emphasized that changes in Western society resulted in the gradual separation of the public institution of work and the community from the private sphere of the family. Middle-class family life since the nineteenth century has been distinguished by this removal from the community setting. And the American suburb has continued to foster this privatizing process.

Many sociologists see the privatization of the middle-class family as antithetical to women's independence. More specifically, the spatial segregation of residence from home and the development of the single-family house led to the increased dependence of women on income-earning husbands. In addition, and most significantly, the house became the setting that required the full involvement of women. As Ruth Schwartz Cowan (1983) and Susan Strasser (1982) have demonstrated, women's domestic labor paradoxically increased with the development of mechanized techniques, e.g., vacuum cleaners and sewing, washing, and dishwashing machines that were designed supposedly for efficiency's sake but in fact have set new housekeeping standards. In addition, the automobile fostered the end of home delivery services for all kinds of goods and services, thus requiring that families own an automobile to perform these services. These new tasks included driving spouses to commuter transportation stations, picking up and delivering children to school and after-school activities, and taking sick family members to doctors, who no longer made house calls.

One technological advance that ran counter to the prevailing "more work for mother" pattern was the residential telephone (Fischer, 1988). Historically, the residential telephone has been used by women to foster gender-linked social relationships and involvements. Often, women used the telephone for what Micaela di Leonardo (Reading 5) calls "kin-work." Kin-work involves kinship contact across households and is as much a part of domestic labor as housework. It includes maintaining kinship ties, organizing holiday gatherings, and the creation and sustaining of kinship relationships. Kin-work is seen to fuse both the labor perspective and the domestic network categories of female work. The concern of di Leonardo's article is examining kin-work in the context of the interrelationships between women's kinship and economic lives of Italian American women who work in the labor market and at home.

In contrast to the relative separation of the nuclear family from extended kinship ties and community involvement with middle-class suburbia, is the family life of working class and ethnic groups. Di Leonardo's article provides one such illustrative example. So does Reading 6, "Mexican American Women Grassroots Community Activists: 'Mothers of East Los Angeles.'" In this article, Mary Pardo discusses the community activities of a group called the Mothers of East Los Angeles (MELA). It demonstrates how women use their family networks and family roles as the basis for political action that includes the building of new schools and safe work sites.

Pardo's work, as well as the research by Mark Hutter (Reading 2) and Nazli Kibria (Reading 7), demonstrates that the family structures of many immigrant and ethnic family groups in the United States are characterized by a developed social network comprising extended kin and neighbors. This social support structure is often an important mediating factor in a given family's involvement with the larger community.

Reading 7 is concerned with newly arrived Vietnamese refugees in Philadelphia. The author, Nazli Kibria, argues that it is not solely the cultural orientation of this group that explains this latest "immigrant success story." Rather, to understand their story it is necessary to examine the economic diversity of the Vietnamese American population within the context of a given family's household structure and family ideology. By focusing on the dynamics of the immigrant family household one can get a better sense of the ways in which cultural factors and external structural conditions shape its economic life.

References

Bellah, Robert N., Richard Madsen, William M. Sullivan, Ann Swidler, and Steven M. Tipton. 1985. *Habits of the Heart: Individualism and Commitment in American Life.* New York: Perennial Library, Harper & Row.

Cowan, Ruth Schwartz. 1983. *More Work for Mother: The Ironies of Household Technology from the Open Hearth to the Microwave.* New York: Basic Books.

Engels, Friedrich. 1972. *The Origins of the Family, Private Property, and the State.* New York: Pathfinder Press. (Originally published in 1884.)

Fischer, Claude S. 1988. "Gender and the Residential Telephone: 1890–1940." *Sociological Forum* 3(2):211–233.

Strasser, Susan. 1982. *Never Done: A History of American Housework.* New York: Pantheon.

1

The Changing Family: History and Politics

Reading 1   Where Are the Good Old Days?*

STEPHANIE COONTZ

The American family is under siege. To listen to the rhetoric of recent months, we have all fallen down on the job. We're selfish; too preoccupied with our own gratification to raise our children properly. We are ungrateful; we want a handout, not a hand.

If only we'd buckle down, stay on the straight and narrow, keep our feet on the ground, our shoulder to the wheel, our eye on the ball, our nose to the grindstone. Then everything would be all right, just as it was in the family-friendly '50s, when we could settle down in front of the television after an honest day's work and see our lives reflected in shows like *Ozzie and Harriet* and *Father Knows Best.*

But American families have been under siege more often than not during the past 300 years. Moreover, they have always been diverse, both in structure and ethnicity. No family type has been able to protect its members from the roller-coaster rides of economic setbacks or social change. Changes that improved the lives and fortunes of one family type or individual often resulted in losses for another.

A man employed in the auto industry, for example, would have been better off financially in the 1950s than now, but his retired parents would be better off today. If he had a strong taste for power, he might prefer Colonial times, when a man was the undisputed monarch of the household and any disobedience by wife, child, or servant was punishable by whipping. But woe betide that man if he wasn't born to property. In those days, men without estates could be told what to wear, where to live, and whom to associate with.

His wife, on the other hand, might have been happier in the 1850s, when she might have afforded two or three servants. We can be pretty sure, though, that the black or Irish servants of that day would not have found the times so agreeable. And today's children, even those scarred by divorce, might well want to stay put rather than live in the late 19th century, when nearly half of them died before they reached their late teens.

A HISTORY OF TRADEOFFS

These kinds of tradeoffs have characterized American family life from the beginning. Several distinctly different types of families already

---

*Coontz, Stephanie. 1996. "Where are the Good Old Days?" *Modern Maturity* (May/June): 36–43. Reprinted by permission of the author.

coexisted in Colonial times: On the East Coast, the Iroquois lived in longhouses with large extended families. Small families were more common among the nomadic Indian groups, where marital separation, though frequent, caused no social stigma or loss of access to group resources. African-American slaves, whose nuclear families had been torn apart, built extended family networks through ritual coparenting, the adoption of orphans, and complex naming patterns designed to preserve links among families across space and time.

White Colonial families were also diverse: High death rates meant that a majority spent some time in a stepfamily. Even in intact families, membership ebbed and flowed; many children left their parents' home well before puberty to work as servants or apprentices to other households. Colonial family values didn't sentimentalize childhood. Mothers were far less involved in caring for their children than modern working women, typically delegating the task to servants or older siblings. Children living away from home usually wrote to their fathers, sometimes adding a postscript asking him to "give my regards to my mother, your wife."

A REVOLUTION OF SORTS

Patriarchal authority started to collapse at the beginning of the Revolutionary War: The rate of premarital conception soared and children began to marry out of birth order. Small family farms and shops flourished and, as in Colonial days, a wife's work was valued as highly as her husband's. The revolutionary ferment also produced the first stirrings of feminism and civil rights. A popular 1773 Massachusetts almanac declared: "Then equal Laws let custom find, and neither Sex oppress: More Freedom give to Womankind or to Mankind give less." New Jersey women had the right to vote after the Revolution. In several states slaves won their freedom when they sued, citing the Declaration of Independence.

But commercial progress undermined these movements. The spread of international trade networks and the invention of the cotton gin in 1793 increased slavery's profits. Ironically, when revolutionary commitment to basic human equality went head-to-head with economic dependence on slavery, the result was an increase in racism: Apologists now justified slavery on the grounds that blacks were *less* than human. This attitude spilled over to free blacks, who gradually lost both their foothold in the artisan trades and the legal rights they'd enjoyed in early Colonial times. The subsequent deterioration in their status worked to the advantage of Irish immigrants, previously considered nonwhite and an immoral underclass.

Feminist ideals also faded as industrialization and wage labor took work away from the small family farms and businesses, excluding middle-class wives from their former economic partnerships. For the first time, men became known as breadwinners. By the post-Civil War era of 1870–90, the participation of married women in the labor force was at an all-time low; social commentators labeled those wives who took part in political or economic life sexual degenerates or "semi-hermaphrodites."

WOMEN LOSE; CHILDREN LOSE MORE

As women left the workforce children entered it by the thousands, often laboring in abysmal conditions up to ten hours a day. In the North, they worked in factories or tenement workshops. As late as 1900, 120,000 children worked in Pennsylvania's mines and factories. In the South, states passed "apprentice" laws binding black children out as unpaid laborers, often under the pretext that their parents neglected them. Plantation owners (whose wives and daughters encased themselves in corsets and grew their fingernails long) accused their former female slaves of "loaferism" when they resisted field labor in order to stay closer to home with their children.

So for every 19th-century middle-class family that was able to nurture its women and children comfortably inside the family circle, there was an Irish or German girl scrubbing floors, a Welsh boy mining coal, a black girl doing laundry, a black mother and child picking cotton, and a Jewish or Italian daughter making dresses, cigars, or artificial flowers in a sweatshop.

Meanwhile, self-styled "child-saver" charity workers, whose definition of an unfit parent had more to do with religion, ethnicity, or poverty than behavior, removed other children from their families. They sent these "orphans" to live with Western farmers who needed extra hands—or merely dumped them in a farm town with a dollar and an earnest lecture about escaping the evils of city life.

THE OUTER FAMILY CIRCLE

Even in the comfortable middle-class households of the late 19th century, norms and values were far different from those we ascribe to "traditional" families. Many households took in boarders, lodgers, or unmarried relatives. The nuclear family wasn't the primary focus of emotional life. The Victorian insistence on separate spheres for men and women made male-female relations extremely stilted, so women commonly turned to other women for their most intimate relationships. A woman's diary would rhapsodize for pages about a female friend, explaining how they carved their initials on a tree, and then remark, "Accepted the marriage proposal of Mr. R. last night" without further comment. Romantic friendships were also common among young

middle-class men, who often recorded that they missed sleeping with a college roommate and laying an arm across his bosom. No one considered such relationships a sign of homosexuality; indeed, the term wasn't even invented until the late 19th century.

Not that 19th-century Americans were asexual: By midcentury New York City had one prostitute for every 64 men; the mayor of Savannah estimated his city had one for every 39. Perhaps prostitution's spread was inevitable at a time when the middle class referred to the "white meat" and "dark meat" of chicken to spare ladies the embarrassment of hearing the terms "breast" or "thigh."

THE ADVENT OF THE COUPLE

The early 20th century brought more changes. Now the emotional focus shifted to the husband and wife. World War I combined with a resurgence of feminism to hasten the collapse of Victorian values, but we can't underestimate the role the emergence of a mass consumer market played: Advertisers quickly found that romance and sexual titillation worked wonders for the bottom line.

Marriage experts and the clergy, concerned that longer lifespans would put a strain on marriages, denounced same-sex friendships as competitors to love; people were expected to direct all their emotional, altruistic and sensual impulses into marriage. While this brought new intimacy and sexual satisfaction to married life, it also introduced two trends that disturbed observers. One was an increased dissatisfaction with what used to be considered adequate relationships. Great expectations, social historian Elaine Tyler May points out in her book of the same name, could generate great disappointments. It's no surprise that the U.S. has had both the highest consumption of romance novels and the highest divorce rates in the world since the early part of the 20th century.

The second consequence of this new cult of married bliss was the emergence of an independent and increasingly sexualized youth culture. In the late 19th century, middle-class courtship revolved around the institution of "calling." A boy was invited to call by the girl or her parents. It was as inappropriate then for a boy to hint he'd like to be asked over as it was in the 1950s for a girl to hint she'd like to be asked out. By the mid-1920s, calling had been almost totally replaced by dating, which took young people away from parental control but made a girl far more dependent on the boy's initiative. Parents especially worried about the moral dangers the automobile posed—and with reason: A middle-class boy was increasingly likely to have his first sexual encounter with a girlfriend rather than a prostitute.

The early part of the century brought a different set of changes to America's working class. In the 1920s, for the first time, a majority of children were born to male-breadwinner, female-homemaker families. Child labor laws and the spread of mass education allowed more parents to keep their children out of the workforce. Numerous immigrant families, however, continued to pull their offspring out of school so they could help support the family, often arousing intense generational conflicts. African-American families kept their children in school longer than other families in those groups, but their wives were much more likely to work outside the home.

THERE GOES THE FAMILY

In all sectors of society these changes created a sense of foreboding. *Is Marriage on the Skids?* asked one magazine article of the times; *What Is the Family Still Good For?* fretted another. Popular commentators harkened back to the "good old days," bemoaning the sexual revolution, the fragility of nuclear-family ties, the cult of youthful romance, and the threat of the "emancipated woman."

The stock market crash, the Great Depression, and the advent of World War II moved such fears to the back burner. During the '30s and '40s, family trends fluctuated from one extreme to another. Depression hardship—contrary to its television portrayal on *The Waltons*—usually failed to make family and community life stronger. Divorce rates fell, but desertion and domestic violence rose sharply; economic stress often translated into punitive parenting that left children with emotional scars still apparent to social researchers decades later. Murder rates in the '30s were as high as in the 1980s; rates of marriages and births plummeted.

WWII started a marriage boom, but by 1946 the number of divorces was double that in 1941. This time the social commentators blamed working women, interfering in-laws and, above all, inadequate mothers. In 1946, psychiatrist Edward Strecker published *Their Mothers' Sons: The Psychiatrist Examines an American Problem,* which argued that women who were old-fashioned "moms" instead of modern "mothers" were emasculating American boys.

Moms, he said disapprovingly, were immature and unstable and sought emotional recompense for the disappointments of their own lives. They took care of aging parents and tried to exert too much control over their children. Mothers, on the other hand, put their parents in nursing homes and derived all their satisfaction from the nuclear family while cheerfully urging independence on their children. Without motherhood, said the experts, a woman's life meant nothing. Too much mothering, though, would destroy her own marriage and her son's life. These new values put women in an emotional double-bind, and it's hardly surprising that tranquilizers, which came on the scene in the '50s, were marketed and prescribed almost exclusively to housewives.

THE '50s: PARADISE LOST?

Such were the economic and cultural ups and downs that created the 1950s. If that single decade had actually represented the "tradition" it would be reasonable to argue that the family has indeed collapsed. By the mid 1950s, the age of marriage and parenthood had dropped dramatically, divorce rates bottomed out and the birthrate, one sociologist has recently noted, "approached that of India." The proportion of children in Ozzie-and-Harriet type families reached an all-time high of 60 percent.

Today, in contrast, a majority of mothers, including those with preschool children, work outside the home. Fifty percent of children live with both biological parents, almost one quarter live with single parents and more than 21 percent are in stepfamilies. Three quarters of today's 18–24-year-olds have never been married, while almost 50 percent of all first marriages—and 60 percent of remarriages—will end in divorce. Married couples wait longer to bear children and have fewer of them. For the first time there are more married couples without children than with them. Less than one quarter of contemporary marriages are supported by one wage earner.

Taking the 1950s as the traditional norm, however, overstates both the novelty of modern family life and the continuity of tradition. The 1950s was the most atypical decade in the entire history of American marriage and family life. In some ways, today's families are closer to older patterns than were '50s families. The median age at first marriage today is about the same as it was at the beginning of the century, while the proportion of never-married people is actually lower. The number of women who are coproviders and the proportion of children living in step-

families are both closer to that of Colonial days than the 1950s. Even the ethnic diversity among modern families is closer to the patterns of the early part of this century than to the demographics of the 1950s. And the time a modern working mother devotes to childcare is higher than in Colonial or Revolutionary days.

The 1950s family, in other words, was not at all traditional; nor was it always idyllic. Though many people found satisfactions in family life during that period, we now know the experiences of many groups and individuals were denied. Problems such as alcoholism, battering, and incest were swept under the rug. So was discrimination against ethnic groups, political dissidents, women, elders, gays, lesbians, religious minorities and the handicapped. Rates of divorce and unwed motherhood were low, but that did not prevent 30 percent of American children from living in poverty, a higher figure than at present.

IT'S ALL RELATIVE

Why then, do many people remember the 1950s as so much easier than today? One reason is that after the hardships of the Depression and WWII, things *were* improving on many fronts. Though poverty rates were higher than today, they were falling. Economic inequality was also decreasing. The teenage birthrate was almost twice as high in 1957 as today, but most young men could afford to marry. Violence against African-Americans was appallingly widespread, yet many blacks got jobs in the expanding manufacturing industries and for the first time found an alternative to Southern agriculture's peonage.

What we forget when politicians tell us we should revive the 1950s family is that the social stability of that period was due less to its distinctive family forms than to its unique socio-economic and political climate. High rates of unionization, heavy corporate investment in manufacturing, and generous government assistance in the form of public-works projects, veterans' benefits, student loans and housing subsidies gave young families a tremendous jump start, created predictable paths out of poverty, and led to unprecedented increases in real wages. By the time the "traditional male breadwinner" reached age 30, in both the 1950s and '60s, he could pay the principal and interest on a median-priced home on only 15–18 percent of his income. Social Security promised a much-needed safety net for the elderly, formerly the poorest segment of the population. These economic carrots combined with the sticks of McCarthyism and segregation to keep social dissent on the back burner.

THE NEW TRENDS

Because the '60s were a time of social protest, many people forget that families still made economic gains throughout the decade. Older workers and homeowners continued to build security for their retirement years. The postwar boom and government subsidies cut child poverty in half from 1949 to 1959. It was halved again, to its lowest levels ever, from 1959 to 1969. The high point of health and nutrition for poor children came in 1970, a period that coincided with the peak years of the Great Society, not the high point of the '50s family.

Since 1973, however, a new phase has emerged. Some things have continued to improve: High school graduation rates are at an all-time high; minority test scores rose steadily from 1970 to 1990; poverty rates among the elderly have continued to fall while life expectancy has risen.

Other trends show mixed results: The easy availability of divorce has freed individuals from oppressive or even abusive marriages, but many divorces have caused emotional and economic suffering for both children and adults. Women have found new satisfaction at work, and there's considerable evidence that children can benefit from having a working mother, but the failure of businesses—and some husbands—to adjust to working mothers' needs has caused much family stress and discord.

In still other areas, the news is quite bleak. Children have now replaced seniors as the poorest segment of the population; the depth and concentration of child poverty has increased over the past 20 years so it's now at 1965 levels. Many of the gains ethnic groups made in the 1960s and '70s have been eroded.

History suggests that most of these setbacks originate in social and economic forces rather than in the collapse of some largely mythical traditional family. Perhaps the most powerful of these sources is the breakdown of America's implicit postwar wage bargain with the working class, where corporations ensured labor stability by increasing employment, rewarding increased productivity with higher wages, and investing in jobs and community infrastructure. At the same time, the federal government subsidized home ownership and higher education.

Since 1973, however, real wages have fallen for most families. It increasingly requires the work of two earners to achieve the modest upward mobility one could provide in the 1950s and '60s. Unemployment rates have risen steadily as corporations have abandoned the communities that grew up around them, seeking cheap labor overseas or in nonunionized sectors of the South. Involuntary part-time work has soared. As Time magazine noted in 1993, the predictable job ladders of the '50s and '60s have been sawed off: "Companies are portable, workers are throwaway." A different article in the same issue found, "Long-term commitments…are anathema to the modern corporation."

During the 1980s the gap between the rich and middle-class widened in 46 states, and each year since 1986 has set a new postwar record for the gap between rich and poor. In 1980 a CEO earned 30 to 40 times as much as the average worker; by 1994 he earned 187 times as much. Meanwhile, the real wages of a young male high school graduate are lower today than those earned by his 1963 counterpart.

These economic changes are not driven by the rise in divorce and unwed motherhood. Decaying wage and job structures—not changing family structures—have caused the overwhelming bulk of income redistribution. And contrary to what has been called a new bipartisan consensus, marriage is not the solution to poverty. According to sociologist Donald J. Hernandez, Ph.D., formerly with the U.S. Census Bureau, even if every child in America were reunited with both biological parents, two thirds of those who are poor today would still be poor.

OUR UNCERTAIN FUTURE

History's lessons are both positive and negative. We can take comfort from the fact that American families have always been in flux and that a wide variety of family forms and values have worked well for different groups at different times. There's no reason to assume that recent changes are entirely destructive. Families have always been vulnerable to rapid economic change and have always needed economic and emotional support from beyond their own small boundaries. Our challenge is to grapple with the sweeping transformations we're currently undergoing. History demonstrates it's not as simple as returning to one or another family form from the past. Though there are many precedents for successfully reorganizing family life, there are no clear answers to the issues facing us as we enter the 21st century.

Reading 2   Immigrant Families in the City*

MARK HUTTER

The period of time from 1880 to 1924, when immigration laws placed severe limitation on movement into the United States, witnessed a massive exodus of people from southern and eastern Europe. This "new" immigration was from countries like Austria-Hungary, Greece, Italy, Poland, Rumania, Russia, and Serbia (now a part of Yugoslavia). Immigrants from these countries were joined by others from China and Japan, Mexico, French Canada, and the West Indies. It contrasts with the peoples of the "old" immigration, those who arrived between 1820 (when federal statistics of origin were first recorded) and 1880. That was made up almost entirely of northwest Europeans who came from countries such as England, Ireland, Scotland, France, Germany, Norway and Sweden.

Total immigration in the three decades before the Civil War totaled five million. Between 1860 and 1890 that number doubled, and between 1890 and the beginning of the first world war in 1914, it tripled. The peak years of immigration were in the early twentieth century, with over a million people entering annually in 1905, 1906, 1907, 1910, 1913, and 1914. The main explanation for this massive movement of people to the United States was that the countries of origin of the "new" immigrants were experiencing population explosions and dislocations. By the later part of the nineteenth century, the

pressures of overpopulation, combined with the prospects of economic opportunity in the United States and the availability of rapid transportation systems that included railroads and steamships, set the wheels of world migration moving. Maldwyn Allen Jones, whose study *American Immigration* (1960) has been a standard work on the subject, comments on the shared motives of the culturally diversified im-migrants for coming to America:

> *The motives for immigration . . . have been always a mixture of yearning— for riches, for land, for change, for tranquillity, for freedom, and for something not definable in words. . . . The experiences of different immigrants groups . . . reveal a fundamental uniformity. Whenever they came, the fact that they had been uprooted from their old surroundings meant that they faced the necessity of coming to terms with an unfamiliar environment and a new status. The story of American immigration is one of millions of enterprising, courageous folk, most of them humble, nearly all of them unknown by name to history. Coming from a great variety of backgrounds, they nonetheless*

*Hutter, Mark. 1986–1987. "Immigrant Families in the City." *The Gallatin Review* 6(Winter): 60–69.

resembled one another in their will-
ingness to look beyond the horizon
and in their readiness to pull up
stakes in order to seek a new life.
(Jones 1960, pp. 4–5)

There was a great deal of variation in immigrant family migration arrangements. Some
immigrant groups coming from Scandinavian
societies and from Germany came as nuclear
families responding to America's needs to settle
and farm the vast lands of middle western America. For these groups settlement often meant the
almost complete reconstitution of Old World
rural village life and family patterns in rural
America (Hareven and Modell 1980). One
extreme example of this practice were the Hut-
terites, a German religious group that lived in
Russia and migrated to the United States in the
late nineteenth century. They settled in isolated
rural agricultural sections in order to maintain
their distinctive family patterns. These include
early marriage, exceptionally high fertility, and
near universal remarriage after widowhood. The
Hutterite community was a highly cooperative
family economy ruled by a family patriarch that
operated through kinship affiliations created by
the high fertility and strict laws of intermarriage.
This isolated group could and has maintained
itself until today because of its ability to find
marriage partners within the group.

As agricultural opportunities in rural America declined and as the demand for skilled and
especially unskilled urban workers grew, the
"new" immigrations from southern and eastern
Europe concentrated in the industrial cities of
the Northeast and the Midwest. It was in these
urban areas where job opportunities were plentiful and where the chances of success were greatest. Young unattached males became the main-
stay of the migration population. The ethnic
historian Thomas J. Archdeacon (1983) reports
that, in the decades between 1840 and 1899,

males constituted 58 to 61 percent of the arrivals.
By contrast, the importance of single males
accounts for the statistic that 70 percent of the
newcomers between 1900 and 1909 and that two
out of every three between 1910 and 1914 were
males. The proportion of males to females did
not take place evenly across the immigrant
nationalities. Jews displayed the best balance
with an almost fifty-fifty split. Southern Italians,
on the other hand, had more than three times as
many males as females. The sex ratio among
Greeks, the most extreme group, indicated that
for every one Greek female there were 11 Greek
men. Such sex ratio imbalances obviously set
limits on the possibility of family life during this
time period.

The ultimate success of an immigrant group
depended in large part on its ability to reestablish
a normal pattern of family life in America. This
initially proved quite difficult. Severe problems
confronted the immigrant families in America.
The huge influx of immigrants to the American
cities gave new meaning and visibility to urban
poverty. Ghetto housing was awful; inadequate
buildings were cheaply and quickly built to meet
immediate needs, which proved to be inadequate. People lived in overcrowded, dirty, unsan-
itary, and poorly ventilated and poorly heated
apartment dwellings that were still expensive
because of the demand. Boarders and lodgers
were numerous and helped provide some of the
needed monies to pay the rent. It was not uncommon for beds to be used around the clock, with
day-shift workers using them at night and night-
shift workers using them during the day.

The horrible living conditions were dramatically exposed in the muckraking works of such
novelists as Upton Sinclair, whose famous novel
The Jungle exposed the grinding poverty in the
Slavic communities in Chicago located within
the stench of the blood and entrails of cattle
being slaughtered in the neighborhood stock-
yards, and also of the journalistic accounts of

newsmen like Lincoln Steffens whose book, *The Shame of the Cities,* refers to the ghetto slums as literally looking like hell. The journalist Jacob Riis, himself an immigrant from Denmark, wrote and photographed the urban poverty of New York's ghetto life in his classic work, *How the Other Half Lives.* His graphic descriptions of the barren and filthy firetraps of New York's tenements startled the nation. The following passage from his book is typical of what life was like in one of these buildings:

—*Cherry Street. Be a little careful please. The hall is dark and you might stumble over the children.... Not that it would hurt them; kicks and cuffs are their daily diet. They have little else. Here where the hall turns and dives into utter darkness is a step, and another, another. A flight of stairs. You can feel your way, if you cannot see it. Close? Yes! What would you have? All the fresh air that ever enters these stairs comes from the hall-door that is forever slamming, and from the windows of dark bedrooms that in turn receive from the stairs their sole supply of the elements God meant to be free, but man deals out with such niggardly hand.... The sinks are in the hallway, that all the tenants may have access—and all be poisoned alike by their summer stenches.... Hear the pumps squeak! It is the lullaby of tenement house babies. In summer, when a thousand thirsty throats pant for a cooling drink in this block, it is worked in vain. But the saloon, whose open door you passed in the hall, is always there. The smell of it has followed you up. Here is a door. Listen! That short hacking cough, that*

tiny, helpless wail—what do they mean? They mean ... a sadly familiar story—before the day is at an end. The child is dying with measles. With half a chance it might have lived; but it had none. That dark bedroom killed it. (Riis, 1890/1957, pp. 33–34).

A common theme in the popular literature of that time were stories of wives forgotten in the old country and of families torn asunder by the clash of the old ways of life with the new. The editorial columns of the immigrant press frequently reported on the life struggles of its readers. Many newspapers had "advice" columns with its editors serving as lay clergy, social worker, friend, and relative to those who had nowhere else to turn. The "Bintel Brief" ("Bundle of Letters") of the *Jewish Daily Forward* has become the most famous of these advice columns. Through it, readers wrote of their marital and family problems, the impact of poverty on their lives, religious conflicts in terms of attitudes and behavior, and other life concerns. The following two letters, the first from 1906 and the second from 1910, were reprinted in *A Bintel Brief* (Metzker 1971) and are illustrative of such advice columns:

1906

Worthy Mr. Editor,
    I was married six years ago in Russia. My husband had not yet been called up for the military service, and I married him because he was an only son and I knew he would not be taken as a soldier. But that year all originally exempted men were taken in our village. He had no desire to serve Czar Nickolai and since I didn't want that either, I sold everything I could and sent him to London. From there he went to America:
    At first he wrote to me that it was hard for him to find work, so he couldn't

send me anything to live on. I suffered terribly. I couldn't go to work because I was pregnant. And the harder my struggles became, the sadder were the letters from my husband. I suffered from hunger and cold, but what could I do when he was worse off than I?

Then his letters became fewer. Weeks and months passed without a word.

In the time I went to the rabbi of our town and begged him to have pity on a deserted wife. I asked him to write to a New York rabbi to find out what had happened to my husband. All kinds of thoughts ran through my mind because in a big city like New York anything can happen. I imagined perhaps he was sick, maybe even dead.

A month later an answer came to the rabbi. They had found out where my husband was but didn't want to talk with him until I could come to America.

My relatives from several towns collected enough money for my passage and I came to New York, to the rabbi. They tricked my husband into coming there too. Till the day I die I'll never forget the expression on my husband's face when he unexpectedly saw me and the baby.

I was speechless. The rabbi questioned him for me, sternly, like a judge, and asked him where he worked and how much he earned. My husband answered that he was a carpenter and made twelve dollars a week.

"Do you have a wife, or are you single?" the rabbi asked. My husband trembled as he answered, "I have committed a crime," and he began to wipe his eyes with a handkerchief. And soon a detective appeared in the rabbi's house and arrested my husband, and the next day the story appeared in the Jewish newspapers. Then some good women who had pity on me helped me. They found a job for me, took me to lectures and the-

aters. I began to read books I had never realized existed.

In time I adjusted to life here. I am not lonely, and life for me and my child is quite good. I want to add here, too, that my husband's wife came to me, fell at my feet and cried, but my own problems are enough for me.

But in time my conscience began to bother me. I began to think of my husband, suffering behind bars in his dark cell. In dreams I see his present wife, who certainly loves him, and her little boy living in dire need without their breadwinner. I now feel differently about the whole thing and I have sympathy for my husband. I am even prepared, when he gets out of jail, to wish him luck with his new life partner, but he will probably be embittered toward me. I have terrible pangs of conscience and I don't know what I can do. I hope you will print my letter, and answer me.

Cordially,
Z.B.

Answer:

In the answer to this letter, the woman is comforted and praised for her decency, her sympathy for her husband and his second wife. Also it is noted that when the husband is released he will surely have no complaints against her, since he is the guilty one in the circumstances, not she.

1910

Worthy Editor

My husband [here the name was given] deserted me and our three small children, leaving us in desperate need. I was left without a bit of bread for the children, with debts in the grocery store and the butcher's and last month's rent unpaid.

I am not complaining so much about his abandoning me as about the grief and suffering of our little children, who beg for food, which I cannot give them. I am young and healthy. I am able and willing to work in order to support my children, but unfortunately I am tied down because my baby is only six months old. I looked for an institution which would take care of my baby, but my friends advise against it.

The local Jewish Welfare Agencies are allowing me and my children to die of hunger, and this is because my "faithful" husband brought me over from Canada just four months ago and therefore I do not yet deserve to eat our bread.

It breaks my heart but I have come to the conclusion that in order to save my innocent children from hunger and cold I have to give them away.

I will sell my beautiful children to people who will give them a home. I will sell them, not for money, but for bread, for a secure home where they will have enough food and warm clothing for the winter.

I, the unhappy young mother, am willing to sign a contract, with my heart's blood, stating that the children belong to the good people who will treat them tenderly. Those who are willing and able to give my children a good home can apply to me.

Respectfully,
Mrs. P [The full name and
address are given]
Chicago

Answer:

What kind of society are we living in that forces a mother to such desperate straits that there is no other way out than to sell her three children for a piece of bread?

Isn't this enough to kindle a hellish fire of hatred in every human heart for such a system?

The first to be damned is the heartless father, but who knows what's wrong with him? Perhaps he, too, is unhappy. We hope, though, that this letter will reach him and he will return to aid them.

We also ask our friends and readers to take an interest in this unfortunate woman and to help her so that she herself can be a mother to her children. (Metzker 1971, pp. 50–52, 104–105).

In the late nineteenth and early twentieth century as a result of the public outcry generated by the exposures by social-minded individuals like Sinclair, Steffens and Riis, and such tragedies as the Triangle Shirtwaist Factory fire that claimed the lives of one hundred and forty-six people, reforms were directed to change the living and working environments of immigrants. These movements included tenement-house reforms, workmen's compensation, the abolition of child labor, and the protection of women and children in industry.

However, the pervasive poverty in rapidly growing industrial cities led many to the erroneous conclusion that it was the immigrants themselves who were to blame for their poverty. Blame was not placed on the economic circumstances that the immigrants had to confront. This belief led to the development of a wide number of social programs aimed directly at changing the immigrant families themselves. Social reformers created both private and public welfare agencies to help alleviate the problems of the sick, the poor, and the delinquent or criminal. Immigrant families and especially their children became the major targets for discipline and reformation, and programs were designed to intervene in the affairs of immigrant families. The concern was to Americanize them into what they saw as the great American melting pot where the cultural variations of the given immigrant group would be altered to the standard American way of life.

The settlement house, a private social welfare agency, is a typical example of how some of these practices became articulated. The term "settlement" meant giving the immigrant newcomers the wherewithal to survive in a modern industrial city. Located right in the heart of the immigrant communities, it sought to help the immigrant families cope with poverty and improve their living standards. Settlement house workers tried to teach English, American social customs, and, when necessary, the rudiments of household management, health care, and sanitation. They encouraged family member involvement in work and household roles that often conformed to their own middle class standards of family morality. When successful, as in the case of Jane Addams of Chicago's Hull House, they integrated their work without undermining the immigrant's native culture. Unfortunately, much too frequently, workers saw as their primary task the eradication of "non-American" cultural points of view as to family traditions regarding marital roles and parent child relationships.

Education was seen as the key institution to eradicate immigrant cultures and to achieve Americanization. For example, in the years before World War I Henry Ford required all of his foreign workers to attend English school. For a five year period, 1915–1920, the federal Bureau of Education subsidized a Division of Immigrant Education, which encouraged school districts throughout the nation to establish special Americanization programs. The response was favorable and many state governments provided funds for the education of immigrants. During this period and continuing afterwards, numerous public school systems instituted night classes in which foreign students could learn English and gain knowledge of American government to acquire citizenship (Archdeacon 1983).

For the Americanization of immigrant children, the school system became the prime vehicle to help accomplish this task. Education meant more than simply teaching proper English and the three "Rs" of reading, "riting," and "rithmetic," but also meant socializing children to "American" ways of life, habits of cleanliness, good housekeeping, nutrition, and social graces. Children were also graded on their level of acculturation to American values, as measured by behavior in school. State legislation was passed making compulsory attendance laws more stringent to help ensure that children were adequately exposed to the assimilative influences of the schools. Settlement house workers also played a role here by assisting in the supervision of school attendance and observance of child labor laws.

However, it was the immigrants themselves, especially the immigrant family system that was primarily responsible for the success of the "new" immigration in "making it" in America. Let's see how this came about. By 1920 almost sixty percent of the population of cities of more than 100,000 inhabitants were first or second generation ethnic Americans (Sellers 1977). The immigrant settled in ethnic enclaves which people referred to as "Little Italys," "Polanias," "Little Syrias," and "Jewtowns." Each enclave reflected its distinctive ethnic flavor with its own church, stores, newspapers, clothing, and gestural and language conventions. The Chicago newspaper journalist, Mike Royko, reminiscing on his own Slavic community background recalls that you could always tell where you were "by the odors of the food stores and the open kitchen windows, the sound of the foreign or familiar language, and by whether a stranger hit you in the head with a rock" (Seller 1977, p. 112).

The establishment of immigrant "ghettos" in cities reflects a stage in the development of American cities where there was a great need for occupational concentration as a result of the expansion of the industrial economy in the late 19th century (Yancey, Ericksen, and Juliani 1976). Low-paid industrial immigrant workers were forced by economic pressures to live close to their places of work. The particular choice of residence and occupation was strongly influenced by the presence of friends and relatives in a process that has been called "chain migration." Chain migration refers to the connections made between individuals in countries of origin and destination in the process of international migration and to the process in which choices of residence and occupation were influenced by friends and relatives.

Networks of friends and relatives established in America maintained their European kinship and friendship ties and transmitted assistance across the Atlantic. Relatives acted as recruitment, migration, and housing resources, helping each other to shift from the often rural European work background to urban industrial work. A number of social historians (Anderson 1971; Hareven 1975; Yans-McLaughlin 1971) have observed that nineteenth as well as twentieth century migrants chose their residential and occupational destinations in large part because of the presence of kin group members in the new area.

Chain migration can be seen as facilitating transition and settlement. It ensured a continuity in kins contacts, and made mutual assistance in cases of personal and family crises an important factor in the adjustment of immigrants to the new urban American environment. Workers often migrated into the new industrial urban centers keeping intact or reforming much of their kinship ties and family traditions. As previously mentioned, a prevalent practice was for unmarried sons and daughters of working age, or

young childless married couples to migrate first. After establishing themselves by finding jobs and housing they would tend to send for other family members. Through their contacts at work or in the community they would assist their newly arrived relatives or friends with obtaining jobs and housing.

The fact that so many single individuals came to America alone accounts for the fact that turn of the century urban households of immigrants often included people other than the nuclear family. These people were not kinship related but were strangers. These strangers were boarders and lodgers who for various reasons came to America alone and for a period of time lived with fellow immigrants. This practice of taking in boarders and lodgers proved extremely valuable in allowing new migrants and immigrants to adapt to urban living (Hareven 1983).

The family can be seen as being an important intermediary in recruitment of workers to the new industrial society. Family patterns and values often carried over to the urban setting, and provided the individual with a feeling of continuity between one's rural background and new industrial city. Initially, selected individuals migrated, then families migrated in groups, and often entire rural communities reconstituted themselves in ethnic enclaves. They helped recruit other family members and countrymen into the industrial work force. Migration to industrial communities, then, did not break up traditional kinship ties; rather the family used these ties to facilitate their own transition into industrial life. Tamara Hareven (1983) after examining the historical evidence concludes that it is grossly incorrect to assume that industrialization broke up traditional kinship ties and destroyed the interdependence of the family and the community.

In summary, the 50 year dramatic growth period of 1876–1925 of the industrial urban centers of the Northeast and Midwest can be attributed to the social and family organization of the newly arriving immigration groups. Rather than view this period in terms of social disorganization we would argue that insufficient attention has been placed on the nature of social interactional patterns that were developing among the immigrant groups in American cities. We owe the spectacular rise of world cities like New York City to the vitality of the immigrants and their social support structures.

Reading 3   Interpreting the African Heritage in Afro-American Family Organization*

NIARA SUDARKASA

Many of the debates concerning explanations of Black family organization are waged around false dichotomies. The experience of slavery in America is juxtaposed to the heritage of Africa as *the* explanation of certain aspects of Black family structure. "Class" versus "culture" becomes the framework for discussing determinants of household structure and role relationships. Black families are characterized either as "alternative institutions" or as groups whose structures reflect their "adaptive strategies," as if the two viewpoints were mutually exclusive.

Just as surely as Black American family patterns are in part an outgrowth of the descent into slavery (Frazier, 1939 [1966]), so too are they partly a reflection of the archetypical African institutions and values that informed and influenced the behavior of those Africans who were enslaved in America (Herskovits, 1941 [1958]). With respect to "class" and "culture," it is indeed the case that the variations in historical and contemporary Black family organization cannot be explained without reference to the socioeconomic contexts in which they developed (Allen, 1979). But neither can they be explained without reference to the cultural contexts from which they derived (Nobles, 1974a, 1974b, 1978). Whereas Black families can be analyzed as groups with strategies for coping with wider societal forces (Stack, 1974), they must also be understood as institutions with historical traditions that set them apart as "alternative" formations that are not identical to (or pathological variants of) family structures found among other groups in America (Aschenbrenner, 1978).

After more than a decade of rethinking Black family structure (see, for example, Billingsley, 1968; Staples, 1971, 1978; Aschenbrenner, 1973; English, 1974; Sudarkasa, 1975a; Allen, 1978; Shimkin et al., 1978), it is still the case that a holistic theory of past and present Black family organization remains to be developed. Such a theory or explanation must rest on the premise that political-economic variables are *always* part of any explanation of family formation and functioning, but that the cultural historical derivation of the formations in question helps to explain the nature of their adaptation to particular political-economic contexts.

Author's note: I wish to thank Tao-Lin Hwang for his assistance with the research for this chapter, and Bamidele Agbasegbe Demerson for his helpful comments.

Obviously, it is beyond the scope of this chapter to try to set forth such a holistic explanation of Black family organization. Its more modest aim is to take a step in this direction by laying to rest one of the false dichotomies that stand in the way of such an explanation. This review seeks to show how an understanding of African family structure sheds light on the form and functioning of Black American family structure as it developed in *the context of slavery* and later periods. It seeks to elucidate African institutional arrangements and values that were manifest in the family organization of Blacks enslaved in America, and suggests that some of these values and institutional arrangements continue to be recognizable in contemporary formations.

The relationships of causality, correlation, and constraint that exist between the political-economic sphere and that of the family cannot be dealt with here. What the chapter seeks to clarify is why Black familial institutions embrace certain alternatives of behavior and not others. It suggests a cultural historical basis for the fact that Black family organization differs from that of other groups even when political and economic factors are held relatively constant.

Thus, it is suggested that it cannot suffice to look to political and economic factors to explain, for example, the difference between lower-class Anglo- or Italian-American families and lower-class Afro-American families. One has to come to grips with the divergent culture histories of the groups concerned. In other words, one is led back to the institutional heritage stemming from Western Europe on the one hand and from West Africa on the other. Knowledge of the structure and functioning of kinship and the family in these areas helps to explain the structure and functioning of families formed among their descendants in America.

It might appear that this is too obvious a point to be belabored. However, when it comes to the study of Black American families, the scholarly community has historically taken a different view. Whereas it is generally agreed that the history of the family in Europe is pertinent to an understanding of European derived family organization in America (and throughout the world), many—if not most—scholars working on Black American families have argued or assumed that the African family heritage was all but obliterated by the institution of slavery. This view has retained credence, despite the accumulation of evidence to the contrary, in large measure because E. Franklin Frazier (1939), the most prestigious and prolific student of the Black American family, all but discounted the relevance of Africa in his analyses.

This chapter takes its departure from W.E.B. DuBois (1908[1969]), Carter G. Woodson (1936), and M. J. Herskovits (1958), all of whom looked to Africa as well as to the legacy of slavery for explanations of Afro-American social institutions. Herskovits is the best-known advocate of the concept of African survivals in Afro-American family life, but DuBois was the first scholar to stress the need to study the Black American family against the background of its African origins. In his 1908 study of the Black family, DuBois prefaced his discussions of marriage, household structure, and economic organization with observations concerning the African antecedents of the patterns developed in America.

In each case an attempt has been made to connect present conditions with the African past. This is not because Negro-Americans are Africans, or can trace an unbroken social history from Africa, but because there is a distinct nexus between Africa and America which, though broken and perverted, is nevertheless not to be neglected by the careful student [DuBois, 1969: 9].

Having documented the persistence of African family patterns in the Caribbean, and of African derived wedding ceremonies in Alabama, DuBois noted:

> Careful research would doubtless reveal many other traces of the African family in America. They would, however, be traces only, for the effectiveness of the slave system meant the practically complete crushing out of the African clan and family life [p. 21].

With the evidence that has accumulated since DuBois wrote, it is possible to argue that even though the constraints of slavery did prohibit the replication of African lineage ("clan") and family life in America, the principles on which these kin groups were based, and the values underlying them, led to the emergence of variants of African family life in the form of the extended families which developed among the enslaved Blacks in America. Evidence of the Africanity to which DuBois alluded is to be found not only in the relatively few "traces" of direct *institutional transfer* from Africa to America, but also in the numerous examples of *institutional transformation* from Africa to America.

No discussion of the relevance of Africa for understanding Afro-American family organization can proceed without confronting the issue of the "diversity" of the backgrounds of "African slaves" (read "enslaved Africans") brought to America. Obviously for certain purposes, each African community or each ethnic group can be described in terms of the linguistic, cultural, and/or social structural features which distinguish it from others. At the same time, however, these communities or ethnic groups can be analyzed from the point of view of their similarity to other groups.

It has long been established that the Africans enslaved in the United States and the rest of the Americas came from the Western part of the continent where there had been a long history of culture contact and widespread similarities in certain institutions (Herskovits, 1958: chs. 2 and 3). For example, some features of kinship organization were almost universal. Lineages, large co-resident domestic groups, and polygynous marriages are among the recurrent features found in groups speaking different languages, organized into states as well as "segmentary" societies, and living along the coast as well as in the interior (Radcliffe-Brown, 1950; Fortes, 1953; Onwuejeogwu, 1975).

When the concept of "African family structure" is used here, it refers to those organizational principles and patterns which are common to the different ethnic groups whose members were enslaved in America. These features of family organization are known to have existed for centuries on the African continent and are, therefore, legitimately termed a part of the African heritage.

AFRICAN FAMILY STRUCTURE: UNDERSTANDING THE DYNAMICS OF CONSANGUINITY AND CONJUGALITY

African families, like those in other parts of the world, embody two contrasting bases for membership: *consanguinity,* which refers to kinship that is commonly assumed or presumed to be biologically based and rooted in "blood ties," and *affinity,* which refers to kinship created by law and rooted "in-law." *Conjugality* refers specifically to the affinal kinship created between spouses (Marshall, 1968). Generally, all kinship entails a dynamic tension between the operation of the contrasting principles of consanguinity and affinity. The comparative study of family organization led Ralph Linton (1936: 159–163) to observe that in different societies families tend to be built either around a conjugal core or around a consanguineal core. In either case, the other principle is subordinate.

According to current historical research on the family in Europe, the principle of conjugality appears to have dominated family organization in the Western part of that continent (including Britain) at least since the Middle Ages, when a number of economic and political factors led to the predominancy of nuclear and/or stem families built around married couples. Certainly for the past three or four hundred years, the conjugally based family has been the ideal and the norm in Western Europe (Shorter, 1975; Stone, 1975; Tilly and Scott, 1978). Whether or not the European conjugal family was a structural isolate is not the issue here. The point is that European families, whether nuclear or extended (as in the case of stem families), tended to emphasize the conjugal relationship in matters of household formation, decision making, property transmission, and socialization of the young (Goody, 1976).

African families, on the other hand, have traditionally been organized around consanguineal cores formed by adult siblings of the same sex or by larger same-sex segments of patri- or matrilineages. The groups which formed around these consanguineally related core members included their spouses and children, and perhaps some of their divorced siblings of the opposite sex. This co-resident *extended family* occupied a group of adjoining or contiguous dwellings known as a compound. Upon marriage, Africans did not normally form new isolated households, but joined a compound in which the extended family of the groom, or that of the bride, was already domiciled (Sudarkasa, 1980: 38–49).

African extended families could be subdivided in two ways. From one perspective, there was the division between the nucleus formed by the consanguineal core group and their children and the "outer group" formed by the in-marrying spouses. In many African languages, in-marrying

spouses are collectively referred to as "wives" or "husbands" by both females and males of the core group. Thus, for example, in any compound in a patrilineal society, the in-marrying women may be known as the "wives of the house." They are, of course, also the mothers of the children of the compound. Their collective designation as "wives of the house" stresses the fact that their membership in the compound is rooted in law and can be terminated by law, whereas that of the core group is rooted in descent and is presumed to exist in perpetuity.

African extended families may also be divided into their constituent conjugally based family units comprised of parents and children. In the traditional African family, these conjugal units did not have the characteristics of the typical "nuclear family" of the West. In the first place, African conjugal families normally involved polygynous marriages at some stage in their developmental cycle. A number of Western scholars have chosen to characterize the polygynous conjugal family as several distinct nuclear families with one husband/father in common (Rivers, 1924: 12; Murdock, 1949: 2; Colson, 1962). In the African conception, however, whether a man had one wife and children or many wives and children, his was *one* family. In the case of polygynous families, both the husband and the senior co-wife played important roles in integrating the entire group (Fortes, 1949: chs. III and IV; Sudarkasa, 1973: ch. V; Ware, 1979). The very existence of the extended family as an "umbrella" group for the conjugal family meant that the latter group differed from the Western nuclear family. Since, for many purposes and on many occasions, *all* the children of the same generation within the compound regarded themselves as brothers and sisters (rather than dividing into siblings versus "cousins"), and since the adults assumed certain responsibilities toward their "nephews" and "nieces" (whom they term sons and daughters) as well as toward their own offspring, African conjugal families did not have the rigid boundaries characteristic of nuclear families of the West.

The most far-reaching difference between African and European families stems from their differential emphasis on consanguinity and conjugality. This difference becomes clear when one considers extended family organization in the two contexts. The most common type of European extended family consisted of two or more nuclear families joined through the parent-child or sibling tie. It was this model of the stem family and the joint family that was put forth by George P. Murdock (1949: 23, 33, 39–40) as the generic form of the extended family. However, the African data show that on that continent, extended families were built around consanguineal cores and the conjugal components of these larger families differed significantly from the nuclear families of the West.

In Africa, unlike Europe, in many critical areas of family life the consanguineal core group rather than the conjugal pair was paramount. With respect to household formation, I have already indicated that married couples joined existing compounds. It was the lineage core that owned (or had the right of usufruct over) the land and the compound where families lived, farmed, and/or practiced their crafts. The most important properties in African societies—land, titles, and entitlements—were transmitted through the lineages, and spouses did not inherit from each other (Goody, 1976).

Within the extended family residing in a single compound, decision making centered in the consanguineal core group. The oldest male in the compound was usually its head, and all the men in his generation constituted the elders of the group. Together they were ultimately responsible for settling internal disputes, including those that could not be settled within the separate conjugal families or, in some cases, by the

female elders among the wives (Sudarkasa, 1973, 1976). They also made decisions, such as those involving the allocation of land and other resources, which affected the functioning of the constituent conjugal families.

Given the presence of multiple spouses within the *conjugal* families, it is not surprising that decision making within them also differed from the model associated with nuclear family organization. Separate rather than joint decision making was common. In fact, husbands and wives normally had distinct purviews and responsibilities within the conjugal family (Sudarkasa, 1973; Oppong, 1974). Excepting those areas where Islamic traditions overshadowed indigenous African traditions, women had a good deal of control over the fruits of their own labor. Even though husbands typically had ultimate authority over wives, this authority did not extend to control over their wives' properties (Oppong, 1974; Robertson, 1976; Sudarkasa, 1976). Moreover, even though women were subordinate in their roles as wives, as mothers and sisters they wielded considerable authority, power, and influence. This distinction in the power attached to women's roles is symbolized by the fact that in the same society where wives knelt before their husbands, sons prostrated before their mothers and seniority as determined by age, rather than gender, governed relationships among siblings (Sudarkasa, 1973, 1976).

Socialization of the young involved the entire extended family, not just the separate conjugal families, even though each conjugal family had special responsibility for the children (theirs or their relatives') living with them. It is important to note that the concept of "living with" a conjugal family took on a different meaning in the context of the African compound. In the first place, husbands, wives, and children did not live in a bounded space, apart from other such units. Wives had their own rooms or small dwellings, and husbands had theirs. These were not necessarily adjacent to one another. (In some matrilineal societies, husbands and wives resided in separate compounds). Children ordinarily slept in their mothers' rooms until they were of a certain age, after which they customarily slept in communal rooms allocated to boys or girls. Children usually ate their meals with their mothers but they might also eat some of these meals with their fathers' co-wives (assuming that no hostility existed between the women concerned) or with their grandmothers. Children of the same compound played together and shared many learning experiences. They were socialized by all the adults to identify themselves collectively as sons and daughters of a particular lineage and compound, which entailed a kinship, based on descent, with all the lineage ancestors and with generations unborn (Radcliffe-Brown and Forde, 1950; Uchendu, 1965; Sudarkasa, 1980).

The stability of the African extended family did not depend on the stability of the marriage(s) of the individual core group members. Although traditional African marriages (particularly those in patrilineal societies) were more stable than those of most contemporary societies, marital dissolution did not have the ramifications it has in nuclear family systems. When divorces did occur, they were usually followed by remarriage. Normally, all adults other than those who held certain ceremonial offices or who were severely mentally or physically handicapped lived in a marital union (though not necessarily the same one) throughout their lives (for example, Lloyd, 1968). The children of a divorced couple were usually brought up in their natal compound (or by members of their lineage residing elsewhere), even though the in-marrying parent had left that compound.

Several scholars have remarked on the relative ease of divorce in some traditional African societies, particularly those in which matrilineal descent was the rule (for example, Fortes, 1950:

283). Jack Goody (1976: 64) has even suggested that the rate of divorce in precolonial Africa was higher than in parts of Europe and Asia in comparable periods as a corollary of contrasting patterns of property transmission, contrasting attitudes toward the remarriage of women (especially widows), and contrasting implications of polygyny and monogamy. If indeed there was a higher incidence of divorce in precolonial Africa, this would not be inconsistent with the wide-ranging emphasis on consanguinity in Africa as opposed to conjugality in Europe.

Marriage in Africa was a contractual union which often involved long-lasting compassionate relationships, but it was not expected to be the all-encompassing, exclusive relationship of the Euro-American ideal type. Both men and women relied on their extended families and friends, as well as on their spouses, for emotionally gratifying relationships. Often, too, in the context of polygyny women as well as men had sexual liaisons with more than one partner. A woman's clandestine affairs did not necessarily lead to divorce because, in the absence of publicized information to the contrary, her husband was considered the father of all her children (Radcliffe-Brown, 1950). And in the context of the lineage (especially the patrilineage), all men aspired to have as many children as possible.

Interpersonal relationships within African families were governed by principles and values which I have elsewhere summarized under the concepts of respect, restraint, responsibility, and reciprocity. Common to all these principles was a notion of commitment to the collectivity. The family offered a network of security, but it also imposed a burden of obligations (Sudarkasa, 1980: 49–50). From the foregoing discussion, it should be understandable that, in their material form, these obligations extended first and foremost to consanguineal kin. Excepting the gifts that were exchanged at the time of marriage, the material obligations entailed in the conjugal relationship and the wider affinal relationships created by marriage were of a lesser magnitude than those associated with "blood" ties.

AFRO-AMERICAN FAMILY STRUCTURE: INTERPRETING THE AFRICAN CONNECTION

Rather than start with the question of what was *African* about the families established by those Africans who were enslaved in America, it would be more appropriate to ask what was *not* African about them. Most of the Africans who were captured and brought to America arrived without any members of their families, but they brought with them the societal codes they had learned regarding family life. To argue that the trans-Atlantic voyage and the trauma of enslavement made them forget, or rendered useless their memories of how they had been brought up or how they had lived before their capture, is to argue from premises laden with myths about the Black experience (Elkins, 1963: 101–102; see also Frazier, 1966: ch. 1).

Given the African tradition of multilingualism and the widespread use of lingua francas (Maquet, 1972: 18–25)—which in West Africa would include Hausa, Yoruba, Djoula, and Twi—it is probable that many more of the enslaved Africans could communicate among themselves than is implied by those who remark on the multiplicity of "tribes" represented among the slaves. As Landman (1978: 80) has pointed out:

> In many areas of the world, individuals are expected to learn only one language in the ordinary course of their lives. But many Africans have been enculturated in social systems where multiple language or dialect acquisition have been regarded as normal.

The fact that Africans typically spoke three to five languages also makes it understandable why they quickly adopted "pidginized" forms of European languages as lingua francas for communicating among themselves and with their captors.

The relationships which the Blacks in America established among themselves would have reflected their own backgrounds *and* the conditions in which they found themselves. It is as erroneous to try to attribute what developed among them solely to slavery as it is to attribute it solely to the African background. Writers such as Herbert Gutman (1976), who emphasize the "adaptive" nature of "slave culture" must ask what it was that was being adapted as well as in what context this adaptation took place. Moreover, they must realize that adaptation does not necessarily imply extensive modification of an institution, especially when its structure is already suited (or "preadapted") to survival in the new context. Such an institution was the African extended family, which had served on that continent, in various environments and different political contexts, as a unit of production and distribution; of socialization, education, and social control; and of emotional and material support for the aged and the infirm as well as the hale and hearty (Kerri, 1979; Okediji, 1975; Shimkin and Uchendu, 1978; Sudarkasa, 1975b).

The extended family networks that were formed during slavery by Africans *and their descendants* were based on the institutional heritage which the Africans had brought with them to this continent, and the specific forms they took reflected the influence of European-derived institutions as well as the political and economic circumstances in which the enslaved population found itself.

The picture of Black families during slavery has become clearer over the past decade, particularly as a result of the wealth of data in Gutman's justly heralded study. Individual households were normally comprised of a conjugal pair, their children, and sometimes their grandchildren, other relatives, or non-kin. Marriage was usually monogamous, but polygynous unions where the wives lived in separate households have also been reported (Gutman, 1976: 59, 158; Blassingame, 1979: 171; Perdue et al., 1980: 209).

Probably only in a few localities did female-headed households constitute as much as one-quarter of all households (Gutman, 1976: esp. chs. 1–3). The rarity of this household type was in keeping with the African tradition whereby women normally bore children within the context of marriage and lived in monogamous or polygynous conjugal families that were part of larger extended families. I have tried to show elsewhere why it is inappropriate to apply the term "nuclear family" to the mother-child dyads within African polygynous families (Sudarkasa, 1980: 43–46). In some African societies—especially in matrilineal ones—a small percentage of previously married women, or married women living apart from their husbands, might head households that were usually attached to larger compounds. However, in my view, on the question of the origin of female-headed households among Blacks in America, Herskovits was wrong, and Frazier was right in attributing this development to conditions that arose during slavery and in the context of urbanization in later periods (Frazier, 1966; Herskovits, 1958; Furstenberg et al., 1975).

Gutman's data suggest that enslaved women who had their first children out of wedlock did not normally set up independent households, but rather continued to live with their parents. Most of them subsequently married and set up neolocal residence with their husbands. The data also suggest that female-headed households developed mainly in two situations: (1) A woman whose husband died or was sold off the plantation might head a household comprised of her children and perhaps her grandchildren born to an unmarried daughter; (2) a woman who did not marry after having one or two children out of wedlock but continued to have children (no doubt often for the "master") might have her own cabin built for her (Gutman, 1976: chs. 1–3).

It is very important to distinguish these two types of female-headed households, the first being only a phase in the developmental cycle of a conjugally headed household, and the second being a case of neolocal residence by an unmarried female. The pattern of households headed by widows was definitely not typical of family structure in Africa, where normally a widow married another member of her deceased husband's lineage. The pattern of neolocal residence by an unmarried woman with children would have been virtually unheard of in Africa. Indeed, it was also relatively rare among enslaved Blacks and in Black communities in later periods. Before the twentieth-century policy of public assistance for unwed mothers, virtually all young unmarried mothers in Black communities continued to live in households headed by other adults. If in later years they did establish their own households, these tended to be tied into transresidential family networks.

The existence during slavery of long-lasting conjugal unions among Blacks was not a departure from African family tradition. Even with the relative ease of divorce in matrilineal societies, most Africans lived in marital unions that ended only with the death of one of the spouses. In the patrilineal societies from which most American Blacks were taken, a number of factors, including the custom of returning bridewealth payments upon the dissolution of marriage, served to encourage marital stability (Radcliffe-Brown, 1950: 43–54). Given that the conditions of slavery did not permit the *replication* of African families, it might be expected that the husband and wife as elders in the household would assume even greater importance than they had in

Africa, where the elders within the consanguineal core of the extended family and those among the wives would have had major leadership roles within the compound.

When the distinction is made between family and household—and, following Bender (1967), between the composition of the co-resident group and the domestic functions associated with both households and families—it becomes apparent that the question of who lived with whom during slavery (or later) must be subordinate to the questions of who was doing what for whom and what kin relationships were maintained over space and time. In any case, decisions concerning residence per se were not always in the hands of the enslaved Blacks themselves, and space alone served as a constraint on the size, and consequently to some extent on the composition, of the "slave" cabins.

That each conjugally based household formed a primary unit for food consumption and production among the enslaved Blacks is consistent with domestic organization within the African compound. However, Gutman's data, and those reported by enslaved Blacks themselves, on the strong bonds of obligation among kinsmen suggest that even within the constraints imposed by the slave regime, transresidential cooperation—including that between households in different localities—was the rule rather than the exception (Gutman, 1976: esp. 131–138; Perdue et al., 1980: esp. 26, 256, 323). One might hypothesize that on the larger plantations with a number of Black families related through consanguineal and affinal ties, the households of these families might have formed groupings similar to African compounds. Certainly we know that in later times such groupings were found in the South Carolina Sea Islands and other parts of the South (Agbasegbe, 1976, 1981; Gutman, 1976; Johnson, 1934: ch. 2; Powdermaker, 1939: ch. 8).

By focusing on extended families (rather than simply on households) among the enslaved

Blacks, it becomes apparent that these kin networks had many of the features of continental African extended families. These Afro-American groupings were built around consanguineal kin whose spouses were related to or incorporated into the networks in different degrees. The significance of the consanguineal principle in these networks is indicated by Gutman's statement that "the pull between ties to an immediate family and to an enlarged kin network sometimes strained husbands and wives" (1976: 202; see also Frazier, 1966: pt. 2).

The literature on Black families during slavery provides a wealth of data on the way in which consanguineal kin assisted each other with child rearing, in life crisis events such as birth and death, in work groups, in efforts to obtain freedom, and so on. They maintained their networks against formidable odds and, after slavery, sought out those parents, siblings, aunts, and uncles from whom they had been torn (Blassingame, 1979; Genovese, 1974; Gutman, 1976; Owens, 1976). Relationships within these groups were governed by principles and values stemming from the African background. Respect for elders and reciprocity among kinsmen are noted in all discussions of Black families during slavery. The willingness to assume responsibility for relatives beyond the conjugal family and selflessness (a form of restraint) in the face of these responsibilities are also characteristics attributed to the enslaved population.

As would be expected, early Afro-American extended families differed from their African prototypes in ways that reflected the influence of slavery and of Euro-American values, especially their proscriptions and prescriptions regarding mating, marriage, and the family. No doubt, too, the Euro-American emphasis on the primacy of marriage within the family reinforced conjugality among the Afro-Americans even though the "legal" marriage of enslaved Blacks was prohibited. As DuBois noted at the turn of the century, African corporate lineages could not survive intact during slavery. Hence, the consanguineal core groups of Afro-American extended families differed in some ways from those of their African antecedents. It appears that in some of these Afro-American families membership in the core group was traced bilaterally, whereas in others there was a unilineal emphasis without full-fledged lineages.

Interestingly, after slavery, some of the corporate functions of African lineages reemerged in some extended families which became property-owning collectivities. I have suggested elsewhere that "the disappearance of the lineage principle or its absorption into the concept of extended family" is one of the aspects of the transformation of African family organization in America that requires research (Sudarkasa, 1980: 57). Among the various other issues that remain to be studied concerning these extended families are these: (1) Did members belong by virtue of bilateral or unilineal descent from a common ancestor or because of shared kinship with a living person? (2) How were group boundaries established and maintained? (3) What was the nature and extent of the authority of the elder(s)? (4) How long did the group last and what factors determined its span in time and space?

CONCLUSION

At the outset of this chapter it was suggested that a holistic explanation of Black family organization requires discarding or recasting some of the debates which have framed discussions in the past. I have tried to show why it is time to move beyond the debate over whether it was slavery *or* the African heritage which "determined" Black family organization to a synthesis which looks at institutional transformation as well as institutional transfer for the interplay between Africa and America in shaping the family structures of Afro-Americans.

Obviously, Black families have changed over time, and today one would expect that the evidence for African "retentions" (Herskovits, 1958: xxii–xxiii) in them would be more controvertible than in the past. Nevertheless, the persistence of some features of African family organization among contemporary Black American families has been documented for both rural and urban areas. Although this study cannot attempt a full-scale analysis of these features and the changes they have undergone, it is important to make reference to one of them, precisely because it impacts upon so many other aspects of Black family organization, and because its connection to Africa has not been acknowledged by most contemporary scholars. I refer to the emphasis on consanguinity noted especially among lower-income Black families and those in the rural South. Some writers, including Shimkin and Uchendu (1978), Agbasegbe (1976; 1981), Aschenbrenner (1973; 1975; 1978; Aschenbrenner and Carr, 1980) and the present author (1975a, 1980, 1981) have dealt explicitly with this concept in their discussions of Black family organization. However, without labelling it as such, many other scholars have described some aspects of the operation of consanguinity within the Black family in their discussions of "matrifocality" and "female-headed households." Too often, the origin of this consanguineal emphasis in Black families, which can be manifest even in households with both husband and wife present, is left unexplained or is "explained" by labelling it an "adaptive" characteristic.

In my view, historical realities require that the derivation of this aspect of Black family organization be traced to its African antecedents. Such a view does not deny the adaptive significance of consanguineal networks. In fact, it helps to clarify why these networks had the flexibility they had and why they, rather than conjugal relationships, came to be the stabilizing factor in Black families. The significance of this principle of organization is indicated by the list of Black family characteristics derived from it. Scrutiny of the list of Black family characteristics given by Aschenbrenner (1978) shows that 12 of the 18 "separate" features she lists are manifestations of the overall strength and entailments of consanguineal relationships.

Some writers have viewed the consanguineally based extended family as a factor of *instability* in the Black family because it sometimes undermines the conjugal relationships in which its members are involved. I would suggest that historically among Black Americans the concept of "family" meant first and foremost relationships created by "blood" rather than by marriage. (R. T. Smith [1973] has made substantially the same point with respect to West Indian family organization.) Children were socialized to think in terms of obligations to parents (especially mothers), siblings, and others defined as "close kin." Obligations to "outsiders," who would include prospective spouses and in-laws, were definitely less compelling. Once a marriage took place, if the demands of the conjugal relationship came into irreconcilable conflict with consanguineal commitments, the former would often be sacrificed. Instead of interpreting instances of *marital* instability as prima facie evidence of family instability, it should be realized that the fragility of the conjugal relationship could be a consequence or corollary of the *stability* of the consanguineal family network. Historically, such groups survived by nurturing a strong sense of responsibility among members and by fostering a code of reciprocity which could strain relations with persons not bound by it.

Not all Black families exhibit the same emphasis on consanguinity relationships. Various factors, including education, occupational demands, aspirations toward upward mobility, and acceptance of American ideals concerning marriage and the family, have moved some (mainly middle- and upper-class) Black families toward conjugally focused households and conjugally centered extended family groupings. Even when such households include relatives other than the nuclear family, those relatives tend to be subordinated to the conjugal pair who form the core of the group. This contrasts with some older type Black families where a senior relative (especially the wife's or the husband's mother) could have a position of authority in the household equal to or greater than that of one or both of the spouses. Children in many contemporary Black homes are not socialized to think in terms of the parent-sibling group as the primary kin group, but rather in terms of their future spouses and families of procreation as the main source of their future emotional and material satisfaction and support. Among these Blacks, the nuclear household tends to be more isolated in terms of instrumental functions, and such extended family networks as exist tend to be clusters of nuclear families conforming to the model put forth by Murdock (1949: chs. 1 and 2).

For scholars interested in the heritage of Europe as well as the heritage of Africa in Afro-American family organization, a study of the operation of the principles of conjugality and consanguinity in these families would provide considerable insight into the ways in which these two institutional traditions have been interwoven. By looking at the differential impact of these principles in matters of household formation, delegation of authority, maintenance of solidarity and support, acquisition and transmission of property, financial management, and so on (Sudarkasa, 1981), and by examining the political and economic variables which favor the predominance of one or the other principle, we will emerge with questions and formulations that can move us beyond debates over "pathology" and "normalcy" in Black family life.

Reading 4   Family Decline in America*

DAVID POPENOE

As a social institution, the family has been "in decline" since the beginning of world history, gradually becoming weaker through losing social functions and power to other institutions such as church, government, and school. Yet during the past 25 years, family decline in the United States, as in other industrialized societies, has been both steeper and more alarming than during any other quarter century in our history. Although they may not use the term "decline," most family scholars now agree, with a growing tinge of pessimism, that the family during this period has undergone a social transformation. Some see "dramatic and unparalleled changes" while others call it "a veritable revolution."[1]

Agreement about the dramatic nature of family change over the past few decades, together with a pessimistic assessment of it, represent a recent shift of viewpoint on the part of many scholars. In the 1970s, in sharp contrast to the prevailing mood of the general public, the outlook of many family experts was one of complacency. For example, in their 1981 book *What's Happening to the American Family?*, economists Sar Levitan and Richard Belous noted that "currently fashionable gloom and doom scenarios miss the essential process of adjustment and

change" and that "a critical analysis of the evidence does not paint such a dire picture, and thus a heartfelt 'hurrah' is in order."[2]

Yet after reviewing the events of the 1980s, their optimistic mood shifted strikingly. The second edition of this book, published in 1988, contains much apprehensive talk of "radical changes in family structure." The authors conclude, with some apologies for the "more sanguine scenario" of the earlier edition, that "American families are besieged from all sides" and "widespread family breakdown is bound to have a pervasive and debilitating impact not only on the quality of life but on the vitality of the body politic as well."[3]

The recent social transformation of the family has been so momentous that, in my opinion, we are witnessing the end of an epoch. Today's societal trends are bringing to a close the cultural dominance of what historians call the modern (I will use the term "traditional") nuclear family, a family situated apart from both the larger kin group and the workplace; focused on the procreation of children; and consisting of a legal, lifelong, sexually exclusive, heterosexual, monogamous marriage, based on affection and companionship, in which there is a sharp division of labor, with the female as full-time housewife and

*Popenoe, David. 1990. "Family Decline in America." Pp. 39–51, from *Rebuilding the Nest: A New Commitment to the American Family,* edited by David Blakenhorn et al., Lewiston, NY: Manticore Publishers. Copyright 1990. Reprinted by permission.

the male as primary provider and ultimate authority. Lasting for only a little more than a century, this family form emphasized the male as "good provider," the female as "good wife and mother," and the paramount importance of the family for child rearing. (Of course, not all families were able to live up to these cultural ideals.) During its cultural heyday, the terms "family," "home," and "mother" ranked extraordinarily high in the hierarchy of cultural values.[4]

In certain respects, this family form reached its apogee in the middle of the 20th century. By the 1950s—fueled in part by failing maternal and child mortality rates, greater longevity, and a high marriage rate—it is probably the case that a higher percentage of children than ever before were growing up in stable, two-parent families.[5] Similarly, this period witnessed the highest ever proportion of women who married, bore children, and lived jointly with their husbands until at least age 50.[6]

FLIGHT FROM THE NUCLEAR FAMILY

In the 1960s, however, four major social trends emerged to signal a widespread "flight" from both the ideal and the reality of the traditional nuclear family: rapid fertility decline, the sexual revolution, the movement of mothers into the labor force, and the divorce revolution. None of these changes was new to the 1960s; each represented a tendency that was already evident in earlier years. However, a striking acceleration of these trends occurred in the 1960s, which was made more dramatic by the fact that during the 1950s these trends had leveled off and in some cases even reversed their directions.[7]

The Decline in Fertility

First (taking up these four trends without reference to their relative importance or causal prior-

ity), fertility declined in the United States by almost 50% between 1960 and 1989, from an average of 3.7 children per woman to only 1.9. Although fertility has been gradually diminishing for several centuries (the main exception being the two decades following World War II), the level of fertility during the past decade was the lowest in U.S. history and below that necessary for the replacement of the population. As a percentage of the total population, children over the past 25 years have dropped from more than a third to about one-fourth.[8]

Growing dissatisfaction with parenthood is now evident among adults in our culture, along with a dramatic decrease in the stigma associated with childlessness.[9] Some demographers now predict that between 20% and 25% of today's young women will remain completely childless, and nearly 50% will be either childless or have only one child.[10]

The Sexual Revolution

Second, what is often called the sexual revolution has shattered the association of sex and reproduction.[11] The erotic has become a necessary ingredient of personal well-being and fulfillment, both in and outside marriage, as well as a highly marketable commodity. The greatest change has been in the area of premarital sex: from 1971 to 1982, the proportion of unmarried girls in the United States aged 15–19 who engaged in premarital sexual intercourse jumped from 28% to 44%.[12] This behavior reflects a widespread change in values: in 1967, 85% of Americans "condemned premarital sex as mortally wrong," compared with only 37% in 1979.[13] The sexual revolution has been a major contributor to the striking increase in unwed parenthood. Nonmarital births jumped from 5% of all births in 1960 (22% of births among blacks) to 22% in 1985 (60% of births among blacks). This is the highest rate of nonmarital births ever recorded in the United States.

Working Married Mothers

Third, although unmarried women have long been in the labor force, the past quarter century has witnessed a striking movement into the paid work force of married women with children.[14] In 1960, only 19% of married women with children younger than 6 were in the labor force (39% with children between 6 and 17); by 1986, this figure had climbed to 54% (68% of those with older children).[15]

Increased Divorce Rate

Fourth, the divorce rate in the United States over the past 25 years (as measured by the number of divorced persons per 1,000 married persons) has nearly quadrupled, increasing from 35 to 130. This increase has led many to refer to a divorce revolution.[16] A landmark of sorts was passed in 1974, when for the first time in American history more marriages ended in divorce than in death.[17] The probability that a marriage contracted today will end in divorce ranges from 44% to 66%, depending upon the method of calculation.[18]

Reshaped Family Experience

These four trends signal a widespread retreat from the traditional nuclear family in its terms of a lifelong, sexually exclusive unit, focused on children, with a separate-sphere division of labor between husband and wife. Unlike most previous family change, which reduced family functions and diminished the importance of the kin group, the family change of the past 25 years has tended to break up the "nucleus" of the family unit—the bond between husband and wife. Nuclear units, therefore, are losing ground to single-parent families, serial and stepfamilies, and unmarried and homosexual couples.[19]

The number of single-parent families, for example, has risen sharply as a result not only of marital breakup, but also of marriage decline (fewer persons who bear children are getting married) and widespread abandonment by males. In 1960, only 9% of children in the United States younger than 18 were living with one parent; by 1986, this figure had climbed to nearly one-fourth of all children. (The comparable figures for blacks are 22% and 53%, respectively.) Of children born between 1950 and 1954, only 19% of whites (48% of blacks) had lived in a single-parent family by the time they reached age 17. But for children born in 1980, the figure is projected to be 70% (94% for blacks).[20]

During the past quarter century there has also been a retreat from family living in general. For instance, the percentage of "nonfamily" households (households other than those containing two or more persons living together and related by blood, marriage, or adoption) has nearly doubled, from 15% to 28% of all households. Approximately 85% of these new households consist of a person living alone.[21]

To summarize the state of the family today compared with that of 25 years ago:

- fewer persons are marrying and they are marrying later in life
- those marrying are having fewer children
- more marriages end in divorce

Trends such as these have dramatically reshaped people's lifetime family experiences, that is, their connectedness to the institution of the family. The proportion of an average person's adult life spent with spouse and children was 62% in 1960, the highest in our history. Today it has dropped to 43%, the lowest point in our history.[22]

In the United States, the changing family structure has helped to continue, and in some ways exacerbate, the tragedy of child poverty. Since 1974, the poverty rate among children has exceeded that among the elderly, and 40% of all poor people in this nation today are children.[23] According to a recent estimate, one out of every four American preschoolers in 1987 was living below the poverty line.[24]

In addition to family structural change, the psychological character of the marital relationship has also changed substantially over the years.[25] Traditionally, marriage has been understood as a social obligation—an institution designed mainly for economic security and procreation. Today, marriage is understood mainly as a path toward self-fulfillment: self-development is seen to require a significant other, and marital partners are picked primarily to be personal companions. Put another way, marriage is becoming deinstitutionalized. No longer comprising a set of norms and social obligations that are widely enforced, marriage today is a voluntary relationship that individuals can make and break at will. As one indicator of this shift, laws regulating marriage and divorce have become increasingly more lax.[26]

As psychological expectations for marriage grow ever higher, dashed expectations for personal fulfillment fuel our society's high divorce rate. Divorce also feeds upon itself. The higher the divorce rate, the more "normal" it becomes, with fewer negative sanctions to oppose it, and the more potential partners become available. In general, psychological need, in and of itself, has proved to be a weak basis for stable marriage.

These family trends are all interrelated. They are also evident, in varying degrees, in every industrialized Western country, which suggests that their source lies not in particular political or economic systems but in the broad cultural shift that has accompanied industrialization and urbanization. Although scholars do not agree on all aspects of this shift, clearly an ethos of radical individualism has emerged in these societies, in which personal autonomy, individual rights, and social equality have gained supremacy as cultural ideals. In keeping with these ideals, the main goals of personal behavior have shifted from commitment to social units of all kinds (families, communities, religions, nations) to personal choices, lifestyle options, self-fulfillment, and personal pleasure.[27]

FAMILY CHANGE AS FAMILY DECLINE

Despite the dramatic nature of the recent social transformation of the family, many family experts are still reluctant to refer to the transformation as "family decline." This is unfortunate, because the concept of the family as a declining or weakening institution provides a "best fit" for many of the changes that have taken place. The concept also alerts us to examine the consequences of a rapidly changing institution.

During the past 25 years, the institution of the family has weakened substantially in a number of ways. Individual family members have become more autonomous and less bound by the family group, and the group has become less cohesive. Fewer of its traditional social functions are now carried out by the family; these have shifted to other institutions. The family has lost more power and authority to other institutions, especially to the state and its agencies. The family has grown smaller, less stable, and has a shorter life span; people are therefore family members for a smaller percentage of their life. The outcome of these trends is that people have become less willing to invest time, money, and energy in family life. It is the individual him- or herself, not the family unit, in whom the main investments are increasingly made.[28]

Why, then, are so many family scholars reluctant to speak of family decline? The short answer is that to speak of family decline within the intellectual community in recent years has been to be accused of opposing equality for women.

The dominance of the traditional nuclear family in the 1950s helped to fuel the modern women's movement. Reacting strongly to the lingering patriarchy of this family form, as well as to its separate-sphere removal of women from the labor market, the women's movement came to view the traditional nuclear family in very negative terms.[29] Today those who believe in greater equality for women—and that includes most academics and other intellectuals—favor an egalitarian family form, with substantial economic independence for wives. With respect to these characteristics, the flight from the traditional nuclear family is regarded as progress, not decline.

To speak of decline under these circumstances, therefore, is perceived as being implicitly in favor of a discredited family form, one that oppressed women. Indeed, the term "decline" has been used most forcefully by those conservatives who tend to view every recent family change as negative and who have issued a clarion call for a return to the traditional nuclear family.

But properly used, the term "decline" should not carry such ideological baggage. To empirically conclude that the family is declining should not automatically link one to a particular ideology of family or gender. Moreover, not all decline is negative in its effects; decline is not necessarily the opposite of progress. All sorts of institutional forms that were once fully accepted have declined: theocracies, hereditary monarchies, imperialism. The results of their decline have been by no means merely regressive. It is important to distinguish an empirical trend, such as the weakening of an institution, from both its positive and negative consequences.

THE SOCIAL CONSEQUENCES OF FAMILY DECLINE

How are we to evaluate the social consequences of recent family decline? At the outset, it must be stressed that the issue is extremely complex. Society has been ill-served by the simplistic, either/or terms used by both the political right and left in the national debate.

Certainly, one should not jump immediately to the conclusion that family decline is necessarily bad for our society. A great many positive aspects of the recent family changes stand out as noteworthy. During this same quarter century of family decline, women (and many minorities) have clearly improved their status and probably the overall quality of their lives. Much of women's gain in status has come through their release from family duties and increased participation in the labor force. In addition, given the great emphasis on psychological criteria for choosing and keeping marriage partners, it can be argued persuasively that those marriages today that endure are more likely than ever before to be emotionally rewarding companionships.[30]

This period has also seen improved health care and longevity as well as widespread economic affluence, all of which have produced, for most people, a material standard of living that is historically unprecedented. Some of this improvement is due to the fact that people are no longer so dependent on their families for health care and economic support; they no longer are so imprisoned by social class and family obligation. When in need, they can now rely more on public care and support, as well as self-initiative and self-development.

Despite these positive aspects, the negative consequences of family decline are real and profound. The greatest negative effect, in the opinion of nearly everyone, is on children. Because children represent the future of a society, any negative consequences for them are especially significant. Substantial, if not conclusive, evidence indicates that, partly due to family changes, the quality of life for children in the past 25 years has worsened.[31] Much of the problem is of a psychological nature and thus is difficult to measure quantitatively.

Perhaps the most serious problem is a weakening in many families of the fundamental assumption that children are to be loved and valued at the highest level of priority. The general disinvestment in family life that has occurred has commonly meant a disinvestment in children's welfare. Some refer to this as a national "parent deficit." Yet the deficit goes well beyond parents to encompass an increasingly less child-friendly society. The parent deficit is all too easily blamed on newly working women. But it is men who have left the parenting scene in large numbers, a phenomenon one scholar has called "A disappearing act by fathers."[32] More than ever before, fathers are denying paternity, avoiding their parental obligations, and absent from home (at the same time there has been a slow but not offsetting growth of the "housefather" role).[33] Indeed, a persuasive case can be made that men began to abandon the "good provider" role at about the same time that many women started to relinquish the role of the full-time homemaker.[34] Thus, men and women may have been equally involved in triggering the recent flight from the traditional nuclear family.

The breakup of the nuclear unit has been the focus of much concern. Virtually every child desires two biological parents for life, and substantial evidence exists that child rearing is most successful when it involves two parents, both of whom are strongly motivated for the task.[35] This is not to say that other family forms can not be successful, only that as a group they are not as likely to be successful. This is also not to say that the two strongly motivated parents must be organized in the patriarchal and separate-sphere terms of the traditional nuclear family.

Regardless of family form, a significant change has occurred over the past quarter century in what can be called the social ecology of childhood.[36] Advanced societies are moving ever farther from what many hold to be a highly desirable child-rearing environment consisting of the following characteristics: a relatively large family that does a lot of things together, has many routines and traditions, and provides a great deal of quality contact time between adults and children; regular contact with relatives, active friendships in a supportive neighborhood, and contact with the adult world of work; little concern on the part of children that their parents will break up; and the coming together of all these ingredients in the development of a rich family subculture that has lasting meaning and strongly promulgates family values such as cooperation and sharing.

As this brief sketch of the changing ecology of childhood suggests, not only the family has been transformed, but also the community environment in which families exist. Children are especially sensitive to their local environments; yet adults, too, have a big stake in the quality of their surroundings.

The family has always been a fundamental and probably essential unit of what some call "civil society"—the local society made up of kin and friendship networks, neighborhoods, religious institutions, and voluntary associations. Civil society provides meaning and attachment for people's lives and helps to protect them from the impersonal forces of market and state.[37] As the market and state "megastructures" grow ever more powerful, the need for the mediating structures of civil society becomes that much more compelling, both for psychic survival and political freedom.[38] Although reasonable doubt can be expressed about the empirical accuracy of the common phrase "as the family goes, so goes the nation," I am not so doubtful about the phrase "as the family goes, so goes civil society."

FAMILY DECLINE AND TODAY'S POLICY DEBATE

What should be done to counteract or remedy the negative effects of family decline? This is the most controversial question of all, and the most difficult to answer.

The problems of purposive social action are enormous. In remedying the negative effects, it is never easy to avoid canceling out the positive benefits. Also, if family decline in fact stems from a broad cultural shift, it will not be easy to modify. The underlying trend may simply have to play itself out. It could be, of course, that the problems we are seeing result not from the intrinsic character of the cultural shift, but rather from its extreme rapidity. From this perspective, as the changes become complete and society settles down, we may be able to adjust without great difficulty to the new conditions.

Let us assume, however, that purposive social action is both called for and can have a useful outcome. Among the broad proposals for change that have been put forth, two extremes stand out prominently in the national debate: (1) a return to the structure of the traditional nuclear family characteristic of the 1950s and (2) the development of extensive governmental family policies.

Aside from the fact that it is probably impossible to return to a situation of an earlier time, the first alternative has major drawbacks. Such a shift would require many women to leave the work force and to some extent become "deliberated," an unlikely occurrence indeed. Economic conditions necessitate that even more women take jobs, and cultural conditions stress ever greater equality between the sexes.

In addition to such considerations, the traditional nuclear family form, in today's world, may be fundamentally flawed. As an indication of this, one should realize that the young people who led the transformation of the family during the 1960s and 1970s were brought up in 1950s families. If the 1950s families were so wonderful, why didn't their children seek to emulate them? In hindsight, the 1950s families seem to have been beset with problems that went well beyond patriarchy and separate spheres. For many families the mother–child unit had become increasingly isolated from the kin group, the neighborhood, and community, and even from the father, who worked a long distance away. This was especially true for women who were fully educated and eager to take their place in work and public life. Maternal child rearing under these historically unprecedented circumstances became highly problematic.[39]

Despite such difficulties, the traditional nuclear family is still the family of choice for millions of Americans. They are comfortable with it, and for them it seems to work. It is reasonable, therefore, at least not to place roadblocks in the way of couples with children who wish to conduct their lives according to the traditional family's dictates. Women who freely desire to spend much of their lives as mothers and housewives, outside the labor force, should not be economically penalized by public policy for making that choice. Nor should they be denigrated by our culture as second-class citizens.

The second major proposal for change that has been stressed in national debate is the development of extensive governmental programs offering monetary support and social services for families, especially for the new "nonnuclear" families. In some cases these programs assist with functions that families are unable to perform adequately; in other cases, the functions are taken over, transforming them from family to public responsibilities.

This is the path followed by the European welfare states, but it has been less accepted by the United States than by any other industrialized nation. The European welfare states have been far more successful than the United States in minimizing the negative economic impact of family decline on family members, especially children. In addition, many European nations have established policies making it much easier for women (and increasingly men) to combine work with child rearing.[40] With these successes in mind, it seems inevitable that the United States will (and I believe should) move gradually in the direction of European countries with respect to family policies, just as we are now moving gradually in that direction with respect to medical care.

There are clear drawbacks, however, in moving too far down this road. If children are to be best served, we should seek to make the family stronger, not to replace it. At the same time that welfare states are minimizing some of the consequences of family decline, they may also be causing further decline of the family unit. This phenomenon can be witnessed today in Sweden, where the institution of the family has probably grown weaker than anywhere else in the world.[41] On a lesser scale, the phenomenon has been seen in the United States in connection with our welfare programs. Fundamental to the success of welfare-state programs, therefore, is keeping the ultimate goal of strengthening families uppermost in mind.

A NEW SOCIAL MOVEMENT

Although each of the above alternatives has some merit, I suggest a third alternative, which is premised on the fact that we cannot return to the 1950s family, nor can we depend on the welfare state for a solution. Instead, we should strike at the heart of the cultural shift that has occurred, point up its negative aspects, and seek to reinvigorate the cultural ideals of "family," "parents," and "children" within the changed circumstances of our time. We should stress that the individualistic ethos has gone too far, that children are being woefully shortchanged, and that, in the long run, strong families represent the best path toward self-fulfillment and personal happiness. We should bring again to the cultural forefront the old ideal of parents living together and sharing responsibility for their children and for each other.

What is needed is a new social movement whose purpose is the promotion of families and family values within the new constraints of modern life. It should point out the supreme importance of strong families to society, while at the same time suggesting ways that the family can better adapt to the modern conditions of individualism, equality, and the labor force participation of both women and men. Such a movement could build on the fact that the overwhelming majority of young people today still put forth as their major life goal a lasting, monogamous, heterosexual relationship that includes the procreation of children. It is reasonable to suppose that this goal is so pervasive because it is based on a deep-seated human need.

The reassertion of this personal goal as a highly ranked cultural value is not a legislative alternative; politics necessarily must respond to the obvious diversity in American life. But it is an alternative ideally suited to the leadership of broad-based citizens' groups. The history of recent social movements in America provides good reason for hope that such an initiative can make an impact. Witness the recent cultural shifts toward female and minority-group equality and the current move toward environmental protection, each of which has been led by popular movements focusing on fundamental social values. The time seems ripe to reassert that strong families concerned with the needs of children are, under modern conditions, not only possible but necessary.

The Family, Kinship, and the Community

Reading 5   The Female World of Cards and Holidays: Women, Families, and the Work of Kinship[1]

MICAELA di LEONARDO*

Why is it that the married women of America are supposed to write all the letters and send all the cards to their husbands' families? My old man is a much better writer than I am, yet he expects me to correspond with his whole family. If I asked him to correspond with mine, he would blow a gasket. [LETTER TO ANN LANDERS]

Women's place in man's life cycle has been that of nurturer, caretaker, and helpmate, the weaver of those networks of relationships on which she in turn relies. [CAROL GILLIGAN, In a Different Voice][2]

Feminist scholars in the past fifteen years have made great strides in formulating new under-standings of the relations among gender, kinship, and the larger economy. As a result of this pioneering research, women are newly visible and audible, no longer submerged within their families. We see households as loci of political struggle, inseparable parts of the larger society and economy, rather than as havens from the heartless world of industrial capitalism.[3] And historical and cultural variations in kinship and family forms have become clearer with the maturation of feminist historical and social-scientific scholarship.

Two theoretical trends have been key to this reinterpretation of women's work and family domain. The first is the elevation to visibility of women's nonmarket activities—housework, child care, the servicing of men, and the care of the elderly—and the definition of all these activities as *labor*, to be enumerated alongside and

Many thanks to Cynthia Costello, Rayna Rapp, Roberta Spalter-Roth, John Willoughby, and Barbara Gelpi, Susan Johnson, and Sylvia Yanagisako of *Signs* for their help with this article. I wish in particular to acknowledge the influence of Rayna Rapp's work on my ideas.
*di Leonardo, Micaela. 1987. "The Female World of Cards and Holidays: Women, Families, and the Work of Kinship." *Signs: Journal of Woman in Culture and Society* (12:2):440–453. © 1987 by the University of Chicago. All rights reserved.

counted as part of overall social reproduction. The second theoretical trend is the nonpejorative focus on women's domestic or kin-centered networks. We now see them as the products of conscious strategy, as crucial to the functioning of kinship systems, as sources of women's autonomous power and possible primary sites of emotional fulfillment, and, at times, as the vehicles for actual survival and/or political resistance.[4]

Recently, however, a division has developed between feminist interpreters of the "labor" and the "network" perspectives on women's lives. Those who focus on women's work tend to envision women as sentient, goal-oriented actors, while those who concern themselves with women's ties to others tend to perceive women primarily in terms of nurturance, other-orientation—altruism. The most celebrated recent example of this division is the opposing testimony of historians Alice Kessler-Harris and Rosalind Rosenberg in the Equal Employment Opportunity Commission's sex discrimination case against Sears Roebuck and Company. Kessler-Harris argued that American women historically have actively sought higher-paying jobs and have been prevented from gaining them because of sex discrimination by employers. Rosenberg argued that American women in the nineteenth century created among themselves, through their domestic networks, a "women's culture" that emphasized the nurturance of children and others and the maintenance of family life and that discouraged women from competition over or heavy emotional investment in demanding, high-paid employment.[5]

I shall not here address this specific debate but, instead, shall consider its theoretical background and implications. I shall argue that we need to fuse, rather than to oppose, the domestic network and labor perspectives. In what follows, I introduce a new concept, the work of kinship, both to aid empirical feminist research on

women, work, and family and to help advance feminist theory in this arena. I believe that the boundary-crossing nature of the concept helps to confound the self-interest/altruism dichotomy, forcing us from an either-or stance to a position that includes both perspectives. I hope in this way to contribute to a more critical feminist vision of women's lives and the meaning of family in the industrial West.

In my recent field research among Italian-Americans in Northern California, I found myself considering the relations between women's kinship and economic lives. As an anthropologist, I was concerned with people's kin lives beyond conventional American nuclear family or household boundaries. To this end, I collected individual and family life histories, asking about all kin and close friends and their activities. I was also very interested in women's labor. As I sat with women and listened to their accounts of their past and present lives, I began to realize that they were involved in three types of work: housework and child care, work in the labor market, and the work of kinship.[6]

By kin work I refer to the conception, maintenance, and ritual celebration of cross-household kin ties, including visits, letters, telephone calls, presents, and cards to kin; the organization of holiday gatherings; the creation and maintenance of quasi-kin relations; decisions to neglect or to intensify particular ties; the mental work of reflection about all these activities; and the creation and communication of altering images of family and kin vis-à-vis the images of others, both folk and mass media. Kin work is a key element that has been missing in the synthesis of the "household labor" and "domestic network" perspectives. In our emphasis on individual women's responsibilities within households and on the job, we reflect the common picture of households as nuclear units, tied perhaps to the larger social and economic system, but not to *each other.* We miss the point of telephone and soft drink advertising, of women's magazines' holiday issues, of commentators' confused nostalgia for the mythical American extended family: it is kinship contact *across households,* as much as women's work within them, that fulfills our cultural expectation of satisfying family life.

Maintaining these contacts, this sense of family, takes time, intention, and skill. We tend to think of human social and kin networks as the epiphenomena of production and reproduction: the social traces created by our material lives. Or, in the neoclassical tradition, we see them as part of leisure activities, outside an economic purview except insofar as they involve consumption behavior. But the creation and maintenance of kin and quasi-kin networks in advanced industrial societies is *work;* and, moreover, it is largely women's work.

The kin-work lens brought into focus new perspectives on my informants' family lives. First, life histories revealed that often the very existence of kin contact and holiday celebration depended on the presence of an adult woman in the household. When couples divorced or mothers died, the work of kinship was left undone; when women entered into sanctioned sexual or marital relationships with men in these situations, they reconstituted the men's kinship networks and organized gatherings and holiday celebrations. Middle-aged businessman Al Bertini, for example, recalled the death of his mother in his early adolescence: "I think that's probably one of the biggest losses in losing a family—yeah, I remember as a child when my Mom was alive . . . the holidays were treated with enthusiasm and love . . . after she died the attempt was there but it just didn't materialize." Later in life, when Al Bertini and his wife separated, his own and his son Jim's participation in extended-family contact decreased rapidly. But when Jim began a relationship with Jane Bateman, she and he moved in with Al, and Jim and Jane began to invite his kin over for holidays. Jane single-handedly planned and cooked the holiday feasts.

Kin work, then, is like housework and child care: men in the aggregate do not do it. It differs from these forms of labor in that it is harder for men to substitute hired labor to accomplish these tasks in the absence of kinswomen. Second, I found that women, as the workers in this arena, generally had much greater kin knowledge than did their husbands, often including more accurate and extensive knowledge of their husbands' families. This was true both of middle-aged and younger couples and surfaced as a phenomenon in my interviews in the form of humorous arguments and in wives' detailed additions to husbands' narratives. Nick Meraviglia, a middle-aged professional, discussed his Italian antecedents in the presence of his wife, Pina:

> *Nick:* My grandfather was a very outspoken man, and it was reported he took off for the hills when he found out that Mussolini was in power.
> *Pina:* And he was a very tall man; he used to have to bow his head to get inside doors.
> *Nick:* No, that was my uncle.
> *Pina:* Your grandfather too, I've heard your mother say.
> *Nick:* My mother has a sister and a brother.
> *Pina:* Two *sisters!*
> *Nick:* You're right!
> *Pina:* Maria and Angelina.

Women were also much more willing to discuss family feuds and crises and their own roles in them; men tended to repeat formulaic statements asserting family unity and respectability. (This was much less true for younger men.) Joe and Cetta Longhinotti's statements illustrate these tendencies. Joe responded to my question about kin relations: "We all get along. As a rule, relatives, you got nothing but trouble." Cetta, instead, discussed her relations with each of her grown children, their wives, her in-laws, and her own blood kin in detail. She did not hide the fact that relations were strained in several cases; she was eager to discuss the evolution of problems and to seek my opinions of her actions. Similarly, Pina Meraviglia told the following story of her fight with one of her brothers with hysterical laughter: "There was some biting and hair pulling and choking . . . it was terrible! I shouldn't even tell you. . . ." Nick, meanwhile, was concerned about maintaining an image of family unity and respectability.

Also, men waxed fluent while women were quite inarticulate in discussing their past and present occupations. When asked about their work lives, Joe Longhinotti and Nick Meraviglia, union baker and professional, respectively, gave detailed narratives of their work careers. Cetta Longhinotti and Pina Meraviglia, clerical and former clerical, respectively, offered only short descriptions focusing on factors of ambience, such as the "lovely things" sold by Cetta's firm.

These patterns are not repeated in the younger generation, especially among younger women, such as Jane Bateman, who have managed to acquire training and jobs with some prospect of mobility. These younger women, though, have *added* a professional and detailed interest in their jobs to a felt responsibility for the work of kinship.[7]

Although men rarely took on any kin-work tasks, family histories and accounts of contemporary life revealed that kinswoman often negotiated among themselves, alternating hosting, food-preparation, and gift-buying responsibilities—or

sometimes ceding entire task clusters to one woman. Taking on or ceding tasks was clearly related to acquiring or divesting oneself of power within kin networks, but women varied in their interpretation of the meaning of this power. Cetta Longhinotti, for example, relied on the "family Christmas dinner" as a symbol of her central kinship role and was involved in painful negotiations with her daughter-in-law over the issue: "Last year she insisted—this is touchy. She doesn't want to spend the holiday dinner together. So last year we went there. But I still had my dinner the next day . . . I made a big dinner on Christmas Day, regardless of who's coming—candles on the table, the whole routine. I decorate the house myself too . . . well, I just feel that the time will come when maybe I won't feel like cooking a big dinner—she should take advantage of the fact that I feel like doing it now." Pina Meraviglia, in contrast, was saddened by the centripetal force of the developmental cycle but was unworried about the power dynamics involved in her negotiations with daughters- and mother-in-law over holiday celebrations.

Kin work is not just a matter of power among women but also of the mediation of power represented by household units.[8] Women often choose to minimize status claims in their kin work and to include numbers of households under the rubric of family. Cetta Longhinotti's sister Anna, for example, is married to a professional man whose parents have considerable economic resources, while Joe and Cetta have low incomes and no other well-off kin. Cetta and Anna remain close, talk on the phone several times a week, and assist their adult children, divided by distance and economic status, in remaining united as cousins.

Finally, women perceived housework, child care, market labor, the care of the elderly, and the work of kinship as competing responsibilities. Kin work was a unique category, however, because it was unlabeled and because women felt they could either cede some tasks to kinswoman and/or could cut them back severely. Women variously cited the pressures of market labor, the needs of the elderly, and their own desires for freedom and job enrichment as reasons for cutting back Christmas card lists, organized holiday gatherings, multifamily dinners, letters, visits, and phone calls. They expressed guilt and defensiveness about this cutback process and, particularly, about their failures to keep families close through constant contact and about their failures to create perfect holiday celebrations. Cetta Longhinotti, during the period when she was visiting her elderly mother every weekend in addition to working a full-time job, said of her grown children, "I'd have the whole gang here once a month, but I've been so busy that I haven't done that for about six months." And Pina Meriviglia lamented her insufficient work on family Christmases, "I wish I had really made it traditional . . . like my sister-in-law has special stories."

Kin work, then, takes place in an arena characterized simultaneously by cooperation and competition, by guilt and gratification. Like housework and child care, it is women's work, with the same lack of clear-cut agreement concerning its proper components: How often should sheets be changed? When should children be toilet trained? Should an aunt send a niece a birthday present? Unlike housework and child care, however, kin work, taking place across the boundaries of normative households, is as yet unlabeled and has no retinue of experts prescribing its correct forms. Neither home economists nor child psychologists have much to say about nieces' birthday presents. Kin work is thus more easily cut back without social interference. On the other hand, the results of kin work—frequent kin contact and feelings of intimacy—are the subject of considerable cultural manipulation as

indicators of family happiness. Thus, women in general are subject to the guilt my informants expressed over cutting back kin-work activities.

Although many of my informants referred to the results of women's kin work—cross-household kin contacts and attendant ritual gatherings—as particularly Italian-American, I suggest that in fact this phenomenon is broadly characteristic of American kinship. We think of kin-work tasks such as the preparation of ritual feasts, responsibility for holiday card lists, and gift buying as extensions of women's domestic responsibilities for cooking, consumption, and nurturance. American men in general do not take on these tasks any more than they do housework and child care—and probably less, as these tasks have not yet been the subject of intense public debate. And my informants' gender breakdown in relative articulateness on kinship and workplace themes reflects the still prevalent occupational segregation—most women cannot find jobs that provide enough pay, status, or promotion possibilities to make them worth focusing on—as well as women's perceived power within kinship networks. The common recognition of that power is reflected in Selma Greenberg's book on nonsexist child rearing. Greenberg calls mothers "press agents" who sponsor relations between their own children and other relatives; she advises a mother whose relatives treat her disrespectfully to deny those kin access to her children.[9]

Kin work is a salient concept in other parts of the developed world as well. Larissa Adler Lomnitz and Marisol Pérez Lizaur have found that "centralizing women" are responsible for these tasks and for communicating "family ideology" among upper-class families in Mexico City. Matthews Hamabata, in his study of upper-class families in Japan, has found that women's kin work involves key financial transactions. Sylvia Junko Yanagisako discovered that, among rural Japanese migrants to the United States, the maintenance of kin networks was assigned to women as the migrants adopted the American ideology of the independent nuclear family household. Maila Stivens notes that urban Australian housewives' kin ties and kin ideology "transcend women's isolation in domestic units."[10]

This is not to say that cultural conceptions of appropriate kin work do not vary, even within the United States. Carol B. Stack documents institutionalized fictive kinship and concomitant reciprocity networks among impoverished black American women. Women in populations characterized by intense feelings of ethnic identity may feel bound to emphasize particular occasions— Saint Patrick's or Columbus Day—with organized family feasts. These constructs may be mediated by religious affiliation, as in the differing emphases on Friday or Sunday family dinners among Jews and Christians. Thus the personnel involved and the amount and kind of labor considered necessary for the satisfactory performance of particular kin-work tasks are likely to be culturally constructed.[11] But while the kin and quasi-kin universes and the ritual calendar may vary among women according to race or ethnicity, their general responsibility for maintaining kin links and ritual observances does not.

As kin work is not an ethnic or racial phenomenon, neither is it linked only to one social class. Some commentators on American family life still reflect the influence of work done in England in the 1950s and 1960s (by Elizabeth Bott and by Peter Willmott and Michael Young) in their assumption that working-class families are close and extended, while the middle class substitutes friends (or anomie) for family. Others reflect the prevalent family pessimism in their presumption that neither working- nor middle-class families have extended kin contact.[12] Insofar as kin contact depends on residential proxim-

ity, the larger economy's shifts will influence particular groups' experiences. Factory workers, close to kin or not, are likely to disperse when plants shut down or relocate. Small businesspeople or independent professionals may, however, remain resident in particular areas—and thus maintain proximity to kin—for generations, while professional employees of large firms relocate at their firms' behest. This pattern obtained among my informants.

In any event, cross-household kin contact can be and is effected at long distance through letters, cards, phone calls, and holiday and vacation visits. The form and functions of contact, however, vary according to economic resources. Stack and Brett Williams offer rich accounts of kin networks among poor blacks and migrant Chicano farmworkers functioning to provide emotional support, labor, commodity, and cash exchange—a funeral visit, help with laundry, the gift of a dress or piece of furniture.[13] Far different in degree are exchanges such as the loan of a vacation home, multifamily boating trip, or the provision of free professional services—examples from the kin networks of my wealthier informants. The point is that households, as labor- and income-pooling units, whatever their relative wealth, are somewhat porous in relation to others with those whose members they share kin or quasi-kin ties. We do not really know how class differences operate in this realm; it is possible that they do so largely in terms of ideology. It may be, as David Schneider and Raymond T. Smith suggest, that the affluent and the very poor are more open in recognizing necessary economic ties to kin than are those who identify themselves as middle class.[14]

Recognizing that kin work is gender rather than class based allows us to see women's kin networks among all groups, not just among working-class and impoverished women in industrialized societies. This recognition in turn clarifies our understanding of the privileges and limits of women's varying access to economic resources. Affluent women can "buy out" of housework, child care—and even some kin-work responsibilities. But they, like all women, are ultimately responsible, and subject to both guilt and blame, as the administrators of home, children, and kin network. Even the wealthiest women must negotiate the timing and venue of holidays and other family rituals with their kinswoman. It may be that kin work is the core women's work category in which all women cooperate, while women's perceptions of the appropriateness of cooperation for housework, child care, and the care of the elderly varies by race, class, region, and generation.

But kin work is not necessarily an appropriate category of labor, much less gendered labor, in all societies. In many small-scale societies, kinship is the major organizing principle of all social life, and all contacts are by definition kin contacts.[15] One cannot, therefore, speak of labor that does not involve kin. In the United States, kin work as a separable category of gendered labor perhaps arose historically in concert with the ideological and material constructs of the moral mother/cult of domesticity and the privatized family during the course of industrialization in the eighteenth and nineteenth centuries. These phenomena are connected to the increase in the ubiquity of productive occupations *for men* that are not organized through kinship. This includes the demise of the family farm with the capitalization of agriculture and rural-urban migration; the decline of family recruitment in factories as firms grew, ended child labor, and began to assert bureaucratized forms of control; the decline of artisanal labor and of small entrepreneurial enterprises as large firms took greater and greater shares of the commodity market; the decline of the family firm as corporations—and their managerial work forces—grew beyond the capacities

of individual families to provision them; and, finally, the rise of civil service bureaucracies and public pressure against nepotism.[16]

As men increasingly worked alongside of non-kin, and as the ideology of separate spheres was increasingly accepted, perhaps the responsibility for kin maintenance, like that for child rearing, became gender-focused. Ryan points out that "built into the updated family economy ... was a new measure of voluntarism." This voluntarism, though, "perceived as the shift from patriarchal authority to domestic affection," also signaled the rise of women's moral responsibility for family life. Just as the "idea of fatherhood itself seemed almost to wither away" so did male involvement in the responsibility for kindred lapse.[17]

With postbellum economic growth and geographic movement women's new kin burden involved increasing amounts of time and labor. The ubiquity of lengthy visits and of frequent letter-writing among nineteenth-century women attests to this. And for visitors and for those who were residentially proximate, the continuing commonalities of women's domestic labor allowed for kinds of work sharing—nursing, childkeeping, cooking, cleaning—that men, with their increasingly differentiated and controlled activities, probably could not maintain. This is not to say that some kin-related male productive work did not continue; my own data, for instance, show kin involvement among small businessmen in the present. It is, instead, to suggest a general trend in material life and a cultural shift that influenced even those whose productive and kin lives remained commingled. Yanagisako has distinguished between the realms of domestic and public kinship in order to draw attention to anthropology's relatively "thin descriptions" of the domestic (female) domain. Using her typology, we might say that kin work as gendered labor comes into existence within the domestic domain with the relative erasure of the domain of public, male kinship.[18]

Whether or not this proposed historical model bears up under further research, the question remains, Why do women do kin work? However material factors may shape activities, they do not determine how individuals may perceive them. And in considering issues of motivation, of intention, of the cultural construction of kin work, we return to the altruism versus self-interest dichotomy in recent feminist theory. Consider the epigraphs to this article. Are women kin workers the nurturant weavers of the Gilligan quotation, or victims, like the fed-up woman who writes to complain to Ann Landers? That is, are we to see kin work as yet another example of "women's culture" that takes the care of others as its primary desideratum? Or are we to see kin work as another way in which men, the economy, and the state extract labor from women without a fair return? And how do women themselves see their kin work and its place in their lives?

As I have indicated above, I believe that it is the creation of the self-interest/altruism dichotomy that is itself the problem here. My women informants, like most American women, accepted their primary responsibility for housework and the care of dependent children. Despite two major waves of feminist activism in this century, the gendering of certain categories of unpaid labor is still largely unaltered. These work responsibilities clearly interfere with some women's labor force commitments at certain life-cycle stages; but, more important, women are simply discriminated against in the labor market and rarely are able to achieve wage and status parity with men of the same age, race, class, and educational background.[19]

Thus for my women informants, as for most American women, the domestic domain is not only an arena in which much unpaid labor must be undertaken but also a realm in which one may attempt to gain human satisfactions—and power—not available in the labor market. Anthropologists Jane Collier and Louise Lamphere have written compellingly on the ways in which varying kinship and economic structures may shape women's competition or cooperation with one another in domestic domains.[20] Feminists considering Western women and families have looked at the issue of power primarily in terms of husband-wife relations or psychological relations between parents and children. If we adopt Collier and Lamphere's broader canvas, though, we see that kin work is not only women's labor from which men and children benefit but also labor that women undertake in order to create obligations in men and children and to gain power over one another. Thus Cetta Longhinotti's struggle with her daughter-in-law over the venue of Christmas dinner is not just about a competition over altruism, it is also about the creation of future obligations. And thus Cetta's and Anna's sponsorship of their children's friendship with each other is both an act of nurturance and a cooperative means of gaining power over those children.

Although this was not a clear-cut distinction, those of my informants who were more explicitly antifeminist tended to be most invested in kin work. Given the overwhelming historical shift toward greater autonomy for younger generations and the withering of children's financial and labor obligations to their parents, this investment was in most cases tragically doomed. Cetta Longhinotti, for example, had repaid her own mother's devotion with extensive home nursing during the mother's last years. Given Cetta's general failure to direct her adult children in work, marital choice, religious worship, or even frequency of visits, she is unlikely to receive such care from them when she is older.

The kin-work lens thus reveals the close relations between altruism and self-interest in women's actions. As economists Nancy Folbre and Heidi Hartmann point out, we have inherited a Western intellectual tradition that both dichotomizes the domestic and public domains and associates them on exclusive axes such that we find it difficult to see self-interest in the home and altruism in the workplace.[21] But why, in fact, have women fought for better jobs if not, in part, to support their children? These dichotomies are Procrustean beds that warp our understanding of women's lives both at home and at work. "Altruism" and "self-interest" are cultural constructions that are not necessarily mutually exclusive, and we forget this to our peril.

The concept of kin work helps to bring into focus a heretofore unacknowledged array of tasks that is culturally assigned to women in industrialized societies. At the same time, this concept, embodying notions of both love and work and crossing the boundaries of households, helps us to reflect on current feminist debates on women's work, family, and community. We newly see both the interrelations of these phenomena and women's roles in creating and maintaining those interrelations. Revealing the actual labor embodied in what we culturally conceive as love and considering the political uses of this labor helps to deconstruct the self-interest/altruism dichotomy and to connect more closely women's domestic and labor-force lives.

The true value of the concept, however, remains to be tested through further historical and contemporary research on gender, kinship, and labor. We need to assess the suggestion that gendered kin work emerges in concert with the capitalist development process; to probe the historical record for women's and men's varying and changing conceptions of it; and to research the current range of its cultural constructions and material realities. We know that household boundaries are more porous than we had thought—but they are undoubtedly differentially porous, and this is what we need to specify. We need, in particular, to assess the relations of changing labor processes, residential patterns, and the use of technology to changing kin work.

Altering the values attached to this particular set of women's tasks will be as difficult as are the housework, child-care, and occupational-segregation struggles. But just as feminist research in these latter areas is complementary and cumulative, so researching kin work should help us to piece together the home, work, and public-life landscape—to see the female world of cards and holidays as it is constructed and lived within the changing political economy. How female that world is to remain, and what it would look like if it were not sex-segregated, are questions we cannot yet answer.

Reading 6   Mexican American Women Grassroots Community Activists: "Mothers of East Los Angeles"*

MARY PARDO

The relatively few studies of Chicana political activism show a bias in the way political activism is conceptualized by social scientists, who often use a narrow definition confined to electoral politics.[1] Most feminist research uses an expanded definition that moves across the boundaries between public, electoral politics and private, family politics; but feminist research generally focuses on women mobilized around gender-specific issues.[2] For some feminists, adherence to "tradition" constitutes conservatism and submission to patriarchy. Both approaches exclude the contributions of working-class women, particularly those of Afro-American women and Latinas, thus failing to capture the full dynamic of social change.[3]

The following case study of Mexican American women activists in "Mothers of East Los Angeles" (MELA) contributes another dimension to the conception of grassroots politics. It illustrates how these Mexican American women transform "traditional" networks and resources based on family and culture into political assets to defend the quality of urban life. Far from unique, these patterns of activism are repeated in Latin America and elsewhere. Here as in other times and places, the women's activism arises out of seemingly "traditional" roles, addresses wider social and political issues, and capitalizes on informal associations sanctioned by the community.[4] Religion, commonly viewed as a conservative force, is intertwined with politics.[5] Often, women speak of their communities and their activism as extensions of their family and household responsibility. The central role of women in grassroots struggles around quality of life, in the Third World and in the United States, challenges conventional assumptions about the powerlessness of women and static definitions of culture and tradition.

In general, the women in MELA are long-time residents of East Los Angeles; some are bilingual and native born, others Mexican born and Spanish dominant. All the core activists are bilingual and have lived in the community over thirty years. All have been active in parish-sponsored groups and activities; some have had experience working in community-based groups arising from schools, neighborhood watch associations, and labor support groups. To gain an appreciation of the group and the core activists, I used ethnographic field methods. I interviewed

*Pardo, Mary. 1990. "Mexican American Women Grassroots Community Activists: 'Mothers of East Los Angeles.'" *Frontiers* 11 (1):1–7. FRONTIERS Editorial Collective. Reprinted by permission.

six women, using a life history approach focused on their first community activities, current activism, household and family responsibilities, and perceptions of community issues.[6] Also, from December 1987 through October 1989, I attended hearings on the two currently pending projects of contention—a proposed state prison and a toxic waste incinerator—and participated in community and organizational meetings and demonstrations. The following discussion briefly chronicles an intense and significant five-year segment of community history from which emerged MELA and the women's transformation of "traditional" resources and experiences into political assets for community mobilization.[7]

THE COMMUNITY CONTEXT: EAST LOS ANGELES RESISTING SIEGE

Political science theory often guides the political strategies used by local government to select the sites for undesirable projects. In 1984, the state of California commissioned a public relations firm to assess the political difficulties facing the construction of energy-producing waste incinerators. The report provided a "personality profile" of those residents most likely to organize effective opposition to projects:

> *middle and upper socioeconomic strata possess better resources to effectuate their opposition. Middle and higher socioeconomic strata neighborhoods should not fall within the one-mile and five-mile radii of the proposed site. Conversely, older people, people with a high school education or less are least likely to oppose a facility.[8]*

The state accordingly placed the plant in Commerce, a predominantly Mexican American,

low-income community. This pattern holds throughout the state and the country: three out of five Afro-Americans and Latinos live near toxic waste sites, and three of the five largest hazardous waste landfills are in communities with at least 80 percent minority populations.[9]

Similarly, in March 1985, when the state sought a site for the first state prison in Los Angeles County, Governor Deukmejian resolved to place the 1,700-inmate institution in East Los Angeles, within a mile of the long-established Boyle Heights neighborhood and within two miles of thirty-four schools. Furthermore, violating convention, the state bid on the expensive parcel of industrially zoned land without compiling an environmental impact report or providing a public community hearing. According to James Vigil, Jr., a field representative for Assemblywoman Gloria Molina, shortly after the state announced the site selection, Molina's office began informing the community and gauging residents' sentiments about it through direct mailings and calls to leaders of organizations and business groups.

In spring 1986, after much pressure from the 56th assembly district office and the community, the Department of Corrections agreed to hold a public information meeting, which was attended by over 700 Boyle Heights residents. From this moment on, Vigil observed, "the tables turned, the community mobilized, and the residents began calling the political representatives and requesting their presence at hearings and meetings."[10] By summer 1986, the community was well aware of the prison site proposal. Over two thousand people, carrying placards proclaiming "No Prison in ELA," marched from Resurrection Church in Boyle Heights to the 3rd Street bridge linking East Los Angeles with the rapidly expanding downtown Los Angeles.[11] This march marked the beginning of one of the largest grassroots coalitions to emerge from the Latino community in the last decade.

Prominent among the coalition's groups is "Mothers of East Los Angeles," a loosely knit group of over 400 Mexican American women.[12] MELA initially coalesced to oppose the state prison construction but has since organized opposition to several other projects detrimental to the quality of life in the central city.[13] Its second large target is a toxic waste incinerator proposed for Vernon, a small city adjacent to East Los Angeles. This incinerator would worsen the already debilitating air quality of the entire county and set a precedent dangerous for other communities throughout California.[14] When MELA took up the fight against the toxic waste incinerator it became more than a single-issue group and began working with environmental groups around the state.[15] As a result of the community struggle, AB58 (Roybal-Allard), which provides all Californians with the minimum protection of an environmental impact report before the construction of hazardous waste incinerators, was signed into law. But the law's effectiveness relies on a watchful community network. Since its emergence, "Mothers of East Los Angeles" has become centrally important to just such a network of grassroots activists including a select number of Catholic priests and two Mexican American political representatives. Furthermore, the group's very formation, and its continued spirit and activism, fly in the face of the conventional political science beliefs regarding political participation.

Predictions by the "experts" attribute the low formal political participation (i.e., voting) of Mexican American people in the U.S. to a set of cultural "retardants" including primary kinship systems, fatalism, religious traditionalism, traditional cultural values, and mother country attachments.[16] The core activists in MELA may appear to fit this description, as well as the state-commissioned profile of residents least likely to oppose toxic waste incinerator projects. All the women live in a low-income community. Furthermore, they identify themselves as active and committed participants in the Catholic Church; they claim an ethnic identity—Mexican American; their ages range from forty to sixty; and they have attained at most high school educations. However, these women fail to conform to the predicted political apathy. Instead, they have transformed social identity—ethnic identity, class identity, and gender identity—into an impetus as well as a basis for activism. And, in transforming their existing social networks into grassroots political networks, they have also transformed themselves.

TRANSFORMATION AS A DOMINANT THEME

From the life histories of the group's core activists and from my own field notes, I have selected excerpts that tell two representative stories. One is a narrative of the events that led to community mobilization in East Los Angeles. The other is a story of transformation, the process of creating new and better relationships that empower people to unite and achieve common goals.[17]

First, women have transformed organizing experiences and social networks arising from gender-related responsibilities into political resources.[18] When I asked the women about the first community, not necessarily "political," involvement they could recall, they discussed experiences that predated the formation of MELA. Juana Gutiérrez explained:

Well, it didn't start with the prison, you know. It started when my kids went to school. I started by joining the Parents Club and we worked on different problems here in the area. Like the people who come to the parks to sell drugs to the kids. I got the neighbors to have meetings. I would go knock at the doors, house to house. And I told them that we should stick together with the Neighborhood Watch for the community and for the kids.[19]

Erlinda Robles similarly recalled:

I wanted my kids to go to Catholic school and from the time my oldest one went there, I was there every day. I used to take my two little ones with me and I helped one way or another. I used to question things they did. And the other mothers would just watch me. Later, they would ask me, "Why do you do that? They are going to take it out on your kids." I'd say, "They better not." And before you knew it, we had a big group of mothers that were very involved.[20]

Part of a mother's "traditional" responsibility includes overseeing her child's progress in school, interacting with school staff, and supporting school activities. In these processes, women meet other mothers and begin developing a network of acquaintanceships and friendships based on mutual concern for the welfare of their children.

Although the women in MELA carried the greatest burden of participating in school activities, Erlinda Robles also spoke of strategies they used to draw men into the enterprise and into the networks:[21]

At the beginning, the priests used to say who the president of the mothers guild would be; they used to pick

'um. But, we wanted elections, so we got elections. Then we wanted the fathers to be involved, and the nuns suggested that a father should be president and a mother would be secretary or be involved there [at the school site].[22]

Of course, this comment piqued my curiosity, so I asked how the mothers agreed on the nuns' suggestion. The answer was simple and instructive:

At the time we thought it was a "natural" way to get the fathers involved because they weren't involved; it was just the mothers. Everybody [the women] agreed on them [the fathers] being president because they worked all day and they couldn't be involved in a lot of daily activities like food sales and whatever. During the week, a steering committee of mothers planned the group's activities. But now that I think about it, a woman could have done the job just as well![23]

So women got men into the group by giving them a position they could manage. The men may have held the title of "president," but they were not making day-to-day decisions about work, nor were they dictating the direction of the group. Erlinda Robles laughed as she recalled an occasion when the president insisted, against the wishes of the women, on scheduling a parents' group fundraiser—a breakfast—on Mother's Day. On that morning, only the president and his wife were present to prepare breakfast. This should alert researchers against measuring power and influence by looking solely at who holds titles.

Each of the cofounders had a history of working with groups arising out of the responsibilities usually assumed by "mothers"—the education of children and the safety of the surrounding community. From these groups, they gained valuable experiences and networks that facilitated the formation of "Mothers of East Los Angeles." Juana Gutiérrez explained how preexisting networks progressively expanded community support:

> You know nobody knew about the plan to build a prison in this community until Assemblywoman Gloria Molina told me. Martha Molina called me and said, "You know what is happening in your area? The governor wants to put a prison in Boyle Heights!" So, I called a Neighborhood Watch meeting at my house and we got fifteen people together. Then, Father John started informing his people at the Church and that is when the group of two to three hundred started showing up for every march on the bridge.[24]

MELA effectively linked up preexisting networks into a viable grassroots coalition.

Second, the process of activism also transformed previously "invisible" women, making them not only visible but the center of public attention. From a conventional perspective, political activism assumes a kind of gender neutrality. This means that anyone can participate, but men are the expected key actors. In accordance with this pattern, in winter 1986 an informal group of concerned businessmen in the community began lobbying and testifying against the prison at hearings in Sacramento. Working in conjunction with Assemblywoman Molina, they made many trips to Sacramento at their own expense. Residents who did not have the income to travel were unable to join them. Finally, Molina, commonly recognized as a forceful advocate for Latinas and the community, asked Frank Villalobos, an urban planner in the group, why there were no women coming up to speak in Sacramento against the prison. As he phrased it, "I was getting some heat from her because no women were going up there."[25]

In response to this comment, Veronica Gutiérrez, a law student who lived in the community, agreed to accompany him on the next trip to Sacramento.[26] He also mentioned the comment to Father John Moretta at Resurrection Catholic Parish. Meanwhile, representatives of the business sector of the community and of the 56th assembly district office were continuing to compile arguments and supportive data against the East Los Angeles prison site. Frank Villalobos stated one of the pressing problems:

> We felt that the Senators whom we prepared all this for didn't even acknowledge that we existed. They kept calling it the "downtown" site, and they argued that there was no opposition in the community. So, I told Father Moretta, what we have to do is demonstrate that there is a link (proximity) between the Boyle Heights community and the prison.[27]

The next juncture illustrates how perceptions of gender-specific behavior set in motion a sequence of events that brought women into the political limelight. Father Moretta decided to ask all the women to meet after mass. He told them about the prison site and called for their support. When I asked him about his rationale for selecting the women, he replied:

I felt so strongly about the issue, and I knew in my heart what a terrible offense this was to the people. So, I was afraid that once we got into a demonstration situation we had to be very careful. I thought the women would be cooler and calmer than the men. The bottom line is that the men came anyway. The first times out the majority were women. Then they began to invite their husbands and their children, but originally it was just women.[28]

Father Moretta also named the group. Quite moved by a film, *The Official Story,* about the courageous Argentine women who demonstrated for the return of their children who disappeared during a repressive right-wing military dictatorship, he transformed the name "Las Madres de la Plaza de Mayo" into "Mothers of East Los Angeles."[29]

However, Aurora Castillo, one of the cofounders of the group, modified my emphasis on the predominance of women:

Of course the fathers work. We also have many, many grandmothers. And all this is with the support of the fathers. They make the placards and the posters; they do the security and carry the signs; and they come to the marches when they can.[30]

Although women played a key role in the mobilization, they emphasized the group's broad base of active supporters as well as the other organizations in the "Coalition Against the Prison." Their intent was to counter any notion that MELA was composed exclusively of women or mothers and to stress the "inclusiveness" of the group. All the women who assumed lead roles in the group had long histories of volunteer work in the Boyle Heights community; but formation of the group brought them out of the "private" margins and into "public" light.

Third, the women in "Mothers of East L.A." have transformed the definition of "mother" to include militant political opposition to state-proposed projects they see as adverse to the quality of life in the community. Explaining how she discovered the issue, Aurora Castillo said,

You know if one of your children's safety is jeopardized, the mother turns into a lioness. That's why Father John got the mothers. We have to have a well-organized, strong group of mothers to protect the community and oppose things that are detrimental to us. You know the governor is in the wrong and the mothers are in the right. After all, the mothers have to be right. Mothers are for the children's interest, not for self-interest; the governor is for his own political interest.[31]

The women also have expanded the boundaries of "motherhood" to include social and political community activism and redefined the word to include women who are not biological "mothers." At one meeting a young Latina expressed her solidarity with the group and, almost apologetically, qualified herself as a "resident," not a "mother," of East Los Angeles. Erlinda Robles replied:

When you are fighting for a better life for children and "doing" for them, isn't that what mothers do? So we're all mothers. You don't have to have children to be a "mother."[32]

At critical points, grassroots community activism requires attending many meetings, phone calling, and door-to-door communications—all very labor-intensive work. In order to keep harmony in the "domestic" sphere, the core activists must creatively integrate family members into their community activities. I asked Erlinda Robles how her husband felt about her activism, and she replied quite openly:

> My husband doesn't like getting involved, but he takes me because he knows I like it. Sometimes we would have two or three meetings a week. And my husband would say, "Why are you doing so much? It is really getting out of hand." But he is very supportive. Once he gets there, he enjoys it and he starts in arguing too! See, it's just that he is not used to it. He couldn't believe things happened the way that they do. He was in the Navy twenty years and they brainwashed him that none of the politicians could do wrong. So he has come a long way. Now he comes home and parks the car out front and asks me, "Well, where are we going tonight?"[33]

When women explain their activism, they link family and community as one entity. Juana Gutiérrez, a woman with extensive experience working on community and neighborhood issues, stated:

> Yo como madre de familia, y como residente del Este de Los Angeles, seguiré luchando sin descanso por que se nos respete. Y yo lo hago con bastante cariño hacia mi comunidad. Digo "mi comunidad,"

> porque me siento parte de ella, quiero a mi raza como parte de mi familia, y si Dios me permite seguiré luchando contra todos los gobernadores que quieran abusar de nosotros. (As a mother and a resident of East L.A., I shall continue fighting tirelessly, so we will be respected. And I will do this with much affection for my community. I say "my community" because I am part of it. I love my "raza" [race] as part of my family; and if God allows, I will keep on fighting against all the governors that want to take advantage of us.)[34]

Like the other activists, she has expanded her responsibilities and legitimated militant opposition to abuse of the community by representatives of the state.

Working-class women activists seldom opt to separate themselves from men and their families. In this particular struggle for community quality of life, they are fighting for the family unit and thus are not competitive with men.[35] Of course, this fact does not preclude different alignments in other contexts and situations.[36]

Fourth, the story of MELA also shows the transformation of class and ethnic identity. Aurora Castillo told of an incident that illustrated her growing knowledge of the relationship of East Los Angeles to other communities and the basis necessary for coalition building:

> And do you know we have been approached by other groups? [She lowers her voice in emphasis.] You know that Pacific Palisades group asked for our backing. But what they did, they sent their powerful lobbyist that they pay thousands of dollars to

get our support against the drilling in Pacific Palisades. So what we did was tell them to send their grassroots people, not their lobbyist. We're suspicious. We don't want to talk to a high-salaried lobbyist; we are humble people. We did our own lobbying. In one week we went to Sacramento twice.[37]

The contrast between the often tedious and labor-intensive work of mobilizing people at the "grassroots" level and the paid work of a "high salaried lobbyist" represents a point of pride and integrity, not a deficiency or a source of shame. If the two groups were to construct a coalition, they must communicate on equal terms.

The women of MELA combine a willingness to assert opposition with a critical assessment of their own weaknesses. At one community meeting, for example, representatives of several oil companies attempted to gain support for placement of an oil pipeline through the center of East Los Angeles. The exchange between the women in the audience and the oil representative was heated, as women alternated asking questions about the chosen route for the pipeline:

"Is it going through Cielito Lindo [Reagan's ranch]?" The oil representative answered, "No." Another woman stood up and asked, "Why not place it along the coastline?" Without thinking of the implications, the representative responded, "Oh, no! If it burst, it would endanger the marine life." The woman retorted, "You value the marine life more than human beings?" His face reddened with anger and the hearing disintegrated into angry chanting.[38]

The proposal was quickly defeated. But Aurora Castillo acknowledged that it was not solely their opposition that brought about the defeat:

We won because the westside was opposed to it, so we united with them. You know there are a lot of attorneys who live there and they also questioned the representative. Believe me, no way is justice blind.... We just don't want all this garbage thrown at us because we are low-income and Mexican American. We are lucky now that we have good representatives, which we didn't have before.[39]

Throughout their life histories, the women refer to the disruptive effects of land use decisions made in the 1950s. As longtime residents, all but one share the experience of losing a home and relocating to make way for a freeway. Juana Gutiérrez refers to the community response at that time:

Una de las cosas que me caen muy mal es la injusticia y en nuestra comunidad hemos visto mucho de eso. Sobre todo antes, porque creo que nuestra gente estaba mas dormida, nos atrevíamos menos. En los cincuentas hicieron los freeways y así, sin más, nos dieron la noticia de que nos teníamos que mudar. Y eso pasó dos veces. La gente se conformaba porque lo ordeno el gobierno. Recuerdo que yo me enojaba y quería que los demás me secundaran, pero nadia quería hacer nada. (One of the things that really upsets me is the injustice that we see so much in our community. Above everything else, I believe that our people were less aware; we were less challenging. In the 1950s—they made the freeways and just like that they gave us a notice that we had to move. That happened twice. The people accepted it because the government ordered it. I remember that I was angry and wanted the others to back me but nobody else wanted to do anything.)[40]

The freeways that cut through communities and disrupted neighborhoods are now a concrete reminder of shared injustice, of the vulnerability of the community in the 1950s. The community's social and political history thus informs perceptions of its current predicament; however, today's activists emphasize not the powerlessness of the community but the change in status and progression toward political empowerment.

Fifth, the core activists typically tell stories illustrating personal change and a new sense of entitlement to speak for the community. They have transformed the unspoken sentiments of individuals into a collective community voice. Lucy Ramos related her initial apprehensions:

I was afraid to get involved. I didn't know what was going to come out of this and I hesitated at first. Right after we started, Father John came up to me and told me, "I want you to be a spokesperson." I said, "Oh no, I don't know what I am going to say." I was nervous. I am surprised I didn't have a nervous breakdown then. Every time we used to get in front of the TV cameras and even interviews like this, I used to sit there and I could feel myself shaking. But as time went on, I started getting used to it.

And this is what I have noticed with a lot of them. They were afraid to speak up and say anything. Now, with this prison issue, a lot of them have come out and come forward and given their opinions. Everybody used to be real "quietlike."[41]

She also related a situation that brought all her fears to a climax, which she confronted and resolved as follows:

When I first started working with the coalition, Channel 13 called me up and said they wanted to interview me and I said OK. Then I started getting nervous. So I called Father John and told him, "You better get over here right away." He said, "Don't worry, don't worry, you can handle it by yourself." Then Channel 13 called me back and said they were going to interview another person, someone I had never heard of, and asked if it was OK if he came to my house. And I said OK again. Then I began thinking, what if this guy is for the prison? What am I going to do? And I was so nervous and I thought, I know what I am going to do!

Since the meeting was taking place in her home, she reasoned that she was entitled to order any troublemakers out of her domain:

If this man tells me anything, I am just going to chase him out of my house. That is what I am going to do! All these thoughts were going through my head. Then Channel 13 walk into my house followed by six men I had never met. And I thought,

Oh, my God, what did I get myself into? I kept saying to myself, if they get smart with me I am throwing them ALL out.[42]

At this point her tone expressed a sense of resolve. In fact, the situation turned out to be neither confrontational nor threatening, as the "other men" were also members of the coalition. This woman confronted an anxiety-laden situation by relying on her sense of control within her home and family—a quite "traditional" source of authority for women—and transforming that control into the courage to express a political position before a potential audience all over one of the largest metropolitan areas in the nation.

People living in Third World countries as well as in minority communities in the United States face an increasingly degraded environment.[43] Recognizing the threat to the well-being of their families, residents have mobilized at the neighborhood level to fight for "quality of life" issues. The common notion that environmental well-being is of concern solely to white middle-class and upper-class residents ignores the specific way working-class neighborhoods suffer from the fallout of the city "growth machine" geared for profit.[44]

In Los Angeles, the culmination of postwar urban renewal policies, the growing Pacific Rim trade surplus and investment, and low-wage international labor migration from Third World countries are creating potentially volatile conditions. Literally palatial financial buildings swallow up the space previously occupied by modest, low-cost housing. Increasing density and development not matched by investment in social programs, services, and infrastructure erode the quality of life, beginning in the core of the city.[45] Latinos, the majority of whom live close to the center of the city, must confront the distilled social consequences of development focused solely on profit. The Mexican American community in East Los Angeles, much like other minority working-class communities, has been a repository for prisons instead of new schools, hazardous industries instead of safe work sites, and one of the largest concentrations of freeway interchanges in the country, which transports much wealth past the community. And the concerns of residents in East Los Angeles may provide lessons for other minority as well as middle-class communities. Increasing environmental pollution resulting from inadequate waste disposal plans and an out-of-control "need" for penal institutions to contain the casualties created by the growing bipolar distribution of wages may not be limited to the Southwest.[46] These conditions set the stage for new conflicts and new opportunities, to reform old relationships into coalitions that can challenge state agendas and create new community visions.[47]

Mexican American women living east of downtown Los Angeles exemplify the tendency of women to enter into environmental struggles in defense of their community. Women have a rich historical legacy of community activism, partly reconstructed over the last two decades in social histories of women who contested other "quality of life issues," from the price of bread to "Demon Rum" (often representing domestic violence).[48]

But something new is also happening. The issues "traditionally" addressed by women—health, housing, sanitation, and the urban environment—have moved to center stage as capitalist urbanization progresses. Environmental issues now fuel the fires of many political campaigns and drive citizens beyond the rather restricted, perfunctory political act of voting. Instances of political mobilization at the grassroots level, where women often play a central role, allow us to "see" abstract concepts like participatory democracy and social change as dynamic processes.

The existence and activities of "Mothers of East Los Angeles" attest to the dynamic nature of participatory democracy, as well as to the dynamic nature of our gender, class, and ethnic identity. The story of MELA reveals, on the one hand, how individuals and groups can transform a seemingly "traditional" role such as "mother." On the other hand, it illustrates how such a role may also be a social agent drawing members of the community into the "political" arena. Studying women's contributions as well as men's will shed greater light on the networks dynamic of grassroots movements.[49]

The work "Mothers of East Los Angeles" do to mobilize the community demonstrates that people's political involvement cannot be predicted by their cultural characteristics. These women have defied stereotypes of apathy and used ethnic, gender, and class identity as an impetus, a strength, a vehicle for political activism. They have expanded their—and our—understanding of the complexities of a political system, and they have reaffirmed the possibility of "doing something."

They also generously share the lessons they have learned. One of the women in "Mothers of East Los Angeles" told me, as I hesitated to set up an interview with another woman I hadn't yet met in person,

> *You know, nothing ventured nothing lost. You should have seen how timid we were the first time we went to a public hearing. Now, forget it, I walk right up and make myself heard and that's what you have to do.*[50]

Reading 7 Household Structure and Family Ideologies: The Dynamics of Immigrant Economic Adaptation Among Vietnemese Refugees*

NAZLI KIBRIA

Using materials from an ethnographic study of newly arrived Vietnamese refugees in Philadelphia, this article argues that household structure and family ideology play a critical role in the dynamics of immigrant economic adaptation. The study shows the Vietnamese refugee households that were more heterogeneous in age and gender composition to be more adept at "patchworking" or gathering together a wide variety of resources from diverse social and economic arenas. This "patchworking" strategy mitigates the instability and scarcity of available resources. The economic dynamics of the Vietnamese refugee households are also shaped by an ideology of family collectivism—a set of beliefs about family life that encourage the sharing of individual social and economic resources within the household. Cooperative household economic behavior is also fostered by beliefs that help to generate agreement among household members about household goals. These ideological dimensions of household life are, however, being shaped and in some cases challenged by the migration process.

> What explains their [Indochinese refugees'] success? The values they come with—a dedication to family, education and thrift—are cited as the main reason by people who have observed the refugees (Hume 1985).

In recent years the popular media has often portrayed Vietnamese refugees as the latest "immigrant success story"—a group whose cultural predisposition for hard work, initiative and frugality has enabled them to climb out of poverty. These reports not only conceal the tremendous economic diversity of the Vietnamese American population (Gold and Kibria 1993; Gold 1992), but also suggest a particular model of immigrant economic achievement, one in which the cultural

I would like to thank Eun Mee Kim, Barrie Thorne and Diane Wolf for their comments on earlier drafts.

*Kibria, Nazli. 1994. "Household Structure and Family Ideologies: The Dynamics of Immigrant Economic Adaption Among Vietnamese Refugees." *Social Problems* 41(1): 81–94. © 1994 by The Society for the Study of Social Problems. Reprinted by permission.

orientation of the group in question is critical to its success or failure. By contrast, scholarly analyses have increasingly rejected cultural models in favor of perspectives that focus on the role of external structural conditions in shaping immigrant economic adaptation (e.g., Lieberson 1980; Pedraza-Bailey 1985; Portes and Bach 1985; Portes and Rumbaut 1990; Steinberg 1981).

In this paper I suggest that a conceptual and empirical focus on the immigrant household and family[1] offers a fruitful avenue for exploring the ways in which cultural factors and external structural conditions shape immigrant economic life. There is growing interest in the family as a unit of analysis in migration studies (Grasmuck and Pessar 1990; Massey et al. 1987). Pedraza (1991) argues that the family provides a valuable intermediary level of analysis for migration scholars. That is, a focus on the family avoids the dichotomous extremes of micro- and macro-level approaches, which analyze migration as a process that is either individually or structurally determined. I suggest that the immigrant household and family are valuable dimensions to examine not only migration movements, but also the processes by which immigrants economically adapt to the "host" society. Analyses that focus on variations in household and family organization, both within and across immigrant groups, may be particularly useful in generating explanations for different patterns of economic adaptation.

[1]Whereas households are residential units, families may be defined as kinship groups in which the members do not necessarily live together. As inthe case of a household in which members do not see themselves as kin, it is possible for the household and the family to be units that are entirely distinct. More commonly however, the household and family are vitally connected. As Rapp (1992:51) observes, "families organize households." That is, notions of family tend to define the membership of households as well as relations between household members.

The significance of household and family organization to immigrant economic life is suggested by an ethnographic study of newly arrived Vietnamese refugees in Philadelphia. The findings of my study indicate that household structure and family ideologies play an important role in the economic life of the group. Those Vietnamese American households that were more differentiated in their age and gender composition were more successful in attaining economic goals such as the purchase of a home or the establishment of a small business. Age and gender heterogeneity is advantageous for households because it widens their structure of opportunities. This facilitates attempts to "patchwork," or to bring together diverse resources into the household economy, a strategy that helps to mitigate the instability and scarcity of available resources.

While the household composition affects its collective ability to access resources, it is Vietnamese American ideologies of family life that shape the manner in which household members respond to available opportunities. The Vietnamese American households are organized around an ideology of family collectivism. This encourages cooperative economic behavior—or "patchworking"—by emphasizing the unity of household interests and the economic significance of kinship ties. Cooperative economic behavior is also facilitated for Vietnamese Americans by family ideologies that help to define collective goals, such as the education of the young, for household members.

HOUSEHOLD STRUCTURE, FAMILY IDEOLOGIES AND IMMIGRANT ECONOMIC LIFE

Family-centered studies of the economic behavior of immigrants often view the family as a strategic arena, a social site where individuals can collectively cope with the economic environment to survive and to reach their goals (Dinerman 1978; Massey et al. 1937; Wood 1981).[2] With its focus on the strategic and flexible character of economic behavior, this emphasis on family strategies appears to offer an opportunity for developing a dynamic and processual understanding of immigrant economic adaptation. I suggest, however, that its potential to do so has been constrained by its inattention to household structure and to family ideologies.

The Effects of Household Composition

One of the most basic ways in which households differ is in their composition—who is included within the boundaries of the household. The potential effects of composition on a household's pool of available resources have not been adequately explored in studies of immigrant economic adjustment. I suggest this is largely due to limited definitions of the resources or assets that are pertinent to the household economy. Wage labor is often seen as the sole economic resource of the household, and household composition has accordingly been assessed for its impact on the household's pool of wage labor (Angel and Tienda 1982; Massey et al. 1987; Perez 1986). But this exclusive concern with wage labor neglects other, equally valuable, types of contributions to the household economy. For example, women and children may contribute to the household economy by providing their unpaid labor to the family businesses that have been an important part of the economic experience of some immigrant groups (Aldrich and Waldinger 1990; Portes and Rumbaut 1990).

Besides wages to the household financial pot or labor to the family business, members may also contribute assets of other kinds to the household economy. As current discussions of immigrant economic life suggest, it is not just labor market conditions, but also such contextual factors as "the policies of the receiving government, and the characteristics of their own [immigrants'] ethnic communities" (Portes and Rumbaut 1990: 85) that are relevant to immigrant economic progress. Such assertions suggest that we define the structural environment as not simply the labor market, but also in terms of institutions that potentially provide a range of important social and economic resources for the household. State institutions and bureaucracies may provide facilities and services such as assistance with education, job training, legal protection, health care, and resettlement (Pedraza-Bailey 1985). Groups within the household that are clearly disadvantaged in the labor market, such as children, may even have a better ability than adults to bring in resources from state institutions (e.g., college tuition loans).

The immigrant household economy is also affected by its social embeddedness in ongoing social relations and networks. As suggested by the extensive literature on the adaptive role of social networks and ethnic community ties (e.g., Massey et al. 1987; Min 1988; Morawska 1985; Portes and Bach 1985), for the immigrant group, the ethnic community may be a crucial source of loans, jobs, and information. Once again, recognition of the important economic role played by the ethnic community enhances our ability to consider forms of contribution to the household economy that are hidden by focus on wage labor. For example, the work that immigrant women put into cultivating and sustaining the kinship and friendship ties that socially integrate a family into the ethnic community may be seen as an important form of labor, one that facilitates the access of the household economy to ethnic community resources (di Leonardo 1987; Ewen 1985; Seller 1981).

---

[2]For a review of the literature on family adaptive strategies, see Moen and Wethington 1992.

When the definition of household economy includes relevant resources and institutions, household composition must be considered as well. Instead of assuming that a household membership configuration that maximizes the capacity for wage labor (such as one that is dominated by adult men) is advantageous, it becomes important to consider household composition in light of its repercussions for a wider range of household assets. Resources that appear to have little value when viewed individually may prove to be critical in their economic impact on the household economy when combined with other types of assets.

The Impact of Family ideologies

Another dimension of the household critical to understanding its economic dynamics are the beliefs about family life held by members (Grasmuck and Pessar 1991; Moen and Wethington 1992). These family beliefs or ideologies define norms and expectations about household activities and relations that affect the household economy. For example, beliefs about women's family roles have important implications for the household economy, since they shape women's labor force participation as well as the ability of female household members to control economic resources. In a study comparing the economic activities of single female factory workers in Java and Taiwan, Diane Wolf (1990, 1992) found that the Javanese women, in contrast to their Taiwanese counterparts, often did not contribute their earnings to the family economy. Instead, the Javanese women retained control over their pay, spending it independently of their families. Wolf attributes the Javanese pattern to the relatively high degree of autonomy accorded women in the Javanese kinship system. In this particular case, family ideology concerning women's roles weakened the ability of the

household economy to effectively incorporate the financial resources of its young single female members.

One of the central ways in which family ideology impacts the household economy is through its role in defining normative patterns of economic exchange within the household. That is, family ideology helps to define the economic relationships of household members. It thus influences the extent to which individual household members view their own economic activities and resources as part of the collective household economy. A household economy in which members view their economic life in collectivist terms will differ in its goals and dynamics from one in which the orientation is individualistic. Analyses of immigrant entrepreneurship, for example, suggest that groups with an ideology that emphasizes a collectivist and familial orientation towards economic achievement are more likely to engage in small business than others (Aldrich and Waldinger 1990; Sibley Butler 1991). However, as Aldrich and Waldinger (1990) note, such economic orientations tend to be fluid and responsive to the changing social context, as evidenced by the often radical shifts in the extent of a group's orientation towards entrepreneurship over the course of a few generations.

In general, family ideology must be seen as not only varied across groups, but also as fluid and reactive, constantly shifting in response to changing social contexts. The changing character of family ideology is often downplayed in cultural analyses of immigrant economic adaptation, which tend to portray immigrant cultural traditions as "given" and static (Caplan, Whitmore, and Choy 1989; Glazer and Moynihan 1963; Petersen 1971). The fluidity of familial cultural traditions is highlighted by Geschwender's (1992) analysis of historical changes in women's labor force participation. He describes how women of various ethnicities in the United States entered the labor force out of economic necessity, in a departure from the behaviors prescribed by the "cult of domesticity." The entry of women into the labor force generated normative change among some ethnic groups, whereby women were expected to contribute to the household economy through employment. In brief, structural changes in the economy led to shifts in family ideology concerning women's employment outside the home.

METHODS

During 1983–85, I studied newly arrived Vietnamese refugees in Philadelphia through participant-observation and in-depth interviews (Kibria 1993). I conducted 31 interviews, 15 with women and 16 with men in the ethnic community. The interviews, which were tape-recorded, focused on the respondents' past and current experiences of family life. I also asked my interviewees a series of questions about their employment experiences and household budgeting practices in the United States. Because my knowledge of Vietnamese was minimal, many, but not all, of the interviews took place with the help of Vietnamese language interpreters. I also interviewed 11 Vietnamese American community leaders and social service agency workers in the city about the organizations in which they were involved and the relationship of these organizations to the Vietnamese American population in the city.

I also conducted participant-observation in household and community settings. For more than two years, I regularly visited 12 households in the community. During these visits, I observed and talked informally with household members. I spent time as a participant-observer in the neighborhood of study, in an attempt to gain a better understanding of the informal community life of Vietnamese Americans in the area, and the relationship of community life to household dynamics. Eventually, I focused my time on three popular community gathering places—a restaurant, a grocery store, and a hairdressing shop—all neighborhood businesses run by Vietnamese Americans.

More than 80 percent of the study-participants were from urban middle-class backgrounds in Southern Vietnam. Those men who had been beyond school age in Vietnam had usually been involved in military or government service. Women had worked, often sporadically, in family businesses or in informal, small-scale trading. All had experienced economic and social dislocations following the 1975 political transition to Communist rule in Vietnam. Directly and indirectly, these dislocations were responsible for the decisions of the refugees to undertake the hazardous escape by sea out of Vietnam during the late 1970s and early 1980s. While most of the refugees had been resettled in Philadelphia by social service agencies, others had relocated there from other places in the United States to join with kin or friends, forming households with them. The households in the community tended to be extended in character, containing a variety of kinfolk and friends (cf. Gardner, Bryant, and Smith 1985; Gold 1992).

THE SOCIAL CONTEXT

Critical to understanding the economic dynamics of the Vietnamese refugee households are the conditions they encountered in three social arenas: the labor market, government policies and services, and the Vietnamese ethnic community. These arenas were central axes in the structure of opportunities facing the group, and thus provided the structural parameters for their economic behavior. The discussion shows available resources to be limited and unstable in supply, and restricted in availability to certain segments of the community.

Labor Market

Labor market opportunities for Vietnamese Americans were limited, a reflection of both the conditions of the local economy and the job skills of the group. During the study the Philadelphia city economy was highly polarized, composed of a professional high-income sector and a service sector that provided mainly low-paid, semiskilled or unskilled work. The increasingly limited range of job opportunities, combined with the effects of a nationwide recession, inflated unemployment and poverty rates in the city during the early 1980s (Philadelphia City Planning Commission 1984). Further restricting the group's employment opportunities was its minority ethnic status and lack of suitable job skills for the formal economy. It is not surprising then, that unemployment rates in the community were high; in mid-1984, roughly 35 percent of the adult men in the 12 study households were unemployed.

The jobs that were most easily accessible to the group were low-level service sector positions, such as cleaning and waitressing, which tended to be poorly paid, part-time, unstable, and devoid of benefits and opportunities for advancement.[3] Also available to the group were jobs in the informal economy, particularly in garment assembly, an industry in which the Vietnamese refugee women were far more likely to be involved than the men.

---

[3]Studies of Vietnamese refugee communities in other parts of the country reveal similar employment patterns (Gold 1992; Rumbaut 1989).

Government Policies and Services

The "political refugee" status of the Vietnamese Americans gave legal legitimacy to their presence in the United States, and also provided access to a federal refugee aid and resettlement system (Pedraza-Bailey 1985; Rumbaut 1989a). Voluntary social service agencies (VOLAGS) played a leading role in finding housing for new refugee arrivals, and providing information on services available to refugees such as English language classes, job counseling, and income support. All refugees were eligible for cash assistance and medical benefits through the Refugee Cash Assistance and Refugee Medical Assistance programs. When eligibility (based on length of residence in the United States) for Refugee Cash assistance ran out, those meeting the family composition and income level requirements continued to receive assistance through programs available to U.S. citizens such as AFDC (Aid to Families with Dependent Children), SSI (Supplemental Security Income), Medicaid, Food Stamps and GA (General Assistance). While all of the Vietnamese refugees had some contact with this system of assistance, a few had more sustained contact with the programs than others. Given the eligibility requirements, it is not surprising that those who were elderly, disabled, under the age of 18, and single parents, were more likely to have a long-term relationship with the cash and medical assistance programs.

The cash and medical assistance available to Vietnamese immigrants by virtue of their refugee status has been identified as an important economic boost for the group. What has been less noted, perhaps because it is less visible, is the access provided by the system to valuable social relationships, or "social capital" (cf. Coleman 1988). For example, out of their initial contacts with the resettlement system, some of the refugees developed close relationships with individual social service agency workers or sponsors, relying on them as a source of information about jobs, bank loans, and educational opportunities. In one particular case, members of a church congregation that had collectively sponsored a refugee household helped them to obtain a bank loan that they needed to open a business. Furthermore, sponsors or social service agency officials often provided job referrals for refugees. For some of my respondents, the friends that they had gained through the refugee resettlement system represented their only relationships with persons outside the ethnic community and were thus highly valued as a source of help for dealing with the dominant society's institutions. In some cases these "outside" persons were identified by adults as important role models for their children, who could turn to them for help with homework and other academic matters. In short, the social relationships that households were able to acquire through the resettlement system enhanced the socioeconomic heterogeneity of its social networks.

Households with children under age eighteen had greater access to public education than other households did. Public schools provided the opportunity to gain educational credentials, to learn English, and to acquire other cultural skills important for getting by in the United States. Because of this, households with school-age children had an advantage in dealing with dominant society institutions, since their children could serve as reliable interpreters. In addition, much like the refugee assistance system, the schools were also an arena through which the immigrants were able to develop relationships with teachers and other school officials. Once again, these social relations could be an important source of information and assistance. A high school teacher in the community helped the families of his students fill out home loan mortgage forms, while another teacher provided much-needed information about the complex regulations of the public assistance bureaucracy.

Ethnic Community

Two dimensions of ethnic community life—economic enclaves and ethnic associations—are widely identified by social scientists as important resources for immigrants, at least in the initial process of settlement in the United States. Ethnic economic enclaves are important sources of jobs, training, and opportunities for advancement for immigrant groups (Portes and Bach 1985). Ethnic associations also provide assistance in the form of capital, information about jobs, business ventures, and various aspects of life in the "host" society.

For the Philadelphia Vietnamese community, both ethnic economic enclaves and formal ethnic organizations were under-developed, partly due to the recency of Vietnamese settlement in the area. Ethnic ties did, however, play an extremely important role in the group's economic experiences. The immigrants belonged to ethnic social networks that provided a range of important resources, including financial loans and information about jobs, housing, and welfare (cf. Gold 1992; Hein 1993). While these informal social networks were often based on kinship ties and shared neighborhoods, they were also organized around age, gender and social class background. In other words, the social networks of individuals reflected their status along these variables.

PATCHWORKING AND HOUSEHOLD COMPOSITION

In the structure of opportunities that I have described, the resources potentially available from any one source were limited and unreliable. Available jobs tended to be low-paying and unstable. Payments from the Refugee Cash Assistance and other assistance programs were also restricted and viewed by the Vietnamese refugees as highly temporary and unstable assets that could be terminated abruptly. The immigrants saw social relations in the ethnic community as far more reliable sources of economic and social assistance than either the labor market or government assistance programs. But, given both the economically homogeneous and fairly transient character of the community, even these resources were viewed as inherently scarce and unstable.

Like other economically disadvantaged communities (Bolles 1983; Glenn 1991; Stack 1974), Vietnamese Americans responded to these economic conditions by pooling resources within their domestic groups. But the notion of 'pooling,' which suggests sharing resources, does not adequately convey the Vietnamese American practice of sharing diverse resources.[4] I suggest that this practice is better conveyed by the notion of "patchworking" because the term conjures up an image of jagged pieces of assorted material stitched together in sometimes haphazard fashion.

Patchworking—the bringing together and sharing of diverse resources—is a practice that helps the Vietnamese American households to protect themselves against economic instability, or fluctuations in the supply of resources. The importance of having access to multiple resources was suggested by the experiences of an informant named Binh, a man in his forties who came to the United States with his two teenage sons.

After arriving, the family lived on the government benefits available to newly-arrived refugees. Binh also took English language classes while his sons attended high school. Binh described the household as being economically self-sufficient at this time. Although his sister and her husband lived in the city, Binh did not rely on them for assistance. In fact, priding himself in his-self-sufficiency, he had forbidden his sons to either "give or take money or anything else from other people." After about two years, Binh began looking for work; however, his job search was cut short by a back injury. Despite what he described as debilitating back pain, he was told by social service agency workers that he was no longer eligible for government aid. At the same time, his oldest son, who had just turned nineteen, was also told that he could no longer receive public assistance. These events created a crisis during which the household relied heavily on Binh's sister for food and other household expenses. Binh said his beliefs regarding the viability of self-sufficiency and survival in the United States had radically changed as a result of this unfortunate period. He came to realize that relations with kin were virtually a necessity in the United States. He also recognized the dangers of having only one source of income.

In Binh's case, access to a diverse resource base provided some degree of stability in a risky economic context. In an environment in which the quantity of assets from any one arena was limited, it was also a strategy that enhanced the scope of a household's resource pool. In a household I observed, one member took courses in machine repair at a local technical institute, while another member worked for a sewing contractor at home, also taking care of the young children in the family, and collecting Refugee Cash Assistance payments. Of the other two household members, one worked in an ethnic

[4]The Vietnamese American practice that I observed of bringing diverse resources together extends the concept of income diversification, which has been noted by studies of developing societies to be a common strategy for dealing with risky economic contexts (Agarwal 1992; Perez-Aleman 1992).

business run by friends and the other in a semi-skilled manufacturing job outside the city. Through these various activities, household members brought in wages from the formal and the informal economy, benefits from public assistance programs, and job skills and cultural capital from participation in training programs. Because a member worked in an ethnic business, the household also had access to a variety of ethnic community networks and resources.

The ability to access a wide range of resources was enhanced by a high degree of differentiation among household members. The structure of available resources was scarce, unstable, and restricted, since not all household members had equal access to jobs, welfare, or the ethnic community networks. For example, in many informal sector jobs, such as those in the garment industry, women were more favored as employees than men. Furthermore, age clearly affected access to government assistance programs. Households with children and elderly were more likely to have a sustained and long-term relationship with public assistance programs. Membership in social networks and access to the resources embedded in these networks was also determined by age and gender. Thus, a high degree of status differentiation among household members expanded the household's reach, allowing it to more effectively take advantage of available opportunities and to "patchwork" resources. The economic advantages of internally heterogeneous households were suggested to me by the words of a Vietnamese American man in his thirties who had come to the United States alone:

> After coming to America I realized that my college education from Vietnam doesn't mean anything here. I look around and I see that many of the Vietnamese who do well here are not the ones who have education. If you come here with your family, or maybe your relatives are already here, you're better off because you can live together and save money. The children can go to school and slowly they can help their parents. Maybe they can open a store together, or maybe two people can get jobs and support the family while the rest of the people go to school or the community college.

To further clarify the economic consequences of differentiation in household composition, I will next contrast the economic experiences of three specific households. These three households represent the range of diversity in terms of age and gender composition that I found in my sample. Different degrees of internal diversity resulted in different levels of access to such resources as public assistance and education, and to social networks in the community.

Household One: High Diversity

Household One contained members of varied age and gender. It consisted of seven people: a woman named Thanh[5] in her late fifties, her three adult sons, two daughters, and one son-in-law.

After arriving in the United States, all household members received government aid through refugee assistance programs. But about a year-and-a-half later, the four men in the household were cut off from these programs when social service workers judged them to be capable of economic self-sufficiency. The household economy continued, however, to draw resources from public assistance programs. After receiving Refugee Cash Assistance and Refugee Medical

---

[5]All names have been changed to maintain anonymity.

Assistance for more than two years, Thanh and her daughters were transferred into other aid programs. For Thanh and her youngest daughter (who was fourteen), age was a critical factor in their continued eligibility for government assistance. Due to her status as a low-income elderly person, Thanh was eligible for Supplemental Security Income. The youngest daughter could receive General Assistance because she was under age eighteen, attending school, and a member of a low-income household. Following the birth of her baby, Thanh's older daughter became eligible for Aid to Families with Dependent Children, a program that targets low-income families with young children.

The diverse composition of Household One enabled it to have a sustained relationship with government aid programs. The household's age and gender diversity also gave it access to a wide range of community networks. About five years after arriving in the United States, the household opened a Vietnamese-Chinese restaurant. The household's wide-ranging networks were critical to its ability to open the business since small personal loans from friends and contacts provided the household start-up capital. The success with which the household was able to obtain these loans was related to its diversity. For example, Thanh was able to borrow money from her circle of friends, which was composed of elderly Vietnamese refugee men and women. Without Thanh, the household would not have had access to these financial resources. Similarly, Thanh's older daughter was able to prevail on her own group of woman friends for small loans. Thanh's three sons were also able to obtain funds from their friendship networks of young single men. In addition, Thanh's son-in-law, who was a member of the household, was able to tap into his own separate kinship networks in New York to obtain loans. In short, the household worked to obtain a large number of small personal loans

to open the business. The age and gender diversity of the household contributed to the success of this strategy.

Household Two: Medium Diversity

Household Two represents the middle range in terms of age and diversity of the households in my study. The household consisted of six persons: a married couple named Hung and Lien, Hung's three younger brothers, and a male friend. Not only was the household numerically dominated by men, but it was also marked by age homogeneity. All of the household members were in their late teens or early twenties.

The household's homogeneous composition contributed to its somewhat weaker links to the public assistance system, compared to Household One. Two of Hung's younger brothers collected General Assistance payments, which they were eligible to receive because they were under age eighteen, and attending school. Hung and Lien had also attended school and received public assistance for about three years after arriving in the United States. But neither of them had been able to complete high school before turning eighteen. The household's access to public assistance did strengthen, however, after the birth of Hung and Lien's daughter. As a low-income mother, Lien became eligible for Aid to Families with Dependent Children.

Government assistance resources available to the household were crucial to its economic survival. All household members had trouble finding stable jobs. Hung and the two other young men who were not attending school worked sporadically, usually in janitorial jobs in restaurants. Lien often supplemented the household income by sewing garments at home or working as a waitress in one of the area's Chinese or Vietnamese restaurants. Further compounding the paucity of household economic resources was the fact that, unlike the first household, it was not connected to a set of diverse and wide-ranging social networks. The similar age of household members was a critical factor in the household's homogeneous networks. Household members' social circles tended to overlap a great deal since they all socialized with other Vietnamese refugees in the area who were young, unmarried, or newly married.

Household Three: Low Diversity

Household Three was extremely homogeneous in age and gender composition. It consisted of five unrelated men, all single and in their early twenties. All of the men had received Refugee Cash Assistance and Refugee Medical Assistance after arriving in the United States for periods of one to two years. After this, the household was completely cut off from government aid programs. As young, able-bodied, single men, they were unable to meet the programs' core requirement: an inability to financially sustain oneself due to age, illness, or the burden of dependents. All five men had also arrived in the United States at an age (seventeen years or more) preventing them from taking full advantage of public education opportunities.

Like Household Two, the members of Household Three belonged to overlapping social circles. These social circles provided them with referrals and information about jobs as well as other aspects of life in the United States. However, as the young men discovered when they began to investigate the possibility of opening a car repair shop, their social contacts limited their financial capacity. They were unable to borrow enough money from friends and contacts for the venture. This inability reflected the limited range and diversity of the household's social networks, which were composed almost solely of young, single, recently arrived Vietnamese refugee men. Thus, unlike Household One, this household was unable to turn to a diverse set of acquaintances for financial loans.

PATCHWORKING AND FAMILY IDEOLOGIES

While composition structured a household's access to societal resources, the manner in which these resources were utilized or "processed" was critically shaped by the family ideology of household members. Here I examine two ideological dimensions of Vietnamese refugee life that help to explain the "patchworking" strategy of households.

The Ideology of Family Collectivism

A tradition of defining kinship in an inclusive and fluid manner encouraged the members of the Vietnamese refugee households to view each other as kin, regardless of whether or not the relationships fulfilled formal kinship criteria (Kibria 1993; Luong 1984). Thus in the households that I observed, familial expectations of economic participation applied to all household members, both kin and non-kin. Underlying these economic expectations was an ideology of family collectivism, a set of beliefs about the nature and significance of family life. The ideology of family collectivism, which drew on Vietnamese kinship traditions, organized and undergirded the economic patchworking of households in several ways. It advanced the view that economic reliance on family ties was an appropriate and judicious response to the economic demands and opportunities of the migration process. It also helped to promote a collective, cooperative approach towards resources and activities among household members by stressing, and indeed, idealizing the unity of family interests.

Central to the ideology of family collectivism is the notion that the kin group is far more significant than the individual. This dimension of family collectivism drew strength from Confucian family traditions, including the practice of ancestor worship. Family altars that were used to perform rites to honor ancestors were a common sight in the Vietnamese American households that I visited. Ancestor worship affirmed the sacredness and essential unity of the kin group, as well as its permanence in comparison to the transience of the individual. It also highlighted obligation as a key feature of a member's relationship to the kin group. The central obligation of the family member was to place the needs and desires of the kin group over and above any personal ones.

Another component of the ideology of family collectivism is the belief that the family is an individual's most reliable source of support—the only institution that could be counted on for help under all circumstances. Among my informants there was a strong belief that kin ties were an economic safety net, a belief that had been cultivated by the long years of social turmoil in contemporary South Vietnam during which time kin ties had been a source of security for many Vietnamese. Respondents told me several traditional proverbs that stressed the durability and significance of kin over non-kin relations, such as: "A bitter relative is still a relative, a sweet stranger is still a stranger," and "If your father leaves you, you still have your uncle; if your mother leaves you, you can nurse on your aunt's milk."

In a variety of ways, these family beliefs encouraged individuals to maintain close economic ties to the households in which they lived and to participate in "patchworking." The ideology of family collectivism, for example, could be used as a sanction against rebellious household members who refuse to go along with the decisions made by others. One such situation involved a young man named Doan, who was living in a household with three older brothers, their wives and children. Doan's refusal to contribute money towards the collective household

purchase of a family home gave rise to conflict with his older brothers. Doan was planning to use his extra income to sponsor his girlfriend (who was in a refugee camp in Thailand) to the United States. Drawing on notions embedded in the ideology of family collectivism, such as individual obligation to the family, Doan's older brothers interpreted his refusal as evidence of selfishness and lack of concern for the family, as well as lack of respect for his family elders. Doan justified his refusal by arguing that the purchase of a house would serve his brothers' interests far better than his own. Since his brothers were all married and had children (unlike him), it was far more important for them to secure housing that was stable and in a relatively prosperous neighborhood. Unable to resolve the dispute, Doan eventually moved out of the household and into a friend's home.

As this example suggests, households were not always successful in forcing deviant members to conform to established economic decisions. Migration had, in fact, created conditions that made non-compliance to the principles of family collectivism more likely than ever. According to traditional Vietnamese family patterns, authority in the family rested with men and the elderly. But migration to the United States had diminished the power of men and the elderly. This opened opportunities for traditionally less powerful groups to challenge their authority, thus increasing the potential for intrahousehold conflicts over economic decisions. Doan, for example, told me he probably would not have disagreed with his brothers' decision in Vietnam, because the elder status of his brothers had carried more authority there.

The challenge posed by migration to the authority of men over women was particularly striking. The economic power of men in the community had declined with migration, thus weakening the economic basis for male authority (Kibria 1990). In many households, men were periodically or chronically unemployed, with women contributing a major share of the household finances. This economic power shift challenged the traditional authority of men and generated household environments that were ripe for conflicts between men and women. It is not surprising then, that "patchworking" was often accompanied by dissension and negotiation between men and women, particularly over the ways in which money should be spent. But despite these conflicts, the wholesale defection of men and women from the household economy was rare, because most were dependent on it for economic survival and economic mobility. In this sense, the economic conditions of life in the United States, in their Poverty and uncertainty, had reinforced traditional beliefs about the economic significance of kinship ties and how they fulfilled the function of an economic safety net. Thus the conditions of settlement in the United States were simultaneously strengthening and challenging the ability of the ideology of family collectivism to organize the economic life of the Vietnamese American households.

"Making it" Through the Education of the Young

For the Vietnamese Americans, cooperative household economic behavior is also promoted by widely shared goals that helped to generate consensus among members about collective economic investment. One of these goals is the schooling of the young. This is seen as an effective path by which the family as a whole can achieve mobility in the future, a view that encourages the household economy to invest resources in education. This perspective on education reflects the experiences of my informants in pre-1975 South Vietnam, a context in which academic credentials had been deeply valued among the middle class. Education could secure one a high-ranking place in the government bureaucracy or military, or in the professions. Historically, education was seen by the group as an effective method by which to achieve economic prosperity and stability (cf. Ogbu 1978). This understanding of education had been reinforced for the Vietnamese Americans by the comparatively greater opportunities in the United States for obtaining higher education.

A child's education was understood as a venture from which the household as a whole would reap rewards in the future. In the short run, the academic achievements of the young were a source of collective familial status and prestige in the ethnic community. In the informal social gatherings that I attended, it was not unusual for parents or other family elders to pass around and compare the report cards of school-aged children. In the long run, household members expected to gain not only status privileges, but also material rewards. In accordance with the prescriptions of the ideology of family collectivism, the young were expected to pay back their families after completing their education. In fact, many parents explicitly identified the children's education as an investment for their future and for the collective future of the kin group. Although not without ambivalence, these expectations of payback were also shared by many young Vietnamese Americans who often focused on fields that would allow them to more effectively meet family financial obligations. Thus a young Vietnamese American who was studying for a degree in pharmacy (although he would have preferred to study art) told me that he planned to buy a house for his sister and brother-in-law, with whom he was living, as soon as he completed college. Similarly, in a study of Southeast Asian refugee youth conducted by

Rumbaut and Ima (forthcoming), a Vietnamese refugee said the children in his family were all expected to pay a money "tax" to their mother after completing college.

Expectation of future rewards to motivate households to invest in the schooling of the young was vividly highlighted to me by one case in which a young member was actually dissuaded by kin from continuing his education. Kim's mother and aunt discouraged him from taking courses in college, encouraging him instead to find a job that would help the household to amass the savings necessary to purchase a home. The household preferred to channel its educational aspirations into Kim's younger brother, who was seen as more likely to succeed academically, since he was proficient in English and was receiving much better grades.

The rewards of education are not the only means by which Vietnamese Americans collectively approach schooling. Researchers have noted how studying is organized in Vietnamese refugee households as a collective rather than individual task or activity. Children sit down together to study and assist each other with school-related problems (Caplan, Choy, and Whitmore 1992). Rumbaut and Ima (forthcoming) further describe the Vietnamese refugee family as a "mini-school system" with older siblings playing a major role in mentoring and tutoring their younger brothers and sisters.

The manner in which the Vietnamese immigrants view the education of the young helps to explain the well-publicized educational successes of Vietnamese refugee youth as a group (Caplan, Choy, and Whitmore 1992). Perhaps most importantly, the collectivist familial orientation to schooling that I have described results in a situation in which the stakes for doing well at school are extremely high; for the young, it is not only their own future that hinges on their

ability to do well at school, but also that of the family. However, as with other ideological dimensions of Vietnamese American family life, these ideas about education are being challenged in the United States. Perhaps the most significant challenge stems from the diminishing strength of the ideology of family collectivism among young Vietnamese Americans, who are increasingly likely to favor an individualistic rather than collective familial approach to economic activities. For family elders, the cultural assimilation and potential defection of the young from the cooperative family economy raises questions about the education of the young as a collective goal. The "Americanization" of the young endangers the payback that kin hope to receive in the future from their investments in the education of the young.

CONCLUSIONS

In this paper I have argued that the organization of immigrant households and families is useful in examining the role of external structural conditions and cultural factors in shaping immigrant economic life. An ethnographic study of Vietnamese refugees suggests a number of specific ways in which the organization of households and families enter into the dynamics of immigrant economic life. A significant aspect of household structure that I encountered is the degree of age and gender diversity in household composition, which is found to impact the structure of household opportunities. Besides age and gender diversity, there are other variations in household structure—such as size, proportion of kin versus non-kin, lifecycle stage, and membership stability—that may be useful to explore in studies of immigrant economic adaptation (Angel and Tienda 1982; Moen and Wethington 1992; Perez 1986).

The consequences of diversity in household composition may also extend well beyond the access to resources that I have emphasized. Because age and gender are central bases of family inequality, a household that is age and gender diverse is also likely to be hierarchical in its internal relations. Such a household, in which some members have substantial authority over others, may organize its economic activities quite differently than a household that is homogeneous and thus more egalitarian in its relations between members. For example, hierarchical households may be better able to demand economic behavior from members that calls for self-sacrifice and is directed towards familial rather than individual goals.

Our understanding of the economic implications of age and gender diversity in households will also be enhanced by investigations into its consequences across varied social contexts. The economic advantages associated with membership diversity for the Vietnamese refugee households in my study were tied to the specific character of the structural environment that surrounded them. This was an environment in which all household members, regardless of age and gender, tended to have access to valued, although different, resources. It was not an environment in which a particular age and gender group (for example, young men) had *substantially* better access to societal resources than others. An important reason for this relative equality was the access of young and elderly persons to government aid and services (e.g., cash and medical assistance, public schooling). If such programs had not been available, it is possible that age and gender diversity in household composition would not have been a source of economic advantage.

This relationship between government programs and the economic advantages of age and gender diverse households also suggests that internal household differentiation may be an especially significant variable in the economic experiences of refugee immigrant groups. In the contemporary United States, immigrants who enter under the official classification of "refugee" have access to government assistance programs that are unavailable to non-refugee immigrants (Portes and Rumbaut 1990). To the extent that the benefits of household diversity stem from the availability of such programs, diverse households will be particularly advantageous for refugee groups. While they do not focus specifically on the linkages between household composition and government assistance programs, studies of Cuban refugees in the United States have noted the importance of both government aid programs and family structure to the economic adaptation of the group (Pedraza-Bailey 1985; Perez 1986).

While household organization is a useful dimension by which to explore the structural context of immigrant economic life, family ideologies provide an understanding of immigrants' responses to opportunities. Among the Vietnamese refugees of my study, the general response to the structural environment is to engage in cooperative and household-centered "patchworking." "Patchworking" behavior is supported by an ideology of family collectivism as well as beliefs concerning the relationship of the family economy to the education of the young. Structuralist analyses of immigrant economic adaptation tend to neglect such ideological factors, a neglect that weakens their ability to develop convincing explanations of how and why groups respond differently to similar circumstances. Studies that systematically compare the family ideologies of immigrant groups and their impact on economic behavior are needed in order to develop a fuller understanding of the dynamics of immigrant economic adaptation. Such studies must, however, avoid the static view of immigrant cultures that has often marked cultural analyses of immigrant economic adaptation (Caplan, Whitmore, and Choy 1989; Petersen 1971). My study reveals the family ideologies of the Vietnamese refugees to be responsive to shifting social conditions. It is clear that the Vietnamese American ideology of family collectivism is in a state of flux and being molded in often contradictory ways by the migration and resettlement process.

Part II

Gender Relations: Inequality, Sexuality, and Intimacy

Gender relations both within and outside of marriage and the family have been influenced by the ideology of patriarchal authority, which has been deeply entrenched in political, social, and economic institutions. Patriarchy has affected premarital, marital, and familial relationships and has been articulated in attitudes and behavior regarding sexuality, intimacy, power, and privilege.

However, the ideological revolutions regarding marriage and the family combined with the processes of industrialization and urbanization have produced a major reconceptualization of gender role relations within the last two hundred years. Social scientists (Ariès 1962; Shorter 1975; Stone 1977) have observed that prior to that period, the Western European and American nuclear family was not intimate and did not encourage domesticity or privacy. The inseparable and indistinguishable facets of social life were family and community. The notion of family privacy was practically unknown. Indeed, the very concept of the nuclear family did not emerge until the seventeenth century. The low valuation of the family in preindustrial Western society occurred because of the individual's almost total involvement with the community. The general situation was one in which most activities were public and one where people were rarely alone. The lack of privacy attributed to this overwhelming community sociability hindered the development of the family as we know it.

The family in this preindustrial period and extending into much later periods was patriarchal and authoritarian, and demanded deference. Husbands had virtually absolute power and control over wives and children. The relationship between husband and wife was not as intimate or private as it is today. In addition, the status and treatment of women varied with their involvement in economically productive work. When a woman contributed economically, she had more power and control over her own life. When she did not, her life was that of a domestically confined slave, servile and subservient to her master—her husband. The absolute power of the husband held true not only in economic terms but also in moral matters. Both women and children were relegated to subordinate legal positions that were based on the economic and political control of the husbands and fathers.

The rise of the national state, ideological changes that included emerging ideas about liberty and the importance of the individual, combined with the Industrial Revolution all contributed to changes in the way marriage and the family were conceptualized. Traditional patriarchal relations were gradually replaced by romantic love, compassionate marriage, and an affectionate and permissive mode of child rearing. Edward Shorter (1975) labels the changes in the period after 1750 as the "Sentimental Revolution." The Sentimental Revolution ushered in a new emotional component to gender relations in three areas: courtship, the mother-child relationship, and the relationship of the family with the community.

The emergent emphasis on affection, friendship, and the romantic love ideology began to characterize courtship. As a result, marriage became more and more a matter of free choice rather than an arrangement determined by the parents on the basis of economic and social considerations. Attitudes toward children underwent a similar change, with new sentiments of affection and love emerging and neglect and indifference decreasing. An increase in the growth of maternal care and the development of a more loving attitude toward children by their mothers resulted. These shifting sentiments brought about a change in the relationship of the family to the community. Affection and caring tied the husband-wife relationship tighter and began to replace lineage, property, and economic considerations as the foundation of the marriage. Simultaneously, the couple's involvement with the community lessened.

In summary, the historical evidence illustrates two processes at work: the first is the couple's almost complete withdrawal from the community; the second is the corresponding strength of the ties of the couple with each other and with their children and close relatives. Taken together, these processes are often seen to have disturbed the grip of patriarchy on marriage and the family. The readings in this part of the book will investigate whether this has in fact occurred in the areas of dating and courtship (Chapter Three), sexuality, intimacy, and the family (Chapter Four), and in the interrelationship of gender roles, work, and the family (Chapter Five).

Most social historians believe that the modern American family emerged with the American Revolution and formed its major components by 1830. The four predominant characteristics of the American family are marriage based on affection and mutual respect, low fertility, child-centeredness, and what historian Carl Degler (1980) has called the "doctrine of the two spheres." This doctrine held that the primary role of the wife was child care and the maintenance of the household (the private sphere) while the husband's was work outside the home (the public sphere). Anchoring this doctrine was the belief that while the wife may be the moral superior in the relationship, legal and social power rests with the husband. The direct consequence is the subordination of women's roles to their husbands'. To deal with subordination, women carved out a source of power based on the emerging importance of mutual affection, love, and sexuality as integral components of modern marriage. As we shall see, a number of our readings will examine this development within an analysis of dating and courtship processes and in the expressions of sexuality.

An analysis of American courtship processes reflects historical changes that have shifted decision making from parental control to the couple themselves. This shift reflects the emerging nineteenth-century attitude that marriage should be based on personal happiness and the affection of the partners for each other. As marriage began to be equated with love and individualism, the growing acceptance of affection as the primary ground for marriage became an essential factor in the change in women's roles and a potential source of power and autonomy within the family. A woman could appeal to her husband's affection for her, and she, in turn, could manipulate that affection to increase her power or influence within marriage and the household.

Similarly, the expression of sexuality both within and outside of the courtship process took on a power component. The Victorian notion of the "passionlessness" woman can be seen as serving to improve women's status. Nancy Cott (1979) contends that the downplaying of sexuality could be used as a means of limiting male domination. The de-emphasis of feminine sexuality was replaced by an emphasis on women's moral and spiritual superiority over males and was used to enhance their status and widen their opportunities.

The doctrine of the two spheres that developed in the nineteenth century defined the essence of maleness as occupational involvement and the pursuit of worldly and material success. Women, on the other hand, were defined in terms of home—wife and mother—involvement and moral virtue. As a consequence, the idealization of masculine and feminine behavior affected courtship to the extent that romantic love took on greater importance as the criterion for marriage than ever before. Yet, ultimately, the doctrine of the two spheres continued to foster obstacles to friendship between the sexes, often resulting in a reliance on same sex friendships. Further, it severely handicapped the development of emotional bonds within courtship.

The study of dating and courtship patterns on college campuses in the United States has long fascinated sociologists. Perhaps the most famous analysis was conducted by Willard Waller (1937) in his study of what he called the "rating and dating complex," which he observed on the Pennsylvania State University campus in the 1930s. Waller described a mutually exploitative dating system in which male students sought sexual gratification while women sought to enhance their prestige by going out with the more desirable men and being taken to restaurants, theaters, amusements, etc. As a result, dating became a bargaining relationship with exploitative and antagonistic overtones. Waller further speculated that the gender-role antagonisms generated by the dating system were continued in courtship, love, and marriage, and led to undesirable emotional tensions throughout the couples' lives. He conceptualized the "principle of least interest" to describe how unequal emotional involvement could lead to the person with "least interest" exploiting the other throughout their relationship.

Sixty years later, there are persistent reports of the prevalence of a "rape culture"—a set of values and beliefs that provide an environment conducive to date and acquaintance rape—on college campuses. The authors of Reading 8, A. Ayres Boswell and Joan Z.

Spade, see college fraternities as the site where much of this rape culture originates and operates. The structure of campus life and the nature of gender relations are seen as the crucial factors in this development. More specifically, the authors compare "dangerous" places with "safer" places as identified by their informants as the sites where rape culture is and is not prevalent.

Egon Mayer's discussion (Reading 9) of intermarriage between Jews and Christians revolves around the issues of individualism and love versus tradition and family continuity. An underlying issue is the maintenance of ethnic identity in intermarriages and the continuation of that identity in future generations.

The concluding reading (10) in this chapter is Adele Bahn and Angela Jaquez's "One Style of Dominican Bridal Shower." The authors provide an ethnographic account of what, at first glance, seems to be a festive celebration with no serious intent. However, the underlying meaning of bridal showers for these Dominican women living in New York City revolves around the anticipatory socialization of the prospective wife into four roles. The shower is seen to reflect old and new norms that prescribe and reinforce the traditional roles for the bride, including the role of a woman among women, the sexual role, the homemaker role, and the subservient role of the wife vis-a-vis the husband.

Chapter Four, "Sexuality, Intimacy, and the Family," opens with an exploration of how love is defined differently by women and men. Francesca M. Cancian explores the "feminization of love" in Reading 11. The feminized perspective defines love in terms of emotional expressiveness, verbal self-disclosure, and affection. Women are identified with this perspective. In contrast, the definition largely ignores love manifested by instrumental help or the sharing of physical activities that has been identified with masculine behavior. She argues that, by conceptualizing love in this manner, polarized gender-role relationships that contribute to social and economic inequality occur. Cancian calls for an androgynous perspective that rejects the underlying ideology of separate spheres and validates masculine as well as feminine styles of love.

Kath Weston in her book, *Families We Choose,* draws on her ethnographic field research of gays and lesbians in the San Francisco Bay Area to examine the kinship character of the ties among close friends and lovers and the political and ideological battles that were waged so that these ties would receive social and legal recognition. Weston documents how gay men and lesbians developed families and separated parenting and family formation from heterosexual relationships. In this selection from her book, Reading 12, Weston examines the ideological transformation that saw "gay" and "family" as mutually antithetical categories move to one in which these categories are used in combination to describe a particular form of kinship relation.

Chapter 5, "Gender Roles, Work, and the Family," contains three readings focusing on gender relationships in terms of the different allocations and divisions of labor that exist between outside work and the home. Arlie Russell Hochschild (1989) examined the contemporary dual-career family in her widely praised book, *The Second Shift.* Hochschild is concerned with how cultural definitions of "appropriate" domestic roles and labor-force roles affect marital dynamics. She observes that contemporary economic trends have altered women's lives much more than they have altered men's lives.

Women have found themselves in new circumstances: They are working full time in the paid labor force, yet, at the same time, they are seen as primarily involved in domestic work. As a result, women are experiencing a "culture lag" in the larger world and a "gender lag" in the home. There is a lag regarding both attitudes and behavior towards women's paid work and domestic work.

In a recent book, *The Time Bind,* Hochschild (1997) examines the ways in which women are also using work as an escape from domestic duties. Based on this research, Hochschild reports in Reading 13 that the demands of domestic work (shopping, cooking, cleaning, and childcare), especially in light of the fact that both women and men are employed outside the home, have led to a very curious development. Work for many is now becoming the site for refuge. No longer is one's home one's castle; the new "haven in a heartless world" is the work site. The real possibility of child neglect as a consequence of the removal of parents from the home is explored in Hochschild's provocative article.

In-Sook Lim (Reading 14) examines how the "second shift" has been implemented in the homes of Korean immigrant working-class couples. Immigrant Korean women find themselves actively employed in the paid labor market virtually to the same extent as their husbands. However, traditional patriarchal customs still govern their husbands' attitudes and behavior. These women challenge these customs and seek to end the unequal division of family work.

In Reading 15, "Gender, Class, Family, and Migration: Puerto Rican Women in Chicago," Maura I. Toro-Morn provides another illustration of the interrelationship of migration patterns and gender relations within the family. Toro-Morn documents how women who joined their husbands in Chicago either participated in the paid economy or contributed with the reproductive work—the taking care of children, husbands, and families—that supported their husbands and families. She compares working-class to better-educated middle-class Puerto Rican women and examines how both had to confront dual responsibilities for the reproductive work that takes place in the home and the economically productive work that takes place outside the home.

References

Ariès, Philippe. 1962. *Centuries of Childhood: A Social History of Family Life.* Translated by Robert Baldick. New York: Knopf.

Cott, Nancy. 1979. "Passionlessness: An Interpretation of Victorian Sexual Ideology, 1790–1850." Pp. 162–181 in *A Heritage of Her Own,* edited by Nancy F. Cott and Elizabeth H. Pleck. New York: Simon and Schuster.

Degler, Carl N. 1980. *At Odds: Women and the Family in America from the Revolution to the Present.* New York: Oxford University Press.

Hochschild, Arlie (with Anne Machung). 1989. *The Second Shift: Working Parents and the Revolution at Home.* New York: Viking.

Hochschild, Arlie Russell. 1997. *The Time Bind: When Work Becomes Home & Home Becomes Work.* New York: Metropolitan Books.

Shorter, Edward. 1975. *The Making of the Modern Family.* New York: Basic Books.

Stone, Lawrence. 1977. *The Family, Sex and Marriage in England 1500–1800.* Abridged edition. New York: Harper/Colophon Books.

Waller, Willard. 1937. "The Rating and Dating Complex." *American Sociological Review* 2:727–734.

3 | Premarital and Mate Selection Relationships

Reading 8   Fraternities and Collegiate Rape Culture:

Why Are Some Fraternities More Dangerous Places for Women?*

A. AYRES BOSWELL
JOAN Z. SPADE

Social interaction at fraternities that undergraduate women identified as places where there is a high risk of rape are compared to those at fraternities identified as low risk as well as two local bars. Factors that contribute to rape are common on this campus; however, both men and women behaved differently in different settings. Implications of these findings are considered.

Date rape and acquaintance rape on college campuses are topics of concern to both researchers and college administrators. Some estimate that 60 to 80 percent of rapes are date or acquaintance rape (Koss, Dinero, Seibel, and Cox 1988). Further, 1 out of 4 college women say they were raped or experienced an attempted rape, and 1 out of 12 college men say they forced a woman to have sexual intercourse against her will (Koss, Gidycz, and Wisniewski 1985).

Although considerable attention focuses on the incidence of rape, we know relatively little about the context or the *rape culture* surrounding date and acquaintance rape. Rape culture is a set

AUTHORS' NOTE An earlier version of this article was presented at the annual meeting of the American Sociological Association, August 1993. Special thanks go to Barbara Frankel, Karen Hicks, and Jennifer Volchko for their input into the process and final version and to Judith Gerson, Sue Curry Jansen, Judith Lasker, Patricia Yancey Martin, and Ronnie Steinberg for their careful readings of drafts of this article and for many helpful comments.

of values and beliefs that provide an environment conducive to rape (Buchwald, Fletcher, & Roth 1993; Herman 1984). The term applies to a generic culture surrounding and promoting rape, not the specific settings in which rape is likely to occur. We believe that the specific settings also are important in defining relationships between men and women.

Some have argued that fraternities are places where rape is likely to occur on college campuses (Martin and Hummer 1989; O'Sullivan 1993; Sanday 1990) and that the students most likely to accept rape myths and be more sexually aggressive are more likely to live in fraternities and sororities, consume higher doses of alcohol and drugs, and place a higher value on social life at college (Gwartney-Gibbs and Stockard 1989; Kalof and Cargill 1991). Others suggest that sexual aggression is learned in settings such as fraternities and is not part of predispositions or preexisting attitudes (Boeringer, Shehan, and Akers 1991). To prevent further incidences of rape on college campuses, we need to understand what it is about fraternities in particular and college life in general that may contribute to the maintenance of a rape culture on college campuses.

Our approach is to identify the social contexts that link fraternities to campus rape and promote a rape culture. Instead of assuming that all fraternities provide an environment conducive to rape, we compare the interactions of men and women at fraternities identified on campus as being especially *dangerous* places for women, where the likelihood of rape is high, to those seen as *safer* places, where the perceived probability of rape occurring is lower. Prior to collecting data for our study, we found that most women students identified some fraternities as having more sexually aggressive members and a higher probability of rape. These women also considered other fraternities as relatively safe houses, where

a woman could go and get drunk if she wanted to and feel secure that the fraternity men would not take advantage of her. We compared parties at houses identified as high-risk and low-risk houses as well as at two local bars frequented by college students. Our analysis provides an opportunity to examine situations and contexts that hinder or facilitate positive social relations between undergraduate men and women.

The abusive attitudes toward women that some fraternities perpetuate exist within a general culture where rape is intertwined in traditional gender scripts. Men are viewed as initiators of sex and women as either passive partners or active resisters, preventing men from touching their bodies (LaPlante, McCormick, and Brannigan 1980). Rape culture is based on the assumptions that men are aggressive and dominant whereas women are passive and acquiescent (Buchwald et al. 1993; Herman 1984). What occurs on college campuses is an extension of the portrayal of domination and aggression of men over women that exemplifies the double standard of sexual behavior in U.S. society (Barthel 1988; Kimmel 1993).

Sexually active men are positively reinforced by being referred to as "studs," whereas women who are sexually active or report enjoying sex are derogatorily labeled as "sluts" (Herman 1984; O'Sullivan 1993). These gender scripts are embodied in rape myths and stereotypes such as "She really wanted it; she just said no because she didn't want me to think she was a bad girl" (Burke, Stets, and Pirog-Good 1989; Jenkins and Dambrot 1987; Lisak and Roth 1988; Malamuth 1986; Muehlenhard and Linton 1987; Peterson and Franzese 1987). Because men's sexuality is seen as more natural, acceptable, and uncontrollable than women's sexuality, many men and women excuse acquaintance rape by affirming that men cannot control their natural urges (Miller and Marshall 1987).

Whereas some researchers explain these attitudes toward sexuality and rape using an individual or a psychological interpretation, we argue that rape has a social basis, one in which both men and women create and recreate masculine and feminine identities and relations. Based on the assumption that rape is part of the social construction of gender, we examine how men and women "do gender" on a college campus (West and Zimmerman 1987). We focus on fraternities because they have been identified as settings that encourage rape (Sanday 1990). By comparing fraternities that are viewed by women as places where there is a high risk of rape to those where women believe there is a low risk of rape as well as two local commercial bars, we seek to identify characteristics that make some social settings more likely places for the occurrence of rape.

METHOD

We observed social interactions between men and women at a private coeducational school in which a high percentage (49.4 percent) of students affiliate with Greek organizations. The university has an undergraduate population of approximately 4,500 students, just more than one third of whom are women; the students are primarily from upper-middle-class families. The school, which admitted only men until 1971, is highly competitive academically.

We used a variety of data collection approaches: observations of interactions between men and women at fraternity parties and bars, formal interviews, and informal conversations. The first author, a former undergraduate at this school and a graduate student at the time of the study, collected the data. She knew about the social life at the school and had established rapport and trust between herself and undergraduate students as a teaching assistant in a human sexuality course.

The process of identifying high- and low-risk fraternity houses followed Hunter's (1953) reputational approach. In our study, 40 women students identified fraternities that they considered to be high risk, or to have more sexually aggressive members and higher incidence of rape, as well as fraternities that they considered to be safe houses. The women represented all four years of undergraduate college and different living groups (sororities, residence halls, and off-campus housing). Observations focused on the four fraternities named most often by these women as high-risk houses and the four identified as low-risk houses.

Throughout the spring semester, the first author observed at two fraternity parties each weekend at two different houses (fraternities could have parties only on weekends at this campus). She also observed students' interactions in two popular university bars on weeknights to provide a comparison of students' behavior in non-Greek settings. The first local bar at which she observed was popular with seniors and older students; the second bar was popular with first-, second-, and third-year undergraduates because the management did not strictly enforce drinking age laws in this bar.

The observer focused on the social context as well as interaction among participants at each setting. In terms of social context, she observed the following: ratio of men to women, physical setting such as the party decor and theme, use and control of alcohol and level of intoxication, and explicit and implicit norms. She noted interactions between men and women (i.e., physical contact, conversational style, use of jokes) and the relations among men (i.e., their treatment of pledges and other men at fraternity parties). Other than the observer, no one knew the identity of the high- or low-risk fraternities. Although this may have introduced bias into the data collection, students on this campus who read this article before it was submitted for publication commented on how accurately the social scene is described.

In addition, 50 individuals were interviewed including men from the selected fraternities, women who attended those parties, men not affiliated with fraternities, and self-identified rape victims known to the first author. The first author approached men and women by telephone or on campus and asked them to participate in interviews. The interviews included open-ended questions about gender relations on campus, attitudes about date rape, and their own experiences on campus.

To assess whether self-selection was a factor in determining the classification of the fraternity, we compared high-risk houses to low-risk houses on several characteristics. In terms of status on campus, the high- and low-risk houses we studied attracted about the same number of pledges; however, many of the high-risk houses had more members. There was no difference in grade point averages for the two types of houses. In fact, the highest and lowest grade point averages were found in the high-risk category. Although both high- and low-risk fraternities participated in sports, brothers in the low-risk houses tended to play intramural sports whereas brothers in the high-risk houses were more likely to be varsity athletes. The high-risk houses may be more aggressive, as they had a slightly larger number of disciplinary incidents and their reports were more severe, often with physical harm to others and damage to property. Further, in year-end reports, there was more property damage in the high-risk houses. Last, more of the low-risk houses participated in a campus rape-prevention program. In summary, both high- and low-risk fraternities seem to be equally attractive to freshmen men on this campus, and differences between the eight fraternities we studied were not great; however, the high-risk houses had a

slightly larger number of reports of aggression and physical destruction in the houses and the low-risk houses were more likely to participate in a rape prevention program.

RESULTS

The Settings

Fraternity Parties

We observed several differences in the quality of the interaction of men and women at parties at high-risk fraternities compared to those at low-risk houses. A typical party at a low-risk house included an equal number of women and men. The social atmosphere was friendly, with considerable interaction between women and men. Men and women danced in groups and in couples, with many of the couples kissing and displaying affection toward each other. Brothers explained that, because many of the men in these houses had girlfriends, it was normal to see couples kissing on the dance floor. Coed groups engaged in conversations at many of these houses, with women and men engaging in friendly exchanges, giving the impression that they knew each other well. Almost no cursing and yelling was observed at parties in low-risk houses; when pushing occurred, the participants apologized. Respect for women extended to the women's bathrooms, which were clean and well supplied.

At high-risk houses, parties typically had skewed gender ratios, sometimes involving more men and other times involving more women. Gender segregation also was evident at these parties, with the men on one side of a room or in the bar drinking while women gathered in another area. Men treated women differently in the high-risk houses. The women's bathrooms in the high-risk houses were filthy, including clogged toilets and vomit in the sinks. When a brother was told of the mess in the bathroom at a high-risk house, he replied, "Good, maybe some of these beer wenches will leave so there will be more beer for us."

Men attending parties at high-risk houses treated women less respectfully, engaging in jokes, conversations, and behaviors that degraded women. Men made a display of assessing women's bodies and rated them with thumbs up or thumbs down for the other men in the sight of the women. One man attending a party at a high-risk fraternity said to another, "Did you know that this week is Women's Awareness Week? I guess that means we get to abuse them more this week." Men behaved more crudely at parties at high-risk houses. At one party, a brother dropped his pants, including his underwear, while dancing in front of several women. Another brother slid across the dance floor completely naked.

The atmosphere at parties in high-risk fraternities was less friendly overall. With the exception of greetings, men and women rarely smiled or laughed and spoke to each other less often than was the case at parties in low-risk houses. The few one-on-one conversations between women and men appeared to be strictly flirtatious (lots of eye contact, touching, and very close talking). It was rare to see a group of men and women together talking. Men were openly hostile, which made the high-risk parties seem almost threatening at times. For example, there was a lot of touching, pushing, profanity, and name calling, some done by women.

Students at parties at the high-risk houses seemed self-conscious and aware of the presence of members of the opposite sex, an awareness that was sexually charged. Dancing early in the evening was usually between women. Close to midnight, the sex ratio began to balance out with the arrival of more men or more women. Couples began to dance together but in a sexual way (close dancing with lots of pelvic thrusts). Men

tried to pick up women using lines such as "Want to see my fish tank?" and "Let's go upstairs so that we can talk; I can't hear what you're saying in here."

Although many of the same people who attended high-risk parties also attended low-risk parties, their behavior changed as they moved from setting to setting. Group norms differed across contexts as well. At a party that was held jointly at a low-risk house, with a high-risk fraternity, the ambience was that of a party at a high-risk fraternity with heavier drinking, less dancing, and fewer conversations between women and men. The men from both high- and low-risk fraternities were very aggressive; a fight broke out, and there was pushing and shoving on the dance floor and in general.

As others have found, fraternity brothers at high-risk houses on this campus told about routinely discussing their sexual exploits at breakfast the morning after parties and sometimes at house meetings (cf. Martin and Hummer 1989; O'Sullivan 1993; Sanday 1990). During these sessions, the brothers we interviewed said that men bragged about what they did the night before with stories of sexual conquests often told by the same men, usually sophomores. The women involved in these exploits were women they did not know or knew but did not respect, or *faceless victims*. Men usually treated girlfriends with respect and did not talk about them in these storytelling sessions. Men from low-risk houses, however, did not describe similar sessions in their houses.

The Bar Scene

The bar atmosphere and social context differed from those of fraternity parties. The music was not as loud, and both bars had places to sit and have conversations. At all fraternity parties, it was difficult to maintain conversations with loud music playing and no place to sit. The volume of music at parties at high-risk fraternities was even louder than it was at low-risk houses, making it virtually impossible to have conversations. In general, students in the local bars behaved in the same way that students did at parties in low-risk houses with conversations typical, most occurring between men and women.

The first bar, frequented by older students, had live entertainment every night of the week. Some nights were more crowded than others, and the atmosphere was friendly, relaxed, and conducive to conversation. People laughed and smiled and behaved politely toward each other. The ratio of men to women was fairly equal, with students congregating in mostly coed groups. Conversation flowed freely and people listened to each other.

Although the women and men at the first bar also were at parties at low- and high-risk fraternities, their behavior at the bar included none of the blatant sexual or intoxicated behaviors observed at some of these parties. As the evenings wore on, the number of one-on-one conversations between men and women increased and conversations shifted from small talk to topics such as war and AIDS. Conversations did not revolve around picking up another person, and most people left the bar with same-sex friends or in coed groups.

The second bar was less popular with older students. Younger students, often under the legal drinking age, went there to drink, sometimes after leaving campus parties. This bar was much smaller and usually not as crowded as the first bar. The atmosphere was more mellow and relaxed than it was at the fraternity parties. People went there to hang out and talk to each other.

On a couple of occasions, however, the atmosphere at the second bar became similar to that of a party at a high-risk fraternity. As the number of people in the bar increased, they removed chairs and tables, leaving no place to sit

and talk. The music also was turned up louder, drowning out conversation. With no place to dance or sit, most people stood around but could not maintain conversations because of the noise and crowds. Interactions between women and men consisted mostly of flirting. Alcohol consumption also was greater than it was on the less crowded nights, and the number of visibly drunk people increased. The more people drank, the more conversation and socializing broke down. The only differences between this setting and that of a party at a high-risk house were that brothers no longer controlled the territory and bedrooms were not available upstairs.

Gender Relations

Relations between women and men are shaped by the contexts in which they meet and interact. As is the case on other college campuses, *hooking up* has replaced dating on this campus, and fraternities are places where many students hook up. Hooking up is a loosely applied term on college campuses that had different meanings for men and women on this campus.

Most men defined hooking up similarly. One man said it was something that happens

> *when you are really drunk and meet up with a woman you sort of know, or possibly don't know at all and don't care about. You go home with her with the intention of getting as much sexual, physical pleasure as she'll give you, which can range anywhere from kissing to intercourse, without any strings attached.*

The exception to this rule is when men hook up with women they admire. Men said they are less likely to press for sexual activity with someone they know and like because they want the relationship to continue and be based on respect.

Women's version of hooking up differed. Women said they hook up only with men they cared about and described hooking up as kissing and petting but not sexual intercourse. Many women said that hooking up was disappointing because they wanted longer-term relationships. First-year women students realized quickly that hook-ups were usually one-night stands with no strings attached, but many continued to hook up because they had few opportunities to develop relationships with men on campus. One first-year woman said that "70 percent of hook-ups never talk again and try to avoid one another; 26 percent may actually hear from them or talk to them again, and 4 percent may actually go on a date, which can lead to a relationship." Another first-year woman said, "It was fun in the beginning. You get a lot of attention and kiss a lot of boys and think this is what college is about, but it gets tiresome fast."

Whereas first-year women get tired of the hook-up scene early on, many men do not become bored with it until their junior or senior year. As one upperclassman said, "The whole game of hooking up became really meaningless and tiresome for me during my second semester of my sophomore year, but most of my friends didn't get bored with it until the following year."

In contrast to hooking up, students also described monogamous relationships with steady partners. Some type of commitment was expected, but most people did not anticipate marriage. The term *seeing each other* was applied when people were sexually involved but free to date other people. This type of relationship involved less commitment than did one of boyfriend/girlfriend but was not considered to be a hook-up.

The general consensus of women and men interviewed on this campus was that the Greek system, called "the hill," set the scene for gender relations. The predominance of Greek member-ship and subsequent living arrangements segregated men and women. During the week, little interaction occurred between women and men after their first year in college because students in fraternities or sororities live and dine in separate quarters. In addition, many non-Greek upper-class students move off campus into apartments. Therefore, students see each other in classes or in the library, but there is no place where students can just hang out together.

Both men and women said that fraternities dominate campus social life, a situation that everyone felt limited opportunities for meaningful interactions. One senior Greek man said,

> *This environment is horrible and so unhealthy for good male and female relationships and interactions to occur. It is so segregated and male dominated…. It is our party, with our rules and our beer. We are allowing these women and other men to come to our party. Men can feel superior in their domain.*

Comments from a senior woman reinforced his views: "Men are dominant; they are the kings of the campus. It is their environment that they allow us to enter; therefore, we have to abide by their rules." A junior woman described fraternity parties as

> *good for meeting acquaintances but almost impossible to really get to know anyone. The environment is so superficial, probably because there are so many social cliques due to the Greek system. Also, the music is too loud and the people are too drunk to attempt to have a real conversation, anyway.*

Some students claim that fraternities even control the dating relationships of their members. One senior woman said, "Guys dictate how dating occurs on this campus, whether it's cool, who it's with, how much time can be spent with the girlfriend and with the brothers." Couples either left campus for an evening or hung out separately with their own same-gender friends at fraternity parties, finally getting together with each other at about 2 A.M. Couples rarely went together to fraternity parties. Some men felt that a girlfriend was just a replacement for a hook-up. According to one junior man, "Basically a girlfriend is someone you go to at 2 A.M. after you've hung out with the guys. She is the sexual outlet that the guys can't provide you with."

Some fraternity brothers pressure each other to limit their time with and commitment to their girlfriends. One senior man said, "The hill [fraternities] and girlfriends don't mix." A brother described a constant battle between girlfriends and brothers over who the guy is going out with for the night, with the brothers usually winning. Brothers teased men with girlfriends with remarks such as "whipped" or "where's the ball and chain?" A brother from a high-risk house said that few brothers at his house had girlfriends; some did, but it was uncommon. One man said that from the minute he was a pledge he knew he would probably never have a girlfriend on this campus because "it was just not the norm in my house. No one has girlfriends; the guys have too much fun with [each other]."

The pressure on men to limit their commitment to girlfriends, however, was not true of all fraternities or of all men on campus. Couples attended low-risk fraternity parties together, and men in the low-risk houses went out on dates more often. A man in one low-risk house said that about 70 percet of the members of his house were involved in relationships with women, including the pledges (who were sophomores).

Treatment of Women

Not all men held negative attitudes toward women that are typical of a rape culture, and not all social contexts promoted the negative treatment of women. When men were asked whether they treated the women on campus with respect, the most common response was "On an individual basis, yes, but when you have a group of men together, no." Men said that, when together in groups with other men, they sensed a pressure to be disrespectful toward women. A first-year man's perception of the treatment of women was that "they are treated with more respect to their faces, but behind closed doors, with a group of men present, respect for women is not an issue." One senior man stated, "In general, college-aged men don't treat women their age with respect because 90 percent of them think of women as merely a means to sex." Women reinforced this perception. A first-year woman stated, "Men here are more interested in hooking up and drinking beer than they are in getting to know women as real people." Another woman said, "Men here use and abuse women."

Characteristic of rape culture, a double standard of sexual behavior for men versus women was prevalent on this campus. As one Greek senior man stated, "Women who sleep around are sluts and get bad reputations; men who do are champions and get a pat on the back from their brothers." Women also supported a double standard for sexual behavior by criticizing sexually active women. A first-year woman spoke out against women who are sexually active: "I think some girls here make it difficult for the men to respect women as a whole."

One concrete example of demeaning sexually active women on this campus is the "walk of shame." Fraternity brothers come out on the porches of their houses the night after parties and heckle women walking by. It is assumed that these women spent the night at fraternity houses and that the men they were with did not care enough about them to drive them home. Although sororities now reside in former fraternity houses, this practice continues and sometimes the victims of hecklings are sorority women on their way to study in the library.

A junior man in a high-risk fraternity described another ritual of disrespect toward women called "chatter." When an unknown woman sleeps over at the house, the brothers yell degrading remarks out the window at her as she leaves the next morning such as "Fuck that bitch" and "Who is that slut?" He said that sometimes brothers harass the brothers whose girlfriends stay over instead of heckling those women.

Fraternity men most often mistreated women they did not know personally. Men and women alike reported incidents in which brothers observed other brothers having sex with unknown women or women they knew only casually. A sophomore woman's experience exemplifies this anonymous state: "I don't mind if 10 guys were watching or it was videotaped. That's expected on this campus. It's the fact that he didn't apologize or even offer to drive me home that really upset me." Descriptions of sexual encounters involved the satisfaction of men by nameless women. A brother in a high-risk fraternity described a similar occurrence:

A brother of mine was hooking up upstairs with an unattractive woman who had been pursuing him all night. He told some brothers to go outside the window and watch. Well, one thing led to another and they were almost completely naked when the woman noticed the brothers outside. She was then unwilling to go any further, so the brother went outside and yelled at the other brothers and then closed the shades. I don't know if he scored or not, because the woman was pretty upset. But he did win the award for hooking up with the ugliest chick that weekend.

Attitudes toward Rape

The sexually charged environment of college campuses raises many questions about cultures that facilitate the rape of women. How women and men define their sexual behavior is important legally as well as interpersonally. We asked students how they defined rape and had them compare it to the following legal definition: the perpetration of an act of sexual intercourse with a female against her will and consent, whether her will is overcome by force or fear resulting from the threat of force, or by drugs or intoxicants; or when, because of mental deficiency, she is incapable of exercising rational judgment. (Brownmiller 1975, 368)

When presented with this legal definition, most women interviewed recognized it as well as the complexities involved in applying it. A first-year woman said, "If a girl is drunk and the guy knows it and the girl says, 'Yes, I want to have sex,' and they do, that is still rape because the girl can't make a conscious, rational decision under the influence of alcohol." Some women disagreed. Another first-year woman stated, "I don't think it is fair that the guy gets blamed when both people involved are drunk."

The typical definition men gave for rape was "when a guy jumps out of the bushes and forces himself sexually onto a girl." When asked what date rape was, the most common answer was "when one person has sex with another person who did not consent." Many men said, however, that "date rape is when a woman wakes up the next morning and regrets having sex." Some men said that date rape was too gray an area to define. "Consent is a fine line," said a Greek senior man student. For the most part, the men we spoke with argued that rape did not occur on this campus. One Greek sophomore man said, "I think it is ridiculous that someone here would rape someone." A first-year man stated, "I have a problem with the word rape. It sounds so criminal, and we are not criminals; we are sane people."

Whether aware of the legal definitions of rape, most men resisted the idea that a woman who is intoxicated is unable to consent to sex. A Greek junior man said, "Men should not be responsible for women's drunkenness." One first-year man said, "If that is the legal definition of rape, then it happens all the time on this campus." A senior man said, "I don't care whether alcohol is involved or not; that is not rape. Rapists are people that have something seriously wrong with them." A first-year man even claimed that when women get drunk, they invite sex. He said, "Girls get so drunk here and then come on to us. What are we supposed to do? We are only human."

DISCUSSION AND CONCLUSION

These findings describe the physical and normative aspects of one college campus as they relate to attitudes about and relations between men and women. Our findings suggest that an explanation emphasizing rape culture also must focus on those characteristics of the social setting that play a role in defining heterosexual relationships on college campuses (Kalof and Cargill 1991). The degradation of women as portrayed in rape culture was not found in all fraternities on this campus. Both group norms and individual

behavior changed as students went from one place to another. Although individual men are the ones who rape, we found that some settings are more likely places for rape than are others. Our findings suggest that rape cannot be seen only as an isolated act and blamed on individual behavior and proclivities, whether it be alcohol consumption or attitudes. We also must consider characteristics of the settings that promote the behaviors that reinforce a rape culture.

Relations between women and men at parties in low-risk fraternities varied considerably from those in high-risk houses. Peer pressure and situational norms influenced women as well as men. Although many men in high- and low-risk houses shared similar views and attitudes about the Greek system, women on this campus, and date rape, their behaviors at fraternity parties were quite different.

Women who are at highest risk of rape are women whom fraternity brothers did not know. These women are faceless victims, nameless acquaintances—not friends. Men said their responsibility to such persons and the level of guilt they feel later if the hook-ups end in sexual intercourse are much lower if they hook up with women they do not know. In high-risk houses, brothers treated women as subordinates and kept them at a distance. Men in high-risk houses actively discouraged ongoing heterosexual relationships, routinely degraded women, and participated more fully in the hook-up scene; thus, the probability that women would become faceless victims was higher in these houses. The flirtatious nature of the parties indicated that women go to these parties looking for available men, but finding boyfriends or relationships was difficult at parties in high-risk houses. However, in the low-risk houses, where more men had long-term relationships, the women were not strangers and were less likely to become faceless victims.

The social scene on this campus, and on most others, offers women and men few other options to socialize. Although there may be no such thing as a completely safe fraternity party for women, parties at low-risk houses and commercial bars encouraged men and women to get know each other better and decreased the probability that women would become faceless victims. Although both men and women found the social scene on this campus demeaning, neither demanded different settings for socializing, and attendance at fraternity parties is a common form of entertainment.

These findings suggest that a more conducive environment for conversation can promote more positive interactions between men and women. Simple changes would provide the opportunity for men and women to interact in meaningful ways such as adding places to sit and lowering the volume of music at fraternity parties or having parties in neutral locations, where men are not in control. The typical party room in fraternity houses includes a place to dance but not to sit and talk. The music often is loud, making it difficult, if not impossible, to carry on conversations; however, there were more conversations at the low-risk parties, where there also was more respect shown toward women. Although the number of brothers who had steady girlfriends in the low-risk houses as compared to those in the high-risk houses may explain the differences, we found that commercial bars also provided a context for interaction between men and women. At the bars, students sat and talked and conversations between men and women flowed freely, resulting in deep discussions and fewer hook-ups.

Alcohol consumption was a major focus of social events here and intensified attitudes and orientations of a rape culture. Although pressure to drink was evident at all fraternity parties and at both bars, drinking dominated high-risk fraternity parties, at which nonalcoholic beverages usually were not available and people chugged beers and became visibly drunk. A rape culture is strengthened by rules that permit alcohol only at fraternity parties. Under this system, men control the parties and dominate the men as well as the women who attend. As college administrators crack down on fraternities and alcohol on campus, however, the same behaviors and norms may transfer to other places such as parties in apartments or private homes where administrators have much less control. At commercial bars, interaction and socialization with others were as important as drinking, with the exception of the nights when the bar frequented by under-class students became crowded. Although one solution is to offer nonalcoholic social activities, such events receive little support on this campus. Either these alternative events lacked the prestige of the fraternity parties or the alcohol was seen as necessary to unwind, or both.

In many ways, the fraternities on this campus determined the settings in which men and women interacted. As others before us have found, pressures for conformity to the norms and values exist at both high-risk and low-risk houses (Kalof and Cargill 1991; Martin and Hummer 1989; Sanday 1990). The desire to be accepted is not unique to this campus or the Greek system (Holland and Eisenhart 1990; Horowitz 1988; Moffat 1989). The degree of conformity required by Greeks may be greater than that required in most social groups, with considerable pressure to adopt and maintain the image of their houses. The fraternity system intensifies the "groupthink syndrome" (Janis 1972) by solidifying the identity of the in-group and creating an us/them atmosphere. Within the fraternity culture, brothers are highly regarded and women are viewed as outsiders. For men in high-risk fraternities, women threatened their brotherhood; therefore, brothers discouraged relationships and harassed those who treated women as equals or with respect.

The pressure to be one of the guys and hang out with the guys strengthens a rape culture on college campus by demeaning women and encouraging the segregation of men and women.

Students on this campus were aware of the contexts in which they operated and the choices available to them. They recognized that, in their interactions, they created differences between men and women that are not natural, essential, or biological (West and Zimmerman 1987). Not all men and women accepted the demeaning treatment of women, but they continued to participate in behaviors that supported aspects of a rape culture. Many women participated in the hookup scene even after they had been humiliated and hurt because they had few other means of initiating contact with men on campus. Men and women alike played out this scene, recognizing its injustices in many cases but being unable to change the course of their behaviors.

Although this research provides some clues to gender relations on college campuses, it raises many questions. Why do men and women participate in activities that support a rape culture when they see its injustices? What would happen if alcohol were not controlled by groups of men who admit that they disrespect women when they get together? What can be done to give men and women on college campuses more opportunities to interact responsibly and get to know each other better? These questions should be studied on other campuses with a focus on the social settings in which the incidence of rape and the attitudes that support a rape culture exist. Fraternities are social contexts that may or may not foster a rape culture.

Our findings indicate that a rape culture exists in some fraternities, especially those we identified as high-risk houses. College administrators are responding to this situation by providing counseling and educational programs that increase awareness of date rape including campaigns such as "No means no." These strategies are important in changing attitudes, values, and behaviors; however, changing individuals is not enough. The structure of campus life and the impact of that structure on gender relations on campus are highly determinative. To eliminate campus rape culture, student leaders and administrators must examine the situations in which women and men meet and restructure these settings to provide opportunities for respectful interaction. Change may not require abolishing fraternities; rather, it may require promoting settings that facilitate positive gender relations.

Reading 9   Two Can Make a Revolution*

EGON MAYER

Paul's grandmother, Ba Thi Tu, had been cooking for the Bar Mitzvah for days alongside her daughter, Josephine Tu Steinman. The menu included veal with black mushroom sauce, Vietnamese meatballs, beef chow fun, chicken and cashew nuts, rice noodles, and other Oriental delicacies. A dish calling for pork had to be eliminated, along with shellfish dishes, because they were not kosher.

This was no ordinary Bar Mitzvah fare: no chopped herring, stuffed derma, or matzoh ball soup here. This was the home-catered Bar Mitzvah feast of Paul Steinman—the son of Ron Steinman, an executive at NBC-TV News—and Josephine Steinman, formerly Ngoc Suong Tu, a Vietnamese Buddhist who converted to Judaism after she came to the United States with her husband.

That *The New York Times* chose to report on the "Bar Mitzvah with a Vietnamese Flavor" (June 29, 1983) is ample indication, of course, that such ceremonies are far from common. Indeed, such families are far from common. Jews and Vietnamese are generally not found together in large enough numbers to produce more than one or two intermarriages. But the story highlights what have become increasingly common facts of family life for Jews, as well as other minorities, since the early part of the twentieth century. America is blending, and out of its cultural caldron are emerging life-styles and new customs that defy age-old distinctions. When it comes to mate selection and the family forms that follow from it, love triumphs over tradition; inclinations triumph over timeless customs; and even religious rituals are transfigured to meet private needs and desires.

In that simple human interest story in *The Times,* which focused on the menu rather than on the ironies of the occasion, one can see reflected centuries of tension, and the fermenting of cultural forces and contending human drives coming to fruition.

Paul's Hebrew teacher was *kvelling* (rejoicing) at what appeared to her to be the fulfillment of the American dream. "A blending of two ancient cultures have met here today," Ms. Saletsky said. One is almost moved to the clichéd exultation "Love Conquers All." But as we shall see, such simple generalizations are defied by the complex realities of intermarriages.

Here, and in most other cases, too, love is no blind conqueror. It does not vanquish all other bonds or loyalties. Ron Steinman's Jewishness was important enough for him to have Ngoc Suong convert; important enough to have his children raised as Jews and educated in a Hebrew school; and important enough to have his

*Mayer, Egon. 1987. "Two Can Make a Revolution." Pp. 23–58 in *Love and Tradition: Marriage Between Jews and Christians*. New York: Plenum Publishing Corporation. Reprinted by permission.

firstborn son go through the traditional Jewish rite of passage. In subsequent personal conversation with Ron and Josephine, it became apparent that those same Jewish sentiments were not a salient consideration in Ron's mind when he chose to marry the then Ngoc Suong. Moreover, Josephine observed that one of her deeply felt reasons for wanting to become Jewish was her Vietnamese heritage that obliges a married woman to join her fate entirely to her husband and his family. Thus, for her, conversion to Judaism was a traditional wifely obligation. At the same time, for Ron, marriage to a Vietnamese woman was very much a break from his Brooklyn Jewish family tradition. For both, albeit for different reasons and in different ways, love and marriage entailed not following the customary path of their respective families, at least as far as mate selection was concerned.

The modern vocabulary of motives for marriage emphasizes love, compatibility, and mutual fulfillment. It leaves but little room for such considerations as duty, respect for tradition, and responsibility to one's ancestors and parents. Individualism, personalism, and privatism form the cornerstones of contemporary family relationships—at least that is the conventional wisdom. In the light of that wisdom, the very concept—intermarriage—is an anachronism. What should it matter, as the question is often asked, what a person's religious, ethnic, racial, etc., background is? Only one man and one woman are united in a marriage. Ron and Ngoc Suong no doubt underwent such questioning before their marriage; at least in their own minds, if not with one another and their respective parents.

Yet their very life as a modern Reform Jewish family is a testimonial to the persistence of tradition, albeit in modern garb. The fact that she became Jewish, an American, and changed her name to Josephine is an indication of just how important it was for both of them to bridge the cultural and religious differences that many think should not matter any more to modern men and women living in the age of hi-tech.

The brief story of Paul's Bar Mitzvah points to a multitude of insights about what it means to be a Jew in modern America; about what it means to be a member of a religious or ethnic minority in a liberal, pluralistic society; about what it means to be a family today; and, indeed, about the very nature of identity in modern society.

The story symbolizes the simultaneous drive of individuals to pursue their own individual happiness under circumstances that are made unpredictable by the impersonal forces of history (e.g., war). At the same time, the story also symbolizes the deeply rooted tenacity of traditions and the capacity of free individuals to blend and connect the most time-honored traditions in the most unconventional ways. In a sense, the story of Paul's Bar Mitzvah epitomizes the irony of Jewish survival.

The image of love emerging out of the ashes of war has always been one of profound irony. That an American-Jewish bureau chief for NBC, covering the war in Vietnam, should return to the United States with a Buddhist wife who becomes a Jew, and that they should, in turn, raise Jewish children, is truly newsworthy. At least one of the sources of the irony is war itself. That love should emerge from it is somewhat understandable, but that it should leave intact two people's attachments to their heritage, despite their experience of the war and despite their love across vastly different heritages, is remarkable. To be sure, the Steinmans' experience is virtually unique, and hardly generalizable. Yet it recalls for me my own first encounter with Jewish intermarriage as a child, in the person of one of our closest family friends—Allen Feher, or Sándor bácsi, as I called him—in my childhood in Budapest.

Sándor had been one of my father's closest friends, ever since they were teenagers in Komárom (a small town in southwestern Czecho-slovakia). They had attended yeshiva together, both being from Orthodox Jewish families. Sándor had married a few years before World War II and lived a traditional Orthodox Jewish life as a small merchant. When the Nazis entered Hungary in 1944 he happened to be away from home on business. His wife and two children were deported and never returned from the concentration camp. Sándor had gone into hiding in Budapest in the apartment of a Christian friend. There he was befriended by Irene, the daughter of a high-ranking officer in the Hungarian military, naturally, a Christian.

At the end of the war, Sándor and Irene married and had a child. Sándor abandoned his Orthodoxy and even joined the Communist Party—at least for appearance's sake. It helped him advance in the nationalized shop in which he worked. Yet, he continued to cling to a lifelong desire to go to Israel. In Communist Hungary in the late 1940s and early 1950s, that was—for all intents and purposes—a Messianic hope. But Irene, using her family contacts in the government, was able to obtain an exit visa for the three of them. In 1953 (at the close of the Stalinist era), Sándor—an intermarried Jew with a Catholic wife and daughter—immigrated to Israel, the land of his Jewish dreams. Irene never converted. She felt that she had returned to the land of Jesus and continued to live her life as an Israeli Catholic, as did her daughter.

A different war, a different continent and, surely, different personalities, yet one cannot help but feel that the same forces were working their curious chemistry in the lives of the Steinman and the Feher families. Ron and Sándor drew from the same well of tradition. And, for some as yet mysterious reason, Ngoc Suong and Irene both found it to be their desire to link their lives and fates to the ways in which their men would come to grips with their heritages. Ngoc

Suong joined Ron Steinman's religion; Irene joined Allen Feher's nation.

Surely neither couple sought to make a social revolution of any kind and would probably be surprised to see themselves spoken of as "revolutionaries." Yet their relationships, along with the multitude of other similar relationships, continue to exert transformative pressures on the ancient culture of the Jewish people, as well as on the laws of a modern nation-state, Israel.

Allen and Irene's daughter, for example, has remained a Christian, but as a young, dynamic woman, she has also served in the Israeli army. Naturally, she met and socialized with Israeli young men, virtually all of whom were Jews. For her, it was hardly a break with any social convention to fall in love with a Jewish man. But marriage for the two of them in Israel was out of the question, since matrimonial law in Israel is determined by Jewish religious regulations that prohibit such marriages. Ironically, they had to "elope" to Cyprus to marry in a Greek civil ceremony so as to be able to live as a legitimately married couple in Israel. Their case, along with untold others, remains a source of festering tension in Israeli political life.

Bar Mitzvahs like that of the Steinmans' also stretch the meaning of the ancient Jewish ritual. According to the *halacha* (the body of Jewish law made up by the commandments in the *Five Books of Moses* and their rabbinic interpretations in the Talmud and subsequent exigetical texts), Bar Mitzvah refers to the ancient legal status of adulthood at which point an adolescent is obligated to abide by the laws. The term applied only to young men who were regarded as having reached their Bar Mitzvah at the age of thirteen. There had been no comparable status for Jewish women, nor a celebration thereof, until the Conservative movement institutionalized the Bat Mitzvah in the 1920s.

Interestingly enough, the Bar Mitzvah was one of the many observances the Reform movement abandoned in the nineteenth century. The Reform movement, born out of the spirit of the enlightenment and German nationalism at the end of the eighteenth century, sought to do away with all those Jewish religious customs that could not be rendered plausible in the light of modern reason and contemporary life-style. The notion that a pubescent young man at the tender age of thirteen should somehow be regarded as a legal adult responsible for his actions was one of those implausible customs in the eyes of the Reform movement.

Consequently, some of the oldest and most respectable Reform temples in America would not permit Bar Mitzvahs to be performed as late as the 1950s, nor were Bat Mitzvahs permitted.

But ancient traditions die hard, and sometimes not at all. The need on the part of Jewish families to signify to themselves and their communities that their children are part of the Jewish fold through some kind of joyous public ceremony could not be eradicated by rational philosophy. The Bar Mitzvah has gradually made its return into the Reform movement since the 1950s. In fact, with the increasing incidence of marriages between Jews and non-Jews, particularly in the Reform community, the Bar Mitzvah has emerged as the signal Jewish ceremony by which an intermarried family publicly proclaims that their child is being raised as a Jew.

In a twist of modern Jewish family history, the Steinmans, as Reform Jews, were celebrating the Bar Mitzvah, which had lost its apparent meaningfulness for Reform Jews earlier. It now serves a highly potent social and psychological function precisely as a result of intermarriage. To be sure, not all children of intermarriages go through a Bar or a Bat Mitzvah ceremony. Indeed, most do not. My own studies have shown that in those intermarried families in which the

non-Jewish spouse does not convert to Judaism, only about 15 percent of the children will go through that symbolic Jewish life cycle ceremony. In what we call conversionary families, in which the formerly non-Jewish spouse converts to Judaism, as in the case of the Steinmans, nearly 75 percent of the children go through the ceremony; it apparently does not take many to stimulate cultural reforms.

The Steinmans' Bar Mitzvah menu also hints at an unfolding cultural revolution. Although most of America's Jews have relinquished the ethnic distinctiveness of their daily diet over the past few generations (hardly anyone really lives on chopped herring, *gefilte* fish, or *chulent* any more), such Jewish ceremonial occasions as weddings and Bar Mitzvahs are still marked by highly traditional food. For most modern American Jews, that is probably one of the salient features of these occasions: the opportunity to recollect the flavors and images of the past through their palates. But because most typical Jewish homes no longer prepare traditional Jewish foods as part of their normal diet, professional Jewish catering has emerged as an industry in its own right. Ostensibly, the function of the industry is to provide food and style consistent with the middle-class consumer values of American Jews. However, its more subtle, latent function is to serve up a feast of traditions through culinary inventiveness: to blend the taste of the immigrant with the style of the successful American.

In "olden days," it was not the caterer, but rather the women of the family who prepared the food for days and weeks before a Bar Mitzvah or a wedding. One of the objects of the ceremony was to exhibit before the larger invited community the mastery of the family of shared food values. "Look at my *kugel*," or *strudel,* or *gefilte* fish, the proud mother of a Bar Mitzvah boy would exclaim to her friends. And recipes, memories of mothers, and culinary techniques would be exchanged. But who asks a caterer for a recipe or memories of his mother?

Not surprisingly, it was Paul Steinman's Vietnamese grandmother and mother who spent their days cooking in preparation for the Bar Mitzvah. After all, where do you get a kosher caterer who cooks Vietnamese style? And the arousal of sensory memories through food is evidently no less important to the Vietnamese than it is to Jews—even if it is at a Bar Mitzvah. But the irony is this: Given the obvious importance attached to the memories of the palate by both Jews and Vietnamese, and probably all other ethnic Americans as well, what kind of memories are being built into young Paul's palate, and what kind of a Bar Mitzvah feast will he lay out for his own son?

The old adage that an army marches on its stomach may be true, but, at least from the brief account of Paul Steinman's Bar Mitzvah feast, it may also be surmised that cultural revolutions can be instigated in the kitchen.

The ironies of Paul's Bar Mitzvah and the late Sándor bácsi's marriage to Irene and immigration to Israel all point to the historical tension between love and tradition; between the drive of the individual for self-expression and fulfillment and his affinity for the norms and values of his heritage. This tension, of course, is not unique to intermarriages. It is endemic to all modern marriages. It is therefore appropriate and necessary to turn our attention briefly to the role of love and tradition in the making of modern family life.

Modern marriages, generally, and intermarriages, most particularly, are based on the feeling that two people share by being in love. In a brilliantly argued essay, Franceso Alberoni, the Italian sociologist, has suggested that the experience of falling in love is very much akin to the birth of a social movement; it is the moment that signals the birth of a new collective "we."

In an existing social structure, the movement divides whoever was united and unites whoever was divided to form a new collective subject, a "we" which, in the case of falling in love, is formed by the lover-beloved couple.[1]

"No experience of falling in love exists without the transgression of a difference," writes Alberoni, and therefore, "falling in love challenges institutions on the level of their fundamental values."[2] The potential of two individuals to make a revolution is realized through love.

But love, like any other revolutionary force, can only transform people or social institutions if it is harnessed in some kind of ongoing collective enterprise such as marriage. Perhaps for this reason, love had not been allowed to play a significant role in mate selection in most societies until the last 200 years.

In a collection of essays with the title *Romanticism: Definition, Explanation and Evaluation* (1965), the historian John B. Halsted informs us that "the term Romanticism came into currency at the very beginning of the nineteenth century" and referred primarily to the works of poets and writers, later artists and composers, who gave primacy in their works to moods, feelings, passions, and enthusiasms.[3] They saw themselves as rebelling against the structures of Classicism and Rationalism. Historians of the modern family, such as Edward Shorter and Ellen K. Rothman, have shown that at more or less the same time that Romanticism was emerging as a thematic force in the world of the arts, romance—the primacy of empathy and spontaneity as well as sexuality between men and women—was emerging as an ideology on the basis of which couples would seek to form marriages and families.[4] It is in its latter, more layman's sense that we will use the terms *romance* and *romantic*.

Whereas love unites, tradition divides. The feelings of love burst through walls and spill over boundaries of conventionality. The feelings toward a tradition are quite different. No matter how passionately one may be committed to it, the sentiments inspired by tradition can be expressed only in forms and rituals that were established by others long ago. Tradition inspires conformity, just as surely as love inspires inventiveness. Tradition makes careful distinctions in time, in space and, most importantly, between categories of people. Love is oblivious to all that.

In point of fact, modern marriages are not merely based on love. More importantly, they are based on a belief; an ideology of romance that regards the deep psychological and sexual attachments that are experienced as love as socially legitimate and desirable; an adequate basis for the making of a complex relationship called marriage. A related tenet of this ideology of romance is that the social identity or group background of the beloved has no place in the emotional calculus of the loving relationship, nor should it have a role to play in the organization and quality of the marriage that ensues from loving.

But as we shall see . . . , the heritages, traditions, cultural memories, and group identities of individuals who fall in love and marry do continue to play a significant role in the individuals' self-concepts and also in the life-styles of their families.

Thus, love is only the spark that may start a revolution. But real social transformation occurs precisely when the energy of love is harnessed and integrated in the flux of established situations: the family, religion, the state, and the community. That the love of two should have such far-reaching consequences, that is a real revolution.

For all these reasons, love and tradition have never lived comfortably with one another. Tracing the history of love in the West since the time of the ancient Greeks, Morton Hunt—a historian—shows vividly, and with some sense of both its drama and its humor, that the "joining of romantic passion, sensuous enjoyment, friendship and marriage" took nearly 2,000 years to evolve to its modern form.[5]

The general lovelessness of ancient marriages is captured in a somewhat cruel Greek adage of the sixth century before the Christian era: "Marriage brings a man only two happy days: the day he takes his bride to his bed, and the day he lays her in her grave."[6] But as late as our own twentieth century, the fictional Goldie, wife of Sholom Aleichem's *Tevyeh, The Milkman* (popularized in America as *Fiddler on the Roof*), is perplexed when her husband asks her, "Do you love me?" She replies:

> For twenty-five years I've washed your clothes, cooked your meals, cleaned your house, given you children, and milked the cow. After twenty-five years, why talk about love right now?[7]

Goldie's words are virtually a mirror image of the ancient Greek view of matrimony attributed by Morton Hunt to the famous orator Demosthenes: "Mistresses we keep for pleasure, concubines for daily attendance upon our needs, and wives to bear us legitimate children and to be our housekeepers."[8]

Undoubtedly, many more wives and husbands probably loved one another, before, as well as during the course of their married life, than one finds recorded in the annals of history. But it is also true, and far more widely established historically, that love has been but rarely considered an acceptable reason, much less an expected forerunner, of matrimony. If love was to be found at all, it was most often to be found briefly before, and frequently outside of, marriage, generally in forbidden relationships.

Marriage, however, was a moral duty and a social responsibility particularly incumbent upon men. It was through marriage that a family name, the family heritage, and property would be passed, unto posterity. Singlehood was as much frowned upon in the ancient Jewish tradition as it was in the ancient Greek and Roman traditions. Indeed, even in colonial America, bachelors were highly suspect and, in most colonies, were burdened with special taxes and generally kept under the watchful eyes of their neighbors. In Connecticut, William Kephart reports, "every kind of obstacle was put in the way of a bachelor keeping his own house. . . . Unless a bachelor had authority to live alone he was fined one pound (£) a week."[9]

But although marriage was a duty almost universally honored by most adults since ancient times, who actually married whom was not left to the individual. Such decisions were too important to be left in private hands, subject to personal whim or fancy. Given its strong social, moral, and religious objectives, marriages were arranged throughout most of history, in both the East and West, by parents, older siblings, and other guardians of family tradition. They made certain that the marriage partners who were chosen for their young ones were consistent with the needs and values of the family and the larger community. Naturally, under such a controlled mate selection system, marriages between Jews and Christians were virtually out of the question on both sides; only social deviants would intermarry.

To be sure, even under such a system, a son or daughter might be granted veto power by a permissive parent over a particular choice. But it is highly unlikely that more than a rare few ever had the freedom to choose a mate based entirely on their private emotional preference and without due regard to the broad conventional preferences of their families and communities. Those who violated the imperatives of custom or clan, the Romeos and Juliets of history, most often paid the price. In short, for much of our history, the dictates of tradition clearly dominated the inclinations of the heart when it came to marriage. It is more than likely that the ancestors of Ron Steinman—as well as those of his wife, Ngoc Suong Tu—were married off in their early teen years to mates chosen by their parents.

It took several far-reaching revolutions, and about two centuries, to dismantle traditional constraints upon mate selection and to replace them with romantic idealism. By the end of the eighteenth century, writes Edward Shorter, "young people began paying much more attention to inner feelings than to outward considerations, such as property and parental wishes, in choosing marriage partners."[10]

The onset of the Industrial Revolution in the latter half of the seventeenth century began to unsettle the closely bunched lives of people in villages and farms, forcing increasing numbers to leave their highly traditional rural enclaves for larger towns and cities.

The feudal West was beginning to stir, shaking the age-old foundations of family organization. Of course, for most Jews, those early stirrings were barely noticed. They would continue to live in restricted isolation from their Christian neighbors for yet another two centuries. But a few famous "court Jews" were beginning to enter intimate political and economic arrangements with dukes and princes in Germany, which, in due time, would lead to even greater intimacies between their children and grandchildren, as one can see among the illustrious Rothschilds. Selma Stern's colorful account of the adventurous lives of the seventeenth-century court Jews amply hints at the advance of the industrial age that was beginning to pave the way for a growing intimacy between Jews and non-Jews.[11] But whether the intimacy would lead to love and marriage would depend on the relative power of tradition and love in the prevailing social norms.

With the benefit of hindsight, we now know that romanticism followed closely on the heels of the American and French revolutions, the two epoch-making revolutions at the end of the eighteenth century that ushered in the modern era. As Edward Shorter put it, in the years after 1750, "the libido unfroze in the blast of the wish to be free." Gradually the idea gained currency that marriage should be much more than a joining of hands, of fortunes, and of families—that it should be a joining of hearts.

At least as it applies to the making of marriages, the romanticism that followed in the wake of two great political revolutions probably advanced much further in the United States than elsewhere in the West. In a delicately drawn history of courtship in America, Ellen Rothman shows that parents increasingly allowed and expected their children to freely choose their own marriage partners.[12] In turn, young men and women recognized that in order to find a mate, they must first find love. Perhaps Thomas Jefferson himself might be credited (or blamed) for the ascendancy of love. After all, it was he who changed the famous slogan of liberty attributed to John Locke ("Life, Liberty, and Property") to "Life, Liberty, and the Pursuit of Happiness."

In a profound analysis of that Jeffersonian turn of phrase, Jan Lewis, a historian, has shown that the freedom to pursue personal happiness soon became a moral as well as a psychological imperative, with wide-ranging effects on both family life and religion.[13] Put succinctly, "in the decades after the Revolution, the head fell victim to the heart." Marriage was now to grow out of passionate desire and was to lead to mutual emotional fulfillment and inner peace, and not simply to outer stability and respectability.

In their *Manifesto of the Communist Party,* Karl Marx and Friedrich Engels argued that the purely economic forces of capitalism that they saw all around them in the Europe of 1848 were sweeping away age-old customs that had governed religion, family life, and social relations in general. However, a closer look at the surge of Romanticism in that era—be it in the form of sublime poetry read in the drawing rooms of the bourgeoisie or in the form of the unbridled sexuality of the lower classes—suggests that it was not the power of capital alone (or even primarily) that was transforming social norms. Rather, it was the revolutionary new idea that each individual had the right to pursue his or her own personal happiness: that society could be so ordered that people might find true happiness in their choice of mates, and that they might try to exploit their own talents to their best possible advantage.

Today, the unconditional value of conjugal love as both the basis for and the proper object of marriage is so thoroughly taken for granted that it is difficult to imagine that it was ever otherwise, or that any alternate view of that tender emotion might be equally valid. But if such social historians as the Frenchman, Philippe Ariès; or the Canadian, Edward Shorter; or the American, Morton M. Hunt, are correct, the popular infatuation with romantic love and its close connection in the popular mind with marriage is a relatively recent phenomenon. For most of history, men and women were joined in matrimony out of more practical considerations, such as the demands of social conventionality or the needs for security.

Looking back upon traditional patterns of courtship, Shorter writes,

> *All situations in which boys and girls met for the first time were monitored by some larger group.... Young*

women simply did not encounter young men without other people around.[14]

The opportunity for the spontaneous involvement of members of the opposite sex with one another was rigorously controlled so as to prevent undesirable amorous entanglements. The "other people around" were most often parents, older siblings, or even peers who could safeguard the individual against "stepping out" of the bounds of social propriety—emotionally or otherwise. Arranged marriages, which often took place among well-to-do families in Europe, be they Jews or Christians, were the surest way to prevent romance from intruding into the all-important process of family formation. Continuing his backward glance, Shorter continues,

The most important change in the nineteenth- and twentieth-century courtship has been the surge of sentiment. . . . People started to place affection and personal compatibility at the top of the list of criteria in choosing marriage partners. These new standards became articulated as romantic love. And secondly, even those who continued to use the traditional criteria of prudence and wealth in selecting partners began to behave romantically within these limits.[15]

Like stardust in the trail of a comet, the romantic revolution followed in the wake of twin social revolutions of the eighteenth and nineteenth centuries: the industrial and the democratic.

In the United States, love and the pursuit of happiness had yet another major role in transforming the society. It was to be the flame under the melting pot.

What, then, is the American, this new man? He is neither a European, nor the descendant of a European; hence that strange mixture of blood, which you will find in no other country. I could point out to you a family whose grandfather was an Englishman, whose wife was Dutch, whose son married a French woman, and whose present four sons have now four wives of different nations.[16]

This often-quoted passage, from the pen of French-American Jean De Crevocouer in his *Letters from an American Farmer* (1782), presaged by some 120 years the theme if not the title of the Jewish-American Israel Zangwill's play, *The Melting Pot* (1908).[17] As some critics of the period observed, Zangwill captured in a phrase the spirit of the nation.

The Melting Pot was a drama about a romance, a thinly veiled imitation of Shakespeare's *Romeo and Juliet,* only with a happy ending—at least for the couple. David Quixano, a Russian-born Jewish immigrant, falls in love with Vera Revendal, a Russian-born Christian; both work on the Lower East Side of New York—that quintessential immigrant ghetto of the turn of the century. For some reason, Zangwill chose the most un-Russian last names for his principal characters. Perhaps he thought that they would blend better if they were not burdened with more distinctive names. Be that as it may, the young lovers were determined to marry, despite the turbulence of their emotions and opposition of their relatives. They put off their marriage only when it was learned that Vera's father, a colonel in the Tsar's army, was personally responsible for the killing of David's family in the Kishinev *pogrom* of 1903.

However, by the end of the play love prevails over all the sorrow, bitterness, and prejudice. To paraphrase Zangwill, the shadows of Kishinev melt away in the American crucible. The young lovers walk hand in hand into the sunset against the skyline of lower Manhattan, to the background strains of "My Country 'Tis of Thee."

The play opened at the Columbia Theater in Washington, D.C. with President Theodore Roosevelt in attendance. In fact, the play was dedicated to Roosevelt. When the final curtain fell, Arthur Mann, the historian, writes, the President shouted from his box, "That's a great play, Mr. Zangwill! That's a great play!" *The Melting Pot* went on to become a huge popular success, continues Mann.

> After showing in the nation's capital, it ran for six months in Chicago, and then for 136 performances in New York City. Thereafter, for close to a decade, it played in dozens of cities across America. In 1914 it was produced in London, again before full houses and admiring audiences.[18]

The play became a text in high schools and colleges; it was produced by amateur theatrical groups frequently, and its publisher, Macmillan, reprinted it at least once a year until 1917.

One does not need a great deal of historical insight to understand why that play should have become so popular and, particularly, so highly praised by the official champions of American culture. Between 1870 and 1924 (when the Johnson Act finally stemmed the tide of mass immigration), the population of America more than doubled from about 45 million to about 110 million.[19] The growth was fueled by the entry of about 25 million immigrants, overwhelmingly from southern, eastern, and middle Europe: Jews, Slavs, Poles, Italians, Serbs, Croats, etc. In some of the larger American cities, nearly 40 percent of the population was comprised of the foreign-born and recently arrived immigrants: "The tired, the poor, the wretched refuse of the earth," as Emma Lazarus described them on the base of the Statue of Liberty.

Lincoln Steffens voiced the central question of the period in a title of an article, "What Are We Going to Do with Our Immigrants?"[20] Perforce, the answer had to be assimilation. The pervasive and troubling division between blacks and whites, which continues as the single most salient social division in America, inevitably drew all immigrants into the general society and made their gradual assimilation a popular social goal. Ralph Waldo Emerson gave poetic voice to this sentiment.

> As in the old burning of the Temple at Corinth, by the melting and intermixture of silver and gold and other metals a new compound more precious than any, called Corinthian brass, was formed, so in this continent—asylum of all nations—the energy of the Irish, Germans, Swedes, Poles, Cossacks, and all the European tribes—of the Africans, and the Polynesians—will construct a new race, a new religion, a new state, a new literature, which will be as vigorous as the new Europe which came out of the smelting pot of the Dark Ages.[21]

Although social scientists make useful distinctions between such concepts as assimilation, amalgamation, and pluralism, it is clear from all the studies of the great immigration of that period that the process of Americanization was to involve both the relinquishing of many old-world traditions and the acquisition of many new ones.

How rapidly the process would occur in the lives of particular individuals, and in the collective history of one ethnic group or another, was to vary according to biographical and social circumstances. The peddler who found himself in the hinterlands of Pennsylvania was surely Americanized more rapidly than his cousin who manned a pushcart on New York's Lower East Side. But what would ultimately make America a true amalgam—an embodiment of the ideal printed on her coinage, *E Pluribus Unum*—was to be a universal human emotion: love.

Zangwill's play owed its popularity to the fact that it held out a promise that both the masses of immigrants yearning to become full-fledged Americans and the guardians of American culture, trying to cope with the massive influx of foreign multitudes, dearly wished to believe. The fire that was to heat the melting pot was none other than love—not the love of nation or folk, nor the love of abstract ideas, but the entirely private kind of love between a man and a woman.

It was expected that contact between different ethnic groups would lead to acculturation: borrowing a custom here and there, sharing recipes, and the like. The practical necessity of working and living in America would lead to assimilation in such matters as language, education, and political and economic aspirations. But what would forge the blended American, as Roosevelt, Emerson, or Steffens envisioned him, would be none other than marriage—the union of diverse groups through the power of romantic love.

In Jewish communities, the social revolutions of the nineteenth century socially emancipated the individual Jew, thus enabling him to become an equal citizen. As the German historian Heinrich Graetz put it,

The hour of freedom for the European Jews dawned in the revolutions of February and March, 1848, in Paris, Vienna, Berlin, in Italy, and other countries. An intoxicating desire for liberty came over the nations of Europe, more overpowering and marvelous than the movement of 1830. With imperious demands the people confronted their princes and rulers. Among the demands was the emancipation of the Jews. In all popular assemblies and proclamations, the despised Jews of yesterday were admitted into the bond of "Liberty, Equality, and Fraternity" (the slogan of the French Revolution of 1789).[22]

As a result of those revolutions, Jews streamed from confined settlements in backward towns and villages into the capitals of Europe; from narrowly restricted occupations into the full range of modern pursuits that were being opened up by the Industrial Revolution; and into a new kind of relationship with Christians—one that, at least in principle if not in fact, was based on a doctrine of social equality.

Intermarriages between free-thinking Jews and Christians followed on the heels of emancipation in an inexorable sequence. Historians surmise that the salons in the homes of Jewish bankers in Berlin and Vienna offered the first common meeting places for liberated Jews and Christians, and it was from these sociable acquaintanceships that the first intermarriages resulted. First the privilege of only the well-to-do Jews, intermarriage between Jews and Christians gradually became an available option for the broad masses of urban middle-class Jews.

Although statistics on the rate of Jewish intermarriage at the beginning of the modern era are spotty and imprecise, there are some available that clearly buttress the general impressions. In a study of marriage records right after the American Revolution, the historian Malcolm H. Stern found that in 699 marriages of Jews, 201, or about 29 percent, were intermarriages between a Jew and a Christian.[23] Similar patterns are reported by others elsewhere in the Western World.

Citing the work of such early students of Jewish social life as Drachsler, Engelman, Fishberg, and Ruppin, Milton L. Barron reports, for instance, that the percentage of intermarriages as a proportion of all marriages in which Jews were involved increased in Switzerland from 5 percent in 1888 to about 12 percent by 1920; in Hungary, the rate increased from about 5 percent in 1895 to about 24 percent by 1935; and in Germany, the rate increased from about 15 percent in 1901 to about 44 percent by 1933, on the eve of the Nazi rise to power and the passage of the draconian Nuremberg Laws that forbade marriage between Jews and Christians.[24]

Citing the work of the French demographer E. Schnurmann, Moshe Davis similarly reports that in Strasbourg, the rate of intermarriage between Jews and Christians increased from an undetermined "very low rate" to over one-third of all marriages of Jews between 1880 and 1909. The French city of Strasbourg had a substantial Jewish population at the time, so the increase in intermarriage could not be attributed to a dearth of eligible Jewish marriage partners.[25]

Jews were apparently eager to enter the mainstream of modern society through the portals of romance and matrimony with their Christian neighbors, and they were also being more readily accepted in their host societies. The separation of church and state following the revolutions in America and France, and the availability of civil marriage—there as well as in much of the rest of the Western World—further hastened

the incidence of intermarriages that would not have been legal in earlier generations.

Although the statistics are spotty, as we have seen, and not as precise as most social scientists would prefer, their message is unmistakable. Jews were choosing Christian mates (most often a Jewish man choosing a Christian woman), as well as being chosen by them, in ever-increasing number. They were breaking sharply with one of the oldest and most deeply held norms of Jewish life: the norm of endogamy—the *halachic* requirement (based on biblical inductions) that Jews only marry other Jews.

The one sleeping-giant exception to this trend at the turn of the twentieth century was the Jew of Eastern Europe, about half of the world's approximately 8 to 9 million Jews at the time. They lived in the infamous Pale of Jewish Settlement, a territory about the size of Texas on the periphery of Russia and Poland.[26] In these small, isolated, economically backward and politically enfeebled villages, they were barely touched by the great revolutions of the previous two centuries. Whereas the lives of Western Jews had undergone significant transformations since the end of the seventeenth century, particularly rapidly from the mid-eighteenth century, the lives of Eastern European Jews in the 1880s did not differ much from what they might have been in the Middle Ages. Indeed, some might say that they were probably better off in the Middle Ages than they were in the last decades of the nineteenth century.

As described by many writers, in varying hues of pain, humor, and bitterness, as well as some nostalgia, Eastern European Jewry lived a cloistered, virtually medieval existence until the first decades of the twentieth century.

Their language, Yiddish; their religious life, a highly ritualized and fundamentalist form of Orthodox Judaism laced with the mysticism of the Hasidic Jews; their economy, pre-industrial and progressively rendered impoverished by anti-Semitic decrees; their host culture, Polish and Russian peasantry wantonly anti-Semitic and given to periodic orgies of organized violence against Jews; their self-image, a moral kingdom of priests and philosophers who were destined to attain a loftier existence someday. All these features of their life served to erect an almost impregnable barrier between Jews and Christians who lived as neighbors in the villages (or *shtetlach,* as they were called in Yiddish). Social intimacy at the level of friendship was almost non-existent between them. Therefore, the possibility of intermarriage was virtually unthinkable.

And yet, if the story of *Tevyeh, the Milkman* is any indication of social realities, despite those great barriers some Jews and Catholics or Russian Orthodox peasants did fall in love; did go against the prevailing social norms and did marry, although often they did so by eloping to the West. Clearly the inclination of the individual to pursue his or her own personal happiness, even in the face of powerful opposing social norms, could not be entirely suppressed.

Nevertheless, the central point remains—marriages between Jews and Christians were far less common in the ghettoized areas of Eastern Europe than they were for Western Jewry. Arthur Ruppin, one of the early sociologists of world Jewry, has amply documented that, for instance, the proportion of intermarriages in one hundred Jewish marriages was less than 1 percent in Galicia as late as 1929. By contrast, the rate in places like Germany was 23 percent, and it was 13 to 27 percent in Budapest and Vienna. Elsewhere in Eastern Europe—in Latvia, Lithuania, White Russia, and the Ukraine—mixed marriages rarely occurred.[27] Moreover, it stands to reason that they were not any more frequent at the end of the nineteenth century than they were in the first decades of the twentieth.

However, it must be recalled that between the 1880s and the 1920s, about half of the approximately 5 million Jews who lived in Eastern Europe immigrated to the United States. Beginning with the pogroms of 1881, masses of *shtetl* Jews were quite literally chased into the modern world by the whips and swords of Russian Cossacks. Rather than try to bear it stoically, dying martyrs' deaths as their ancestors might have done, millions of Jews from the Pale chose the path of migration to the West, specifically to the United States.

Between 1881 and 1923, approximately 2.8 million Jews entered through Ellis Island, the "golden door" to America. They quickly overwhelmed the 250,000 Jews, mostly of German descent, who had comprised American Jewry up to that time. As is well known from Irving Howe's popular *World of Our Fathers,* the first generation of Eastern European immigrants settled in such densely Jewish ghettos as the Lower East Side in New York, Maxwell Street in Chicago, and similar enclaves in Philadelphia, Baltimore, and Washington, D.C.[28]

Their settlement patterns, their economic circumstances, their dependence on *mame-loschen* (mother tongue, i.e., Yiddish), and the rising tide of anti-Semitism in America soon resulted in the re-establishment of the kind of ghettoized mode of social life that they had all just recently left behind in the Old World. The convergence of all these social factors resulted in a dramatic decline in the overall rate of mixed marriages for American Jews.

In contrast to the approximately 30 percent rate of Jewish mixed marriages discovered by Malcolm Stern among American Jews in the Federal period (when there were no more than 100 thousand Jews in the country, representing about one-quarter of 1 percent of the total population), the proportion of intermarriages among Jews in the first decades of this century (when they were about 3.5 percent of the total U.S. population) was less than 2 percent.[29]

At the very historical moment when Israel Zangwill was rhapsodizing about the power of love, and intermarriage in particular, and as the great emotional fire flamed under the "melting pot," more of his own people were huddling together—as were immigrant Italians, Poles, Irish, Greeks, and Chinese—than they might have been a half century earlier. The tough realities of immigrant life, and traditions of the Old-World culture that most immigrants brought with them, placed a powerful check on the romanticism of the nineteenth century; but not for long.

In a popular compilation of letters to the editor of the *Jewish Daily Forward,* the preeminent Yiddish newspaper in America since 1890, we find that from the earliest times their readers were writing to the illustrious editor of the paper about problems having to do with marriage, particularly between Jews and non-Jews. Isaac Metzker, who published the popular compilation in 1971 under the title *A Bintle Brief (*a bundle of letters), gives us a vivid flavor of some of their concerns.

1908

Worthy Editor:
I have been in America almost three years. I came from Russia where I studied in yeshiva.... At the age of twenty I had to go to America. Before I left I gave my father my word that I would walk the righteous path and be good and pious. But America makes one forget everything.

Here I became a (machine) operator, and at night I went to school. In a few months I entered a preparatory school, where for two subjects I had a gentile girl as teacher.... Soon I realized that her lessons with me were not ordinary...she wanted to teach me without pay.... I began to feel at home in her house... also her parents welcomed me warmly....

Then she spoke frankly of her love for me and her hope that I would love her.

I was confused and I couldn't answer her immediately.... I do agree with her that we are first human beings, and she is a human being in the fullest sense of the word. She is pretty, educated, intelligent, and has a good character. But I am in despair when I think of my parents. I go around confused and yet I am drawn to her. I must see her every day, but when I am there I think of my parents and I am torn by doubt.
Respectfully,
Skeptic from Philadelphia[30]

Reading this poignant letter nearly 80 years after it was written, and with the hindsight of history, one wonders what the nameless correspondent was skeptical about. Was it about his faith, about the wisdom of his parents, or the wisdom of his attachment to them? Was it about his love for the girl or her love for him, or was it perhaps about love itself?

Another correspondent, writing to the editor just about a year later, had other problems, but seemed to be unperturbed by any skepticism.

1909

Dear Editor:
I come from a small town in Russia. I was brought up by decent parents and got a good education. I am now twenty years old and am a custom-peddler in a Southern city. Since my customers here are Colored people, I became acquainted with a young Negro girl, twenty-two years of age, who buys merchandise from me.... She is a teacher, a graduate of a Negro college, and I think she is an honorable person.

I fell in love with the girl but I couldn't go around with her openly because I am White and she is Colored.

However, whenever I deliver her order, I visit with her for awhile.

In time she went away to another city to teach, and I corresponded with her. When she came home for Christmas, I told her I loved her and intended to marry her and take her North to live. But she refused me and gave me no reason. Perhaps it was because I am a White man.

I spoke about my love for her to my friends, who are supposedly decent people, and they wanted to spit in my face. To them it appeared that I was about to commit a crime.

Therefore I would like to hear your answer as to whether I should be condemned for falling in love with a Negro woman and wanting to marry her. And if you can, explain to me also her reason for refusing me.

Respectfully,
Z.B.[31]

One wonders how many young Jewish peddlers, machine operators, and night school students who had recently come to America were having their first taste of the bittersweet pulls and pinches of romance with Italians, Irish, WASPs, and blacks. One wonders, and wishes for more data. But even in the absence of such data, it is safe to say that there were many more such matches, resulting in marriages (and even occasional conversions to Judaism), than there had been in Eastern Europe.

Writing in 1920, Julius Drachsler reported that the rate of intermarriage for Jews in New York City was 2.27 percent between 1908 and 1912. However, the trend was clearly upward as one looked past the immigrant generations and outside the ghettoized areas of Jewish Settlements.[32]

The trend became most clearly defined for American Jews only as recently as 1971. It was in that year that the Council of Jewish Federa-tions and Welfare released its landmark study of the U.S. Jewish population known as the National Jewish Population Study, or NJPS. Table 5.1 succinctly presents the key finding of that study with regard to the intermarriage trend. Although there is some scholarly debate about the precise, most current intermarriage rate, there is no debate about the direction of the trend.

It took about sixty years, or roughly three generations, for the descendants of the Eastern European immigrants (who constitute approximately 75 to 80 percent of the total American Jewish population) to catch up in their rate of mixed marriage with those of their brethren in America and Western Europe who had been modernized in the eighteenth and nineteenth centuries.

The magnitude of the most recent rates, and the speed with which they had increased, rang out like a thunderclap in the Jewish community. In a seminal work, *Assimilation in American Life* (1964), Milton Gordon had argued that "if marital assimilation . . . takes place fully, the minority group loses its ethnic identity in the larger host or core society."[33] The findings of NJPS rang a powerful alarm in the minds of those concerned with Jewish group survival.

TABLE 1   Percentage of Jewish Persons Marrying Someone Who Was Not Born Jewish, out of All Jews Who Married at Given Time Periods

Time period	Jews marrying non-Jews
1900–1920	2.0
1921–1930	3.2
1931–1940	3.0
1941–1950	6.7
1951–1955	6.4
1956–1960	5.9
1961–1965	17.4
1966–1971	31.7

The convergence of Gordon's sociological insights and the statistical patterns discovered by the NJPS led many learned observers to a foreboding conclusion. American Jewry might become an "extinct species" as a result of marital assimilation. At the very least, so it was feared, the size and significance of an already small minority in the American mosaic might be further reduced to ultimate insignificance as a result of intermarriage. In a carefully calculated analysis, Harvard demographer Elihu Bergman cautioned in 1977 that the net effect of the increased rate of intermarriage projected out over a century would be to reduce the size of the American-Jewish population from the approximately 5.7 million in 1976 to as few as about 10 thousand by the time of the American tricentennial, in the year 2076.[34]

Nor have the concerns been based upon Jewish facts alone. In the wake of Vatican Council II, the *Decree on Ecumenism* (1966) proposed that the Catholic Church mitigate its historically rigorous opposition to mixed marriages. By 1970, the Church no longer required in such marriages that the non-Catholic partner promise to raise the children as Catholics—much less to convert to Catholicism. The result of the liberalizing trend in the Church was to see a steady increase in Catholic intermarriages and a corresponding decline in conversions to Catholicism. Indeed, as Andrew Greeley has shown in his *Crisis in the Church* (1979), "by far the largest numbers of those who have disidentified from the Roman Catholic Church have done so in connection with a mixed marriage."[35]

If religious tradition was steadily losing its grip on cupid's arrows, the once restraining influence of ethnic traditions was faring even worse. In an influential article in the *American Sociological Review,*[36] Richard Alba showed that marriage across ethnic lines among Catholics had increased significantly with the coming of age of successive generations of the descendents of immigrants. Ethnic in-group marriage among the immigrant generations of English, Irish, German, Polish, French, and Italian Catholics quickly yielded to ethnic mixing among the second and third generations, according to Alba's deft analysis.

Among Jews, too, the breaching of the previous generations' ethnic divisions was nearly total by the end of the 1950s. As recently as the 1910s, Konrad Bercovici reports, intermarriage between a Sephardic Jew and a Russian Jew was as rare, if not rarer (and more frowned upon), as marriage between a Jew and a non-Jew.[37] Indeed, Bavarian Jews even hesitated to marry German Jews who came from nearer the Polish border, derisively referring to them with the ethnic slur "Pollacks." In turn, the Russian Jews looked down upon the Polish Jews as well as upon the Galicians and would not permit their children to marry them, reports Milton Barron. But by midcentury the inter-ethnic aversions had largely disappeared in the Jewish community, in much the same way as they had among Catholics.

In retrospect, it would seem that the wholesale crossing of ethnic boundaries *within* religious groups paved the way for the crossing of religious boundaries. The walls of tradition were being battered down by sentiment and emotional attachments, one cultural building block at a time. If those trends would continue unabated for even a few successive generations, Israel Zangwill's play about the melting pot would prove to be prophetic. The romantic ideology of the eighteenth and the nineteenth centuries would indeed sweep away the last vestiges of traditional constraint on the individual's choice of a mate. Such a fundamental change in the making of family life would prove a more profound point as well. It would prove that happiness—and, indeed, identity itself—is quite possible in the modern world without any significant rootedness in a shared tradition.

However, alongside the increasing rates of intermarriage for Jews and others, mid-century modernity was marked by other cultural trends as well. Perhaps none is more notable than the Americans' search for their diverse heritages. The period saw a spate of publications, both in the social sciences and popular literature, extolling the virtues of ethnicity and tradition. Opposing Zangwill, Michael Novak heralded *The Rise of the Unmeltable Ethnic* (1972) and the age of "White ethnicity."[38] Earlier, Herbert Gans and Michael Parenti had also seen the signs amidst the suburban and urban transitions of the 1950s and 1960s.[39] Ethnic group ties continued to play a powerful role in shaping the residential as well as friendship preferences of people long after ethnicity had been declared irrelevant in American life by the conventional wisdom.

In popular literature, the enthusiasm for nearly lost heritages reached its crescendo with the publication and subsequent serialization on TV of Alex Haley's *Roots*. It is particularly ironic that Haley dedicated his book to America's bicentennial, since it was published in 1976. The "nation of many nations," in which the culture was to blend and render indistinguishable the diversity of cultures that it comprised, was being greeted, on its bicentennial, with a massive outpouring of interest in ethnic distinctiveness and family heritage. The interest in "roots" spawned a virtual cottage industry in genealogy as a family pastime for several years. It was being fed by such books as Bill R. Linder's *How to Trace Your Family History* (1978) and, for Jews, Arthur Kurzweil's popular *Tracing Your Jewish Roots*.[40] As recently as 1984, no less a personage than the President of the United States, Ronald Reagan, created a significant "media event" by visiting the village in Ireland from whence his ancestors emigrated to the United States in the 1840s.

The "Bar Mitzvah with the Vietnamese flavor" with which this chapter began, now points to an even deeper irony. It purports to blend two cultures, Jewish and Vietnamese, very much in keeping with the American ideal of the melting pot. But it simultaneously speaks to the persistence of an unalloyed attachment to the traditions of those cultures. It particularly speaks to the persistence of Jewish identity and ritual in the lives of people—some born Jewish, some newly so—who, at least on the basis of their choice of marriage partners, would seem to have agreed that love is more important than tradition.

The Steinman Bar Mitzvah underscores the emergence of two apparently contradictory trends among modern American Jews, in particular, and perhaps among all modern ethnic Americans, in general. One is the trend described by Shorter, by Lewis, by Rothman, and by other students of the romanticization of the modern family: the triumph of the heart over the head, of love over tradition in matters of mate selection. The other is the trend of resurgent ethnicity described by Novak, by Parenti, by Glazer and Moynihan, and by others since the 1960s. These two contradictory trends have been made even more puzzling since the mid-1970s with the resurgence of religious emotionalism and fundamentalism among those very segments of society—the young, professional, educated, and middle class—who had been thought to be immune to spiritual matters because of their modern consciousness and life-style.

As do all profound contradictions, these contradictory trends raise several compelling questions that strike at the very core of the meaning of intermarriage. Why do people choose to celebrate particular symbols or rituals of a larger tradition whose main tenets they have rejected? For example, why did Josephine Steinman want her son's Bar Mitzvah to have a "Vietnamese flavor" when she had converted to Judaism and presumably now sees herself as part of the Jewish people? Why did Ron Steinman want his wife to become Jewish, as do tens of thousands of other young Jews who marry Christians, when his sense of equality was such that he was able to fall in love with a woman who was a Buddhist? Why do the hundreds of thousands of Jews and Christians, who marry one another in defiance of their age-old ethnic and religious traditions, persist in memorializing many of those very same traditions in their holiday celebrations, in the way they rear their children, in what they read and what they eat, and in their very concept of themselves as human beings? Particularly among American Jews who have experienced such a great and rapid increase in intermarriages, why has the trend toward intermarriage *not* been accompanied by a comparable trend of disidentification from the Jewish people?

Perhaps Josephine Steinman herself was answering some of those deep questions in her own mind when she commented on the unique Bar Mitzvah menu to *The Times'* reporter, "It was a desire to put on a party in one's own image. That became particularly important with the kind of family we have. After all, there aren't many Vietnamese-Jewish families."

Of course, Mrs. Steinman is right. There aren't many Vietnamese-Jewish families, but, until the 1950s, it is not likely that one would have found culturally blended Jewish families of even less exotic mixture, such as Italian-Jewish or Irish-Jewish, which are far more common. It is not that such marriages did not occur. Of course, they did. Jews have been marrying non-Jews since biblical times. But the social stigma attached to such marriages usually compelled intermarried couples to become more or less socially invisible—at least in the eyes of the Jewish community and often in the eyes of the Christian community as well.

What stands out as remarkable about the Steinman's Bar Mitzvah is that this family has

no desire or need to "pass" as either exclusively Jewish or Vietnamese, or exclusively anything else. They can create a party in their own image, indeed an entire social identity in their own image. Moreover, they can find a Reform Jewish congregation (of which they are members) that seems not only to accept but also to actually delight in this family's ability to express their Jewishness in their own unique idiom.

Rose Epstein, an old friend of the family, is quoted as commenting on the celebration, "It's a new world, isn't it? I can't get over how nice it is when people accept." Her comment is almost liturgical. It recalls the well-known Hebrew song "Hine Ma Tov U'Manaim, Shevet Achim Gam Yachad" (Behold, how good and pleasant it is when brethren dwell in unity).[41] One almost has to pinch one's self to realize that the unity of brethren rhapsodized by the Hebrew poet certainly did not envision the celebration of Bar Mitzvahs with Vietnamese cousins or chicken with cashew nuts.

Some might say the desire, as Josephine put it, to "put on a party in one's own image" proclaims nothing more profound than the contemporary consumerist values of modern upper-middle-class Americans—young, professional urbanites—whose numbers are legion in New York City and other major metropolitan areas. Perhaps they merely reflect the narcissism of the postwar baby-boomers coming of age and expressing their passionate individualism in a traditional idiom. Perhaps tradition here is nothing more than yet another vehicle for their highly personal "ego trip." Perhaps.

But, in fact, Ron and Josephine Steinman went through a long period of searching within themselves, as well as through various Jewish institutions on two continents, before they could arrive at a form of religious identification and affiliation that was harmonious with their view of life. Josephine was searching for the compassion and respect for life she had learned as a child.

Ron wanted to belong to a community that reflected tolerance and social responsibility. Their personal outlooks, although drawn from vastly different cultures, were surprisingly similar. What the two wanted was to be able to link their inner felt similarity to a single tradition; in this instance, the Jewish tradition—to link the personal feelings shared by two to a tradition shared by many. The particular resolutions they have made in dealing with their dual family heritage have come at the cost of great effort and, at times, the suffering of callousness and intolerance from those closest to them.

Their search, and particular resolution, reflects an apparent need on the part of many intermarried couples to not dismiss their heritages, but, rather, to integrate them into some kind of harmonious whole.... The Steinmans are not alone, even if their particular cultural blend is a bit more unusual than that of others.

Amidst the general alarm among American Jews over the increasing rate of intermarriage throughout the 1970s, relatively little attention was paid to the fact that unprecedented numbers of non-Jews were becoming Jewish by choice. The National Jewish Population Study had found that about one-third of the contemporary intermarriages involved the conversion of the non-Jewish partner. My own study of intermarried couples, conducted on behalf of the American Jewish Committee (1976–1977), confirmed those figures and also found that in about 20 percent of the intermarriages in which no conversion to Judaism had taken place, the non-Jewish spouse had more or less "assimilated" into the Jewish community through the Jewishness of the family.

Other demographic studies of Jewish communities, such as those of Floyd Fowler in Boston (1975), of Albert Mayer in Kansas City (1977), of Bruce Phillips in Denver (1982), and of Steve Cohen and Paul Ritterband in New York (1983), all show that the rate of conversion into Judaism has increased along with the increase in intermarriage.[42] In fact, the percentage of conversions from among the intermarriers has tended to run ahead of the rate of intermarriage itself. Taken together, these studies show that the rate of conversion into Judaism during the past thirty years has increased by about 300 percent.

In 1954, Rabbi David Eichhorn published a report estimating that the Reform and Conservative movements were producing between 1,500 to 1,750 "new Jews" each year through conversions.[43] In 1984, Rabbi Sanford Seltzer of the Reform Union of American Hebrew Congregations estimated, in a personal conversation, that his movement was producing between 7,000 to 8,000 "new Jews" each year. Although increases among the Conservative and Orthodox have not been as great, knowledgeable observers in those movements also point to significant increases in their conversion activities—all this, by the way, without any direct efforts by any of the movements thus far to seek out converts actively.

As . . . in the great majority of such conversionary families, a high value is placed on the maintenance of Jewish traditions, as in the Steinman family. But there appears also to be an inclination to express those values in a life-style and cultural idiom that reflects the non-Jewish heritage of the family as well, at least in some respects. In those intermarried families in which no conversion has taken place, considerably less value is placed on the maintenance of Jewish traditions, as one might expect. Yet even in those families, there is a tendency in a great many cases to include certain Jewish traditions in the life-style of the home, along with such non-Jewish traditions as the celebration of Christmas with Christian relatives, and possibly other Christian holidays and life-cycle events.

One Jewish-Catholic couple—the husband had actually studied for the priesthood before he became an agnostic social worker—used the occasion of their honeymoon to travel to some of the small villages of southern Italy to try to trace the husband's ancestors. Yet this couple's son had a Bar Mitzvah thirteen years later. At the time of our meeting in 1980, their home offered a comfortable display of Italian-Catholic memorabilia; reproductions of Gothic portraits of saints alongside Diane's menorah, a reproduction of Chagall's famous fiddler on the roof picture, and Danny's Hebrew books from which he was studying for his Bar Mitzvah. And Frank—who is a master of Italian cuisine—also did much of the cooking for his son's Bar Mitzvah. Apparently the Leone family also wanted a party in their own image, a Bar Mitzvah with an Italian flavor.

Perhaps one has to be a bit narcissistic to make such casual use of divergent cultural symbols to satisfy one's own sense of the good fit between traditional and personal life-style. But such an invidious psychological label as narcissism is hardly adequate to account for the lingering attachments of contemporary intermarrieds to greater or lesser fragments of their ancestral traditions. Nor are the other explanations of intermarriage as helpful as they once might have been. The proverbial power of love, which popularly accounts for the incidence of intermarriage itself, should have rendered all previous tribal loyalties for naught. Or as Zangwill put it,

the melting pot should have so alloyed the couple's traditions that the new amalgam would not betray traces of its origins.

Finally, any understanding of how intermarrieds merge their ancestral traditions with their contemporary life-style must encompass the ways in which modern families, Jewish families especially, incorporate tradition into their lives. After all, the life-styles of all ethnic groups have been greatly influenced by one another, as well as by the general patterns of American culture. Just as "you don't have to be Jewish to love Levy's real Jewish rye bread,"[44] so, too, you don't have to be intermarried to have a Jamaican calypso band at a Jewish wedding or to have kosher Chinese food at a Bar Mitzvah.

At the heart of the matter lies the cardinal principle of modern consciousness: that, in American society as in most other modern societies, the individual enjoys simultaneous membership in a great variety of groups and cliques—from work to community to leisure—and yet is freer from the constraints of any of those memberships than at any previous time in history. But that very freedom impels many to seek linkages with the timeless traditions of their ancestors.

Reading 10 One Style of Dominican Bridal Shower*

ADELE BAHN AND ANGELA JAQUEZ

Unlike American bridal showers, which are used as a means of helping the couple furnish their home, or to give personal gifts to the bride, the Hispanic shower, particularly the Dominican shower, is often the means of socialization for the bride in her future status as wife. Gifts are also presented at the Dominican shower, but gifts are not the primary purpose of the shower. While seemingly frivolous and festive, the customs and activities at showers reveal serious content when analyzed for their underlying meaning—content that reflects the norms and

*Bahn, Adele and Angela Jaquez. 1988. "One Style of Dominican Bridal Shower." Pp. 131–146 in *The Apple Sliced: Sociological Studies of New York City,* edited by Vernon Boggs, Gerald Handel and Sylvia Fava. Prospect Heights, IL: Waveland Press. Reprinted by permission of the editors.

METHODOLOGICAL NOTE: The research reported here was done through observation of bridal showers and interviews with guests, former guests, and women who had given showers.

Seven showers were attended in New York City; the brides were in the age range 19–22. Information was obtained on thirty-two additional showers through open-ended interviews in Spanish with fifty women who described showers they had given or attended in New York City or in the Dominican Republic. The interviews took place, in groups of up to eight women at a time, over coffee or tea in the junior author's apartment. The women were primarily of Dominican background, but some were of Puerto Rican, Cuban, San Salvadoran, or Colombian origin. Invitations to the showers and introductions to the women interviewed were obtained through a "snowball sample."

Our research process illustrates some special approaches needed to study ethnic phenomena in the city to which access is limited by language, sex, and age. The senior author had studied earlier the changes and continuities in the status of American brides, through a content analysis of United States bridal magazines from 1967 to 1977, the decade of the women's movement; British, French, and Italian bridal magazines were also examined. The analysis covered family patterns, marriage customs, sex roles, sexual behavior, birth control and family planning, consumption patterns, images of the wedding, prescriptions for wifehood, concepts of beauty, and symbols and images of the wedding. This provided a framework for the study of Dominican bridal showers in New York City. The senior author participated in some of the interviews when sufficient conversation was in English.

The junior author, a graduate student in sociology, is Dominican in background, bilingual, and in her 20s, characteristics that enabled her to attend the showers and conduct the interviews. She was able to establish rapport and believes that the events and conversations were not significantly affected by her presence. Rarely was she treated as an "outsider," although on one occasion the participants deliberately did not share with the researcher their pornographic pictures and written jokes. In most instances events at the showers were tape recorded and photographed. The interviews were also recorded, transcribed, and later translated into English.

values of society and societal expectations about the young woman about to make the transition from fiancée and bride to wife.

One important factor in Dominican culture is the Roman Catholic church, but just as important are the historical ties with Spain (and thence with Arab culture); these underlie Dominican culture and translate into two basic values that are paramount in the coming nuptials: virginity for the woman and *machismo* (a culturally specific type of virility or manliness) for the man. These values are interrelated and in fact are the reason for the socialization at the shower.

The young woman is expected to be a virgin when she marries. Although some norms are changing, this remains an important one. She is expected to be innocent, virginal, and inexperienced. Although more freedom is allowed her here in this country, and although it varies from one Hispanic culture to another, virginity remains the ideal. Therefore, the shower functions as an introduction and socialization for the bride to a number of her future roles, particularly the sexual role.

> *One is therefore led to think that most of these rites whose sexual nature is not to be denied and which [are] said to make the individual a man or woman or fit to be one—fall into the same category as certain rites of cutting the umbilical cord, of childhood, and of adolescence. These are rites of separation from the sexual world, and they are followed by rites of incorporation into the world of sexuality, and in all societies and all social groups, into a group confined to persons of one sex or the other. This statement holds true especially for girls, since the social activity of a woman is much simpler than that of a man.* [1]

SOCIAL FUNCTIONS OF THE SHOWER

The primary functions of the shower had to do with socialization, socialization to at least four roles that are components of the wifely status in traditional Dominican family life. These are (1) the role of a woman among women, (2) the sexual role, (3) the homemaker role, and (4) the subservient role of the female in the marital relationship. The socialization is both implicit and explicit.

A Woman among Women

The shower itself is attended only by women (although often men are invited to come in at the end of the shower, at which time it becomes a party with music, drinking, and dancing). However, what has happened before the men arrive is kept secret from them, and all sexual decorations and related materials will have been removed.

The women are dressed in their best. Decorations, food, entertainment, and the order of festivities have been planned by women, usually close friends or relatives of the bride. There are limitations on who is invited. No one who is either too young or too old—or too staid—is invited. Often the mother and older aunts of the bride are not invited because it is felt that such guests would put a damper on the activities; the shower would have to be "too respectable." A number of middle-aged women even denied that this type of shower takes place at all! It seems out of consonance with the continuing norms for women of respectability and sexual innocence and indifference. Only women from about sixteen to thirty-five or forty are present at the showers, with the ages of most guests, as might be expected, clustering around the age of the bride.

Some of the women who plan the shower have a consciousness of tradition and duty to the bride: to inform her of what she needs to know and what is likely to happen to her.

Not all the guests are friends of the bride. Sometimes a woman who is particularly adept at being mistress of ceremonies at the shower, or who is known to have had experience at running showers, is invited even though she may not be a particular friend of the bride or even well known to the organizer of the shower, except by reputation. These women take pride in their ability to invent and create activities and decor and to set the order and sequence of the shower.

There may be a handwritten "book," a collection of dirty jokes, sayings, and tricks that is borrowed and lent for showers. New material that is particularly successful is added to the book and it even travels from New York to the Dominican Republic in the luggage of guests invited to showers there. The essence of the book is that it is shared lore passed from women to women. Some of the respondents referred to the "dirty papers" that are part of the collection (for example, the "Memorandum" set forth a little later in this essay). However, some of the women who are particularly adept at organizing showers took pride in *not* using such materials. They felt they were experienced and creative enough not to need it.

Learning the Sexual Role

The Dominican-Spanish term for "bridal shower" is *"despedida de soltera,"* which is literally translated, "Good-bye to singlehood." It is a ceremony that rarely takes place earlier than two weeks prior to the marriage ceremony and is planned by the closest friends of the bride-to-be or her relatives but not by her parents.

Formal invitations are rarely used since the planners prefer to invite the bride-to-be's friends by word of mouth. This gives them the opportunity to make suggestions about bringing some-

thing that is sexually explicit, which will embarrass the bride.

The planners make arrangements to decorate the living room of the apartment where the shower will take place either on a Friday or Saturday evening. An umbrella is affixed to a decorated chair, which is usually placed in the corner of the room. Often pornographic pictures taken from magazines are taped on the walls around the chair. The scenes they depict are both conventional and unconventional, and a number of postures are shown. The balloons that may decorate the room turn out, on closer inspection, to be condoms, blown up and tied to hang satirically from the ceiling and walls.

For the New York shower, special items may have been bought in Times Square sex shops: a plastic banana that, when opened, reveals a pink plastic penis in a constant and impossible state of erection; or a "baby pacifier" that turns out to be a tiny penis.

The refreshments may consist—besides the cakes and sandwiches prepared by friends and relatives of the guest of honor—of sausage and hot dogs arranged to look like the male sex organs and served to the guest of honor. Sometimes a root vegetable, *yautia,* which resembles a long potato, is arranged and decorated with corn silk and two small potatoes to resemble male genitalia. The vegetables are hairy and exaggerated and may also be smeared with condensed milk and ketchup or tomato paste to symbolize the semen and blood that are expected to flow on the bride's wedding night.

The guests arrive at least thirty minutes before the bride-to-be is brought in. While waiting for her, the guests engage in a lively discussion about their first night's experience. When they suspect that she is at the door, they get together in the center of the room and turn off the lights. When she enters, she is surprised. Sometimes one of the guests throws a glass of water on her, which is supposed to give her good luck. From the doorway she is led to the decorated chair, where she remains for the rest of the ceremony. As the shower continues, the bride-to-be is prepared and informed about her future roles as a wife. This includes the giving of gifts that underline her role as a housewife. She is expected to be a virgin and sexually unknowledgeable, and these expectations color the rest of the ceremony. It is also expected that she will blush and show embarrassment, horror, and astonishment at the "dirty jokes," "red tales," and "fresh tricks" that follow.

A "corsage" made of stockings in the shape of male genitalia is pinned to the bride's bosom. A dildo, sausage, or plastic hot dog may also be used. She may be forced to eat the sausage or to keep the plastic effigy in her mouth, She may be undressed to her underwear and told to put on a "baby doll" nightgown.[2] A vibrator may be used on her breast and intimate parts but no penetration occurs. The bride is shown pictures of a variety of sexual scenes and told that this is what she may expect—that this could happen to her, that she must be ready and supply "anything he wants." Typically, one of the participants is dressed like a man and imitates the groom's actions on the wedding night. If no one dresses as a man, a dildo is tied around the waist of one of the guests and this "male impersonator" "attacks" the bride. The dildo is rubbed on her face and all over her body. Aside from these overt "sexual" acts, there are guests who give her "tips" about how to please a man sexually, such as how to perform fellatio successfully.

One respondent tells of a woman dressed as a man with a dildo attached, who jumped out of the closet and enacted a rape scene. The respondent, at whose bridal shower this had occurred, claimed that it had been a valuable experience in that it had "prepared" her for her wedding night,

which had been "rough." But because of these scenes, some of the guests protest that they "don't *ever* want a shower."

At any time during the shower, any of the participants can draw the bride-to-be's attention and tell her a "red joke" or read a litany to her. Litanies are anonymously written poems that use pseudonyms for the saints and contain a great deal of vulgarity. A popular litany that is used at showers both here and in the Dominican Republic is called "A Virgin's Bedside Prayer." The main character of this litany, who is supposed to be the bride-to-be, asks the saints for a man who will be sexually satisfied by her.

Double-entendres are popular at the showers. The following example was obtained from a respondent and had been translated from the Spanish.

MEMORANDUM

For the ultimate goal of maintaining the high standard of social hygiene in our city, the Honorable City Mayor along with the City Council have decreed the following:

TO ALL LOVERS AND COUPLES

As of the 16th September 1980, the Mayor and City Council in a unanimous decision have declared that all lovers and couples caught in a theater, movie, park, beach, street or avenue, empty building or even in an alleyway, committing such acts as mentioned below, will be punished to the fullest extent of the law and fined accordingly:

1. With the hand on the thigh......$ 5.00
2. With the hand on the thing.....$10.00
3. With the thing in the hand......$15.00
4. With the thing in the mouth....$20.00

5. With the mouth on the thing .. $25.00
6. With the thing in the thing $30.00
7. With the thing inside
    the thing $35.00
8. With the thing on the thing $40.00
9. With the thing in the
    front of the thing.................... $45.00
10. With the thing behind
    the thing $50.00

For those who are curious about what "the thing" means:

a. It is not a bat, but it lives most of the time hanging down.
b. It is not an accordion; however, it shrinks and stretches.
c. It is not a soldier, but it attacks in the front and in the back.
d. It does not think, but it has a head.
e. It is not attractive; however, occasionally it's called "beautiful."
f. It is not analgesic, but it can be used as a tranquilizer.
g. It is not a palm tree, but it has nuts.
h. It does not belong to any club or organization; however, it's known as a member.
i. It does not produce music, but is called an organ.
j. It is not a gentleman, but it will stand up for ladies.

Any comments made by the bride-to-be during the shower are recorded or written down by one of the participants. At the end of the shower they are either read aloud or played back for the couple in a private room. The comments that she makes during the ceremony are interpreted sexually. For example, she may be forced to place her finger in a glass of ice cubes for a long time, and she may cry out, "Please take it out!" By this comment, it is understood that she will be saying the same thing to the groom on her wedding night.

Typically, home-made snacks and refreshments are served while the ceremony goes on. As the climax of the shower, the bride is told to open the gifts that she has received. The gifts consist of kitchen utensils, linen, porcelain figurines, and personal items such as nightgowns. When she opens them, she is expected to thank each donor individually and to exhibit the gifts so that the others can see what she has received. Afterward, her best friend helps her to change into her street clothes.

The role of the bride-to-be at the shower is very clear, underscoring the appropriateness of her reaction to the sexual aspects of the proceedings. She is expected to scream and show horror and surprise. The response of the girl is scripted and socially prescribed. She is expected to cry and scream to be let go, and to beg for her mother to rescue her. She is expected to be modest and maidenly. Should the bride not show the proper surprise and horror, the order of festivities changes. The tricks stop and the shower becomes more conventional.[3] Such a bride is believed by many to be perhaps "experienced" and not a virgin.

If a girl is pregnant or is known to have had sexual experience, the shower takes on a more conventional form. There are gifts and some joking, but it is mild. Interestingly, some of the respondents admit that the original purpose of the shower, to socialize and educate for sex and for the anticipated first night, may not be as necessary as before.[4] Still, they feel that it should be done "for the fun of it"—for the sociability.

Homemaker Role

The women at the older edge of the age range who are attending the shower may have a different socializing purpose. Although Dominican girls are taught from an early age to cook and perform domestic tasks at home, it was the duty of the older women at the showers, especially in the Dominican Republic, to give advice on the care of house and husband, particularly the presentation of food and the treatment of the husband in terms of comfort. They may propose the ironing of sheets, for example. Their gifts are more likely to have some relationship with cleaning and housekeeping.

At the showers observed, there was very little discussion of the housekeeper role, but participants at showers in the Dominican Republic mention that it is still a component there. In the Dominican Republic the future bride is advised to talk with her future mother-in-law in order to find out what the future husband likes or dislikes, especially with regard to food. Along similar lines, she is advised to clean the house well, particularly the bedroom and bathroom since these are the two rooms that men use the most. She is advised to serve his meals properly and make sure that he has everything he needs at the table, including toothpicks, napkin, and cold water. She is also told that she should keep herself well groomed in order to hold his interest in her as a woman. She should be tolerant, kind, understanding, show him compassion, and be sweet all the time. This type of premarital conversation with the future mother-in-law does not seem to take place in this country.

The Subservient Status of Women

The marriage is said to be in the bride's hands. She is said to be solely responsible for its success and for the happiness and comfort of her husband. Traditionally, she was dependent upon him for financial and emotional support. It will be her fault if the marriage breaks up. The woman internalizes these norms and is expected to conform. If the man leaves, it is believed that she was responsible. If he strays, that is to be expected: it is "natural" for a man to have others. And as for nagging, or even mentioning the man's misbehavior, that is worse than anything he may do. The proper role is for a wife to act even more loving and understanding.

The internalization of these values is associated with the concept of machismo,[5] the superiority of the male over the female in every area. A frequent theme is the wife's inadequacy as a sexual partner. If the husband is unfaithful and needs an excuse, or is impotent, or feels some dissatisfaction, it is her fault. Her vagina is too big rather than that he is an inept lover. The size of the women's vagina is believed to be critical to the sexual satisfaction of both. She may be told to use ointments that will shrink her vagina temporarily before having sex. The size of the vagina is a subject of conversation among the girls and women and a good deal of anxiety is reflected in the conversation and jokes. There is little acknowledgment that the clitoris is the primary area of female pleasure and that more expert manipulation or adjustment might make sexual satisfaction a reality for both. Blaming the size of the vagina allows the man to say that it is the woman's fault for being "so big"—and she, internalizing his perspective, agrees.

Some respondents speak of the old days in the Dominican Republic when, in the event proof of virginity was lacking, the wife could be sent back to her parents. One respondent, whose husband trained as a physician in the Dominican Republic, notes that even recently operations have been performed, primarily on upper-middle-class women who might have had sexual experience, to restore their hymen or to at least make penetration seem difficult. Another respondent, who was a virgin at the time of her marriage ten years ago but did not bleed, notes that her husband (who is not a Dominican) still mentions it and that it is the last word in any argument they have.

The concept of *machismo* is broader than explicit sexual relations. It also covers the wife's contact with men and women in general. Under the rules of *machismo*:

1. No males are allowed to visit a woman when her husband is not at home.
2. She is not allowed to "hang out" with a group of friends.
3. She is to restrict her friendship to females.
4. She should not be too friendly with others of either sex.

Many jokes told at the shower are forms of reactions to *machismo*. Most jokes are antimale and tend to fall into two categories. The first has to do with sexual inadequacy on the part of the husband. The second has to do with his cuckoldry. In both cases, the women may be expressing the laughter of the oppressed. The jokes are a way to say that which is unsayable, that there is an unequal distribution of power. The jokes constitute an ideological attack on a system, and make manifest another ideology: that the weaker one may also have a weapon; that "he" is not so powerful after all and "she" may have a weapon at her disposal. The antimale joke that follows has been translated from the Spanish:

APARTMENT FOR RENT

A prosperous businessman propositioned a prostitute, and she agreed to spend the night with him for the sum of five hundred dollars. When he departed the following morning, he told her that he didn't carry money with him, but he would tell his secretary to send a check with the indication that the check was for renting an "apartment." On the way to his office, he felt that the "program" did not warrant the fee and was not worth the amount agreed upon, and for that reason he ordered his secretary to send a check for two hundred dollars with the following note:

Dear Mrs.:
I am sending you a check for the renting of your apartment. I am not sending the amount agreed upon because when I rented your apartment, I was under the impression

1. That it had never been used;
2. That it had heat; and
3. That it was small.

But last night, I noticed that it had been used, that it did not have heat, and that it was excessively big.

The prostitute had hardly received the note before she sent back the check with the following note:

Dear Sir:
I am sending back your check of two hundred dollars, since I do not understand how you can have imagined that such a pretty apartment would not have been previously occupied. In reference to the heat, I want to tell you that you didn't know how to turn it on, and as for the size, I am not at fault that you did not have sufficient household goods to fill it.

ETHNIC ADAPTATION IN THE BRIDAL SHOWER

In New York City, the Dominican bridal shower appears in two forms, the "pure" Dominican shower and the American-Dominican shower. A "pure," shower is characterized by Dominican hospitality and warmth shown to people in general. The Dominican tendency to share, to talk, to open themselves up makes everyone feel at home. Fewer commercially purchased items are used. For decorations, pictures taken from pornographic magazines are usually used. The dildoes are all homemade rather than bought in sex-item stores. The snacks and refreshments are personally served and the souvenirs are individually pinned on the guests. This is not always true at American-Dominican showers.

The language spoken at the "pure" Dominican showers is Spanish, whereas at the American-Dominican one, bilingualism is quite prevalent. Here the guests are found forming little social groups who chatter among themselves. They also help themselves to the snacks and refreshments. The difference, it appears, is that the "pure" shower is more strongly characterized by collectivism, while the American adaptation reflects more individualism.

The Americanized bride-to-be seems to show less shock and astonishment at the goings-on than does the "pure" Dominican bride, whose reaction is very strong, spontaneous, and full of tears. The sexually explicit material that is shown her often brings about refusals to look at or to participate in the acts. However, the American-Dominican bride-to-be responds less dramatically and seems to enjoy it all. This "take-it-on-the-chin" attitude of the Americanized bride seems to be the result of having been exposed to much more sexual information, either in school, at work, on television, or at the movies.

Another important distinction between American-Dominican showers and their "pure" counterparts is the integration of different ethnic features in the ceremony. There is a considerable influence of Puerto-Rican and Cuban culture in some showers held in New York City, whether they are "pure" or American-Dominican. This is illustrated by the types of litanies and dirty poems read at the showers. Most of the vulgar words used to describe sexual organs and acts are slang from Puerto Rico or Cuba. For example, the word "*pinga*" is Cuban slang for "penis" and "*chocha*" is a Puerto Rican slang word for "vagina." The Dominican immigrants have learned the words through social interaction with other Hispanic groups domiciled in the city. In fact, many Dominican males were nicknamed "*Chicho*" at home, but are not called that here, since for Puerto Ricans it is the slang word for "sexual intercourse." As has already been noted, vulgarity is not commonly used by Dominican women, but is quite acceptable and indeed pertinent at the showers in both countries.

The showers are rapidly being affected by the technology of modern society. The tape recorder is taking the place of written notes; the film projector is beginning to replace the sex education "classes" held at most ceremonies; and cameras are being used to record these events. This is happening not only here, but also in the Dominican Republic, probably introduced there by Dominican immigrants who travel constantly between the two places.[6]

CONCLUSION

Exploration of the showers suggests that they might be a good indicator of the degree of assimilation to American values of marital egalitarianism, even allowing for class differences within the Dominican family structure, particularly in New York but also perhaps in the Dominican Republic.[7] It used to be that "*New Yorkinas*"—girls who grew up in or came to New York—were seen to be on the track of a loose life: corrupted somehow, nonvirginal, or at least on the way to being that way. But the true "corruption" may be nonacceptance of the traditional subservient role, a major change that immigration has brought. There is a continuous exchange between the Dominican Republic and Dominicans in New York. People go back and forth. When they first came here, the old norms remained strong at first. But changes in the family structure having to do with economic and social life here in New York have changed some of the norms and have at least made others the focus of conflict.

Both men and women work here in New York. In fact, the employment opportunities for women in factories and the garment district may be better than for men. More women go to school than men. Many young women serve as the brokers for their families, dealing with city officials and social agencies and thus gaining experience and autonomy. The broker role, traditional for men in the Dominican Republic, serves here to give women power in their families; but it may also cause conflicts. For example, a woman's fiancée may retain the traditional values of Dominican family life, even though he may be earning no more than she and may be less educated. The shower, whether reflecting old or new norms, prescribes and reinforces some of the traditional roles for the bride. But she, while enjoying the attention her friends are paying her, may be making an adjustment that will not necessarily be helpful to her in her new status as a married woman in a family structure that is in flux. Changes in the social context in which the marriage will be embedded, as well as the urban environment in which she lives, require education, independence, and aggressiveness on the part of both men and women.

A CASE STUDY: MARIA'S SHOWER

José and Maria, who met at a party in Upper Manhattan, have now been going out for eight months. Their relationship had to be approved by Maria's parents, who ultimately agreed that José could visit her regularly at her home. Since they decided to have a steady relationship, it was expected that a formal engagement would follow. José bought Maria an engagement ring and presented it to her in front of her parents. Their next step was to set up a wedding date. Maria decided to get married in spring. Maria's friends and relatives were anxious to learn the exact date of the wedding. Her best friend and her future sister-in-law wanted to give her a shower. They felt that it would be good for her to participate in one, since it would be a time for her to have fun with all her friends before she got married. Two weeks prior to the wedding, the word was spread, at her job, at the church, at the local bodega, and throughout the neighborhood that she was going to have a shower. Nobody was supposed to reveal to Maria that such an event was being planned for her. It could not take place at her home because the preparations might make her suspicious. It would no longer be a surprise, as it is supposed to be. Her best friend offered her apartment in Washington Heights (Manhattan), which she and two other friends cleaned and decorated, particularly the living room. On a Saturday evening in March, one week before the wedding, the shower was held. When the planners invited other friends, they suggested that they bring dirty jokes, "fresh" gifts, and anything else that would amuse and embarrass the bride-to-be. They divided up the work, and two women made kipper and pastelitos; these were the snacks that would be served at the shower along with Pepsi-Cola and orange soda.[8]

One hour before the shower everything was ready. During this time, the guests, all females, arrived and awaited the bride-to-be's entrance at seven o'clock. Thirty-four well-dressed women of all ages, most of them in their twenties, were present at the ceremony. However, one young girl fifteen years of age was in attendance. The living room contained a decorated chair with an umbrella placed above it, a wishing well, and a table with an elaborately decorated pink cake on it. Under the chair was a tape recorder. On the wall were pornographic pictures of nude white men and women with abnormally large genitalia and of couples engaged in various stages of sexual intercourse. In the center of these pictures, a large home-made penis had been placed. It was made by one of the participants out of a nylon stocking and paper. (The woman who made it is Cuban; she stated that she loved to go to bridal showers.) Next to the cake was a doll dressed in pink with a hot dog on its head.

All of the participants were from Latin America. They began discussing their own experiences on their wedding nights. A Dominican said that she almost died of a heart attack when she saw her husband naked for the first time: "He had a big member." Another participant replied, "It's quality not quantity that counts." Some of the women admitted that they were afraid on their wedding night, and others said that they were anxious to find out what it really was like to have sex for the first time. All of the participants engaged in this type of conversation.

At the moment of the bride-to-be's arrival, one of the women said, "She's coming. Silent! Quiet!" There was a lot of tension in the air, as people tried to decide where to place themselves so as to completely surprise the bride. The light was turned off. One of the women was standing in the middle of the room with a glass of water in her hands. When the bride appeared in the doorway, the water was thrown in her face and everyone shouted, "Surprise!" The bride covered her face and began to cry. She said, "José and I have an appointment with the priest right now, but I guess that we will have to go another day."

Everyone was speaking Spanish, telling jokes, and generally having fun. The only words spoken in English were "Okay" and "Nice." A young woman took the penis from the wall and pinned it on the bride as a corsage. The bride-to-be begged, "No, please. It's ugly!" The woman replied, "You have to wear it because from now on, you're always going to have one chasing you and following you around." Another woman asked the bride to put it into her mouth. She refused to do so. Another woman took it and forced it into Maria's mouth. "There's nothing to be afraid of! Just be a good girl. This is harmless in comparison to what you're marrying." Another person asked, "Do you like it the way it is—hard like a rock?" Whenever the bride touched it, other women would say, "Oh, look how she caresses it. I knew you were going to like it."

One woman took a glass filled with ice and forced the bride's finger into it. She had to keep her finger in it until it hurt so that she could beg and scream for them to stop, saying things like, "Please stop doing this to me. I hate you. Are you crazy or something? I didn't know you were going to do this to me." Meanwhile, everything she was saying was being recorded. This was later played back for the groom at the shower's end. The women then said to him, "Listen to all the things she's going to say to you on your wedding night."

A woman picked up a penis that she had made from the protective rubber of her sewing machine and dropped it in Maria's lap, saying, "This thing loves to be between legs. You have to get accustomed to it." Another woman said, "Do you know which number is going to be your favorite? You mark my words, it will be sixty-nine." Another participant showed Maria a red baby-doll nightgown and told her, "Come on and put it on! Take off your panty-hose."

Maria seemed surprised and said, "I am okay in my dress." A woman told her, "No, you have to wear the gown, now." Two women helped her to undress and to put on the nightgown while others applauded and commented, "She is going to look good. Not bad! You're going to drive him crazy. Sexy. That's the way he wants you." A woman picked up the home-made dildo and quickly rubbed it on the bride-to-be's vulva. Another young woman who was standing up said to her, "I am going to show you the woodpecker style, but you have to be drunk to do it." She stuck her tongue in and out and said, "Pick, pick, with the tip of your tongue. Touch his ass simultaneously right in the hole." Everyone laughed, and the bride-to-be, although laughing with them, was amazed. A woman in her late thirties approached Maria, who said to the women, "Look, auntie, what these women are doing to me." Her aunt smiled at her and another woman stood up and said, "Listen to Maria's prayer. She used to say this prayer every night before she met José." A litany was read aloud and everyone laughed at each sentence. The name of the litany was "A Virgin's Bedside Prayer." After the litany had been read, the reader asked the bride-to-be, "Is this true? No, don't answer because we know it's true." Maria told them that they were "a bunch of fresh women." She was beginning to feel more comfortable. Meanwhile a copy of *Playgirl* magazine was being passed around and the women made jokes about the naked men, the size of their penises, etc. Suddenly, someone cried out, "José is coming!" Immediately, a young woman impersonating a man walked in. Everyone began to laugh. She had a home-made penis hanging from the zipper of her pants. She came up to the bride and wiped the penis across her face. Then she took Maria's hand and made her squeeze the penis. "This is yours, my love."

Laughing, the bride pushed her away. Then the young girl with the "penis" began chasing all the women in the room. Everyone was having fun.

A native of Colombia had brought a film projector along to show some X-rated films. Everyone sat on the floor and the first film was shown. It was about two women engaged in a homosexual relationship. Most of the women protested and one of them said, "We don't want to see homosexuals. We want to see the real thing." Finally, the woman changed the film. Another woman said to Maria, "Pay attention, Maria!" The film showed two women engaged in various sexual acts with a man who was in a bathtub. Someone said to Maria, "You have to be ready to do it anywhere at anytime, Maria." The film showed the man ejaculating, and someone said to the bride, "Look at all that milk. You have to get accustomed to it. And look at how vulnerable a man can be when he comes!" The film ended and the kipper and pastelitos were served to the guests by two of the women in attendance.

At the time that this was happening, a thirty-five-year-old Dominican woman was giving Maria advice and telling her to wear something blue, something old, and something new on her wedding day for good luck. (It is part of the Dominican folklore to do this.) Two young women suggested that she should start opening her gifts. The first gift that she opened was a table set. Then she opened a box containing kitchen utensils and other boxes containing bathroom towels, an automatic broom, a nightgown, etc. On the whole, the gifts were household gifts, mainly items for use in the kitchen or bathroom. (There seemed to be a great deal of curiosity about who brought which gift.) The bride thanked everyone for their gifts and at 10 P.M. she was helped into her street clothes and prepared for the arrival of José. Then someone said to her, "Maria, guess who's here?" José shook hands with all the women and some of the male relatives, who came in when it was clear that the shower had ended. No one discussed what had gone on during the shower and at 11 P.M. everyone went home, including the bridal couple.

ACKNOWLEDGMENTS

The authors would like to thank Carmen Salcedo and Altagracia Mejia for the initial invitations and Vernon Boggs for his encouragement of the study.

4 Sexuality, Intimacy, and the Family

Reading 11   The Feminization of Love*

FRANCESCA M. CANCIAN

A feminized and incomplete perspective on love predominates in the United States. We identify love with emotional expression and talking about feelings, aspects of love that women prefer and in which women tend to be more skilled than men. At the same time we often ignore the instrumental and physical aspects of love that men prefer, such as providing help, sharing activities, and sex. This feminized perspective leads us to believe that women are much more capable of love than men and that the way to make relationships more loving is for men to become more like women.[1] This paper proposes an alternative, androgynous perspective on love, one based on the premise that love is both instrumental and expressive.[2] From this perspective, the way to make relationships more loving is for women and men to reject polarized gender roles and integrate "masculine" and "feminine" styles of love.

THE TWO PERSPECTIVES

"Love is active, doing something for your good even if it bothers me" says a fundamentalist Christian. "Love is sharing, the real sharing of feelings" says a divorced secretary who is in love

again. In ancient Greece, the ideal love was the adoration of a man for a beautiful young boy who was his lover. In the thirteenth century, the exemplar of love was the chaste devotion of a knight for another man's wife. In Puritan New England, love between husband and wife was the ideal, and in Victorian times, the asexual devotion of a mother for her child seemed the essence of love.[3] My purpose is to focus on one kind of love: long-term heterosexual love in the contemporary United States.

What is a useful definition of enduring love between a woman and a man? One guideline for a definition comes from the prototypes of enduring love—the relations between committed lovers, husband and wife, parent and child. These relationships combine care and assistance with physical and emotional closeness. Studies of attachment between infants and their mothers emphasize the importance of being protected and fed as well as touched and held. In marriage, according to most family sociologists, both practical help and affection are part of enduring love, or "the affection we feel for those with whom our lives are deeply intertwined."[4] Our own informal observations often point in the same direction: if we consider the relationships that are the prototypes of enduring love, it seems that what we really mean by love is some combination of instrumental and expressive qualities.

Historical studies provide a second guideline for defining enduring love, specifically between a woman and a man.[5] In precapitalist America, such love was a complex whole that included work and feelings. Then it was split into feminine and masculine fragments by the separation of home and workplace. This historical analysis implies that affection, material help, and routine cooperation all are parts of enduring love.

Consistent with these guidelines, my working definition of enduring love between adults is a relationship wherein a small number of people are affectionate and emotionally committed to each other, define their collective well-being as a major goal, and feel obliged to provide care and practical assistance for each other. People who love each other also usually share physical contact; they communicate with each other frequently and cooperate in some routine tasks of daily life. My discussion is of enduring heterosexual love only; I will for the sake of simplicity refer to it as "love."

In contrast to this broad definition of love, the narrower, feminized definition dominates both contemporary scholarship and public opinion. Most scholars who study love, intimacy, or close friendship focus on qualities that are stereotypically feminine, such as talking about feelings.[6] For example, Abraham Maslow defines love as "a feeling of tenderness and affection with great enjoyment, happiness, satisfaction, elation and even ecstasy." Among healthy individuals, he says, "there is a growing intimacy and honesty and self-expression."[7] Zick Rubin's "Love Scale," designed to measure the degree of passionate love as opposed to liking, includes questions about confiding in each other, longing to be together, and sexual attraction as well as

caring for each other. Studies of friendship usually distinguish close friends from acquaintances on the basis of how much personal information is disclosed, and many recent studies of married couples and lovers emphasize communication and self-disclosure. A recent book on marital love by Lillian Rubin focuses on intimacy, which she defines as "reciprocal expression of feeling and thought, not out of fear or dependent need, but out of a wish to know another's inner life and to be able to share one's own."[8] She argues that intimacy is distinct from nurturance or caretaking and that men are usually unable to be intimate.

Among the general public, love is also defined primarily as expressing feelings and verbal disclosure, not as instrumental help. This is especially true among the more affluent; poorer people are more likely than they to see practical help and financial assistance as a sign of love.[9] In a study conducted in 1980, 130 adults from a wide range of social classes and ethnic backgrounds were interviewed about the qualities that make a good love relationship. The most frequent response referred to honest and open communication. Being caring and supportive and being tolerant and understanding were the other qualities most often mentioned.[10] Similar results were reported from Ann Swidler's study of an affluent suburb: the dominant conception of love stressed communicating feelings, working on the relationship, and self-development.[11] Finally, a contemporary dictionary defines love as "strong affection for another arising out of kinship or personal ties" and as attraction based on sexual desire, affection, and tenderness.[12]

These contemporary definitions of love clearly focus on qualities that are seen as feminine in our culture. A study of gender roles in 1968 found that warmth, expressiveness, and talkativeness were seen as appropriate for women and not for men. In 1978 the core features of gender stereotypes were unchanged although fewer qualities were seen as appropriate for only one sex. Expressing tender feelings, being gentle, and being aware of the feelings of others were still ideal qualities for women and not for men. The desirable qualities for men and not for women included being independent, unemotional, and interested in sex.[13] The only component perceived as masculine in popular definitions of love is interest in sex.

The two approaches to defining love—one broad, encompassing instrumental and affective qualities, one narrow, including only the affective qualities—inform the two different perspectives on love. According to the androgynous perspective, both gender roles contain elements of love. The feminine role does not include all of the major ways of loving; some aspects of love come from the masculine role, such as sex and providing material help, and some, such as cooperating in daily tasks, are associated with neither gender role. In contrast, the feminized perspective on love implies that all of the elements of love are included in the feminine role. The capacity to love is divided by gender. Women can love and men cannot.

SOME FEMINIST INTERPRETATIONS

Feminist scholars are divided on the question of love and gender. Supporters of the feminized perspective seem most influential at present. Nancy Chodorow's psychoanalytic theory has been especially influential in promoting a feminized perspective on love among social scientists studying close relationships. Chodorow's argument—in greatly simplified form—is that as infants, both boys and girls have strong identification and intimate attachments with their mothers. Since boys grow up to be men, they must repress this early identification, and in the

process they repress their capacity for intimacy. Girls retain their early identification since they will grow up to be women, and throughout their lives females see themselves as connected to others. As a result of this process, Chodorow argues, "girls come to define and experience themselves as continuous with others; . . . boys come to define themselves as more separate and distinct."[14] This theory implies that love is feminine—women are more open to love than men—and that this gender difference will remain as long as women are the primary caretakers of infants.

Scholars have used Chodorow's theory to develop the idea that love and attachment are fundamental parts of women's personalities but not of men's. Carol Gilligan's influential book on female personality development asserts that women define their identity "by a standard of responsibility and care." The predominant female image is "a network of connection, a web of relationships that is sustained by a process of communication." In contrast, males favor a "hierarchical ordering, with its imagery of winning and losing and the potential for violence which it contains." "Although the world of the self that men describe at times includes 'people' and 'deep attachments,' no particular person or relationship is mentioned. . . . Thus the male 'I' is defined in separation."[15]

A feminized conception of love can be supported by other theories as well. In past decades, for example, such a conception developed from Talcott Parsons's theory of the benefits to the nuclear family of women's specializing in expressive action and men's specializing in instrumental action. Among contemporary social scientists, the strongest support for the feminized perspective comes from such psychological theories as Chodorow's.[16]

On the other hand, feminist historians have developed an incisive critique of the feminized perspective on love. Mary Ryan and other social historians have analyzed how the separation of home and workplace in the nineteenth century polarized gender roles and feminized love.[17] Their argument, in simplified form, begins with the observation that in the colonial era the family household was the arena for economic production, affection, and social welfare. The integration of activities in the family produced a certain integration of expressive and instrumental traits in the personalities of men and women. Both women and men were expected to be hard working, modest, and loving toward their spouses and children, and the concept of love included instrumental cooperation as well as expression of feelings. In Ryan's words, "When early Americans spoke of love they were not withdrawing into a female byway of human experience. Domestic affection, like sex and economics, was not segregated into male and female spheres." There was a "reciprocal ideal of conjugal love" that "grew out of the day-to-day cooperation, sharing, and closeness of the diversified home economy."[18]

Economic production gradually moved out of the home and became separated from personal relationships as capitalism expanded. Husbands increasingly worked for wages in factories and shops while wives stayed at home to care for the family. This division of labor gave women more experience with close relationships and intensified women's economic dependence on men. As the daily activities of men and women grew further apart, a new worldview emerged that exaggerated the differences between the personal, loving, feminine sphere of the home and the impersonal, powerful, masculine sphere of the workplace. Work became identified with what men do for money while love became identified with women's activities at home. As a result, the conception of love shifted toward emphasizing tenderness, powerlessness, and the expression of emotion.[19]

This partial and feminized conception of love persisted into the twentieth century as the division of labor remained stable: the workplace remained impersonal and separated from the home, and married women continued to be excluded from paid employment. According to this historical explanation, one might expect a change in the conception of love since the 1940s, as growing numbers of wives took jobs. However, women's persistent responsibility for child care and housework, and their lower wages, might explain a continued feminized conception of love.[20]

Like the historical critiques, some psychological studies of gender also imply that our current conception of love is distorted and needs to be integrated with qualities associated with the masculine role. For example, Jean Baker Miller argues that women's ways of loving—their need to be attached to a man and to serve others—result from women's powerlessness, and that a better way of loving would integrate power with women's style of love.[21] The importance of combining activities and personality traits that have been split apart by gender is also a frequent theme in the human potential movement.[22] These historical and psychological works em-phasize the flexibility of gender roles and the inadequacy of a concept of love that includes only the feminine half of human qualities. In contrast, theories like Chodorow's emphasize the rigidity of gender differences after childhood and define love in terms of feminine qualities. The two theoretical approaches are not as inconsistent as my simplified sketches may suggest, and many scholars combine them;[23] however, the two approaches have different implications for empirical research.

EVIDENCE ON WOMEN'S "SUPERIORITY" IN LOVE

A large number of studies show that women are more interested and more skilled in love than men. However, most of these studies use biased measures based on feminine styles of loving, such as verbal self-disclosure, emotional expression, and willingness to report that one has close relationships. When less biased measures are used, the differences between women and men are often small.

Women have a greater number of close relationships than men. At all stages of the life cycle, women see their relatives more often. Men and women report closer relations with their mothers than with their fathers and are generally closer to female kin. Thus an average Yale man in the 1970s talked about himself more with his mother than with his father and was more satisfied with his relationship with his mother. His most frequent grievance against his father was that his father gave too little of himself and was cold and uninvolved; his grievance against his mother was that she gave too much of herself and was alternately overprotective and punitive.[24]

Throughout their lives, women are more likely to have a confidant—a person to whom one discloses personal experiences and feelings. Girls prefer to be with one friend or a small group, while boys usually play competitive games in large groups. Men usually get together with friends to play sports or do some other activity, while women get together explicitly to talk and to be together.[25]

Men seemed isolated given their weak ties with their families and friends. Among blue-collar couples interviewed in 1950, 64 percent of the husbands had no confidants other than their spouses, compared to 24 percent of the wives.[26] The predominantly upper-middle-class men interviewed by Daniel Levinson in the 1970s were no less isolated. Levinson concludes that "close friendship with a man or a woman is rarely experienced by American men."[27] Apparently, most men have no loving relationships besides those with wife or lover; and given the

estrangement that often occurs in marriages, many men may have no loving relationship at all.

Several psychologists have suggested that there is a natural reversal of these roles in middle age, as men become more concerned with relationships and women turn toward independence and achievement; but there seems to be no evidence showing that men's relationships become more numerous or more intimate after middle age, and some evidence to the contrary.[28]

Women are also more skilled than men in talking about relationships. Whether working class or middle class, women value talking about feelings and relationships and disclose more than men about personal experiences. Men who deviate and talk a lot about their personal experiences are commonly defined as feminine and maladjusted.[29] Working-class wives prefer to talk about themselves, their close relationships with family and friends, and their homes, while their husbands prefer to talk about cars, sports, work, and politics. The same gender-specific preferences are expressed by college students.[30]

Men do talk more about one area of personal experience: their victories and achievements; but talking about success is associated with power, not intimacy. Women say more about their fears and disappointments, and it is disclosure of such weaknesses that usually is interpreted as a sign of intimacy.[31] Women are also more accepting of the expression of intense feelings, including love, sadness, and fear, and they are more skilled in interpreting other people's emotions.[32]

Finally, in their leisure time women are drawn to topics of love and human entanglements while men are drawn to competition among men. Women's preferences in television viewing run to daytime soap operas, or if they are more educated, the high-brow soap operas on educational channels, while most men like to watch competitive and often aggressive sports. Reading tastes show the same pattern. Women read novels and magazine articles about love, while men's magazines feature stories about men's adventures and encounters with death.[33]

However, this evidence on women's greater involvement and skill in love is not as strong as it appears. Part of the reason that men seem so much less loving than women is that their behavior is measured with a feminine ruler. Much of this research considers only the kinds of loving behavior that are associated with the feminine role and rarely compares women and men in terms of qualities associated with the masculine role. When less biased measures are used, the behavior of men and women is often quite similar. For example, in a careful study of kinship relations among young adults in a southern city, Bert Adams found that women were much more likely than men to say that their parents and relatives were very important to their lives (58 percent of women and 37 percent of men). In measures of actual contact with relatives, though, there were much smaller differences: 88 percent of women and 81 percent of men whose parents lived in the same city saw their parents weekly. Adams concluded that "differences between males and females in relations with parents are discernible primarily in the subjective sphere; contact frequencies are quite similar."[34]

The differences between the sexes can be small even when biased measures are used. For example, Marjorie Lowenthal and Clayton Haven reported the finding, later widely quoted, that elderly women were more likely than elderly men to have a friend with whom they could talk about their personal troubles—clearly a measure of a traditionally feminine behavior. The figures revealed that 81 percent of the married women and 74 percent of the married men had confidants—not a sizable difference.[35] On the other hand, whatever the measure, virtually all such studies find that women are more involved in close relationships than men, even if the difference is small.

In sum, women are only moderately superior to men in love: they have more close relationships and care more about them, and they seem to be more skilled at love, especially those aspects of love that involve expressing feelings and being vulnerable. This does not mean that men are separate and unconcerned with close relationships, however. When national surveys ask people what is most important in their lives, women tend to put family bonds first while men put family bonds first or second, along with work.[36] For both sexes, love is clearly very important.

EVIDENCE ON THE MASCULINE STYLE OF LOVE

Men tend to have a distinctive style of love that focuses on practical help, shared physical activities, spending time together, and sex.[37] The major elements of the masculine style of love emerged in Margaret Reedy's study of 102 married couples in the late 1970s. She showed individuals' statements describing aspects of love and asked them to rate how well the statements described their marriages. On the whole, husband and wife had similar views of their marriage, but several sex differences emerged. Practical help and spending time together were more important to men. The men were more likely to give high ratings to such statements as: "When she needs help I help her," and "She would rather spend her time with me than with anyone else." Men also described themselves more often as sexually attracted and endorsed such statements as: "I get physically excited and aroused just thinking about her." In addition, emotional security was less important to men than to women, and men were less likely to describe the relationship as secure, safe, and comforting.[38] Another study in the late 1970s showed a similar pattern among young, highly educated couples. The husbands gave greater emphasis to feeling responsible for the partner's well-being and putting the spouse's needs first, as well as to spending time together. The wives gave greater importance to emotional involvement and verbal self-disclosure but also were more concerned than the men about maintaining their separate activities and their independence.[39]

The difference between men and women in their views of the significance of practical help was demonstrated in a study in which seven couples recorded their interactions for several days. They noted how pleasant their relations were and counted how often the spouse did a helpful chore, such as cooking a good meal or repairing a faucet, and how often the spouse expressed acceptance or affection. The social scientists doing the study used a feminized definition of love. They labeled practical help as "instrumental behavior" and expressions of acceptance or affection as "affectionate behavior," thereby denying the affectionate aspect of practical help. The wives seemed to be using the same scheme; they thought their marital relations were pleasant that day if their husbands had directed a lot of affectionate behavior to them, regardless of their husbands' positive instrumental behavior. The husbands' enjoyment of their marital relations, on the other hand, depended on their wives' instrumental actions, not on their expressions of affection. The men actually saw instrumental actions as affection.[40] One husband who was told by the researchers to increase his affectionate behavior toward his wife decided to wash her car and was surprised when neither his wife nor the researchers accepted that as an "affectionate" act.

The masculine view of instrumental help as loving behavior is clearly expressed by a husband discussing his wife's complaints about his lack of communication: "What does she want?

Proof? She's got it, hasn't she? Would I be knocking myself out to get things for her—like to keep up this house—if I didn't love her? Why does a man do things like that if not because he loves his wife and kids? I swear, I can't figure what she wants." His wife, who has a feminine orientation to love, says something very different: "It is not enough that he supports us and takes care of us. I appreciate that, but I want him to share things with me. I need for him to tell me his feelings."[41] Many working-class women agree with men that a man's job is something he does out of love for his family,[42] but middle-class women and social scientists rarely recognize men's practical help as a form of love. (Indeed, among upper-middle-class men whose jobs offer a great deal of intrinsic gratification, their belief that they are "doing it for the family" may seem somewhat self-serving.)

Other differences between men's and women's styles of love involve sex. Men seem to separate sex and love while women connect them,[43] but, paradoxically, sexual intercourse seems to be the most meaningful way of giving and receiving love for many men. A twenty-nine-year-old carpenter who had been married for three years said that, after sex, "I feel so close to her and the kids. We feel like a real family then. I don't talk to her very often, I guess, but somehow I feel we have really communicated after we have made love."[44]

Because sexual intimacy is the only recognized "masculine" way of expressing love, the recent trend toward viewing sex as a way for men and women to express mutual intimacy is an important challenge to the feminization of love. However, the connection between sexuality and love is undermined both by the "sexual revolution" definition of sex as a form of casual recreation and by the view of male sexuality as a weapon—as in rape—with which men dominate and punish women.[45]

Another paradoxical feature of men's style of love is that men have a more romantic attitude toward their partners than do women. In Reedy's study, men were more likely to select statements like "we are perfect for each other."[46] In a survey of college students, 65 percent of the men but only 24 percent of the women said that, even if a relationship had all of the other qualities they desired, they would not marry unless they were in love.[47] The common view of this phenomenon focuses on women. The view is that women marry for money and status and so see marriage as instrumentally, rather than emotionally, desirable. This of course is at odds with women's greater concern with self-disclosure and emotional intimacy and lesser concern with instrumental help. A better way to explain men's greater romanticism might be to focus on men. One such possible explanation is that men do not feel responsible for "working on" the emotional aspects of a relationship, and therefore see love as magically and perfectly present or absent. This is consistent with men's relative lack of concern with affective interaction and greater concern with instrumental help.

In sum, there is a masculine style of love. Except for romanticism, men's style fits the popularly conceived masculine role of being the powerful provider.[48] From the androgynous perspective, the practical help and physical activities included in this role are as much a part of love as the expression of feelings. The feminized perspective cannot account for this masculine style of love; nor can it explain why women and men are so close in the degrees to which they are loving.

NEGATIVE CONSEQUENCES OF THE FEMINIZATION OF LOVE

The division of gender roles in our society that contributes to the two separate styles of love is reinforced by the feminized perspective and leads to political and moral problems that would be mitigated with a more androgynous approach to love. The feminized perspective works against some of the key values and goals of feminists and humanists by contributing to the devaluation and exploitation of women.

It is especially striking how the differences between men's and women's styles of love reinforce men's power over women. Men's style involves giving women important resources, such as money and protection that men control and women believe they need, and ignoring the resources that women control and men need. Thus men's dependency on women remains covert and repressed, while women's dependency on men is overt and exaggerated; and it is overt dependency that creates power, according to social exchange theory.[49] The feminized perspective on love reinforces this power differential by leading to the belief that women need love more than do men, which is implied in the association of love with the feminine role. The effect of this belief is to intensify the asymmetrical dependency of women on men.[50] In fact, however, evidence on the high death rates of unmarried men suggests that men need love at least as much as do women.[51]

Sexual relations also can reinforce male dominance insofar as the man takes the initiative and intercourse is defined either as his "taking" pleasure or as his being skilled at "giving" pleasure, either way giving him control. The man's power advantage is further strengthened if the couple assumes that the man's sexual needs can be filled by any attractive woman while the woman's sexual needs can be filled only by the man she loves.[52]

On the other hand, women's preferred ways of loving seem incompatible with control. They involve admitting dependency and sharing or losing control, and being emotionally intense.

Further, the intimate talk about personal troubles that appeals to women requires of a couple a mutual vulnerability, a willingness to see oneself as weak and in need of support. It is true that a woman, like a man, can gain some power by providing her partner with services, such as understanding, sex, or cooking; but this power is largely unrecognized because the man's dependency on such services is not overt. The couple may even see these services as her duty or as her response to his requests (or demands).

The identification of love with expressing feelings also contributes to the lack of recognition of women's power by obscuring the instrumental active component of women's love just as it obscures the loving aspect of men's work. In a culture that glorifies instrumental achievement, this identification devalues both women and love.[53] In reality, a major way by which women are loving is in the clearly instrumental activities associated with caring for others, such as preparing meals, washing clothes, and providing care during illness; but because of our focus on the expressive side of love, this caring work of women is either ignored or redefined as expressing feelings. Thus, from the feminized perspective on love, child care is a subtle communication of attitudes, not work. A wife washing her husband's shirt is seen as expressing love, even though a husband washing his wife's car is seen as doing a job.

Gilligan, in her critique of theories of human development, shows the way in which devaluing love is linked to devaluing women. Basic to most psychological theories of development is the idea that a healthy person develops from a dependent child to an autonomous, independent adult. As Gilligan comments, "Development itself comes to be identified with separation, and attachments appear to be developmental impediments."[54] Thus women, who emphasize attachment, are judged to be developmentally retarded or insufficiently individuated.

The pervasiveness of this image was documented in a well-known study of mental health professionals who were asked to describe mental health, femininity, and masculinity. They associated both mental health and masculinity with independence, rationality, and dominance. Qualities concerning attachment, such as being tactful, gentle, or aware of the feelings of others, they associated with femininity but not with mental health.[55]

Another negative consequence of a feminized perspective on love is that it legitimates impersonal, exploitive relations in the workplace and the community. The ideology of separate spheres that developed in the nineteenth century contrasted the harsh, immoral marketplace with the warm and loving home and implied that this contrast is acceptable.[56] Defining love as expressive, feminine, and divorced from productive activity maintains this ideology. If personal relationships and love are reserved for women and the home, then it is acceptable for a manager to underpay workers or for a community to ignore a needy family. Such behavior is not unloving; it is businesslike or shows a respect for privacy. The ideology of separate spheres also implies that men are properly judged by their instrumental and economic achievements and that poor or unsuccessful men are failures who may deserve a hard life. Levinson presents a conception of masculine development itself as centering on achieving an occupational dream.[57]

Finally, the feminization of love intensifies the conflicts over intimacy between women and men in close relationships. One of the most common conflicts is that the woman wants more closeness and verbal contact while the man withdraws and wants less pressure.[58] Her need for more closeness is partly the result of the feminization of love, which encourages her to be more emotionally dependent on him. Because love is feminine, he in turn may feel controlled during intimate contact. Intimacy is her "turf," an area where she sets the rules and expectations. Talking about the relationship as she wants, may well feel to him like taking a test that she made up and that he will fail. He is likely to react by withdrawing, causing her to intensify her efforts to get closer. The feminization of love thus can lead to a vicious cycle of conflict where neither partner feels in control or gets what she or he wants.

CONCLUSION

The values of improving the status of women and humanizing the public sphere are shared by many of the scholars who support a feminized conception of love; and they, too, explain the conflicts in close relationships in terms of polarized gender roles. Nancy Chodorow, Lillian Rubin, and Carol Gilligan have addressed these issues in detail and with great insight. However, by arguing that women's identity is based on attachment while men's identity is based on separation, they reinforce the distinction between feminine expressiveness and masculine instrumentality, revive the ideology of separate spheres, and legitimate the popular idea that only women know the right way to love. They also suggest that there is no way to overcome the rigidity of gender roles other than by pursuing the goal of men and women becoming equally involved in infant care. In contrast, an androgynous perspective on love challenges the identification of women and love with being expressive, powerless, and nonproductive and the identification of men with being instrumental, powerful, and productive. It rejects the ideology of separate spheres and validates masculine as well as feminine styles of love. This viewpoint suggests that progress could be made by means of a variety of social changes, including men doing child care, relations at work becoming more personal and nurturant, and cultural conceptions of love and gender becoming more androgynous. Changes that equalize power within close relationships by equalizing the economic and emotional dependency between men and women may be especially important in moving toward androgynous love.

The validity of an androgynous definition of love cannot be "proven"; the view that informs the androgynous perspective is that both the feminine style of love (characterized by emotional closeness and verbal self-disclosure) and the masculine style of love (characterized by instrumental help and sex) represent necessary parts of a good love relationship. Who is more loving: a couple who confide most of their experiences to each other but rarely cooperate or give each other practical help, or a couple who help each other through many crises and cooperate in running a household but rarely discuss their personal experiences? Both relationships are limited. Most people would probably choose a combination: a relationship that integrates feminine and masculine styles of loving, an androgynous love.

Reading 12   Is "Straight" to "Gay" as "Family" Is to "No Family"?*

KATH WESTON

For years, and in an amazing variety of contexts, claiming a lesbian or gay identity has been portrayed as a rejection of "the family" and a departure from kinship. In media portrayals of AIDS, Simon Watney (1987:103) observes that "we are invited to imagine some absolute divide between the two domains of 'gay life' and 'the family,' as if gay men grew up, were educated, worked and lived our lives in total isolation from the rest of society." Two presuppositions lend a dubious credence to such imagery: the belief that gay men and lesbians do not have children or establish lasting relationships, and the belief that they invariably alienate adoptive and blood kin once their sexual identities become known. By presenting "the family" as a unitary object, these depictions also imply that everyone participates in identical sorts of kinship relations and subscribes to one universally agreed-upon definition of family.

Representations that exclude lesbians and gay men from "the family" invoke what Blanche Wiesen Cook (1977:48) has called "the assumption that gay people do not love and do not work," the reduction of lesbians and gay men to sexual identity, and sexual identity to sex alone. In the United States, sex apart from heterosexual marriage tends to introduce a wild card into social relations, signifying unbridled lust and the limits of individualism. If heterosexual intercourse can bring people into enduring association via the creation of kinship ties, lesbian and gay sexuality in these depictions isolates individuals from one another rather than weaving them into a social fabric. To assert that straight people "naturally" have access to family, while gay people are destined to move toward a future of solitude and loneliness, is not only to tie kinship closely to procreation, but also to treat gay men and lesbians as members of a nonprocreative species set apart from the rest of humanity (cf. Foucault 1978).

It is but a short step from positioning lesbians and gay men somewhere beyond "the family"—unencumbered by relations of kinship, responsibility, or affection—to portraying them as a menace to family and society. A person or group must first be outside and other in order to invade, endanger, and threaten. My own impression from fieldwork corroborates Frances FitzGerald's (1986) observation that many heterosexuals believe not only that gay people have gained considerable political power, but also that the absolute number of lesbians and gay men (rather than their visibility) has increased in recent years. Inflammatory rhetoric that plays on fears about the "spread" of gay identity and of AIDS finds a disturbing parallel in the imagery used by fascists to describe syphilis at mid-century, when "the healthy" confronted "the degenerate" while the fate of civilization hung in the balance (Hocquenghem 1978).

A long sociological tradition in the United States of studying "the family" under siege or in various states of dissolution lent credibility to charges that this institution required protection from "the homosexual threat." Proposition 6 (the Briggs initiative), which appeared on the ballot in California in 1978, was defeated only after a massive organizing campaign that mobilized lesbians and gay men in record numbers. The text of the initiative, which would have barred gay and lesbian teachers (along with heterosexual teachers who advocated homosexuality) from the public schools, was phrased as a defense of "the family" (in Hollibaugh 1979:55):

> One of the most fundamental interests of the State is the establishment and preservation of the family unit. Consistent with this interest is the State's duty to protect its impressionable youth from influences which are antithetical to this vital interest.

Other anti-gay legislative initiative campaigns adopted the slogans "save the family" and "save the children" as their rallying cries. In 1983 the *Moral Majority Report* referred obliquely to AIDS with the headline, "Homosexual Diseases Threaten American Families" (Godwin 1983). When the *Boston Herald* opposed a gay rights bill introduced into the Massachusetts legislature, it was with an eye to "the preservation of family values" (Allen 1987).

Discourse that opposes gay identity to family membership is not confined to the political arena. A gay doctor was advised during his residency to discourage other gay people from becoming his patients, lest his waiting room become filled with homosexuals. "It'll scare away the families," warned his supervisor (Lazere 1986). Discussions of dual-career families and the implications of a family wage system usually render invisible the financial obligations of gay people who support dependents or who pool material resources with lovers and others they define as kin. Just as women have been accused of taking jobs away from "men with families to support," some lesbians and gay men in the Bay Area recalled coworkers who had condemned them for competing against "people with families" for scarce employment. Or consider the choice of words by a guard at that "all-American" institution, Disneyland, commenting on a legal suit brought by two gay men who had been prohibited from dancing with one another at a dance floor on the grounds: "This is a family park. There is no room for alternative lifestyles here" (Mendenhall 1985).

Scholarly treatments are hardly exempt from this tendency to locate gay men and lesbians beyond the bounds of kinship. Even when researchers are sympathetic to gay concerns, they may equate kinship with genealogically calculated relations. Manuel Castells' and Karen Murphy's (1982) study of the "spatial organization of San Francisco's gay community," for instance, frames its analysis using "gay territory" and "family land" as mutually exclusive categories.

From New Right polemics to the rhetoric of high school hallways, "recruitment" joins "reproduction" in allusions to homosexuality. Alleging that gay men and lesbians must seduce young people in order to perpetuate (or expand) the gay population because they cannot have children of their own, heterosexist critics have conjured up visions of an end to society, the inevitable fate of a society that fails to "reproduce."[1] Of course, the contradictory inferences that sexual identity is "caught" rather than claimed, and that parents pass their sexual identities on to their children, are unsubstantiated. The power of this chain of associations lies in a play on words that blurs the multiple senses of the term "reproduction."

Reproduction's status as a mixed metaphor may detract from its analytic utility, but its very ambiguities make it ideally suited to argument and innuendo.[2] By shifting without signal between reproduction's meaning of physical procreation and its sense as the perpetuation of society as a whole, the characterization of lesbians and gay men as nonreproductive beings links their supposed attacks on "the family" to attacks on society in the broadest sense. Speaking of parents who had refused to accept her lesbian identity, a Jewish woman explained, "They feel like I'm finishing off Hitler's job." The plausibility of the contention that gay people pose a threat to "the family" (and, through the family, to ethnicity) depends upon a view of family grounded in heterosexual relations, combined with the conviction that gay men and lesbians are incapable of procreation, parenting, and establishing kinship ties.

Some lesbians and gay men in the Bay Area had embraced the popular equation of their sexual identities with the renunciation of access to kinship, particularly when first coming out. "My image of gay life was very lonely, very weird, no family," Rafael Ortiz recollected. "I assumed that my family was gone now—that's it." After Bob Korkowski began to call himself gay, he wrote a series of poems in which an orphan was the central character. Bob said the poetry expressed his fear of "having to give up my family because I was queer." When I spoke with Rona Bren after she had been home with the flu, she

told me that whenever she was sick, she relived old fears. That day she had remembered her mother's grim prediction: "You'll be a lesbian and you'll be alone the rest of your life. Even a dog shouldn't be alone."

Looking backward and forward across the life cycle, people who equated their adoption of a lesbian or gay identity with a renunciation of family did so in the double-sided sense of fearing rejection by the families in which they had grown up, and not expecting to marry or have children as adults. Although few in numbers, there were still those who had considered "going straight" or getting married specifically in order to "have a family." Vic Kochifos thought he understood why:

> It's a whole lot easier being straight in the world than it is being gay.... You have built-in loved ones: wife, husband, kids, extended family. It just works easier. And when you want to do something that requires children, and you want to have a feeling of knowing that there's gonna be someone around who cares about you when you're 85 years old, there are thoughts that go through your head, sure. There must be. There's a way of doing it gay, but it's a whole lot harder, and it's less secure.

Bernie Margolis had been sexually involved with men since he was in his teens, but for years had been married to a woman with whom he had several children. At age 67 he regretted having grown to adulthood before the current discussion of gay families, with its focus on redefining kinship and constructing new sorts of parenting arrangements.

> I didn't want to give up the possibility of becoming a family person. Of

having kids of my own to carry on whatever I built up. . . . My mother was always talking about she's looking forward to the day when she would bring her children under the canopy to get married. It never occurred to her that I wouldn't be married. It probably never occurred to me either.

The very categories "good family person" and "good family man" had seemed to Bernie intrinsically opposed to a gay identity. In his fifties at the time I interviewed him, Stephen Richter attributed never having become a father to "not having the relationship with the woman." Because he had envisioned parenting and procreation only in the context of a heterosexual relationship, regarding the two as completely bound up with one another, Stephen had never considered children an option.

Older gay men and lesbians were not the only ones whose adult lives had been shaped by ideologies that banish gay people from the domain of kinship. Explaining why he felt uncomfortable participating in "family occasions," a young man who had no particular interest in raising a child commented, "When families get together, what do they talk about? Who's getting married, who's having children. And who's not, okay? Well, look who's not." Very few of the lesbians and gay men I met believed that claiming a gay identity automatically requires leaving kinship behind. In some cases people described this equation as an outmoded view that contrasted sharply with revised notions of what constitutes a family.

Well-meaning defenders of lesbian and gay identity sometimes assert that gays are not inherently "anti-family," in ways that perpetuate the association of heterosexual identity with exclusive access to kinship. Charles Silverstein (1977), for instance, contends that lesbians and gay men may place more importance on maintaining family ties than heterosexuals do because gay people do not marry and raise children. Here the affirmation that gays and lesbians are capable of fostering enduring kinship ties ends up reinforcing the implication that they cannot establish "families of their own," presumably because the author regards kinship as unshakably rooted in heterosexual alliance and procreation. In contrast, discourse on gay families cuts across the politically loaded couplet of "pro-family" and "anti-family" that places gay men and lesbians in an inherently antagonistic relation to kinship solely on the basis of their nonprocreative sexualities. "Homosexuality is not what is breaking up the Black family," declared Barbara Smith (1987), a black lesbian writer, activist, and speaker at the 1987 Gay and Lesbian March on Washington. "Homophobia is. My Black gay brothers and my Black lesbian sisters are members of Black families, both the ones we were born into and the ones we create."

At the height of gay liberation, activists had attempted to develop alternatives to "the family," whereas by the 1980s many lesbians and gay men were struggling to legitimate gay families as a form of kinship. When Armistead Maupin spoke at a gathering on Castro Street to welcome home two gay men who had been held hostage in the Middle East, partners who had stood with arms around one another upon their release, he congratulated them not only for their safe return, but also as representatives of a new kind of family. Gay or chosen families might incorporate friends, lovers, or children, in any combination. Organized through ideologies of love, choice, and creation, gay families have been defined through a contrast with what many gay men and lesbians in the Bay Area called "straight," "biological," or "blood" family. If families we choose were the families lesbians and gay men created for themselves, straight family represented the families in which most had grown to adulthood.

What does it mean to say that these two categories of family have been defined through contrast? One thing it emphatically does not mean is that heterosexuals share a single coherent form of family (although some of the lesbians and gay men doing the defining believed this to be the case). I am not arguing here for the existence of some central, unified kinship system vis-à-vis which gay people have distinguished their own practice and understanding of family. In the United States, race, class, gender, ethnicity, regional origin, and context all inform differences in household organization, as well as differences in notions of family and what it means to call someone kin.[3]

In any relational definition, the juxtaposition of two terms gives meaning to both.[4] Just as light would not be meaningful without some notion of darkness, so gay or chosen families cannot be understood apart from the families lesbians and gay men call "biological," "blood," or "straight." Like others in their society, most gay people in the Bay Area considered biology a matter of "natural fact." When they applied the terms "blood" and "biology" to kinship, however, they tended to depict families more consistently organized by procreation, more rigidly grounded in genealogy, and more uniform in their conceptualization than anthropologists know most families to be. For many lesbians and gay men, blood family represented not some naturally, given unit that provided a base for all forms of kinship, but rather a procreative principle that organized only one possible *type* of kinship. In their descriptions they situated gay families at the opposite end of a spectrum of determination, subject to no constraints beyond a logic of "free" choice that ordered membership. To the extent that gay men and lesbians mapped "biology" and "choice" onto identities already opposed to one another (straight and gay, respectively), they polarized these two types of family along an axis of sexual identity.[5]

The chart below recapitulates the ideological transformation generated as lesbians and gay men began to inscribe themselves within the domain of kinship.

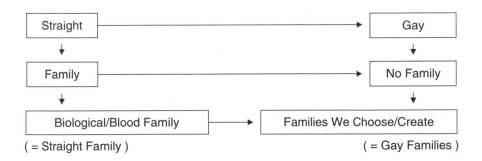

What this chart presents is not some static substitution set, but a historically motivated succession.[6] To move across or down the chart is to move through time. Following along from left to right, time appears as process, periodized with reference to the experience of coming out. In the first opposition, coming out defines the transition from a straight to a gay identity. For the person who maintains an exclusively biogenetic notion of kinship, coming out can mark the renunciation of kinship, the shift from "family" to "no family" portrayed in the second opposition. In the third line, individuals who accepted the possibility of gay families after coming out could experience themselves making a transition from the biological or blood families in which they had grown up to the establishment of their own chosen families.

Moving from top to bottom, the chart depicts the historical time, that inaugurated contemporary discourse on gay kinship. "Straight" changes from a category with an exclusive claim on kinship to an identity allied with a specific kind of family symbolized by biology or blood. Lesbians and gay men, originally relegated to the status of people without family, later lay claim to a distinctive type of family characterized as families we choose or create. While dominant cultural representations have asserted that straight is to gay as family is to no family (lines 1 and 2), at a certain point in history gay people began to contend that straight is to gay as blood family is to chosen families (lines 1 and 3).

What provided the impetus for this ideological shift? Transformations in the relation of lesbians and gay men to kinship are inseparable from sociohistorical developments: changes in the context for disclosing a lesbian or gay identity to others, attempts to build urban gay "community," cultural inferences about relationships between "same-gender" partners, and the lesbian baby boom associated with alternative (artificial) insemination.... If Pierre Bourdieu (1977) is correct, and kinship is something people use to act as well as to think, then its transformations should have unfolded not only on the "big screen" of history, but also on the more modest stage of day-to-day life, where individuals have actively engaged novel ideological distinctions and contested representations that would exclude them from kinship.

Chapter 5

Gender Roles, Work, and the Family

Reading 13 There's No Place Like Work*

ARLIE RUSSELL HOCHSCHILD

It's 7:40 a.m. when Cassie Bell, 4, arrives at the Spotted Deer Child-Care Center, her hair half-combed, a blanket in one hand, a fudge bar in the other. "I'm late," her mother, Gwen, a sturdy young woman whose short-cropped hair frames a pleasant face, explains to the child-care worker in charge. "Cassie wanted the fudge bar so bad, I gave it to her," she adds apologetically.

"Pleeese, can't you take me with you?" Cassie pleads.

"You know I can't take you to work," Gwen replies in a tone that suggests that she has been expecting this request. Cassie's shoulders droop. But she has struck a hard bargain—the morning fudge bar—aware of her mother's anxiety about the long day that lies ahead at the center. As Gwen explains later, she continually feels that she owes Cassie more time than she gives her—she has a "time debt."

Arriving at her office just before 8, Gwen finds on her desk a cup of coffee in her personal mug, milk no sugar (exactly as she likes it), pre-pared by a co-worker who managed to get in ahead of her. As the assistant to the head of public relations at a company I will call Amerco, Gwen has to handle responses to any reports that may appear about the company in the press—a challenging job, but one that gives her satisfaction. As she prepares for her first meeting of the day, she misses her daughter, but she also feels relief; there's a lot to get done at Amerco.

Gwen used to work a straight eight-hour day. But over the last three years, her workday has gradually stretched to eight and a half or nine hours, not counting the E-mail messages and faxes she answers from home. She complains about her hours to her co-workers and listens to their complaints—but she loves her job. Gwen picks up Cassie at 5:45 and gives her a long, affectionate hug.

At home, Gwen's husband, John, a computer programmer, plays with their daughter while Gwen prepares dinner. To protect the dinner "hour"—8:00–8:30—Gwen checks that the

---

Over three years, I interviewed 130 respondents for a book. They spoke freely and allowed me to follow them through "typical" days, on the understanding that I would protect their anonymity. I have changed the names of the company and of those I interviewed, and altered certain identifying details. Their words appear here as they were spoken. —A. R. H.

Hochschild, Arlie Russell. 1997. "There's No Place Like Work." *The New York Times Magazine* (April 20): 51–55, 81, 84. Copyright © 1997 by Arlie Russell Hochschild. Reprinted by permission of Georges Borchardt, Inc. for the author.

phone machine is on, hears the phone ring during dinner but resists the urge to answer. After Cassie's bath, Gwen and Cassie have "quality time," or "Q.T.," as John affectionately calls it. Half an hour later, at 9:30, Gwen tucks Cassie into bed.

There are, in a sense, two Bell households: the rushed family they actually are and the relaxed family they imagine they might be if only they had time. Gwen and John complain that they are in a time bind. What they say they want seems so modest—time to throw a ball, to read to Cassie, to witness the small dramas of her development, not to speak of having a little fun and romance themselves. Yet even these modest wishes seem strangely out of reach. Before going to bed, Gwen has to E-mail messages to her colleagues in preparation for the next day's meeting; John goes to bed early, exhausted—he's out the door by 7 every morning.

Nationwide, many working parents are in the same boat. More mothers of small children than ever now work outside the home. In 1993, 56 percent of women with children between 6 and 17 worked outside the home full time year round; 43 percent of women with children 6 and under did the same. Meanwhile, fathers of small children are not cutting back hours of work to help out at home. If anything, they have increased their hours at work. According to a 1993 national survey conducted by the Families and Work Institute in New York, American men average 48.8 hours of work a week, and women 41.7 hours, including overtime and commuting. All in all, more women are on the economic train, and for many—men and women alike—that train is going faster.

But Amerco has "family friendly" policies. If your division head and supervisor agree, you can work part time, share a job with another worker, work some hours at home, take parental leave or use "flex time." But hardly anyone uses

these policies. In seven years, only two Amerco fathers have taken formal parental leave. Fewer than 1 percent have taken advantage of the opportunity to work part time. Of all such policies, only flex time—which rearranges but does not shorten work time—has had a significant number of takers (perhaps a third of working parents at Amerco).

Forgoing family-friendly policies is not exclusive to Amerco workers. A 1991 study of 188 companies conducted by the Families and Work Institute found that while a majority offered part-time shifts, fewer than 5 percent of employees made use of them. Thirty-five percent offered "flex place"—work from home—and fewer than 3 percent of their employees took advantage of it. And an earlier Bureau of Labor Statistics survey asked workers whether they preferred a shorter workweek, a longer one or their present schedule. About 62 percent preferred their present schedule; 28 percent would have preferred longer hours. Fewer than 10 percent said they wanted a cut in hours.

Still, I found it hard to believe that people didn't protest their long hours at work. So I contacted Bright Horizons, a company that runs 136 company-based child-care centers associated with corporations, hospitals and Federal agencies in 25 states. Bright Horizons allowed me to add questions to a questionnaire they sent out to 3,000 parents whose children attended the centers. The respondents, mainly middle-class parents in their early 30's, largely confirmed the picture I'd found at Amerco. A third of fathers and a fifth of mothers described themselves as "workaholic," and 1 out of 3 said their partners were.

To be sure, some parents have tried to shorten their hours. Twenty-one percent of the nation's women voluntarily work part time, as do 7 percent of men. A number of others make under-the-table arrangements that don't show up on surveys. But while working parents say they need more time at home, the main story of their lives does not center on a struggle to get it. Why? Given the hours parents are working these days, why aren't they taking advantage of an opportunity to reduce their time at work?

The most widely held explanation is that working parents cannot afford to work shorter hours. Certainly this is true for many. But if money is the whole explanation, why would it be that at places like Amerco, the best-paid employees—upper-level managers and professionals—were the least interested in part-time work or job sharing, while clerical workers who earned less were more interested?

Similarly, if money were the answer, we would expect poorer new mothers to return to work more quickly after giving birth than rich mothers. But among working women nationwide, well-to-do new mothers are not much more likely to stay home after 13 weeks with a new baby than low-income new mothers. When asked what they look for in a job, only a third of respondents in a recent study said salary came first. Money is important, but by itself, money does not explain why many people don't want to cut back hours at work.

A second explanation goes that workers don't dare ask for time off because they are afraid it would make them vulnerable to layoffs. With recent downsizings at many large corporations, and with well-paying, secure jobs being replaced by lower-paying, insecure ones, it occurred to me that perhaps employees are "working scared." But when I asked Amerco employees whether they worked long hours for fear of getting on a layoff list, virtually everyone said no. Even among a particularly vulnerable group—factory workers who were laid off in the downturn of the early 1980's and were later rehired—most did not cite fear for their jobs as the only, or main,

reason they worked overtime. For unionized workers, layoffs are assigned by seniority, and for nonunionized workers, layoffs are usually related to the profitability of the division a person works in, not to an individual work schedule.

Were workers uninformed about the company's family friendly policies? No. Some even mentioned that they were proud to work for a company that offered such enlightened policies. Were rigid middle managers standing in the way of workers using these policies? Sometimes. But when I compared Amerco employees who worked for flexible managers with those who worked for rigid managers, I found that the flexible managers reported only a few more applicants than the rigid ones. The evidence, however counterintuitive, pointed to a paradox: workers at the company I studied weren't protesting the time bind. They were accommodating to it.

Why? I did not anticipate the conclusion I found myself coming to: namely, that work has become a form of "home" and home has become "work." The worlds of home and work have not begun to blur, as the conventional wisdom goes, but to reverse places. We are used to thinking that home is where most people feel the most appreciated, the most truly "themselves," the most secure, the most relaxed. We are used to thinking that work is where most people feel like "just a number" or "a cog in a machine." It is where they have to be "on," have to "act," where they are least secure and most harried.

But new management techniques so pervasive in corporate life have helped transform the workplace into a more appreciative, personal sort of social world. Meanwhile, at home the divorce rate has risen, and the emotional demands have become more baffling and complex. In addition to teething, tantrums and the normal developments of growing children, the needs of elderly parents are creating more tasks for the modern family—as are the blending, unblending, reblending of new stepparents, stepchildren, exes and former in-laws.

This idea began to dawn on me during one of my first interviews with an Amerco worker. Linda Avery, a friendly, 38-year-old mother, is a shift supervisor at an Amerco plant. When I meet her in the factory's coffee-break room over a couple of Cokes, she is wearing blue jeans and a pink jersey, her hair pulled back in a long, blond ponytail. Linda's husband, Bill, is a technician in the same plant. By working different shifts, they manage to share the care of their 2-year-old son and Linda's 16-year-old daughter from a previous marriage. "Bill works the 7 a.m. to 3 p.m. shift while I watch the baby," she explains. "Then I work the 3 p.m. to 11 p.m. shift and he watches the baby. My daughter works at Walgreen's after school."

Linda is working overtime, and so I begin by asking whether Amerco required the overtime, or whether she volunteered for it. "Oh, I put in for it," she replies. I ask her whether, if finances and company policy permitted, she'd be interested in cutting back on the overtime. She takes off her safety glasses, rubs her face and, without answering my question, explains: "I get home, and the minute I turn the key, my daughter is right there. Granted, she needs somebody to talk to about her day.... The baby is still up. He should have been in bed two hours ago, and that upsets me. The dishes are piled in the sink. My daughter comes right up to the door and complains about anything her stepfather said or did, and she wants to talk about her job. My husband is in the other room hollering to my daughter, 'Tracy, I don't ever get any time to talk to your mother, because you're always monopolizing her time before I even get a chance!' They all come at me at once."

Linda's description of the urgency of demands and the unarbitrated quarrels that await her homecoming contrast with her account of arriving at her job as a shift supervisor: "I usually come to work early, just to get away from the house. When I arrive, people are there waiting. We sit, we talk, we joke. I let them know what's going on, who has to be where, what changes I've made for the shift that day. We sit and chitchat for 5 or 10 minutes. There's laughing, joking, fun.

For Linda, home has come to feel like work and work has come to feel a bit like home. Indeed, she feels she can get relief from the "work" of being at home only by going to the "home" of work. Why has her life at home come to seem like this? Linda explains it this way: "My husband's a great help watching our baby. But as far as doing housework or even taking the baby when I'm at home, no. He figures he works five days a week; he's not going to come home and clean. But he doesn't stop to think that I work seven days a week. Why should I have to come home and do the housework without help from anybody else? My husband and I have been through this over and over again. Even if he would just pick up from the kitchen table and stack the dishes for me, that would make a big difference. He does nothing. On his weekends off, he goes fishing. If I want any time off, I have to get a sitter. He'll help out if I'm not here, but the minute I am, all the work at home is mine."

With a light laugh, she continues: "So I take a lot of overtime. The more I get out of the house, the better I am. It's a terrible thing to say, but that's the way I feel."

When Bill feels the need for time off, to relax, to have fun, to feel free, he climbs in his truck and takes his free time without his family. Largely in response, Linda grabs what she also calls "free time"—at work. Neither Linda nor Bill Avery wants more time together at home, not as things are arranged now.

How do Linda and Bill Avery fit into the broader picture of American family and work life? Current research suggests that however hectic their lives, women who do paid work feel less depressed, think better of themselves and are more satisfied than women who stay at home. One study reported that women who work outside the home feel more valued at home than housewives do. Meanwhile, work is where many women feel like "good mothers." As Linda reflects: "I'm a good mom at home, but I'm a better mom at work. At home, I get into fights with Tracy. I want her to apply to a junior college, but she's not interested. At work, I think I'm better at seeing the other person's point of view."

Many workers feel more confident they could "get the job done" at work than at home. One study found that only 59 percent of workers feel their "performance" in the family is "good or unusually good," while 86 percent rank their performance on the job this way.

Forces at work and at home are simultaneously reinforcing this "reversal." The lure of work has been enhanced in recent years by the rise of company cultural engineering—in particular, the shift from Frederick Taylor's principles of scientific management to the Total Quality principles originally set out by W. Edwards Deming. Under the influence of a Taylorist world view, the manager's job was to coerce the worker's mind and body, not to appeal to the worker's heart. The Taylorized worker was de-skilled, replaceable and cheap, and as a consequence felt bored, demeaned and unappreciated.

Using modern participative management techniques, many companies now train workers to make their own work decisions, and then set before their newly "empowered" employees moral as well as financial incentives. At Amerco, the Total Quality worker is invited to feel recognized for job accomplishments. Amerco regularly strengthens the familylike ties of co-workers by holding "recognition ceremonies" honoring particular workers or self-managed production teams.

Amerco employees speak of "belonging to the Amerco family," and proudly wear their "Total Quality" pins or "High Performance Team" T-shirts, symbols of their loyalty to the company and of its loyalty to them.

The company occasionally decorates a section of the factory and serves refreshments. The production teams, too, have regular get-togethers. In a New Age recasting of an old business slogan— "The Customer Is Always Right"—Amerco proposes that its workers "Value the Internal Customer." This means: Be as polite and considerate to co-workers inside the company as you would be to customers outside it. How many recognition ceremonies for competent performance are being offered at home? Who is valuing the internal customer there?

Amerco also tries to take on the role of a helpful relative with regard to employee problems at work and at home. The education-and-training division offers employees free courses (on company time) in "Dealing With Anger," "How to Give and Accept Criticism," "How to Cope With Difficult People."

At home, of course, people seldom receive anything like this much help on issues basic to family life. There, no courses are being offered on "Dealing With Your Child's Disappointment in You" or "How to Treat Your Spouse Like an Internal Customer."

If Total Quality calls for "re-skilling" the worker in an "enriched" job environment, technological developments have long been de-skilling parents at home. Over the centuries, store-bought goods have replaced homespun cloth, homemade soap and homebaked foods. Day care for children, retirement homes for the elderly, even psychotherapy are, in a way, commercial substitutes for jobs that a mother once did at home. Even family-generated entertainment has, to some extent, been replaced by television, video games and the VCR. I sometimes watched

Amerco families sitting together after their dinners, mute but cozy, watching sitcoms in which television mothers, fathers and children related in an animated way to one another while the viewing family engaged in relational loafing.

The one "skill" still required of family members is the hardest one of all—the emotional work of forging, deepening or repairing family relationships. It takes time to develop this skill, and even then things can go awry. Family ties are complicated. People get hurt. Yet as broken homes become more common—and as the sense of belonging to a geographical community grows less and less secure in an age of mobility—the corporate world has created a sense of "neighborhood," of "feminine culture," of family at work. Life at work can be insecure; the company can fire workers. But workers aren't so secure at home, either. Many employees have been working for Amerco for 20 years but are on their second or third marriages or relationships. The shifting balance between these two "divorce rates" may be the most powerful reason why tired parents flee a world of unresolved quarrels and unwashed laundry for the orderliness, harmony and managed cheer of work. People are getting their "pink slips" at home.

Amerco workers have not only turned their offices into "home" and their homes into workplaces; many have also begun to "Taylorize" time at home, where families are succumbing to a cult of efficiency previously associated mainly with the office and factory. Meanwhile, work time, with its ever longer hours, has become more hospitable to sociability—periods of talking with friends on E-mail, patching up quarrels, gossiping. Within the long workday of many Amerco employees are great hidden pockets of inefficiency while, in the far smaller number of waking weekday hours at home, they are, despite themselves, forced to act increasingly time-conscious and efficient.

The Averys respond to their time bind at home by trying to value and protect "quality time." A concept unknown to their parents and grandparents, "quality time" has become a powerful symbol of the struggle against the growing pressures at home. It reflects the extent to which modern parents feel the flow of time to be running against them. The premise behind "quality time" is that the time we devote to relationships can somehow be separated from ordinary time. Relationships go on during quantity time, of course, but then we are only passively, not actively, wholeheartedly, specializing in our emotional ties. We aren't "on." Quality time at home becomes like an office appointment. You don't want to be caught "goofing off around the water cooler" when you are "at work."

Quality time holds out the hope that scheduling intense periods of togetherness can compensate for an overall loss of time in such a way that a relationship will suffer no loss of quality. But this is just another way of transferring the cult of efficiency from office to home. We must now get our relationships in good repair in less time. Instead of nine hours a day with a child, we declare ourselves capable of getting "the same result" with one intensely focused hour.

Parents now more commonly speak of time as if it is a threatened form of personal capital they have no choice but to manage and invest. What's new here is the spread into the home of a financial manager's attitude toward time. Working parents at Amerco owe what they think of as time debts at home. This is because they are, in a sense, inadvertently "Taylorizing" the house—speeding up the pace of home life as Taylor once tried to "scientifically" speed up the pace of factory life.

Advertisers of products aimed at women have recognized that this new reality provides an opportunity to sell products, and have turned the very pressure that threatens to explode the home into a positive attribute. Take, for example, an ad promoting Instant Quaker Oatmeal: it shows a smiling mother ready for the office in her square-shouldered suit, hugging her happy son. A caption reads: "Nicky is a very picky eater. With Instant Quaker Oatmeal, I can give him a terrific hot breakfast in just 90 seconds. And I don't have to spend any time coaxing him to eat it!" Here, the modern mother seems to have absorbed the lessons of Frederick Taylor as she presses for efficiency at home because she is in a hurry to get to work.

Part of modern parenthood seems to include coping with the resistance of real children who are not so eager to get their cereal so fast. Some parents try desperately not to appease their children with special gifts or smooth-talking promises about the future. But when time is scarce, even the best parents find themselves passing a system-wide familial speed-up along to the most vulnerable workers on the line. Parents are then obliged to try to control the damage done by a reversal of worlds. They monitor mealtime, homework time, bedtime, trying to cut out "wasted" time.

In response, children often protest the pace, the deadlines, the grand irrationality of "efficient" family life. Children dawdle. They refuse to leave places when it's time to leave. They insist on leaving places when it's not time to leave. Surely, this is part of the usual stop-and-go of childhood itself, but perhaps, too, it is the plea of children for more family time, and more control over what time there is. This only adds to the feeling that life at home has become hard work.

Instead of trying to arrange shorter or more flexible work schedules, Amerco parents often avoid confronting the reality of the time bind. Some minimize their ideas about how much care a child, a partner or they themselves "really need." They make do with less time, less attention, less understanding and less support at home than they once imagined possible. They *emo-*

tionally downsize life. In essence, they deny the needs of family members, and they themselves become emotional ascetics. If they once "needed" time with each other, they are now increasingly "fine" without it.

Another way that working parents try to evade the time bind is to buy themselves out of it—an approach that puts women in particular at the heart of a contradiction. Like men, women absorb the work-family speed-up far more than they resist it; but unlike men, they still shoulder most of the workload at home. And women still represent in people's minds the heart and soul of family life. They're the ones—especially women of the urban middle and upper-middle classes—who feel most acutely the need to save time, who are the most tempted by the new "time saving" goods and services—and who wind up feeling the most guilty about it. For example, Playgroup Connections, a Washington-area business started by a former executive recruiter, matches playmates to one another. One mother hired the service to find her child a French-speaking playmate.

In several cities, children home alone can call a number for "Grandma, Please!" and reach an adult who has the time to talk with them, sing to them or help them with their homework. An ad for Kindercare Learning Centers, a for-profit child-care chain, pitches its appeal this way: "You want your child to be active, tolerant, smart, loved, emotionally stable, self-aware, artistic and get a two-hour nap. Anything else?" It goes on to note that Kindercare accepts children 6 weeks to 12 years old and provides a number to call for the Kindercare nearest you. Another typical service organizes children's birthday parties, making out invitations ("sure hope you can come") and providing party favors, entertainment, a decorated cake and balloons. Creative Memories is a service that puts ancestral photos into family albums for you.

An overwhelming majority of the working mothers I spoke with recoiled from the idea of buying themselves out of parental duties. A bought birthday party was "too impersonal," a 90-second breakfast "too fast." Yet a surprising amount of lunchtime conversation between female friends at Amerco was devoted to expressing complex, conflicting feelings about the lure of trading time for one service or another. The temptation to order flash-frozen dinners or to call a local number for a homework helper did not come up because such services had not yet appeared at Spotted Deer Child-Care Center. But many women dwelled on the question of how to decide where a mother's job began and ended, especially with regard to baby sitters and television. One mother said to another in the break-room of an Amerco plant: "Damon doesn't settle down until 10 at night, so he hates me to wake him up in the morning and I hate to do it. He's cranky. He pulls the covers up. I put on cartoons. That way, I can dress him and he doesn't object. I don't like to use TV that way. It's like a drug. But I do it."

The other mother countered. "Well, Todd is up before we are, so that's not a problem. It's after dinner, when I feel like watching a little television, that I feel guilty, because he gets too much TV at the sitter's."

As task after task falls into the realm of time-saving goods and services, questions arise about the moral meanings attached to doing or not doing such tasks. Is it being a good mother to bake a child's birthday cake (alone or together with one's partner)? Or can we gratefully save time by ordering it, and be good mothers by planning the party? Can we save more time by hiring a planning service, and be good mothers simply by watching our children have a good time? "Wouldn't that be nice!" one Amerco mother exclaimed. As the idea of the "good mother" retreats before the pressures of work and the expansion of motherly services, mothers are in fact continually reinventing themselves.

The final way working parents tried to evade the time bind was to develop what I call "potential selves." The potential selves that I discovered in my Amerco interviews were fantasy creations of time-poor parents who dreamed of living as time millionaires.

One man, a gifted 55-year-old engineer in research and development at Amerco, told how he had dreamed of taking his daughters on a camping trip in the Sierra Mountains: "I bought all the gear three years ago when they were 5 and 7, the tent, the sleeping bags, the air mattresses, the backpacks, the ponchos. I got a map of the area. I even got the freeze-dried food. Since then the kids and I have talked about it a lot, and gone over what we're going to do. They've been on me to do it for a long time. I feel bad about it. I keep putting it off, but we'll do it, I just don't know when."

Banished to garages and attics of many Amerco workers were expensive electric saws, cameras, skis and musical instruments, all bought with wages it took time to earn. These items were to their owners what Cassie's fudge bar was to her—a substitute for time, a talisman, a reminder of the potential self.

Obviously, not everyone, not even a majority of Americans, is making a home out of work and a workplace out of home. But in the working world, it is a growing reality, and one we need to face. Increasing numbers of women are discovering a great male secret—that work can be an escape from the pressures of home, pressures that the changing nature of work itself are only intensifying. Neither men nor women are going to take up "family friendly" policies, whether corporate or governmental, as long as the current realities of work and home remain as they are. For a substantial number of time-bound parents, the stripped-down home and the neighborhood devoid of community are simply losing out to the pull of the workplace.

There are several broader, historical causes of this reversal of realms. The last 30 years have witnessed the rapid rise of women in the workplace. At the same time, job mobility has taken families farther from relatives who might lend a hand, and made it harder to make close friends of neighbors who could help out. Moreover, as women have acquired more education and have joined men at work, they have absorbed the views of an older, male-oriented work world, its views of a "real career," far more than men have taken up their share of the work at home. One reason women have changed more than men is that the world of "male" work seems more honorable and valuable than the "female" world of home and children.

So where do we go from here? There is surely no going back to the mythical 1950's family that confined women to the home. Most women don't wish to return to a full-time role at home—and couldn't afford it even if they did. But equally troubling is a workaholic culture that strands both men and women outside the home.

For a while now, scholars on work-family issues have pointed to Sweden, Norway and Denmark as better models of work-family balance. Today, for example, almost all Swedish fathers take two paid weeks off from work at the birth of their children, and about half of fathers and most mothers take additional "parental leave" during the child's first or second year. Research shows that men who take family leave when their children are very young are more likely to be involved with their children as they grow older. When I mentioned this Swedish record of paternity leave to a focus group of American male managers, one of them replied, "Right, we've already heard about Sweden." To this executive, paternity leave was a good idea not for the U.S. today, but for some "potential society" in another place and time.

Meanwhile, children are paying the price. In her book "When the Bough Breaks: The Cost of Neglecting Our Children," the economist Sylvia Hewlett claims that "compared with the previous generation, young people today are more likely to "underperform at school; commit suicide; need psychiatric help; suffer a severe eating disorder; bear a child out of wedlock; take drugs, be the victim of a violent crime." But we needn't dwell on sledgehammer problems like heroin or suicide to realize that children like those at Spotted Deer need more of our time. If other advanced nations with two-job families can give children the time they need, why can't we?

Reading 14   Korean Immigrant Women's Challenge To Gender Inequality at Home:

The Interplay of Economic Resources, Gender, and Family*

IN-SOOK LIM

Based on in-depth interviews with 18 Korean immigrant working couples, this study explores Korean immigrant working wives' ongoing challenge to male dominance at home and to the unequal division of family work. A main factor in wives' being less obedient to their husbands is their psychological resources such as pride, competence, and honor which they gain from awareness of their contribution to the family economy. Under immigrant family circumstances in which working for family survival is prioritized, wives feel that their negligence of family work, rejection of the superwoman ideal, and perceived right to demand their husbands' help with family work, is legitimized. However Confucian patriarchal beliefs lead these wives to place limits on the degree of challenge. The findings highlight the interplay of wives' psychological resources, gender norms, and the social standing of being immigrant families in affecting wives' challenge to gender inequality at home. Differences in effects among Korean immigrant families are explored.

Previous research has found that Korean immigrant husbands rarely participate in family work and are dominant over their wives; they demonstrate that Korean immigrant families are not gender egalitarian. However, one study reveals that Korean immigrants point to male dominance and men's nonparticipation in family work as Korean cultural traits that they need to modify (Hurh and Kim 1984); it suggests that Korean immigrant wives are aware of gender inequality at home and may attempt to challenge it.

This study aims to explore the stability and changes in gender inequality among Korean immigrant working couples by examining wives' challenges to their husbands' dominance and the unequal division of family work. Ideologies and structures of patriarchy are still powerful enough to hinder possible changes in the status quo of

I would like to thank Christine L. Williams, Norval D. Glenn, Pierrette Hondagneu-Sotelo, and the anonymous reviewers for their helpful comments on earlier drafts of this article.

*Lim, In-Sook. 1997. "Korean Immigrant Women's Challenge to Gender Equality at Home: The Interplay of Economic Resources, Gender, and Family, *Gender & Society* 11(1): 31–51. Copyright © 1997 by Sociologists for Women in Society. Reprinted by permission of Sage Publications, Inc.

158

gender hierarchy, and women may not have yet succeeded in bringing about gender equality at home. Nevertheless, some changes may have occurred. Accordingly, this study analyzes the nature of Korean immigrant working wives' desire for change, their attempts to change marital relations, their tendency to resign themselves to their status quo, and husbands' responses to their wives' challenges.

A broader purpose of this study is to explore the interplay of Korean immigrant wives' economic resources, patriarchal cultural traditions, and immigrant family circumstances in facilitating or hindering wives' challenges. Resource theory suggests that working women attain the ability to challenge gender inequality at home through their participation in the paid labor force. However, gender theories suggest that the increase in women's economic resources does not necessarily guarantee more power for them because patriarchal gender norms and beliefs constrain women from maximizing their power and options. Furthermore, research on racial-ethnic minority or immigrant families suggests that despite the universal presence of patriarchy, men exercise varying degrees of power and women resist in diverse ways (Baca Zinn et al. 1986; Collins 1990; Hondagneu-Sotelo 1992).

This study examines the changes as well as stability in gender inequality among Korean immigrant families by exploring the following issues: how Korean immigrant working wives experience the shift in their relative economic resources in the United Stairs; how wives' employment affects their desire to challenge male dominance and the unequal division of family work; how Korean immigrants' strong attachment to patriarchal tradition constrains women from challenging gender inequality at home; and how being immigrant families affects wives' challenge and resignation to the status quo.

In-depth interviews with 18 Korean immigrant working couples in the United States were conducted for the analysis. The data collected from both spouses in this study reveal gender dynamics more vividly than the data in previous research that focused on one spouse only. Interviews of both Korean immigrant husbands and wives also show their differential perceptions of the same marriage. This study, which integrates Korean immigrants' unique cultural traditions such as Confucian ideologies with their social standing as immigrants, also highlights the importance of contextual understanding of gender.

BACKGROUND OF THE STUDY

Korean Immigrant Family

Korean immigrants are characterized by strong ethnic attachment to the native culture, which is typically attributed to racial-ethnic segregation in the United States (Hurh and Kim 1984; Min 1995). High levels of affiliation with ethnic churches (around 67 percent in a 1986 survey in Los Angeles), which play the role of a "pseudoextended family" for Korean immigrants, are one example of Korean immigrants' efforts to preserve their ethnicity (Kim 1981, 199). While Ferree (1979) claimed that assimilation to Western culture, which entails more egalitarian values, creates some variation in the patterns of division of labor among immigrant families, Korean immigrants' strong attachment to the high level of patriarchal tradition may constrain women from challenging gender inequality at home.

Gender inequality in Korea was intensified during the Chosun Dynasty (1392–1910), which adopted Confucianism as a ruling ideology of the era. Confucian patriarchy was characterized by the Rule of Three Obedience, which emphasized women's subordination to men: A woman should obey her father before her marriage, her husband after marriage, and her son(s) after her husband's death (Cho 1988). Therefore, women's assertiveness and disobedience were discouraged. A wife could be divorced if she was talkative or rebellious toward her parents-in-law, which included talking back to them. Since the principle of Distinction between Man and Woman was emphasized, even children over six years old were not expected to mix with the other gender. The principle of Distinction between Wife and Husband also demanded separate living and work spheres and accented the gendered power difference. Under these circumstances, a man ran the risk of losing face by participating in family work since the female work was regarded as degrading to men's prestige and dignity. These notions and principles were more strongly emphasized and more frequently practiced among the ruling class of the time.

Despite contemporary increases in women's employment and some men's participation in family work, the traditional notions are still pervasive in Korea. A comparative study reports that 71 percent of Korean married women agree with the statement "The husband should be the breadwinner, while the wife stays at home;" 34 percent of American women, 14 percent of Swedish women, and 71 percent of Japanese women agree (Korean Survey [Gallup] Polls Ltd. 1987). Therefore, Korean women still face strong resistance from men to participate in family work. While Korean working women spend four and a half hours per day on family work, men participate only 38 minutes. Consequently, Korean women work at both family work and paid work two months a year more than men, while American women work one month a year more than American men (Hochschild 1989).

In addition, unique social characteristics of Korean immigrant families may operate as factors hindering gender equality at home. The majority of Korean immigrants are engaged in small family businesses, which are run by a wife and husband without employees. Forty-five percent of Korean workers in Los Angeles, 61 percent of married males, and 49 percent of married females in New York City were in family businesses in the 1980s (Min 1991). Research on Chinese Americans in family business (Glenn 1983) found that collectivity is emphasized over the individual and a high premium is placed on cooperation rather than self-expression, which may precipitate conflicts. Furthermore, Korean immigrant women in family businesses may not accumulate their own individual resources because they are unpaid workers regardless of their significant contribution to the family income. Considering that female control over income is a more important determinant of marital power than their employment or earnings (Blumberg 1991; Hertz 1986), Korean immigrant women in family businesses may be disadvantaged from the beginning in bargaining with their husbands.

Women's Economic Resources, Gender, and Family

Previous theory and research findings suggest the interplay of working wives' economic resources, gender norms, and family circumstances in wives' challenging gender inequality at home. According to resource theory, the relative resources of the spouse, such as education, income, or occupational status, are more viable determinants of marital power relations than the normative factor—that is, the husband's authority—in contemporary marriage (Blood and Wolfe 1960). The resources possessed by each spouse provide "leverage" in bargaining and negotiation between spouse, and affect marital power. A study by Blumstein and Schwartz (1983) revealed that the amount of money a spouse earns establishes relative power in any kind of relationship, except among lesbians.

As for the gender division of family work, resource theorists maintain that those members with greater resources can compel those with fewer resources to undertake the onerous work of the household (Berk 1985). Husbands' participation in family work is highest when spouses' incomes are similar (Haas 1987; Hood 1983; Scanzoni 1979). According to Ferree (1987), when women make a relatively substantial financial contribution to the family, this leads them to define their husbands' share of housework as too low and to articulate a desire for change. If this is the case, racial-ethnic minority or immigrant women may have a greater potential to challenge gender inequality at home. In these families, which experience racial discrimination and oppression in the job market, wives' earnings are more essential to their families, and the gap between a wife's earnings and husband's earnings is smaller than in dominant groups (Baca Zinn 1990; Glenn 1987). Therefore, these women have an advantage in the relative economic resources of spouses, which may allow them a greater potential for bargaining to cope with male dominance in the family than other women.

However, the causal relationship between relative resources and bargaining power may be overly simplistic. Resource theory does not explain why some women are careful not to exploit their greater potential power to the fullest, despite their increased economic resources, consequently resulting in no significant change in gender relations (Hood 1983; Wallace and Wolf 1991).

Introducing the notion of patriarchy, gender theories explain how normative expectations in marriage operate as a form of subtle coercion that undermines the relationship between women's resources and their power in marriage (Komter 1989). In a society in which breadwinning is a social representation of manhood, wives whose husbands are not good providers often submit to their husbands' dominance because they feel guilty for contributing to their husbands' sense of failure. Hochschild (1989) found that wives whose husbands are underemployed, less ambitious, or earned less than their wives do not press their husbands to do more housework to establish

a "balance." Rather, they attempt to soothe their husbands' threatened male ego, and they bolster their husbands' sense of self-worth. In these marriages, women's earnings are not considered a resource but a burden for the husband, and thus it does not influence marital power (Pyke 1994). Furthermore, as long as either the husband or the wife endorses the notion of "male-breadwinning and manhood," the husband is more powerful, regardless of his income (Blumstein and Schwartz 1983). Findings suggest that women still negotiate and adapt to the set of patriarchal rules that guide and constrain gender relations (Kandiyoti 1988).

Some women's challenge to gender inequality at home also may be constrained by their family circumstances. For example, among immigrant families who face a precarious economic environment wives' employment is not a means for achieving independence from their husbands. Rather, it is an obligation for family survival and sacrifice necessary for the collective interests of the family (Ferree 1979; Glenn 1987; Kibria 1990). The members of immigrant families may perceive their families as a source of support in resisting oppression from outside institutions rather than a locus of gender conflict; any conflicts among family members may therefore be muted. For example, in a study of Vietnamese immigrants, Kibria (1990) found that the patriarchal family system is too valuable to give up because it adds income earners and extends resources. Furthermore, Vietnamese immigrant women find a fundamental appeal in the traditional patriarchal bargain—the authority to wield influence over the lives of the young.

These theories and research evidence led me to two research questions in this study. Firstly, I explore the changes as well as stability in gender inequality among Korean immigrant working couples by examining the challenge by wives to their husbands' dominance and unequal division of family work as well as their resignation to the status quo. Secondly, I explore how Korean immigrant working wives' economic resources, traditional gender norms, and the social standing of being immigrant families operate in these wives' challenges to gender inequality at home.

METHODOLOGY

Selecting the Sample and Characteristics of the Sample

In-depth interviews were conducted with 18 Korean immigrant working couples between December 1993 and August 1994 in Austin and Dallas, Texas. I contacted possible respondents using snowball sampling techniques and by random visits to Korean ethnic stores. Fifteen couples were obtained through the first method, while 3 couples were included through the second. In choosing couples to interview, several factors were considered that might be related to motivations, meanings, feelings, and justifications for wives' employment and husbands' family work: age, education, occupation, family income, years of marriage, years in the United States, the number and age of children, and helper(s) at home.

The four professional couples in this study have higher class characteristics in terms of family annual income, occupational prestige, and education levels than the three nonprofessional wage-earner couples and the family business couples. Among the latter were seven couples in which the wife and husband work full-time in the business and four couples in which the spouse works in his/her own business with part-time help of the other spouse who has a separate wage-earning job. Husbands of professional couples have a master's degree or higher and work in occupations such as engineer and publisher of a

Korean ethnic newspaper. Wives of professional couples tend to graduate from a university and work as engineers, technicians, or nurses. Their family annual income ranges from $60,000 to $130,000. Family business couples work in a shoe-repair shop, restaurants, laundries, a flea market, a video rental shop, a wig shop, or a used appliance shop. Nonprofessional wage-earner couples work as building cleaners, technicians, or clerks. The family business couples and nonprofessional wage-earner couples tend to be high school graduates. Their family annual income ranges from $30,000 to $70,000. Wives and husbands range in age from 30 to 60 years.

There are recognizable distinctions in breadwinner role expectations between professional couples and the other couples. Professional couples still hold the traditional belief that breadwinning for their families is a husband's responsibility, while the nonprofessional couples emphasize that in the immigrant families, both a wife and a husband should share the breadwinning responsibility for their families. Wives of the former couples are secondary breadwinners, while wives of the latter couples play the role of equal breadwinners in their everyday lives. However, these distinctions are not salient in their attitudes toward and practices of homemaking among them. Both groups believe in the traditional notion that family work is generally a wife's responsibility and show no significant changes in men's participation in family work on a behavioral level. Even husbands whose wives equally contribute to the family economy do not necessarily share family work more than other husbands whose wives are secondary breadwinners.

Interviewing Procedures and Analysis

Interview schedules consisted of four parts. First, I asked interviewees a series of background questions about their family, jobs, marriage, and immigration. Second, I ascertained the practical experiences associated with breadwinning and homemaking in interviewees' families by asking who financially supported their families and who did what kinds of family work and to what extent. The third part focused on two themes: the meanings and feelings of wives working outside the home and husbands participating in family work, and the perceptions and feelings of changes in their marital relations. The interviews were conducted in a semistructured format, based on a series of open-ended questions. Finally, general attitudes toward the responsibility of the breadwinner/homemaker role were examined.

One may wonder whether my being a woman affected the levels of comfort of male interviewees, consequently affecting rapport building and the quality of this research. I do not believe that it did. Husbands were candid enough to reveal their fears of and complaints against wives' changes, their sense of relative deprivation of wives' services and caring, and their beliefs in traditional marital hierarchy. This exposure of these thoughts and feelings are a good indication of the successful rapport established between myself and male interviewees. As for female interviewees, I believe the interviews were good for these wives in that they offered women new meanings and perspectives on taken-for-granted aspects of their marriage. During the interviews, many wives became aware and surprised at their husbands' nonparticipation and insensitivity when they responded to my questions of what kinds of family work their husbands perform. Many of them then expressed their feelings of anger, frustration, and resignation with marital relations.

Interviews were conducted at respondents' workplaces, houses, or the offices of several Korean ethnic churches. Husbands and wives were interviewed separately. All interviews were conducted in Korean because the majority of interviewees were first-generation immigrants and felt more comfortable speaking in Korean than in English. With permission from the interviewees, I taped each interview of approximately 90 minutes. Because of exposure of their private lives, I guaranteed my respondents anonymity and confidentiality, promising them to use pseudonyms in my study to protect their identity. I also assured interviewees that I would not discuss any of what they told me with their spouses. With an awareness of the inherent power imbalance between researchers and participants, I told my interviewees that they need not discuss topics that made them feel anxious or under stress (Gilgun, Daly, and Handel 1992). I reciprocated interviewees' time with a gift (an alarm clock to each couple valued at $15.00).

All interviews were transcribed from the audiotape in Korean. Then, I read and coded the interview transcripts carefully to catch major themes as well as unique aspects of interview content. To avoid misrepresentation of interviewees' responses, three follow-up calls were made when I needed clarification on what a respondent stated.

FINDINGS

Wives' New Self-Expression and Marital Conflicts

Korean immigrant husbands in this study expressed consistent fears of wives' challenge to male dominance at home. Three factors contribute to the husbands' fears. One is the stereotypical image of America to Koreans. America has been portrayed as a Western society in which women enjoy equal rights and freedom. Therefore, Korean immigrant husbands have speculated that an exposure to Western culture will lead their wives to desire more power at home. Secondly, husbands whose wives change from a full-time homemaker to a working wife (nine wives in this study) have been afraid that their wives may bargain for new marital relations based on their newly derived earning power. Thirdly, newly immigrant husbands have often been warned by other Korean immigrant husbands, "Watch out for your wife. She may change a lot in the U.S. enough to think little of you." Therefore, they have been afraid that their wives will not be the same as they used to be in Korea.

Those husbands who have not yet found any change in their wives feel fortunate, while they do not hide their hostility against other wives who they feel use their moneymaking as an excuse to look down on their husbands. Those husbands who have already experienced their wives' changes express their displeasure. Choe, who is in his fifties and works with his wife in a shoe-repair and alteration shop, finds she is no longer the obedient wife she was in Korea. He is displeased with his wife's new "self-assertion":

After she started working her voice got louder than in the past. Now, she says whatever she wants to say to me. She shows a lot of self-assertion. She didn't do that in Korea. Right after I came to the U.S., I heard that Korean wives change a lot in America. Now, I clearly understand what it means. However, it's wrong for women to think that they can control men in their own ways.

Choe's wife is in her forties and was a full-time housewife in Korea. She admits that since she has begun working in the United States, her "self-expression" has increased. Her comments imply that, with a growing sense of not being totally dependent on her husband for money, she no longer assumes a position of submission toward her husband. When she felt dependent on her husband as a full-time housewife, she obeyed her husband voluntarily. However, as she identifies herself as a working wife who contributes to her family as much as her husband, she has a different view of her marital relationship. She describes her changes:

In Korea, wives tend to obey their husbands because husbands have financial power and provide for their families. However, in the U.S., wives also work to make money as their husbands do, so women are apt to speak out at least one time on what they previously restrained from saying.

The above statements by the Choe couple indicate that there is a gender difference in perception about the extent of wives' change. Choe feels that she does not speak out yet about all the things that she wants to say to her husband, while her husband perceives his wife's change as so evident that she says "whatever she wants to say." Yang, who is in his forties and runs an appliance repair shop, also claims that his wife is no longer naive in that she does not completely follow his orders as she did when she was a full-time housewife. He feels his decision-making power has become less secure since his wife began earning money. As she has worked hard to make a living, Yang's wife admits, she has become more aggressive and stronger than she was as a full-time housewife. She has a part-time job as an operator and helps in his repair shop. However, she claims that there is no great change in marital power since she still permits her husband to make final decisions in family matters. These findings suggest that even a little change in the marital power relation may not be perceived as trivial to husbands.

In addition to increasing self-expression, wives feel all right about spending money without their husbands' permission. This change is evident when Chung, who is in her thirties and runs a Japanese restaurant with her husband, says, "I feel differently spending money when I earn it. I have come to think I deserve to spend the money when I pick up something for my family. I feel honorable even when I send a gift to my own parents." Although wives feel that they can spend money in their own ways, they tend to buy things for children or family members rather than for themselves. With tight family budgets and the pooled family accounting system, wives say, there is little discrete money that husbands as well as wives control for their own interests. In the case of family business couples, husbands often manage general spending related to the business. However, the control of money flow in their business is perceived not as a right of husbands but as a mental labor that demands a struggle with stringent budgets.

As Korean immigrant wives increasingly express their opinions, speak out against their husbands, or spend money without husbands' permission, marital conflicts increase. This is more evident among family business couples. Yu, a thirty-year-old who works with her husband in a laundry shop, says, "After we began working together in this business, we came to quarrel about even trivial things almost every day. I don't think it is desirable for both husband and wife to work together." Chung's husband understands the meaning of an old saying, "Don't be a business partner with a close person," through his experiences of working together with his wife.

Frequent conflicts among family business couples are related to both wives' newly acquired psychological resources and working conditions. Wives in family business are more likely to be defined as equal breadwinners by themselves and their husbands than their counterparts. As these wives are aware that they contribute to their family economy as much as their husbands, wives gain a sense of being honorable, fair, worthy, and proud, all of which allow them to express themselves actively. Since these immigrant families set a priority on income-generating work for family survival and value those who are involved in the work, wives feel competent as equal breadwinners. Bonacich, Hossain, and Park (1987) pointed out an ambiguity in the wife's position as co-operator of a family business-namely, she is both a co-owner and her husband's employee without even the benefit of a paycheck. They recognized that for many immigrant women, the latter role predominates and that their husbands could be exploiters of their wives' labor. However, wives of family business couples in this study think of themselves as co-owners of their business rather than unpaid employees of their husbands. Husbands also fully admit their wives' efforts to shoulder half of the burden of providing for their families by saying, "My wife also works as much as I do. Half and half, we contribute to the family economy."

The physically demanding work of family business couples also causes marital conflict to increase. As family business couples define their everyday lives as "nothing except eating, sleeping, and working," they feel so tired or stressed that they get easily angry at others. Also, the working condition, in which a wife and husband do similar work side by side in a small place, often leads them to meddle with each other. For example, a husband may question why his wife asks less money from her customers than he thinks she should or why she is not more efficient. However, these couples also mention merits of the working condition that allow the couples to share advice or consolation when they face difficulties with their business. In short, being coworkers offers the couples a sense of psychological interdependence as well as a source of conflict.

Wives' new self-expression and consequent marital conflicts suggest that Korean immigrant wives attempt to make a change in their husbands' dominance at home. However, it is important to recognize that Korean immigrant wives limit their attempts to change unequal marital relations. Although they try to check their husbands' monopoly at home, they do not intend to subvert the traditional sense of marital hierarchy itself. They believe that the authority of men as family heads should remain unchallenged for the family order. The distinction between attemptable change and avoided change is clear in the case of Yang. She reports her change from being a typical Korean wife who obeyed her husband "one hundred percent" into being a bold and competent woman after she had a job. However, she is still willing to defer to her husband's authority. When asked why, she replies:

> I don't think it is desirable for a woman to henpeck her husband even though she works outside the home. I want men to lead everything in his family. I think the authority of a family head needs to be secure at home.

The gap between a wife and husband in job prestige and earnings cannot explain her deference to her husband. Rather, her belief in the authority of the husband as a family head justifies the power difference in her marriage, consequently restraining her from challenging the overall system of male domination. Shin, who

no longer perceives herself as a submissive wife, explicitly said, "I work just because I should. With my moneymaking, I do not covet a better position at home." In fact, among the majority of family business couples, wives' employment is regarded as a responsibility for the family, which they perceive as a "system of coexistence." For Korean immigrant families in this study, family survival often means not only securing food to eat, shelter, and clothes to wear, but also providing their children with the best education possible. Many immigrant wives cannot pass the buck to their husbands when they feel breadwinning is a joint responsibility of parents for their children. The notion of marital equality is never expressed directly by these wives.

Wives' Attempts to Change Husbands' Family Work

The majority of interviewees (30 out of 36) still believe that wives are responsible for family work in principle. However, the old belief that family work is unmanly and degrading to men's prestige is no longer dominant among them. Proudly reporting their attitudinal change toward family work in the United States, a husband states, "Nobody thinks that it is shameful for a husband to enter the kitchen because we live in the U.S. where wives as well as husbands have jobs." All but one wife depart from the traditional notion that family work should be done exclusively by themselves. While wives no longer take their husbands' insensitivity and nonparticipation in family work for granted, they perceive a right to demand that their husbands participate in family work.

The attitudinal change among Korean immigrant wives is linked to their awareness of their contribution to the family economy. As wives recognize that they share the traditional male activity, breadwinning, with their husbands, they think there should be a transformation in their husbands' family work. Emphasizing the differences in breadwinning experiences between working wives and full-time housewives, these wives tend to say, "In the case of wives as full-time housewives, family work is totally wives' work. But in the case of wives with jobs, husbands need to help their wives with family work."

The wives' reasoning does not necessarily imply that wives think their husbands should help them with family work to compensate for their inability to be sole breadwinners. Husbands also do not think that wives can demand their husbands to do family work with wives' money-making as an excuse. Husbands' family work is mainly framed in terms of family cooperation or an adjustment to their employment. Family cooperation is understood to be the basis of survival and security for immigrant families, who begin rootless lives in a new land and face a precarious economic situation. Therefore, as wives work outside the home to reduce their husbands' burden of breadwinning, their husbands are expected to respond to wives' time shortage and fatigue.

Since husbands' outright resistance to sharing family work is no longer taken for granted as it used to be in Korea, resistant husbands are now perceived as selfish men who try to avoid another burden while wives bear two burdens: family work and a job. Under these circumstances, wives feel they work twice as hard as their husbands when they find their husbands' reluctance to share family work regardless of their employment. A sense of unfairness develops when they feel their lives relatively more burdened than their husbands.

With a sense of injustice, wives attempt to change the unequal division of family work by demand or appeal to their husbands. Kim de-

manded that her husband help her with the family work. Kim, who is in her forties, financially supported her family by herself for five years when her family came to the United States for her husband's study for a Ph.D. degree. She had a hard time managing both family work and job because her husband rarely participated in family work. She passionately describes how she claimed her husband's help:

> I had always told him, "Isn't it ethical and humanistic for you to help me with family work when I feel tired? I can't manage it. Of course, I know that women are responsible for it. But I have to leave home to make money. I am doing the things men are responsible for. However, when I return from work to see family work left undone, as it was when I left home, I have to work twice as hard as you do."

Contrary to Kim, however, other wives do not actively defend the right to demand that their husbands participate in family work. When they try to introduce husbands to family work, they often use the "politics of appeal." They politely ask their husbands to help out by claiming their fatigue or time shortage due to their employment: "I am so tired. Will you please do the vacuuming?"; "Would you help me by taking out the garbage?" The politics of appeal, whereby women use stereotypical feminine traits, such as weakness and cautiousness, instead of assertiveness, is a strategy to change the unequal division of family work.

Wives' awareness that hurting men's self-respect or authority is ineffective to their interests factors into the politics of appeal. Wives are aware that when they demand that their husbands do something, their husbands may feel ordered about by a female, consequently damaging their pride. Husbands also admit that they tend to refuse their wives' requests for family work when they feel that their wives treat them without respect. Because doing family work traditionally means that women are "doing their gender" (Berk 1985), husbands try to show their wives the fundamental difference between men and women by rejecting family work. For example, Yu withdraws his participation in family work, saying, "No, how dare you think that men and women are the same!" to reclaim his authority as a man when he feels his wife hurt it. Through experiences, wives have known that their husbands respond more to their appeals than to demands.

Furthermore, wives are aware that their demands may lead husbands to think that they lord their earning power over them. In Korea, the traditional notion that "only a stupid man makes his wife leave home to make money" is still pervasive, despite the increasing rate of women's employment. However, most men I interviewed did not reveal much feeling of shame at being dependent on their wives' earnings, since they regard the situation not as a consequence of personal failure but as an unavoidable reality that any immigrant family must face. Nonetheless, wives sense that their husbands' self-respect is not quite secure when the men are no longer sole breadwinners. Therefore, they try not to get on their husbands' nerves.

Wives also think it more wise for a wife to take care of most of the family work, at least in the presence of others, than to push her husband into the kitchen. As an old Korean saying goes, "If women or hens of a family run wild and speak with an air, the family will be ruined." There are ample warnings against female dominance and assertiveness among Korean immigrants, and because wives are aware of the social stigma attached to being dominant wives, they

are careful not to give others the impression that they control their husbands. They also do not want their husbands to lose face; the women do not want to be ridiculed for emasculating their husbands publicly.

Women's Resignation to Unequal Division of Family Work

While all but one wife perceive that they have a right to demand their husbands' participation in family work, they do not necessarily try to defend this right in their everyday lives. Rather, these Korean immigrant wives expressed resignation to the unequal division of family work. Patriarchal gender ideas and immigrant family circumstances hinder women's attempts to challenge gender inequality at home.

The Belief in Women's Endurance and Sacrifice

Some wives' resignation to unequal division of family work is due to their deep-seated belief that women should endure any marital relations no matter how unfair they perceive them to be. Although they recognize the current unequal division of labor at home as unfair, they frame it as their "destiny" that they must embrace because they are women. Whenever they get irritated with their constant feelings of being rushed and fatigued with both a job and family work, they feel their lives more burdened than their husbands'. However, they say, "There is no other way. This is the life given to me." These wives tend to have been married for more than 20 years and are in their late forties or older.

When these wives recognize that younger husbands help their wives with family work, they express envy. However, the older women feel they cannot change the status quo. Rather, they regard their husbands' resistance against sharing family work as understandable. Their reasoning is that Korean men of their generation are not used to doing family work since they have been taught that family work is fundamentally a female obligation. Therefore, they think that it is not easy for husbands to change themselves all of a sudden.

The patriarchal belief in women's sacrifice for their families also contributes to wives' resignation. Those wives who experienced marital conflicts over the division of family work or other matters now want to avoid further conflict by resigning themselves to the status quo. For example, Lee's husband, who made less money than Lee for several years in the early stages of their immigration, constantly initiated quarrels and made Lee's life in the United States unbearable. Therefore, Lee gave up requesting her husband's help, because she felt it might create ill temper and result in more marital conflict, which would make her children unhappy.

This pattern parallels previous research on American women that reveals that women's low level of desire for men's participation in family work may reflect their resignation and wish to avoid marital conflict (Berheide 1984; Hochschild 1989; Komter 1989). However, there is a subtle difference between Korean immigrant women and American women in general. American women live in a society in which more than half of the marriages end in divorce, which is a primary factor in the increased impoverishment of women. Fears of divorce and a declining standard of living restrain them from demanding that their husbands help with family work (Hochschild 1989). However, fear of divorce is less salient among Korean immigrant women, who still have a low divorce rate.

Understanding Husbands' Time Shortage and Fatigue

As long as wives regard men's family work as a matter of help rather than a matter of responsibility, they cannot demand that their husbands help

unless the men have extra time and energy. Therefore, husbands' absolute or relative time shortages and fatigue, which Korean immigrant wives recognize, affect the extent of their resignation.

Wives of family business couples, who work more than 13 hours per day at physically demanding jobs, admit that their husbands as well as they themselves have little time to do family work. These wives reveal sympathy for their husbands, saying, "I know how tired he is because I experience the same thing." The wives explicitly state that both their husbands and they themselves need to rest rather than spend their time doing family work. Their statements suggest that for Korean immigrant families, working for family survival is a priority that takes precedence over the matter of division of family work. Consequently, their husbands can limit their participation in family work to the extent that they put the dishes in the sink and put leftovers in the refrigerator after eating alone. The wives reveal that they also lower the quality and quantity of family work that they perform.

The findings suggest that working conditions of family business couples provide both an opportunity and a constraint for these wives' challenge to gender inequality at home. All but two wives of family business couples earn the title of equal breadwinners by working as much as their husbands in labor-intensive family businesses and are in a better position to bargain for new marital power than wives who are secondary breadwinners. However, the tough working conditions limit these wives' attempts to change the unequal division of family work.

The relative time shortage of husbands is more likely to be a reason for professional wives' giving up achieving husbands' help. Whang, who works part-time as a engineering consultant while her husband works as an engineer full-time, thinks it is fair for her to take care of most of the family work without her husband's help because she has relatively more time at home than her husband. Furthermore, she believes that her husband may be excused from family work because he needs to spend his time on his own work for career advancement. Instead of expecting help from her husband, she often gets household help from a maid.

Gatekeeping of Mothers/Mothers-in-Law

Some wives' resignation to the unequal division of family work is due to the presence of mothers or mothers-in-law at home. All of the mothers in this study (four mothers-in-law and two mothers) moved into the houses of respondents to help with child rearing and household tasks. In fact, four out of six families have children under seven years old. These grandmothers take care of most of the everyday child rearing. All but one do the everyday cooking and cleaning except on weekends when their daughters or daughters-in-law do not go to work. Therefore, these mothers are significant helpers. However, they are also gatekeepers who try to maintain the traditional way of doing family work. For these mothers, family work has been a culturally designated female job, obligating women to take care of it. They believe that when a wife is not able to do family work, she should manage it anyway with other women's help. Therefore, the mothers do not complain about their doing family work instead of their daughters or daughters-in-law. But they restrain their daughters or daughters-in-law from asking their husbands to help with family work, as the following comments of Park, who is in her forties, reveal: "My mother shouts at me and scolds me for making my husband do the family work, saying 'Why do you demand that your husband do family work even though there are two women in this house?'"

These mothers also do not want their sons to do family work at the demand of their daughters-in-law because they perceive that the daughters-

in-law control their sons in their own way. According to Hong, who works at a building-cleaning job and flea market with his wife, their parents do not care about his voluntary participation in family work because they know that their son is a good cook and that he enjoys cooking. However, he cannot help being conscious of his parents when he tries to help his wife with family work at the request of his wife. He perceives that his mother does not like her daughter-in-law to be aggressive enough to demand that her son do something. At the same time, his wife recognizes that her mother-in-law expects her to be strong and aggressive enough to deal with employment in the United States. Hong's wife, a woman in her thirties who was a full-time housewife in Korea, recalls feeling pushed into working by her mother-in-law who had worked for more than 10 years in the United States. She feels that she was brainwashed by her mother-in-law, who repeatedly said, "From now on, never dream about living like a princess as you did in Korea. Here, in the U.S., women should be more aggressive and stronger than men."

These mothers also try to keep their sons or sons-in-law from doing family work, arguing that men lose face and self-respect when they are involved in traditionally female work. According to Chung, her mother-in-law interrupts her husband who tries to do dishes on Sunday, saying to him, "Leave it. Both of us [Chung and the mother-in-law] will take care of it. It's not good for men to do family work too much. You worked hard all week. You just take a rest you look tired." However, the task is often done by Chung because she feels that it is proper for her as a daughter-in-law to take care of family work at least when she does not go to work.

As Chung's case reveals, some wives do recognize their mother-in-law's differential treatment of them and their husbands. Regardless of identical working hours and fatigue of their son and daughter-in-law, in the eyes of their daughters-in-law, mothers-in-law seem to care about only their own sons' fatigue. The mothers-in-law seem to believe that no matter how tired their daughters or daughters-in-law are, the exhaustion does not release them from family work responsibility. While wives feel differential treatment by their mothers-in-law, they do not argue against them. This is especially the case when the wives really appreciate the mothers for reducing their burden of family work and when they know it is disobedient for a daughter-in-law to talk back to parents-in-law.

Will women interviewed in this study be more generous to their future daughters-in-law than their mothers-in-law? When asked how she feels about her son helping her future daughter-in-law with family work, many wives say, "It's OK. No longer should women suffer lives as I did." Some wives emphasize that they ask their sons to do household chores so that the sons can naturally learn family work from an early stage in their lives. However, the ways in which family work is assigned to their children follows the traditional distinction between family work for men and family work for women. Sons older than 10 years perform such tasks as vacuuming, laundry, gardening, and taking out garbage by themselves or with their siblings, while doing the dishes or cooking are mainly performed by daughters. And a few wives admit a subtle difference between their feelings about their own sons' family work and that of their future sons-in-law. They may feel thankful to their future sons-in-law for helping their daughters with family work, while they may feel sorry for their sons' having a hard time with family work. These wives ambivalently desire change in men.

Husbands' Reluctance

Despite attitudinal change in men's family work, few husbands practice what they preach. Only one husband I interviewed voluntarily participates in family work, and if a husband participates in a household task, he is more likely to do it at his wife's request. Even when some men accept their wives' requests, they tend to control the time they are involved in family work. "Leave it undone. I will do it later" is a typical response of husbands' to wives' requests. If wives push their husbands, the latter often argues, "Can't you do it, if you think it is really urgent?" The task is often done by wives who feel they cannot leave the task undone until the husbands do it. Husbands also control the task that they may accept at their wives' request. Korean immigrant husbands are most likely to vacuum, take out garbage, and do the gardening because they regard this as male work in that it occurs outside the house or it demands more or less physical strength. In contrast, they strongly resist doing laundry, cooking, and doing the dishes because they believe that these tasks are typical indoor work, related to women.

Facing their husbands' constant reluctance and resistance, some wives finally give up demanding help from their husbands. These wives recall the anger and frustration they felt begging for their husbands' help. Once they define their husbands as men who will never change, they feel further appeals to their husbands are just tiresome and meaningless. Kim, who says that the unequal division of family work has been the sole reason for marital conflict for 14 years of her marriage, declares her final resignation. Since her family can now afford it, she quit her full-time job, cutting back her work hours as a solution to her double burden of family work and job.

Husbands explain their reluctance to share family work in terms of the persistent influence of Korean traditions. They feel that since they are "Korean men" who used to take for granted strict gender division of work and patriarchal privileges of men, it is not easy to change themselves.

Even after 16 years in the United States, Lee, who is in his sixties, still mentions his difficulty with being engaged in tasks that are traditionally defined as nonmasculine, His reluctance to change contrasts with his wife' fast change from a full-time housewife to a working wife two days after her arrival.

Being "immigrant men" also serves as an excuse for husbands' reluctance to change. Husbands mention their hardships as immigrants and consequent stresses; they have often felt depressed, angry, tired, and frustrated with the language barrier, underemployment, or racial discrimination. This is evident when Lee explains why he rejects his wife's requests:

I will say "No" when I am not in the mood. How really tiring physically and psychologically the immigrant life in the U.S. is! I am always full of stress. It will burst into flames if anybody touches it.

The status of immigrant offers Lee elective affinity in viewing the changes in traditional marital roles. Since he perceived wives' employment as a required part of immigrant womanhood, he took his wife's change into a breadwinner for granted. However, the stress, anxiety, and tension that he feels as an immigrant man operate as excuses for his reluctant change into a sharing partner of family work.

No Longer Superwomen

As a coping strategy to combine their jobs and family work, most Korean immigrant wives in this study choose to neglect the quality and/or quantity of family work. This coping strategy is a self-resolution, with no significant changes occurring in their husbands' behaviors. Nonethe-

less, this is an indication of Korean immigrant women's attempt to change their share of family labor in that women's relinquishment of some family work is a step for them toward bargaining for equal sharing of household work with their husbands (Hood 1983).

For most wives (15 out of 18), what they neglect is not the types of family work they do but the standards they apply to their family work. These wives still take care of most household chores that are related to family sustenance, such as cooking, grocery shopping, and doing the dishes and the laundry. However, laundry is often delayed until clean socks are no longer available, the house is often messy, and just one side dish is prepared for dinner. Other wives neglect not only the standard of family work but also the kinds of family work. For example, Yu, who feels exhausted after 15 hours of hard work in a newly opened laundry, rarely does family work except grocery shopping. The only thing that Kong does is cooking dinner. Yu and Kong's abandoned tasks are taken over by her mother and her grown children (a 14-year-old daughter and an 18-year-old son), respectively.

These wives try to give up being a good housewife who always serves her family, regardless of her employment. Without hesitation, Kong, who runs a used appliance store with her husband, says, "I turn off the switch for family work. I now concern myself only with the business." As this quote suggests, Korean immigrant working wives reject the superwoman ideal, which their counterparts in Korea are still socially expected to follow.

A socially acknowledged priority of immigrant families, building a secure economic base as soon as possible, offers these wives a valid excuse for their neglect of family work. The notion that wives' employment is secondary and a matter of choice, which offers a basis for the Superwoman ideal, is convincing to only affluent Korean immigrant families. Professional husbands in this study insist that their wives' first priority be their children and family work, while they do not oppose their wives having a job. However, husbands of family business couples or low-wage-earner couples admit that more commitment of wives to their jobs than to family work is unavoidable. Therefore, these wives are not afraid of the social stigmas attached to being absent mothers or having a poorly kept house.

With an awareness of their contribution to the family economy, these women also believe that their great effort and consequent hardships for family survival can compensate for their reduced effort in homemaking. Choe reveals that "In Korea, it might have been absurd for me to treat my husband to a humble dish when he came home from work. However, in the U.S., with the excuse that I am busy, it is natural for me to make my family a simple dinner. Under these circumstances I work as much as my husband does, there is no other way to this." Therefore, they do not feel sorry for their husbands, though they regret their limited time in caring for their children.

Their husbands also admit that they cannot complain about wives' reduced family work because they know it is unavoidable. However, there is a contradiction between what husbands think they "should feel" and what they "really feel" about their wives' reduced services and caring (Hochschild 1989). Husbands cannot help feeling deprived of their wives' full-time services in the United States, which they enjoyed in Korea and which their counterparts in Korea may still enjoy. This feeling of relative deprivation is, according to these husbands, the cost that they have to pay for by not being sole breadwinners. This is well illustrated by the following comments of Kang. He has spent most of the daytime for several years alone at home because he and his wife work on different shifts. He grieves about his misfortune:

> I just gave up on [my wife's services] rather than understand her. I can't help resigning. This is my life. I wish I lived in Korea because at least a husband is able to provide for his family with only his earnings, whatever job he has.

DISCUSSION

Korean immigrant wives in this study no longer take for granted husbands' dominance at home and relief from family work. Many wives become less obedient to their husbands by expressing their opinions or speaking out against them, consequently resulting in marital conflicts. With an awareness of their contribution to the family economy, wives also believe that they deserve their husbands' help with family work. Most wives also believe that their great efforts toward family survival legitimize their own decreased effort in homemaking. Therefore, they do not practice the superwoman ideal and feel no guilt about this. These findings suggest an ongoing challenge by wives to gender inequality at home.

Resource theory, which explains the relationship between spouses' economic resources and bargaining power in a marriage, is confirmed in this study. However, it is important to recognize that the increase in wives' negotiating power is not a result of the increases in that amount of money that wives have or in their control over their earnings. In fact, few Korean immigrant wives in this study accumulate their own individual money to control because some are unpaid workers in family businesses and the majority of family accounting systems are pooled rather than discrete. Instead, psychological resources such as pride and honor, which Korean immigrant wives gain as they are aware of their contribution to the family, are more viable driving forces of wives' challenge.

These positive feelings are related to the immigrant family circumstances under which the hierarchy of paid work and unpaid family work is intensified. Among immigrant families who prioritize working for survival, wives recognize that their contribution to their families as working wives or mothers will never be trivialized by other family members. The socially acknowledged priority of immigrant families offers these wives a valid excuse for their neglect of family work. As immigrant women, who work as hard and as many hours as their husbands at labor-intensive jobs for family survival, many wives earn the title of equal breadwinners and thus gain a foothold to challenge gender inequality at home. While family cooperation is an emphasized ethos among these families that put a priority on family survival, it does not make wives keep silent. In the context of unequal marital relations, many Korean immigrant families are the loci of conflict as well as cooperation.

It is important to recognize a difference between a wife's feeling about her job itself and her feeling about what she does for her family through the job. Those wives who work intensively at a laundry, flea market, or shoe-repair shop may not find satisfaction in their jobs. With physical hardships such as fainting spells, cramps in their legs, bloody noses, or emotional stress, they wish they could have a little recess or work at more comfortable jobs. Nonetheless, through their employment, they recognize themselves as fair contributors to their families and feel proud of themselves. Though these wives did not begin their jobs to secure a base of independence from their husbands, they find a new sense of not being totally dependent on their husbands through employment, consequently perceiving new rights to a voice at home and to demands for help from their husbands. This is a main reason that all but one wife in this study desire to remain in the labor force even if their families no longer needed their earnings, thus confirming Ferree's (1984) assertion that having to work for the family does not preclude wanting to work.

In the process of challenge to gender inequality at home, Korean immigrant wives still draw boundaries that are not to be crossed, although they are stretching those lines. The goal of their ongoing challenge is not to subvert the marital hierarchy itself. The Confucian patriarchal ideology, that women should submit to their husbands' authority and protect male morale as heads of families, restrains women from protesting against marital hierarchy itself. The patriarchal beliefs in women's unconditional endurance in a marriage and sacrifice for the family also overwhelm some wives' perceived right to demand men's change in family work. With an awareness of the social stigma against female dominance and their husbands' insecure self-esteem, wives often apply the "politics of appeal" as a strategy to induce their husbands to participate in family work. This is a "patriarchal bargain," in which women maximize their power within patriarchy (Kandiyoti 1988; Kibria 1990).

The findings highlight the interplay of Korean immigrant wives' psychological resources, traditional patriarchal ideas, and immigrant family circumstances in affecting their challenge to gender inequality at home. However, it is important to recognize a difference in the effects of wives' economic resources and immigrant family circumstances on wives' challenges among Korean immigrant families. The effects are most salient among family business couples and non-professional wage-earner couples in this study, in which a family priority is still put on family survival and being immigrants operates as an overriding status to legitimate their changes in the traditional marital roles. This is far less so among professional couples.

Reading 15   Gender, Class, Family, and Migration:

Puerto Rican Women in Chicago*

MAURA I. TORO-MORN

Using in-depth interviews with women in the Puerto Rican community of Chicago, this article explores how migration emerged as a strategy for families across class backgrounds and how gender relations within the family mediate the migration of married working-class and middle-class Puerto Rican women. The women who followed their husbands to Chicago participated in another form of labor migration, since some wives joined their husbands in the paid economy and those who did not contributed with the reproductive work that supported their husbands and families. This article also explores how Puerto Rican women confront the basic duality of reproductive and productive work.

Recently, there has been a surge of scholarly interest about immigrant women (Diner 1983; Ewen 1983; Glenn 1986; Hondagneu-Sotelo 1992; Lamphere 1987; Simon and Brettell 1986; Weinberg 1988). Although women have always participated in population movements (Tyree and Donato 1986), suddenly newspaper reports are calling women the "new immigrants." Initial attempts at making immigrant women visible owe much to the efforts of feminist researchers of the 1960s and 1970s (Morokvasic 1983). The first wave of research on immigrant women helped to fill in the gaps by calling attention to the presence of women in migratory movements and by providing the much needed descriptive detail on the employment status and family situations of particular groups, but, according to Morokvasic (1983), this early research did not break with the traditional individualist approach so pervasive in immigration research. It continued to analyze women as if their decisions to migrate were determined by their individual motives and desires; consequently, important questions were left unanswered: How do we account for women's migration and should the migration of women be treated in the same conceptual framework as male migrants or do they require separate analysis? Recently, a new

I am indebted to Judith Wittner, Loyola University of Chicago, for her invaluable assistance and suggestions during the early stages of this work and to *las mujeres del barrio* for sharing their experiences with me. I would also like to thank Margaret Andersen and the anonymous reviewers for their comments and suggestions.

*Toro-Morn, Maura I. 1995. "Gender, Class, Family, and Migration: Puerto Rican Women in Chicago." *Gender & Society* 9(6): 712–726. Copyright © 1995 by Sociologists for Women in Society. Reprinted by permission of Sage Publications, Inc.

wave of research has begun to correct some of the problems unresolved by the earlier research. Scholars have begun to move beyond the additive approach to articulate how gender affects and shapes the migration process (Hondagneu-Sotelo 1992; Kibria 1990). This new research shows that immigrant women's relationship to market and nonmarket conditions is unique. The place of immigrant women in the labor market is shaped by class and their statuses as immigrants and racial/ethnic minorities; this intersection creates a particular and distinct experience (Glenn 1986).

Much empirical research has been done linking the entrance of women into labor migrations because of the emergence of export-led manufacturing zones in the Caribbean, Mexico, and Asia (Fernandez-Kelly 1983; Sassen-Koob 1984). In addition, studies have examined the incorporation of immigrant women into the labor force (Garcia-Castro 1985; Prieto 1986) and the consequent labor market outcomes in terms of occupational distribution and income differences from native populations (Boyd 1986; Simon and DeLey 1986; Sullivan 1984; Tienda, Jensen, and Bach 1984). Still, much empirical work remains to be done to explain how these processes differ by race and ethnicity.

This article examines how working-class and better-educated middle-class Puerto Rican women enter the migration process, how gender relations shape their move, and how women adapt to their new homes in the United States. Specifically, I focus on the experiences of married working-class and middle-class women. My interviews suggest that while both groups migrated to the United States as part of what sociologists have called a "family stage migration," there are important differences between them that challenge our understanding of women's migration. In the first part of this article, I explore how working-class and middle-class Puerto Rican women moved to the United States. I

pay particular attention to the language women used to describe this process. While middle-class women talked about their migration as motivated by professional goals, working-class Puerto Rican women talked about how they came to take care of their children, husbands, and families. When confronted with these answers, I found that the experiences of married working-class women did not fit the traditional explanations found in the migration literature. Here, I draw on the feminist construct of productive and reproductive work, to argue that our current definition of "labor migration" is too narrow. Not all labor migrations need to relate to productive activities (i.e., the entrance of immigrant women in the labor market). One very important aspect of labor migrations should include the work of women who migrate and do not necessarily join the labor force, but stay and do the reproductive work that supports families and immigrant communities. Within this category, there are women who migrate as wives, as grandmothers, or as relatives, and whose major responsibility is to help with the reproductive tasks—be they housework or child care—of their own families and/or their extended families.

The second part of this article explores how, once in the United States, both working-class and middle-class Puerto Rican women had to confront the duality of being responsible for the reproductive work that takes place at home and the productive work outside the home. The interviews indicate that both working-class and middle-class Puerto Rican women tried to provide as much continuity in the process of forming and re-creating family life. Again, important class differences emerged when comparing married working-class and middle-class migrants. interviews suggest that working-class husbands may have accommodated to their wives temporary employment, but that did not change the traditional division of labor within the household. Instead, working-class women had to develop strategies to accommodate their roles as working wives. Middle-class women developed strategies both as family members and as individuals in the process of adjusting to life in Chicago. The strategies they devised, however, reflected their class position. When juggling family and work responsibilities, educated and professional women gave career goals equal standing alongside family obligations.

METHODOLOGY

From March 1989 to July 1990, I interviewed women in the Puerto Rican community of Chicago, which covers the areas of West Town, Humboldt Park, and Logan Square. I participated in community activities and attended cultural events. These activities allowed me to meet the women of the community and, through informal snowball sampling techniques, to select interviewees. The interviews took place in the homes of the informants and lasted between one to three hours. Interviews were conducted in Spanish. The interview questions were organized around a series of themes, ranging from their migration history to family, work, and community experiences.

The sample of married women consisted of 17 informants. Eleven were mostly working class, with little education, who came to Chicago in the early 1950s and 1960s. Generally, at the time of migration, they were married—or were soon to be married—and most had children. The six professional and educated women in the sample had all migrated in the late 1960s and had over 14 years of education at the time of their move. Most educated informants described themselves as predominantly middle class and from urban backgrounds in Puerto Rico. At the time of the interview, two informants had earned doctorate degrees. Ten respondents were in their

sixties; seven were in their forties and fifties. Different respondents will be identified by pseudonyms.

Being Puerto Rican and bilingual, I was able to establish rapport with informants. Most of the older migrant women spoke little English, and conducting the interviews in Spanish facilitated the exchange. By the same token, being fluent in English allowed women to use the language with which they felt most comfortable. Sometimes the interview started in Spanish and ended in English. On other occasions, women switched back and forth.

GENDER, CLASS, AND MIGRATION

The most significant movement of Puerto Ricans to the United States took place at the end of World War II (Dietz 1986; Falcon 1990; History Task Force 1979; Pantojas-Garcia 1990). In the late 1940s, the impact of U.S. investment and modernization of the economy transformed Puerto Rico from a predominantly agricultural to an industrial economy. Operation Bootstrap, as the development model became popularly known in Puerto Rico, attracted labor intensive light manufacturing industries such as textiles and apparel to Puerto Rico by offering tax incentives, cheap labor, and easy access to U.S. markets (Dietz 1986; Pantojas-Garcias 1990). These changes in Puerto Rico's economy had profound consequences for Puerto Rican families. The development model was unable to create enough jobs, and working-class Puerto Ricans began to leave the island, heading for familiar places like New York City and new places like Chicago. News about jobs spread quickly throughout the island, as informal networks of family members, friends, and relatives told people of opportunities and helped families migrate.

My interviews suggest that working-class women and their families used migration as a strategy for dealing with economic problems. Married working-class women, in particular, talked about migration as a family project. For them, migration took place in stages. Husbands moved first, secured employment and housing arrangements, and then sent for the rest of the family. Even single men frequently left their future brides in Puerto Rico, returning to the island to get married as their employment and economic resources permitted. Some women came as brides-to-be, as they joined their future husbands in Chicago. For example, Rosie's mother came to Indiana in order to join her husband working in the steel mills. He had been recruited earlier, along with other workers in Puerto Rico. Once at the mills in Indiana, these men often found better jobs and moved on. They went back to Puerto Rico, got married, and returned to Indiana. Others arranged for the future brides to join them in Chicago. Alicia's explanation indicates how these decisions took place within the family context.

> My husband and I were neighbors in San Lorenzo. Before he left to come to Chicago, he had demonstrated an interest in me. Initially, I did not accept him, because I did not want to get married so young. We started corresponding and I agreed to the relationship.... In one letter, he asked me to marry him and come to live with him in Chicago. I told him that he needed to ask my father's permission.... He wrote to my father but my father did not agree...it took some convincing by my cousins who were coming to Chicago so that he would let me come and get married.

> My cousin took it upon himself to be responsible for me and that's how I came. Within two weeks of getting here, we got married.

Alicia's experience suggests that even within the constraints of a patriarchal society, single women were active in negotiating their moves to Chicago.

Married working-class women left the island to be with their husbands and families, even though some reported to have been working before leaving. Lucy and Luz were working in apparel factories in Puerto Rico when their unemployed husbands decided to move. Economic opportunities seemed better for their husbands in the United States and they both quit their jobs to move. For others, like Teresa and Agnes, both husband and wife were looking for work, when news about job opportunities came via relatives visiting the island. Similarly, Agnes also came with her husband in the 1970s after a cousin who was visiting from Chicago convinced them that there were better job opportunities for both of them.

Working-class women also talked about the struggles over the decision to move. Fear of the unknown bothered Lucy. In addition, with a baby in her arms and pregnant with a second child, Lucy did not have anyone to help her in Chicago, but accompanied by her sister and her youngest child, Lucy followed her husband. Shortly after her migration, Lucy's mother and her sister-in-law arrived to care for the children while Lucy worked. Asuncion's husband could not find work in Puerto Rico either, so he migrated to Chicago with his relatives. Asuncion took a vacation from work and came to visit. Her family

> started talking about how they were recruiting case workers in the welfare

*office that could speak Spanish. They
all had connections there and could
very easily help me get a job. In fact,
I went just to try it.*

Asuncion gave in to the pressure and started working while still holding her job in Puerto Rico:

*I worked for six months, but I had so
many problems, I wanted to go back.
Life here [in Chicago] is really different when compared to the Island's. I
was really confused. I cried a lot. I
had left my children behind and I
missed them a lot.*

In fact, Asuncion went back to Puerto Rico because she missed her daughters; she was uncertain about what would happen to her marriage.
She remembered how she felt when her husband
took her to the airport:

*I really did not know whether I was
going to see him again. He wanted to
stay here and start a new life. I really
did not care about what would happen to us and our relationship; I
thought about my daughters. I owe it
to my mother that my marriage was
saved. After I returned to Puerto Rico,
she sat me down and told me that my
place was to be with my husband.
That he was a good man and that my
place was next to him. That I had to
think about my children growing up
without a father, so I returned again.*

As Asuncion's case illustrates, she struggled between her husband's needs in Chicago
and those of her children on the Island. Ultimately, moving to Chicago meant maintaining
the family and saving her marriage.

Victoria's story is somewhat similar. She
was living in her hometown of Ponce when she
fell in love with the son of a family visiting from
Chicago. She became pregnant and, in keeping
with Puerto Rican culture, she was forced to
marry him. Without consulting with Victoria, the
young man's parents sent him a ticket so that he
could return to Illinois. Once in Chicago, he expected she would follow.

*I did not want to come....One day
he sent me a ticket for me and my
baby girl. I sent it back because I did
not want to come. But he send it
back again. So I had to come....I had
no idea where I was going, I had
lived all my life in Ponce and had
never left Ponce. I was so scared....*
In 1966, she followed her husband
to Chicago against her will.

The emotional and cultural shock was very
strong:

*I cried my eyes out. In Puerto Rico,
you are always outside and carefree.
Here, we lived in small apartments,
we could not go outside. We could
not open the windows. We did not
know the language.*

When her second child was to be born, Victoria was so intimidated with the city that she
asked her mother to send a plane ticket so that she
might give birth in Puerto Rico. Within less than
a year, she had returned to Puerto Rico. Eventually her husband joined her also, but he was not
happy. Soon he began to disappear and neglect
his responsibilities as a father. In one of his escapades, he went back to Chicago. Once again, he
sent for her. This time, however, Victoria began
to analyze the situation in different ways.

In Puerto Rico, I did not have any money to pay rent, electricity, and other bills or even feed my babies. I recognized it was a difficult situation, but I thought to myself that if I stayed I had less opportunities to do something with my life. So, I thought that if I returned and brought my other brother with me they could help me and eventually even my mother could come and I could get myself a job. I had noticed that there were factories close to where we lived and my sister-in-law had offered to help as well. My brother who had moved with me the first time had gotten married and brought his wife with him.

Victoria had changed; as a married woman who followed her husband to Chicago, she began to develop her own agenda and use migration as a way for its realization.

Of the women who followed their husbands to Chicago, only two (Luz and Rita) complained that their husbands failed to fulfill their end of the bargain, forcing them to use migration as a way to assert their claims as wives. Lucy's husband had just returned from the military when he began talking about migrating to Chicago. Initially he went to Indiana where some relatives helped him find a job. When he was laid off, he learned through other friends that there were job opportunities in Illinois. He then moved to Chicago, promising to send for the family once he secured employment. But, according to Luz, he had been working for quite a while and had not sent for her and the children. Also, he was not sending any money to support the family. Instead, her husband kept putting off sending for her, and she was forced to confront him. Finally, Lucy left Arecibo in 1951 to join her husband

and save her marriage. Rita was also forced to confront her husband by letter, reminding him of his promise to bring the rest of the family to Chicago. Even though it was over 20 years ago, Rita stated with emotion that she

had to write him a letter. Because it had been over a year and he didn't send for me. I had three babies and I was alone. When he left, he said that he was going to send for me shortly and it had been a year and I was still waiting.

He replied that he did not want her to come, because living in Chicago was hard and she and the children would not be able to get used to the weather. She replied, "either you send the ticket or send me the divorce papers." Apparently, this was a typical problem for Puerto Rican women when their husbands preceded them in migration. Juarbe (1988) reported that Puerto Rican women migrants in New York experienced similar problems. Juarbe's (1988) informant, Anastacia, stated that after her husband had migrated, he did not want her to come. He had been living and working for over three months. He wrote occasionally but did not send any money. Apparently, she had some money saved and was able to buy the ticket without his knowledge. Anastacia wrote him a letter announcing her arrival.

Middle-Class Migrants

The migration of educated and professional middle-class Puerto Ricans to Chicago remains an unanswered empirical question. Sanchez-Korrol's (1986) study of migration to New York City hints at the possibility that middle-class Puerto Ricans had been involved in the migration process; furthermore, surveys by the Planning Office in Puerto Rico between 1957 and 1962 found higher literacy levels and English proficiency among migrants than among the population as a whole (Rodriguez 1989). Pantojas-Garcia (1990) comes closest to analyzing the changing political economy in Puerto Rico and its impact on middle-class and educated workers. He points out that skilled and professional workers have increasingly joined semiskilled and unskilled workers in the migration process. As Pedraza (1991) points out, despite the growing importance of the "brain drain" as a type of migration, from a gender perspective, it remains the least understood.

In contrast to working-class migrants, moving was a joint family project for married middle-class women. In addition, the language this group used to describe the move differs from that of the working-class married woman. Middle-class women came with their husbands and had an agenda of their own. Aurea met her husband while attending the University of Puerto Rico. Initially, the couple moved from San Juan to Boston to enable her husband to take a university position. In 1971, a new job opportunity brought them to Chicago. In fact, Aurea talked about moving as a mutual arrangement between her and her husband. She saw the move to Chicago as an opportunity to join community and political struggles. Shortly after arriving in the city, they bought a house—something that took years for working-class families to accomplish.

Brunilda had just completed her bachelor's degree and was working as a field researcher for the University of Puerto Rico when she was asked to work with a group of American scholars who came to Puerto Rico to conduct research in the 1970s. The researchers were very pleased with her work and offered her a position if she would relocate to Chicago. They promised they would help her to make the transition. She had just been married when the job offer came, and she felt that was a big problem:

My husband did not want to come, he said that he did not know English. He just did not want to come. I told him that there were no doubts in my mind as to what that job meant for me. It was a great opportunity, and I was not going to let it go. If he did not want to come, then I guess that was it, I knew I was coming with him or without him.

In this case the roles changed. It was the husband who was asked to follow his wife; initially he resisted, but the job meant so much to Brunilda that she was willing to sacrifice her marriage. Brunilda, therefore, moved within a professional rather than a family network. In addition, she did not live close to other Puerto Ricans in Chicago because the research team found her a place to stay closer to the university. After completing her work with the university researchers, Brunilda started graduate studies at a local university. She went to school full time for a year and in 1971 started working as a community organizer in the south side of Chicago.

Vilma moved from San Juan to Wisconsin to go to graduate school. While in Madison, she met her future husband and they moved in together. They had completed their degrees when he was offered a job in Chicago. In 1986, they both relocated to Chicago. Vilma described her move

as very traditional in terms that I had just finished my masters and was looking for a job when my "compañero" (living in boyfriend) got a job offer in Chicago. I followed him to Chicago, but I came not only for him, but also knowing that in Madison there was no professional future for me.

Comparing the migration of married working-class and middle-class Puerto Rican women offers some insights into how gender and class shapes the migration process. As my interviews suggest, both working-class and middle-class Puerto Rican women found themselves migrating as part of a family migration. Married working-class women came to support their husbands and be with their families. In other words, their roles as mothers and wives compelled them to migrate. The narratives suggest that some women struggled over the decision to move. In contrast, educated married middle-class women were less encumbered by such relations of authority. They shared in the decision making and were less dependent on other family members to make the move. As Vilma's and Brunilda's stories indicate, these middle-class migrants clearly had professional agendas of their own. How does each confront the problem of balancing family and work responsibilities?

GENDER, FAMILY, AND WORK

In Puerto Rican culture, there is a gender-specific division of labor consisting of men's work (*trabajo de hombre*) as the providers and women's work (*trabajo de mujer*) as the caretakers of the home and children. Underlying this gender division of labor is a patriarchal ideology, machismo, emphasizing men's sexual freedom, virility, and aggressiveness, and women's sexual repression and submission (Acosta-Belen 1986). Machismo represents the male ideal and plays an important role in maintaining sexual restrictions and the subordination of women. This ideology rationalizes a double standard where a woman can be seen as *una mujer buena o una mujer de la casa* (a good woman or a good homemaker) or as *una mujer mala o una mujer de la calle* (a bad woman or a woman of the streets). A man has to show that *él lleva los pantalones en la casa* (he

is the one who wears the pants in the family) and that he is free to *echar una canita al aire* (literally meaning, blow a gray hair to the wind; culturally, it means to have an affair).

The counterpart of machismo is *marianismo* in which the Virgin Mary is seen as the role model for women (Sanchez-Ayendez 1986, 628). Within this context, a woman's sexual purity and virginity is a cultural imperative. Motherhood, in Puerto Rican culture, lies at the center of such ideology. A woman is viewed in light of her relationship to her children and, as Carmen, one of my informants, put it, in her ability "dar buenos ejemplos" (to provide a good role model).

Among working-class Puerto Ricans, gender roles are very rigid (Safa 1984). Although industrialization and the entrance of women in the labor force completely contradicts this ideal of *la mujer es de la casa* (women belong to the home), in Puerto Rico the domestic role of working class remains intact. Working mothers are primarily responsible for the care of the home and the children.

In Chicago, in keeping with this ideology surrounding family values, some working-class husbands resisted their wives working. The men would take a double shift so that wives could stay home, take care of the children, and do housework. Carmen stayed home to care for her children and was very proud of her accomplishments as a mother, but economic necessity obliged other husbands to conform to women's work outside the home. Like Lucy said, "I did not come here to work, but I had to." Alicia elaborates, "in those days one paycheck was like nothing. We put together both paychecks and there were times that he had very little next to nothing left. By that time there were other relatives living with us and there were lots of mouths to feed."

The same network of family and friends that helped in the process of migration helped working wives find employment in Chicago factories. Josefa, Lucy, Luz, Rita, and Teresa all reported working in factories. Chicago's political economy in the 1950s allowed these women to find factory jobs with relative ease; however, most working-class married women viewed employment as a temporary necessity. The way women talked about their work experiences reflected this attitude. Josefa and her husband worked not only to meet the family needs but also to take care of the medical expenses of their child. When her daughter started going to school, she stopped working. Alicia worked in a factory prior to getting pregnant; after having the baby, she stopped working. When the family wanted to buy a house, Alicia went back to work for two years. After her second child, she stopped working altogether. Brunilda started working in a factory immediately upon arriving from Puerto Rico, but when she became pregnant, she stopped. Lucy was the only married respondent who stayed in the factory for a prolonged period of time. Eventually, she stopped working when she got sick.

Although most working-class married women gave in to their husbands wishes for them to stay home, Rita illustrates how a woman resisted those traditional roles and even sought to change them. Rita's husband did not want her to work. According to Rita:

After I got to Chicago, my husband didn't want me to work. But I wanted to work. I wanted to work because you can meet people, learn new things, and one can also leave the house for a while. I saw all the women in the family, his sisters and cousins, working and earning some money, and I wanted to work too. They used to tell me that I should be working. But I had four children, and who was going to take care of them?

Rita succumbed to the pressure and started working secretly for about three months. When asked how she managed to work without her husband knowing about it, Rita replied that

since he left to work very early, I found someone to take care of my smallest child, and the others went to school. My work hours were from 9:00 to 3:30, so by the time my husband got home, I had everything done. I had the house clean, the children were cleaned and had eaten, and I was all put together. My husband did not like when I was not put together.

Rita eventually told her husband about her work escapades because she did not like doing things *a la escondida* (in hiding); however, her husband's traditionalism prevailed, and Rita was forced to give up working. To relent was a blow, because the money she had earned had gone to clothe the children and to purchase a sewing machine. Note the tone of pride:

With the money I earned I was able to buy my sewing machine and I felt so proud of myself that I was able to buy it with my own money. We saved a lot of money afterwards. I sew for the family; I felt so proud.

Although she gave in to her husband's traditionalism, Rita found a source of pride and accomplishment even within the confines of the house. She may have stopped working, but her contributions to the household continued as she was able to sew her children's clothing and other items for the house and the family.

Others reported that they stopped working for wages, but continued to contribute to the family's income by working in their husbands' neighborhood stores. They used the word "helped," but, in reality, they actually ran the stores while their husbands worked elsewhere.

Puerto Rican men may have accommodated to the wife's employment, but the traditional division of labor within the family did not change. Lucy best articulated the working woman's problem:

> It was very hard work because I had to take care of the house, the children, and the store. Since my husband never learned how to drive, I had to learn to drive. I had to go to the warehouse, do the bookkeeping, everything. In the store, I used to do everything. My husband helped, but I was practically in charge of everything.

Puerto Rican working mothers, regardless of whether they worked outside the home or with their husbands in the family business, were still responsible for the care of the children and housework. Child care first became a problem at the time of migration since families could not afford to travel all at once. A strategy women used to deal with this problem was to leave the children in Puerto Rico in the care of grandparents. This arrangement was a widespread practice in the Island for many years.

Once the family was in Chicago, women developed short-term arrangements to deal with the daily problems of child care. Shift work represented one strategy that couples used to allow these women to stay home with the children. The husband could work the day shift, and the wife worked at night. Haydee's father worked the day shift in a factory, while her mother worked the evening shift as a cook in a hotel. Josefa worked the night shift in a candy store; her husband worked the day shift. I asked Josefa if they ever switched, where he worked nights and she worked days. She replied that working at night allowed her to take care of her daughter during the day.

When children were school age, both husband and wife might be able to work during the day. For wives, however, there was always the added responsibility of returning home to care for the children and do the household chores. Here, girls were introduced to the household responsibilities very early and were left to care for younger brothers and sisters. When Claudia reached nine years, she acquired household responsibilities. She was given keys to the apartment, and after school she was expected to clean the kitchen, pick up around the house, and start dinner. This was also a way mothers trained their daughters in the traditional gender roles.

Given the ease of migration, other working-class women brought over relatives with them to help care for the children, suggesting that women can get involved in the migration process to do the reproductive work, allowing other women to do work outside the home. Lucy and Daniela brought their mothers, and Teresa brought a younger sister to Chicago to help take care of the children. Teresa's sister stayed home and took care of her children until she met a fellow and got married. That was when Teresa then turned to a woman in her building who took care of them for a small fee. Teresa gave her $12.00 weekly for the two girls and provided their food.

Sanchez-Korrol (1983, 98) found the same kind of informal child care practices in the early "colonias" in New York City in which "childcare tasks previously undertaken by relatives defaulted to friends and acquaintances outside the kinship network who provided the services in exchange for a prearranged fee." This grassroots system served both employed women and women who had to stay at home. The arrangement usually consisted of bringing the child, food, and additional clothing to the "mother-substitute" and collecting the child after work. This system provided a practical way to increase family earnings and was an extralegal system with advantages not found in established child care institutions. These informal child care arrangements allowed children to be cared for in a familiar environment, where there was mutual trust, agreement between the adults involved, and flexibility. Children were cared for in a family setting where the language, customs, and Puerto Rican traditions were reinforced.

When Teresa stopped working, she became a child care provider for the women in her building. Now, she no longer cares for other people's children, but instead cares for her own grandchildren. Teresa's history represents an example of the cycle of care that women provided. Such a cycle may begin when a woman places her children with a neighbor while she works. Then she may care for other neighbor's children while they work and, finally, care for her own children's children.

Middle-Class Migrants

Middle-class women placed their career goals equally alongside their family responsibilities. Rosa talked about how she had managed to work full time in Puerto Rico and go to school to acquire an associate's degree because her extended family helped take care of the children and the household chores. In Chicago, since they did not have their extended family, they had to adjust differently. Shortly after arriving in the city, Rosa, had given birth to her youngest child, who opted to stay home with her children until they were of school age. Rosa recognized that she wanted to be with her children, but she also wanted to stay active.

When I arrived, I saw a lot of possibilities, but I chose to stay home with my baby because I wanted to be with my

children. When the baby was three years old, I started thinking what can I do to keep myself busy? In Puerto Rico, I had always worked, and I was not used to be a full-time mom. I was very independent. I was very active. So I started helping the church. I started just because I wanted to get out of the house.

Eventually it became a full-time job. Then, when she started working full time, her husband took on more household responsibilities:

Here he has learned all kinds of domestic chores. At times I get home from work and he has everything ready, I don't have to do a thing in the house. Other times, we decide to go out for dinner.

Brunilda could not have made it without her husband, who helped her take care of the children as she pursued both her educational goals and, later, her political activism:

My husband was very understanding of my goals and political interest. We shared many of the household responsibilities.... I have to admit that I spent a lot of time outside of the house during my children's childhood; for that I am a little bit sorry.

Later on she elaborated on her struggles and how she resolved them:

When you are a professional, you face what Americans call "conflicting priorities." It's like I want to be everywhere at the same time. For me, community work has always inter-

ested me, whereas being a housewife has always been secondary. I feel more gratification in my role as a professional.

At the time of the interview, Brunilda worked as a professor in a local university. Aurea too placed her community activism (which was her professional orientation) alongside her family responsibilities:

For me, both are part of the same process. I define my family network beyond the nuclear family, or better yet, beyond the traditional American concept of the nuclear family. My family is part of my social activism.

I asked whether this brought about any conflicts. She replied:

Without doubt, my husband is part of this sexist society and obviously expects privileges that this society accords men, but we have worked and negotiated these roles quite successfully; moreover, we both made a political pact. It worked rather well because he shares the same vision of the world and social change as I do.

CONCLUSION

Evidence from this research has only begun to show how, in the context of changing political economy, migration emerged as a strategy for families across class backgrounds. Initially, migration was a strategy working-class families, used to deal with shrinking economic opportunities for the men in the family, but eventually middle-class better-educated men and women joined working-class Puerto Ricans in the migration process.

The political economy that rendered working-class husbands unemployable forced women to migrate to Chicago as part of a family strategy. Gender relations within the family were a major factor shaping the migration of married working-class women to Chicago. Some married women went willingly, thinking that the move would improve their families' financial situation. Others resisted, but ultimately their roles as mothers and wives compelled them to follow their husbands to Chicago.

Whether working class or middle class Puerto Rican women, like other immigrant women, confronted a basic duality in family and work. Families provided economic and emotional support. They see the family as the only area where people are free to be themselves, and where people come for affection and love, but the family is also an institution that has historically oppressed women (Glenn 1986). When individuals and families confront economic deprivation, legal discrimination, and other threats to their survival, conflict within the context of the family is muted by the pressure of the family to unite against assaults from the outside. The focus on the family as a site of resistance often underestimates how certain family arrangements can be oppressive to women. Often misunderstood by scholars is the reproductive work of women on behalf of the family and the benefits such work brings to the men (Glenn 1987, 192).

Working-class women saw themselves in keeping with Puerto Rican culture as primarily *mujeres de la casa*, but many found themselves working, albeit temporarily, given the family's economic situation. Here, families accommodated to the wives' temporary employment, but in ways that did not challenge the traditional patriarchal structure in the family. Wives were still responsible for cooking, cleaning, and child care. Given this situation, working-class married women developed strategies to accommodate their roles as working wives.

The area of child care best reflects the resourcefulness of working-class Puerto Rican women migrants in developing accommodating strategies. Some women left their children behind in Puerto Rico, others brought relatives from Puerto Rico to help them. Still others turned to older daughters as helpers. Some became involved in a cycle of child care similar to the one developed by Puerto Rican women migrants in New York City.

Married working-class Puerto Rican women adapted to life in Chicago in ways that did not disturb traditional family arrangements. They also developed strategies to resist some arrangements. Some sought to change their husbands' view about work outside the home and created networks to help accomplish their goals. Other stopped working for wages, but continued contributing as mothers, giving them influence and power within the family. In addition, some women remained active in income-generating activities, such as working in the family business. When husbands neglected their responsibilities as fathers, women took charge of the household, providing for their children and family.

Although middle-class women felt differently about work and family obligations, they also struggled over their roles as mothers and wives. They rejected traditional ideologies about women's roles and saw no conflict in doing both. Some husbands supported them, but when husbands resisted, they also negotiated the work and family responsibilities. Their class position afforded them options, such as staying home until they were ready to return to work, hiring help, postponing having children, and organizing their schedule around their children's schooling. This study has only begun to explore a very small slice of the Puerto Rican experience in Chicago, namely that of married working-class and middle-class women. Much empirical work needs to be done to fully understand how gender shapes the migration process for other groups of Puerto Rican women in different family arrangements and across class backgrounds.

Part III

Generational Relationships

Part II of this reader was largely devoted to examining the marriage and family dynamics of gender relationships. We now shift our attention to readings that study relationships between family members of different ages.

All human societies are differentiated on the basis of age and sex. Throughout history, the social roles of men and women have been separate, as have the roles of children, adults, and the aged. The family is composed of members of various ages who are differentially related. Most sociological accounts of the family have emphasized how age differentiation of family members enhances their solidarity. The interdependence of family members has been seen to foster emotional attachments, structural solidarity, and family cohesion. Yet, inherent in this differential age structure is the potential for conflict and tension.

Differential age structures have always been linked to status discrepancies in power, privilege, and prestige. Just as a power dimension is often articulated in gender relationships, families can be viewed in terms of hierarchical social structures in which older generations or older siblings hold positions of power, authority, and prestige over their younger counterparts. There are various degrees of family stratification by age. But the universal tendency is for the elders to exercise control over younger family members.

The articles contained in the two chapters that make up this part of the book will examine how families define sets of people according to age. These age categories influence family members' relations to one another. Distinguishing family members by age also has implications for the conceptualization of persons placed in particular age groups. The conceptualizations of childhood and adolescence, adulthood, and the aged reflect conceptualizations of the family, and they should be seen in terms of cultural diversity and social-historical context.

Philippe Ariès in his classic study, *Centuries of Childhood: A Social History of Family Life* (1962), put forth the striking theme that Western ideas about childhood and family life have changed and developed from the Middle Ages to modern times. Ariès sought to document how in medieval life the child was integrated into the community. It was not until the development of bourgeois capitalist society that the segregation of children occurred. He argued that, in the earlier period, children were treated as small adults. As soon as they were capable of being without their mothers, children interacted in the adult world, sharing the same world of work and play. By the age of seven or eight, they were treated as if they had the same mental capacities for understanding and feeling as their adult counterparts.

The lack of awareness of the particular nature of childhood and the full participation of children in adult life is associated with the nature of the family and the community. Ariès depicted the medieval community as intense; no one was left alone because the high density of social life made isolation virtually impossible. This sociability practically nullified the reality and the conceptualization of the private home and the private family. The distinct sense of privacy so characteristic of modern-day families was absent.

Ariès saw the transition to the modern conceptualization of the child beginning to emerge during the seventeenth century. Economic changes led to a revival of interest in education. This, in turn, introduced the idea that a period of special preparation was necessary before individuals could assume their place as adults. Children began to be treated differently, they were expected to behave differently, and their nature was viewed as being different. Children were now coddled, and a greater interest and concern for their moral welfare and development became common.

Ariès emphasized that this emerging concept of childhood developed and was given expression in the emergence of the bourgeois family. He argued that, from a relatively insignificant institution during the Middle Ages, there developed a growing belief in the virtue of the intimate and private nuclear family. The rise of the private family and the growth of the sentimental bonds among its members consequently came about at the expense of the public community.

The continued inward development of the family and its creation of a private sphere of life removed from the outside world was intertwined with the increased importance given to children. The outside community came to be viewed with suspicion and indifference. Proceeding into the industrial era, the family began to withdraw its nonproductive members, women and children, from involvement with the surrounding community. The increased division of labor of family members and the consequent isolation of women and children within the home resulted.

Here again, the broad historical survey of Western patterns of parenthood and child-rearing needs to be modified through an examination of the experiences of racial ethnic families in the United States. In Chapter Six, "Patterns of Parenthood, Childhood, and Adolescence," Patricia Hill Collins (Reading 16) does just that. Collins observes that motherhood must be seen both in its historical context and in the context of the interlocking structures of race, class, and gender. Collins argues that the feminist perspective has often failed to recognize the diversity of patterns of motherhood. It takes the experience of white, middle-class women as universal. This has led to two fundamental assumptions on motherhood that are erroneous. The first is the belief that work and family have always been separate spheres. The second relates to women's identity conceptualizations as seeing themselves in search of personal autonomy. Let's briefly summarize Collins's line of thought here.

The "separate spheres" doctrine relegated women to household work characterized by childbearing, child rearing, and domestic labor, or "reproductive work." This model was based on patriarchal authority in which men's economic activities allowed them to control the family. Women, while having few legal rights, were protected under the umbrella of patriarchy in their designated roles as wives, mothers, and daughters. This model was essentially the pattern prevalent among white middle-class women. Collins observes that the circumstances of racial ethnic women were quite different.

Similarly, women of color were concerned with working for the physical survival of themselves, their children, and their community. Motherhood was not centered on the search for personal autonomy (as with their white middle-class counterparts) but with helping to teach their children how to construct their individual and collective racial identity to help them survive in an often hostile cultural climate. Collins's social-historical analysis of Native American, African American, Hispanic, and Asian American patterns of motherhood demonstrates the necessity for the recontextualization of motherhood from multiple perspectives. This is what she means by the title of her essay "Shifting the Center."

Elaine Bell Kaplan (Reading 17) examines the relationship between Black teenage mothers and their mothers. She reports in her study of twenty-two teenage mothers that they felt that their mothers did not support them emotionally. Their mothers, in turn, concurred in this belief. They felt that their daughters' early motherhood reflected badly on them and threatened their held moral values. In this essay we are shown, once again, how relational problems must be seen through linking socioeconomic conditions with gender, race, and class inequalities.

We opened this part of the book by discussing how age conceptualizations reflect conceptualizations of the family. Reading 18, by Frances K. Goldscheider and Calvin Goldscheider, discusses how young American adults are increasingly setting up a household alone or with housemates. This is a relatively new pattern. Until recently, children lived in their parents' homes until they were married and ready to start their own families. Why this change has occurred is the center of concern for Goldscheider and Goldscheider.

To provide background for this reading it would be advisable to say something about the changing nature of adolescence and young adulthood. In the eighteenth and nineteenth centuries, the American family acted as a self-sufficient economic unit. Boys and girls were involved in work activities on the farm and in the home. They participated in the growing and harvesting of crops, the storing and cooking of foods, the caring of domestic animals, and the making of clothes. In short, the children were an economic asset contributing to the economic well-being of the family. Children not only were able to pay their own way by working but also were expected to be the chief source of their parents' support when they got older. There was no government old-age assistance such as Social Security.

By the end of the nineteenth century, the family economy was disappearing, giving way to a cash industrial economy. Industrialization meant the loss of economic participation by young people in the labor force. Having once assumed economically viable positions in the family, they now can no longer be counted on to provide such an economic resource and are instead an economic liability.

This historical change in the character of childhood and adolescence captures our attention. Modern children and adolescents are faced by a dilemma: the desire for the development of personal freedom and autonomy in the face of dependency situations, both in the home and in social institutions. Goldscheider and Goldscheider are concerned with whether living independently from parents well before marriage represents a new life course requirement. They observe how independent living may come at the expense of financial investment in education and family responsibilities. Independent living may also reflect changes in the parent-child relationship and roles in the parental home. Finally, Goldscheider and Goldscheider examine whether independent living replaces marriage as the symbol of adult status. Differences in nonfamily living are examined in the contexts of the communities that these groups of young adults represent and the family attitudes, values, and environments that they share. The authors consider Asian Americans, African Americans, and Hispanics as well as fundamentalist Protestants, Catholics, and Jews, and they compare young men and women as they integrate marriage and residential independence into their transition into adulthood.

Chapter Seven, "The Family and the Elderly," is concerned with the nature of generational relationships between the elderly and the family. Earlier, we commented that the universal tendency has been for elders to exercise control over younger family members. Indeed in more traditional societies that are less susceptible to social change, the elderly have been seen as the repositories of strategic knowledge and religious custom, controlling the ownership of property, and having major influence over kinship and extended family rights and obligations. But, with the movement toward modernization, individualism, and the private family there has been a significant decline in the influence, power, and prestige that the elderly have in the family. The elderly have relatively little importance in an industrial society that emphasizes individual welfare, social and economic progress and change, and that is opposed to the ideology of family continuity and tradition.

The first article in this chapter examines the elderly's loss of family importance and high status by looking at one ethnic group that at one time and place epitomized the crucial and significant role of the elderly in the family. Florentius Chan (Reading 19) reports on the experiences of elderly Asian and Pacific Islanders, many of whom are foreign-born and are newly arrived immigrants or refugees. The popular image is of the veneration of elders by Asians and Pacific Islanders. However, as Chan observes, problems of cultural adjustment and the shattering of support networks in the United States result in very disruptive family and social patterns for these people.

The significant decline in the mortality rate, especially in the last decades of the twentieth century, has fundamentally changed the character of the relationship between elders and their mature children, grandchildren, and great-grandchildren. This decline has given contemporary grandparenthood (the children of the elders) new meaning associated with the rise of the four-generation family. This demographic change has greatly increased the potential for family interaction across more than two generations.

The relationships between members of these different generations can be quite problematic. Some of the difficulty stems from the fact that the great-grandparent generation is composed of old people whom society views as residuals and somewhat useless. Our society has deprived old people both of responsibility and of function. By so doing, it has provided the basis for the roleless position of the elderly.

Often the one place that old people can find refuge and have a role is within the family. Yet that role is not clearly defined, and often the great-grandparent generation is found to strain the emotional as well as economic resources of their children in the family. Particularly caught in the middle is this grandparent generation. Known in the popular literature as the "sandwich generation," they are sandwiched between their children and their parents, both of whom need care. They often are asked to assist their children as they enter early adulthood and married and family life, while at the same time they are expected to care for their aged parents. People in this sandwich generation are experiencing stresses associated with their own stage in life and the family life cycle. Many are contemplating their own aging as they face retirement and perhaps their own financial and health problems. This generation has the brunt of generational responsibility thrust on it.

Women within the sandwich generation are the ones who often take on a disproportionate share of the time and emotional involvement with their elderly parents. For many of them, the "mommy track" is being replaced by the "daughter track." The shift is from balancing work, career, and child rearing to balancing work, career, and elder-caring. Indeed, these women are often working mothers and caretakers. They provide both for their parents and for their children while often holding down a full-time job.

However, what happens to the elderly when their adult children cannot take care of them and when they no longer can take care of themselves? This is the concern of Reading 20. The editor of this anthology, Mark Hutter, reports on a family situation when this occurs. His analysis goes beyond the examination of the relationship of adult children and their parents to an examination of the web of relationships that emerge when a paid health care worker—the "intimate stranger"—enters the picture.

REFERENCES

Ariès, Philippe. 1962. *Centuries of Childhood: A Social History of the Family.* New York: Knopf.

6

Patterns of Parenthood, Childhood, and Adolescence

Reading 16   Shifting the Center: Race, Class, and Feminist Theorizing About Motherhood*

PATRICIA HILL COLLINS

I dread to see my children grow, I know not their fate. Where the white boy has every opportunity and protection, mine will have few opportunities and no protection. It does not matter how good or wise my children may be, they are colored.

—an anonymous African-American mother
in 1904, reported in Lerner, 1972 p. 158.

For Native American, African-American, Hispanic, and Asian-American women, motherhood cannot be analyzed in isolation from its context. Motherhood occurs in specific historical situations framed by interlocking structures of race, class, and gender, where the sons and daughters of white mothers have "every opportunity and protection," and the "colored" daughters and sons of racial ethnic mothers "know not their fate." Racial domination and economic exploitation profoundly shape the mothering context, not only for the ethnic women in the United States, but for all women.[1]

Despite the significance of race and class, feminist theorizing routinely minimizes their im-portance. In this sense, feminist theorizing about motherhood has not been immune to the decontextualization of Western social thought overall.[2] While many dimensions of motherhood's context are ignored, the exclusion of race and/or class from feminist theorizing generally (Spelman 1988), and from feminist theorizing about motherhood specifically, merit special attention.[3]

Much feminist theorizing about motherhood assumes that male domination in the political economy and the household is the driving force in family life, and that understanding the struggle for individual autonomy in the face of such domination is central to understanding motherhood (Esenstein 1983).[4] Several guiding principles

*Collins, Patricia Hill. 1986. "Shifting the Center: Race, Class, and Feminist Theorizing About Motherhood." Pp. 45–65, from *Mothering: Ideology, Experience, and Agency*, edited by Evelyn Nakano Glenn et al., New York: Routledge. Reprinted by permission of the author.

frame such analyses. First, such theories posit a dichotomous split between the public sphere of economic and political discourse and the private sphere of family and household responsibilities. This juxtaposition of a public, political economy to a private, noneconomic and apolitical domestic household allows work and family to be seen as separate institutions. Second, reserving the public sphere for men as a "male" domain leaves the private domestic sphere as a "female" domain. Gender roles become tied to the dichotomous constructions of these two basic societal institutions—men work and women take care of families. Third, the public/private dichotomy separating the family/household from the paid labor market shapes sex-segregated gender roles within the private sphere of the family. The archetypal white, middle-class nuclear family divides family life into two oppositional spheres—the "male" sphere of economic providing and the "female" sphere of affective nurturing, mainly mothering. This normative family household ideally consists of a working father who earns enough to allow his spouse and dependent children to withdraw from the paid labor force. Due in large part to their superior earning power, men as workers and fathers exert power over women in the labor market and in families. Finally, the struggle for individual autonomy in the face of a controlling oppressive, "public" society, or the father as patriarch, comprises the main human enterprise.[5] Successful adult males achieve this autonomy. Women, children, and less successful males, namely those who are working-class or from racial ethnic groups, are seen as dependent persons, as less autonomous, and therefore as fitting objects for elite male domination. Within the nuclear family, this struggle for autonomy takes the form of increasing opposition to the mother, the individual responsible for socializing children by these guiding principles (Chodorow 1978; Flax 1978).

Placing the experiences of women of color in the center of feminist theorizing about motherhood demonstrates how emphasizing the issue of father as patriarch in a decontextualized nuclear family distorts the experiences of women in alternative family structures with quite different political economies. While male domination certainly has been an important theme for racial ethnic women in the United States, gender inequality has long worked in tandem with racial domination and economic exploitation. Since work and family have rarely functioned as dichotomous spheres for women of color, examining racial ethnic women's experiences reveals how these two spheres actually are interwoven (Glenn 1985; Dill 1988; Collins 1990).

For women of color, the subjective experience of mothering/motherhood is inextricably linked to the sociocultural concern of racial ethnic communities—one does not exist without the other. Whether because of the labor exploitation of African-American women under slavery and its ensuing tenant farm system, the political conquest of Native American women during European acquisition of land, or exclusionary immigration policies applied to Asian-Americans and Hispanics, women of color have performed motherwork that challenges social constructions of work and family as separate spheres, of male and female gender roles as similarly dichotomized, and of the search for autonomy as the guiding human quest. "Women's reproductive labor—that is, feeding, clothing, and psychologically supporting the male wage earner and nurturing and socializing the next generation—is seen as work on behalf of the family as a whole, rather than as work benefiting men in particular," observes Asian-American sociologist Evelyn Nakano Glenn (1986, p. 192). The locus of conflict lies outside the household, as women and their families engage in collective effort to create and maintain family life in the face of forces that undermine family integrity. But this "reproductive labor" or "motherwork" goes beyond ensuring the survival of one's own biological children or those of one's family. This type of motherwork recognizes that individual survival, empowerment, and identity require group survival empowerment, and identity.

In describing her relationship with her "Grandmother," Marilou Awiakta, a Native American poet and feminist theorist, captures the essence of motherwork.

> *Putting my arms around the Grandmother, I lay my head on her shoulder. Through touch we exchange sorrow, despair that anything really changes.*

Awiakta senses the power of the Grandmother and of the motherwork that mothers and grandmothers do.

> *"But from the presence of her arms I also feel the stern, beautiful power that flows from all the Grandmothers, as it flows from our mountains themselves. It says, "Dry your tears. Get up. Do for yourselves or do without. Work for the day to come."* (1988, p. 127)

Awiakta's passage places women and motherwork squarely in the center of what are typically seen as disjunctures, the place between human and nature, between private and public, between oppression and liberation. I use the term "motherwork" to soften the existing dichotomies in feminist theorizing about motherhood that posit rigid distinctions between private and public, family and work, the individual and the collective, identity as individual autonomy and identity growing from the collective self-determination of one's group. Racial ethnic women's mothering and work experiences occur at the boundaries demarking these dualities. "Work for the day to come," is motherwork, whether it is on behalf of one's own biological children, or for the children of one's own racial ethnic community, or to preserve the earth for those children who are yet unborn. The space that this motherwork occupies promises to shift our thinking about motherhood itself.

SHIFTING THE CENTER: WOMEN OF COLOR AND MOTHERWORK

What themes might emerge if issues of race and class generally, and understanding of racial ethnic women's motherwork specifically, became central to feminist theorizing about motherhood? Centering feminist theorizing on the concerns of white, middle-class women leads to two problematic assumptions. The first is that a relative degree of economic security exists for mothers and their children. The second is that all women enjoy the racial privilege that allows them to see themselves primarily as individuals in search of personal autonomy, instead of members of racial ethnic groups struggling for power. It is these assumptions that allow feminist theorists to concentrate on themes such as the connections among mothering, aggression, and death, the effects of maternal isolation on mother-child relationships within nuclear family households, maternal sexuality, relationships among family members, all-powerful mothers as conduits for gender oppression, and the possibilities of an idealized motherhood freed from patriarchy (Chodorow and Contratto 1982; Eisenstein 1983).

While these issues merit investigation, centering feminist theorizing about motherhood in the ideas and experiences of African-American, Native American, Hispanic, and Asian-American women might yield markedly different themes (Andersen 1988; Brown 1989). This stance is to be distinguished from one that merely adds racial ethnic women's experiences to preexisting feminist theories, without considering how these experiences challenge those theories (Spelman 1988). Involving much more than simply the consulting of existing social science sources, the placing of ideas and experiences of women of color in the center of analysis requires invoking a different epistemology. We must distinguish between what has been said about subordinated groups in the dominant discourse, and what such groups might say about themselves if given the opportunity. Personal narratives, autobiographical statements, poetry, fiction, and other personalized statements have all been used by women of color to express self-defined standpoints on mothering and motherhood. Such knowledge reflects the authentic standpoint of subordinated groups. Therefore, placing these sources in the center and supplementing them with statistics, historical material, and other knowledge produced to justify the interests of ruling elites should create new themes and angles of vision (Smith 1990).[6]

Specifying the contours of racial ethnic women's motherwork promises to point the way toward richer feminist theorizing about motherhood. Themes of survival, power, and identity form the bedrock and reveal how racial ethnic women in the United States encounter and fashion motherwork. That is to understand the importance of working for the physical survival of children and community, the dialectical nature of power and powerlessness in structuring mothering patterns, and the significance of self-definition in constructing individual and collective racial identity is to grasp the three core themes characterizing the experiences of Native American, African-American, Hispanic and Asian-American women. It is also to suggest

how feminist theorizing about motherhood might be shifted if different voices became central in feminist discourse.

MOTHERWORK AND PHYSICAL SURVIVAL

When we are not physically starving we have the luxury to realize psychic and emotional starvation. (Cherrie Moraga 1979, p. 29.)

Physical survival is assumed for children who are white and middle-class. The choice to thus examine their psychic and emotional well-being and that of their mothers appears rational. The children of women of color, many of whom are "physically starving," have no such choices however. Racial ethnic children's lives have long been held in low regard: African-American children face an infant mortality rate twice that for white infants; and approximately one-third of Hispanic children and one-half of African-American children who survive infancy live in poverty. In addition racial ethnic children often live in harsh urban environments where drugs, crime, industrial pollutants, and violence threaten their survival. Children in rural environments often fare no better. Winona LaDuke, for example, reports that Native Americans on reservations often must use contaminated water. And on the Pine Ridge Sioux Reservation in 1979, thirty-eight percent of all pregnancies resulted in miscarriages before the fifth month, or in excessive hemorrhaging. Approximately sixty-five percent of all children born suffered breathing problems caused by underdeveloped lungs and jaundice (1988, p. 63).

Struggles to foster the survival of Native American, Hispanic, Asian-American, and African-American families and communities by ensuring the survival of children comprise a fundamental dimension of racial ethnic women's motherwork. African-American women's fiction contains numerous stories of mothers fighting for the physical survival both of their own biological children and of those of the larger Black community.[7] "Don't care how much death it is in the land, I got to make preparations for my baby to live!" proclaims Mariah Upshur, the African-American heroine of Sara Wright's 1986 novel *This Child's Gonna Live* (p. 143). Like Mariah Upshur, the harsh climates which confront racial ethnic children require that their mothers "make preparations for their babies to live" as a central feature of their motherwork.

Yet, like all deep cultural themes, the theme of motherwork for physical survival contains contradictory elements. On the one hand, racial ethnic women's motherwork for individual and community survival has been essential. Without women's motherwork, communities would not survive, and by definition, women of color themselves would not survive. On the other hand, this work often extracts a high cost for large numbers of women. There is loss of individual autonomy and there is submersion of individual growth for the benefit of the group. While this dimension of motherwork remains essential, the question of women doing more than their fair share of such work for individual and community development merits open debate.

The histories of family-based labor have been shaped by racial ethnic women's motherwork for survival and the types of mothering relationships that ensued. African-American, Asian-American, Native American and Hispanic women have all worked and contributed to family economic well-being (Glenn 1985; Dill 1988). Much of their experiences with motherwork, in fact, stem from the work they performed as children. The commodification of children of color, starting with the enslavement of African children who were legally "owned" as property, to the subsequent treatment of children as units of labor in agricultural work, family businesses, and industry, has been a major theme shaping motherhood for women of color. Beginning in slavery and continuing into the post-World War II period, Black children were put to work at young ages in the fields of Southern agriculture. Sara Brooks began full-time work in the fields at the age of eleven, and remembers, "we never was lazy cause we used to really work. We used to work like men. Oh, fight sometime, fuss sometime, but worked on" (Collins 1990, p. 54).

Black and Hispanic children in contemporary migrant farm families make similar contributions to their family's economy. "I musta been almost eight when I started following the crops," remembers Jessie de la Cruz, a Mexican-American mother with six grown children. "Every winter, up north. I was on the end of the row of prunes, taking care of my younger brother and sister. They would help me fill up the cans and put 'em in a box while the rest of the family was picking the whole row" (de la Cruz 1980, p. 168). Asian-American children spend long hours working in family businesses, child labor practices that have earned Asian Americans the dubious distinction being "model minorities." More recently, the family-based labor of undocumented racial ethnic immigrants, often mother-child units doing piecework for the garment industry, recalls the sweatshop conditions confronting turn-of-the-century European immigrants.

A certain degree of maternal isolation from members of the dominant group characterizes the preceding mother-child units. For women of color working along with their children, such isolation is more appropriately seen as reflecting a placement in racially and class stratified labor systems than as a result of a patriarchal system. The unit may be isolated, but the work performed by the mother-child unit closely ties the mothering experiences to wider political and economic issues. Children, too, learn to see their work and that of their mother's not as isolated from wider society, but as essential to their family's survival. Moreover, in the case of family agricultural labor or family businesses, women and children work alongside men, often performing the same work. If isolation occurs, the family, not the mother-child unit, is the focus of such isolation.

Children working in close proximity to their mothers receive distinctive types of mothering. Asian-American children working in urban family businesses, for example, report long days filled almost exclusively with work and school. In contrast, the sons and daughters of African-American sharecroppers and migrant farm children of all backgrounds have less access to educational opportunities. "I think the longest time I went to school was two months in one place," remembers Jessie de la Cruz. "I attended, I think, about forty-five schools. When my parents or my brothers didn't find work, we wouldn't attend school because we weren't sure of staying there. So I missed a lot of school (de la Cruz 1980, p. 167–8)." It was only in the 1950s in fact, that Southern school districts stopped the practice of closing segregated Black schools during certain times of the year so that Black children could work.

Work that separated women of color from their children also framed the mothering relationship. Until the 1960s, large numbers of African-American, Hispanic, and Asian-American women worked in domestic service. Even though women worked long hours to ensure their children's physical survival, that same work ironically denied mothers access to their children. Different institutional arrangements emerged in these mothers' respective communities, to resolve the tension between maternal separation due to employment and the needs of dependent children. The extended family structure in African-American communities endured as a flexible institution that mitigated some of the effects of maternal separation. Grandmothers are highly revered in Black communities, often because grandmothers function as primary caretakers of their daughters' and daughter-in-laws' children (Collins 1990). In contrast, exclusionary immigration policies that mitigated against intergenerational family units in the United States led Chinese-American and Japanese-American families to make other arrangements (Dill 1988).

Some mothers are clearly defeated by the demands for incessant labor they must perform to ensure their children's survival. The magnitude of their motherwork overwhelms them. But others, even while appearing to be defeated, manage to pass on the meaning of motherwork for survival to their children. African-American feminist June Jordan remembers her perceptions of her mother's work:

As a child I noticed the sadness of my mother as she sat alone in the kitchen at night.... Her woman's work never won permanent victories of any kind. It never enlarged the universe of her imagination or her power to influence what happened beyond the front door of our house. Her women's work never tickled her to laugh or shout or dance. (Jordan 1985, p. 105)

But Jordan also sees her mother's work as being essential to individual and community survival.

She did raise me to respect her way of offering love and to believe that hard work is often the irreducible factor for survival, not something to avoid. Her woman's work produced a reli-

able home base where I could pursue the privileges of books and music. Her woman's work invented the potential for a completely new kind of work for us, the next generation of Black women: huge, rewarding hard work demanded by the huge, different ambitions that her perfect confidence in us engendered. (Jordan 1985, p. 105)

MOTHERWORK AND POWER

Jessie de la Cruz, a Mexican-American migrant farm worker, experienced firsthand the struggle for empowerment facing racial ethnic women whose daily motherwork centers on issues of survival.

How can I write down how I felt when I was a little child and my grandmother used to cry with us 'cause she didn't have enough food to give us? Because my brother was going barefooted and he was cryin' because he wasn't used to going without shoes? How can I describe that? I can't describe when my little girl died because I didn't have money for a doctor. And never had any teaching on caring for sick babies. Living out in labor camps. How can I describe that? (Jessie de la Cruz 1980, p. 177)

A dialectical relationship exists between efforts of racial orders to mold the institution of motherhood to serve the interests of elites, in this case, racial elites, and efforts on the part of subordinated groups to retain power over motherhood so that it serves the legitimate needs of their communities (Collins 1990). African-American,

Asian-American, Hispanic, and Native American women have long been preoccupied with patterns of maternal power and powerlessness because their mothering experiences have been profoundly affected by this dialectical process. But instead of emphasizing maternal power in dialectical with father as patriarch (Chodorow 1978; Rich 1996), or with male dominance in general (Ferguson 1989), women of color are concerned with their power and powerlessness within an array of social institutions that frame their lives.

Racial ethnic women's struggles for maternal empowerment have resolved around three main themes. First is the struggle for control over their own bodies in order to preserve choice over whether to become mothers at all. The ambiguous politics of caring for unplanned children has long shaped African-American women's motherwork. For example, the widespread institutionalized rape of Black women by white men, both during slavery and in the segregated South, created countless biracial children who had to be absorbed into African-American families and communities (Davis 1981). The range of skin colors and hair textures in contemporary African-American communities bears mute testament to the powerlessness of African-American women in controlling this dimension of motherhood.

For many women of color, choosing to become a mother challenges institutional policies that encourage white, middle-class women to reproduce, and discourage and even penalize low-income racial ethnic women from doing so (Davis 1981). Rita Silk-Nauni, an incarcerated Native American woman, writes of the difficulties she encountered in trying to have additional children. She loved her son so much that she only left him to go to work. "I tried having more after him and couldn't," she laments.

"I went to a specialist and he thought I had been fixed when I had my son.

He said I would have to have surgery in order to give birth again. The surgery was so expensive but I thought I could make a way even if I had to work 24 hours a day. Now that I'm here, I know I'll never have that chance." (Brant 1988, p. 94).

Like Silk-Nauni, Puerto Rican and African-American women have long had to struggle with issues of sterilization abuse (Davis 1981). More recent efforts to manipulate the fertility of women dependent on public assistance speaks to the continued salience of this issue.

A second dimension of racial ethnic women's struggles for maternal empowerment concerns the process of keeping the children that are wanted, whether they were planned for or not. For mothers like Jessie de la Cruz whose "little girl died" because she "didn't have money for a doctor," maternal separation from one's children becomes a much more salient issue than maternal isolation with one's children within an allegedly private nuclear family. Physical and/or psychological separation of mothers and children, designed to disempower individuals, forms the basis of a systematic effort to disempower racial ethnic communities.

For both Native American and African-American mothers, situations of conquest introduced this dimension of the struggle for maternal empowerment. In her fictional account of a Native American mother's loss of her children in 1890, Brant explores the pain of maternal separation.

It has been two days since they came and took the children away. My body is greatly chilled. All our blankets have been used to bring me warmth. The women keep the fire blazing. The men sit. They talk among them-

selves. We are frightened by this sudden child-stealing. We signed papers, the agent said. This gave them rights to take our babies. It is good for them, the agent said. It will make them civilized (1988, p. 101).

A legacy of conquest has meant that Native American mothers on "reservations" confront intrusive government institutions such as the Bureau of Indian Affairs in deciding the fate of their children. For example, the long-standing policy of removing Native American children from their homes and housing them in reservation boarding schools can be seen as efforts to disempower Native American mothers. For African-American women, slavery was a situation where owners controlled numerous dimensions of their children's lives. Black children could be sold at will, whipped, or even killed, all without any recourse by their mothers. In such a situation, getting to keep one's children and raise them accordingly fosters empowerment.

A third dimension of racial ethnic women's struggles for empowerment concerns the pervasive efforts by the dominant group to control the children's minds. In her short story, "A Long Memory," Beth Brant juxtaposes the loss felt by a Native American mother in 1890 whose son and daughter had been forcibly removed by white officials, to the loss that she felt in 1978 upon losing her daughter in a custody hearing. "Why do they want our babies?" queries the turn-of-the-century mother. "They want our power. They take our children to remove the inside of them. Our power" (Brant 1988, p. 105). This mother recognizes that the future of the Native American way of life lies in retaining the power to define that worldview through the education of children. By forbidding children to speak their native languages, and in other ways encourage children to assimilate into Anglo culture, external agencies challenge the power of mothers to raise their children as they see fit.

Schools controlled by the dominant group comprise one important location where this dimension of the struggle for maternal empowerment occurs. In contrast to white, middle-class children, whose educational experiences affirm their mothers' middle class values, culture, and authority, the educational experiences of African-American, Hispanic, Asian-American and Native American children typically denigrate their mothers' perspective. For example, the struggles over bilingual education in Hispanic communities are about much more than retaining Spanish as a second language. Speaking the language of one's childhood is a way of retaining the entire culture and honoring the mother teaching that culture (Morago 1979; Anzaldua 1987).

Jenny Yamoto describes the stress of continuing to negotiate with schools regarding her Black-Japanese sons.

> *I've noticed that depending on which parent, Black mom or Asian dad, goes to school open house, my oldest son's behavior is interpreted as disruptive and irreverent, or assertive and clever…. I resent their behavior being defined and even expected on the basis of racial biases their teachers may struggle with or hold…. I don't have the time or energy to constantly change and challenge their teacher's and friends' misperceptions. I only go after them when the children really seem to be seriously threatened. (Yamoto 1988, p. 24).*

In confronting each of these three dimensions of their struggles, for empowerment, racial ethnic women are not powerless in the face of racial and class oppression. Being grounded in a strong, dynamic, indigenous culture can be central in these women's social constructions of motherhood. Depending on their access to traditional culture, they invoke alternative sources of power.[8]

"Equality, per se, may have a different meaning for Indian women and Indian people," suggests Kate Shanley. "That difference begins with personal and tribal sovereignty—the right to be legally recognized as people empowered to determine our own destinies" (1988, p. 214). Personal sovereignty involves the struggle to promote the survival of a social structure whose organizational principles represent notions of family and motherhood different from those of the mainstream. "The nuclear family has little relevance to Indian women," observes Shanley. "In fact, in many ways, mainstream feminists now are striving to redefine family and community in a way that Indian women have long known" (p. 214).

African-American mothers can draw upon an Afrocentric tradition where motherhood of varying types, whether bloodmother, othermother, or community othermother, can be invoked as a symbol of power. Many Black women receive respect and recognition within their local communities for innovative and practical approaches not only to mothering their own "blood" children, but also to being othermothers to the children in their extended family networks, and those in the community overall. Black women's involvement in fostering Black community development forms the basis of this community-based power. In local African-American communities, community othermothers can become identified as powerful figures through their work in furthering the community's well-being (Collins 1990).

Despite policies of dominant institutions that place racial ethnic mothers in positions where they appear less powerful to their children, mothers and children empower themselves by understanding each other's position and relying on each other's strengths. In many cases, children, especially daughters, bond with their mothers instead of railing against them as symbols of patriarchal power. Cherríe Moraga describes the impact that her mother had on her. Because she was repeatedly removed from school in order to work, by prevailing standards Moraga's mother would be considered largely illiterate. But she was also a fine storyteller, and found ways to empower herself within dominant institutions. "I would go with my mother to fill out job applications for her, or write checks for her at the supermarket," Moraga recounts.

> We would have the scenario worked out ahead of time. My mother would sign the check before we'd get to the store. Then, as we'd approach the checkstand, she would say—within earshot of the cashier—"oh, honey, you go 'head and make out the check,'" as if she couldn't be bothered with such an insignificant detail. (1979, p. 28)

Like Cherríe Moraga and her mother, racial ethnic women's motherwork involves collaborating to empower mothers and children within structures that oppress.

MOTHERWORK AND IDENTITY

> Please help me find out who I am. My mother was Indian, but we were taken from her and put in foster homes. They were white and didn't want to tell us about our mother. I have a name and maybe a place of birth. Do you think you can help me? (Brant 1988, p. 9)

Like this excerpt from a letter to the editor, the theme of lost racial ethnic identity and the struggle to maintain a sense of self and community many of the stories, poetry and narratives in Beth Brant's volume, *A Gathering of Spirit*. Carol Lee Sanchez offers another view of the impact of the loss of self "Radicals look at reservation Indians and get very upset about their poverty conditions," observes Sanchez.

> But poverty to us is not the same thing as poverty is to you. Our poverty is that we can't be who we are. We can't hunt or fish or grow our food because our basic resources and the right to use them in traditional ways are denied us. (Brant 1988, p. 165)

Racial ethnic women's motherwork reflects the tensions inherent in trying to foster a meaningful racial identity in children within a society that denigrates people of color. The racial privilege enjoyed by white, middle-class women makes unnecessary this complicated dimension of the mothering tradition of women of color. While white children can be prepared to fight racial oppression, their survival does not depend on gaining these skills. Their racial identity is validated by their schools, the media, and other social institutions. White children are socialized into their rightful place in systems of racial privilege. Racial ethnic women have no such guarantees for their children; their children must first be taught to survive in systems that oppress them. Moreover, this survival must not come at the expense of self-esteem. Thus, a dialectical relationship exists between systems of racial oppression designed to strip subordinated groups of a sense of personal identity and a sense of collective peoplehood, and the cultures of resistance extant in various racial ethnic groups that resist the oppression. For women of color, motherwork for identity occurs at this critical juncture (Collins 1990).

"Through our mothers, the culture gave us mixed messages," observes Mexican-American poet Gloria Anzaldua. "Which was it to be—strong, or submissive, rebellious or conforming?" (1987, p. 18). Thus women of color's motherwork requires reconciling contradictory needs concerning identity. Preparing children to cope with and survive within systems of racial oppression is extremely difficult because the pressures for children of racial ethnic groups to assimilate are pervasive. In order to compel women of color to participate in their children's assimilation, dominant institutions promulgate ideologies that belittle people of color. Negative controlling images infuse the worlds of male and female children of color (Tajima 1989; Collins 1990; Green 1990). Native American girls are encouraged to see themselves as "Pocahontases" or "squaws"; Asian-American girls as "geisha girls" or "Suzy Wongs"; Hispanic girls as "Madonnas" or "hot-blooded whores"; and African-American girls as "mammies", "matriarchs" and "prostitutes." Girls of all groups are told that their lives cannot be complete without a male partner, and that their educational and career aspirations must always be subordinated to their family obligations.

This push toward assimilation is part of a larger effort to a second dimension of the mothering tradition involves equipping children with skills to confront this contradiction and to challenge systems of racial oppression. Girls who become women believing that they are only capable of being maids and prostitutes cannot contribute to racial ethnic women's motherwork.

Mothers make varying choices in negotiating the complicated relationship of preparing children to fit into, yet resist, systems of racial domination. Some mothers remain powerless in the face of external forces that foster their children's assimilation and subsequent alienation from their families and communities. Through fiction, Native American author Beth Brant again explores the grief felt by a mother whose children had been taken away to live among whites. A letter arrives giving news of her missing children.

This letter is from two strangers with the names Martha and Daniel. They say they are learning civilized ways. Daniel works in the fields, growing food for the school. Martha is being taught to sew aprons. She will be going to live with the schoolmasters wife. She will be a live-in girl. What is live-in girl? I shake my head. The words sound the same to me. I am afraid of Martha and Daniel. These strangers who know my name. (Brant 1988, pp. 102–103)

Other mothers become unwitting conduits of the dominant ideology. Gloria Anzalduce (1987, p. 16) asks:

How many time have I heard mothers and mothers-in-law tell their sons to beat their wives for not obeying them, for being hociconas *(big mouths), for being* callajeras *(going to visit and gossip with neighbors), for expecting their husbands to help with the rearing of children and the housework, for wanting to be something other than housewives?*

Some mothers encourage their children to fit in, for reasons of survival. "My mother, nursed in the folds of a town that once christened its black babies Lee, after Robert E., and Jackson, after

Stonewall, raised me on a dangerous generation's old belief," remembers African-American author Marita Golden.

> *Because of my dark brown complex-ion, she warned me against wearing browns or yellow and reds…and every summer I was admonished not to play in the sun "cause you gonna have to get a light husband anyway, for the sake of your children."* *(Golden 1983, p. 24)*

To Cherrie Moraga's mother,

> *On a basic economic level, being Chicana meant being "less." It was through my mother's desire to protect her children from poverty and illiter-acy that we became "anglocized"; the more effectively we could pass in the white world, the better guaran-teed our future. (1979, p. 28).*

Despite their mothers' good intentions, the costs to children taught to submit to racist and sexist ideologies can be high. Raven, a Native Ameri-can woman, looks back on her childhood:

> *I've been raised in white man's world and was forbade more or less to con-verse with Indian people. As my mother wanted me to be educated and live a good life, free from pov-erty. I lived a life of loneliness. Today I am desperate to know my people. (Brant 1988, p. 221)*

To avoid poverty, Raven's mother did what she thought best, but ultimately, Raven experienced the poverty of not being able to be who she was.

Still other mothers transmit sophisticated skills to their children, enabling them to appear to be submissive while at the same time to be able to challenge inequality. Willi Coleman's mother used a Saturday-night hair-combing rit-ual to impart a Black women's standpoint to her daughters:

> *Except for special occasions mama came home from work early on Sat-urdays. She spent six days a week mopping, waxing and dusting other women's houses and keeping out of reach of other women's husbands. Saturday nights were reserved for "taking care of them girls'" hair and the telling of stories. Some of which included a recitation of what she had endured and how she had triumphed over "folks that were lower than dirt" and "no-good snakes in the grass." She combed, patted, twisted and talked, saying things which would have embarrassed or shamed her at other times. (Coleman 1987, p. 34)*

Historian Elsa Barkley Brown captures this del-icate balance that racial ethnic mothers negotia-te. Brown points out that her mother's behavior demonstrated the "need to teach me to live my life one way and, at the same time, to provide all the tools I would need to live it quite differently" (1989, p. 929).

For women of color, the struggle to main-tain an independent racial identity has taken many forms: All reveal varying solutions to the dialectical relationship between institutions that would deny their children their humanity and in-stitutions that would affirm their children's right to exist as self-defined people. Like Willi Cole-man's mother, African-American women draw upon a long-standing Afrocentric feminist worldview, emphasizing the importance of self-definition, self-reliance, and the necessity of demanding respect from others (Terborg-Penn 1986; Collins 1990).

Racial ethnic cultures, themselves, do not always help to support women's self-definition. Poet and essayist Gloria Anzaldua, for example, challenges many of the ideas in Hispanic cultures concerning women. "Though I'll defend my race and culture when they are attacked by non*mexicanos*,... I abhor some of my culture's ways, how it cripples its women, *como burras, our strengths used against us*" (1987, p. 21). Anzaldua offers a trenchant analysis of the ways in which the Spanish conquest of Native Americans fragmented women's identity and produced three symbolic "mothers." *La Virgen de Guadalupe,* perhaps the single most potent religious, political and cultural image of the Chicano people, represents the virgin mother who cares for and nurtures an oppressed people. *La Chingada (Malinche)* represents the raped mother, all but abandoned. A combination of the other two, *La Llorona* symbolizes the mother who seeks her lost children. "Ambiguity surrounds the symbols of these three 'Our Mothers,'" claims Anzaldua.

In part, the true identity of all three has been subverted—Guadalupe, to make us docile and enduring, la Chingada, to make us ashamed of our Indian side, and la Llorona to make us a long-suffering people. 1987, p. 31)

For Anzaldua, the Spanish conquest, which brought racism and economic subordination to Indian people, and created a new mixed-race Hispanic people, simultaneously devalued women:

No, I do not buy all the myths of the tribe into which I was born. I can understand why the more tinged with Anglo blood, the more adamantly my colored and colorless sisters glorify their colored culture's values—to offset the extreme devaluation of it by the white culture. It's a legitimate reaction. But I will not glorify those aspects of my culture which have injured me and which have injured me in the name of Protecting me. (Anzaldua 1987, p. 22)

Hispanic mothers face the complicated task of shepherding their children through the racism extant in dominant society, and the reactions to that racism framing cultural beliefs internal to Hispanic communities.

Many Asian American mothers stress conformity and fitting in as a way to challenge the system. "Our parents are painted as hard workers who were socially uncomfortable and had difficulty expressing even the smallest opinion," observes Japanese-American Kesaya Noda, in her autobiographical essay "Growing Up Asian in America" (1989, p. 246). Noda questioned this seeming capitulation on the part of her parents: "'Why did you go into those camps,' I raged at my parents, frightened by my own inner silence and timidity. 'Why didn't you do anything to resist?'" But Noda later discovers a compelling explanation as to why Asian-Americans are so often portrayed as conformist:

I had not been able to imagine before what it must have felt like to be an American—to know absolutely that one is an American—and yet to have almost everyone else deny it. Not only deny it, but challenge that identity with machine guns and troops of white American soldiers. In those circumstances it was difficult to say, "I'm a Japanese-American." "American" had to do. (1989, p. 247)

Native American women can draw upon a tradition of motherhood and woman's power inherent in Native American cultures (Allen 1986; Awiakta 1988). In such philosophies, "water, land, and life are basic to the natural order," claims Winona LaDuke.

All else has been created by the use and misuse of technology. It is only natural that in our respective struggles for survival, the native peoples are waging a way to protect the land, the water, and life, while the consumer culture strives to protect its technological lifeblood. (1988, p. 65)

Marilou Awiakta offers a powerful summary of the symbolic meaning of motherhood in Native American cultures. "I feel the Grandmother's power. She sings of harmony, not dominance," offers Awiakta. "And her song rises from a culture that repeats the wise balance of nature: the gender capable of bearing life is not separated from the power to sustain it" (1988, p. 126). A culture that sees the connectedness between the earth and human survival, and sees motherhood as symbolic of the earth itself, holds motherhood as an institution in high regard.

CONCLUDING REMARKS

Survival, power and identity shape motherhood for all women. But these themes remain muted when the mothering experiences of women of color are marginalized in feminist theorizing.

Feminist theorizing about motherhood reflects a lack of attention to the connection between ideas and the contexts in which they emerge. While such decontexualization aims to generate universal "theories" of human behavior, in actuality, it routinely distorts, and omits huge categories of human experience.

Placing racial ethnic women's motherwork in the center of analysis recontexualized motherhood. While the significance of race and class in shaping the context in which motherhood occurs remains virtually invisible when white, middle-class women's mothering experiences assume prominence, the effects of race and class on motherhood stand out in stark relief when women of color are accorded theoretical primacy. Highlighting racial ethnic mothers' struggles concerning their children's right to exist focuses attention on the importance of survival. Exploring the dialectical nature of racial ethnic women's empowerment in structures of racial domination and economic exploitation demonstrates the need to broaden the definition of maternal power. Emphasizing how the quest for self-definition is mediated by membership in different racial and social class groups reveals how the issues of identity are crucial to all motherwork.

Existing feminist theories of motherhood have emerged in specific intellectual and political contexts. By assuming that social theory will be applicable regardless of social context, feminist scholars fail to realize that they themselves are rooted in specific locations, and that the specific contexts in which they are located provide the thought-models of how they interpret the world. While subsequent theories appear to be universal and objective, they actually are partial perspectives reflecting the white, middle-class context in which their creators live. Large segments of experience, specifically those of women who are not white and middle-class, have been excluded (Spelman 1988).

Feminist theories of motherhood are thus valid as partial perspectives, but cannot be seen as *theories* of motherhood generalizable to all women. The resulting patterns of partiality inherent in existing theories, such as, for example, the emphasis placed on all-powerful mothers as conduits for gender oppression, reflect feminist theorists' positions in structures of power. These theorists are themselves participants in a system of privilege that awards them for not seeing race and class privilege as being important.

Theorizing about motherhood will not be helped by supplanting one group's theory with that of another, for example, by claiming that women of color's experiences are more valid than those of white, middle-class women. Varying placement in systems of privilege, whether race, class, sexuality, or age, generates divergent experiences with motherhood; therefore, examination of motherhood and mother-as-subject from multiple perspectives should uncover rich textures of difference. Shifting the center to accommodate this diversity promises to recontextualize motherhood and point us toward feminist theorizing that embraces difference as an essential part of commonality.

Reading 17   Black Teenage Mothers and Their Mothers: The Impact of Adolescent Childbearing on Daughters' Relations With Mothers*

ELAINE BELL KAPLAN

The popular view assumes that Black families condone teenage motherhood. This study argues that this assumption is incorrect, finding instead that teenage motherhood can produce long-term conflict both in family relations and structure. The 22 teenage mothers interviewed for this qualitative study believed that their mothers did not support them emotionally. Interviews with nine adult mothers[1] of the teenagers substantiated this belief: Their daughters' early motherhood threatened their deeply held moral values as well as their reputations in the community. This study concludes that sociologists need to address these relational problems through linking these mothers' socioeconomic conditions with gender, class, and race inequalities.

> Well, my momma said to me, "You shouldn't have gotten pregnant. You ain't married. You don't have no job. You ain't this and you ain't that" (16-year-old Susan).

> Susan should give the baby up to foster care, to someone who can take care of it (37-year-old Janet).

As these quotes suggest, relations between teenage mothers and their mothers can be complex and disturbing: Teenage motherhood serves as a source of conflict for everyone involved. Social scientists who study teenage motherhood have engaged in an on-going theoretical and, many times, politicized debate about these mother-daughter relationships. Embedded in some theoretical posi-

A version of this paper was presented at the 1994 annual meeting of the American Psychological Association. A special thanks to Gwyneth Kerr Erwin. Eun Mee Kim, Mike Messner, Pierrette Hondagneu-Sotelo, Barrie Thorne, and the anonymous reviewers for *Social Problems* for their comments on an earlier draft. The material in this study was taken from a larger study, "'Not Our Kind of Girl' Black Teenage Motherhood: Realities Hiding Behind the Myths" (forthcoming).

tions is a culture-of-poverty notion that Black, female-headed families produce more of their kind: that is, teenage girls with few values—a slap in the face of the central ideas of America's "family values" (Moynihan 1965). In this theory it is the rule of the father (and not the mother) that establishes the family's mainstream values and behavior.

Wilson (1987) responds to this position by arguing that economic restructuring during the 1960s created havoc for Black families—high unemployment rates for Black men, which in turn led to high divorce rates or fewer marriages. These changes produced a population of Black mothers who live in depleted and hostile inner-city neighborhoods. In such neighborhoods, Black mothers watch their sons seek shelter in gang involvement while their daughters seek significance in motherhood. While Wilson (1987) shows how family life is changed by economic conditions and how people's sense of their lives is mitigated by their structural conditions, his theory does not pay sufficient attention to the way gender ideology contributes to family dynamics, nor does he directly tackle the thorny question: Do teenage mothers and their mothers share values that are antithetical to mainstream values?

I argue that these political debates have limited our view of Black teenage mothers. Rather, they have produced stereotypical portrayals of Black teenage mothers and their mothers, obscuring both the way in which Black women's norms and values are actually shaped by mainstream ideology and the complex nature of their obligations as mothers, especially when their adolescent daughters become young mothers.

So far, the research focusing specifically on relations between mothers and daughters suggests that it is common for mothers and daughters to struggle over issues of independence and identity during the daughters' adolescent years (Rich 1990; Fischer 1986; Gilligan 1990). However, most of these studies primarily focus on white middle-class daughter-mother relationships; therefore they limit the ability to theorize about how Black teenage mothers and their mothers might respond to a crisis such as teenage motherhood.

There are studies that focus on the relationships of Black daughters and mothers (George and Dickerson 1995; Mayfield 1994; Rogers and Lee 1992; Apfel and Steiz 1991; Collins 1987; Burton and Bengston 1985; Ladner and Gourdine 1984; Furstenberg 1980). But these studies do not sufficiently discuss the conflict between teenage mothers and their mothers. Some find that "baby getting" and "baby keeping" are cultural survival strategies (Stack 1974) that do not have a long-term negative effect on the mother (Geronimus 1990). Ladner and Gourdine (1984) studied Black mothers and daughters' relationships to find that adult mothers do not condone their daughters' pregnancies. While this study shows that adult mothers feel themselves swept up in a "tide of circumstances with few options available to them" (p. 23), it does not sufficiently articulate the underlying mothering obligation, nor its subsequent conflicts. These studies do not link gender, race, and class in their analyses.

Collins (1990), who explores the institution of motherhood from the standpoint of Black mothers, argues that Black motherhood as an institution is both dynamic and dialectical. Collins argues that an ongoing tension exists between the dominant society's efforts to mold the institution of Black motherhood to benefit systems of race, gender, and class oppression and efforts by Black women to define and value their motherhood experiences (also see Brewer 1995).

My study explores gender, racial, and economic oppressions by examining how Black teenage mothers and their daughters cope with teenage motherhood. Gender ideology in U.S. society has been crucial to the notion that motherhood is the primary task for women of all racial and class backgrounds. In the literature on women's obligations as mothers, Russo (1976) argues that, in U.S. society's view, it is the women, but not the men, who are charged with caring for others. Further, being a good mother carries the responsibility of providing moral training to their children, supporting their children regardless of one's own needs, and spending all one's time and energy on children, even getting them out of difficult life experiences (Russo 1976). Russo's (1976) theory of motherhood directly connects the family structure to patriarchy—fathers provide the economic leadership and authority, while mothers are responsible for the reproduction of children's mainstream values and behavior. Especially during a child's early and teenage years, a mother's role in reproducing these values in children is considered to be crucial.

Similarly, racism and economic inequality are key factors in creating high numbers of Black mothers raising teenage daughters who are also mothers and in limiting the financial and emotional support they receive from others (see Bell Kaplan forthcoming; Wilson 1987). The key to understanding the dynamics between the teen and adult mothers lies in the gender, race, and class inequities wherein poor, Black women are positioned at the bottom of the labor market. These inequalities are present in systems of discrimination wherein Black women, but not Black men, are punished, or expect to be punished, for stepping outside the traditionally assigned middle-class norms and values regarding teenage parenthood.

This study offers a sample of 22 teen mothers and 9 adult mothers of the teen mothers, using their perceptions of experiences to elucidate the complexities, contradictions, and conflicts arising within family relationships as the result of teenage pregnancy. The families in this study do not reveal a deviant culture. Nor are they the super-strong women who can cope without

needing support (Myers 1980). Indeed, these teen mothers thought that motherhood would provide them with some kind of control over their lives. By contrast, the adult mothers thought their daughters' motherhood would further erode the little control adult mothers already had over their family life. The pivotal question is: What happens to family relationships when adolescent girls and their families have to deal with the pressures created by teenage motherhood?

I suggest the conflict between daughters and mothers can be traumatic for both if the daughters, as 15- or 16-year-old mothers, find themselves abandoned by the school system, their fathers, and the babies' fathers and feel that their mothers are their only source of support. What happens to these relationships when the mothers of teenage mothers themselves feel vulnerable, especially if they are young, single, have limited resources, and are in need of support themselves? These relationships may be further complicated if the adult mothers believe that their daughter's pregnancy is a reflection of lower-class behavior. These adult mothers may feel that they are also affected because the daughters' pregnancy is not their fault, but they will be perceived by others to be responsible for their daughters' situation. The adult mothers distance themselves from their daughters' behavior and align themselves with conventional expectations about teen mothers by linking themselves to traditional culture in unique ways (see Stokes and Hewitt 1976). In this study, when the daughters became pregnant, both daughters and mothers were angry and resentful of the other. That anger and resentment was debilitating and had long-term consequences on the mothers' relationships with their mothers.

SAMPLE AND METHODOLOGY

The interviews involved in this study are taken from a larger three-year study on Black teenage mothers who lived in Oakland and Richmond, California, between 1986 and 1989. This paper focuses on interviews with 22 teen mothers who lived in single-parent/mother only households. I also interviewed nine adult single-parent mothers of teenage mothers.

I met 12 of these teen mothers and 9 of their mothers through volunteer consulting work at a nonprofit teen parenting service agency in Oakland. The rest were drawn from a snowball sample in which the teen mothers provided me with names of other teen mothers. I gave the teen

mothers written and verbal information on the research and asked their permission to interview their mothers. All mother were interviewed for two to two-and-one-half hours, usually in their homes. (See Tables 1 and 2 for the demographic characteristics of the teen and adult mothers' samples.)

To gain the trust of the women in this study, I tried to create a nonhierarchical interview setting and a casual interview atmosphere. Also, being of the same race and gender, having my little boy accompany me on some visits, sharing

TABLE 17.1 Teenage Mothers' Demographic Characteristics

Name	Age	Age at Birth	Educational Background	Source of Income	Family Origin	Age of Mom at First Birth
Dana	21	15	D	AFDC	F	16
DeLesha	17	15	D	Emp.	2p.	20
Denise	25	18	HSG.	Emp.	F	15
De Vonya	17	15	11 grd.	AFDC	F	16
Diane	20	17	S.C.	AFDC	F	22
Evie	43	17	C.Deg.	Disab.	2p.	23
Georgia	16	15	11 grd.	AFDC	F	15
Irene	21	18	D	Unemp.	F	16
Jackie	17	15	11 grd.	AFDC	F	15
Jasmine	17	16	10 grd.	Pt. Emp.	F	17
Joanne	25	14	D	Emp.	F	21
Junie	15	14	9 grd.	Mom	F	24
LaShana	17	15	D	AFDC	F	22
Lenora	20	15	D	Emp.	2p.	16
Lois	27	15	D	AFDC	2p.	15
Margaret	35	15	S.Col.	Emp.	F	22
Mamie	16	15	D	AFDC	2p.	20
Melanie	17	15	11 grd.	AFDC	2p.	20
Terry	20	16	D	AFDC	F	16
Tracy	16	16	10 grd.	AFDC	F	16
Shana	17	16	D	AFDC	F	15
Susan	16	15	D	Mom	F	21

Key:
Education Level: D = high school dropout. HSG = high school graduate. C. Deg. = college degree. S. Col. = Some College. Income Source.: Disab. = Workers' Compensation Insurance. Family Origin Type: F = Female Headed Household. 2p. = Two parent household.

TABLE 17.2   Adult Mothers of Teenage Mothers' Demographic Characteristics

Name (Daughter)	Age	Marital status	Educational Back-ground	Source of Income	Annual** Income
Middle-Class Status Sliders					
Marie (Evie)	66	M	C.Deg.	Retired	$45,000
Alma (Diane)	42	W	C.Deg.	Emp.	32,000
Selma (Joanne)	46	M	C.Deg.	Emp.	25,000
Salina (Jackie)	32	S	HSG.	Emp.	23,000
Working-Class and Poor High Aspirers					
Martha (Margaret)	57	S	D.	Emp.	$13,000
Janet (Susan)	37	S	S.C.	Emp.	11,000
Jessie (Marnie)	36	S	D	AFDC	8,000
Mary (De Vonya)	54	S	D	Disab.	7,000
Ruth (Junie)	39	S	D	AFDC	6,500

Key:
Education Level: D = high school dropout. HSG = high school graduate. C. Deg. = college degree. S. Col. = Some College. Income Source.: Disab. = Workers' Compensation Insurance. Family Origin Type: F = Female Headed Household. 2p. = Two parent household. Marital Status: M = married. S = Single. W = widower. **Approximation of income.

with them my own similar family and class background, may have helped me establish rapport with the mothers (see Reinharz 1992).

Using Goffman's (1963) stigma analysis as a frame of reference, I suggest that discredited people will often act to cover whatever stigma they believe discredits them so that they can appear like others. With this in mind, I asked the teen and adult mothers about their attitudes and reactions to teenage motherhood. I wanted to know how they reorganized and redefined themselves within a context of difficult economic circumstances. Along with asking the teen mothers such questions as, "Who was the 'most' and 'least' supportive before, during, and after your pregnancy?" I asked adult mothers, "How did you respond to the news of your daughter's pregnancy?" and "Did your relationship with your daughter change after her pregnancy?" The interviews aptly illustrate both entrenched and emerging patterns in these daughter-mother relationships.

BLACK TEENAGE MOTHERS AND THEIR MOTHERS

All of the teen and adult mothers lived in economically depressed inner-city areas of Oakland and Richmond in the midst of a visible drug and gang culture. Several of the teen mothers lived in neighborhoods where, "over 40 percent of the families were headed by single mothers and virtually all the single mothers received AFDC" (Oakland City Council Report 1988). Sixteen of the twenty-two teen mothers and their babies were living with their mothers. Two of these teen mothers were ineligible for welfare assistance because their mothers' annual income exceeded the family eligibility limits. The rest were receiving welfare assistance and living on their own.

Susan serves as an example of the teen mothers who were living with their mothers. Susan, a 16-year-old mother who dropped out of the ninth grade when she learned she was pregnant, lived with her mother and two sisters in a cramped two bedroom apartment in East Oakland. Her baby's father was serving a two-year term in a youth camp facility. Susan's father, who left the family when she was very young and moved to Oklahoma, refused to pay child support and seldom visited his children. To make matters worse, Susan said, her mother's nurses' aide income of $11,000 disqualified Susan for welfare assistance.

According to Susan, her mother, Janet, was resentful and constantly complaining to Susan about the additional money it cost her to support her family since the baby's birth. Janet said she was indeed shocked when she learned that her daughter was pregnant. She thought that Susan (the first person in her family to become a teenage mother) was too young and had a too "irresponsible nature" to be a good mother. These problems exacerbated the hostility between the mother and daughter, and their arguments escalated until they fell over tables and chairs trying to hit each other.

Twelve teen mothers qualified for welfare assistance. The rest were employed. Many thought they could resolve their problems by moving out of their mothers' homes. However, only a few of the older teenage mothers were able to establish stable households. Younger teen mothers had to count on friends to lend them sleeping space; sometimes, it was on the floor. Generally, the teen mothers couldn't stay longer than a week before they would have to look for new arrangements (see Elliott and Krivo 1991). For example, 16-year-old De Vonya, the youngest of six siblings, recalled moving into her friend's home after an argument with her mother when she told her she was pregnant. De Vonya did find her own apartment in a housing complex, a hangout for drug dealers. Within two weeks of moving in, faced with mounting expenses she couldn't afford, De Vonya moved out, leaving no forwarding address or telephone number.

De Vonya's mother, Mary, a single mother who depended on monthly Social Security checks, had trouble coping with De Vonya since the baby's birth. Mary said she wanted her daughter to do something with her life other than follow in her footsteps by being a teenage welfare mother. Mary was angry, hurt, and resentful that her youngest child, De Vonya, would repeat a family cycle of teenage pregnancy that began when her own mother gave birth to Mary at age sixteen. De Vonya's father, who stopped speaking to her for several months after he learned she was pregnant, refused to offer her much in the way of support. De Vonya's reaction was: "Sometimes he gets on my nerves." Losing his support was extremely difficult for De Vonya, especially since her baby's father also broke off their relationship shortly after she became pregnant.

Most of the teen and adult mothers had poor educational skills, while some were educated and employed. But even those who were employed felt afraid that they could lose it all "in the wink of an eye," said 32-year-old Salina, mother of 16-year-old Jackie. As a result, they didn't see much of a future for themselves. When I asked the teen mothers (and adult mothers who had been teen mothers) why they became mothers so young, most responded like 16-year-old De Vonya: "Maybe I'll feel loved by having my own child." Being a mother was something she could do to feel good about herself, perhaps feeling she could be a mother even if she didn't have other options. All of the teen mothers agreed that they were only beginning to comprehend the impact of teenage motherhood on all aspects of their lives.

THE ISSUE OF GENDER: MOTHERS' OBLIGATIONS

First, teenage mothers reported that being teenage mothers placed great stress on their relations with their mothers, who strongly believed that their daughters had failed to adhere to the gendered norms about girls' sexual behavior. Second, these teen mothers were also adolescents, a period during which girls are often experiencing anxiety and confusion as they strive for maturity and are striving to develop trust and make connections with others.

Third, further complicating the challenges felt by these teen mothers is that, like all children, they felt their mothers were obligated to care for them, regardless of the mothers' own problems. The teen and adult mothers' comments in this study underscore a crucial element of the norm concerning the mothering obligation: Mothers should be able to exert control over their daughters' sexual behavior. The teen mothers also reveal the daughters' expectations that their mothers be good mothers, offering unconditional love, understanding, and forgiveness. If mothers withdraw support, they are failing. These teen mothers idealized the concept of "a good mother" and became angry when their mothers didn't conform. These adult mothers are caught in an impossible dilemma. If a mother offers support, chances are others will pass on the stigma of her daughter's deviant status to her (see Goffman 1963): The family has "slipped" in its community standing. It was common, the adult mothers said, to hear neighbors say, "These girls have no guidance" in judging their mothers' maternal abilities.

Compounding these challenges were problems caused by the break-up of important relationships: the babies' fathers disappearing from their lives, "so-called" friends gossiping about them, as one teen mother put it—abandonments that caused the teen mothers to turn to their mothers for increased emotional and financial support, only to find both unavailable. At the same time, they were having to learn how to be mothers.

Fourth, the adult mothers, many of whom were barely making enough money to support their existing families, reported that teenage motherhood ran counter to their values about marriage and motherhood. The adult mothers, overwhelmed by their new situations, negatively evaluated their daughters' actions, fearing they would be held responsible for their grandchildren's welfare. Not only did the adult mothers not appreciate their daughters' pregnancies, they took adversarial positions, often failing to be supportive of their daughters. They also felt at risk both economically and morally.

The adult mothers developed impression management strategies that distanced them from their daughters' actions. These strategies are juxtaposed against the daughters' impression management strategies that linked them to their babies and motherhood. These critical feelings led to new tensions between mothers and daughters, or exacerbated old ones.

Negotiating the Status Transition

Mothers and daughters often mark transitions in their relationships by struggling to negotiate new ways of dealing with the changes in their status (Fischer 1986). In this regard, the teen mothers demonstrate how a disproportionate amount of negotiation occurs between daughters who are moving from non-mother to mother status and mothers who are moving on to being grandmothers—all of which is occurring at an inappropriate time in their lives.

These struggles emerge in the teen mothers' responses to the first research question, "Who was most or least supportive of you before, during, and after your pregnancy?" Before pregnancy, most of the teens had fights with their mothers over time allocated to television viewing, cleaning their rooms, and doing their homework—all typical family issues. Once pregnancy was established, 6 of the 22 teens had mothers who continued being supportive of them. Sixteen-year-old Georgia typified these mothers when she said her mother (who had also been a teen mother) helped her by sharing her own experiences. Another teen mother, Terry, gave her mother credit for being emotionally supportive of her and for giving her helpful information about her own pregnancy. Her mother often told Terry how happy she was when Terry was born.

For 16 teen mothers, the family fights took on a new edge when pregnancy occurred. Only a third of these teenagers expected their mothers not to react negatively to the news of their pregnancies. Many anticipated a fight. Several said they were "scared" and feared their mothers' reactions when they were told the news, so they tried to hide their pregnancies from their mothers as long as possible. Seventeen-year-old Jasmine's story demonstrates this untenable strategy: "I didn't show until I was six months. I kept it in. Then I got sick. So my mother took me to the hospital for an examination and they told her."

The most compelling stories come from teen mothers responding to my question: "Who was the least supportive of you?" Sixteen teen mothers said that they left or were leaving their mothers' homes because of ongoing fights with their mothers. Seventeen-year-old De Vonya said:

She asked me whether I was going to keep it and who's the father and where were I going to stay. I told her, "Yeah, I'm going to stay." And she said "How do you know that I want you here? I've already raised my kids."

De Vonya's expectations illustrate the norms and roles associated with the mothering obligation: Mothers should always be available and supportive of their children and never waver in that support regardless of their own problems. De Vonya expected her mother to mother her again and to continue previous levels of support, despite the extra demands an additional child would make on her mother. Her mother, who had her own set of problems, worried that the responsibility for her grandchild would fall on her shoulders. Why was she worried? I suggest two reasons: First, she was the only parent available to care for her grandchild; second, she knew that her daughter expected her to offer all of her resources to help her grandchild.

Sixteen teen mothers associated the news of their pregnancies with a decline in their mothers' support. To Diane, from a middle-class family, her mother's feelings about status superceded her love for her daughter: "She looks down on people on AFDC, it's the same thing with teenage mothers." When Diane told her mother she had been pregnant for a month, her mother said she had to have an abortion right away, or she couldn't live in her house anymore. Diane was surprised by this strong reaction; until then, she and her mother had been fairly close. She moved out that night, stayed at a motel for a few days, and applied for emergency welfare aid. "This is not the life I had in mind," the young mother said.

Most teen mothers with unsupportive mothers said their mothers assailed their characters: "My mother called me a bitch and a whore." Their mothers' epithets apparently continued throughout the pregnancies, as illustrated by 15-year-old Junie, whose revelations about her mother's reactions are especially poignant:

When I was pregnant, she used to call me, "You're a whore, you're a tramp." I remember she was talking to a friend and calling me a whore and a tramp to her friends. I ran to my room and started crying. I left. When I got back, she said, "You big fat blimp, you don't need to be having this baby. You're too young."

Junie, like most teen mothers, was confused by her mother's negative labeling of her. These teen mothers, knowing other sexually active girls who were not pregnant, saw themselves as no different from those other girls. For the first time, many of the teenage mothers had to deal with a powerful negative label, one that was imbedded in the minds of others about Black girls who become mothers.

The Anti-Abortion Stand as an Affirmation of Motherhood

All but one of the adult mothers demanded that their daughters have abortions. While adult mothers demanded abortions, and an abortion could have resolved the issue of impending motherhood, the teens chose not to. A typical response by both sets of mothers came to light during these interviews. Junie said her mother called everyone in the family, including the teen's long-absent father, to garner support for her daughter having an abortion. In lieu of abortion, her mother wanted her to marry the baby's father. Junie said she wouldn't marry a man who refused to acknowledge his baby's existence.

Even mothers who themselves had been teen mothers wanted their daughters to have abortions. For example, Terry, whose mother was supportive of her, said she planned on having an abortion because her mother demanded it. Her plans fell through when the baby's father left town without giving her the agreed-upon half of the abortion fee. "Anyway," she justified her decision, "I'm glad I didn't. I wouldn't know what to do if I didn't have my baby."

When asked why they refused to have abortions, the teen mothers responded in "us against them" terms. Seventeen-year-old Melanie said with moral conviction: "My mother didn't get rid of me." Margaret, whose baby's father moved to a southern state shortly after she became pregnant, remembered thinking at the time, "I'm going to have my baby. It's going to be rough but we'll make it."

At issue in this teen mother's statements about abortion and motherhood, is what C. Wright Mills (1956:5) would call, "Matters that transcend those local environments of the individuals and the range of [their] inner life." Melanie (like the others), did not consider herself particularly religious. But the moral convictions revealed in her comments may reflect the general religiosity of the Black community. Along with these moral beliefs, Melanie's and Margaret's comments also reveal that motherhood provided a coping strategy: a way to gain control over their lives and a way of fulfilling both social expectation and personal desire. Ironically, these teen mothers, who according to the popular view, do not have mainstream family values, were choosing a traditional model of women—motherhood. It didn't matter if their mothers approved or disapproved of their pregnancies, these teen mothers, who lived in depressed neighborhoods where there were few successful role models for girls, were driven by the desire to fit into the norms of the larger society.

LINKING GENDER AND RACE: THE LIMITED SUPPORT OF EXTENDED FAMILY

At one time, Black mothers could rely on their extended families as a resource when faced with a crisis (Stack 1974). Today, many of these Black families are too poor to help other family members (Staples 1994). De Vonya's interview provides a powerful example of a large Black family with little to offer in way of support to the teenage mother. Of De Vonya's five siblings, one brother was in jail, the other brother had disappeared years ago, and her three sisters were all single parents on welfare. Her aunts and uncles worked at odd jobs or were unavailable to offer any support. Other mothers had similar stories, confirming that the extended Black family system has declined in recent years (Staples 1994).

I asked the teen mothers who else offered them support during and after they became pregnant. Fathers and other kin were virtually nonexistent in the teen mothers' assessments. Most teen mothers either did not know their fathers or know much about them. Two teen mothers said their fathers were "somewhat supportive." Twenty said that they counted primarily on one or two women friends for financial support. Only two of the teen mothers and adult mothers said they could rely on what Stack (1974) refers to as a mutual exchange system. Twenty-seven-year-old Lois, who became a mother at fifteen, lived with her grandmother and sister and considered her immediate family and a few women friends her family support system. But, the help she received from them was not consistent, since they had their own money problems. For two teen mothers, it was a matter of pride. As 16-year-old Tracy explained, "I was just too embarrassed to ask anyone [for help]."

Despite the lack of family support, these interviews illuminate the teens' expectations that nothing in the relationship with family, especially adult mother, should change—the norms and values associated with the way women mother would require that their mothers follow through with the needed support. The daughters perceived their mothers' refusals to be repudiations of this obligation rather than statements of economic powerlessness. The teens' ideas legitimize the wider society's view that mothering is women's essential nature.

Conforming to Cultural Norms

Before we discuss further specific aspects of the interviews with the adult mothers, we should consider why adult mothers in this study reacted so strongly to their daughters' pregnancies. Most adult mothers were deeply disappointed with their daughters; they all expected that their daughters would graduate from high school and go on to college. According to Furstenberg (1980), the mother who nurtures a teen girl in her early years could be the same person who, acting from her own needs, punishes the child she sees as immoral especially when feeling challenged by someone whom she considers under her authority.

In this study, the mothers were reacting to the breaking of at least three strongly held gender expectations or norms about childbearing and sexuality. The mothers' negative labeling of their daughters reveals their adherence to the first of these norms: Young girls should not have babies before reaching adult status, and certainly not before marriage. In a study of Black mothers who have teenage daughters, Burton and Bengtson (1985:34) find that, "The off-time accession to the lineage role creates," for many young mothers, conflicts in their view of themselves and in their families' systems of cohesion and social support.

For example, when 16-year-old Susan's baby was born, the tension between daughter and mother became unbearable, often dissolving into swinging matches. During one of my visits with Susan's mother, Janet—an attractive woman with two younger children who said she didn't think of herself as a grandmother—she threatened to put her daughter into a foster home. Susan fought back by warning her mother that she neglected her own children. Janet believed her daughter to be a lazy mother whose baby should be taken away from her because, "She stays out late, leaves the baby with me all the time, doesn't do any work around the house, and sleeps late every day." Both mothers' comments reflect the increasing frustrations intrinsic in any relationship that has to adjust to sudden changes.

The second social norm aggravating the conflict between daughters and mothers is the cultural taboo against age inappropriate sexual behavior. Most of the adult mothers, including those who were themselves teen mothers, found it difficult to acknowledge that their 14- or 15-year-old daughters were sexually active. After the daughters' admissions, the mothers had to deal with the stigma (see Goffman 1963) and deviancy associated with Black teenage mothers:

> I know she was only 14 when she got pregnant and some of my church friends couldn't stop blaming me for what happened to my daughter. Like I can follow her around everywhere to stop her from getting pregnant.

Forty-three-year-old Evie recalled her mother's reaction 25 years ago as if it just happened. With a trace of bitterness, she remembered:

> The bigger I got during my pregnancy, the more my mother hated me. By the time I reached my seventh month she'd look at me, and close the door to my bedroom. So I finally left.

This vignette also illustrates the longevity of conflict between nine former teen mothers and their mothers. Evie's mother Marie said:

> I wanted her to really be something, to go on and finish school, and I wanted to send her to Europe, to just be something other than a mother.

Despite Evie returning to school to earn a college degree in social work, her mother continued to imply she has failed: "My mother insinuates I could have done so much more, but I've ruined my chances for a good marriage and career." Evie believed her mother was concerned only about damage to her own reputation. Evie cried softly as she recalled old memories, "My mother hated me for it. I was just alone."

The third norm surfacing in these interviews is that "successful" mothering obligates one to pass on society's social values to children. Therefore, when a teen becomes pregnant, her mother's (but not her father's) abilities to socialize the daughter gain in significance. Mothers fear their daughters' failure may be linked to them: If the adult mother has been a teen mother herself her daughter's failure will be perceived as her own ongoing moral failure; if she is middle-class, others will think she doesn't properly control her daughter. By criticizing the daughter, the mother affirms her place in the world of convention: "Why am I being blamed? it's her fault," said one mother, distancing herself from the stigma of her daughter's sexual behavior.

The daughters' interviews bore out their mothers' concerns that friends were gossiping about them. Joanne, a 30-year-old former teen mother, provides an example. At the time of her teen pregnancy, she became estranged from her mother when church members threatened her mother's status in the community. Joanne's mother, Selma, carried herself as a model of moral virtues and taught her daughter to do the same. Joanne shared her mother's moral beliefs until she became pregnant, "I wanted to be married and to not have a baby at an early age."

Joanne describes how her mother's set of moral values affected her ability to grapple with Joanne's pregnancy. Her mother saw her family disgraced by ugly talk about her daughter:

*My mother thought she had failed.
She, as well as me, was being talked
about. That was the first sign in my
family that all was not well.*

Her mother grew increasingly concerned with
the gossip, "My mother could not overcome her
moral sense, and this had a tremendous impact
on our relationship." Selma says Joanne's pregnancy was an indication that, "I didn't have control over her; she was irresponsible and didn't
have control over herself."

ADULT MOTHERS:
VARIATIONS BY CLASS

In considering the logic of the culture of poverty's perspective of the Black matriarchal family structure and the circumstances of the teens'
adult mothers, what become significant are the
meanings these adult mothers gave to their
daughters' situations in concert with the daughters' perceptions of their mothers. The daughters' expectation that their mothers be available
and approachable at all times (See Fischer
1986), collided with the mothers' expectation
that their daughters would follow the traditional
path to motherhood, by marrying first. Exacer-
bating the conflict was that the adult mothers
were young themselves and still raising other
children.

Adding weight to these meanings was the
influence of the adult mothers' economic status:
Three of the nine adult mothers had incomes of
$6,500 to $8,000 a year, two working-class
mothers earned yearly incomes of $11,000 to
$13,000; four of the mothers were middle-class
professionals with yearly incomes of $23,000 to
$45,000. Neither class variation nor the mothers'
status as former teen mothers illustrated marked
differences in the problems they had with their
teenage daughters. But, as we shall see, class

variations and status did impact the meaning the
adult mothers made of their daughters' pregnancies, affecting the way they justified their coping
strategies. Further, as we shall see, the adult
mothers in this study shared certain common
characteristics.

Before describing the adult mothers' perceptions of their daughters, I want to make an
analytical contrast between sliders and aspirers.
Both concepts refer to the aspirations people
have regarding their dreams, abilities, and sense
of place within the economic structure (see MacLeod 1987). Class sliders wanted to preserve
their-hard-won middle-class status for themselves
(and their daughters). Class aspirers wanted their
daughters to pull them up the class ladder by attaining a higher class status than they themselves
had achieved.

MIDDLE-CLASS
STATUS "SLIDERS"

Four of the mothers were employed in middle-
class professions: Two were school teachers, one
was employed in a supervisory civil service occupation, and another worked as an insurance
agent. Three were the first in their families to
earn college degrees. I refer to this group as
"class sliders." All of these mothers expressed
concerns that their daughters' pregnancies would
change their middle-class image for the worse;
they linked teenage pregnancy to lower-class behavior, so they tried to distance themselves from
their daughters. On the practical level, as the sole
financial providers for their families, they had to
be concerned about financially supporting another child, a burden that could spell downward
economic mobility for them.

Alma, an elementary school teacher, said that
teenage mothers have "ghettoized mentalities."
Only low-class teenage girls, living in poor families where teenage pregnancy is a way of life,

become pregnant. In line with this reasoning, when her daughter Diane became the first teenage welfare mother in her family, Alma felt that Diane gave the family a "ghetto" image, thereby creating distance between the mother and daughter.

Evie's mother, a retired high school teacher, thought of her daughter's pregnancy as a "stigma." Evie's mother's inability to "forgive" Evie 25 years later demonstrates the long-term affect teenage motherhood can have on these mother-daughter relationships.

Another adult mother, Martha, a Deaconess in the church and moral authority in the family, demanded her 15-year-old pregnant daughter, Margaret, confess her "sin" to the church congregation, asking for forgiveness. Margaret did so but moved out of her mother's home. When Margaret, now 35 and a re-entry pre-law student, told her mother she had just registered for college, her mother didn't believe her, she doubted her daughter could do anything well.

WORKING-CLASS AND POOR ADULT MOTHER "CLASS ASPIRERS"

Unlike the middle-class mothers, four of the five "class aspirer" mothers had been teenage mothers, two were still raising small children and on disability, welfare, or employed in low-wage service occupations. Notions of upward mobility echoed throughout these mothers' interviews, stressing their wish that their daughters lead the good life, climb the class ladder, and help the family do so as well. Sadly, the adult mothers tried to put their views across by putting themselves down: They felt that the only way to handle their experiences was to serve as negative role models for their daughters, as Ruth told me, of "what not to do." A 36-year-old mother of four, Ruth was disappointed with 15-year-old Junie: "She wanted to go to college. Now she be like me."

Ruth was afraid of being stigmatized as a "bad mother" who passed on "low moral standards" to her daughter. Often, this fear drove adult mothers like Ruth to act harshly toward their daughters. When 54-year-old Mary learned that De Vonya was pregnant, she refused to help her. Her own life had been "pure drudgery:" her daughter's pregnancy made it all the worse: "I wanted her to go to college, because this is what she keeps talking about."

Thirty-six-year-old Jessie, whose mother was fifteen when she was born, wanted her teenage daughter, Marnie, also pregnant at fifteen to "go to school and be a doctor or something." When her daughter became pregnant, she was "so hurt I can't describe it." Marnie, who expected compassion, was confused by her mother's lack of support, "After all, it happened to her. Instead of helping me she called me a bunch of names and still does."

Many of the daughters of "class aspirers" thought their mothers were punishing them. According to 17-year-old Shana, "She didn't really want me to have the baby, and she was given' me a hard time." Sixteen-year-old Marnie had a similar story:

> [My mother] told me, "You do everything. No company, no telephone. The rest of the [children] can go out." She was punishing me for having my baby.

Was Marnie's mother punishing her daughter or merely assigning her daughter household tasks as many parents do? Each adult mother made different meanings of these experiences. Marnie's mother was afraid she would have to raise her grandchild, something she wasn't financially or emotionally prepared to do. The same was true for Mary, De Vonya's mother:

This is my daughter's responsibility. This is her mistake. It's not mine. It's not like I'm trying to punish her. But her baby days are over.

Mary saw her daughter's new motherhood as a signal of adult status (see Apfel and Seitz 1991). But whatever Mary's intentions, De Vonya, like Marnie, saw the housework assignments as a punishing strategy, creating friction between daughter and mother: "I can't stand her attitude and she can't stand mine," De Vonya declared. Shortly after the baby was born, De Vonya moved out of her mother's home. When 14-year-old Junie became pregnant, her mother, Ruthie, didn't know how to handle the news: "So I called her a bunch of names. I made her stay in her room for weeks at a time—I was so angry." As Stokes and Hewitt (1976:842) argue, when people confront a situation that seems "culturally inappropriate" they "organize their conduct, individually and jointly to get it back on track." One way the adult mothers could reorganize their lives was to develop impression management strategies that allowed them to cope with their daughters' "appalling" situation.

IMPRESSION MANAGEMENT STRATEGIES

The adult mothers' interviews reveal the use of several impression management strategies in an effort to defend themselves against their daughters' "soiled identity" as Goffman (1963:65) would say, keeping the spotlight off themselves. According to Goffman's discussion of stigmatized people:

The issue is not that of managing tension generated during social contacts, but rather that of managing information about their failing: "To

display or not to display; to tell or not to tell; to let on or not to let on; to lie or not to lie; and in each case, to whom, how, when, and where to disclose discrediting information about the self (1963:63).

A number of adult mothers used a "covering" strategy (Goffman 1963) as a way to distance themselves from the stigma associated with their daughters: adding a few years to their ages or to that of their daughters. Even now, one mother pretends that her 25-year-old daughter is older than her actual age. Evie, the daughter, said of her mother: "She didn't tell anybody she had a grandchild until he was three years old."

Another strategy most of the adult mothers used, I call "redirecting the gaze." Feeling the need to criticize a daughter during the interview, Alma, like other adult mothers, said she tried to raise her daughter well: "What can you do when she wants to hang out all day with those characters from the school? She's just like them." For this adult mother (as with most class sliders and aspirers), labeling her daughter worked as an impression management strategy. It allowed her to place, measure, and compare the obvious sign of her daughter's sexual behavior with other teenage girls' sexual and non-sexual involvements in explaining her daughter's pregnancy and to remove any issue of her responsibilities as a mother, detaching herself from her daughter's stigma.

In attempting to get their lives "back on track," the daughters developed their own impression management strategies. Most tried to shift the perception of themselves as problem daughters to that of good mothers. Tracy, a 16-year-old mother using this strategy, said she was a "regular old lady" who devoted all of her time to her baby, implying that the baby's birth gave her maturity and, in turn, made her a good mother. These young women also tended to deny they were having problems with their own lives. What they said about their home life, relations with their fathers and babies' fathers, along with my own observations of their living arrangements, tell another story. For example, Tracy, who was attending school, was inclined to say that everything was going well, despite having to study at the same time she was having to care for her child. She was failing in school. Another way to see the teen mothers' denial strategies is to understand that these are adolescent girls, and as such, they tend to want to fit in with others and appear as if they are in control of their situation.

SUMMARY AND DISCUSSION

Consequences for Teen Mothers and Their Mothers

These interviews suggest the importance of understanding women's interactions with each other, along with how they confront a threatening situation, noting when these problems are structured by gender, race, and class. Affluent white middle-class mothers may find themselves encountering fewer severely critical events like their teenage daughter's motherhood. When they do, they usually have the children's fathers in the home who provide adequate financial resources (Fischer 1986). In this study, both teen and adult mothers made note of absent adult fathers and babies' fathers (see Wilson 1987). Mary, De Vonya's mother, compared her life with that of her husband's:

> My husband, he leaves. Where would I find the money to leave? Where would I go? How would I live? And what would people say about me if I left like he did?

Mary's words convey a sense of being trapped by her daughter's (and her other children's) difficulties, touching on the real problems within these daughter-mother relations. Neither teen nor adult mother has others who can provide them with the resources they need to deal with serious problems such as teenage motherhood. Even Alma, with a middle-class professional job, had to handle all of her daughter's problems alone. The absence of the fathers, or other supportive people, meant that these mother-daughter relationships became riddled with unresolvable dependency needs.

Health Problems

The friction and anger voiced by both teen and adult mothers must be understood on a deeper level than the typical struggle between mothers and daughters that ends when the daughters grow up. The lack of adequate support has serious consequences for adult mothers like Alma, Janet, and Mary. Studies of low income Black families (Allen and Britt 1984; Ladner and Gourdine 1984) find that they experience low levels of social support and high levels of acute stress. In this study, examples of such stress emerged as teen and adult mothers talked about their health problems. They experienced a disproportionate amount of anxiety and depression as indicated by a number of accidents, heart attacks (Evie had two), hypertension (six adult mothers), and back problems (two adult mothers). Many adult and teen mothers were involved in car accidents (five each), job-related injuries (seven adult mothers), and physical abuse (three teens/four adult mothers).

The adult mothers recognized the problems their daughters would bring to their already depleted lives. As Collins (1987) notes in her study of Black mothers, the mothering tasks can be so overwhelming for women who have so little that often they can't offer even motherly affection.

The daughters in this study, angry and confused adolescents, looked at their mothers without understanding the socioeconomic problems forcing their mothers to take such a strong stance.

CONCLUSION: DEBUNKING THE MORAL VALUE ARGUMENT

While this study is small and is limited to a particular region of the country, the findings do suggest that teenage motherhood stings as it stigmatizes both teenage and adult mothers, causing problems for them. To say that these adult mothers have deviant values they pass on to their daughters, thereby failing as mothers, ignores the obvious: Their capacity to be good mothers was tested by the severity of the problems they faced as Black mothers. But to suggest that Black mothers are superhuman—a common tendency in the literature—and can go it alone, is to suggest also that gender inequality, racism, and money problems do not affect them.

This study adds complexity to the structural perspective, providing rich evidence that Black mothers are not the "other," as the literature suggests. Rather, they are women with complex perceptions and problems. This research supports other findings (Bell Kaplan, forthcoming; Fischer 1986; Ladner and Gourdine 1984) that daughters and mothers may reevaluate each other as daughters move into early motherhood. They tend to confront and negatively sanction each other when they have to deal with such realities. Therefore, this study refutes the current idea (McGron, 1994) that, "Illegitimacy has pretty much lost its sting in certain ghetto neighborhoods" (McGrory 1994:25), and, "We need to stigmatize it again" (p. 25).

We need to develop a more sophisticated understanding of the way in which gender relations and socioeconomic conditions transform daughter-mother relationships and the way society's beliefs about moral values influence the perception of these relationships.

The issue of moral values is an extremely important one for these mothers, since the image of deviant mothers raising deviant daughters incites politicians to call for the end of welfare and other social policies. In the current political climate, welfare opponents argue that taxpayers should not support social policies for "immoral" Black mothers and their "immoral" teenage daughters. This study proposes that just such a need—the creation of family policies to assist teenage mothers and their adult mothers—is vital to the well-being of these mothers (and, ultimately, society), as evidenced by the number of health problems they report and by my findings that socioeconomic strains only multiply these problems.

These findings are also important because they indicate the need to place the causes of these family problems (and the causes of teenage pregnancies in the first place), within their historical, social, and economic context (Hardy and Zabin 1991; Ladner and Gourdine 1984). We need to understand that mothering as an ideology can and does exist apart from the practice of mothering. The Black mothers in this study adhered to the same ideology as white mothers in that they feel responsible for raising children, for the way children turn out, and for the values children espouse. Since these Black women, as compared to white women, are often raising teenage daughters alone, such mothering can become a daunting task.

Relational problems between daughters and mothers will persist, even increase, if politicians and social welfare agencies do not adequately address these mothers' social and economic problems. The adult mothers' needs are undercut by the stereotyped perceptions of them as failed mothers or as super-strong women who can cope with all kinds of hardship—a conservative ideology that assumes Black women have such unfailing personal character that they need little support from people in power. These mothers' economic realities, buttressed by wrongheaded sociological stereotypes, reinforce hostile conservative views and harmful political agendas.

As the teen mother interviews show, the real tragedy is that these teenagers have to expend energy on activities other than complex adolescent developmental issues. When adolescence is skipped, as it is for teenage mothers, girls may not learn how to develop their confidence and independence: to do as adolescents learn to do, move away from mothers, and then move back again as adults. Instead, much like sexually abused girls (see Musick 1987), they have problems making the leap across the developmental gap and become involved in defining themselves only in relation to the trauma inherent in being teenage mothers.

Older women's interviews, like Evie's for example, show that even women who find some measure of success in their adult lives find their success undermined by having been teenage mothers, especially when they have no way of understanding that experience other than from the moral perspective. The problem becomes more egregious when adult mothers are not able to offer them the kind of emotional and financial support they need to feel safe and secure as they handle teenage motherhood at the same time they must deal with adolescent issues.

FUTURE PROBLEMS

Several candid teen mothers revealed another relationship problem. Terry, a 19-year-old mother

with a three-year-old son, said she liked babies until they reached the age of two, when they became problems. When I asked 16-year-old De Vonya if she had any advice for other teenage girls, she yelled into the microphone, "Don't have no babies!" These teen mothers' reactions are more realistic than the "regular old lady" comment made earlier by 16-year-old Tracy. The dilemma for these mothers is that at this age and stage of adolescent development, a teen mother may not be able to push aside her own need to be mothered in order to adequately mother her child. Yet at the time these teenage daughters need "to become daughters again" (Fischer 1986), adult mothers can't afford to keep mothering their teenage daughters, economically, socially, or emotionally,

Negative messages about teenage and adult mothers' moral character also threaten the positive development of the teenage mothers' children, who need both mothers and grandmothers, since men are absent from their lives. Without financial resources and family policies providing support, without rebuilding the extended-family social support system, we may expect increased alienation within these families. The tragic consequence may be the further erosion of the already fragile social fabric of Black mother-headed families. As this study demonstrates, we can develop a complex and beneficial sociological framework if a comprehensive understanding incorporating a gender, race, and class perspective is used to find solutions to the problems experienced by young mothers, helping us discover preventative alternatives to teenage pregnancy.

Reading 18   Nonfamily Living in Context:

Households, the Life Course, and Family Values*

FRANCES K. GOLDSCHEIDER AND CALVIN GOLDSCHEIDER

Residential independence before marriage has emerged from these analyses as a complex new phenomenon, one that is negotiated between parents and their maturing children over the transition to adulthood. Fundamentally, nonfamily living is about whether *marriage* and new family formation should continue to be the primary basis for adulthood and residential independence. As such, leaving home before or at marriage reflects key values about the meaning of families and the family roles of young adults in the late twentieth century.

What should be the status of young adults in their late teen years or twenties when they are *unmarried*? Should they be dependent "children" in the parental home? This is the situation implied for those who expect residential independence for themselves or for their children to occur only at the time they marry.[1] Or should unmarried young persons be considered autonomous adults who incidentally happen not to be married? If so, young people should pursue residential independence, and their parents should facilitate it—and/or insist on it—at an early age. These are very different views of early adulthood, which may link to a wide range of personal, family, and social issues and have a powerful impact on the later stages of the life course.

…(T)he second definition of independence, which separates it from marriage, has begun to take precedence in the last decades of the twentieth century in the United States. A high proportion of young adults expect and plan for residential independence for some period before marriage (70%). However, it is likely to be a new definition, since barely half their parents subscribe to it. It is also a fuzzy definition, since it is unclear when, in the period between high school graduation and marriage, it should begin. There is a wide range of expected ages at residential independence, both by parents and children, although most expected the young adult to achieve residential independence within six years after high school. It is thus not surprising, given its newness and its fuzziness, that it is also a *fragile* definition, since many return to residential dependence sometime during young adulthood, and the return to the parental home is primarily from nonfamily living, not marriage. Despite the growing fragility of marriage in young adulthood, nonfamily living is much, much more fragile.

As an emergent, normatively "required" stage in young adulthood, nonfamily living may have greater costs than most have considered. As the capstone defining the transformation of young adulthood, it is a direct substitute for marriage as the quintessential symbol of autonomy and independence. In addition to the effect of nonfamily living on decreasing the likelihood of marriage, particularly for young women (Goldscheider and Waite 1991), we have shown that those planning for it are more likely to end schooling prematurely. Young people may be ranking immediate residential independence higher than these other, longer-run uses of resources, since nonfamily living, family formation, and education beyond high school all involve considerable financial expenditures. The continuing trade-offs between residential independence, education, and marriage in the transition to adulthood are areas where clearly more research is needed.

PARENTS AND NONFAMILY LIVING

Increasingly, parents may be aiding and abetting this new definition of young adulthood, often by using their scarce resources to increase their own privacy. An important result of our analysis is that parents play a key role in young people's expectations and particularly in their decisions about residential independence, indicating that the decision about when and under what circumstances young adults leave their parents' home to establish one of their own is not simply the private calculation of the young adult. While parental characteristics, such as social class and ethnicity, have fairly weak direct effects on young people's expectations, they have a much stronger impact on the expectations of the parents. In turn, parents' expectations matter even more for most elements of young people's residential decisions than do the expectations of the young people themselves. Young adults' expectations about nonfamily living have an important effect on whether they subsequently experience it; when parents have the same expectations about the sequence of marriage and residential independence that their child holds, their support greatly strengthens the link between expectations and later behavior. Most young adults who became residentially independent followed the route they expected of themselves and that their parents expected for them.

However, when parents and their children disagree about the role of marriage in residential independence, that is, when either only the parents expect their child to leave home before marriage or only the young people do, the evidence shows that while the route taken out of the household is largely unaffected, the *timing* of residential independence is greatly altered. When parents expect residential independence *prior* to marriage but their child does not, very early residential independence occurs. In some of these families, young people marry very early, and in others, young people leave home before marriage. This combination suggests that parents who expect their children to leave home before marriage really want independence from their children and achieve it one way or the other. They either facilitate early nest leaving even if their children are not expecting it or do little to prevent early marriages, if that is what their children are planning. In contrast, when parents expect residential independence to wait until marriage but their children were expecting to leave home before marriage, intergenerational coresidence is prolonged. Parents are comfortable with this outcome, since they expect coresidence to continue, even if they had not expected it for so long, but a rupture is prevented, presumably at the risk of some discomfort on the part of the young adults.

These results confirm that living arrangements decisions are really household-level rather than individual-level decisions. As such, research should consider the points of view of the relevant decision makers in the household. There are a wide range of living arrangements decisions, from marital and parent-child to roommate arrangements, that involve at least two parties. Few studies of living arrangements take more than one point of view, and not many more collect much information from the respondent about others in the household.[2] The need for considering the variety of points of view is particularly acute for living arrangements decisions in which, as in this case, one of the parties (the parents) has been traditionally defined as the responsible authority vis-á-vis the behavior and well-being of the others (their children).

The active role parents have in the nest-leaving process is further evidenced by the impact of parental contributions on residential independence. Although parental education, not income, was the critical element of parental socioeconomic status in young people's likelihood of expecting and experiencing nonfamily living (among parents with low levels of education, increased parental income actually decreased the likelihood that their children left home before marriage), when parents actually transfer part of their resources to children for education, the child is more likely to leave home before marriage, either in conjunction with or after schooling.

The importance of parental decisions in their children's move to residential independence also appeared in the powerful impact of parental marital history on their children's later behavior. Parents who remarry, introducing a stepparent into the household and their child's life, strongly increased the likelihood that the child would leave home, both before and at marriage. This is one of the strongest effects to emerge in our study, and it is one that merits much more detailed and focused research. It is particularly interesting in light of the fact that things would have been very different if a remarriage had not occurred: a parent raising children alone can anticipate that while their children will in most cases leave home prior to marriage, this is not likely to occur very early in adulthood. Marriage for those growing up in one-parent families occurs later than in intact families, while when a remarriage occurs, the marriage of the younger generation is accelerated. Evidently, things can change fast in families, with considerable impact on both generations involved.

EXPECTATIONS AND BEHAVIOR OVER THE LIFE COURSE

The vast majority of the factors that we examined to explain variation in nonfamily living influenced the expectations of the young adults (and those of their parents), as well as their subsequent behavior, in much the same ways. This was surprising, given the extent of change in the lives of these young adults during the four to six years after their high school senior year and given the newness of the phenomenon we were examining. This overall result suggests that the analysis of measures of expectations, at least those expressed during a salient segment of the life course, can be a valuable proxy for measures of behavior for researchers trying to understand the forces underling variation in some behaviors. Evidently, the end of high school is a good point in the life course for measuring these expectations. Few young adults had yet *become* residentially independent, but many had already given it some thought and were evidently making plans on which basis they could form expectations about the sequence they were likely to follow.[3]

Part of the connection between expectations and behavior results from the fact that the same factors were influencing both. But this result also reflects the fact that young people's expectations are important direct predictors of their later behavior. Indeed, one of the strongest measures predicting whether young adults will leave home before marriage was the expectation young adults expressed about it, measured in most cases quite a few years before the actual behavior took place.

It is important to realize, however, that the similarity of patterns explaining expectations and behavior was increased by taking marriage timing into account. Marriage age can distort patterns of residential independence by providing more time to leave home while unmarried, so that even those who did not expect it often fall into it while pursuing some of the other items on the agenda of young adulthood, such as a career ladder job. Similarly, those who marry early need to be examined within the small window prior to their marriage, to see whether they use it to experience nonfamily living or for continued residential dependence.

Of course, these expectations were not very good *absolute* predictors in many ways, and the result noted above should not be overinterpreted. Many individuals who expected one route to residential independence actually took the other. Further, both the parents and (particularly) the young adults underestimated *how long* it would take them to become residentially independent. Expectations cannot be used to predict precisely *who* will take one or the other pathway, and guesses about *when* leaving home will occur should be treated with even greater skepticism. It is likely that part of the slippage for this cohort of young adults reflects the rapid changes that were taking place in the U.S. economy during the early 1980s, when these young people were first beginning to navigate into the responsibilities of adulthood. This decade began with a sharp recession, which had barely begun to ease by 1986 (Levy 1987). The period was marked by

rapidly increasing housing costs, which neither generation could have predicted when they were first asked about their expectations about residential independence.

Further, not all factors influenced expectations and behavior in the same way. Many young adults responded to factors in their immediate environment that turned out not to matter in the longer run. Others did not take into account at least some of the forces that would later become important influences on their behavior.

The factors that influenced expectations but not behavior were almost entirely attitudinal and were primarily associated with religion. Those who indicated that they had no religious denominational affiliation (None), did not consider themselves religious, or rarely if ever attended religious services also indicated a strong orientation toward nonfamily living but did not follow through. Either religious orientations and behavior are essentially unrelated to residential autonomy, however much they influence expectations about it, or else these elements of religiosity are themselves volatile at these ages. Religiosity and religious self-identification are likely to vary over the life course,[4] so to understand the effect of personal religious orientations on nonfamily living requires indicators taken much closer in time to the decision to establish an independent residence. Given the importance of religious affiliation both for expectations and behavior, the connection between religiosity and nonfamily living needs to be carefully disentangled. Longitudinal data measuring changes in living arrangements over the life course need also to assess changes in religious intensity, particularly around the time of new family formation.

The reverse pattern, in which some factors influenced behavior but were not taken into account by young adults in forming their expectations, was linked entirely with parental socioeconomic status and resources. In forming their expectations, young people did not appear to consider carefully the extent to which parental social class (whose influence turned out to be based primarily on parental education) or their parents' contributions to their education[5] would influence their likelihood of actually leaving home before marriage. Other evidence of the relatively small effect of financial resources on nonfamily living is our finding that social class did not help young adults carry through on their expectations in the way one would have expected; expectations for nonfamily living were much more important for actually experiencing it than having a lot of resources.

The social class results also suggest that the effect of parental education is felt disproportionately on the extent to which parents *propel* their children to residential independence, not on the extent to which the young people have internalized their parents' values in forming their own expectations. Even more important, these findings about the weakness of social class and resources in predicting residential independence before marriage shift our attention to isolating and identifying the "taste" factors and the structure of noneconomic preferences that emerge as so important in shaping these patterns.

Overall, the factors that we examined were consistent in their influence on both behavior and expectations. Our measures of parental family structure and, in particular, *all* our measures of ethnicity and ethnic group membership, as well as those relating to religious affiliation, were consistent in their effects on both expectations and behavior. The family structure results are not too surprising. The changes in the household that result from parental divorce and possible remarriage have, if anything, been greatly exaggerated in the personal and public consciousness. It would have been untenable to find family structure having no effect on the emerging patterns of expectations and behavior of young persons in this family-household decision. However, the lack of impact of financial resources, as discussed above, and the sustained effect of values were not anticipated.

VALUES

The power and consistency of the ethnic and religious group membership effects, as well as those of the ethnic process variables (foreign language use, generation, and residential concentration), present a challenge for future research. Many scholars have dismissed these factors as transitional, indicators of social class, or irrelevant in the secular world of American young adults. Such was not the case in this analysis of expectations and decisions about the route to residential independence. Most research of living arrangements changes has highlighted the increase in resources—the rise in affluence over time—far more than changes brought by decreased familism or secularization. Our results suggest that affluence is much less important than values, since they show few and weak relationships between resources and nonfamily living and unambiguously document that nonfamily living has simply not been as well accepted in more familistic ethnic groups and more familistic religious denominations as it has been in the dominant, largely secular culture.

Every measure of the strength of these groups that operates at the group level (unlike the personal religiosity measures) shows strong effects on both the expectations to leave home before marriage and actual nonfamily living. The use of an ethnic language, closeness to the foreign-born generation (even among high school students in the 1980s, most of whom are at least second-generation Americans), and ethnic residential group cohesiveness (even when crudely measured by the data available) all reduce the likelihood that ethnic group members expect and experience nonfamily living. And the more these differentiating factors weaken, particularly when they weaken together (e.g., among those who are both more distant from their immigrant roots and only use English), the more nonfamily living is expected and experienced. These processes characterized both the relatively recent arrivals in the United States (Asians and Hispanics) and some of the older ethnic groups (whites from southern and eastern Europe). However, they were less evident among African-Americans (even the few who were close to their foreign-born roots) or among those from elsewhere in Europe.

Religious affiliation also displayed strong effects on both expectations and behavior. However, it was necessary to subdivide both Protestants and Catholics to discern this result, indicating that these two great world religions are too heterogeneous to be treated as single communities. It was also necessary to parcel out the effects of the distinctive Catholic marriage pattern, which for most Catholics results in the relatively late marriage ages that, other things being equal, allow for nonfamily living to occur somewhat by default. The difference between the results for religious affiliation and for personal religiosity suggests that denominational affiliation is the key to the effects of religious differentiation, one that produces either strongly limiting structures or enduring values. And despite the wealth of studies on denominational change, it seems likely that denominational affiliation is more nearly constant than are indicators of personal religiosity and religious service attendance, at least in the transition to adulthood.

The key to many of these ethnic and religious results is likely to be some aspect of familism. This conclusion is reinforced directly by the "attitude" measures of familism that we examined, which strongly influenced both the expectations and experience of nonfamily living. One

measure was the personal statement about the importance of being close to family, which had a strong effect on the extent of nonfamily living in young adulthood. It did not mediate the effects of family structure but was closely linked to several of the ethnic patterns that emerged. The other "familism" attitude, which indexed the importance of nonfamily roles for women, told much the same story. This latter attitude had even stronger effects on nonfamily living than on expectations, and it was much less limited to women in its impact than was the case for gender role attitudes, which focused on gender equality *in* the family.

PROFILES

The patterns we have described apply to young adults as a whole graduating from high school in the early 1980s. More specifically, they apply to white Protestant young adults, the dominant group in American society (and sometimes even more specifically to nonfundamentalist Protestants). Given the strength of ethnic and religious variation throughout this analysis, we profile the various other groups, contrasting them with the dominant group—and often with each other—to see how residential independence strategies tie in with other subgroup patterns in the transition to adulthood.

These profiles do not simply reflect the overlap of race/ethnicity with the social class or the regional concentration of these groups, their characteristic marriage timing, or some other obvious differentiating characteristic, although group differentiation works in some cases through one or more of these axes to produce a special configuration. It is best to understand differences in nonfamily living in the contexts of the communities that these groups represent and the family attitudes, values, and environments that they share. We consider Asian-Americans, African-Americans, and

Hispanics as well as Catholics and Jews. Then, although they normally inhabit the same communities, we compare young men and women as they integrate marriage and residential independence into their "separate spheres" over the transition to adulthood.

Asian-Americans

Asian-Americans emerge from these analyses as the most cohesively familistic group we examined, with strong two-parent family structures supporting young adults, an emphasis on the value of living close to parents and relatives (which has a powerfully negative effect on nonfamily living), and, as a result, a generally very low level of expected and experienced nonfamily living for both young men and young women. Perhaps because of this strong family support, the plans of these young Asian-Americans are very likely to be carried through, as reflected in the strong links between nonfamily living expectations and behavior. Change cannot easily enter the system with such a strong array of social supports to act as checks. Asian-Americans very rarely marry earlier than they expected, become parents before they expected, or drop out of school before they expected. And when earlier than planned parenthood occurs, it overwhelmingly occurs within the context of marriage, contributing to the strength of family structure in the next generation.[6] Even generational change is largely missing, with generation in America making essentially no difference in the likelihood young Asian-Americans expect or experience nonfamily living.

Like other racial/ethnic groups, convergence toward high levels of nonfamily living occurs as a result of increased use of English and of residential mobility out of the dominant area of settlement (in this case, the Pacific region). But Asian-Americans' armor of familism is also breached in several ways distinctive to them.

When the parental marital structure did not hold, there was a very strong movement toward leaving home before marriage, particularly when there was a parental remarriage. In this case, the strong pattern of intergenerational control may backfire, with the younger generation escaping a paternalism that they feel is both personally alien and un-American, resulting in nonfamily living and perhaps a real break from their families. But these cases are rare.

Much more important is the strong effect of increases in socioeconomic status, particularly for young people's expectations about nonfamily living. At the highest levels of socioeconomic status, there are few differences in expectations for nonfamily living between young Asian-Americans and the white Protestant majority. Whether this is a form of emancipation from their group's super-familism or simply a temporary correlate of going away to college (very rare among Asian-Americans, who are likely to commute [Goldscheider and DaVanzo 1989]) would require more detailed analysis to unravel. It is likely that the Asian form of familism can survive distance among its members, as the rich research literature on multinational Asian family corporations, lending societies, and other forms of family coordination suggests (Waldinger, Aldrich, and Ward 1990; Light and Bonacich 1988).

Finally, the Asian community may find itself backing into nonfamily living because of its very late age at marriage. This phenomenon originally created a complex puzzle for our analysis. It appeared that Asian-Americans were unlikely to expect nonfamily living but more likely than average to experience it. It turned out that while nonfamily living is rare among Asian-Americans, it is just not so rare as marriage during the six years of observation included in our survey. Only by taking this characteristic into account could we show the underlying avoidance of nonfamily living. Like increased socioeconomic status, the consequences of delayed marriage are real. Young people observe more of their peers becoming residentially independent before they marry during the early years of adulthood. There is unlikely to be a move toward marriage at younger ages to prevent this effect, since early marriage is not consistent with their other characteristic patterns, particularly longer school enrollment. Simple exposure time among unmarried young Asian-Americans may well contribute to increased nonfamily living among Asian-Americans in the future.

Hispanic-Americans

While not quite as powerfully familistic as Asian-Americans, Hispanics are the least likely to expect and experience nonfamily living of all the ethnic groups that we examined. Hispanic parents are particularly unlikely to expect nonfamily living for their children. So there is a generational gap, but both generations are at relatively low levels of anticipating nonfamily living compared with others of their generation. They maintain this distinctively low level by continuing high use of Spanish and continued residential concentration (in the Southwest for Mexicans; in Florida and New York for Cubans). Maintaining family closeness as a valued goal also contributes importantly to their intergenerational coresidence. Rating family closeness highly has an unusually strong impact in reducing the likelihood of expecting and experiencing nonfamily living, much as it does for Asian-Americans. Among Hispanics, Cubans stand out as the least likely to experience and expect nonfamily living, but the general Hispanic pattern is consistent across groups, particularly when their relatively late marriage ages—at least compared with white Protestants—are taken into account.

Like Asian-Americans, increased English use and moving away from their ethnic region enhance the likelihood that young adults will leave home before they marry. However, Hispanics are also experiencing rapid generational change, particularly among the group that is most highly foreign born, the Cubans.[7]

Hispanics also lack the powerful family structure of Asian-Americans. Although there may be strong sanctions for deviant marital behavior (and in fact, Hispanics, like Asian-Americans, are particularly likely to couple early childbearing with early marriage), parental family structure, with average levels of one-parent families and stepfamilies, is not distinctive. This may be related to the high levels of unexpectedly early transitions to marriage and parenthood and from school that characterize Hispanic communities. While family disruption is disapproved, too many have placed themselves at risk of it to keep levels very low.

In the context of the familism revolutions under way in the United States, Hispanics may be particularly vulnerable on one axis—parent-child—because they are under such pressure on another—gender. Gender differences in nonfamily living are unusually large for Hispanics, in contrast to Asians. This means that although both groups are patriarchal in their sex role attitudes, holding gender-linked attitudes can have very different implications. Asians, unlike Hispanics, deny premarital residential independence to both their sons and their daughters and therefore are under less pressure from the gender revolution among young people.

The nature of familism also appears to be different for these two groups. Familism among Asians appears to include commitment to extended family and strong family support for the children's education and mobility. Over time, this may involve leaving home before marriage, if that is what is needed to achieve the group's educational and career goals. In contrast, Hispanics have a distinctive pattern reinforcing avoidance of nonfamily living—a high level of financial contribution *from* young adults to parents—which also likely serves to reduce social and economic mobility. In ways that are not totally clear, this pattern appears to be linked to early marriage. If Hispanics converge to the general pattern of low to no financial contributions from adult children as well, an additional barrier to nonfamily living will fall.

African-Americans

The patterns for African-Americans are quite different from those of both Asian-Americans and Hispanic-Americans. It appears that the major basis for group cohesion for this group is not familism at all but the powerfully unifying effect of discrimination and racism, so that race creates its own distinctiveness, blurring all others. Factors that lead to variation in nonfamily living arrangements in the nonblack community have been shown over and over again in these chapters to have little or no effect among blacks. Living in the South, using a foreign language, being Catholic, Protestant, or of some other religious affiliation, being the child of a foreign-born parent, and even gender make little difference in nonfamily living among young African-Americans. Similarly, expressing feelings about the importance of living close to parents and relatives and growing up in a one-parent or stepparent family had no effect on the likelihood of expecting or experiencing nonfamily living. There are a few exceptions to this pattern, for example, attendance at Catholic schools seems to mark young blacks as it does others, although its effects are different, leading to a convergence of blacks and whites.

Nevertheless, of all the race and ethnic groups that we examined, blacks are most likely to expect and most likely to actually experience premarital residential autonomy as their route out of the parental home. The key factor that helps place the black pattern into perspective is their very late expected and actual age at marriage. Once age at marriage is taken into account, the black pattern of nonfamily living relative to whites reverses itself. Blacks are less likely to expect or experience nonfamily living at a given age than white young adults. Just as for Asians, leaving home before marriage is not common among blacks; it is just not as rare as marriage. In the African-American case, the combination appears to be the result of weak family patterns: low rates of marriage lead eventually to nonfamily living by default.

Viewing this pattern as evidence of weak, not strong, family structures is reinforced by the low levels young adults report for feeling it important to live close to parents and relatives as well as by the high level of fragmentary or disrupted parental families, with much higher proportions living in both mother-only and step-families at the end of high school than any of the other groups we studied. Marriage is only weakly connected to parenthood in the younger generation as well, since blacks who become parents at ages earlier than expected are less likely to marry than others who have this experience. This picture of weak family structure is also consistent with the fact that young African-Americans are very unlikely to be able to carry out their planned route to residential independence—at or before marriage. This pattern may indicate a very low level of parental support for their plans—whichever ones they have—since the black parents in this study were much less likely to expect their children to leave home before marriage than their children expected; the level of parent-child conflict in expectations at the family level is also considerably greater among blacks than among any other group (Goldscheider and Goldscheider 1989).

However, young black adults can evidently draw strength from outside their own families in ways that do not appear for other groups. The best evidence for this is the absence of a family structure effect on nonfamily living, indicating that the losses nonblacks experience in this situation are somehow made up within the black community. In addition, ratings of family closeness are not important for nonfamily living among blacks, suggesting that even those who report that family closeness is not of particular importance to them are as comfortable remaining home until marriage—no matter how long it is delayed—as those who rate it highly.

These contrasts with white Protestants would not be complete without considering the two religious groups normally grouped with them as the major religions in the United States[8] as well as the special communities of Protestants. Although our initial glance revealed very little difference in nonfamily living expectations among Protestants, Catholics, and Jews, a closer examination of religious groups, defined more sharply as communities than as categories, particularly taking into account the very different marriage patterns of Protestants, allowed the differences to emerge more clearly.

Fundamentalist Protestants

Our primary finding for this group was that they were less likely to expect and actually experience nonfamily living than are other Protestants. This was particularly the case when their younger marriage age was taken into account. The difference between the two groups was quite large: less than half of the more fundamentalist Protestants actually left home before marriage compared with two-thirds of the more liberal Protestants.

Although fundamentalist Protestants are more likely to describe themselves as religious and to attend religious services more regularly, the supports for nonfamily living seem to be less individual and more embedded in the social structures to which they belong. Unlike for Protestants in more liberal denominations, neither the

level of personal religious feelings nor the level of service attendance had any effect on the actual patterns of leaving home before marriage.

Fundamentalist Protestant denominations are among the least studied religious groups in the United States. While the effects that we documented take into account differences in social class and region, our profile of them is less complete than those of most other groups. We only focused on them in the context of specifying the religious factor in the living arrangements of young adults and did not consider whether other factors—for example, socioeconomic status, family structure, or parental expectations—influenced their orientations toward nonfamily living differently from other groups. Yet while Protestants all have some distinctive traits, in particular, earlier marriage than any other of the white religious groups or the other racial or ethnic groups, our results for fundamentalist Protestants suggest that for most purposes, taking all Protestants together as a group is not adequate.

Catholics

Recent research on the family-related behavior of American Catholics has shown convergence to the more general (i.e., Protestant) pattern. Despite continuing doctrinal differences and increasingly vocal pronouncements descending the hierarchy from Rome, Catholics in the United States no longer have larger families than non-Catholics and have lost most of their distinctive contraceptive and abortion patterns (Goldscheider and Mosher 1991, Jones and Westoff 1979; see also Alba 1990). Their propensity to divorce is also rapidly approaching the Protestant level. Other research that has focused on the values and beliefs of American Catholics has documented continuing differences from Protestants, in part reflecting broader orientations that are religiously and institutionally based (Greeley 1989).

The results of our analysis are consistent with findings documenting the general lack of Catholic distinctiveness within marriage but show at the same time that important differences remain in family building prior to marriage, as do differences in parent-child relationships. Each of these has important implications for nonfamily living. It is also clear from the evidence we presented that these differences are re-inforced by specifically Catholic institutions, schools and churches.

Catholics expect to marry a full year later, on average, than do Protestants, and they follow through, with a distinctively lower likelihood of marriage at each age during the six years after high school. This is reinforced among those attending Catholic schools. This pattern is most distinctive among Catholics who are not from southern Europe, suggesting that the Irish pattern of very late marriage still continues (Kennedy 1972, Kobrin and Goldscheider 1978), at least to some extent, more than a century after the major wave of immigration from Ireland.

But this very distinctiveness appears to be opening the way to a rapid increase in nonfamily living and perhaps to a period of conflict in parent-child relationships. The "generation gap" in expectations is very large among Catholics, with far fewer Catholic than Protestant parents expecting nonfamily living for their children. Nevertheless, the traditional late marriage age (which their parents also expect for their children) has allowed this generation of young Catholics who have established an independent residence to experience nonfamily living in almost exactly the same proportions as non-Catholics. If the marriage age of Catholics was the same as for non-Catholics, nonfamily living patterns between the groups would have been significantly different. So the very distinctiveness in one area (marriage age) has resulted in

greater similarities between Catholics and non-Catholics in other areas (living arrangements).

Jews

Young Jewish adults expect and experience nonfamily living more than any other white group in this study and are most distinctive in having *parents* who are most likely to expect it for them as well. As with Catholics, part of this is the result of very late marriage, but there the resemblance ends. Late marriage (and nonfamily living) is paired among Jews with a distinctive pattern of planning efficacy, so that not only do few marry, become parents, or drop out of school earlier than expected but plans for leaving home are also unusually well carried out. In a tantalizing finding, we also documented that Jews who were finding conditions unfavorable to carrying out their planned age *at parenthood* were nevertheless marrying. Jews do not need to marry late to defer childbearing (as many Catholics do) but can combine marriage with delayed childbearing within marriage to achieve educational and career goals (particularly for women).

However, most of our results for Jews were weakened by the very small number of cases in our final analytical sample. It is a population that has been characterized as extremely cohesive, yet it is undergoing rapid change (Goldscheider 1986). The indicators of change available for other groups in the sample (living in an ethnic region, generation, and language use) did not work well for them. Part of the key may lie in religious denominational shifts (from Orthodox to Conservative to Reform), in affiliation with other specifically Jewish organizations, or in other indicators of group cohesiveness, none of which can be examined with these data. Nevertheless, the data reveal that nonfamily living among Jews receives the support of parents and is consistent with their educational and family goals. Together, these patterns imply that familism and family commitments among Jews are consistent with high levels of nonfamily living, probably because living independently is part of a broader family-supported life course trajectory.

Young Men and Young Women

Comparing the transitions to adulthood of young men and women normally focuses our attention on the fact that young women are more family oriented than young men. This reflects in part their earlier age at marriage and in part the fact that most consider family roles to be more critical for young women than for young men, since they shape women's financial well-being, social status, and niche in society.[9] It is true that young women in this study expect to, and actually, marry earlier than young men and that this has some impact on young men's greater likelihood of experiencing nonfamily living. But what is fascinating in all these results is that this difference is extraordinarily fragile and that there are many circumstances in which young women's likelihood of nonfamily living approaches and even surpasses that of young men. Young women are much more responsive than young men to variation in the attitudinal and social factors we measure—ethnicity, religion, social class—and hence are much more heterogeneous in their expectations about, and experiences of, nonfamily living as a route to residential independence.

The picture that emerges from a wide range of results can be illustrated with the following example: among families at low levels of socioeconomic status, the likelihood that females will expect or experience nonfamily living is much less than that of males, but at high levels of socioeconomic status there is very little gender difference. To the extent that family socioeconomic status is increasing, then, this cross-sectional finding predicts convergence in the residential patterns of young men and women. Similarly, there is a strikingly consistent pattern linking ethnicity and religion with gender differences. The route to residential independence differs most between young men and women among those speaking a foreign language and among those who live in the region where most of their ethnic group live. These findings suggests that the process of linguistic and residential integration into the broader American society reduces gender differentiation. Similarly, religion reinforces gender differences: young men and women who consider themselves very religious, who frequently attend religious services, and who were enrolled in Catholic school varied more in their nonfamily living patterns than more secular young adults. Hence the forces that are leading to increased affluence and secularism and to decreased familism are also increasing the similarities between the early transition to adulthood of young men and women, that is, egalitarianism.

Nevertheless, substantial gender differences in nonfamily living remain, suggesting that young women who want to experience nonfamily living have to overcome the resistance of their ethnic communities and religious teachers. They also have to deal with parents who make larger gender distinctions than their own generation does. The importance of parents was apparent in the evidence about the parents' expectations, directly (although the generational differences were not great) as well as in the effect of parental contributions to their children's education, which had a stronger effect on the expectations and experience of their daughters than on their sons.

Even so, there was substantial evidence that young women could overcome these structural and family barriers through their own actions. Planning for a later than average marriage age had much more impact on young women's likelihood of nonfamily living than on young men's, greatly reducing the differences between them. And planning directly to leave home before marriage, as evidenced by their expectations at the end of high school, was very successful in increasing young women's likelihood of actually experiencing nonfamily living as their route to residential independence—far more so than such plans did for young men.

This finding should also encourage us to think somewhat more about the lives of young men. They planned for nonfamily living, but their plans had little effect on their attaining it. In the midst of the wealth of studies on how the plans and expectations of women are changing, there is a great paucity of research on men, as they grope their way to adulthood under circumstances of changed male-female roles. Negotiating within these changes may be particularly problematic when the traditional route to male independence, via economic prowess, has been compromised (Easterlin et al. 1992).

However, many young women were also not successful in following through on their plans in young adulthood, and it may be that even for those who were, the costs of nonfamily living were greater than for young men. Daughters were much more likely than sons to experience marriage and parenthood earlier than they expected, which perhaps should not surprise us, given the forces arrayed against any alternative plans by many of their families and religious/ethnic communities. And while the closer linkage between dropping out of school and marriage for females than males is also not surprising, it was also the case that young women were more likely to leave home before marriage by dropping out of school than were young men. This further suggests that the costs of nonfamily living in terms of long-run educational attainment are greater for young women

than for young men. Egalitarianism is clearly unfolding in the generation of the 1980s; but there is still a way to go before young men and women proceed in the transition to adulthood without the liabilities and costs of gender.

THE CONTEXTS OF NONFAMILY LIVING

What these results—particularly the group profiles—suggest is that nonfamily living is highly variable across social contexts. It is virtually taken for granted among highly educated Protestants and Jews, both parents and young adults (and hence, most family scholars as well), but it is much less clear among other communities and in other circumstances. The newness of the phenomenon, the fuzziness about when it should start (and end), and its fragility, together with the lack of consensus between parents and children on what are appropriate residential sequences in young adulthood, show that it is not yet clearly institutionalized as a waystation in young adulthood.

It is also likely, although here our evidence is less clear, that the rules underlying the alternative to nonfamily living—the continued coresidence of parents and unmarried children past their late teens and into their twenties—are also becoming fuzzy. It may be that these changes are increasing the pressure on young adults and their parents toward nonfamily living, since parents rarely attempt to incorporate young adults as contributors and responsible persons in the household, while at the same time they resent their "freeloading." Increasing the involvement and responsibilities of children in the parental household—and beginning this process prior to adulthood—could relieve the pressure. This would allow the parental home to serve more extensively as a resource allowing for greater investment for later adulthood, promoting young people's remaining in school longer, increasing the accumulation of human capital, and otherwise saving for an adult future.

Both these paths into young adulthood need further research. We need to learn how young adults feel about the homes they are expecting to establish prior to marriage, and we need to learn more about the domestic basis of parent-child relationships, the strains this imposes, and how these strains can be reduced. We need to go much further to understand the forces underlying the growth in nonfamily living and the costs and benefits the various pathways to residential independence impose on both generations, now and in the future.

Chapter 7

The Family and the Elderly

Reading 19 To Be Old and Asian: An Unsettling Life in America*

FLORENTIUS CHAN

The 1980 census reported that there were 211,736 older Asian and Pacific Islanders aged 65 and over living in the United States. This figure is expected to increase significantly by 1990. The majority of these elderly are foreign-born and many of them are newly arrived immigrants or refugees. Like most of the Asians in this country, they usually live in or near big cities such as San Francisco, Los Angeles and New York.

The Asian elderly who were born in this country have experiences similar to those of other elderly Americans. Typically, they live by themselves and have fairly regular contact with their grown-up children.

The situation of elderly immigrants and refugees, however, is quite different, as is now well known to the mental health professionals who assist them with their problems of adjustment to life in America. Most of the refugees and immigrants who came to this country when already elderly did not intend to come here in the first place. They accompanied children who migrated to this country or followed later when their children sponsored their entry to the United States. They did not know very much about this country and were not well prepared for the changes about to confront them.

As they left their home countries these elderly persons experienced a series of significant losses. Their support networks of relatives and friends were shattered by war or were left behind when they departed. Their status in society and family changed dramatically, along with cultural and financial changes that deeply affected every aspect of their lives.

Elderly refugees from Vietnam, Cambodia and Laos faced additional problems. Unlike most other immigrants, they could not reasonably expect to be able to return to their countries of origin if adjustment to life in the United States proved too difficult.

Severe adjustment problems often induce in the elderly Asians a sense of having lost control over their lives and daily events, increasing their dependency and depression.

Most elderly Asian persons have great difficulty learning English. Except for those who live in Chinatowns or other ethnic communities, English is a necessity if they are to engage in even simple conversations with neighbors, take

*Chan, Florentius. 1988. "To Be Old and Asian: An Unsettling Life in America." *Aging* 358:14–15. Reprinted with permission. In the balance of this article, the term Asian refers to immigrants and refugees from Asia and the Pacific Islands.

buses, read newspapers, understand TV programs and carry on the ordinary activities of everyday life. The language problem may keep them at home with little to do, making them dependent on their children or others as interpreters and intermediaries.

Lack of transportation is another major problem. Very few Asian elderly own cars or have drivers' licenses, and if they can't read street signs or subway maps, they probably can't use public transportation. Even keeping appointments with doctors or welfare agencies may be very difficult. The expression "no legs" is commonly used by the Asian elderly who complain of severe handicaps due to lack of transportation.

Problems of cultural adjustment tend to underlie all the other difficulties that Asian elderly immigrants and refugees face. In their home countries they were generally respected and consulted for their wisdom and experience. They usually lived with their adult children and grandchildren and received any care they needed from them. They participated actively in making household decisions and disciplining grandchildren, while enjoying a position of authority in the home.

Their position in this country, however, may be quite different. Although they often live with their children or relatives, the older generation's knowledge may be considered obsolete and their wisdom may be ignored by the younger family members. The elders' religious practices, such as burning paper money and sacrificing live chickens, may seem totally out of place here. They may be allowed to play little role in household decisions. When they get sick they may be regarded as a burden, especially if they do not have health insurance or Medicaid coverage.

Elderly Asian men often come to feel bored and useless because they have few friends and activities and cannot get involved in household events. Elderly Asian women may be challenged on their childrearing practices when they babysit their grandchildren. Their methods and thinking may seem old-fashioned or unsuitable.

Arguments and disagreements tend to erupt more when they are living with their daughters-in-law than when with their sons-in-law. They complain that their daughters-in-law do not live up to traditional virtues and expectations. And the daughters-in-law tend to find the elderly women too bossy and stubborn.

Following are some notes from case histories illustrating some of the difficulties Asian elderly persons face:

• A homeless, divorced 80-year-old Filipino man came to the community mental health clinic complaining of sleep disturbance, poor memory and anxiety. He has four children but refuses to live with them, saying they do not respect him and mistreat him. Social Security disability income is his main financial resource. He carries his bags of belongings from place to place and has been mugged several times.

• A 63-year-old married Vietnamese woman sought help at the mental health clinic for depression. She and her husband came to the United States in 1985, sponsored by one of their sons. They have five children, two in Vietnam, one in a Thai camp, and two in the United States. They stayed with the son who lived in California until he rejected them because his wife didn't want them in her home any longer. The other married son who lives in Texas also refused to accept them. The couple is now dependent on general relief funds and has very serious financial problems.

• A healthy 84-year-old Vietnamese widow has lived in this country since 1978. She was a wealthy business woman in Vietnam. She does not want to live with her children because she does not get along well with them. Currently she lives alone and is able to take care of herself. A devout Buddhist, she maintains an altar with a statue of the Buddha and burns incense there every day. She is extremely concerned that if she should die in this country her soul would never rest. Her children would not visit her burial place often, she believes, and would not burn money there, as is the tradition—they would probably only bring flowers. She speaks of returning to Vietnam in four more years. In Vietnam her soul could rest in peace, she feels. Her greatest fear is that she may die suddenly before returning to Vietnam. Sometimes she goes to the community social services agency to ask for help with a translation or local transportation. At those times she usually tells the community worker she has no friends and feels very lonely.

Such problems and conflicts are not unique, of course, to Asian immigrants and refugees. But they do call for culturally-sensitive assistance of a special kind, tailored to the needs of the older Asians and the process of adjustment they are undergoing.

Reading 20 Intimate Strangers: The Elderly and Home-Care Worker Relationships*

MARK HUTTER

Ours is an aging society. Demographic trends reveal that there will be a sharp rise in the elderly population in the foreseeable future. In 1900, around 3 million people in the United States were over the age of 65. They represented 4 percent of the population. In 1980 there were 25.5 million people over 65 years old. This was a 28 percent increase since 1970. Ten years later, in 1990, 31.7 million people representing 12.7 percent of the population was in this age group. This group is expected to increase to nearly a quarter of the population by the year 2050. The median age, at which half the population is younger and half is older, rose in the decade that ended in 1990 from 30 years to 32.7 years. The factors accounting for this rise were that the proportion of people age 65 or over is increasing while the proportion of people under the age of 15 is decreasing (Thorson, 1995). These statistics indicate a sharply rising median age over the next three decades and have major implications for the elderly, for families, and for society.

The age of grandparents covers much of the human life span—from the early 30s to the 100s. Obviously, there will be a great variation in generational relationships depending on the respective ages. Much of the research is on the three-generation family that covers the period when the senior generation is from 50 to 70 years of age, the middle generation 30 to 50, and the youngest generation from birth to teenage years. However, four-generation families are becoming more common.

Cherlin and Furstenberg (1986) observe that the revolution in the health conditions of the elderly, combined with their economic independence, enable them to pursue independent lives and live apart from the family. The title of their book, *The New American Grandparent,* and its subtitle, *A Place in the Family, A Life Apart,* characterizes the role of the grandparent generation during this stage of the life cycle when they are still relatively healthy. But, what happens when the oldest generation becomes older and moves into their 70s, 80s, 90s, and beyond? Often this proves to be a very difficult period in the lives of family members in all three generations, and problems can be exacerbated when the grandchildren become parents.

Some of the difficulty stems from the fact that the elder generation is composed of old people whom society views as residuals and somewhat useless. Irving Rosow (1976) has astutely observed that our society has deprived old peo-

*A version of this paper was presented at the Couch/Stone Society for the Study of Symbolic Interaction Symposium, February 20–22, 1998, Houston, Texas.

ple both of responsibility and of function; by so doing, it has provided the basis for the roleless position of the elderly. In Rosow's terms, the lives of the elderly are "socially unstructured" (1976:466); that is, these people in their 70s, 80s, and 90s have no role models and no role prescriptions that they can use to fashion their own present-day roles.

For adult children, and especially women, changing role expectations both in career and familial involvements complicate matters. These people are known in the popular literature as the "sandwich generation" because they are sandwiched between their own children who need care and their older parents who also need care. These people experience stress associated with their own stage in the family life cycle (Thorson, 1995). Many are contemplating their own aging as they face retirement and perhaps their own financial and health problems. This generation has the brunt of generational responsibility thrust on it. They often are asked to assist their own children as they enter early adulthood and married and family life, while at the same time they are expected to care for their aged parents. Ethel Shanas (1980) quotes a woman who speaks for this generation: "I've raised my family. I want to spend time with my husband or my wife. I want to enjoy my grandchildren. I never expected that when I was a grandparent, I'd have to look after my parents" (1980:14).

It is not accidental that the above quote is by a woman. Women within that sandwich generation are the ones who often take on a disproportionate share of the time and emotional involvement with their elderly parents. In 1988, a U.S. House of Representatives report observed that the average woman will spend even more years (18 years) taking care of elderly parents than they did (17 years) raising their children. Commenting on this fact, *Newsweek* (1990) observes that the "mommy track" is being replaced by a "daughter track." The shift is from balanc-

ing work, career, and child rearing to balancing work, career, and elder-caring. Indeed, often these women are working mothers and caregivers. They provide both for their parents and for their children while holding down full-time jobs.

Elaine Brody of the Philadelphia Geriatric Center has found that among her clientele, working wives are taking on the same responsibilities as nonemployed women. "They don't give up caring for their parent. They don't slack off on responsibility to their jobs or their husbands. They take it out of their own hides" (Brody quoted in Gelman et al., 1985:68). The gender role and family literature often talks about the "double burden" or "dual roles" of women. For these women, we can now see a "triple burden." And yet, as Brody laments, there is little attention paid to the problems of these women by the government, industry, or the women's movement.

The research on adult children taking care of their parents is growing. Much of that research reports that it is a daughter who is usually the family member who takes on the responsibility of caring for aging parents and other elderly kin (Brody, 1990). Elaine M. Brody and her associates (1992) have investigated the effects of women's marital status on their parent care experience. They found that the stress of caregiving was lessened for women who had husbands, had more socio-emotional and instrumental support, and were financially well-off and thus experienced less financial strain from caregiving. Brody and her coauthors found that the changing lifestyles of women—higher divorce rates and higher rates of not ever marrying—increase the difficulties of the parent care years. A never-married daughter expresses the concerns and anxieties of these women without extensive kin involvements but who have taken on the major responsibility of parental care: "It's an awesome responsibility. It's scary to think what would happen if anything happens to me" (Brody et al., 1992:65).

Sandra J. Litvin (1992), a colleague of Brody's, is concerned with elderly care receivers' status transitions, that include the loss of good health and declining social activities with friends and family members. She is also concerned with the effect that these status transitions have on the caregivers. Such a status transition can cause considerable fear and anxiety over the future for both the care receiver and the caregiver. This relationship itself is susceptible to breakdown.

Litvin observed that the caregiver experienced role conflict when the care receiver had a lack of social participation with family and friends. Many of these caregivers perceived their care receivers as being in better health and participating more in social activities than did the care receivers. Litvin explains, "If caregivers can rationalize that their infirm elderly kin are independent and have adequate social interaction with family and friends, then the burden is temporarily lifted from their shoulders" (Litvin, 1992). For the caregiver knows that if their elderly kin participate less with others, then they will focus more of their expectations on increased emotional and instrumental support on the caregiver.

Litvin observes that as the aging population continues to grow, and where a major part of this growth is among the very old (those in their 80s and 90s and beyond), it becomes essential to understand the changing nature of intergenerational relationships when status transitions occur. Litvin calls for the need for more studies to examine variations in the caregiving/care receiving experience by race, gender, and social class.

In this paper I am concerned with the relationships that develop when an "intimate stranger"—a home-care worker—comes to provide care for an elderly person who, for whatever reasons, cannot maintain their own everyday independence and family members and friends cannot aid them to do so. My particular focus is on the relationships surrounding one elderly individual—a close relation.

THE HOME-CARE WORKER

While at least two-thirds of home care for the elderly is still provided by relatives and other non-paid caregivers, that figure is growing smaller (Conover, 1997). It is the growing dilemma of our age. In an increasingly mobile society, grown children seldom live a short commuting distance from their parents. Of the estimated 25 million Americans who serve as caregivers to an elder, more than a quarter are doing it long distance. And that number is expected to grow as more baby boomers take on the heartwrenching task of mothering and fathering their parents. Further, as the baby boomers in turn age, an even larger number of their children will find themselves in the same position in the years ahead. In 1980 there were 25.6 million Americans over the age of 65. By the year 2030 it is estimated that that population will more than double to around 70 million people.

Many elders are managing their own lives. Those that are more affluent live in retirement communities and senior citizen homes. Others live in their own homes. An estimated 75 percent of the old remain in independent living situations. Another 18 percent live with an adult child. A relatively small number live in isolation. About 80 percent of older people see a close relative every week, according to Dr. Franklin Williams, director of the National Institute on Aging (Gelman et al., 1985).

The support and helping patterns between adult children and aged parents are most likely to occur when the elder generation is still relatively healthy and economically independent. Unfortunately, it is in circumstances when the elders become dependent (whether because of illness or financial matters) that adult children find themselves in a most difficult situation. This would especially be the case when there is a potential for conflict between adult children's career, spousal, and parental commitments and their concerns and commitments to their aged parents. As the elder generation ages, they increasingly find that they cannot meet their own everyday needs, and often their adult children cannot provide the necessary aid.

As they move into the new "age frontier," the elderly are confronted with a dazzling array of services from home health aides to community-living facilities (*Newsweek,* 1997). Instead of nursing homes, seniors are increasingly choosing either assisted-living facilities or continuing-care retirement communities (CCRCs). The former, which charge anywhere from several hundred to several thousand dollars a month, offer residents meals, housekeeping services, and help with basic tasks such as dressing and bathing. CCRCs offer a wider range of living choices, enabling tenants to move from apartments to nursing facilities within the same complex. They cost more as well. For a one-bedroom apartment, entry fees alone run as high as $87,000, with monthly rents of $1,000 and up (*Newsweek,* 1997).

Despite these options, many seniors—even those confined to wheelchairs—prefer to stay in their own homes. As a result, home health care services are booming. The home health care industry has grown phenomenally since the early 1980s. The number of certified home-care agencies has nearly doubled since 1989. This boom reflects a response to the cost of assisted-living facilities and CCRCs as well as the desire to spend their final years at home. The home provides a familiar setting and the situational context where the person is best able to exercise self-determination and maintain ties and relationships with friends and neighbors.

The rise of the American home health care industry began in the early 1980s as a response

to the increasing number of people over the age of 65 and to the cost of nursing-home care. *The New York Times Magazine* (Conover, 1997) reports that 7 million people now receive some form of paid home care. Medicare and Medicaid began to provide funding in 1967 and 1971, respectively. For those over 65 needing skilled recuperative care after an acute illness, Medicare will pay up to 4 hours a day, 7 days a week for 40 days or so. For the poor, Medicaid pays for ongoing home care for those with chronic maladies. When the cost for such care reaches 90 percent of the cost of a nursing home, the patient is usually sent to such a facility.

In the coming years, the home-care field is expected to be one of the fastest-growing industries. The Bureau of Labor Statistics predicts a 119 percent increase in jobs for home-care aides from 1994 to 2005 (cited in Conover, 1997). Today, there are over 1,000 geriatric-care-management businesses; in the New York City metropolitan area alone there are three dozen. These firms oversee all aspects of the care of an aging person including scheduling of doctor appointments and providing accounting help for monthly bills. These agencies—and others that are not as comprehensive in their management facilities—often arrange for health care aides to take care of the everyday needs of elderly people. They may work for a few hours a day, or they may provide 24-hour around-the-clock help 7 days a week.

As Conover observes (1997), the quality and experience of these aides varies widely; many have little or no formal training. They are not there to provide the care that only a registered nurse can provide. Rather, they are people who provide companionship along with light housekeeping that includes grocery shopping, cooking, and cleaning for those elderly that need little else. For those elderly who require help in bathing, dressing, and the taking of medicine, a licensed home health aide with at least 75 hours of training is required.

Conover, in his *New York Times Magazine* cover story on the "new nanny," reports:

> *You see it on the sidewalks and in the parks and lobbies of neighborhoods throughout cities like New York: elderly people, often white, assisted or simply accompanied by younger women, usually black or Hispanic. As our parents and grandparents live longer, and spend fewer and fewer of their final years with us, a caring woman from the Caribbean—her face, her voice, her touch—will very likely be the last human contact many of them will have. (1997:127)*

AN INTIMATE STRANGER RELATIONSHIP CASE STUDY

A close relation, Ben N., died January 2, 1998, 6 months to the day after he was diagnosed with pancreatic cancer. At the time of diagnosis, his physician informed his two daughters that he had between 3 to 6 months to live. While his death was predictable, events in the unfolding time period would prove problematic. The focus of this case study is on the last 2 months of his life and the relationships that developed—not so much between Ben and his home-care worker, Georgette, but rather between Georgette and Ben's companion of 5 years, Mary; between Georgette and Ben's two daughters, Phyllis and Judith; and between Mary and the two sisters.

Ben was 87 when he died. He was married for 52 years. His wife, Freida, died in 1992. Shortly thereafter he began an intimate relationship with Mary, a woman 15 years his junior. Mary was a widow whose only child died in early adulthood. She had no immediate relatives

that she interacted with on an everyday basis. During the 5 years that they were companions, they kept separate apartments in a cooperative apartment house complex in Brooklyn. Blessed with good health, Ben continued the pattern of autonomy from his children and their families that characterized his retirement years with Freida. He saw them periodically, and they kept in touch weekly by telephone. He and Mary spent much of their time together relatively uninvolved with other family members, friends, or neighbors.

Ben's grandparenthood role follows Cherlin and Furstenburg's observation that many grandparents prefer to have "a place in the family, [and] a life apart." This characterized Ben's relationship with his children and grandchildren both during the period when Freida was alive and after he was with Mary.

In turn, Ben's daughters also had their own separate involvements. Phyllis lives in the Philadelphia metropolitan area, 100 miles away from her father. She is employed full-time as a special education teacher. Her sister Judith lives in Suffolk County, Long Island, New York, and she and her self-employed husband own a second home in Florida to which they commute on a regular basis. Both daughters have adult children who are on their own but remain in constant contact either through daily phone chats or frequent visits.

Following the schema developed by Herbert Gans (1962), both sisters' conjugal families fall into the "adult directed" category characteristic of the upper-middle class. Predominantly college educated, this family type is interested in and participates in the activities of the larger world. Its activities are not confined to the local community. Extended kinship ties and the home are given low priority. Frequently, the wife pursues a career prior to having children and is either working or has aspirations to work as the children are growing. Domestic household activities are alleviated to some extent through the employment of service help or the sharing of activities by both spouses. Children serve as a common focal point of interest and concern. These upper-middle-class couples are concerned with the intellectual and social development of their children. They are highly motivated to provide direction in the lives of their children, so that family life is child centered as well as adult centered.

In contrast, Ben and Freida's family pattern through most of their marriage can be characterized, utilizing Gans's schema, as "adult centered." Here the husband and wife live gender-segregated. roles. They have separate family roles and engage in little of the companionship typically found in the middle class. The husband is predominantly the wage earner and the enforcer of child discipline. The wife's activities are confined to household tasks and child rearing. Children are expected to follow adult rules and are required to act "grown up"; they are disciplined when they act childish. Family life is centered around the desires and interests of the adults and does not cater to the demands of the children. This was Ben and Freida's parental pattern. Gans also observes that husbands and wives are frequently involved with extended kin and with neighbors and friends, albeit different ones for each. In Ben and Freida's case this did not hold true; they were minimally involved with such others.

This "adult centered" pattern continued throughout their marriage. Soon after Freida's death, Ben developed a companionship relationship with Mary that essentially took on the same pattern. Ben's independence from his family continued until his complaint of abdominal pain was diagnosed as pancreatic cancer on July 1997. Ben, although not told of the full implications of his illness, was now confronted with the realization that he would need medical care in the short term (chemotherapy), and that he would need full-time care in the not-to-distant future. He also

knew that Mary would be unable to provide that help. Further, he knew that his daughters' own concerns and involvements would prevent them from providing full-time care.

The daughters realized that they were faced with a dilemma common in our geographically mobile society. They would have to become increasingly more involved in the day-to-day life of their father to ensure his well-being, yet they did not live in easy commuting distance from him. Further, their own personal and professional commitments would have to temper that involvement.

It was in July that Ben underwent a 10-week chemotherapy treatment. Judith and her husband took him and Mary to the treatment center each week. The chemotherapy weakened him, but it had the positive effect of minimizing pain. He was beginning the process of slow physical decline and was getting progressively more tired and weak. Yet, his desire for independence and to be on his own strongly motivated his behavior. He continued to drive, albeit on shorter trips. Rather than walk to the neighborhood diner, he drove; he also drove to the doctor. And on a day that he felt particularly strong, he and Mary took a 1-day bus excursion to the casinos in Atlantic City.

But the signs were clear. When he fell going to the bathroom one night and had difficulty getting up, he realized that he would need everyday help. In the fourth month into his terminal illness, it was decided among Ben, Judith, and Phyllis that Mary should not and could not take care of him as he started slipping into a steady health decline. A home-care aide would help provide the round-the-clock personal care that Ben required. The aide would also be able to take on light housekeeping duties such as grocery shopping and cooking. It was in early October that a home health care agency was contacted.

After the hiring of two unsatisfactory aides, Georgette was hired. Like many other aides,

Georgette was from Jamaica, in the Caribbean. Health care is one of the few careers traditionally open to women in Jamaica—a fact that dovetails nicely with Americans' growing needs (Conover, 1997). Extended family relationships are strong for many people of the Caribbean, and the integration of elderly people into the nuclear family is common. Such involvements and experience make it relatively easy to transfer that caring relationship to strangers. One Jamaican woman home-care giver asserts:

> *In the countryside, we always take care of old people ourselves, Lorna says. And frankly, she feels, it is superior to the American system. When you do it yourself, "You give them more love, you understand much more about them. You make them more happy." That happiness is important, she says, because "you have some old people who just give up on their life." (Conover, 1997:127)*

However, many such women often find themselves in a sense victimized by the global economy. The pressing needs of the elderly in the United States provides them with economic opportunities to move to this country and fill a gap in the health care of the elderly. But paradoxically, at the same time that they provide service to the elderly, they often find themselves forced to leave their own parents and children. That was the case for Georgette. Her 7-year-old son, Robert, was cared for by her mother in Jamaica. Much of the money she earned was earmarked for her family back home. If financially feasible, between jobs she tried to return to Jamaica to see her family. In the meantime she lived with the elders and, when she did have time off she had space in her aunt's apartment.

For Ben, Georgette proved to be an ideal employee. She was young, attractive, and more importantly, had a warm personality and was quick to smile and laugh. Arlie Hochschild talks of "emotion work," and this was an essential feature of Georgette's work. She took care of the home—cleaned, grocery shopped, and did some cooking. Most importantly, she allayed Ben's increasing fear of dependency.

Intimacy became an integral part of their relationship. The literature on the dying observes that because an aide tends to spend the most time with the dying patient, the relationship may become intimate (Marrone, 1996). Similarly, Tracy X. Karner (1998), in a study of home-care workers with elderly care recipients, found that a sphere of intimacy often develops between the care recipient and the caregiver that takes the form of a familial relationship. She observes that the home-care worker may be "adopted" as "fictive kin." Fictive kin is defined as individuals who are not related by blood but by choice. These adopted family members accept the affection, obligations, and duties of actual kin.

The two sisters fully appreciated how important Georgette's supportive and expressive role behavior was for both Ben and for themselves. She could provide the everyday care and attentiveness that the sisters were unable to provide. During the 2-month period that Georgette lived with Ben, the sisters felt comforted by the fact that Ben was not alone. This stranger was providing an emotional haven that helped Ben cope with his increasingly debilitating illness. During the numerous times that they called each day, Georgette would answer the phone and give the current progress report on Ben's behavior: what and how much he ate, if he went outside for a brief stroll, if he slept through the night, etc. Judith would visit one day during the week, and Phyllis would come on a weekend day to check on things and to spend time with her father.

Mary, however, had a different relationship with both Georgette and the sisters after Georgette's arrival. Mary realized the need for such an aide; she was not capable, emotionally or physically, of providing the 24-hour care that Ben increasingly required. At the same time, she did not relish another woman entering Ben's everyday life. From the outset, Mary responded antagonistically to Georgette's work efforts. She constantly complained to the two sisters as well as to Ben of her belief that Georgette was not performing her duties in a satisfactory manner. She felt that the aide was not looking after Ben in a way the she would have and that the aide did not devote sufficient attention to him. It was the very intimate nature of the relationship between Georgette and Ben that Mary found most upsetting and threatening. Jealousy—for no other word seems appropriate—governed Mary's perception of Georgette. That Ben was developing a beneficial attachment to Georgette was interpreted by Mary as a threat to her relationship with Ben and his daughters.

At the end of November, around Thanksgiving, Ben had to go into the hospital for a medical procedure to relieve some of his discomfort. Georgette spent the full day with Ben. Mary visited for a few hours each day. When either sister went to the hospital to visit, Mary would express her dissatisfaction with Georgette. Both were more concerned with their father's health and mental outlook than they were with Mary's insistence that Georgette was doing things wrong. They had to admonish Mary on separate occasions to control her dislike for Georgette because it was only upsetting them and their father. The relationship between Mary and the sisters was becoming more and more strained.

Ben returned home a week later, and the home-care pattern continued. Georgette continued to fulfill her role, and Mary took every opportunity to demean it. At times, Mary threat-

ened not to visit, but she continued to see Ben. On New Year's Eve, Ben had to go into the hospital for another medical procedure. He died on January 2. Mary saw him that morning and left. Georgette spent the day with him. Phyllis and her husband and their daughter visited him in the afternoon. He got up to go to the bathroom, collapsed, and died.

After Ben's death, Judith telephoned Mary. Mary's response was a hysterical diatribe against Georgette—that through Georgette's negligence Ben died much sooner than he should have. Rather than expressing her grief at his death, she castigated Judith and, in turn, Phyllis, for (as she perceived it) their inattentiveness toward Ben during the last months of his life.

Lyn Lofland (1992), citing the literature on loneliness, observes that there is considerable social isolation of men and women following the death of their spouses or the breakdown of their marriages. She quotes Helena Lopata, who relates this phenomena to widows:

> *Many wives enjoy company parties, golf, couple-companionate dinners, and such events, and will not engage in them after the husband dies or have them no longer available* since it was his presence which formed the connecting link in the first place. *(Lopata, 1969, p. 253 [italics added] cited in Lofland, 1992:165)*

Similarly, in the case of a companion, this social isolation is even more likely to occur. The relationship of a companion with the children of her partner is quite tenuous. Indeed, the relationship that existed between Mary and Ben's daughters can at best be defined as courteous, and by no means did an emotional bond develop. Mary was invited as a matter of course to all family gatherings, including Judith's eldest son's wedding.

One would suspect that Mary feared that with the death of Ben her relationship with the daughters would also die. Through her actions, a self-fulfilling prophecy occurred.

At the funeral, Mary refused to go to the cemetery with the family. Georgette was also at the funeral, and she expressed her regrets. The sisters subsequently wrote a letter of recommendation and personally thanked her for the comfort that she provided for their father. They have not spoken to or been in contact with Mary since the funeral.

CONCLUSION

Of crucial concern in the years ahead is the increasing number of people over the age of 65 and the increasing number who will live beyond 85. The prospects, then, are of an aging population taking care of a very old population, with all the consequent emotional and financial strains. Given these demographic trends, the problems of the elderly and the sandwich generation will multiply in ways that we are only just beginning to comprehend.

Shanas (1980) cautions that we still know relatively little about the quality of the living arrangements of the elderly. "In much the same way, we do not know whether the visits between older parents and their children and relatives are brief or lengthy, friendly and warm, or acrimonious and hostile" (Shanas, 1980:13). We know that they do occur and that there is social exchange, but "[t]he nature of such an exchange may just be, as people say, 'a visit,' or it may involve actual help and services between the generations" (1980:13).

This observation can be extended to the elderly–home-care aide relationship. The study by Karner (1998) observes that the reconstruction of the care recipient and home-care worker relationship from a professional and task-oriented relationship to a fictive kin relationship has positive consequences for both recipient and the caregiver. Defining the relationship in this manner allows the elder to feel more comfortable in accepting and expecting care from an individual outside of the family. For the home-care worker, much of their job (such as performing basic household tasks like cleaning, shopping, and meal preparation, and personal care like bathing and grooming) is often routine and tedious. Defining the relationship "as one of fictive kin with all the attendant responsibilities and obligations of blood relations…" allows "the homecare worker a means to negotiate the devaluation and lack of status of her employment" (Karner, 1998:80).

Conover (1997), however, cautions that while there are many case studies of positive relationships that have developed between the home health care aide and the elderly, there are many case studies that report on negative relationships. These include abusive relationships with both the elderly abusing the aide and the aide abusing the elderly. There are reports of wholesale theft. More systematic research needs to be done on this relationship.

Further, what little research there is on the relationship between the elderly and the health care worker there are virtually no studies on the relationship between the health care worker and the elderly's family members, companions, and friends. In one of the few studies done, Davis (1992) reports that when home-care worker services are delivered in conjunction with family caregiving, the relationship may result in "interpersonal triangles" involving the elderly, the worker, and family members. The impact of these relationships on the well-being of the elderly has not been studied.

The government has done little to regulate and examine this relationship of intimate strangers in any systematic detail. The case study relationships reported here were positive for Ben and

Georgette and for Georgette and the two sisters and quite negative for Mary in her dealings with Georgette and the two sisters. Other relationships may have strikingly different outcomes.

There is an obligation for cooperation between the government and the family to care for the elderly. Home health care, nursing care and nursing homes will become even more significant in the future as more elderly people find that they do not or cannot live with their families. The cost for such care, as well as the increased share of the national budget needed to be devoted to health care for the elderly, must be confronted now. Further, and most important, the quality of that care must be secured; yet, we find little systematic governmental attention to this future problem.

Shanas is optimistic that the four-generation family and the emerging kinship ties will con-

tinue to demonstrate the amazing resiliency that they have through the centuries. "They may be different for old people in the future from what they are now, but they will continue to provide safe harbor for their members however long they may live" (Shanas, 1980:14). Gelman, in his 1985 *Newsweek* article concludes:

> *If a society can be judged by the way it treats its elderly, then we are not without honor—so far. But as we all grow older, that honor will demand an ever higher price. (Gelman et al., 1985:68)*

Part IV

Families in Crisis and Change

In this part of the reader, we examine two problematic aspects of marriage and family life. The ensuing selections will illustrate how patriarchy has been a major contributor to marital and familial tensions and problems. Patriarchal ideology supported by economic, social, political, and religious institutions often enables men to exert the upper hand in many aspects of marital and family relationships. Similarly, the domination of older family members over younger ones has often been the consequence of age stratification processes operating in family systems. In Chapter Eight, "Family Stress, Crisis, and Violence," the first two deal with the ultimate abuse of marital and familial patterns of stratification and power—family violence.

Intimate violence, whether it takes the form of wife battering or child abuse, can be seen as an irrational outgrowth of the excesses of patriarchal authority. The legitimation of male prerogatives, privilege, authority, and power can be abused, and in the case of wife battering, it is. This results in the severe mistreatment of women. Contemporary American society has just recently discovered the prevalence of marital abuse, which has been hidden from history because the belief that "normal" marriages are happy and well adjusted and that violence is an aberration has led to the underestimation of such abuse. This misunderstanding has further led to the treatment of marital abuse erroneously as a psychologically determined pathology and not as a social phenomenon.

Similarly, child abuse can be seen as a negative consequence of the conceptualization of children and adolescents as essentially inferior and subordinate human beings. Structural characteristics of the private nuclear family also play important contributory roles. Governmental policies and the underlying assumptions of the helping professions, too, often work against the best interests of children.

John M. Johnson and Kathleen J. Ferraro, two sociologists who work out of the symbolic interaction perspective of social psychology, are concerned with how individuals continually adapt to situations and how these adaptations affect self concepts. In Reading 21,

Johnson and Ferraro study the experiences of battered women, who find themselves living through episodic outbursts of violence from their mates. The consequences of that victimization on their sense of identity is the focus of their concern.

In the next reading (22), Murray A. Straus discusses the ten myths that are seen to perpetuate corporal punishment. This reading comes from Straus's larger study, *Beating the Devil Out of Them* (1994). Straus is concerned with spanking and its widespread prevalence. He demonstrates how taken-for-granted notions, religious admonitions, child-rearing advice books, and legal statutes all permit and often encourage the use of corporal punishment in response to a child's misbehavior. As a consequence, a "conspiracy of silence" has prevailed whose effect has prevented the investigation of potentially harmful effects of corporal punishment on children. Straus observes that in recent years there has been a cultural debate that centers on questioning such beliefs as: spanking works better, spanking is needed as a last resort, spanking is harmless, and if you don't spank, your child will be spoiled or run wild. Straus calls these "myths that perpetuate corporal punishment." In five European countries—Finland, Sweden, Norway, Denmark, and Austria—legislation has been passed that has outlawed physical punishment of children, including spanking. In the United States, Straus sees the beginning of a social trend that seeks to redefine expected parental behavior into reprehensible behavior.

The concluding reading (23) in this chapter examines the effects of homelessness on family relationships. The homeless family became a visible phenomena on the American scene in the 1980s. Government figures on the number of homeless range from 350,000 to 2,000,000. Advocates of the homeless put the figure much higher, into the double digits— 10 to 20 million. The variation in these estimates is attributable to the difficulty in getting accurate assessments of people who are highly transient and often unwilling to be counted. Who are these homeless people? The evidence that has been collected indicates that they vary greatly from the "old" homeless who populated the nation's Skid Rows of the 1950s and 1960s who were almost all white males with an average age of around fifty years. The new homeless are characterized by extreme poverty and little family support. They are much younger—around thirty years of age—25 percent are women, and proportionately, African Americans and Hispanics constitute an increasing number of them (Rossi, 1994).

The primary reason for the upsurge in homelessness is related to the structural changes occurring in the economy as it moves from a manufacturing base with large numbers of low-skill manual jobs to a service base requiring higher educational attainment and greater occupational skills (Rossi, 1994). The deteriorating value of AFDC payments and the crisis in affordable housing are contributing factors. The most significant change in the demographic composition of the new homeless was the appearance of homeless families. These families are identified as being single-parent, mostly young mothers in their twenties, with very young children. How these economic changes have impacted on families is given a human dimension in the excerpt (Reading 23) from Steven Vanderstaay's (1992) *Street Lives: An Oral History of Homeless Americans.* "Karla" is the oral history of a woman with two children; Mark and Linda Armstrong are the parents of teenage children.

The final chapter of the book, Chapter Nine, "Divorce, Remarriage, and the Future of the Family," contains four readings. Divorce is a major form of marital dissolution. It represents an ultimate manifestation of marital and familial instability. Divorce has been viewed by some as an indicator of the breakdown of the American family and as a reflection of societal decline. Conversely, others see it as the outcome of a positive individual act, ultimately beneficial to all members and, as such, a sign of societal strength.

Terry Arendell, in an examination of divorce research, observes that while attention has been paid predominantly to mothers and children, fathers have been relatively neglected. In her ethnographic monograph, *Fathers and Divorce* (1995), she examines a group of divorced fathers and their views and behavior on a wide range of topics from noncustodial parenting to relationships with their former spouses to fathers' rights. Arendell refers to the views of these fathers as a "masculinist discourse of divorce." In an earlier article, "The Social Self as Gendered: A Masculinist Discourse of Divorce" (Reading 24), Arendell developed this perspective.

She observes that to understand this shared discourse, we must see it in terms of the larger context of gender arrangements and identities. That is, to understand how men perceive, recognize, and act toward divorce and divorce relationships we must put this masculinist discourse in the larger context of men's views of gender, marriage, parenthood, and the family.

The effects of divorce on children and adolescents has long been a concern of sociologists. These effects have become an even more urgent matter in light of the continued high divorce rate in the United States and the fact that an increasing number of children are affected. In 1960 the number of children involved in divorce was 500,000; thirty years later it doubled to more than 1 million. It is estimated that nearly half of all children under the age of eighteen will experience divorce in the 1990s. Paul R. Amato (Reading 25) provides us with a comprehensive examination of the life-span adjustment of children to their parents' divorce. He states that these children exhibit more conduct problems, more symptoms of psychological maladjustments, lower academic achievement, more social difficulties, and poorer self-concepts compared to children who live in continuously intact two-parent families. Some of the key factors that relate to children's adjustment include the amount and quality of contact with noncustodial kin, the custodial parents' psychological adjustment and parenting skills, the level of inter-parental conflict before and after divorce, the degree of economic hardship that children are exposed to, and the number of stressful events that accompany and follow divorce. He believes that these factors can be used as guides to assess the probable impact of various legal and therapeutic interventions to improve the well-being of children of divorce.

The study of remarriage has increasingly become an interest of sociologists who study the family. There is a myth surrounding remarriage that says the second marriage is more successful than the first—that "love is better the second time around." According to popular opinion, this is so because remarried individuals are now older, wiser, and more mature. Also, it is assumed that divorced persons who remarry will work harder to ensure a more

successful second marriage. Yet Andrew Cherlin (1978), in a much-cited article, reported
that the divorce rate for remarried parents was higher than for persons married for the first
time. According to this researcher, insufficient institutional supports and guidelines to ensure
optimal success of these marriages account for the high rate of divorce among remarried people with children. Cherlin observed that family members of such remarriages faced unique
problems that do not exist in first-marriage families. He believes that the origins of these
problems lie in the complex structure of remarried families and the normative inadequacies
to define these familial roles and relationships. Cherlin's seminal article pointed out the necessity for a more systematic investigation of remarriage. In 1994 Cherlin, along with a colleague, Frank F. Furstenberg, Jr. (Reading 26), did just that.

In Reading 26, Cherlin and Furstenberg examine remarriage by examining the changing demography of divorce and remarriage; new forms of kinship and family organization;
the process of building a stepfamily; the effects of remarriage on children; and the public
policy implications and the suggested directions for new research.

In the concluding reading (27) of this anthology, Marvin B. Sussman, a major researcher in the study of the family for many years, writes on families in the future. He provides a global perspective by looking at such concerns as overpopulation; aging and the
aged; energy; continuous global conflict; climate and food; the global system; AIDS,
chronic illness, and care; the economy; religious awakening; and the gender revolution.
Sussman observes that the anticipated changes in the immediate future will have long-range
implications on the family, and the family must be willing to meet the risks and challenges
by moving out of "encrusted old patterns and encapsulated egos."

References

Arendell, Terry 1995. *Fathers and Divorce.* Berkeley: University of California Press.
Cherlin, Andrew. 1978. "Remarriage as an Incomplete Institution." *American Journal of Sociology* 84(3):634–650.
Rossi, Peter H. 1994. "Troubling Families: Family Homelessness in America." *American Behavioral Scientist* 37 (January) 3:342–395.
Straus, Murray A. Straus. 1994. *Beating the Devil Out of Them: Corporal Punishment in American Families.* New York: Lexington Books.
Vanderstaay, Steven. 1992. *Street Lives: An Oral History of Homeless Americans.* Philadelphia, PA: New Society Publishers.

8 Family Stress, Crisis, and Violence

Reading 21 The Victimized Self: The Case of Battered Women*

JOHN M. JOHNSON AND KATHLEEN J. FERRARO

In existential sociology the self is not fixed but continually changes and adapts to new situations. The self is essentially open to the world of experience, both positive and negative. When the existential self is confronted with challenging or taxing circumstances, it does not usually recoil or shatter. Instead, it struggles to incorporate new experiences into its evolving reality. Battered women provide an excellent example of this. The victimization experienced by battered women illustrates how the existential self moves from one identity to another under varying conditions.[1] Contrary to much of the research and mass-media reporting about battered women, they do not become victims simply by being the recipients of physical violence. In fact, many women live their entire lives experiencing episodic outbursts of violence from their mates without developing the feelings and identity of a victimized self.[2]

The victimized self is a complex mixture of feelings and thoughts based on the individual's overriding feeling of having been violated, exploited, or wronged by another person or persons. It develops when an individual feels a fundamen-tal threat to his or her very being or existence. The actions or situations people interpret as funda-mental threats are varied. Some women feel deeply threatened by verbal assaults, while others may come close to death regularly without feeling themselves to be victims (Ferraro 1979).

THE VICTIMIZATION PROCESS

Women who experience repeated violence or abuse without feeling victimized make use of ra-tionalizations and belief systems that allow them to maintain a feeling of being in a good, normal, or at least acceptable marriage. For example, some women play the role of a "caring wife" and view situations of violence as occasions for taking re-sponsibility to "save" their husbands. Others deny the injuries done to them, even relatively serious ones, and act as if the violence had not occurred. Some will acknowledge the existence of the abuse but reject the husband's responsibility, blaming in-stead external factors, such as unemployment, al-coholism, or mental illness. Others may feel they "had it coming," an attitude commonly based on

*Johnson, John M. and Kathleen J. Ferraro. 1984. "The Victimized Self: The Case of Battered Women." Pp. 119–130 in *The Existential Self in Society,* edited by Joseph A. Kotarba and Andrea Fontana. Chicago: University of Chicago Press. © 1984 by The University of Chicago. All rights reserved. Reprinted by permission.

feelings of submission to the husband's traditionally defined absolute dominance in the home. And some appeal to higher or institutional loyalties, such as religion, the church, or the sanctity of family life. All of these rationalizations are used by individuals to make sense of their feelings, to make rational what might otherwise be seen as irrational. For some women, these rationalizations can sustain a marriage through a lifetime of violence or abuse. Some may go to their graves believing in them, as did over 3,600 victims of family homicides in 1980 (Ferraro 1982).

Some battered women experience a turning point when the violence or abuse done to them comes to be felt as a basic threat, whether to their physical or social self or to both. Such turning points may stem from dramatic events or crises. They may additionally originate from progressive, gradual realizations by women. In all cases, however, the experience of the turning point produces retrospective interpretations of past events, where individuals creatively seek out new understandings of "what went wrong." What had been rationalized as acceptable is recast as dangerous, malicious, perhaps life-threatening. Before this point, many women may have felt guilt concerning their own complicity in their family situations and perhaps hopefulness that things would improve over time. But these feelings commonly change to feelings of fear and despair. The experience of the turning point produces changes in feelings and interpretations. A new sense of self emerges to meet these emergent conditions. While the development of a victimized self is commonly temporary for individuals, at this juncture the self becomes organized around the perceived facts of victimization. Once women develop a victimized self—a new feeling of being exploited and a new interpretation of the causes and consequences of this exploitation—they may become sufficiently motivated to leave violent situations.

An individual's adoption of a victimized self is all-consuming. For the immediate present it tends to override (but not necessarily destroy) other aspects of the self. It becomes an organizing perspective by which all other aspects of life are interpreted or reinterpreted. It has some similarities to what Everett C. Hughes termed "master status," and indeed, for some rare individuals, the victimized self may assume such importance for long periods of time, perhaps even for the remainder of the person's life. But for most, the victimized self is temporary. After leaving a violent relationship a woman soon begins to take practical steps toward recovery and the rebuilding of her life. She must either set up a new, independent household, arrange for marriage counseling, or return to the marriage with renewed optimism that things will be different. These actions militate against continuance of the individual's sense of victimization. Thus, the victimized self tends to be temporary, certainly for those who mobilize their personal and social resources for change.

The victimized self emerges during moments of existential threat, and it dissolves when one takes actions to construct new, safer living conditions. The victimized self emerges when the rationalizations of violence and abuse begin to lose their power; it becomes the all-consuming basis for however long it takes to transcend this period of crisis and threat. It tends to dissolve, over time, for those who change their lives in new, creative ways, although the sense of victimization never disappears altogether. For all who experience it, it becomes incorporated into an individual's biography as lived experience.

CATALYSTS IN THE VICTIMIZATION PROCESS

When the process of victimization begins, events that previously had been defined as acceptable, although unpleasant, aspects of the relationship begin to take on new meanings. Violence, which had been rationalized as either insignificant in its consequences, beyond the abuser's control, or necessary to the relationship or some other value, is now redefined as abuse or battering.

Changing the definition of events is not an isolated process. It is linked to other aspects of the relationship, and, when these aspects change, specific events within the relationship undergo retrospective reinterpretation. As in cases of nonviolent divorce, what was previously accepted as part of the marriage becomes a focus for discontent (see Rasmussen and Ferraro 1979).

There are a number of catalysts that can trigger this redefinition process. Some authors have noted that degree of severity is related to a woman's decision to leave a violent situation (Gelles 1976). However, it is known that women can suffer extremely severe violence for many years without leaving (Pagelow 1981). What does seem significant is a sudden change in the *level of severity*. Women who suddenly realize that their lives are literally in danger may begin the victimization process. At the point where death is imminent, rationalizations to protect the relationship often lose their validity. Life itself is more important to maintain than the relationship. A woman beaten by an alcoholic husband severely over many years explained her decision to leave on the basis of a direct threat to her life:

> *It was like a pendulum. He'd swing to the extremes both ways. He'd get drunk and beat me up, then he'd get sober and treat me like a queen. One day he put a gun to my head and pulled the trigger. It wasn't loaded. But that's when I decided I'd had it. I sued for separation of property. I knew what was coming again, so I got out. I didn't want to. I still loved the guy, but I knew I had to for my own sanity.*

Of course, many homicides do occur, and in such cases the wife has obviously not correctly interpreted increases in severity as a threat to her life. Increases in severity do not guarantee a reinterpretation of the situation, but they may play a part in the process.

Another catalyst for changing one's definition of violence may be a *change in its visibility*. Creating a web of rationalizations in order to overlook violence is accomplished more easily if no outsiders are present to question their validity. Since most violence between couples occurs in privacy, victims do not have to cope with conflicting interpretations from outsiders. In fact, they may have difficulty in convincing others that they have a problem (Martin 1976; Davidson 1979). However, if the violence does break through the bounds of privacy and occur in the presence of others, it may trigger a reinterpretation process. Having others witness the degradation of violence is humiliating, for it is a public statement of subordination and powerlessness. It may also happen that an objective observer will apply a different definition to the event than what is consistent with the victim's prior rationalizations, and the mere existence of this new definition will call into question the victim's ideas.

The effect of external definitions on a battered woman's beliefs about her situation varies with the source and form of external definitions. The opinions of those who are highly regarded by the victim, either by virtue of a personal relationship or an occupational role, will be the most influential. Disbelief or an unsympathetic response from others tends to suppress a woman's belief that she has been victimized and to encourage her to accept what has happened as normal. However, when outsiders respond with unqualified support and condemnation of the abuser, their definitions can be a potent catalyst toward victimization. Friends and relatives who show genuine concern for the woman's well-being may initiate an awareness of danger that contradicts previous rationalizations. As one woman reported:

> My mother-in-law knew what was going on, but she wouldn't admit it.... I said, "Mom, what do you think these bruises are?" and she said, "Well, some people just bruise easy. I do it all the time, bumping into things.". . . and he just denied it, pretended like nothing happened . . . but this time, my neighbor knew what happened, she saw it, and when he denied it, she said, "I can't believe it! You know that's not true!" . . . and I was so happy that finally somebody else saw what was goin' on, and I just told him that this time I wasn't gonna come home!

Shelters for battered women are one source of external definitions that contribute to the victimization process. They offer refuge from a violent situation, a place where a woman may contemplate her circumstances and what she wants to do about them. Within a shelter she will come into contact with counselors and other battered women, who are familiar with the rationalization process and with the reluctance to give up the image of a good marriage. In counseling sessions, rap groups, and informal conversations with other residents, women will hear horror stories from others who have already defined themselves as victims. They will be encouraged to express anger over their abuse and to reject responsibility for the violence. A major goal of many shelters is to help women overcome feelings of guilt and inadequacy so that they will make choices in their own best interests. In this atmosphere, violent incidents are reexamined and defined as assaults in which the woman was *victimized* (Ferraro 1981).

The emergence of shelters as a place to escape from violent marriages has also established a catalyst for the victimization process simply by providing a *change in resources.* When there is no practical alternative to remaining married, there is no advantage in defining oneself as a victim. When resources become available, however, it may be beneficial to reassess the value of remaining in the marriage. Roy (1979) found that the most commonly stated reason for remaining in a violent marriage was having no place else to go. Certainly, a change in resources, then, would alter one's response to violence. Not only shelters, but a change in personal circumstances, such as having the last child leave home, getting a grant for school, or finding a job, can be the catalyst for beginning to think differently about violence.

Apart from external influences, there may be *changes in the relationship itself* that initiate the victimization process. Walker (1979), in her discussion of the stages of a battering relationship, has noted that violent incidents are usually followed by periods of remorse and solicitude. Such phases can be very romantic and thus bind the woman to her husband. But as the battering progresses, this phase may shorten or disappear altogether, eliminating the basis for maintaining a positive outlook on the marriage. When the man realizes that he can get away with violence, he may view it as his prerogative and no longer feel and express remorse. Extended periods devoid of any show of kindness or love may alter the woman's feelings toward her attacker so that she eventually begins to define herself as a victim. One shelter resident described her disenchantment with her marriage this way:

> At first, you know, we used to have so much fun together. He has kind've, you know, a magnetic personality, he can be really charming. But it isn't fun anymore. Since the baby came,

it's changed completely. He just wants me to stay at home, while he goes out with his friends. He doesn't even talk to me, most of the time. . . . No, I don't think I really love him anymore, not like I did.

Changes in the nature of the relationship may result in a loss of hope that things will get better and lead to feelings of despair. As long as a woman can cling to a hope that the violence will stop, she can delude herself about it. But when these hopes are finally destroyed and she feels only despair, she may begin to interpret violence as victimization. The Al-Anon philosophy, which is designed for spouses of alcoholics, who are often also victims of abuse, emphasizes the importance of "hitting bottom" before a person can make real changes in his or her life. The director of an Al-Anon-organized shelter explained hitting bottom to me:

Before the Al-Anon program can really be of benefit, a woman has to hit bottom. When you hit bottom, you realize that all of your own efforts to control the situation have failed; you feel helpless and lost and worthless and completely disenchanted with the world. Women can't really be helped unless they're ready for it and want it. Some women come here when things get bad, but they aren't really ready to be committed to Al-Anon yet. Things haven't gotten bad enough for them, and they go right back. We see this all the time.

She stressed that it is not the objective level of violence that determined hitting bottom but, rather, the woman's feelings of despair. Before one can develop a real, effective sense of victimization, it is necessary to feel that the very foundations of the self have been threatened or attacked, that one's very life or social being is endangered. It isn't until that primordial threat has been experienced that it is likely that the individual will be mobilized for effective action, the kind sufficient to break love-bounds or to change external circumstances. Many do not reach this point. In 1980 over 3,600 persons were killed in family homicides. This figure alone indicates that the interpretive processes discussed here are problematic ones for individuals. Violence may never be interpreted as life-threatening even if it eventually has mortal consequences.

THE TURNING POINT

The victimization process involves redefining past events, their meanings, and one's role in them. Violent incidents must be interpreted as violations of one's rights, as unjustified attacks on one's self, and as the responsibility of the attacker in order for a victimized self to emerge. Whatever the original context of the violence, it is now viewed as the most explicit expression of a generalized pattern of abuse. The positive aspects of the relationship fade into the past, the interactional subtleties and nuances become blurred, and the self becomes organized around victimization.

For some, the awareness of the victimized self may begin with a relatively dramatic event, a "turning point," perhaps similar to what anthropologists have termed "culture shock," that heightened existential awareness associated with meeting persons from foreign cultures, when attempts at communication lay bare the artificiality of social conventions. For others, the process may be more gradual. In either case, the result is similar: for the individual, an awareness of the social reality previously taken for granted. For all individuals, almost all of the time, daily life has a certain obdurate, taken-for-granted quality to it. The substance of what is taken for granted varies from culture to culture, even between individuals within a given culture, whether one is an artist or a hod carrier. But for all persons, most of their lives have this taken-for-granted quality, which is occasionally interrupted or broken by crises of one sort or another. The effect of such crises is to reacquaint the individual with the precariousness of this taken-for-granted reality. This is a time of heightened self-consciousness, when things and events, previously assumed to have an "objective" character, seem to be merely human in their nature. Individuals who experience this crisis in their daily life commonly begin elaborate reconstructions and reinterpretations of past events and individuals in their lives. Different features of events are highlighted. Individuals previously idealized are now "demonized," as Jack Douglas has termed it, as facts of their (putative) character are fashioned in such a manner as to make sense of their evil victimizing. For some persons, perhaps only a few major portions of their lives are reinterpreted (such as the meanings of one's courtship and marriage, following a subsequent reinterpretation of battering), while for others the reinterpretation may be "global," encompassing all aspects of one's life and identity, which are now cast in a new light and subject to new understandings. Such a global reconstruction rarely occurs quickly. It commonly takes months, even years. But initiation of the process involves temporarily adopting a victimized self as a "master status" (Hughes 1958), an interpretive frame that overrides all others in importance for the person and provides the foundation for all lesser interpretations. "Being a victim" is a way of relating to the world, a way of organizing one's thoughts and feelings about daily events and persons. Old things are seen in a new way. Old feelings are felt differently now. Old meanings are experienced in a different light. A woman who discussed her marriage while staying at a shelter illustrates this process of reinterpreting the past:

> *When I look back on it now, of course, I can see how all along he'd do anything to control me. First it was little things, like wanting me not to wear makeup, then it got so he criticized everything I did. He wouldn't let me drive or handle our money. He wouldn't even let me buy the kids' Christmas presents. I think he wanted me to be his slave, and so he started beating on me to make sure I was scared of him.*

Achieving a new sense of a victimized self commonly prepares the way for practical action. While it is true that some individuals seem to find solace and comfort in their interpretations of victimization as such, this is not true for most of those who feel victimized. Feeling victimized threatens one's self, one's sense of competence, and this is usually related to practical actions to see that the victimization stops or does not reoccur. The practical actions taken by individuals vary greatly. One battered woman might leave her husband, establish an independent existence, and perhaps undergo counseling to change relationship patterns that had become habitual over the years. Another might return to the marriage, accepting the husband's claims that he has changed and that he will never hurt her again. Some of those who are victimized join together with others for many purposes, such as setting up self-help groups (e.g., Al-Anon), or for social-movement organization and action. The feeling of victimization underlies social-movement participation in many cases and some political actions as well. Wars, revolutions, and many social movements have started with the feelings of the victimized self.

THE EMOTIONAL CAREER OF THE VICTIMIZED SELF

The cognitive aspects of accepting a victimized self, such as rejecting rationalizations and reinterpreting the past, are tied to the feelings that are created by being battered: The emotional career of the victimized self begins with guilt, shame, and hopefulness, moves to despair and fear, shock and confusion, and finally to relief and sometimes even elation. These feelings are experienced by women who first rationalize violence, then reach a turning point, and finally take action to escape. At any point in her emotional career a woman may decide to cling to rationalizations and a violent marriage. Only about half of the women who enter shelters actually progress along this emotional career to the point of feeling relief that they are no longer in danger. The career path, then, should be viewed as a continuum rather than a fixed sequence through which all battered women pass.

When men beat their wives, they usually have some explanation for their violence even if that explanation seems nonsensical to outsiders. Women are told that their abuse is a natural response to their inadequacies. They are made to feel that they are deficient as women, since they are unable to make their husbands happy. Battered women often feel quite guilty about their marital problems. They feel largely responsible for their husbands' violence and make efforts to control anything that might trigger their displeasure. They feel that the violence is a reflection of their own incompetence or badness. Feelings of guilt and shame are part of the early emotional career of battered victims. At the same time, however, they feel a kind of hopefulness that things will get better. Even the most violent man

is nonviolent much of the time, so there is always a basis for believing that violence is exceptional and that the "real" man is not a threat.

> *First of all, the first beatings, you can't believe it yourself. I'd go to bed, and I'd cry, and I just couldn't believe this was happening, and I'd wake up the next morning thinking, that couldn't have happened, or maybe it was my fault, it's so unbelievable, that this person that you're married to and you love would do that to you, but yet you can't leave either because ya know, for the other 29 days of the month that person loves you and is with you.*

These feelings of guilt and shame mixed with hopefulness give way to despair when the violence continues and the relationship loses all semblance of a loving partnership. At the point of despair, the catalysts described above are most likely to influence a battered woman to make a change.

The turning point in the victimization process, when the self becomes organized around a fundamental threat, is characterized by a penetrating fear. Women who do see their husbands' actions as life-threatening experience a fear that consumes all thoughts and energies. It is felt physiologically in general body achiness, a pain in the pit of the stomach, and tension headaches. There is physical shaking, chills, and inability to eat or sleep. Sometimes the fear is expressed as a numbed shock, in which little is felt or communicated. The belief that her husband is intent on inflicting serious bodily harm explodes the prior self, which is built on rationalizations and the myth of a "good marriage." The self is left without a reality base, in a crisis of ambiguity. The woman is no longer the wife she defined herself to be, but she has not had time to create new meanings for her life. She feels afraid, alone, and confused.

> *At that point, I was just panicked, and all I kept thinking was, "Oh God, he's gonna kill me." I could not think straight, I was so tired and achey, I couldn't deal with anything, find a place to move and all that. Thank God my friends took me in and hid me. They took me by the hand and led me through the motions for a few days, just took care of me, because I really felt just sick.*

The victimized self is highly vulnerable. Battered women escaping violent situations depend on the nurturance and support of outsiders, sometimes strangers in shelters, to endure the period of fear and shock that follows leaving the marriage. In cases where women do not feel the support of others, an abuser's pleas to come home and try again are especially appealing and often effective. People in great pain and confusion will turn to those who offer warmth. If a violent husband is the only person who appears to offer that warmth, a battered woman will probably return to the relationship. However, if she is able to find and accept a temporary refuge with friends, relatives, or a shelter, she will be in a situation much more conducive to the relief that follows in the wake of a crisis endured. Once situated in a safe location, with supportive people, fear for her life subsides. Then, perhaps, she will feel relieved to lay down a burden she has carried for months or years. She will be free of the continuous concern to prevent violence by controlling all potentially disturbing events. This sudden relief sometimes turns to feelings of elation and exhilaration when women who have repressed their own desires find themselves free to do as they please. Women in shelters often

rejoice at such commonplace events as going shopping, getting their hair done, or taking their children to the park without worrying about their husbands' reactions.

> *Boy, tomorrow I'm goin' downtown, and I've got my whole day planned out, and I'm gonna do what I wanna do, and if somebody doesn't like it, to Hell with them! You know, I'm having such a good time, I shoulda done this years ago!*

The elation that accompanies freedom serves as a wellspring of positive action to begin a new life. The difficult tasks of finding a new home, getting divorced, and, often, finding a job are tackled with energies that had previously been directed toward "keeping the peace." As these activities begin, however, the self moves away from victimization. Active involvement with others to obtain one's own desires is inconsistent with the victimized self. The feelings and perceptions of self required to leave a violent marriage wither away as battered women begin to build a new self in a new situation.

CONCLUSION

Feeling victimized is for most individuals a temporary, transitory stage. There are good reasons for this. While it is of great importance for victimized individuals to achieve and create new understandings of their present and past, and while this itself alleviates some of the sufferings of victimization, there are certain incompatibilities between feeling victimized and being oriented toward practical actions to change one's situation in the world. Feeling victimized implies, for most persons, significant passivity in accepting external definitions and statuses. To change such a situation involves the individual in active, purposive, creative behavior. Since victimization represents a primordial threat to the self, individuals are highly motivated to change these circumstances, and these actions by themselves diminish the sense of victimization. The specific time frame for this transitory period varies. For most wars, revolutions, and social movements, it may be a matter of months or years. For individuals caught in the throes of a violent marriage for decades, the process may take longer, even the remainder of their lives. It makes little difference, however, whether or not the practical actions achieve "success," whether success is defined in terms of revolutionary victory, the success of a social-movement organization, or moving into a new relationship in which violent or abusive acts are absent. The very process of taking practical action inevitably diminishes the individual's sense of victimization and in many cases even brings the emotional career of the victimized self to an end.

There are both similarities and differences between the form of victimization described here and other forms. Battered children, for example, often reinterpret childhood abuse when they reach adulthood; these reinterpretations thus do not occur as the by-product of a turning point in the course of the abuse, as is the case in violent marriages. Those who are assaulted by strangers, such as victims of muggings or rapes, may experience the existential threat to the self in much the same way as battered women do, but there is no prior relationship to reinterpret as a consequence of assuming a victimized self. The feelings and perceptions of these other victimized selves remain largely unexplored. Future studies, detailing the cognitive and emotional experiences of various types of victims, would make possible a more complete, generalized analysis of the victimized self than can be gained by focusing only on battered women.

Reading 22   Ten Myths That Perpetuate Corporal Punishment*

MURRAY A. STRAUS

Hitting children is legal in every state of the United States and that 84 percent of a survey of Americans agreed that it is sometimes necessary to give a child a good hard spanking. Almost all parents of toddlers act on these beliefs. Study after study shows that almost 100 percent of parents with toddlers hit their children. There are many reasons for the strong support of spanking. Most of them are myths.

MYTH 1: SPANKING WORKS BETTER

There has been a huge amount of research on the effectiveness of corporal punishment of animals, but remarkably little on the effectiveness of spanking children. That may be because almost no one, including psychologists, feels a need to study it because it is assumed that spanking is effective. In fact, what little research there is on the effectiveness of corporal punishment of children agrees with the research on animals. Studies of both animals and children show that punishment is *not* more effective than other methods of teaching and controlling behavior. Some studies show it is less effective.

Ellen Cohn and I asked 270 students at two New England colleges to tell us about the year they experienced the most corporal punishment. Their average age that year was eight, and they recalled having been hit an average of six times that year.[1] We also asked them about the percent of the time they thought that the corporal punishment was effective. It averaged a little more than half of the times (53 percent). Of course, 53 percent also means that corporal punishment was *not* perceived as effective about half the time it was used.

LaVoie (1974) compared the use of a loud noise (in place of corporal punishment) with withdrawal of affection and verbal explanation in a study of first- and second-grade children. He wanted to find out which was more effective in getting the children to stop touching certain prohibited toys. Although the loud noise was more effective initially, there was no difference over a longer period of time. Just explaining was as effective as the other methods.

A problem with LaVoie's study is that it used a loud noise rather than actual corporal punishment. That problem does not apply to an experiment by Day and Roberts (1983). They studied three-year-old children who had been given "time out" (sitting in a corner). Half of the mothers were assigned to use spanking as the mode of correction if their child did not comply and left the corner. The other half put their noncomplying child behind a low plywood barrier and physically enforced the child staying there. Keeping the child behind the barrier was just as

*Straus, Murray A. Straus. 1994. Ten Myths That Perpetuate Corporal Punishment. Chapter 10 in *Beating the Devil Out of Them: Corporal Punishment in American Families.* New York, NY: Lexington Books. Reprinted by permission of the author.

268

effective as the spanking in correcting the misbe-havior that led to the time out.

A study by Larzelere (1994) also found that a combination of *non*-corporal punishment and reasoning was as effective as corporal punish-ment and reasoning in correcting disobedience.

Crozier and Katz (1979), Patterson (1982), and Webster-Stratton et al. (1988, 1990) all stud-ied children with serious conduct problems. Part of the treatment used in all three experiments was to get parents to stop spanking. In all three, the behavior of the children improved after spanking ended. Of course, many other things in addition to no spanking were part of the intervention. But, as you will see, parents who on their own accord do not spank also do many other things to man-age their children's behavior. It is these other things, such as setting clear standards for what is expected, providing lots of love and affection, ex-plaining things to the child, and recognizing and rewarding good behavior, that account for why children of non-spanking parents tend to be easy to manage and well-behaved. What about parents who do these things and also spank? Their chil-dren also tend to be well-behaved, but it is illog-ical to attribute that to spanking since the same or better results are achieved without spanking, an also without adverse side effects.

Such experiments are extremely important, but more experiments are needed to really under-stand what is going on when parents spank. Still, what Day and Roberts found can be observed in almost any household. Let's look at two examples.

In a typical American family there are many instances when a parent might say, "Mary! You did that again! I'm going to have to send you to your room again." This is just one example of a nonspanking method that did *not* work.

The second example is similar: A parent might say, "Mary! You did that again! I'm going to have to spank you again." This is an example of spanking that did *not* work.

The difference between these two examples is that when spanking does not work, parents tend to forget the incident because it contradicts the al-most-universal American belief that spanking is something that works when all else fails. On the other hand, they tend to remember when a *non*-spanking method did not work. The reality is that nothing works all the time with a toddler. Parents think that spanking is a magic charm that will cure the child's misbehavior. It is not. There is no magic charm. It takes many interactions and many repetitions to bring up children. Some things work better with some children than with others.

Parents who favor spanking can turn this around and ask, If spanking doesn't work any better, isn't that the same as saying that it works just as well? So what's wrong with a quick slap on the wrist or bottom? There are at least three things that are wrong:

- Spanking becomes less and less effective over time and when children get bigger, it becomes difficult or impossible.
- For some children, the lessons learned through spanking include the idea that they only need to be good if Mommy or Daddy is watching or will know about it.
- As the preceding chapters show, there are a number of very harmful side effects, such as a greater chance that the child will grow up to be depressed or violent. Parents don't perceive these side effects because they usu-ally show up only in the long run.

MYTH 2: SPANKING IS NEEDED AS A LAST RESORT

Even parents and social scientists who are op-posed to spanking tend to think that it may be needed when all else falls. There is no scientific evidence supporting this belief, however. It is a myth that grows out of our cultural and psycho-logical commitment to corporal punishment. You can prove this to yourself by a simple exercise with two other people. Each of the three should, in turn, think of the most extreme situation where spanking is necessary. The other two should try to think of alternatives. Experience has shown that it is very difficult to come up with a situation for which the alternatives are not as good as spanking. In fact, they are usually better.

Take the example of a child running out into the street. Almost everyone thinks that spanking is appropriate then because of the extreme danger. Although spanking in that situation may help *parents* relieve their own tension and anxiety, it is not necessary or appropriate for teaching the child. It is not necessary because spanking does not work better than other methods, and it is not appropriate because of the harmful side effects of spanking. The only physical force needed is to pick up the child and get him or her out of danger, and, while hugging the child, explain the danger.

Ironically, if spanking is to be done at all, the "last resort" may be the worst. The problem is that parents are usually very angry by that time and act impulsively. Because of their anger, if the child rebels and calls the parent a name or kicks the parent, the episode can escalate into physical abuse. Indeed, most episodes of physical abuse started as physical punishment and got out of hand (Kadushin and Martin, 1981). Of course, the reverse is not true, that is, most instances of spanking do not escalate into abuse. Still, the danger of abuse is there, and so is the risk of psychological harm.

The second problem with spanking as a last resort is that, in addition to teaching that hitting is the way to correct wrongs, hitting a child impulsively teaches another incorrect lesson—that being extremely angry justifies hitting.

MYTH 3: SPANKING IS HARMLESS

When someone says, I was spanked and I'm OK, he or she is arguing that spanking does no harm. This is contrary to almost all the available research. One reason the harmful effects are ig-

nored is because many of us (including those of us who are social scientists) are reluctant to admit that their own parents did something wrong and even more reluctant to admit that we have been doing something wrong with our own children. But the most important reason may be that it is difficult to see the harm. Most of the harmful effects do not become visible right away, often not for years. In addition, only a relatively small percentage of spanked children experience obviously harmful effects.

The delayed reaction and the small proportion seriously hurt are the same reasons the harmful effects of smoking were not perceived for so long. In the case of smoking, the research shows that a third of very heavy smokers die of lung cancer or some other smoking-induced disease. That, of course, means that two-thirds of heavy smokers do *not* die of these diseases (Mattson et al., 1987). So most heavy smokers can say, I've smoked more than a pack a day for 30 years and I'm OK. Similarly, most people who were spanked can say, My parents spanked me, and I'm not a wife beater or depressed.

Another argument in defense of spanking is that it is not harmful if the parents are loving and explain why they are spanking. The research does show that the harmful effects of spanking are reduced if it is done by loving parents who explain their actions. However, a study by Larzelere (1986) shows that although the harmful effects are reduced, they are not eliminated. The harmful side effects include an increased risk of delinquency as a child and crime as an adult, wife beating, depression, masochistic sex, and lowered earnings.

In addition to having harmful psychological effects on children, hitting children also makes life more difficult for parents. Hitting a child to stop misbehavior may be the easy way in the short run, but in the slightly longer run, it makes the job of being a parent more difficult. This is because spanking reduces the ability of parents to influence their children, especially in adolescence when they are too big to control by physical force. Children are more likely to do what the parents want if there is a strong bond of affection with the parent. In short, being able to influence a child depends in considerable part on the bond between parent and child (Hirschl, 1969). An experiment by Redd, Morris, and Martin (1975) shows that children tend to avoid caretaking adults who use punishment. In the natural setting, of course, there are many things that tie children to their parents. I suggest that each spanking chips away at the bond between parent and child.

Part of the process by which corporal punishment eats away at the parent-child bond is shown in the study of 270 students mentioned earlier. We asked the students for their reactions to "the first time you can remember being hit by one of your parents" and the most recent instance. We used a check list of 33 items, one of which was "hated him or her." That item was checked by 42 percent for both the first and the most recent instance of corporal punishment they could remember. The large percentage who hated their parents for hitting them is important because it is evidence that corporal punishment does chip away at the bond between child and parent.

Contrary to the "spoiled child" myth, children of non-spanking parents are likely to be easier to manage and better behaved than the children of parents who spank. This is partly because they tend to control their own behavior on the basis of what their own conscience tells them is right and wrong rather than to avoid being hit (see Chart 22-1).[2] This is ironic because almost everyone thinks that spanking "when necessary" makes for better behavior.

MYTH 4: ONE OR TWO TIMES WON'T CAUSE ANY DAMAGE

The evidence indicates that the greatest risk of harmful effects occurs when spanking is very frequent. However, that does not necessarily mean

that spanking just once or twice is harmless. Unfortunately, the connection between spanking once or twice and psychological damage has not been addressed by most of the available research. This is because the studies seem to be based on this myth. They generally cluster children into "low" and "high" groups in terms of the frequency they were hit. This prevents the "once or twice is harmless" myth from being tested scientifically because the low group may include parents who spank once a year or as often as once a month. The few studies that did classify children according to the number of times they were hit by their parents show that even one or two instances of corporal punishment are associated with a slightly higher probability of later physically abusing your own child, slightly more depressive symptoms, and a greater probability of violence and other crime later in life. The increase in these

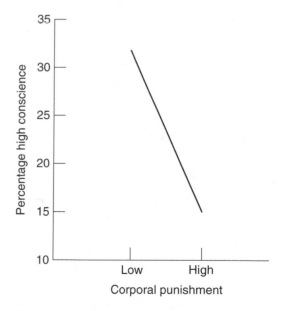

CHART 22-1   **Few children of parents who use a lot of corporal punishment have a well-developed conscience.**

harmful side effects when parents use only moderate corporal punishment (hit only occasionally) may be small, but why run even that small risk when the evidence shows that corporal punishment is no more effective than other forms of discipline in the short run, and less effective in the long run.

MYTH 5: PARENTS CAN'T STOP WITHOUT TRAINING

Although everyone can use additional skills in child management, there is no evidence that it takes some extraordinary training to be able to stop spanking. The most basic step in eliminating corporal punishment is for parent educators, psychologists, and pediatricians to make a simple and unambiguous statement that hitting a child is wrong and that a child *never,* ever, under any circumstances except literal physical self-defense, should be hit.

That idea has been rejected almost without exception everytime I suggest it to parent educators or social scientists. They believe it would turn off parents and it could even be harmful because parents don't know what else to do. I think that belief is an unconscious defense of corporal punishment. I say that because I have never heard a parent educator say that before we can tell parents to never *verbally* attack a child, parents need training in alternatives. Some do need training, but everyone agrees that parents who use *psychological* pain as a method of discipline, such as insulting or demeaning, the child, should stop immediately. But when it comes to causing *physical* pain by spanking, all but a small minority of parent educators say that before parents are told to stop spanking, they need to learn alternative modes of discipline. I believe they should come right out, as they do for verbal attacks, and say without qualification that a child should *never* be hit.

This is not to say that parent education programs are unnecessary, just that they should not be a precondition for ending corporal punishment. Most parents can benefit from parent education programs such as The Nurturing Program (Bavolek, 1983 to 1992), STEP (Dinkmeyer and McKay, 1989), Parent Effectiveness Training (Gordon, 1975), Effective Black Parenting (Alvy and Marigna, 1987), and Los Ninos Bien Educado Program (Tannatt and Alvy, 1989). However, even without such programs, most parents already use a wide range of non-spanking methods, such as explaining, reasoning, and rewarding. The problem is that they also spank. Given the fact that parents already know and use many methods of reaching and controlling, the solution is amazingly simple. In most cases, parents only need the patience to keep on doing what they were doing to correct misbehavior. Just leave out the spanking! Rather than arguing that parents need to learn certain skills *before* they can stop using corporal punishment, I believe that parents are more likely to use and cultivate those skills if they decide or are required to stop spanking.

This can be illustrated by looking at one situation that almost everyone thinks calls for spanking: when a toddler who runs out into the street. A typical parent will scream in terror, rush out and grab the child, and run to safety, telling the child, No! No! and explaining the danger—all of this accompanied by one or more slaps to the legs or behind.

The same sequence is as effective or more effective *without the spanking.* The spanking is not needed because even tiny children can sense the terror in the parent and understand, No! No! Newborn infants can tell the difference between when a mother is relaxed and when she is tense (Stern, 1977). Nevertheless, the fact that a child understands that something is wrong does not guarantee never again running into the street;

just as spanking does not guarantee the child will not run into the street again.

If the child runs out again, nonspanking parents should use one of the same strategies as spanking parents—repetition. Just as spanking parents will spank as many times as necessary until the child learns, parents who don't spank should continue to monitor the child, hold the child's hand, and take whatever other means are needed to protect the child until the lesson is learned. Unfortunately, when non-spanking methods do not work, some parents quickly turn to spanking because they lose patience and believe it is more effective: But spanking parents seldom question its effectiveness, they just keep on spanking.

Of course, when the child misbehaves again, most spanking parents do more than just repeat the spanking or spank harder. They usually also do things such as explain the danger to the child before letting the child go out again or warn the child that if it happens again, he or she will have to stay in the house for the afternoon, and so on. The irony is that when the child finally does learn, the parent attributes the success to the spanking, not the explanation.

MYTH 6: IF YOU DON'T SPANK, YOUR CHILDREN WILL BE SPOILED OR RUN WILD

It is true that some non-spanked children run wild. But when that happens it is not because the parent didn't spank. It is because some parents think the alternative to spanking is to ignore a child's misbehavior or to replace spanking with verbal attacks such as, Only a dummy like you can't learn to keep your toys where I won't trip over them. ·The best alternative is to take firm action to correct the misbehavior without hitting. Firmly condemning what the child has done and explaining why it is wrong are usually enough. When they are not, there are a host of

other things to do, such as requiring a time out or depriving the child of a privilege, neither of which involves hitting the child.

Suppose the child hits another child. Parents need to express outrage at this or the child may think it is acceptable behavior. The expression of outrage and a clear statement explaining why the child should never hit another person, except in self defense, will do the trick in most cases. That does not mean one such warning will do the trick, any more than a single spanking will do the trick. It takes most children a while to learn such things, whatever methods the parents use.

The importance of how parents go about teaching children is clear from a classic study of American parenting—*Patterns of Child Rearing* by Sears, Maccoby, and Levin (1957). This study found two actions by parents that are linked to a high level of aggression by the child: permissiveness of the child's aggression, namely ignoring it when the child hits them or another child, and spanking to correct misbehavior. The most aggressive children in Chart 22–2 are those at the upper right. They are children of parents who permitted aggression by the child and who also hit them for a variety of misbehavior. The least aggressive children are at the lower left. They are children of parents who clearly condemned acts of aggression and who, by not spanking, acted in a way that demonstrated the principle that hitting is wrong.

There are other reasons why, on the average, the children of parents who do not spank are better behaved than children of parents who spank:

- Non-spanking parents pay more attention to their children's behavior, both good and bad, than parents who spank. Consequently, they are more likely to reward good behavior and less likely to ignore misbehavior.
- Their children have fewer opportunities to get into trouble because they are more likely

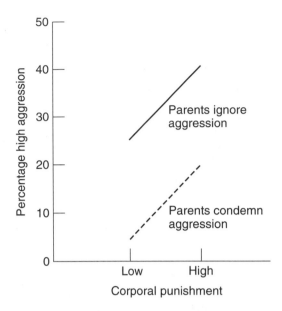

CHART 22-2   Children of parents who use a lot of corporal punishment tend to be aggressive, especially if the parents ignore their aggression.

to child-proof the home. For older children, they have clear rules about where they can go and who they can be with.

- • Non-spanking parents tend to do more explaining and reasoning. This teaches the child how to use these essential tools to monitor his or her own behavior, whereas children who are spanked get less training in thinking things through.

- • Non-spanking parents treat the child in ways that tend to bond the child to them and avoid acts that weaken the bond. They tend to use more rewards for good behavior, greater warmth and affection, and fewer verbal assaults on the child (see Myth 9). By not spanking, they avoid anger and resentment over spanking. When there is a strong

bond, children identify with the parent and want to avoid doing things the parent says are wrong. The child develops a conscience and lets that direct his or her behavior. That is exactly what Sears et al. found (see Chart 22–1).

MYTH 7: PARENTS SPANK RARELY OR ONLY FOR SERIOUS PROBLEMS

Contrary to this myth, parents who spank tend to use this method of discipline for almost any misbehavior. Many do not even give the child a warning. They spank before trying other things. Some advocates of spanking even recommend this. At any supermarket or other public place, you can see examples of a child doing something wrong, such as taking a can of food off the shelf. The parent then slaps the child's hand and puts back the can, sometimes without saying a word to the child. John Rosemond, the author of *Parent Power* (1981), says, "For me, spanking is a first resort. I seldom spank, but when I decide...I do it, and that's the end of it."

The high frequency of spanking also shows up among the parents described in this study. The typical parent of a toddler told us of about 15 instances in which he or she had hit the child during the previous 12 months. That is surely a minimum estimate because spanking a child is generally such a routine and unremarkable event that most instances are forgotten. Other studies, such as Newson and Newson (1963), report much more chronic hitting of children. My tabulations for mothers of three- to five-year-old children in the National Longitudinal Study of Youth found that almost two-thirds hit their children during the week of the interview, and they did it more then three times in just that one week. As high as that figure may seem, I think that daily spanking is not at all uncommon. It has not been documented because the parents who do it usually don't realize how often they are hitting their children.

MYTH 8: BY THE TIME A CHILD IS A TEENAGER, PARENTS HAVE STOPPED

Parents of children in their early teens are also heavy users of corporal punishment, although at that age it is more likely to be a slap on the face than on the behind. More than half of the parents of 13 to 14-year-old children in our two national surveys hit their children in the previous 12 months. The percentage drops each year as children get older, but even at age 17, one out of five parents is still hitting. To make matters worse, these are minimum estimates.

Of the parents of teenagers who told us about using corporal Punishment, 84 percent did it more than once in the previous 12 months. For boys, the average was seven times and for girls, five times. These are minimum figures because we interviewed the mother in half the families and the father in the other half. The number of times would be greater if we had information on what the parent who was not interviewed did.

MYTH 9: IF PARENTS DON'T SPANK, THEY WILL VERBALLY ABUSE THEIR CHILD

The scientific evidence is exactly the opposite. Among the nationally representative samples of parents in this book, those who did the least spanking also engaged in the least verbal aggression.

It must be pointed out that non-spanking parents are an exceptional minority. They are defying the cultural prescription that says a good parent should spank if necessary. The depth of their involvement with their children probably results from the same underlying characteristics that led them to reject spanking. There is a danger that if more ordinary parents are told to never spank, they might replace spanking by ignoring misbehavior or by verbal attacks. Consequently, a campaign to end spanking must also stress the importance of avoiding verbal attacks as well as physical attacks, and also the importance of paying attention to misbehavior.

MYTH 10: IT IS UNREALISTIC TO EXPECT PARENTS TO NEVER SPANK

It is no more unrealistic to expect parents to never hit a child than to expect that husbands should never hit their wives, or that no one should go through a stop sign, or that a supervisor should never hit an employee. Despite the legal prohibition, some husbands hit their wives, just as some drivers go through stop signs, and a supervisor occasionally may hit an employee.

If we were to prohibit spanking, as is the law in Sweden (Deley, 1988; and Haeuser, 1990), there still would be parents who would continue to spank. But that is not a reason to avoid passing such a law here. Some people kill even though murder has been a crime since the dawn of history. Some husbands continue to hit their wives even though it has been more than a century since the courts stopped recognizing the common law right of a husband to "physically chastise an errant wife" (Calvert, 1974).

A law prohibiting spanking is unrealistic only because spanking is such an accepted part of American culture. That also was true of smoking. Yet in less than a generation we have made tremendous progress toward eliminating smoking. We can make similar progress toward eliminating spanking by showing parents that spanking is dangerous, that their children will be easier to bring up if they do not spank, and by clearly saying that a child should *never,* under any circumstances, be spanked.

WHY DO THESE MYTHS PERSIST?

Some of the myths we just presented are grounded in society's beliefs that spanking is effective and relatively harmless. Let's turn to some of the reasons these two types of myths persist.

The Myth of Effectiveness

There are a number of reasons why almost everyone overestimates the effectiveness of spanking, but a central reason is what has been called "selective inattention." This occurs when people do not remember the times when spanking fails because it contradicts what they believe to be true, namely, that spanking works. On the other hand if someone knows that the parents do *not* spank, it is assumed that the child must be spoiled or wild. So there is a tendency to overlook the good behavior of the child and to attribute the inevitable instances of misbehavior to the lack of spanking. This provides the evidence that parents who don't spank "when necessary" have spoiled children. These all-too-human errors in information processing create the perception that spanking is much more effective than it really is. This error may be the main reason for the persistence of the effectiveness myth. The reality is that although all children misbehave, the behavior of children who are not spanked, although far from perfect, is on the average better than the behavior of children whose parents spank.

The idea of selective inattention raises the question of why the "necessity" of spanking is such a deeply held belief. Why do most Americans have a vested interest in defending spanking? The following are some of the possible reasons:

- Almost all have been spanked as children, so it is part of their normal life experience.
- Even if someone is suffering from one of the harmful side effects, such as depression, he

or she may not realize that having been spanked may be one of the reasons why. He or she continues to believe that spanking is harmless.
- Almost all parents slap or spank toddlers. So, if a parent accepts the idea that spanking is wrong, it implies that he or she is a bad parent, at least in this respect. That is difficult to admit.
- Almost everyone has been hit by his or her parents. So, to say corporal punishment is wrong is to condemn your own parents. Few people are comfortable doing that.
- These beliefs and attitudes have been crystallized as part of American culture and the American view of what a good parent owes a child. There is abundant evidence that people tend to misperceive things that are contrary to basic tenants of their culture and beliefs (Higgins and Bargh, 1987).
- Most spanking occurs when parents are frustrated and angry. In that context parents tend to get emotional release and satisfaction from spanking, which is confused with effectiveness in changing the child's behavior.

There is almost always a kernel of truth behind myths and stereotypes. The belief in the usefulness of spanking is no exception. The truth is that some parents who do not spank also do not attempt to correct misbehavior. As explained earlier, children of these extremely permissive or neglectful parents do tend to be out of control. However, such parents are a minority of nonspanking parents. Their children tend to be difficult to deal with or sometimes even to be around. These few and unrepresentative cases get burned into memory.

The Myth of Harmlessness

Probably the most important reasons for the myth of harmlessness are because the harmful effects do not become visible right away, often not for years, and because only a relatively small percentage of spanked children experience obviously harmful effects.

It is now widely accepted that smoking causes lung cancer, but that fact was hotly disputed only a generation ago. The research on spanking children associates it with delinquency, wife beating, depression, and other problems later in life. But just as the research on smoking a generation ago, the evidence is not conclusive. These favoring spanking can dismiss it, just as those favoring smoking dismissed the early inconclusive evidence.

When there is more conclusive evidence on the harmful effects of spanking, it may be harder to get people to give up spanking than it was for them to give up smoking. Spanking may be more firmly entrenched because almost everyone was spanked or is a spanker, but not everyone was a smoker.

Another reason spanking will be hard to eliminate is because the chance of falling victim to one of the harmful effects of spanking is much lower than the risk of experiencing the harmful effects of smoking. For example, spanked children are about four times more likely to be highly aggressive and about twice as likely to hit their spouses later in life. These are large risks, but the effects of smoking are much larger. A high rate of smoking tends to increase the chances of lung cancer by 34 times, even though two-thirds of very heavy smokers do not die of a smoking-related disease (Mattson et al., 1987).

Spanking is associated with a two-to-four-times greater rate of harmful behavior, whereas smoking increases the lung cancer rate by 34 times. Therefore, it can be argued that smoking is a much more serious problem. On the other hand, it also can be argued that spanking is the more serious problem of the two because almost all parents spank, and spanking puts entire generations at risk of harm. There is no need to decide if spanking is worse than smoking. Both are harmful, both need to be eliminated, and both can be eliminated. In the case of spanking, even though it may increase the probability of harm "only" two to four times, it is an unnecessary risk because children are more likely to be well-behaved if parents do not spank.

Reading 23　Karla and the Armstrongs: Two Oral Histories of Homeless American Families*

STEVEN VANDERSTAAY

KARLA—ST. LOUIS, MISSOURI

*"We'll start with what happened,"
Karla begins. Young, bright, a mother
of two children, she is part of a
growing phenomenon: single-parent
mothers on assistance who cannot
afford a place to live.*

*Cities handle such families differ-
ently. New York City houses many
women like Karla in so-called welfare
hotels, while other cities place them
in barracks-style emergency shelters
or housing projects. Karla could find
nowhere to go.*

*Karla is an African American in
her twenties. We met at a Salvation
Army shelter for homeless families.*

I was working up until the time I had my
second baby. I lived with my mom but we
weren't getting along. She took care of the first
child but the second, that was too much. Then
she felt that once I had the children . . . well, her
words were, "Two grown ladies can never manage in the same house." So I got on AFDC and
went to stay with my littlest girl's aunt.

Well, three weeks ago now, her landlord
called and said the building didn't pass inspection. See, the building was infested with bugs
and mice.

I didn't have any money saved 'cause I was
spending all the AFDC and food stamps on us. I
do have qualifications for a lot of jobs, but
they're all $3.35. And it's not worth getting a job
where you have no medical or dental insurance,
not if you have kids. It's not worth giving up
welfare. I would work at $3.35 if they let me
keep Medicaid and the food stamps, but they
don't. They'll cut you off.

But AFDC's not enough to live on either. I
started looking for another place but all the
apartments I could afford were just like the one
we were living in. It wasn't worth leaving one
condemnation to go to another.

Then my daughter's aunt, she moved in with
her sister. There was no way I could afford an
apartment on my own, not and eat too—and like I
said, they were all as bad as the first place. So me
and the kids—I have a 3-year-old and a 9-month-
old—we just stayed in the building. They boarded
it up but we got in through the back window.

There was this older lady that lived next
door. We were friends and if she could have

*Vanderstaay, Steven. 1992. "'Karla' & 'The Armstrongs, Mark and Linda.'" Pp. 170–176 in *Street Lives: An Oral His-
tory of Homeless Americans.* Philadelphia, PA: New Society Publishers, 4527 Springfield Ave., Phila., PA. Reprinted
with permission.

helped me she would have. But she already had her four grown kids, plus their kids, livin' with her in a two-bedroom apartment. There's a lot of that these days.

She gave us blankets, though, and I wrapped us up in them. We'd stay outside all day, do something—go to the library or I'd take 'em to the museum. Something. Nights we'd go back into the apartment, light candles, and sleep.

Then it rained real bad. And it was cold. The electrical was off, the gas was off, we were going by candlelight. Mice and rats came out really bad. I woke up one morning and there was a mouse on my 9-month-old's head...we couldn't stay in there.

So we went outside, walked around all day. Night came and we slept in a car I found. We were wet and both my kids caught a cold real bad. I took 'em to the emergency room and we slept at the hospital.

The next night we were in this laundromat ...it was so awful. I was crying, the kids were still sick. And my oldest, Robert, he asked a lot of questions. "Momma, why did we sleep in the car? Why are we outside? It's raining, Momma, I'm cold. I don't feel good."

I couldn't explain. And we had been out for the last three days, never being able to rest. He hadn't eaten anything that night 'cause I didn't have any more money.

Then the man at the laundromat, he gave me $4 to get Robert something to eat. And I stole my baby a can of milk.

THE ARMSTRONGS, MARK AND LINDA— SEATTLE, WASHINGTON

The Armstrongs lived in Bellevue, a young, largely affluent city east of Seattle, until a medical emergency and the sudden loss of Mark's job forced the family to seek emergency housing.

Since Bellevue has little emergency housing, the Armstrongs were advised to seek shelter in nearby Seattle. Eventually, the family was moved to a large public housing project in the city's Central District. Each morning they awake at 5:00 for the long bus ride back to Bellevue for work and school.

Mark and Linda both work, as do their teenage children. Speaking to them, I am struck that they are the quintessential American family: hardworking, supportive, patriotic, loving. And now homeless. The Armstrongs' difficulties—underemployment, housing, grocery bills, health costs, insurance problems—mirror those of other homeless families driven from affluent communities.

They are African Americans in their early thirties.

Mark:

I designed and built conveyor belts, and was good at it. I was making over $15 an hour. And I can go back there right now and get you a letter of recommendation from the company and let you read what they wrote about me. That in itself tells you what kind of worker I am.

The company went out of business. Bang! Didn't even know it was coming. I was between jobs three or four months. I could have found work right away if I wanted to make minimum wage, but I got pretty high standards for myself. I don't even want to make what I'm making now. We could barely afford rent then, how can we now? But when you got kids to feed and bills to pay, you have to do the best you can.

But minimum wage—that's insulting. I don't knock it for high school students. They're getting training, learning about working, making their pocket money. That's fine. But you take a person...I got six kids. $3.35, $4 an hour, I spend more than that wage in a day's time on a grocery bill. I mean you can accept some setbacks, but you can't tell a person, "I don't care if you've been making $15 something an hour, the minimum is what you've got to make now." If I hand you this letter, give you my resumé, my military record, show you the kind of worker I am, talk about my family, how can you degrade me by offering me the minimum wage?

Then we had trouble with the house we were renting. And, well, the biggest part of it was hospital bills. My son had to have emergency surgery. Since the company was going out of business it let the insurance lapse, so I got stuck with the bill. Spent every penny we had saved and there's still fourteen hundred dollars on it. You would think by being medical that it wouldn't affect the credit, but it does.

Now I'm working with Safeway's warehouse. I work in the milk plant. Swing shift. Sometimes I'm off at 12:30, 1:00 at night, and then turn right around and go back at 8:30 the next morning. Yeah, it's hard sometimes. I'm not making half of what I used to. I'm a helper—I used to have people working for me. I'd worked my way up through the ranks. But like I was saying, you adjust, you do what you have to do. I'm the kind of person, I get with a company I want to stay, be a part of it. I like to get along with people and work, get my hands dirty. See something accomplished. I'm low man on the totem pole but I'll stay and work my way up.

The warehouse, it's refrigerated on one end and kind of hot on the other. They make their own milk cartons out of plastic so you have to deal with heat and cold. You have to know how to dress 'cause you're dealing with both extremes.

Linda:

I've been a custodian, nurse's aid; now I work at K-Mart. I still have to bus back to the East side [Bellevue] every day. It's okay but I'm looking for something else. You know, it's $4 an hour, and there's no benefits, no discounts at the store, nothing like that.

And I'm in school now, too. I'm going for business training, probably computers or administration. When school starts I'll either bring the little ones there with me or have one of the older ones bring them home.

Working full-time and going to school. Six kids, seventeen on down to twelve. Three in high school, three in grade school. Two of them work at Jack in the Box. They've been working the same shift but my oldest, he's on the football team, so he might be working at a different time than my daughter. And then there's the church, and those football games. Yes we're busy! Just an all-American family. One that's hit a string of bad luck, that's all.

The hardest thing is getting up early enough to bus back over there. As soon as school gets started that's really going to be a problem. It might be a couple of hours, both ways. And if they find out our kids are living here they'll want them in school in Seattle. But they like the schools there and I like them. They're better. And that's where we've lived, that's where we work.

But we get by. The kids, they cook, they clean, they wash and iron their own clothes. And the older ones, they all work. We're so proud of them. Oh, we have the same problems everybody else has, with teenagers and so forth. But we get through 'em. Just thank God they're not on drugs. That's the biggest problem here.

Mark:

When we had to move and lost the house, when I lost my job, we told the kids the truth, the flat out truth. With no misconception; none whatsoever. Kids are not dumb. If you lie to kids, why should they be honest with you? They know exactly what we're going through and they know why.

Same thing when we moved here—six kids, three rooms, writing all over the walls, the drugs and crime. We tried to avoid the move but we didn't have any choice. They knew exactly where we were moving to, as best as I could explain it. We told them we didn't want to come, but if it came down to it we were coming. And we did.

Now my worst fear...there's so much drugs in this area. And people think every apartment in the projects is a drug house. They knock on the doors, knock on the windows—they stop me out there and ask where it is. It's here, so close to us all the times. And all the shooting and fighting...you can look out the window any given night and see the police stopping people and searching everyone.

If I can't look out my door and see my kids, I send for 'em. And I'm afraid when I can't see 'em. 'Cause when they get to shootin' and fightin' and carryin'-on a bullet don't got no names on it. Sometimes when I come in from work, three, four o'clock in the morning, I wonder just when they're going to get me. But my worst fear, my worst fear is the kids.

Linda:

Over in Bellevue they think if you can't afford it then you shouldn't be there. You know, who cares if you work there.

The first house that we had, we were the first blacks in the neighborhood. When I moved over there I said, "Where the black people?" [laughs, then moves her head from side to side as if searching]...no black people? Then the neighbors, they got to looking, came out, they were surprised, too. "Oooh, we got black people over here now" [laughs]. The kids were the only black kids around.

Mark:

People don't want to rent to a family. And you know the kind of rent they're asking over there in Bellevue, that's not easy to come up with. And you need first, last month's rent, security.... And then people automatically assess, they stereotype you. Maybe sometimes it's 'cause we're black—I'm not saying this is true, I'm saying that sometimes I *felt* that the reason we didn't get a place was because we were black. But most of the time it's the family. People would rather you have pets than kids these days.

One guy, he had six bedrooms in this house. But he didn't want a family. Why would you have six bedrooms if you didn't want to rent to a family? May not be legal, but they do that all the time.

Now there is some validity in what they say about children tearing up things. But the child is only as bad as you let him be. You're the parent, he's going to do exactly what you let him do and get away with. If my kids tear something up I'll pay for it. But me, I tell my kids that if I have to replace something they've destroyed, then one of their sisters or brothers isn't going to get something they need. And when they do something they answer to me.

I'm not bitter...I mean I'm somewhat so. I'm not angry bitter. It's just that I don't like dragging my kids from one place to the next, and I don't think we've been treated right. We had to take places sight-unseen, just to get 'em. We paid $950 a month, and during the wintertime $300, $400 a month for electric and gas bills. Then bought food, kept my kids in clothes. How you supposed to save to get ahead with all that?

And the house, when we moved in the landlords said they'd do this and that, fix this and that. Said we would have an option to buy it. We said, "Okay, and we'll do these things." We had an agreement.

We never got that chance to buy, and they never fixed those things. But we kept paying that $950 a month. They had a barrel over us: we needed some place to go. And they made a small fortune those years. A month after we moved out we went by: all those things they wouldn't do were done.

Before that the guy decided to sell his house, just like that, and we had to move. It was December, wintertime. For a while we were staying with her mother in a two-bedroom. Nine people. We had to be somewhere so we took that second place before we had even seen it.

Everybody has to have a place to live. And people will do what they have to do to survive. A lot of things that you see going on around here are for survival [he sweeps his hand, indicating the housing projects]. I'm not taking up for them, there's a lot of things happening here that I oppose. But where there's a will there's a way, you know.

9   Divorce, Remarriage, and the Future of the Family

Reading 24   The Social Self as Gendered: A Masculinist Discourse of Divorce*

TERRY ARENDELL

Divorce functions as a prism, making available for examination an array of issues. Pulled into question are the shape and dictates of extra-familial institutions and practices, such as the juridical and economic; and the character of family life, parenting and domestic arrangements. Also brought into view are matters of interpersonal relations and gender identity: it is "unfamiliar situations" which call forth "taken as given identities" and present opportunities to observe the effects of identity upon behavior (Foote 1981, p. 338):

> "Establishment of one's own identity to oneself is as important in interaction as to establish it for the other. One's own identity in a situation is not absolutely given but is more or less problematic" (Foote 1981, p. 337).[1]

Thus investigation of participants' perspectives on and responses to divorce and the postdivorce situation can illumine processes not only of interactional adjustment in the context of change but also of identity maintenance and alteration.

Family and identity transitions are located within a broader sociocultural context: the gender hierarchy and belief system and gender roles are being questioned and altered, although at broadly discrepant rates (Hochschild 1989; Pleck 1985). Specifically, the conventions of masculinity—"those sets of signs indicating that a person is a 'man', or 'not a woman' or 'not a child'" (Hearn 1987, p. 137) and which are "the social reality for men in modern society" (Clatterbaugh 1990, p. 3)—are being challenged (Hearn 1987; Clatterbaugh 1990; Kimmel 1987). Indeed, Kimmel (1987, p. 153) has concluded that contemporary men, like men in other

This paper is a revision of one presented at the 1991 Gregory Stone Symposium held at the University of California, San Francisco, and the research was funded in part by a PSC-CUNY grant. Appreciation is extended to Joseph P. Marino, Jr., for the many useful and provocative discussions regarding this work; Arlie R. Hochschild for her thoughtful commentary on an earlier draft; and to the anonymous reviewers for their constructive remarks on earlier drafts of the paper.

*Arendell, Terry. 1992. "The Social Self as Gendered: A Masculinist Discourse of Divorce." *Symbolic Interaction* 15(2): 151–181. Reprinted by permission of Jai Press Inc.

periods characterized by dramatic social and economic change, "confront a crisis in masculinity." Divorce both exemplifies and prompts a crisis in gender identity (Riessman 1990; Vaughan 1986).

Men's perspectives on, actions in, and adjustments to divorce have been relatively neglected in divorce research. Yet they are significant for understanding contemporary social arrangements and processes as well as for broadening understanding of men's lives: how men define their situations and act in divorce points to their positions in a gender-structured society and to their understandings of the nature of social practices, relationships, and selves. To paraphrase an argument made with regard to the study of a gendered division of labor in families, the ways in which divorced fathers "use motive talk [Mills 1940] to account for [Scott and Lyman 1968], disclaim [Hewitt and Stokes 1975], and/or neutralize [Sykes and Matza 1957] their behavior or changes in their behavior need to be more fully explored and developed" (Pestello and Voyandoff 1991, p. 117).

METHODOLOGY

Based on data obtained through intensive interviews examining postdivorce situations, experiences, and feelings with a sample 75 divorced fathers (Arendell forthcoming), this paper explores the problem of the social self as gendered, and specifically, the nature of the masculinist self. All participants were volunteers who responded to notices and advertisements placed in newsletters, magazines, and newspapers or to referrals from other participants. The men ranged in age from 23 to 59 years with a median age of 38.5 years. Sixty-four interviewees were white, three were black, four Hispanic, two Asian-American, and two Native American. All respondents were residents of New York State, had one or more minor children, and had been divorced or legally separated for at least 18 months. The median time divorced or separated was 4.8 years. At the time they were interviewed, 18 men were remarried, 5 were living with a woman in a marital-like relationship, and the others were unmarried. Nearly half of the sample had some college education with over one-third having completed college and approximately one-sixth having earned a graduate or professional degree. Occupationally, one-third of the employed respondents worked in blue-collar and two-thirds worked in white-collar positions. Six men were unemployed at the time of the interview, three by choice.

The respondents were fathers to a total of 195 children ranging in age from 2 to 25 with a median age of 9.5 years. The number of children per father ranged from one to six; the mean number of children was 2.6 and the median was 2. Child custody arrangements varied among the men: six fathers had primary physical custody, five had co- or shared physical custody with their former wives, and 64 were noncustodial fathers. Two of those categorized as noncustodial fathers actually had split custody arrangements; each had one child living with him and another two children living with their mothers. A total of eleven fathers were "absent" fathers, meaning that they had no contact with any of their children for at least the past twelve months; another four fathers were "absent" from one or more but not all of their children. The sample over-represents "involved" fathers; for example, only 15 percent were "absent" compared to the national figure of about 50 percent (Furstenberg et al. 1987) and 85 percent were noncustodial parents compared to a national figure of 90 percent (USBC 1989). Additionally, with only a few exceptions, the nonresidential fathers repeatedly maintained that they desired increased access to and involvement with their children; many wished for more satisfying relations with their children.

Interviews were open-ended, tended to be long, lasting between two and five hours, and were conducted primarily in 1990 with some occurring in late 1989 and early 1991. Seven respondents participated in follow-up interviews. An interview instrument, initially developed and revised on the basis of 15 earlier interviews in another state, was used as a reference to insure that certain areas were covered during the discussions. All interviews were tape recorded and transcribed. Data were analyzed using the constant comparative method and coding paradigm developed in works on grounded theory (Glaser and Strauss 1967; Strauss 1989).

A MASCULINIST DISCOURSE OF DIVORCE

What the data in this study of divorce provide is a richly descriptive testimony of the men's perspectives on and actions in family and divorce. These divorced fathers, largely irrespective of variations in custody, visitation, marital, or socioeconomic class status, shared a set of dispositions, practices, and explanations with which they managed their identities, situations, and emotional lives. They held in common a body of *gender strategies:* plans of action "through which a person tries to solve problems at hand given the cultural notions of gender at play" and through which an individual reconciles beliefs and feelings with behaviors and circumstances (Hochschild 1989, p. 15). In similar ways, they accounted for past and present actions and described and implied intended future lines of activity, including, significantly, the probable meanings of such movement. The participants shared a *discourse*—particular "matrix of perceptions, appreciations, and actions" (Bourdieu 1987:83). More specifically, they shared a *masculinist discourse of divorce.*

That these men, with their unique personal and family histories, participated in a common divorce discourse points to its complexity. It is not simply an expression of individual men's intentions, pointing to "men we disapprove of and good guys" (Schwenger 1989, p. 101). Rather, the shared discourse points to the collective character and force of gender arrangements and identities: gender is institutionalized (Rubin 1975; Daniels 1987), buttressed by ideology (Jaggar 1983; Hochschild 1989) and internalized, a fundamental aspect of the social self (Chodorow 1978). The acting self, performance, and social stage are braced and shaded by the structures and ideologies of gender.

While very definite patterns prevailed in the men's accounts, organized around central themes and largely involving a turn to and reliance upon conventional gender definitions and practices—the processes of *traditionalization* (LaRossa and LaRossa 1989)—inconsistencies existed both within and across accounts. Having particular significance, a small group, consisting of nine fathers, varied from the others in certain actions and attitudes in largely uniform ways. Characterized as postdivorce "androgynous" fathers, these men were distinctive principally in the ways in which they had, according to their perceptions and explanations, appropriated parental behaviors and postures characterized typically as "feminine" ones, involving especially an emphasis on nurturing activities.[2] Where they perceived they could, they "departed from traditional formulations of men's lives" (Cohen 1989, p. 228).

Considered specifically in this paper are the interviewees' understandings and definitions of family, encompassing issues of gender differences and a *broken* family and the processes of devaluation of the former wife. Then examined is the related use of a rhetoric of *rights*. Following this is a brief discussion and analysis of the contrasting perspectives and actions of the divergent group, the postdivorce "androgynous" fathers. Lastly, several of the implications of the findings are specified.

DEFINITION OF FAMILY

Gender Differences

The family was shown to be a threshold of masculinity in these men's accounts; it was the primary social group (Cooley 1981) that conveyed and reinforced the constructs of gender. The family of origin served as the nursery and early classroom of gender acquisition, and the family of procreation (that formed through marriage) served as a workshop where gender identity was continuously retooled). Then, as the marriage ended and the postdivorce situation entered, the family and its changes evoked a questioning of masculine identity. Made particularly evident in the divorcing process was that beneath the jointly created and shared reality of married life (Berger and Kellner 1964) were distinctive experiences and understandings, organized according to and understood in terms of gender—the "his" and "hers" of married life (Bernard 1981; Riessman 1990). Nearly all of the respondents expressed a belief that gender differences had been at play in their marriages and divorces; while some regretted the consequences of the differences and attributed marital problems to them (see also Riessman 1990), most nonetheless expressed confidence that, compared to their former wife's, their own experiences and perceptions had been, to use their terms, the more valid, reasonable, logical, reliable, or objective ones.

Communication patterns and conversational styles in their marriages varied along gender lines, reflecting and reinforcing gender differences. The men usually expected and reported themselves to be less expressive and self-disclosing in marriage than their former wives; they also claimed to have felt pressured during marriage to be otherwise (see also Tannen 1990; Riessman 1990; Cancian 1987). One participant, in a remark about the differences between men and women which was similar in substance to most others' comments about gender differences, noted:

> *Men compartmentalize. It's just a different pattern of doing things, it has to do with the differences between men and women. I think men are always a few months, a few steps, behind women in a relationship. And men don't talk to each other the way women do to each other so men don't know what's going on outside of the things they are already most familiar with. They are at a disadvantage, they usually don't know what's going on.*

Despite its gendered and therefore problematic character, marriage, for a large majority of these men, was essential to family; indeed, family was predicated upon the enduring "successful marriage." The "successful" and desired marriage, however, was defined in a paradoxical way as being both the traditional marriage and the companionate marriage. That is, on the one hand, most of these men wanted a marital arrangement in which they were ultimately, even if largely benignly, the dominant spouse, befitting men in relationship with women according to the conventions of masculinity. On the other hand, these men wanted a relationship in which they were equal copartners, forging mutually a high degree of intimacy and seeking reciprocally to meet the other's needs and desires. This next person, a co-custodial parent who had opted to leave his marriage two years earlier but was now hoping for a marital reconciliation, explained his position:

> *I'm not talking about a marriage and family with a patriarchal model, but the priority of the relationship between a man and a woman as a husband and wife. I want an equal relationship, a partnership. But let me word it this way, I would like her to be able to trust me to be the leader of the family. When there are times we can't sit down at the table and make decisions cooperatively, then I will make the decisions and she will trust me. I want to be able to do that in a marriage. What I need and want is the trust from her to be able to be the leader of the family. I want her to be the first one to say: 'we've talked about it and I'll let you decide.' I guess I expect her to relinquish the control of the situation first.*

The improbability, even impossibility, of having simultaneously both types of marriage was largely obscured by the gender assumptions held. By conceiving of themselves as more rational, logical, and dependable than their wives, for example, assertions repeated in various ways throughout their accounts of marriage and divorce, these men were able to make claims to both types of marriage without acknowledging the contradictions or tensions between them.

The explanation for the failure to have the desired and lasting companionate marriage was the existence of fundamental differences between themselves as *men* and their former wives as *women*. In specifying these differences, the men rehearsed and reinforced the cultural stereotypes of gender and their expectations that they be the dominant partner. The problem in achieving the companionate marriage, unrecognized by these divorced men, was summarized by Riessman (1990, p. 73):

> *"The realization of the core ingredients of the companionate marriage— emotional intimacy, primacy and companionship, and mutual sexual fulfillment—depends on equality between husbands and wives. Yet institutionalized roles call for differentiation: neither husbands nor wives have been socialized to be equals."*

Perceiving themselves to be fundamentally dissimilar from women had enabled these men to objectify their wives during marriage, at least as their retrospective accounts indicated, and to thereby discount or reconstruct the meanings of their communications in particular ways. Although this process is not limited to husbands in divorce (Vaughan 1986), the objectification of another has distinctive configurations when done by men rather than women given their respective gender socialization and placement (Glenn 1987). Accepting the conventional beliefs in gender differences and asserting the preeminence of their levels of rationality and insight served to strengthen the respondents' identities as masculine selves. For example:

> *I just mostly stayed rational and reasonable during the months we considered separation but she just got crazier and crazier through the whole thing. I should have been prepared for that, I always knew during*

the marriage not to take her too seriously because she could be so illogical. I mean, you know, it's men's rationality that keeps a marriage together to begin with.

Likewise, having dismissed or redefined a wife's expression of marital discontent was justified through claims to basic superiority. One man noted:

She kept saying she was unhappy, that I worked too much and was never home, and that I neither listened to or appreciated her, that I didn't help out with the kids, maybe even didn't care about them. But I insisted she was just depressed because her father had died. It just made sense but I couldn't get her to see it.

By redefining a wife's expressed feelings of discontent with the marriage or him as a partner, an individual could rationalize and discount his own participation in the demise of the marriage. Through such disclaimers (Hewitt and Stokes 1981), the estranged husband reinforced his definitions of the situation and of self. Additionally, the assault on identity resulting from the perception that divorce was a personal failure made public (Arendell forthcoming; see also Riessman 1990), a view held even by those who had been the partner most actively seething the divorce, was countered.

A wife's sentiments about and assessments of their marriage could be discounted; entering into the wife's point of view, or attempting to "take the role of the other"—defined by Mead (1934, p. 254) as a uniquely human capacity which "assumes the attitude of the other individual as well as calling it out in the other"—was not a constitutive element of a husband's range

of activities in the conventional marital relationship. Women spoke a "different language," as one man summed up the differences between men and women which lead to divorce, a language not to be taken too seriously, or at least not as seriously as one's own as a *man*.[3] This posture toward a wife's perspectives and feelings carried over into the postdivorce situation where differences and conflicts of interest were typically highlighted and multiplied.

A "Broken Family"

Family, within the masculinist discourse of divorce, was understood to be a *broken family*, consisting essentially of two parts: the male-self and the wife-and-children or, as referred to, " 'me' and 'them'." Even men who had sought the divorce, about one-third of the group, and several of those who had primary or shared custody of children, understood and discussed the post-divorce family as being a *broken* one. Most of the noncustodial fathers perceived themselves to have been marginalized from the family, and nearly all felt stigmatized as divorced fathers. For instance:

You're not part of the family, part of the society anymore. You really don't have a proper place, a place where you have input into what goes on in your life. You're treated as if you're just scum, that's what you are really.

One father, using the language of *broken* family explicitly, summed up the dilemma he faced, suggesting that with the fracturing of the family went a loss of power and authority:

I guess I'm sort of at a loss in all of this; I just don't know what to do to fix a broken family. I can't say I didn't want the divorce, it was a mutual decision. But I just hadn't under-

stood before how it would break the family into pieces. It's really become them and me and I don't know what to do. I keep thinking of the rhyme: 'Humpty Dumpty sat on a wall, Humpty Dumpty had a great fall. All the king's horses and all the king's men, couldn't put Humpty together again.' I ran it by my ex last week and asked her if she had any Super-Glue but she didn't think it was funny.

The definition of the postdivorce family as a *broken* one had several sources, including the belief that family is predicated on the marriage. Other sources of the view were: acceptance of the conventional definition that masculinity is the measure of mature adulthood in comparison to both femininity and childhood (Broverman et al. 1970; Phillips and Gilroy 1985),[4] meaning, therefore, that men are different in distinctive ways from women and children, and of the ideology, if not the actual practice, of a traditional gender-based family division of labor: child-rearing and caretaking are the responsibilities primarily of women, whether or not they are employed, and economic providing is the responsibility primarily of men (Hochschild 1989; Cohen 1989).[5]

Another and related factor in the view that the postdivorce family consisted of 'me' and 'them' was the understanding that the respective parent–child relationships differed, a perception shared by divorced mothers as well, according to other studies (Arendell 1986; Hetherington et al. 1976). Mother–child relationships were distinctive and separate from father–child relationships. The holding of this view was independent of children's ages and was reinforced by, and arguably based in, the dominant sociocultural ethos linking children to their mothers (Chodorow 1978; Coltrane 1989) and the predominance of maternal custody after divorce (USBC 1989). In

contrast to the unique and independent mother–child unit, the father–child relationship was mediated in varying ways by the wife, consistent with her marital role as emotional worker (Hochschild 1983; 1989), and so was dependent on her actions. One father, who had read extensively about the psychological effects of divorce on children, compared the outcomes of his two divorces:

I would have to say that my children's primary attachment really was with their mother. I think that's typical in families, mothers are just better trained, maybe it's an instinct for parenting. Maybe fathers just don't make the effort. Anyway, even after my first divorce, I found that my ex-wife was vital to my relationship with the child of our marriage: she thought it was important that he maintain contact with me and that I be a part of his life. So she really encouraged him to do this and so it continued to be a relationship. She ran a kind of interference between us. He's 21 now and we have a good, solid relationship, but my children of this last marriage are essentially withdrawn from me. Their mother, my second wife, never really facilitated our relationship.

The retreat by former wives from the activity of facilitating the relationship between children and their fathers after divorce was interpreted as a misuse of power, and often as an overt act of hostility or revenge. In addition to the use and misuse of their psychological power in interpersonal relations (see also Pleck 1989), former wives exercised power by interfering with visitation, denigrating them as fathers and men to their children, provoking interpersonal conflicts, being uncooperative in legal matters, and demanding additional money. Their power in the postdivorce situation was viewed as being wholly disproportionate and undue: former wives were seen as not only holding center-stage position but as directing the production, if not actually writing the script, in the postdivorce drama. Nearly all of the men had an acute sense that their own power and authority in the family had been seriously eroded through divorce (Arendell 1992, forthcoming; see also Riessman 1990). This perception was central to the crisis in gender identity and was not limited to noncustodial fathers: more than half of the primary or co-custodial fathers argued that their former wives had usurped power illegitimately and at their expense, Moreover, former spouses had attained or appropriated dominance only partly through their own actions: the judiciary and legal system and the institutional and informal gender biases of both were accomplices and even instigators.

The legal system is such a crock, I can't believe it. The legal system is so for the woman and so against the man, it's just incredible. And the result is that all of these women get to go around screwing their ex-husbands.

Another person explained:

When we went to court after the divorce was over because of disagreements over support and visitation, the court did nothing. The situation is as it is today [with the mother interfering with his visitation] because the judge did nothing except hold meeting after meeting, delay after delay. The judge even said she was an unfit mother. She violated every aspect of the agreement, she obstructed. But they let her do it.

In support of their assertions about the unjustness of the system, numerous men cited the lack of a legal presumption in favor of joint child custody in New York State. Over half of the fathers argued (erroneously) that joint custody is not allowed in New York State (*Family Law* 1990) and nearly all of the noncustodial fathers, most of whom were granted what they called the "standard visitation arrangement"—every other weekend and one evening a week—complained bitterly about their limited access to their children.

Consistent with the categorization of 'me' and 'them', the perceived centrality of the former wife, and their own limited parental involvement, children most often were talked about as if they were extensions of their mothers rather than separate, unique persons. Thus, identity as a divorced father was intermixed with identity as a former spouse, adding further ambiguity and uncertainty to their place and activities in the changed family. Further, nearly all of the noncustodial and a third of the custodial fathers viewed their children as being instruments of their mothers in the postdivorce exchanges between the parents. A case in point was this father who discussed his young-adolescent daughter's reluctance to have contact with him even though her brother continued to have regular involvement. He attributed the tensions between him and his daughter to both his former wife's actions and essential gender differences:

My daughter was always more resistant, she really didn't want to see me and she always seemed somewhat resistant. Many instances of this kind. How to put it? She's very hard to get along with this kid. She's very bright, thinks she knows everything and she's a real pain in the ass. She's a whiner about everything and we used to get into these terrible fights, just like her mother and I used to have. I can't relate to girls as well as I can relate to boys in that I don't understand a lot of what they think. I never even understood anything about women anyway until after I was divorced. I tried to stay away from my daughter because I thought what I would do is hit her, that's what I thought I would do because I'm angry. I'm less angry now. But where the hell does this little bitch get off trying to dictate everything to her father? I mean, she's not the one who's supposed to set the terms. Obviously she's just become the stand-in for her mother: her mother can't aggravate me much, directly anyway, anymore, but her daughter sure can. I worry about them. What kind of life is that?

Fathers tended to merge their children with their former wives in other ways as well. In explaining their motives for or the consequences of actions, the majority of men frequently shifted from their children as the subject to their former wife. For instance,

I wanted the kids to have a house. So it remains as it is, with them [the kids] living in it, until the youngest is 18. But that was my biggest mistake. I should have had the house sold. Then I could have really gotten away from her [the former wife] and had no ties to her at all.

The approach of not disaggregating the children from the former wife served varying func-

tions. On the one hand, this approach bolstered the primacy of the former spouse in the postdivorce situation, granting her a position of centrality and augmenting the charges against her, and, on the other hand, it reduced her status by categorizing her with the children. Children's experiences and feelings could be discounted more easily than if they were respected as independent persons, thus creating more emotional distance between them. Distancing themselves from unfamiliar and identity-threatening feelings was a primary mechanism for reasserting control of their situations and of themselves and was relied upon particularly by "absent" and "visiting" fathers; one outcome of this gender strategy was the common acceptance of postdivorce father absence as an acceptable line of action under certain conditions (Arendell 1992). Not surprisingly, then, fathers satisfied with their parent–child relations were the exception: they included the postdivorce "androgynous" fathers and eight others. The majority were discontented with and disconcerted by the nature of their interactions with, emotional connections to, and levels of involvement with their children. Most characterized their relations with their children as being strained or superficial, distrustful, and unfulfilling.

Devaluing a Wife's Family Activities

Most of the respondents specifically devalued the family activities done both during and after marriage by the former wife (see also Riessman 1990). Through deprecating the former partner's activities, the men were able to buttress various assertions, including that they had been the dominant spouse and had been mistreated badly by the divorce settlement. Over a third of the fathers contended that they had been exceptional men in their marriages—a "superman," as several fathers quipped, in contrast to the popularized notion of "superwoman"—carrying the major share of income-earning and participating equally or near equally in caretaking activities. These particular fathers especially generalized their critique of their former wife's activities to a broad indictment of women's family roles, thus further reinforcing their beliefs in male superiority. As one noncustodial father, whose career development had demanded exceptionally long work weeks and whose former wife had stayed home during the marriage with the children, said:

> After all, I was able to do it [work and family] all, while she did next to nothing, so I don't see what these women are complaining about.

The devaluing of a former wife's activities also helped sustain the perception that, at least in retrospect, her economic dependence during marriage had been unfair, as was any continued exchange of resources after divorce. The implicit marriage contract operative during marriage, involving a culturally defined and socially structured gender-based division of labor and exchange (Weitzman 1985), was to be terminated upon divorce. Child support was viewed as a continuation of support for the undeserving former spouse. Of the 57 fathers (three-quarters of the sample) who were paying child support consistently or fairly regularly, almost two-thirds were adamant in their assertions that men's rights are infringed upon by the child support system.[6] One man, in a representative statement, said:

> I, a hard-working family man, got screwed, plain and simple. The court, under the direction of a totally biased judge, dictated that she and her children, our children, can relate to me simply as a money machine: 'just push the buttons and out comes the money, no strings attached'. And

> leave me without enough money even to afford a decent place to live.

"Adding insult to injury," as one irate father put it, was the demonstrated and undeniable reality that each time money defined as child support was passed to her, the former wife gained discretionary authority over its use, being accountable to neither the former husband or any institutional authority. Resentment over the child support system and the former wife's unwarranted power over his earnings was the explanation for various actions of resistance. Such common behaviors included: refusing to pay support, providing a check without funds in the bank to cover it, and neglecting to pay on time so that the former spouse was pushed into having to request the support check. Other actions were more idiosyncratic; for example, one father of three described his strategy for protesting the payment of child support:

> I put the check in the kids' dirty clothes bag and send it home with them after they visit. I used to put it in the clean clothes but now I put it in the dirty clothes bag. One woman told me her husband sent back the kids' clothes with a woman's sock, then the next time a woman's bra. I won't go that far, it's too low. But I suspect even this keeps her angry and off-balance and she can't say a word to me about it. She knows I can simply withhold it, refuse to pay it.

The respondents deflned their postdivorce situations and actions primarily in terms of the former wife, and a preoccupation with her was sustained whether or not there was continued direct interaction. Contributing were overlapping factors: lingering feelings about her, characterized generally by ambivalence, frustration and anger and remaining intense for over a third of the men (see also Wallerstein 1989); the perception that she held a position of dominance in the postdivorce milieu together with the processes of devaluing her significance; and the continuing relevance of issues pertaining to their children and finances.

A Rhetoric of Rights

A rhetoric of *rights* was interspersed throughout the men's accounts: it was basic to their understanding of family and their place in it and to their postdivorce actions, perspectives, and relationships. Attitudes held towards *rights* and its use were largely independent of particular experiences. Men satisfied with their divorce and postdivorce experiences spoke of *rights* in ways analogous to those men who were intensely dissatisfied with nearly every aspect of their divorce, the general exception being the small group characterized as "androgynous" fathers.

As used by the men in the study, the rhetoric of *rights* encompassed the ethics of individualism and autonomy and cultural views about choice, control, and authority, each of which is also central to the dominant beliefs about masculinity (Jaggar 1983; Pateman 1990). The rhetoric of *rights,* appropriated largely from political and legal theory and practice, was widely available in the culture at large. Specifically, for example, numerous respondents made reference to newspaper articles or television news spots over the course of the past several years which covered divorce-related issues (and particularly the implementation of the 1989 New York Child Support Standards Act) as ones involving rights. Attorneys were another source of the language of *rights* as was the law itself since the statutory approach to family relations, evidenced in family law codes, is one of rights and obligations (i.e., *Family Law 1990*).

That *rights* were to be secured in relation to another, and primarily the former wife, demystified the assertions and implications that what was at issue were matters of abstract principles of justice. Central among the various issues framed within the rhetoric of *rights* were the privileges of position of husband and father as held, or expected to be held, in the family prior to separation and divorce. As one father referring to the dominant pattern in which mothers receive custody and fathers pay child support pointedly said,

> *Divorce touches men in the two most vulnerable spots possible: rights to their money and rights to their children.*

The rhetoric of *rights* had a distinctive and complex connotation: that which was expected, desired, and believed to be deserved as a *man.* This person, for example, insisted repeatedly and explicitly throughout much of his account that his *rights* had been continuously violated. He had obtained primary custody of their children after "forcing my wife out of our home" and claiming that "she deserted us" in response to her request for a divorce:

> *The legal system abuses you as a man. You know: you have no rights. That is, you're treated as a nonperson or as a second, third, fourth or fifth class citizen. They look at us: you know, 'who is that guy with the mother?' Suddenly we're just sperm donors or something. We're a paycheck and sperm donors and that's our total function in society. The legal bias for the mother is incredible. You pull your hair and spend thousands of dollars and say, 'aren't I a human being?' I mean I saw on tv: gay rights,*

pink rights, blue rights, everybody has rights and they're all demonstrating. I said, 'don't men have rights too? Aren't these my children? Isn't this my house? Don't they bear my name?' I mean I was the first one to hold each of them when they were first born. I was there for it all. What will they do sometime later on in their lives when they are in a crisis—a divorce, job loss, whatever—and they don't have an identity? If I haven't been there to lay the foundation, what kind of identity will they have? Their foundation is to a large extent the result of my input. Don't I have a say as to their fate? I mean, did I have this thing backwards or something? You have to stop believing in the American way: truth and justice and all of that, that's not what happens. That only happens in books. And tv shows. None of my rights were protected, but had I been a woman, you can bet that if I were a female, I'd have had these things automatically, without any fight at all. I was fighting desperately for them because if I had lost my kids, I would have probably turned out to be one of those fathers who says I can't live with myself. I would have lost my identity, my self-respect, my future. I had already failed at marriage; she had insisted on ending it. I wasn't about to let them do this to me.

This father remained locked in a power struggle with his former wife, especially as he actively resisted her involvement with the children. Like many of the men in the study and even though he was a custodial parent, his relations with his children were continuously filtered through his relations and feelings about their mother.

Threats to rights were attributed to, most commonly, the former wife and some attorneys. Conflicts with the former spouse were common experiences among the men participating in the study irrespective of their general level of satisfaction with the postdivorce situation. Dissension involved matters carried over from the marriage as well as issues specific to the divorce settlement and the custody, living arrangements, care, and financial support of children. Resistance or disagreement from the former wife were characterized as "being intended to deny me my rights." Yet, while former wives posed the most tangible threats to their rights by their actions regarding children and finances, the challenge involved a complex meeting of family, cultural, and social changes. For example, in discussing his divorce experience, a noncustodial, "visiting" father of two referred to broader changes which had adversely affected his marriage and position in the family:

Our [his and his former wife's] fighting is just part of the package. We're involved in gender wars here. The women's movement has wimpified men—everywhere, the family, at work. Just look at the reverse discrimination for jobs: women get onto the police force down in New York City with lower scores than men. And it's dangerous, people will die because women are less qualified. Police in New York have been wimpified by the lowering of the scores for women and minorities. There's a loss of integrity for females too. And it's a violation of the taxpayer who doesn't get what he's paid for. It's going to take an all-out assault by men to protect men, to restore men's rights. There's been too much favoring of women, it's time

*for the pendulum to swing back now.
And men's rights are about custody,
about visitation, about genetic ties.*

Feminists were also frequently mentioned as
sources of threats to rights but were only vaguely
defined. Often attributed to the actions of "feminists," for example, were the development and
implementation of the New York Standard Child
Support Guidelines.

A large number of respondents used the language of *fathers' rights,* most often in relation to
the former wife and not the children. This stance
was reinforced by legal codes pertaining to divorce: children were a kind of property, over
which custody was to be authorized, if the divorcing parents were in agreement, or assigned,
if they were not.[7] And the determination of child
custody was related to the parents' family activities. As men they were penalized in divorce for
having invested their energies and efforts primarily in income-earning rather than in child-
caretaking. The institutional and cultural biases
against them in divorce as men in families took
on even greater dimensions for them because
they devaluated women's parenting activities.
One custodial father explained his determination
to obtain and then retain custody of his young
children, who were 14 and 25 months at the time
his wife left the marital home:

*They're my children, that's how I got
custody. I've been challenged nine
times for custody. But they're my
kids. I love them. I wanted them living with me. I couldn't see living on
my own without the little guys [a son
and a daughter] around. You know,
she's capable, I never denied that.
She just wants everybody to bend to
her. She wants to be boss. I didn't
claim that she was an unfit mother.
That's what everybody told me to do:*

*'claim she's an unfit mother and
maybe you've got a chance. That's
what everybody does.' But I said,
'no.' I believed I was the better parent, that I was more emotionally
capable at the time. My first attorney
kept pointing out that she had been
a full-time mother while I was working, but that was only because I had
to work. Why should that make me
lose my rights to my kids? If anything, it should give me more rights.
I was supporting them, and her for
that matter.*

The notion of *fathers' rights* was used also
by some men to explain their efforts to control
their children's behaviors; for example, adhering
to a position of inflexibility with regard to the
visitation schedule:

*I've made it clear to my kids that visi-
tation is not negotiable: 'I expect you
here: this is my time with you. This is
our time together. I expect you here
and when you're with me, this is your
home.' I can be a dictator! So my kids
come over. They waffle here and
there, they've got stuff to do and that
sort of thing, they're teenagers now
with lots of activities. But they are to
come and they do. It's nonnegotiable.
I'm their father. These are my rights. I
didn't let attorneys or social workers
tell me what to do, I don't let their
mother tell me what to do, and I don't
let these kids tell me what to do.*

Several fathers characterized the actions of
their young children as having violated their
rights as fathers; infractions included not demanding and arranging greater amounts of visitation, initiating telephone calls, or aligning with

them in disagreements between the parents. But what was primarily to be secured within the context of *fathers' rights* was a position of control and authority. This man explained his return of their child to his former wife after having fought mightily for custody:

> I am a strong advocate for fathers' rights, for men's rights. I had to fight for my rights as a father; and it cost me over twenty thousand dollars to win the custody fight. But I had to show my ex that I was still in control here, that she couldn't deny me my basic rights just because she got the divorce she wanted. By winning the custody battle, I showed her that I was still in charge. But I knew all along that I would let my son go back to live with his mother once this was over.

Because *rights* were integral to identity, the securing of them was fundamentally important and entailed a process loaded with urgency. The largely adversarial character, whether implicit or explicit, of the legal divorce process reinforced their sense of being both engaged in a competition and, because of the loss of power attendant to divorce, positioned continuously on the defensive. Their response was, as one characterized it, "to go on the offensive since the best defense is a strong offense."[8] Thus, their participation in the negotiations, whether informal between the estranged spouses or formal, involving legal representation, was often intense; exaggerated demands, especially involving child custody or support issues, were made in the anticipation that less than what was being sought would actually be obtained. Seeking to intimidate the former wife was a commonly described, preferred strategy. For instance,

> The truth is that whenever she brings up changing, increasing, the Child Support Order—she'd have to go and get an Order of Modification— all I have to do is 'alright, just go ahead, and I'll be right behind you seeking a change of custody.' I will too. I'll call up my buddy, Bill, in Albany, the guy [family law attorney] who's been winning all of these cases for fathers and we'll get sole custody.

These men's relations to the legal system and assessments of their legal experiences, framed within the context of *rights,* were paradoxical. On one hand, the juridical institution was perceived as being a tool, available for their use. Men expressed pride in the aggressiveness of *their* attorneys, often referring to them by first name, and claimed to share with them, to cite one respondent, "a certain degree of rationality, efficiency, and intelligence." Such perceptions and assertions of commonality empowered them in their interactions, settlement negotiations, and self-evaluations. Legal procedures themselves were characterized as being masculine—aggressive, competitive, tough, and significant.

On the other hand, the law, attorneys, and judges were viewed with disdain and distrust. One man stated that family attorneys are "nothing but today's carpetbaggers." Another said,

> I have nothing but contempt for the system. I don't give a damn what the law says, what the legal system says. I don't give a damn what their psychologists and counselors say. I know best. I know better, these are my kids. Do you know what the legal system does? It tries to emasculate you.

Legal professionals were blamed for the formal divorce-related actions of former wives; such as, efforts to secure sole child custody, obtain financial support, dictate the visitation schedule, and establish the terms of the property settlement.

Thus, some attorneys and judges were allies and others were opponents, and movement between the camps was common. Attorneys were hired, directed, and fired in succession. The authority of the judiciary was conditional, to be voluntarily conceded or withheld: child support could be held back, children "snatched" from their custodial mothers (as nine fathers reported having done), and former wives harassed legally through formalized, legal procedures. Such actions were explicable within the logic of securing one's *rights* in an unjust system.

That the system inherently discriminates against men in divorce was a shared belief irrespective of personal experiences with or assessments of the legal system: whatever the extent of their actual involvement with the legal system, the men shared the beliefs that they were "bargaining in the shadow of the law" (Mnookin and Kornhauser 1979) and that the shadow was darkened with bias against them. Even the men expressing pride in their legal successes, those giving fairly innocuous assessments of their encounters with the system, and those having little direct dealings with it were convinced that women are favored in divorce law and proceedings. One father, for instance, critiqued the legal system in a representative way:

> *The practices of the legal system today infringe upon and revoke our rights as men to make even the most fundamental family decisions. We are systematically being displaced.*

Although about a quarter of the men made references to women acquaintances who had been unjustly treated by divorce and its outcome, such cases were defined as exceptional; no one suggested that his own former wife had been treated unfairly.

The legal divorcing process was viewed as a highly charged contest, the outcome of which carried high stakes. Nearly everyone talked about the legal divorce settlement as evidence of winning or losing and military and sports metaphors, prevalent throughout their overall accounts, were particularly evident in the men's discussions of their legal experiences. *Rights* had either been secured or unjustly lost. Moreover, participation itself in the legal processes of divorce exemplified for many a loss of power and authority in their family lives; the *right* to self-determination in what were viewed as private matters prior to divorce was usurped by the legal and judicial institutions (see also Folberg and Milne 1988), and in some instances, by social service agencies operating at the direction of the judiciary. Made public, and sometimes scrutinized, were such issues as marital relations; childrearing practices and parental involvement; and earning, spending and saving patterns.

The rhetoric of *rights* then was multifaceted, consisting of complex and overlapping themes pertaining to self-identity and involving issues of personal efficacy, dominance, and control. It served to define, reaffirm, and reassert a masculine self. *Rights* was a euphemism for male privilege within the family and the stratified gender system generally, and provided a means for characterizing one's place and experiences in the social order and in divorce. *Rights* then provided a framework for defining the self in relation to others, a particularly important function in a context characterized by rapid changes and ambiguity, and for explaining the changing locus of power and various actual or threatened losses.

Adding yet further complexity to the use of *rights* was its use as a gender strategy (Hochschild 1989): framing their experiences, actions, and relationships as matters of *rights* served as a way to manage feelings and shore up self-identity. This strategy or line of activity empowered them in their assertions that they remained "in control" both of themselves and their situations, despite the unfamiliar, complicated, and usually emotionally stressful postdivorce circumstances. Fears of losing one's children and feelings of confusion, loss, and grief about either or both their children and former wife were reconstructed to be matters of *rights*. Defining a situation as a threat to or an assault on one's rights allowed the emotions experienced to be interpreted as, or to be channeled into, ones of anger (Arendell 1992). Anger was allowed, even expected, within the conventions of masculinity.

Consistent with the view that the postdivorce family was a broken family, the rhetoric of *rights* fostered an objectifying of relationships and an intensification of a perception of a self as autonomous and separate. Moreover, in its framing of relationships, actions, and feelings, *rights* promoted and reinforced competitive and aggressive lines of action even as it reaffirmed, in the unfamiliar postdivorce circumstance, a confident rather than a confused or uncertain self. The rhetoric of *rights* within the gendered divorce discourse abetted and justified their engagement in the processes of traditionalization (LaRossa and LaRossa 1989).

But gendered identity and social arrangements were not deterministic and the processes of traditionalization not universal. As with the role transitions "in becoming a husband and a father" analyzed elsewhere (Cohen 1989, p. 225), some fathers took on new responsibilities, expanded roles, and sought alternative definitions.

"ANDROGYNOUS" FATHERS

The "androgynous" fathers, 9 out of the 75 fathers in the study, differed from the majority in broadly consistent ways. Variations in postdivorce custody status alone did not account for the differences between this small group of fathers and the others. Three of these fathers had primary custody of their children and two shared custody with their former spouses (which in their cases involved dividing equally the time spent with and caring for their children). The other four men were noncustodial fathers who were extensively involved with their children. Only one had remarried, a noncustodial father.

Eight of these men, and two of the others, marveled at how they had "learned to become a father only after divorcing." Six had found it necessary to make major alterations in their behaviors and priorities in order to become involved, nurturing fathers. For example, this postdivorce "androgynous" father assumed his role as a custodial parent of three young children suddenly when his wife left:

> It was terrifying at first, just terrifying. I remember the night she walked out the door. And I cried at the thought of it: I said to myself, 'how in the hell am I going to do this?' I was raised in a stereotypically way, stereotypically male. I did not cook. I did not particularly clean. I was working a lot so it was 'come home and play with the baby.' The youngest was just a year and a half, one was going towards three, and the oldest one was just about four. So it was like playtime. I didn't have any responsibility for their daily care. I'd hardly changed a diaper before. I didn't know what parenting was about, really. I mean,

who teaches us how to parent? I really didn't know how to ask for help. I don't truly remember the first year. It was day by day by day. After about a year, I managed to figure out that I had my act together. But it goes deeper than all of that. I had to learn to relate to them.

After describing in some detail his strategies for coping in the new and stressful situation, he assessed the personal changes:

I actually think I'm a better person, to be honest with you, and certainly a far better parent than I ever would have been had she not left. Not that it would be by choice [single parenting], but however you'd like it to be, I would rather have done what I've done. What happened by becoming single is that I was forced into all of this. Now I admit I lost the playtime when they were little, and that's my greatest regret, and all of that. And it's been very hard financially because I'm always limited in how much I can work and I felt I couldn't change jobs. But I've shared so much more with them than any other father I know, they just don't even know what I'm talking about. Now I can't imagine what life will be like when they're grown and leave home. I feel like I'll be starting all over. I thought I had this ball game all figured out.

The postdivorce family was not characterized as a *broken* one by these fathers. Comparatively little use was made of the language of *rights* to frame experiences, relations, or feelings, although fundamental legal issues were sometimes intrinsic

to their experiences also. The postdivorce family context was not characterized as a battleground on which the struggle for *rights* was actively fought and there was no talk of divorce or gender wars. Instead, family was represented in various ways as a network of relationships which, as a result of the divorce, necessitated changes in assumptions and interactions.

The areas in which these men were particularly unique were their positive assessments of their relations with their children, overall level of sustained postdivorce parental involvement, and perceptions that the postdivorce father–child relationship depended centrally on their own actions. Interactions with the former wife were aimed primarily at fostering and maintaining cooperation and open communication; the objective was to view and relate to her primarily as the other parent, the mother of the children, and not as the former wife. Thus, issues of the relationship and interpersonal tensions between them were generally subordinated to those regarding their children's well-being and their own parenting. Unlike the majority, for example, the "androgynous" fathers had little if anything to say about postdivorce father absence other than that they neither understood it nor perceived it to be an optional line of action, regardless of the extent of tensions or differences with the former wife (Arendell 1992).

Minimizing conflict with the children's mother was viewed as essential to the fostering and protecting of a positive, stable, and sustained father-child relationship regardless of the specific residential arrangements or the nature and scope of their feelings about the former spouse. These men viewed themselves as having a particular and greater burden for preventing or reducing conflict than their former spouse. In ways similar to the other men, they believed that women have within their grasp and at their discretion the support of the legal system and divorce law generally. Primary and co-custodial fathers feared that their custody status could be revoked and noncustodial fathers feared that access to their children could be impeded.

At the same time, however, the moderate or conciliatory attitude toward the former wife went beyond a pragmatic assessment of their circumstances as divorced fathers. For example, rather than devaluing the former wife's mothering or other family activities, these men typically acknowledged the significance of her past and present efforts, even if they held some negative feelings about her in other regards. This person, for example, continued to feel some resentment, which he also characterized as betrayal, about his wife's decision to end the marriage:

> We never had a custody fight and I never threatened her with one. We were in agreement that it [maternal custody] was probably the best thing we could do. I just work too many hours, there was no way I could care for the kids all the time. The kids were too young. Why do that to the kids? I mean, 'you can see your mother ever other weekend?' And just for some reason it seemed to me that it was better, easier, that they stay with their mother at their young ages. They were just three and five years old. And she'd been a full-time mother, she hadn't been employed while I was building my career. She was always there for them. We'd been in agreement about that. And she's a good mother. There are times when I wished I could have them, I would just love to have them everyday. You know, if she would give them to me, I'd take them.

With only one exception, the postdivorce "androgynous" fathers viewed their postdivorce parenting activities as being part of a team effort, done collaboratively with the former spouse. They were part of a *parenting partnership.*[9]

Integral to these men's accounts but generally absent in the others' was the notion of parental or paternal obligation; child support, for example, was discussed primarily in terms of children's needs rather than in terms of conflicts with the former wife. Even so, these men also had some ambivalence about the relationship between child support payments and the former wife as the direct recipient. This father, for example, discussed the settlement process and his child support obligation:

> So the divorce, when you come down to it, didn't involve any true battles or fights or anything. We both worked to keep it on an even keel even though we were upset. It was basically a moderate process, based on agreements and an equal division of everything, although it took longer than it probably needed to because of the slowness of the lawyers. We just had the house, the cars, some furniture, and a few monetary assets. Obviously, she wanted more child support and I would have paid less. But it's what we ended up with. It was a reasonable amount. The point is that the state guidelines were the exact amount I had been paying for two and a half years without even knowing what the formula would be. It just hit it right on the head. We sat down and worked out what seemed right. So it was just what I could afford to pay her. I have financial responsibility for the children, no

doubt about that. But I had some funny feelings about it all for awhile, there was this small financial issue because I felt like 'I'm giving her a lot of money per year.' I had this tendency to think 'why should I pay her all this money when she's probably just going to go out and marry another guy who's making money? Like where do I get my income when I'm paying for the child support?' I have no other worldly manner in my life to get additional money to cover that. But it wasn't that she didn't deserve it or anything like that. They need the money.

As suggested by this participant, the "androgynous" fathers shared with most of the men in the study the assumption that their former spouses would remarry, if they had not already, and be economically supported by another man (even though all but five of their former spouses had some kind of employment), and that this financial change would benefit their children. With the exception of issues regarding finances, however, the "androgynous" fathers viewed their children as unique persons who were distinct from their mothers and siblings and who had particular perceptions of and feelings about the family situation. Also, according to these fathers, while children's understandings and behaviors were affected by the actions and expectations of both parents, they were not determined by either of them. At the same time, both parents were obliged to forego any efforts aimed at polarizing their children.

Issues of gender identity were present, in significant ways, however, for this subset of men also. Although they raised questions about and challenged the conventions of masculinity, its constraints and consequences, they too were

agents of and participants in the masculinist discourse of divorce by virtue of their gender identity, status, and experiences in a gendered-structured society. Because the postdivorce adaptive strategies and attitudes they adopted were often inconsistent with the major themes of the gendered divorce discourse, extensive intra-gender conflict was experienced (Rosenblum 1990). Reflective about and deliberately rejecting of what they perceived to be the typical behaviors and explanations of fathers after divorce, these men "paid a price" for their divergence (see also Coltrane 1989). They were beset with doubts about their actions and motives. Seeking alternative lines of action, they too, nonetheless, used as their measure of self, the norms of masculinity. One custodial father who was struggling with questions of motive and objective said,

I just have to keep asking myself: 'Why are you doing this?' I need to constantly ask myself if I'm doing this for my child or for some other reason. Am I trying to prove something?

Self-doubt was reinforced by inexperience and a sense of isolation: they were largely unprepared for parenting in the postdivorce context and had found few, if any, adequate male role models for their situations as divorced parents. In lamenting the lack of a male role model, four of these fathers observed that their exemplar for parenting was their mother, two noted that theirs was their former wife, and another credited his sister. Persistent questions of identity confronted these men: both they and others around them defined their actions and perspectives as being appropriations of "women's activities and experiences" or "mothers' lives":

I have tried to be a mother, tried to be the image of what their mother

should be, do with them in given times what a mother would do, provide a lot of the emotions she would give them, etc., etc.

In not conforming more fully to the conventions of masculinity, the men found themselves subject to question and even ridicule, especially from male co-workers and relatives: certain performance of gender carry more status and power than others and theirs were defined as deviant. As one man noted, in describing his lingering uncertainty about his decisions "to find another way,"

Even my father and brother told me to get on with my life, to start acting 'like a man' and to let this child go, that my involvement with him would just interfere with my work and future relationships with women. They told me that other people were going to think I was a wimp, you know, unmanly, for not standing up to my former wife.

Interpersonal and cultural pressures to conform to gender conventions were reinforced by structural practices and arrangements. The traditional gender-based division of labor, persisting not only in the domestic but also in the employment arena, hindered these fathers' attempts to act in ways generally deemed to be unconventional for men. Impediments included work schedules and demands, the gender wage gap, cultural definitions of male career success, and perceived, if not real, gender biases in the legal system as well as the culture. Individually confronting the conventions of masculinity and challenging the relevance in their situations of gender prescriptions did not alter dominant ide-

ologies or institutionalized arrangements or constraints (see also Risman 1989; Cohen 1989).

CONCLUSION AND IMPLICATIONS

The masculinist discourse of divorce, constructed and anchored in interaction and reinforced by the stratified social order, made available a set of practices and dispositions that prescribed and reaffirmed these men's gendered identities. But the template of familial relations and interpersonal interactions offered was a restricted one, often unsuited for the ambiguous and emergent character of the postdivorce circumstance. Even as the altered, and often stressful, situation called for continued interactional adjustments, negotiations, and alignment, lines of action were aimed instead primarily at repair and reassertion of self as autonomous, independent, and controlling. Those few men who sought out and engaged in some alternative behaviors also were both agents in and constrained by the gendered divorce discourse.

The implications of the findings from this exploratory study are numerous and can only be touched on here. The perspectives on and actions in family and divorce provided by the participants in this exploratory study invite further investigation into various postdivorce paternal behaviors, including, for example: noncompliance with child support orders (USBC 1989) and limited other forms of parental support (Teachman 1991); father absence after divorce (Furstenberg et al. 1987; Furstenberg 1988); repeat child custody challenges (Weitzman 1985); and the phenomenon of "serial fathering" (Furstenberg 1988). While often counterproductive to the development and sustaining of mutually satisfying father-child relationships, these behaviors, nonetheless, may be understood by the actors as meaningful and appropriate responses given their perspectives and circumstances. The points of view, explanations, and motives underlying such behaviors warrant further investigation and analysis. So too do the findings that men typically are less satisfied with divorce than are women (Riessman 1990; Wallerstein 1989).

Clearly much more study of divorce is called for since divorce as a common event appears to be here to stay. Careful attention must be given to the voices and viewpoints of all participants in divorce—children, women, and men. A fundamental part of the research agenda needs to be consideration of the effects of gender on divorce outcomes because divorce, like marriage, is not gender neutral. But a focus on individuals' definitions of and adjustments to divorce must be coupled with investigation of the effects of institutional practices and arrangements and cultural biases.

Professionals intervening in or advising about family situations and processes in divorce must be sensitized to the effects of gender on interactions and perspectives, and to their own gender biases and identity issues. Legal processes and practices which promote and augment rather than alleviate conflict between divorced parents need to be quickly abandoned and alternatives put in their place. Mediation must be available to assist parents in working through their differences, conflicts of interest, and emotional responses to the ending of their marriage so that they can focus on the postdivorce circumstances and exigencies. Education of divorcing parents is essential: specifically, parents need to be informed of their options, prerogatives, and obligations. They need to be encouraged to seek common ground in order to develop parenting arrangements satisfactory to both and beneficial to their children. A new way of thinking and behaving after divorce needs to be promoted: that a negotiated postdivorce parenting partnership is

both appropriate and necessary and, although it requires communication and good faith efforts, can take a variety of forms. Men and women need to made aware that, although their responses may differ, they actually share many of the same fears and uncertainties in divorce, particularly with regard to their parenting status and activities (Arendell 1986; forthcoming).

Even while divorce reforms continue, and alternative, more constructive, and innovative practices and processes explored, other fundamental social reforms must proceed. As Kay (1990, p. 29) asserted, "if we have learned anything from the work of Weitzman, Marcus, and others, it is that we cannot expect to remedy the defects of marriage at the point of divorce." Specifically required, for example, are the elimination of institutional constraints on and cultural attitudes against both men's more total engagement in family life, especially in parenting and childrearing activities, and women's full and equitable participation in the employment and political arenas. Individuals, including our youth, must receive much more education about marriage and family, parenting, divorce, and gender even as a broad rethinking of these institutions, practices, and underlying ideologies occurs. The "stalled revolution" (Hochschild 1989) in transformations and related institutional reforms must be stirred; social movement must seek to insure gender justice together with the protecting of children in divorce. Called for then, in brief, are continual assessments of what is transpiring in the lives of families; a conscious revisiting of our assumptions about family and the relations between married and former spouses, and parents and children; and a recasting of society aimed at empowering individuals to move beyond the constraints of gender roles and, most significantly, the constraints of gender identity.

Reading 25   Life-Span Adjustment of Children to Their Parents' Divorce*

PAUL R. AMATO

Children have always faced the threat of family disruption. In the past, death was more likely to disrupt families than was divorce. Around the turn of the century in the United States, about 25% of children experienced the death of a parent before age 15, compared with 7% or 8% who experienced parental divorce.[1] As a result of the increase in longevity, the proportion of dependent children who lost a parent through death decreased during this century; currently, only about 5% of children are so affected. But the divorce rate increased over this same period, and at current rates, between two-fifths and two-thirds of all recent first marriages will end in divorce or separation.[2] The high rate of marital dissolution means that about 40% of children will experience a parental divorce prior to the age of 16.[3] Although a substantial risk of family disruption has always been present, today it is much more likely to be caused by divorce than by death.

Americans traditionally have believed that a two-parent family is necessary for the successful socialization and development of children. Consequently, it was assumed that parental death leads to many problems for children, such as delinquency, depression, and even suicide in later life—assumptions that appeared to be confirmed by early research.[4]

More recent studies indicate that, although parental death disadvantages children, the long-term consequences are not as severe as people once believed.[5] Nevertheless, many social scientists assumed that children who "lost" a parent through divorce experienced serious problems similar to those experienced by children who lost a parent through death. Furthermore, whereas the death of a parent is usually unintended and unavoidable, marital dissolution is freely chosen by at least one parent. Consequently, the question of the impact of divorce on children took on moral overtones. These concerns, combined with the dramatic increase in the rate of divorce during the last few decades, resulted in a proliferation of studies on the effects of divorce on children.

This research literature does not always lead to firm conclusions. Many gaps exist in our knowledge, and weaknesses in study methodology mean that many findings are tentative at best. Nevertheless, a consensus is beginning to emerge among social scientists about the consequences of divorce for children. And, in spite of its limitations, this knowledge can help to inform

*Amato, Paul R. 1994. "Life-Span Adjustment of Children to Their Parents' Divorce." *The Future of Children*, 4 (Spring): 143–164. Adapted with permission of the David and Lucile Packard Foundation.

policies designed to improve the well-being of children involved in parental marital dissolution.

HOW DO RESEARCHERS STUDY CHILDREN AND DIVORCE?

To understand how divorce affects children, social scientists predominately rely on two research designs: cross-sectional and longitudinal.[6] In a cross-sectional study,[7] researchers compare children from divorced and continuously intact two-parent families at a single point in time.[8] In a longitudinal study, researchers follow children over an extended period of time following marital dissolution.[8] Longitudinal studies usually include a comparison group of children from two-parent families as well. Although both types of research designs have methodological advantages and disadvantages, they provide useful information about adjustment.[6,8,9] Cross-sectional studies provide a "snapshot" that shows how children of divorce differ from other children, whereas longitudinal studies allow us to understand how children adjust to divorce over time.

In addition to studies of children, social scientists have studied the long-term consequences of divorce by comparing adults who experienced divorce as children with those who grew up in continuously intact families. Researchers also have carried out a small number of longitudinal studies in which children of divorce are followed into early adulthood.[10]

Three types of samples appear in the literature.[11] *Clinical samples* consist of children or adults who are in therapy or counseling. Clinical samples are useful in documenting the kinds of problems presented by offspring who adjust poorly to divorce, but these results cannot be generalized to the broad majority of people who never receive professional attention. Researchers obtain *convenience samples* of children or adults through community organizations (such as single-parent support groups) or other local sources. Convenience samples are relatively easy and inexpensive to obtain, but people in these groups may be atypical in unknown ways. Researchers select *random samples* of children or adults in a scientific manner such that the sample represents a clearly defined population within known limits.[12] These samples may be obtained from schools, court records, or households. Random samples allow us to make valid generalizations about the majority of children who experience divorce.[13] Unfortunately, these types of samples are also the most difficult and expensive to obtain.

Researchers match (or statistically equate) children or adults in the two samples (divorced and intact) on key variables known to be associated with both divorce and adjustment.[14] For example, parents of low socioeconomic status are more likely than other parents to divorce and to have children who exhibit behavioral and academic problems. Consequently, it is necessary to make sure that the socioeconomic backgrounds of parents in the two groups are comparable.

Researchers then select outcome measures that reflect children's and adults' functioning, or well-being. Common outcome measures for children include academic achievement, conduct, psychological adjustment, self-concept, social adjustment, and the quality of relations with parents. Common outcome measures for adults include psychological adjustment, conduct, use of mental health services, self-concept, social well-being, marital quality, separation or divorce, single parenthood, socioeconomic attainment, and physical health.

Social scientists gather information about children by interviewing one or both parents, questioning the child's teachers, administering tests to the child, or directly observing the child's behavior. Information is usually obtained from adults by interviewing them. Researchers then compare outcomes for those in the divorced and the continuously intact family groups.

Statistical criteria are used to judge if differences in outcome measures are large enough to rule out the possibility of their being attributable to chance alone. Observed differences that are too large to be attributable to chance are assumed to be caused by divorce, or at least, by some factor(s) associated with divorce.

Unfortunately, because these studies are correlational, it is difficult to know for certain if divorce is responsible for observed differences between groups. It is always possible that groups might differ in ways that researchers cannot anticipate, measure, and control. For example, an unspecified parental personality characteristic might increase the risk of both divorce and child maladjustment. Firm conclusions about causation require experimentation; because we cannot randomly assign children to divorced and nondivorced families, our beliefs about the causal impact of divorce remain tentative.

HOW DO CHILDREN OF DIVORCE DIFFER FROM OTHER CHILDREN?

Those who delve into the published literature on this topic may experience some frustration, as the results vary a good deal from study to study. Many studies show that children of divorce have more problems than do children in continuously intact two-parent families.[15] But other studies show no difference,[16] and a few show that children in divorced families are better off in certain respects than children in two-parent families.[17] This inconsistency results from the fact that studies vary in their sampling strategies, choice of what outcomes to measure, methods of obtaining information, and techniques for analyzing data.

A technique known as *meta-analysis* was recently developed to deal with this very situation.[18] In a meta-analysis, the results of individual studies are expressed in terms of an "effect size" which summarizes the differences between children in divorced and intact groups on each outcome. Because these effect sizes are expressed in a common unit of measure, it is possible to combine them across all studies to determine whether significant effects exist for each topic being reviewed. It is also possible to examine how design features of studies, such as the nature of the sample, might affect the conclusions.[19]

In 1991, Amato and Keith pooled the results for 92 studies that involved more than 13,000 children ranging from pre-school to college age.[20] This meta-analysis confirmed that children in divorced families, on average, experience more problems and have a lower level of well-being than do children in continuously intact two-parent families.[21] These problems include lower academic achievement, more behavioral problems, poorer psychological adjustment, more negative self-concepts, more social difficulties, and more problematic relationships with both mothers and fathers.[22]

To determine if there are also differences in adjustment when children of divorce grow into adulthood, Amato and Keith carried out a second meta-analysis of 37 studies in which they examined adult children of divorce.[23] These results, based on pooled data from 80,000 adults, suggest that parental divorce has a detrimental impact on the life course.[24] Compared with those raised in intact two-parent families, adults who experienced a parental divorce had lower psychological well-being, more behavioral problems, less education, lower job status, a lower standard of living, lower marital satisfaction, a heightened risk of divorce, a heightened risk of being a single parent, and poorer physical health.[25]

The view that children adapt readily to divorce and show no lingering negative consequences is clearly inconsistent with the cumulative research in this area. However, several qualifications temper the seriousness of this conclusion. First, the average differences between children from divorced and continuously intact families are small rather than large. This fact suggests that divorce is not as severe a stressor for children as are other things that can go wrong during childhood. For example, a recent meta-analysis of studies dealing with childhood sexual abuse revealed average effect sizes three to four times larger than those based on studies of children of divorce.[26] Second, although children of divorce differ, on average, from children in continuously intact two-parent families, there is a great deal of overlap between the two groups.

To illustrate these points, the results of a hypothetical but typical study are shown in Figure 1. This figure shows the distribution of well-being scores (on a representative measure of well-being) for children in divorced and nondivorced families. The height of the curve represents the frequency with which children score at various levels of well-being. Lower scores on the left side of the figure indicate poorer outcomes, whereas higher scores on the right side of the figure indicate better outcomes.

The average for each group of children is represented by the highest point in each curve. Note that the average score of children in the divorced group is lower than the average score of children in the nondivorced group, indicating a lower level of well-being. At the same time, a large proportion of children in the divorced group score *higher* than the average score of children in the nondivorced group. Similarly, a large proportion of children in the nondivorced group score *lower* than the average score of children in the divorced group. This overlap reflects the diversity of outcomes for children in both groups. Although the figure is described in terms of children, the same conclusions apply to studies dealing with adults from divorced and intact families of origin.

This diversity helps us to understand why the *average* effects of divorce are relatively weak. Divorce may represent a severe stressor for some children, resulting in substantial impairment and decline in well-being. But for other children, divorce may be relatively inconsequential. And some children may show improvements following divorce. In other words, to inquire about the effects of divorce, as if all children were affected similarly, is to ask the wrong question. A better question would be, "Under what conditions is divorce harmful or beneficial to children?" This point is returned to below.

Variations by Gender of Child

Some researchers are interested in measuring differences in adjustment between children of divorce and children in intact families based on such variables as gender, ethnicity, age, and cohort membership in attempts to identify groups that may respond differently to divorce. Summarized below are the major findings with regard to the relationship between these variables and adjustment.

Several early influential studies found that boys in divorced families had more adjustment problems than did girls.[15] Because these studies have been widely cited, many have come to accept this finding as incontrovertible. Given that boys usually live with their mothers following family disruption, the loss of contact with the same-sex parent could account for such a difference. In addition, boys, compared with girls, may be exposed to more conflict, receive less support from parents and others (because they are believed to be tougher), and be picked on more by custodial mothers (because they resemble their fathers). Other observers have suggested that boys may be more psychologically vulnerable than girls to a range of stressors, including divorce.[27] However, a number of other studies have failed to find a gender difference in

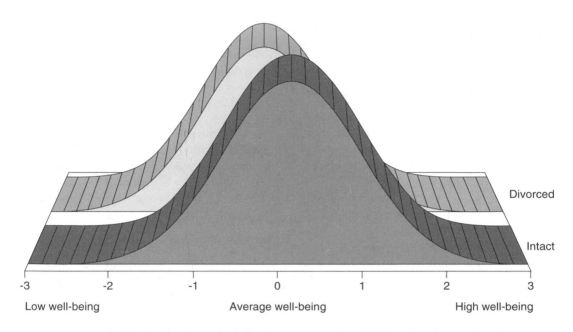

-3   -2   -1   0   1   2   3

Low well-being   Average well-being   High well-being

FIGURE 1   Typical Distribution of Well-Being Scores for Children in Divorced and Intact Families

children's reactions to divorce,[17,28] and some studies have found that girls have more problems than do boys.[29]

Amato and Keith tried to clarify this issue in their meta-analytic studies by pooling the results from all studies that reported data for males and females separately.[20,23] For children, the literature reveals one major gender difference: the estimated negative effects of divorce on social adjustment are stronger for boys than for girls. Social adjustment includes measures of popularity, loneliness, and cooperativeness. In other areas, however, such as academic achievement, conduct, or psychological adjustment, no differences between boys and girls are apparent. Why a difference in social adjustment, in particular, should occur is unclear. Girls may be more socially skilled than boys, and this may make them

less susceptible to any disruptive effects of divorce. Alternatively, the increased aggressiveness of boys from divorced families may make their social relationships especially problematic, at least in the short term.[30] Nevertheless, the meta-analysis suggests that boys do not always suffer more detrimental consequences of divorce than do girls.

The meta-analysis for adults also revealed minimal sex differences, with one exception: although both men and women from divorced families obtain less education than do those from continuously intact two-parent families, this difference is larger for women than for men. The reason for the greater vulnerability of women is somewhat unclear. One possibility is that noncustodial fathers are less likely to finance the higher education of daughters than sons.[31]

Variations by Ethnicity of Child

There is a scant amount of research on how divorce affects nonwhite children of divorce. For example, because relatively little research has focused on this population, Amato and Keith were unable to reach any conclusions about ethnic differences in children's reactions to divorce.[20] The lack of information on how divorce affects nonwhite children is a serious omission in this research literature.

With regard to African-American children, some research has suggested that academic deficits associated with living with a single mother are not as pronounced for black children as for white children.[32]

In relation to adults, Amato and Keith show that African Americans are affected less by parental divorce than are whites. For example, the gap in socioeconomic attainment between adults from divorced and nondivorced families of origin is greater among whites than among African Americans. This difference may have to do with the fact that divorce is more common, and perhaps more accepted, among African Americans than among whites. Also, because extended kin relations tend to be particularly strong among African Americans, single African-American mothers may receive more support from their extended families than do single white mothers.[33] Alternatively, given the large number of structural barriers that inhibit the attainment of African Americans, growing up in a divorced single-parent family may result in relatively little additional disadvantage.

We need additional research on divorce in different racial and ethnic groups, including African Americans, Asian Americans, Hispanics, and Native Americans. In addition to the adjustment of children of divorce, we need information on relationships between children and custodial and noncustodial parents, the role of extended kin in providing support, and, in general, how culture moderates the impact of marital dissolution on children.

Variations by Age of Child

Some of the best descriptions of how divorce affects children of different ages come from the work of Wallerstein and Kelly, who conducted detailed interviews with children and parents.[34] Although their sample appears to have overrepresented parents who had a difficult time adjusting to divorce, many of their conclusions about age differences have been supported by later studies. Observation of children during the first year after parental separation showed that pre-school age children lack the cognitive sophistication to understand the meaning of divorce. Consequently, they react to the departure of one parent with a great deal of confusion. Because they do not understand what is happening, many become fearful. For example, a child may wonder, "Now that one parent is gone, what is to stop the other parent from leaving also?" Young children also tend to be egocentric, that is, they see themselves at the center of the world. This leads some children to blame themselves for their parents' divorce. For example, they may think, "Daddy left because I was bad." Regression to earlier stages of behavior is also common among very young children.

Children of primary school age have greater cognitive maturity and can more accurately grasp the meaning of divorce. However, their understanding of what divorce entails may lead them to grieve for the loss of the family as it was, and feelings of sadness and depression are common. Some children see the divorce as a personal rejection. However, because egocentrism decreases with age, many are able to place the blame elsewhere—usually on a parent. Consequently, older children in this age group may feel a great deal of anger toward one, or sometimes both, parents.

Adolescents are more peer-oriented and less dependent on the family than are younger children. For this reason, they may be impacted less directly by the divorce. However, adolescents may still feel a considerable degree of anger toward one or both parents. In addition, adolescents are concerned about their own intimate relationships. The divorce of their parents may lead adolescents to question their own ability to maintain a long-term relationship with a partner.

The work of Wallerstein and Kelly suggests that children at every age are affected by divorce, although the nature of their reactions differs. But are these reactions more disturbing for one group than for another? Wallerstein and Kelly found that preschool children were the most distressed in the period following parental separation. However, 10 years later, the children of preschool age appeared to have adjusted better than children who were older at the time of family disruption.[35]

Many other studies have examined age at the time of divorce to see if it is associated with children's problems. However, these studies have yielded mixed and often inconsistent results, and the meta-analyses of children[20] and adults[23] were unable to cast much light on these issues.[36] A common problem in many data sets is that age at divorce and time since divorce are confounded. In other words, for a group of children of the same age, the younger they were at the time of divorce, the more time that has elapsed. But if we examine children whose parents all divorced at about the same time, then the more time that has passed, the older children are at the time of the study. Similarly, if we hold constant the age of the child at the time of divorce, then length of time and current age are perfectly correlated. In other words, it is impossible to separate the effects of age at divorce, length of time since divorce, and current age. Given this problem, it is not surprising that re-search findings are unclear. Nevertheless, it is safe to say that divorce has the potential to impact negatively on children of all ages.

Year of Study

One additional noteworthy finding that emerged from the meta-analyses by Amato and Keith[20,23] concerns the year in which the study was conducted. These researchers found that older studies tended to yield larger differences between children from divorced and intact families than studies carried out more recently. This tendency was observed in studies of children (in relation to measures of academic achievement and conduct) and in studies of adults (in relation to measures of psychological adjustment, separation and divorce, material quality of life, and occupational quality).[23,37] The difference persisted when the fact that more recent studies are more methodologically sophisticated than earlier studies was taken into account.

This finding suggests that more recent cohorts of children are showing less severe effects of divorce than earlier cohorts. Two explanations are worth considering. First, as divorce has become more common, attitudes toward divorce have become more accepting, so children probably feel less stigmatized. Similarly, the increasing number of divorces makes it easier for children to obtain support from others in similar circumstances. Second, because the legal and social barriers to marital dissolution were stronger in the past, couples who obtained a divorce several decades ago probably had more serious problems and experienced more conflict prior to separation than do some divorcing couples today. Furthermore, divorces were probably more acrimonious before the introduction of no-fault divorce. Thus, children of divorce in the past may have been exposed to more dysfunctional family environments and higher levels of conflict than were more recent cohorts of children.

WHY DOES DIVORCE LOWER CHILDREN'S WELL-BEING?

Available research clearly shows an association between parental divorce and children's well-being. However, the causal mechanisms responsible for this association are just beginning to be understood. Most explanations refer to the absence of the noncustodial parent, the adjustment of the custodial parent, interparental conflict, economic hardship, and life stress. Variations in these factors may explain why divorce affects some children more adversely than others.

Parental Absence

According to this view, divorce affects children negatively to the extent that it results in a loss of time, assistance, and affection provided by the noncustodial parent. Mothers and fathers are both considered potentially important resources for children. Both can serve as sources of practical assistance, emotional support, protection, guidance, and supervision. Divorce usually brings about the departure of one parent—typically the father—from the child's household. Over time, the quantity and quality of contact between children and noncustodial parents often decreases, and this is believed to result in lower levels of adjustment for these children as compared with children from intact families.[38]

The parental absence explanation is supported by several lines of research. For example, some studies show that children who experience the death of a parent exhibit problems similar to those of children who "lose" a parent through divorce.[39] These findings are consistent with the notion that the absence of a parent *for any reason* is problematic for children. Also consistent with a parental absence perspective are studies showing that children who have another adult (such as a grandparent or other relative) to fill some of the functions of the absent parent have fewer problems than do children who have no substitute for the absent parent.[40] In addition, although the results of studies in the area of access to the noncustodial parent and adjustment are mixed,[41] in general, studies show that a close relationship with both parents is associated with positive adjustment after divorce. One circumstance in which high levels of access may not produce positive adjustment in children is in high-conflict divorces. When conflict between parents is marked, frequent contact with the noncustodial parent may do more harm than good.[42]

Custodial Parental Adjustment and Parenting Skills

According to this view, divorce affects children negatively to the extent that it interferes with the custodial parents' psychological health and ability to parent effectively. Following divorce, custodial parents often exhibit symptoms of depression and anxiety. Lowered emotional well-being, in turn, is likely to impair single parents' child-rearing behaviors. Hetherington and colleagues found that, during the first year following separation, custodial parents were less affectionate toward their children, made fewer maturity demands, supervised them less, were more punitive, and were less consistent in dispensing discipline.[43]

Research provides clear support for this perspective. Almost all studies show that children are better adjusted when the custodial parent is in good mental health[44] and displays good child-rearing skills.[45] In particular, children are better off when custodial parents are affectionate, provide adequate supervision, exercise a moderate degree of control, provide explanations for rules, avoid harsh discipline, and are consistent in dispensing punishment. Also consistent with a parental adjustment perspective are studies showing that, when custodial parents have a good deal of social support, their children have fewer difficulties.[46]

Interparental Conflict

A third explanation for the effects of divorce on children focuses on the role of conflict between parents. A home marked by high levels of discord represents a problematic environment for children's socialization and development. Witnessing overt conflict is a direct stressor for children. Furthermore, parents who argue heatedly or resort to physical violence indirectly teach children that fighting is an appropriate method for resolving differences. As such, children in high-conflict families may not have opportunities to learn alternative ways to manage disagreements, such as negotiating and reaching compromises. Failure to acquire these social skills may interfere with children's ability to form and maintain friendships. Not surprisingly, numerous studies show that children living in high-conflict two-parent families are at increased risk for a variety of problems.[47] It seems likely, therefore, that many of the problems observed among children of divorce are actually caused by the conflict between parents that precedes and accompanies marital dissolution.

Studies show that children in high-conflict intact families are no better off—and often are worse off—than children in divorced single-parent families.[48] Indeed, children in single-parent families may show improvements in well-being following divorce if it represents an escape from an aversive and dysfunctional family environment. Furthermore, a study by Cherlin and colleagues shows that many, but not all, of the difficulties exhibited by children of divorce, such as behavioral problems and low academic test scores, are present *prior* to parental separation, especially for boys.[49] This finding is consistent with the notion that the lowered well-being of children is partly attributable to the conflict that precedes divorce. In addition, conflict may increase around the time of the separation, and parents often continue to fight long after the divorce is final. Indeed, many studies show that children's adjustment is related to the level of conflict between parents following divorce.[50,51] It should be noted here that postdivorce adjustment may also be influenced by residual effects of conflict that occurred during the marriage.

Economic Hardship

Divorce typically results in a severe decline in standard of living for most custodial mothers and their children.[52] Economic hardship increases the risk of psychological and behavioral problems among children[53] and may negatively affect their nutrition and health.[54] Economic hardship also makes it difficult for custodial mothers to provide books, educational toys, home computers, and other resources that can facilitate children's academic attainment. Furthermore, economically pressed parents often move to neighborhoods where schools are poorly financed, crime rates are high, and services are inadequate.[55] Living under these circumstances may facilitate the entry of adolescents into delinquent subcultures. According to this view, divorce affects children negatively to the extent that it results in economic hardship.

Studies show that children's outcomes—especially measures of academic achievement—are related to the level of household income following divorce. For example, Guidubaldi and colleagues found that children in divorced families scored significantly lower than children in intact two-parent families on 27 out of 34 outcomes; taking income differences into account statistically reduced the number of significant differences to only 13.[56] Similarly, McLanahan found that income accounted for about half of the association between living in a single-parent family and high school completion for white students.[57] However, most studies show that, even when families are equated in terms of income, children of divorce continue to experience an increased risk of problems. This suggests that economic disadvantage, although important, is not the sole explanation for divorce effects.

Life Stress

Each of the factors noted above—loss of contact with the noncustodial parent, impaired child rearing by the custodial parent, conflict between parents, and a decline in standard of living—represents a stressor for children. In addition, divorce often sets into motion other events that may be stressful, such as moving, changing schools, and parental remarriage. And of course, parental remarriage brings about the possibility of additional divorces. Multiple instances of divorce expose children to repeated episodes of conflict, diminished parenting, and financial hardship.[58] For some children of divorce, stress accumulates throughout childhood.

Research generally supports a stress interpretation of children's adjustment following divorce. Divorces that are accompanied by a large number of other changes appear to have an especially negative impact on children.[59] Furthermore, parental remarriage sometimes exacerbates problems for children of divorce,[17,60] as does a second divorce.[61]

A General Perspective on How Divorce Affects Children

All five explanations for the effects of divorce on children appear to have merit, and a complete accounting for the effect of divorce on children must make reference to each. Because of variability in these five factors, the consequences of divorce differ considerably from one child to the next.

Consider a divorce in which a child loses contact with the father, the custodial mother is preoccupied and inattentive, the parents fight over child support and other issues, the household descends abruptly into poverty, and the separation is accompanied by a series of other uncontrollable changes. Under these circumstances, one would expect the divorce to have a substantial negative impact on the child. In contrast, consider a divorce in which the child continues to see the noncustodial father regularly, the custodial mother continues to be supportive and exercises appropriate discipline, the parents are able to cooperate without conflict, the child's standard of living changes little, and the transition is accompanied by no other major disruptions in the child's life. Under these circumstances, one would predict few negative consequences of divorce. Finally, consider a high-conflict marriage that ends in divorce. As the level of conflict subsides, the previously distant father grows closer to his child, and the previously distracted and stressed mother becomes warmer and more attentive. Assuming no major economic problems or additional disruptive changes, this divorce would probably have a positive impact on the child.

Overall, to understand how divorce affects children, it is necessary to assess how divorce changes the total configuration of resources and stressors in children's lives.[62] The five factors described above should also be considered when evaluating policy alternatives aimed at improving the well-being of children of divorce.

WHAT INTERVENTIONS MIGHT BENEFIT CHILDREN OF DIVORCE?

Concern for the well-being of children of divorce leads to a consideration of how various policies and interventions might reduce the risk of problems for them. The most commonly discussed interventions include lowering the incidence of divorce, joint custody, child support reform, enhancing the self-sufficiency of single mothers, and therapeutic programs for children and parents. Interventions suggested in this article are considered in the light of available research evidence.

Lowering the Incidence of Divorce

In the United States during the twentieth century, divorce became increasingly available as the result of a series of judicial decisions that widened the grounds for divorce. In 1970, no-fault divorce was introduced in California; presently it is available in all 50 states.[63] Under most forms of no-fault divorce, a divorce can be obtained without a restrictive waiting period if one partner wants it even if the other partner has done nothing to violate the marriage contract and wishes to keep the marriage together. This fact raises an interesting question: If the law were changed to make marital dissolution more difficult to obtain, and if doing so lowered the divorce rate, would we see a corresponding improvement in the well-being of children?

Several considerations suggest that this outcome is unlikely. First, although legal divorces occurred less often in the past, informal separations and desertions were not uncommon, especially among minorities and those of low socioeconomic status.[64] From a child's perspective, separation is no better than divorce. If the legal system were changed to make divorce more difficult, it would most likely increase the proportion of children living in separated but nondivorced families. It would also increase the proportion of people who spend their childhoods in high-conflict two-parent families. As noted above, high-conflict two-parent families present just as many problems for children as do divorced single-parent families, perhaps more so. Given that the legal system cannot stop married couples from living apart or fighting, changing the legal system to decrease the frequency of divorce is unlikely to improve the well-being of children.

Is it possible to lower the frequency of divorce by increasing marital happiness and stability? The government could enact certain changes toward this end, for example, by changing the tax code to benefit married parents. It is possible that such a policy would enhance the quality and stability of some marriages; however, providing these benefits to married-couple families would increase the relative disadvantage of single parents and their children, an undesirable outcome. Alternatively, the government could take steps to promote marriage preparation, enrichment, and counseling. Increasing the availability of such services would probably help to keep some marriages from ending in divorce. However, as Furstenberg and Cherlin suggest, the rise in divorce is the result of fundamental changes in American society, including shifts in personal values and the growing economic independence of women, factors that cannot be affected easily by government policies.[65] As such, any actions taken by government to strengthen marriage are likely to have only minor effects on the divorce rate.

Increasing the Incidence of Joint Physical Custody

The history of custody determination in the United States has changed over time primarily in response to societal influences. In the eighteenth century, fathers usually were awarded custody of their children as they were considered the dominant family figure and were most likely to have the financial means to care for them. In the nineteenth century, the preference for custody moved toward women. The reason for this shift was probably occasioned, in part, by the industrial revolution and the movement of men from the home to the workplace to earn a living. Women, in this circumstance, were needed to care for the children while men were at work and became the primary caretakers of children. At this time, child developmental theorists also focused on the importance of the mother-child relationship, and the assumption was that the children were usually better off under the custody of their mother. Recently, society has moved toward a dual-earner family, and child developmentalists have emphasized the importance of both parents to the child. These changes are currently reflected in the law which emphasizes the importance of maintaining relationships with both parents.[66] The result has been an increased interest in joint custody, which is now available as an option in most states.[59] *Joint physical custody* provides legal rights and responsibilities to both parents and is intended to grant children substantial portions of time with each parent. *Joint legal custody,* which is more common, provides legal rights and responsibilities to both parents, but the child lives with one parent.[66]

Joint legal custody may be beneficial to the extent that it keeps both parents involved in their children's lives. However, studies show few differences between joint legal and mother-custody families in the extent to which fathers pay child support, visit their children, and are involved in making decisions about their children, once parental income, education, and other predivorce parental characteristics are taken into account.[66,67] Although joint legal custody may have symbolic value in emphasizing the importance of both parents, it appears to make little difference in practice.

In contrast, joint physical custody is associated with greater father contact, involvement, and payment of child support.[68] Fathers also appear to be more satisfied with joint physical custody than with mother custody. For example, Shrier and colleagues found in 1991 that joint-custody fathers were significantly more satisfied than sole-maternal-custody fathers in two areas, including their legal rights and responsibilities as a parent and their current alimony and child support financial arrangements.[66,69] Joint physical custody may be beneficial if it gives children

frequent access to both parents. On the other hand, residential instability may be stressful for some children. Although few studies are available, some show that children in joint physical custody are better adjusted than are children with other custody arrangements,[70] and other studies show no difference.[71]

However, these results may present a picture that is too optimistic. Courts are most likely to grant joint physical custody to couples who request it. A large-scale study by Maccoby and Mnookin in California showed that couples with joint physical custody, compared with those who receive sole custody, are better educated and have higher incomes; furthermore, couples who request joint custody may be relatively less hostile, and fathers may be particularly committed to their children prior to divorce.[66,72] These findings suggest that some of the apparent positive "effect" of joint custody is a natural result of the type of people who request it in the first place.

It is unlikely that joint physical custody would work well if it were imposed on parents against their will. Under these conditions, joint custody may lead to more contact between fathers and their children but may also maintain and exacerbate conflict between parents.[73] Maccoby and Mnookin found that, although conflict over custody is relatively rare joint custody is sometimes used to resolve custody disputes. In their study, joint custody was awarded in about one-third of cases in which mothers and fathers had each initially sought sole custody; furthermore, the more legal conflict between parents, the more likely joint custody was to be awarded. Three and one-half years after separation, these couples were experiencing considerably more conflict and less cooperative parenting than couples in which both had wanted joint custody initially. This finding demonstrates that an award of joint custody does not improve the relationship between hostile parents.

As noted above, studies show that children's contact with noncustodial parents is harmful if postdivorce conflict between parents is high. To the extent that joint physical custody maintains contact between children and parents in an atmosphere of conflict, it may do as much (or more) harm than good.[74] Joint custody, therefore, would appear to be the best arrangement for children when parents are cooperative and request such an arrangement. But in cases where parents are unable to cooperate, or when one parent is violent or abusive, a more traditional custody arrangement would be preferable.

Does research suggest that children are better adjusted in mother- or father-custody households? From an economic perspective, one might expect children to be better off with fathers, given that men typically earn more money than do women. On the other hand, children may be cared for more competently by mothers than fathers, given that mothers usually have more child care experience. Studies that have compared the adjustment of children in mother- and father-custody households have yielded mixed results, with some favoring mother custody, some favoring father custody, and others favoring the placement of the child with the same-sex parent.[36]

A recent and thorough study by Downey and Powell,[75] based on a large national sample of children, found little evidence to support the notion that children are better off with the same-sex parent. On a few outcomes, children were better off in father-custody households. However, with household income controlled, children tended to be slightly better off with mothers. This finding suggests that the higher income of single-father households confers certain advantages on children, but if mothers earned as much as fathers, children would be better off with mothers. The overall finding of the study, however, is that the sex of the custodial parent has little to do with children's adjustment. In general then, it does not appear that either

mother or father custody is inherently better for children, regardless of the sex of the child.

Child Support Reform

It is widely recognized that noncustodial fathers often fail to pay child support. In a 1987 study by the U.S. Bureau of the Census, about one-third of formerly married women with custody had no child support award. And among those with an award, one-fourth reported receiving no payments in the previous year.[76] In the past, it has been difficult for custodial mothers to seek compliance with awards because of the complications and expense involved. New provisions in the 1988 Family Support Act allow for states to recover child support payments through the taxation system.[77] Starting in 1994, all new payments will be subject to automatic withholding from parents' paychecks.

Child support payments represent only a fraction of most single mothers' income, usually no more than one-fifth.[78] As such, stricter enforcement of child support payments cannot be expected to have a dramatic impact on children's standard of living. Nevertheless, it is usually highly needed income. As noted above, economic hardship has negative consequences for children's health, academic achievement, and psychological adjustment. Consequently, any policy that reduces the economic hardship experienced by children of divorce would be helpful. Furthermore, the extra income derived from child support may decrease custodial mothers' stress and improve parental functioning, with beneficial consequences for children. Consistent with this view, two studies show that regular payment of child support by noncustodial fathers decreases children's behavior problems and increases academic test scores.[79] Furthermore, in these studies, the apparently beneficial effect of child support occurred in spite of the fact that contact between fathers and children was not related to children's well-being.

Research indicates that the majority of fathers are capable of paying the full amount of child support awarded; in fact, most are capable of paying more.[66] Based on these considerations, it would appear to be desirable to increase the economic support provided by noncustodial fathers to their children. This would include increasing the proportion of children with awards, increasing the level of awards, and enforcing child support awards more strictly. A guaranteed minimum child support benefit, in which the government sets a minimum benefit level and assures full payment when fathers are unable to comply, would also improve the standard of living of many children.[80]

Requiring fathers to increase their economic commitment to children may also lead them to increase visitation, if for no other reason than to make sure that their money is being spent wisely. A number of studies have shown that fathers who pay child support tend to visit their children more often and make more decisions about them than do fathers who fail to pay.[81] If increasing the level of compliance increases father visitation, it may increase conflict be-tween some parents. On the other hand, some children may benefit from greater father involvement. Over-all, the benefits of increasing fathers' economic contribution to children would seem to outweigh any risks.

Economic Self-Sufficiency for Single Mothers

As noted above, stricter enforcement of child support awards will help to raise the standard of living of single mothers and their children. However, even if fathers comply fully with child support awards, the economic situation of many single mothers will remain precarious. To a large extent, the economic vulnerability of single mothers reflects the larger inequality between men and women in American society. Not only do women earn less than men, but many married women sacrifice future earning potential to care for children by dropping out of the paid labor force, cutting back on the number of hours worked, taking jobs with more flexible hours, or taking jobs closer to home. Thus, divorcees are disadvantaged both by the lower wages paid to women and by their work histories. In the long run, single mothers and their children will achieve economic parity with single fathers only when women and men are equal in terms of earnings and time spent caring for children.

In the short term, however, certain steps can be taken to allow single mothers receiving public assistance to be economically self-sufficient. These steps would include the provision of job training and subsidized child care.[82] Although these programs operate at government expense, they are cost-effective to the extent that women and children become independent of further public assistance. Furthermore, many single mothers are "penalized" for working because they lose government benefits, such as health care and child care. Welfare reform that removes work disincentives by allowing women to earn a reasonable level of income without losing health care and child care benefits would be desirable. In fact, changes in these directions are being implemented as part of the Family Support Act of 1988.[83] Given that the employment of single mothers does not appear to be harmful to children and can provide a higher standard of living for children than does welfare, and given that economic self-sufficiency would probably improve the psychological well-being of single mothers, it seems likely that these changes will benefit children.

Therapeutic Interventions for Children

According to Cherlin, there are still no firm estimates on the proportion of children who experience harmful psychological effects from parental divorce.[2] Research suggests that, in many cases, children adjust well to divorce without the need for therapeutic intervention. However, our current understanding is that a minority of children do experience adjustment problems and are in need of therapeutic intervention. The type of therapeutic intervention suited for children varies according to the type and severity of the adjustment problems and the length of time they are expressed by the child. The major types of therapeutic interventions include child-oriented interventions and family-oriented interventions.[84]

Child-oriented interventions attempt to help children by alleviating the problems commonly experienced by them after divorce. Some intervention programs include private individual therapy. However, many single parents are unable to afford private therapy for their children and may enroll them in programs in which counselors work with groups of children.

Typically, in these sessions, children meet on a regular basis to share their experiences, learn about problem-solving strategies, and offer mutual support. Children may also view films, draw, or participate in role-playing exercises. Small groups are desirable for children of divorce for several reasons. Not only can they reach large numbers of children, but the group itself is therapeutic: children may find it easier to talk with other children than with adults about their experiences and feelings. Most group programs are located in schools; such programs have been introduced in thousands of school districts across the United States.

Evaluations of these programs have been attempted, and in spite of some methodological limitations, most are favorable: children from divorced families who participate, compared with those who do not, exhibit fewer maladaptive attitudes and beliefs about divorce, better classroom behavior, less anxiety and depression, and improved self-concept.[85] Although much of the evidence is positive, it is not entirely clear which components of these programs are most effec-

tive. For example, improvement may be brought about by a better understanding of divorce, newly acquired communication skills, or the support of other students. Although more evaluation research is needed, the evidence is positive enough to warrant further development and introduction of therapeutic programs for children.

In addition to child-focused interventions, there are *family-focused interventions* including both educational and therapeutic programs. These programs are aimed at divorcing parents, with the intention of either improving parenting skills or reducing the level of conflict over children.[86] In principle, therapeutic interventions that improve parental child-rearing skills or decrease the level of conflict between parents should benefit children, although this effect has not yet been demonstrated.

WHAT DIRECTIONS SHOULD FUTURE RESEARCH TAKE?

All things being equal, existing research suggests that a well-functioning nuclear family with two caring parents may be a better environment for children's growth and development than a divorced single-parent family. Children of divorce, as a group, are at greater risk than children from intact families, as a group, for many psychological, academic, and social problems. And adults raised in divorced single-parent families, as a group, do not achieve the same level of psychological and material well-being as those raised in continuously intact two-parent families. However, we need to keep in mind that many children are better off living in single-parent households than in a two-parent families marked by conflict. Furthermore, we need to recognize that most single parents work hard to provide their children with a loving and structured family life. Many single-parent families function well, and most children raised in these settings develop into well-adjusted adults. Blaming single parents as a group for the problems experienced by children of divorce is a pointless exercise.

At this time, our knowledge about children and divorce needs to be expanded in certain directions. The long-term effect of divorce on children is the basic question that needs to be addressed. The answers to this question will inform social policy and the court system, shape models of intervention, and influence parental decision making. This type of information should be obtained from longitudinal and longitudinal-sequential designs. Needed are studies that begin prior to divorce, as well as studies that follow children of divorce through adolescence and into adulthood.[87]

Also needed are data on how a variety of factors—relations with parents, parental adjustment, economic well-being, conflict, and exposure to stressors—combine to affect children's response to divorce. This research should make it possible to determine which children lose the most through divorce, which children are relatively unaffected, and which children benefit.

Information on how divorce affects children in different racial and ethnic groups is another area of research that would be informative from the standpoint of both clinical and economic intervention.[33] And more evaluation of various interventions, both legal (joint custody, mediation, child support reform) and therapeutic, are also needed.

It is important to focus on establishing policies that will help narrow the gap in well-being between children of divorce and children from intact families. High divorce rates and single-parent families are facts of life in American society. If it is impossible to prevent children from experiencing parental divorce, steps must be taken to ease the transition.

Reading 26   Stepfamilies in the United States: A Reconsideration*

ANDREW J. CHERLIN AND FRANK F. FURSTENBERG, JR.

This paper discusses five themes related to the formation and functioning of stepfamilies. The first section examines how demographic trends, particularly changing marriage and remarriage rates and rising levels of cohabitation, are affecting post-marital family arrangements. The second section looks at the creation of new forms of kinship associated with remarriage and cohabitation. The third and fourth parts of the paper explore issues related to the social organization of stepfamilies and the consequences for children. The final section of the paper takes up the question of whether and why remarried persons are at higher risk of divorce. We discuss some implications of research for public policy and current theoretical debates about the status of the American family.

INTRODUCTION

In the late 1970s, when rates of divorce and remarriage were at historical high points in the United States, each of us separately reviewed the surprisingly small number of studies on stepfamily life. In our reviews, we presented an agenda of ideas that guided our individual and collaborative investigations over the next one and one half decades. Cherlin's review noted the striking absence, of well-defined rules for family life among households formed by remarriage (Cherlin 1978). He hypothesized that higher rates of separation and divorce might be linked to the structural anomalies of this "incompletely institutionalized" family form. Furstenberg observed that the process of "recycling the family" replaced the nuclear family with a distinctively different family form (Furstenberg 1979, Furstenberg & Spanier 1984). He was especially concerned with the ways that remarried couples thought differently about marriage and family life after divorce and the implications of remarriage for the workings of the American kinship system.

In this article, our intention is not to summarize all of the recent literature that has been produced since our early reviews. Several recent books and articles provide excellent introductions to the current research (Pasley & Ihinger-Tallman 1987, Hetherington & Arasteh 1988,

This paper was prepared while Frank Furstenberg was a Fellow at the Center for Advanced Study in the Behavioral Sciences. He is grateful for financial support provided by the John D. and Catherine T. MacArthur Foundation, Grant No. #8900078

Beer 1988, Coleman & Ganong 1990). Our objective is more modest. We want to revisit some of the topics that we raised in our earlier papers and books; and we wish to examine subsequent research on these topics. For convenience, we have grouped our comments into five sections:

1. The changing demography of divorce and remarriage.
2. The construction of new forms of kinship among members of stepfamilies.
3. Studies of stepfamily "process": the daily interactions through which individuals build a stepfamily life.
4. The effects on children of living in a stepfamily.
5. The risk of divorce among remarried persons.

We believe that remarriage and stepfamily life constitute a strategic site for research on the family. The daily dilemmas of creating and conducting family life after divorce lead one to ask: what is a family, what are the obligations of parenthood, and how are bonds of kinship formed and maintained? There are, of course, no definitive answers to these questions; but our task as social scientists is to discover how answers are being formulated by those who experience divorce and remarriage and by those who devise policies and practices for dealing with the consequences of family change.

THE CHANGING DEMOGRAPHY OF DIVORCE AND REMARRIAGE

Among developed nations, the United States has unusually high rates of divorce and remarriage. Close to a third of all Americans will marry, divorce, and remarry. But informal, cohabiting unions also are increasingly common. The substitution of cohabitation for marriage makes it more difficult to follow remarriage trends and to describe stepfamily life. This trend toward the deinstitutionalization of marriage may be partly a response to the high risks of divorce and the complexities of stepfamily life.

Until the 1960s, the remarriage rate and the divorce rate in the United States rose and fell in parallel—when the divorce rate increased, so did the rate of remarriage. It seemed that divorced people were not rejecting the ideal of being married, they were just rejecting their own first marriages and trying again, Starting in the 1960s, however, the annual rate of remarriage (the number of remarriages in a given year divided by the number of previously married persons age 15 and older in the population) fell even though the divorce rate began to rise. The fall has continued ever since. At current rates, only about two thirds of separated and divorced women would ever remarry, compared to three fourths in the 1960s; the corresponding figure for men is about three fourths compared to more than four fifths in the 1960s.[1]

There are distinct variations in the propensity to remarry among subgroups of Americans. These variations reflect both choice and opportunity. For example, one study found that women who marry in their teenage years or early twenties are more likely to remarry than are women who married later; the authors speculate that women who married young may have less experience in, and less of a preference for, living independently.[2] Among women who choose to remarry, some may have more difficulty finding suitable spouses than others. Women who have three or more children, for instance, have a lower likelihood of remarrying, probably because they have a harder time finding a desirable partner willing to share the responsibilities of supporting a large family. And older women face a shrinking marriage market because of most men's preference for younger partners. Consequently, women who divorce at younger ages are more likely to remarry than are those who divorce at older ages.

In addition, remarriage is far more likely among non-Hispanic whites than among Hispanics or African-Americans. According to one estimate from 1980 US Census Bureau data, about half of all non-Hispanic white women will remarry within five years of their separation, compared to one third of Mexican-American women, and one fifth of African-American women (Sweet & Bumpass 1987). These differences occur, in part, because remarriage rates are lower for the poor than for the non-poor. With few assets and little property to pass on to children, people with low incomes have less need for the legal protection marriage brings. Yet lower incomes do not account for the entire difference. The low remarriage rates for African-Americans also are consistent with the lesser place of marriage in the African-American family.

Cohabitation

The overall decline in remarriage, however, is deceptive. As remarriage rates have declined, cohabitation among the formerly married has increased. Figure 1 shows the change. It is based on data from the National Survey of Families and Households, conducted in 1987 and 1988. Individuals were asked to recall their personal history of union formation and dissolution. The bars on the left hand side represent the situation in approximately 1970, according to the retrospective histories given by the respondents. Forty-nine percent of persons had remarried within five years after they separated from their spouses. In addition, some had cohabited with a partner without marrying. When those who cohabited without remarrying are added to those who remarried, the sum is the number who were ever in a union—marital or cohabiting—within five years of separating. As can be seen, 58% had ever been in a union in 1970. By 1984, only 42% had remarried within five years of separating, reflecting the drop in the remarriage rate. But the percentage who had ever been in a union had increased from its 1970 level to 62% in 1984. In the interim, cohabitation had become so widespread among the previously married that its increase had more than compensated for the decrease in remarriage (Bumpass et al 1991).

Divorced persons, in other words, have not reduced their propensity to live with someone; rather, they have substituted cohabitation for remarriage. We interpret this pattern as an indication that remarriage, like first marriage, is becoming less obligatory and socially regulated. It follows that informal unions are generally less stable and secure arrangements. About one out of seven people who eventually remarry live with a different partner between marriages (Bumpass & Sweet 1989). Indeed, the provisional nature of informal unions may be part of their appeal for individuals who may be hesitant, at least temporarily, to recommit to formal marriage. So the velocity of transitions into and out of unions has surely increased since cohabitation became more widely acceptable in the United States. Accordingly, official marriage statistics are rapidly becoming unreliable indicators of patterns of family formation and reconstitution.

To the extent that we are witnessing a trend toward the deinstitutionalization of remarriage, the rules and roles of family life are probably becoming more discretionary and less uniform. Much of what we discuss in later sections of this paper follows from the premise that for a large segment of the United States population, family life is becoming less predictable, more varied, and more complex. This trend has important implications for both the social organization of family life and the way that family members interpret and enact kinship obligations, the topic of our next section. Later on we mention how the growing precariousness of postmarital arrangements may be affecting children's development and well-being.

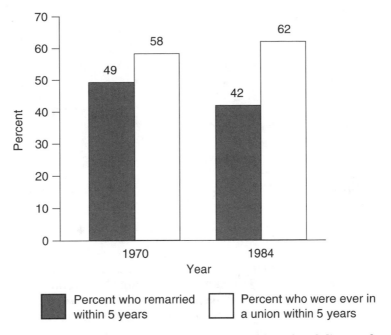

FIGURE 26-1   Percentage of maritally separated and divorced persons who remarried within 5 years, and who were ever in a union (marital or cohabitating) within 5 years, in or about 1970 and in or about 1984.

Source: Retrospective union histories provided by respondents in the National Survey of Families and Households, 1987–1988, as reported in "The Role of Cohabitation in Declining Rates of Marriage," Larry L. Bumpass, James A Sweet, and Andrew Cherlin, *J. Marriage Fam.* 53(1991):913–27.

NEW FORMS OF KINSHIP AND FAMILY ORGANIZATION

One of the taken-for-granted aspects of family life in the West has been that the parents and children in the conjugal family will live in the same household until the children grow up. Until the last few decades, that assumption was justified. The increases, first, in divorce and remarriage and, more recently, in cohabitation and out-of-wedlock childbearing, have made this assumption problematic. Only 59% of American children lived with both biological parents in 1992.[3] Divorce splits the conjugal family into two households—one that typically contains a custodial parent (usually the mother) and the children and a second that contains the noncustodial parent (usually the father).

Remarriage can bring a multitude of ties across households, creating what one of us has called "the new extended family" (Furstenberg 1987). In 1992 11.2% of all children were living with one biological parent and one stepparent. Consider one set of family ties studied by Anne

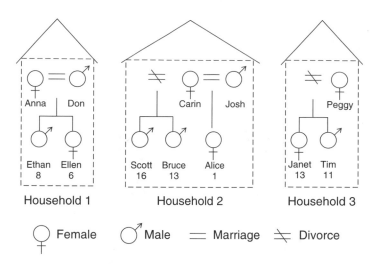

Household 1   **Household 2**   **Household 3**

◯ Female   ◯ Male   ═ Marriage   ≠ Divorce

FIGURE 26-2   Kinship ties due to divorce and remarriage in a network, reported by Anne C. Bernstein, "Unraveling the Tangles: Children's Understanding of Stepfamily Kinship," pp. 83–111. In *Relative Strangers: Studies of Stepfamily Processes,* **ed. William R. Beer.totowa, NJ: & Littlefield.**

Bernstein (1988) and diagrammed in Figure 2. This set of family ties is centered on the marriage of Carin and Josh, who reside in household 2. They have a mutual child, Alice. Josh previously was married to Peggy, with whom he had two children, Janet and Tim, who live with Peggy in household 3. Carin previously was married to Don, with whom she had two children, Scott and Bruce, who still live with her. Her former husband Don then remarried Anna and had two more children, Ethan and Ellen, who live with Anna and him in household 1. Here is how Bruce described his family:

Tim and Janet are my stepbrother and sister. Josh is my stepdad. Carin and Don are my real parents, who are divorced. And Don married Anna and together they had Ethan and

Ellen, my half-sister and -brother. And Carin married Josh and had little Alice, my half-sister (Bernstein 1988, p. 101).

How are we to make sense of this admixture? How many families are involved? What are their boundaries? The relationships spill over the sides of households, with children providing the links from one to the next. Let us suggest that there are two ways to define families in this context. The first is to focus on a household, even though ties extend beyond it. The advantage of this strategy is that in developed Western societies, we are accustomed to thinking of immediate families as being contained within households. We define a stepfamily household as a household that contains a parent with children from a previous union and that parent's current partner.

The children from the previous union are the stepchildren, and the current partner is the step-parent. The household can be even more complex: both partners may have children from previous unions and they also may have a new, mutual child from the current union. But the defining criterion is that they all reside in the same household. (Although there are three households in Figure 2, only household 2 is a stepfamily household. Household 1 has no children from previous unions living there; and household 3 has children from a previous union but no current spouse or partner.) In fact, there is little research comparing the similarities and differences between these expanded households and their simpler nuclear counterparts regarding the exercise of authority, the allocation of time and resources, the bonding of members, routines and rituals, and the like (Hetherington & Jodl 1993).

Note that we have not restricted our purview to families where biological and nonbiological parents are currently married, or even previously married. We want to include the large and growing number of stepfamilies that are formed when previously-married people cohabit, or when an unmarried woman bears a child and later moves in with a man who is not the biological father. This latter kind of stepfamily, in which there was no prior marriage but rather an out-of-wedlock birth, has received little attention, although as we have already observed, it has become common (Beer 1988).

The second way to define families is to ignore household boundaries and to focus instead on the chains that extend from one household to another. The links of the chains are children from previous unions. They connect a divorced woman and her new partner with her ex-husband and his new partner. Anthropologist Paul Bohannan (1971) called these pathways "divorce chains." But it is probably more accurate to refer to them as remarriage chains, as illustrated by the complicated network of ties among the three households depicted in Figure 2.

In fact, if you asked any of the members of the households in Figure 2 who was in their family, you likely would get a different answer from almost every one of them. To be sure, full siblings such as Bruce and Scott probably would name the same chain. Otherwise, each person has his or her own distinctive chain. Consequently, the only way to specify the members of a remarriage chain is to define it in reference to a particular person—not a household.

Remarriage chains can serve as support and exchange networks, when ex-spouses and new spouses give and request favors (Keshet 1988). This system depends on the quality of relations and cooperation of all involved and can easily be disrupted. In extended kin networks centered on conjugal families or on "blood" relatives (see below), people might extend favors based on goodwill and a sense of shared purpose. In remarriage chains that sense of goodwill is limited, and decisions are more likely to be made using the calculus of self-interest. It is best thought of as a system with weak rather than strong ties, a distinction between systems of support made by Granovetter (1973). Remarriage chains are more likely to provide information and referrals than direct material and emotional assistance (Furstenberg 1981, Johnson 1988, White 1993).

So we might expect to discover far more variability and instability in the kinship networks of stepfamilies than is typical in nuclear households. And it is largely unknown how these networks operate when the quasi-stepparents in cohabiting units are involved. Do family alliances become even more improvised and unpredictable when the roles of members are less clearly specified? In family systems where membership is fluid, a sense of kinship can be invoked easily; but a sense of kinship also can be withdrawn easily. We return to this point when we discuss the consequences of divorce and remarriage later in the paper.

Doing the Work of Kinship

When Americans think about kinship, they tend to think about people related through either "blood" or marriage (Schneider 1980). Mere existence of a blood tie, however, does not necessarily make two people think of each other as kin. Kinship is achieved by establishing a "relationship," seeing each other regularly, corresponding, giving or receiving help—at is, by making repeated connections. The absence of a relationship may mean that even a blood relative may not be counted as family. To be sure, almost everyone considers their parents and their children to be kin even if they have not seen them in a long time. But Americans would understand what someone meant if she said, "My father left home when I was three and I never saw him again; he's not part of my family. My stepfather is really the person I consider to be my father." And similarly a person might not regard a cousin as a relative if he never met her.

To be a relative, you must do the work of creating and maintaining kinship. Among parents and children, this happens almost automatically—so much so that we rarely think about it. But among stepparents and stepchildren it does not happen automatically. For one thing, a stepparent in a remarriage that has followed a divorce does not replace the stepchild's nonresident parent, as was the case when most remarriages followed a death. [See also Johnson's (1988) study of the indicators of kinship ties following divorce.] Rather, the stepparent adds to the stepchild's stock of potential kin. If both biological parents are still involved in the stepchild's life, it is not clear what role the stepparent is supposed to play. There are few guidelines, few norms. This situation is what led one of us to conclude that the role of the step-

parent is incompletely institutionalized (Cherlin 1978).

In fact, there is great variability in how stepparents and stepchildren view each other. In a 1981 national survey, children ages 11 to 16 and their parents both were asked who they specifically included in their family. Although only 1% of parents did not mention their biological children, 15% of those with stepchildren in the household did not mention them. Among children, 31% of those in stepfamily households omitted the stepparent who was living with them; and 41% failed to mention a stepsibling (Furstenberg 1987).

What, then, determines how stepchildren and stepparents view each other? A key factor is how old the child was when the stepparent joined the household: the younger the child, the more likely he or she is to consider the stepparent to be a "real" parent (Marsiglio 1992). The evidence isn't precise enough to establish an age cut-off for emotional bonding. Still, we suspect that if the stepparent arrives during the preschool years (before the child is five), it is possible to establish a parent-like relationship; but if the stepparent arrives much later, strong bonds form much more rarely. Research shows that children establish strong bonds of attachment to their parents, whom they rely on for security, within their first year or two. Children's attachments become somewhat reduced after the preschool years (Parkes & Hinde 1982). A second factor is how frequently the stepchild sees his or her nonresident parent; the less frequent their interaction, the easier it is for a stepparent to take on a parent-like role (Marsiglio 1992). A third factor is the quality of the relationship between the stepparent and the biological parent in the home. The more satisfactory that relationship, the more authority the stepparent has to take on a parental role. Finally, there is probably individual variation depending on the child's temperament. Some children may be more welcoming to new parents than others. So there may be differences in the quality of relations among children in the same family.

The kinship terms used by children to designate their parents are one measure of the bonding process. There is no agreed upon direct term of reference for a stepparent (Cherlin 1978). For example, few if any children call their stepfather "Step-Dad." and, it would be equally rare for children to refer to him formally as "Mr. Jones." Instead, some will call him "Dad" but many will use the stepparent's first name. In the absence of empirical research that relates the use of terminology to bonding, we are inclined to think that the use of the first name suggests a relationship that is neither parent nor stranger, but somewhere in between. If children do not address stepparents using the parental term for the biological parent, their children may not grant stepparents the reciprocal rights and obligations ordinarily accorded to so-called "real" parents.

Residential and nonresidential biological parents often have a strong interest in the use of names (Furstenberg & Spanier 1984). A custodial mother may urge her children to call her new husband "dad" in order to replace the role of the noncustodial father. And the latter, in turn, may contest this effort to supplant him with a surrogate. Some members of a group of inner-city African Americans interviewed by one of us (Furstenberg) made a distinction between "Fathers" and "Daddies"—the men who propagate the children and the men who care for them (Furstenberg et al 1992). "Fathers" are the biological parents of the child, but "Daddies" are the men who assume responsibility for their children—who play the role of father to them. The group of African Americans hardly ever talked about having a stepfather. It may be that

among African Americans, fatherhood is earned rather than accorded by birth or marriage. As we argue later on, this sort of cultural reasoning may actually be spreading more broadly in the United States as union instability increases. There is even greater variability in how more distant stepkin relate to the stepchildren. When the two of us carried out a national study of grandparents, we asked them about relationships with stepgrandchildren. Once again, the younger that children were when their parents remarried, the more that grandparents reported feeling that the children were "like biological grandchildren." One stepgrandmother, who had not acquired her stepgrandchildren until they were teenagers, was asked what they called her.

Harriet, I insisted on that. They started by calling me Mrs. Scott.... But from the beginning, you realize, these children were in their teens, and it was hard to accept somebody from an entirely different family, and they didn't know me from Adam.... Now if they were smaller—you know, younger—it would have made a difference (Cherlin & Furstenberg 1992, p. 158).

It also made a big difference where the stepgrandchildren were living: for example, it made a difference whether they resided with the grandparents' adult children (as when a son married a woman who had custody of children from a previous marriage) or were living most of the time in another household (as when a daughter married a man whose children lived with his former wife except for every other weekend and a month in the summer). Within these constraints, the closeness of the relationship depended on how much effort the stepgrandparents and their adult children put into creating the relationship. Being a steprelative depends on doing the work of kinship.

In other words, remarriage is making parenthood and kinship an achieved status rather than an ascribed status, to use the classic distinction in anthropology and sociology (Davis 1948, Eisenstadt 1966). Traditionally being a father or a mother had been a status ascribed to individuals at the birth of their child, which generally occurred only after the couple married. To be sure, people marry and have children through their own efforts; nevertheless, one did not have to do anything else to be a parent, nor could one easily resign from the job, especially in a family system that strongly discouraged divorce. In this sort of stable family system, being a grandparent was similarly ascribed. Those rules still apply to the majority of children who are born to two married parents.

Remarriage after divorce, though, adds a number of other, potential kinship positions. Whether these positions are filled depends on the actions of the individuals involved. The most obvious positions are stepfather and stepmother. We have discussed the wide variation in the roles that stepparents play. Some are parent-like figures who are intensely involved with their stepchildren. Many others are more like friends or uncles and aunts. Others, particularly stepparents who don't live with their stepchildren every day, may be like distant cousins—available for a kinship relation but, in fact, rarely assuming an important position in the child's network. In all cases, how much like a family member a stepparent becomes depends directly on his or her efforts to develop a close relationship with stepchildren. Kinship relations in stepfamilies belong to the broader category of in-law relationships—ties created by marriage or marriage-like arrangements. Such ties are characteristically discretion-

ary and even more so in the absence of marriage. In fact, in France, the current term for stepparent, beau-parent, also means parent-in-law.

Intergenerational ties to stepgrandparents are even more voluntary; they range from no contact to a kin-like role, depending in large part on the investment the stepgrandparents make. Our research on grandparents, in fact, reveals considerable variation in the role played by stepgrandparents in children's lives. To a large extent, remarriage restores a measure of balance between the maternal and paternal lines in the networks of kinship. However, there is reason to suspect that unless remarriage occurs early in the child's life, kinship exchanges over the long-term are strongly tilted toward the (custodial) mother's side of the family. The diminishing importance of legal marriage may accentuate this trend. It seems likely to us that cohabitation will undermine the sense of obligation to extended family that is created by matrimony. For example, the quasi-in-laws of cohabiting couples are even less likely than the in-laws created by a remarriage to form and maintain enduring bonds. But, as we noted before, research on the consequences of cohabitation is scarce.

STEPFAMILY "PROCESS": BUILDING A STEPFAMILY

After divorce, single-parents and their children establish, often with some difficulty, agreed-upon rules and new daily schedules. They establish ways of relating to each other that may differ from the pre-disruption days. A daughter may become a special confidante to her mother. A son may take out the garbage, wash the car, and perform other tasks his father used to do. Put another way, single-parents and children create a new family system. Then, into that system, with its shared history, intensive relationships, and agreed-upon roles, walks a stepparent. It can be difficult for the members of the stepfamily household to adjust to his or her presence.

Recent research suggests that the adjustment can take years to complete. One family therapist argues that the average stepfamily takes about seven years to finish the process (Papernow 1988). That is a long time, considering that more than one fourth of all remarriages disrupt within five years (Martin & Bumpass 1989). At the start, the stepparent is an outsider, almost an intruder in the system. At first, the stepparent may view himself naively as a healer who will nurse the wounded family back to health (Papemow 1988). But his initial efforts may hurt rather than help him attain his goal: a stepdaughter may resent the intimacy and support a new stepfather provides to her mother; a son may not wish to relinquish washing the car to a well-meaning stepfather who thinks he is just doing what fathers are supposed to do. As the two of us wrote, "stepparents quickly discover that they have been issued only a limited license to parent." The wiser ones among them accept the limits of their job description and wait for their time to arrive (Furstenberg & Cherlin 1991, p. 85).

According to recent articles, family therapists seem to agree that for a stepfamily household to be successful, the remarried couple must build a boundary around themselves and work together to solve problems. This process is made more complicated by the negative images of stepparents. In the larger culture (Ganong et al. 1990) and their weak status in our legal system (Fine & Fine 1992). Their own marriage, rather than the relationship between the biological parent and the child, must become the dominant sub-system within the stepfamily household (Keshet 1988, Papernow 1988, Spanier & Furstenberg 1987). To do so, they must reserve time for each other, even if that means sometimes deferring the de-

mands of others. The task of the remarried couple is to create a shared conception of how their family is to manage its daily business. They cannot rely on generally accepted norms, as adults in first marriages can, because few norms exist. They must draw the blueprints themselves and then construct the family. And, depending on their age, children must be brought into taking an active part in the construction of a new family (Hetherington & Jodl 1993).

During this process of family building, research suggests, it can be harder to be a stepmother than a stepfather (White 1993). In the typical remarriage chain, the children live with their biological mother and a stepfather; they visit their biological father and his new wife, who is their stepmother. Consequently, the typical stepmother does not live with her stepchildren; rather, she must establish a relationship during the visits. She usually is seeing children whose primary tie is to their biological mother, with whom she must compete. In contrast, stepfathers compete with noncustodial fathers, many of whom see little of their children (Seltzer 1991). Moreover, in the minority of cases in which the children live with the stepmother and the biological father, other difficulties can arise. In these atypical cases, the children may have been subject to a custody battle, or they may have been sent to live with the father because the mother could not control their behavior (Ihinger-Tallman & Pasley 1987). And mothers who are noncustodial parents visit their children and telephone them more often than do noncustodial fathers, creating competition with the stepmother (Furstenberg & Nord 1985, White 1993).

Stepfathers, in other words, often can fill a vacuum left by the departed biological father. Stepmothers, in contrast, must inhabit the space already occupied by the biological mother. Moreover, stepmothers may judge themselves according to the culturally dominant view that mothers should play the major role in rearing children; if so, they may fall short of these high standards. Stepfathers, in contrast, may hold themselves to the lower standard, namely, that fathers are supposed to provide support to the mother but let her do most of the hands-on child-drearing. If so, they may feel satisfied with their role performance, even if they are doing less than many dissatisfied stepmothers (Keshet 1988, White 1993).

One critical area of family building that has not received much attention is the merging of economic systems. Of course, nuclear families must integrate economic resources and devise a system of allocating funds. Still, it is obvious that divorce complicates this process. Often, the chains of connections that we referred to in Figure 2 signify not only emotional connections but also economic claims. The unemployment of a former partner has consequences for the household economy of his or her current spouse. Also, there are the inevitable problems of dividing the expenses of childrearing between current and former partners. These economic dilemmas extend to kin outside the family. Does divorce obliterate economic exchange among extended kin? Does remarriage automatically require it? These questions become even more murky when couples cohabit instead of remarrying. How do the quasi-stepparents in cohabiting unions recognize their obligations to their partner's children or to the relatives of their partner, their quasi-in-laws? Hardly any research has been done on these topics.

We do not want to leave the impression that stepfamily life in the United States is an interminable struggle. Most stepparents report that they are happy with their roles and their new families. In the 1981 survey, a large majority of parents and children in stepfamily households rated their households as "relaxed," "orderly." and "close"; and less than one third found them "tense" or "disorganized." Nevertheless, the ratings of persons in stepfamily households were slightly but consistently less positive than the ratings of persons in first marriage households (Furstenberg 1987). Moreover, the studies suggest that there is a wide variation in the roles stepparents play (White 1993). In a 1987–1988 national survey, half of all stepfathers disagreed with the statement, "A stepparent is more like a friend than a parent to stepchildren"; one third agreed; and the rest were neutral (Marsiglio 1992). Often, those stepparents who manage to integrate themselves into the stepfamily household successfully play a role somewhere between that of a parent and of a trusted friend—what Papernow calls an "intimate outsider (Papernow 1988)."

EFFECTS ON CHILDREN

Fifteen years ago, the two of us thought that remarriage would improve the overall well-being of children whose parents had divorced. For one thing, when a single-mother remarries, her household income usually rises dramatically because men's wages are so much higher, on average, then are women's wages. One national study found that 8% of children in mother-stepfather households were living below the poverty line, compared to 49% of children in single-mothers households (Bachrach 1983). Consequently, if a divorce causes a decline in household income that hurts the well-being of children, then an increase in household income after the mother remarries should improve children's well-being. In addition, the stepparent adds a second adult to the home. He or she can provide support to the custodial parent and reinforce the custodial parent's monitoring and control of the children's behavior. A stepparent also can provide an adult role model for a child of the same gender.

Despite these advantages, many studies now show that the well-being of children in stepfamily households is no better, on average, than the well-being of children in divorced, single-parent households. Both groups of children show lower levels of well-being than do children in two-biological-parent families. For example, psychologists Mavis Hetherington, Glenn Clingempeel, and several collaborators studied about 200 white households, divided into three groups: nondivorced two-parent households; divorced, single-mother households in which the mothers had been divorced for about four years, on average; and stepfamily households that had just formed (four months average duration) and in which the wife was the biological parent and the husband was the stepparent. The sample was not selected randomly but rather recruited by such means as advertisements, examining marriage records, and sending notices to community organizations. All households had at least one child between nine and thirteen years old; these early adolescents were the main focus of the study. Households were evaluated using multiple methods, including personal interviews with the parents and children, standardized tests given to the children, and videotaped family problem-solving sessions. Evaluations were conducted three times: at the start of the study, again about a year later, and yet again another nine months later (Hetherington & Clingempeel 1992).

At all three evaluations, the children from both the single-mother and remarried households were not faring as well as the children in the nondivorced households. For example, all the mothers were asked which items on a list of behavior problems applied to their early-adolescent child. Scores above a certain level on this widely used behavior problems checklist are said to indicate serious difficulties that might warrant the assistance of mental health professionals. Even at the last assessment, about 25 to 30% of the children in the single-mother households and the stepfamily households were above this level. As opposed to 10% or less of the children in nondivorced households. There was little difference between the former two groups (Maccoby 1992).

A national health survey of 15,000 children in 1981 produced similar results. Children in stepfamily households and in single-parent households both received higher average scores on a checklist of behavior problems than did children in nondivorced, two parent households. When parents were asked questions about the need for psychological help for their children, 3% of nondivorced parents said that their child needed help or had received help in the previous year, compared to 10% in single-mother households and 10% in mother-stepfather households. Both of the latter groups had children who were more likely to have repeated a grade in school than did children from nondivorced households. On all of these indicators, there was little difference between the children in single-parent households and in stepfamily households (Zill 1988).

There is conflicting evidence as to whether children of different ages or genders adjust differently to the arrival of a stepparent. Several studies, conducted mostly with younger children, have found that girls had a more difficult time adjusting to the presence of a stepfather than boys did adjusting to a stepmother (Bray 1988, Hetherington 1987). Some of the authors speculated that girls tend to form close bonds to their divorced mothers and that these bonds are disrupted by the arrival of a stepfather. In support of this idea, at least two studies found that daughters showed poorer adjustment when their mothers and stepfathers reported greater cohesion and bonding in their marriage; conversely, they showed better adjustment when there was less cohesion in the marriage (Brand et al 1988, Bray 1988). It is as if the daughters' sense of well-being falls at least temporarily when their mothers turn some attention and affection toward their new husbands.

However, the 1981 national health survey showed few differences by either age or gender. Neither did Hetherington & Clingempeel's recent joint study find differences between the early-adolescent girls and boys in their study, despite the expectations of the authors, each of whom had reported gender differences among pre-adolescent children in prior studies. Instead, Hetherington & Clingempeel now speculate that it is difficult for early adolescents of either gender to adjust to a remarriage. This period is when children must come to terms with their own burgeoning sexuality; it may be disconcerting to have an adult sexual partner of the parent move into the house—especially one for whom the traditional incest taboos do not hold.[4] Alternatively, the number of family transitions might impair the adjustment of children in stepfamilies. Having coped with a divorce, and possibly with the introduction of a live-in partner, these children must now cope with another major change in their family system. Some studies have found a relationship between the number of family transitions a child has experienced, on the one hand, and behavior problems, on the other hand (Wu & Martinson 1993, Capaldi & Patterson 1991). Finally, children and parents with unmeasured personal characteristics that impair family cohesion could be disproportionately represented in the population of divorced and remarried families. No study to our knowledge has done an adequate job of examining how much of the effect of marriage is due to selection.

Only one finding is well-established concerning the long-term effects on children of having lived in a stepfamily household. Children in stepfamily households—particularly girls—leave their households at an earlier age than do children in single-parent households or in two-parent households. They leave earlier to marry; and they also leave earlier to establish independent house-

holds prior to marrying. An analysis of a large, six-year, national study of high school students showed this pattern for girls (Goldscheider & Goldscheider 1993). In a British study, 23-year-olds who had left their parental homes were asked the main reason why they left. Demographer Kathleen Kiernan (1992) reported that those who had lived in stepfamily households were substantially more likely to say that they left due to "friction at home" than were those who had not lived in stepfamily households. Again, the differences were greater for girls. An analysis of a 1987–1988 American national survey found that girls who had lived in a stepfamily household were more likely to have left home by age 19 to marry or to live independently than were girls who had lived with single parents or with two parents; the differences were much weaker for boys. If a girl also had lived with stepsiblings, her likelihood of leaving home by age 19 was even higher (Aquilino 1991).

Interviews in 1980 and 1983 with a national sample of currently married persons suggested that tensions between stepchildren and their parents and stepparents cause the early home-leaving. Those who had stepchildren in their households reported more family problems involving children. The authors hypothesize that one way these problems are resolved is by encouraging, or arranging for, the stepchildren to leave the household. During the three years between interviews, 51% of all the teenage stepchildren had left the households, compared to 35% of all the teenage biological children. Some may have chosen to live with their other parent, some may have been forced to do so, and some may have left to go to school, establish their own residence, cohabit, or marry (White & Booth 1985). If this effect is indeed more pronounced for girls, it suggests that the "friction" in the household may be due to the disruption of the mother-daughter bond or to the presence of the mother's male sexual partner, whose relationship to the daughter is ambiguous.

Only a small amount of recent research on the consequences of children's experience in stepfamilies has looked at long-term effects. Even less of this literature has sorted out the complementary, compounding, and sometimes competing effects of divorce and remarriage/ cohabitation. From evidence already discussed, it seems likely that kinship bonds in stepfamilies are more fragile, less permanent, and not as significant. A thorough review of the literature by White (1993) provides a wealth of evidence showing that intergenerational ties between children and their stepparents are less robust than ties between children and biological parents. Nonetheless, a good deal of variation exists depending on conditions such as the length of time in stepfamilies, the quality of relations between the biological parents and their offspring, and the gender of the stepparent. In short, as White demonstrates, the effects of stepfamily life are far from uniform, and some portion of the presumed effect may be due to divorce rather than remarriage.

It is important to recognize that some stepparents manage to build relations with their partner's children, though rarely so if their remarriage dissolves. Still, the odds of building durable and intimate bonds that resemble the strong ties that often occur among biological parents and children are relatively low. The discretionary quality of in-law relationships—especially relationships that have a legacy of conflict or emotional distance—often seems to dictate the kinship bonds in later life.

It strikes us that the comparison of stepchildren and biological offspring is not always the most appropriate one. Perhaps it is more reasonable to contrast the sense of obligations that

stepparents and their adult children experience toward one another to obligations assumed by sons and daughters-in-law. By that standard, we may find that relations between stepchildren and their parents are not so impoverished. It would also be interesting to examine the relatively small number of stepchildren who were adopted by their parents (who become treated like "blood" relatives) with adopted children whose membership in the family was not gained through divorce and remarriage.

The structural comparisons of family types also need to be supplemented with qualitative research on the circumstances under which parents and children socially construct family bonds and how those constructions change over time. Clearly, some parents and children experience their steprelations as similar to ties with blood relatives. How do these individuals manage to ignore the signals of a culture that places strong values on blood ties? In the conclusion, we argue that such individuals may become more common in the future. The significance of blood bonds may wane to some degree if the institution of marriage continues to weaken.

THE RISK OF RE-DIVORCE

Throughout this commentary on the research literature about stepfamily life, we have repeatedly referred to the cultural, structural, and emotional complexities associated with family formation after divorce, particularly for couples with children. As mentioned in the introductory section, Cherlin's 1978 article suggested that the everyday problems associated with building and maintaining a stepfamily might generate marital strains, accounting for the higher risk of divorce among remarried persons.

Recent studies confirm that remarriages are somewhat more likely to end in divorce than are first marriages. After ten years, about 37% of re-marriages have dissolved, compared to about 30% of first marriages (Sweet & Bumpass 1987). The difference is concentrated in the first several years, during which time people in remarriages have substantially higher rates of divorce than do people in first marriages. Cherlin's hypothesis has been the source of some debate among re-searchers. One of the first researchers to raise questions about the thesis that "incomplete insti-tutionalization" of remarriage led to higher rates of divorce was Furstenberg, who, along with Graham Spanier, suggested an alternative expla-nation for the higher rates of divorce among re-marriers. Remarried people, they argued, have ipso facto demonstrated a willingness to resort to divorce when unsatisfied in marriage; in contrast, many people in first marriages are reluctant to divorce regardless of their discontents with the relationship. Moreover, Furstenberg & Spanier argued that the experience of divorce may make individuals less inclined to remain in an unhappy remarriage. So remarriage, they assert, involves a select group of people who may differ from first-marriers in their propensity to divorce (Furstenberg & Spanier 1984).

Research published during the 1980s pro-vides evidence that supports both views. For example, support for the Furstenberg-Spanier selection hypothesis was presented by Teresa Castro Martin and Larry Bumpass. They found that a majority of remarried people had begun their first marriages as teenagers (Martin & Bumpass 1989). They speculate that a teenage first marriage may be a sign of personality char-acteristics or other difficulties that make it harder for a person to choose a good spouse or to maintain a marriage. (It is known that first mar-riages begun in the teenage years have a high di-vorce rate.) In any case, Martin & Bumpass found that the greater number of teenage first-marriers in the remarried population accounted

for much of the higher divorce rate among the re-married. Another recent national study found support for both views: In a three-year longitudi-nal study, Alan Booth and John Edwards (1992) found that both the presence of stepchildren (a measure of stepfamily complexity) and a teen-age first marriage (a measure of the selection of particular kinds of people into remarriage) ac-counted for portions of the higher divorce rate among the remarried.

The debate that we helped to stimulate must now be reformulated to consider the growing number of couples who avoid marriage altogether. As we have repeatedly observed, the distinctions between first married, remarried, and never-married may be blurring as the link between mar-riage and childbearing becomes more tenuous and as more couples elect to cohabit before (or instead of) marrying again. These changes make it harder still to detect the sources of instability in patterns of family reconstitution.

IMPLICATIONS FOR RESEARCH AND PUBLIC POLICY

From the perspective of children, these demo-graphic changes increase the odds of experienc-ing substantial family flux during childhood. A near-majority of children growing up in the United States today are likely to encounter mul-tiple parent figures. Many must negotiate chang-ing relations with these parent-figures as the children or their parents move in and out of their households. The children will be situated in complex and changing kinship networks that in-volve the loss and acquisition of relationships. On average, children in stepfamilies and quasi-stepfamilies exhibit more problems on average than do children who grow up in nuclear fami-lies. Nevertheless, many children experiencing the divorce and remarriage of their parents ap-pear to do well.

Research on children whose family experiences include divorce and remarriage is just beginning to identify some of the family processes that make a difference for children's long-term well-being. It seems likely to us that the same processes that make for successful development of children in two-biological-parent families are likely to apply to children who grow up in stepfamilies. Some of these processes reside in the child, some in the parenting system, and some in the resources of the larger family system and community in which parent and child are embedded. The task for researchers is to map these specific sources of influence and to describe how they work in combination. This is a daunting challenge for developmentalists and family sociologists.

The family changes that we have discussed in this paper represent part of a profound cultural transformation in the American kinship system. Elsewhere, separately and together, we have provided a fuller description of the sources and consequences of this transformation. Here we can only make a few observations that are especially relevant to the concerns of researchers.

During the past several years, Americans have witnessed on television and in the newspapers a steady stream of dramatic custody battles between biological and nonbiological parents. Not all involve conflicts resulting from divorce and remarriage, but in nearly every case the same issue recurs: Do blood ties have legal primacy over bonds created by the emotional investment of a nonbiological parent?

David Chambers, a legal scholar who has written about this issue, describes a court case that involved a boy named Danny, who was raised by his stepfather from the age of one, after his mother died. His biological father had not asked for custody initially. However, when Danny was seven, his older brother decided to live with the biological father. The father than

sued for custody of Danny on the grounds that siblings should not be separated. A lower court ruled that Danny should be allowed to stay with his stepfather, who had been the primary parent for six of the seven years of Danny's life. But a higher court overruled this decision, referring to the stepparent as merely a "third party" who should not be allowed to interfere with the rightful interest of the biological parent.

Concerning the dismissive treatment of stepparents by the courts, Chambers wrote that the ruling in Danny's case almost certainly exposes "society's conflicting and unresolved attitudes about stepparents." In fact, the legal doctrine that persists can be traced back to a longstanding belief that biological parents are better equipped to care for their children. Probably, too, it reflects the idea that children are the property of their biological parents.

These legal assumptions evolved from, and helped to sustain, a family system that was culturally and socially designed to reenforce the primacy of biological ties. Or, to put it differently, these assumptions emphasize ascriptive affiliations as opposed to earned or achieved affiliations. Throughout this paper, we have argued that the justification for giving such heavy weight to ascriptive ties is being seriously undermined by now patterns of family formation. It may be time to reconsider the doctrine that family is largely determined by "blood" and to assign, rather, a higher importance to the emotional, social, and material resources that parents, biological and nonbiological, provide. In other words, perhaps we should regard parenthood both as an achieved and an ascribed status. Perhaps we should require that parents earn rights to their children by assuming responsibilities in caretaking and support. Of course, biological parents must be given an opportunity, indeed they must be expected, to assume those responsibilities. Perhaps, however, we should also accept the possibility that other parent-figures may supplant biological parents when circumstances permit or require their involvement (Woodhouse 1993).

Of course, we are aware that multiple parent-figures complicate both the legal system and the parenting system. But the idea that two parents per household is the standard and the only acceptable family form is giving way to a more diverse set of family arrangements that are not so neatly confined to a single household. The change in family forms that we have been tracing introduces a host of anomalies. We see little evidence that remarriage (formal and informal) has become more institutionalized since the two of us first began to write about this growing phenomenon. We see some troubling indications that the cultural, legal, and social anomalies associated with "recycling the family" place a considerable burden on a growing number of children—even if most children seem capable of managing that burden without serious effects.

To describe this new family system is not necessarily to endorse it. But neither can we say that the old order is invariably to be preferred. Moreover, even if we believed that the old order were preferable, we cannot imagine how it could be easily restored without considerable costs to all.

Reading 27   Families in Time to Come: Taking a Position on Trends and Issues*

MARVIN B. SUSSMAN

Writing on families in the future is intellectual play. The substance of the messages stimulates the neural pathways of the brain. For a short time the right side of the brain is stimulated. From deep in the unconscious, there arise strong feelings and emotions on what the future world will and should be like and what this means for families.

I am aware of the pathologies of human societies and cultures and multitudinous frailties of humankind. Depressing as these are, in tandem with their increasing incidence in societies of growing complexity I feel strongly that partial, and in some instances complete solutions, to current pathologies are possible. Consequently, this paper is an upbeat statement on solutions. Each perceived pathology is juxtaposed with a positive and often optimistic set of options. Judgments on what is have well-established empirical referents. The prognostications of the future are more problematic.

OVERPOPULATION

Overpopulation of the world will be a continuous phenomenon. Among the many societal consequences are reduced standards of living, frequent migrations, internal and external conflicts, and increased hunger, starvation, and morbidity within afflicted societies. Expanded population growth has been associated with high levels of misery and human suffering.

The United States will not experience a sharp rise in the growth of population in the 21st Century. Small size families will be the predominant norm with cultural minorities such as Hispanics and Blacks being the exceptions. Worldwide population growth will enhance migration and create pressures to change USA immigration policies. Families of diverse cultural, racial, ethnic, and class backgrounds will challenge existing practices of social and economic separation.

Marvin B. Sussman is UNIDEL Professor of Human Behavior, Emeritus, University of Delaware, and member of Core Faculty, Union Graduate School, Union Institute, Cinncinati, OH.

Individuals and families use their views of the future in committing to action. Dr. Hanks and Dr. Settles asked Dr. Sussman, the Senior Scholar among the editors, to provide his own assessment for the immediate future of families.

A new paradigm focused on coalescing minority cultures around superordinate goals will eventually become normative. Superordinate goals are those which are highly desired by two or more competitive groups but are unobtainable unless joint cooperation is obtained. Such collaborative undertakings do not guarantee peace and harmony among diversified ethnic and cultural groups. The potential to interact towards a resonated common goal, however, is a beginning to deconstruct the *in* versus *out* group norms and values that create conflict, tension, and often violence between groups and their members.

AGING AND THE AGED

Characteristic of societies of increasing complexity is the rising incidence of persons dependent for their lifeways upon the economically productive members of the society. This is especially the case of the older retired population and the very young. Reported for worldwide industrialized societies is the increasing earlier age of retirement from the workforce and the extension of time for the education and socialization of children. The burden of support is upon the workforce, aged 15–65, those who contribute to the gross national product. Consequences of this burdening of the gainfully employed, are society wide transfers of economic value including: (1) increased taxation; (2) demands for higher productivity at lower labor costs; and (3) reduction or dismantling of various entitlement social service and health programs, e.g., Medicaid, Medicare, Headstart, in the United States.

In the coming years, members of families will be asked to spend more of their time, energy, and income to care for the chronically ill and disabled relatives. Laws determining filial responsibility have been enacted in 43 states and such legislation will occur within the next few years in the remaining jurisdictions. While such laws are not being vigorously enforced, they will be undoubtedly in the future as governmental bodies search frantically for monies to care for dependent populations.

Caring for one's own has had a long history and persists today in both expectations and practice. Family members are the major caregivers to their dependent members. The growing requests for care receivers come at a time when there is a paucity of women to assume traditional caregiving roles, because they are settled in careers and jobs. Also, fewer caregivers will be available as a consequence of the lower birthrate of the post World War II baby boom cohort. Ethical, moral, and legal issues regarding the extension of life of the older population; living without quality; care of the ill and disabled; best investment of dollars in medical care and social services will be assiduously debated in the following years.

ENERGY

As we move into the 21st century, the best guesses are that there will be very limited new sources of energy and that major savings will come from conservation. Population growth makes the energy issue one of the most critical ones in the coming decades. Even if new energy sources are found, there is likely to be difficulty in their use and distribution, because of the continuous conflicts over the possession and use of such resources.

The family's love of the automobile may be drastically modified. Currently, we may not be that far away from the rationing of fuel as during World War II or the shortages that occurred in the 1970s as a result of the fixed pricing by Middle Eastern cartels and Middle East conflicts. Families can go beyond relearning the paradigm of conservation. In addition to cutting back on the use of fuels, they can educate and socialize their members into the norm of parsimony, in the use of automobiles. Family education will include greater use of mass transit systems. New technologies will make such travel more energy efficient, convenient and enjoyable.

CONTINUOUS GLOBAL CONFLICT

The energy issue is only one of the basic components of ongoing conflicts between the have and have-not nations. Highly developed societies are the major consumers of energy and most recently the Persian Gulf Conflict was motivated by the great need and concern for continuous cheap oil to power the needs of these societies. In addition to oil, the control and use of diminishing world water sources will catalyze nation state conflicts in the immediate future. Predictably the reduction or loss of water resources in any section of the globe will drastically affect the food chain and any development of human capacities. For example, in Jordan and Israel, the future growth of the population with any quality of life for families depends on the available water supply.

Conflict between ethnic and racial groups attests to the strong identity and ideology of members of such groups. During the period of the early 1990s the horrors inflicted on innocent individuals and families are beyond comprehension. The major victims of such conflicts are families, innocent ones, caught and trapped in undreamed carnage. Unfortunately, the leaders in power, scientific and professional elites, and protagonists of family well-being and values have offered little or no solutions to the wholesale destruction of families. The one and perhaps only solution of those families able to escape death and destruction is to migrate. The stories of such families uprooted and cast adrift, and often unwelcome by their host countries, are among the most tragic stories of this century.

The "ethnic cleansing" is no more than developing new in-groups, to solidify, to organize, and to prepare for future conflicts with other ethnic distillations called out-groups. Unfortunately what is occurring today is highly duplicative of tribal warfare that has occurred throughout all of human history. It appears that humanity lives on the verge of readiness to kill. The task for the humanistically oriented social scientist is to work and experiment with ways to enable ethnic and racial minorities to live with themselves and with others. This may not stop the killing, but it might make a difference. Even if a handful of families are saved, it is worth the effort.

CLIMATE AND FOOD

For the first time in many lifetimes, more and more individuals are becoming concerned about the occurring climatic changes. Questions have arisen on how human uses of the land, water, air, and other nature's bounties create and affect such climatic changes. The destruction of the rain forest, the weakening of the ozone layer, the increasing incidence of high rates of pollution found in our urban areas have become central issues for debate, legislation, and even international accords.

The consequences for families are obvious. Farmers in Iowa who have experienced drought for four or five years are beginning to ask questions about this unexpected phenomenon, e.g., is it due to the depletion of the rain forest in Brazil? Some decide not to seek scientific answers but give up the farm and move to towns or cities in search of work in businesses and factories.

Climatic changes affect the oceans and the tides. An increase of even one to two feet will heap destruction on our coastlines as well as our inland lakes and rivers. The warming of the Arctic and Antarctic icecaps will result in the warming of the earth and severe temperature changes that will require complex and multitudinous changes in housing, lifestyles, and new behaviors for survival.

Foreseen is a continuous conflict between the advocates of an exportable worldwide sane environmental policy and those who speak for jobs by continuous exploitation of our natural resources. Families will be torn over their options attempting to live with this unique paradox. If we destroy our environment, jobs will be few. If we protect our environment, the economy may suffer. If we change the paradigm and integrate the best environmental practices with creation of industries using our high technology, the paradox of economy and environment can be sustained.

Changes in climate are obviously related to modifications of the food chain. Unfortunately, due to variations in climate and limited food supply, especially in its distribution, coupled with high fertility rates, the result will be rising hunger and starvation for tens of millions of families each year in the future. Major activities to modify this condition are (1) coordinated efforts to distribute food supplies through the emerging global economy; and (2) continuous and strengthened programs of child spacing and birth control.

A related program to be expanded would be health maintenance, especially pre-natal care. Pre-natal care is vital to enhance the survival of children. Such survival is critical beyond economic sustenance of family members in old age and is embellished in spiritual and ancestral worship systems involving members over generational time.

Another related concern is gainful and steady employment of providers in families. Security in jobs and possibilities for occupational advancement is another condition that lessens the need for a large sized family.

In sum, hunger can be reduced and families worldwide can experience some quality of life if food redistribution can occur through a global economy matrix; if fertility rates can be reduced; if health programs can be initiated to ensure the survival of children in small-sized families; and if steady jobs can be found for family providers.

THE GLOBAL SYSTEM

The world in the 1990s moved from being bipolar to being multipolar. Early political historians divided the world into component parts where nations like the United States, one-time Soviet Union, Germany and England had hegemony over less powerful nations. In this late period of the 20th century, there is a similar concentration of societies who are organizing around economic and other interests. The difference from previous times is that one nation may not be in power, controlling and dominating other nations in their geographical areas,

This multi-polar world is moving towards an impenetrable global system mainly due to improved and heightened worldwide communication. The communication revolution of the last two decades has effected rising expectations in all societies where there is increasing use of radio and television. The exchange and adoption and integration of cultural forms and soon to be followed, values, are a global process in spite of the efforts to isolate and secularize nation states. The earth has become a living organism; what happens in one part of the globe affects one, then two, then three...n events, organizations, economies. For families the concept of this process in mind-boggling. To grasp it requires acknowledging and understanding that one's own problems and those found in the larger society cannot be solved from a perspective of isolation. The earth, and before too long the cosmos, will have to be accounted as being part of our understanding and solution of the issues and problems. Families must overcome their cynicism about existing social institutions and begin to create new ones that have as their benchmark a global perspective. To be able to participate in this new world order will require renewed respect for science and technology and for demands on the part of families to have greater say in the use and outcomes of the discoveries of science and its endemic technology.

AIDS, CHRONIC ILLNESS, AND CARE

The incidence and prevalence of AIDS will rise each year into the future involving individuals and families of all racial and ethnic groups worldwide. The ultimate cure may be long in coming and foci will be upon prevention and treatment of this life threatening disease. It appears from the results of current research that appropriate treatment of the disease will postpone the deaths of AIDS victims. This prolongation of life will place increasing burdens on caregiving organizations and families.

The medical care system today with its current responsive idcology of viewing and treating physical dysfunctions as pathologies is unprepared to work with life threatening conditions that have strong social causation. Moreover, the heavy involvement of non-medical persons in the care and treatment of AIDS patients, especially family members and other significant service providers such as friends and lovers, portends serious conflicts and alienation between medical and non-medical caregivers. The current model of control empowers the physician who traditionally is in a superordinate position in the treatment hierarchy. The involvement of so many non-medical individuals in the treatment, care, and lifestyles of the afflicted individual requires a new model of care. It is difficult to determine at this point the best model. Suggested forms are partnership structures in which all those involved collectively determine the best

program of care. Another possibility is to empower the victim of the life-threatening disease to the point where he or she can make the final decision on the treatment modalities and endemic care.

AIDS is but one example of chronic illness and attendant disability that are increasing in prevalence and incidence worldwide. We are entering the period of extended survival of individuals with severe disabilities who for the most part are dependent upon the gainfully employed population of the society. The increasingly negative evaluation of expanding institutional resources for the care of ill populations is noticeable in the United States. Government elites both here and in other developed societies hold the position that the society has reached its absorptive capacity for expansion of institutional organizations' services. They turn toward utilization of family members and other volunteers to do the day-to-day care with minimal financial support from societal institutions. Such individuals give of their time and energies without direct cost to the society, expend their own resources and those of the afflicted individuals. There reaches a point in the trajectory of the chronic illness and disability when such resources cannot meet the needs and tasks of care for the ailing individual, and the individual requires hospital care, including intensive care.

Nurturing a humanistic value embedded deep in our culture is to exercise heroic deeds to save the life of individuals at any age. No matter how deficient persons are in "normal" human abilities and function, the expectation is to love and care for these individuals knowing that few will experience a quality of life usually attained by individuals who are not so afflicted.

The moral and ethical issues of sustaining the life of humans severely limited in their normal functions will be a basic and critical issue in our society in the coming years and as we move into the 21st century. Concern and even modification of current moral and ethical postures on caring for the disabled and chronically ill may occur more quickly than we realize if the current economic patterns of federal and state support should change.

The availability and distribution of economic resources will affect the debates on the ethics and moral issues of such care. Families will enter into these discussions, especially when it appears that the resources accumulated over a lifetime are completely lost to pay for the costs of a few days of care or when the family will become bankrupt and radically alter its lifestyle because of the chronic illness of a member. They will look for resources outside the family such as provided by health care organizations in order to complement their primary care activities. If a health care insurance system is developed that will control costs and provide sufficient care, families will not lose their economic resources.

THE ECONOMY

In the remaining years of this decade, the economic and political system continues to be out of control with a burdensome debt and slow economic growth. Coupled with this inability to provide jobs for an increasing number of young people trying to enter the labor market will be soaring crime rates. These situations cast a shadow upon the future but can be opened to new values, paradigms, and practices vis-a-vis the creation of new scenarios.

In 1992 President Bill Clinton resonated the notion that the government should invest in jobs and not just in the bail-out of service and loan institutions. His scenario is to invest in rural and urban work corps in order to rebuild the infrastructure of our cities, rural areas, parks, and woodlands. Such work groups would be similar to those created during the Roosevelt administration, aimed to provide needed repairs of our roads, parks, bridges, and other public structures and also to stimulate the economy by increasing the demands for goods and services of participants in groups resembling Work Progress Administration.

Another scenario would involve an increasingly large number of citizens through political processes and "action in the streets" attempting to enhance and preserve our environment. Educational techniques of such groups usually are spontaneously formed and decentralized, working assiduously in their own or nearby communities. As we approach the 21st century action to preserve our forests, to reduce pollution, to eliminate radiation, could be aimed to create ecological sensitivity, and maintain respect and honor for the environment. Involving families of varied ethnic, racial, economic, and cultural backgrounds would become a potent political force in the coming years. The environmental movement is an example of a pattern of decentralization of power and increasing ability to implement well-reasoned objectives.

RELIGIOUS AWAKENING

Two dominant patterns of religious behavior for America have emerged during the 20th century. The first was a conservative fundamentalist movement whose members believe in the infallibility of the Bible and whose leaders were highly successful in using the mass media, especially television. Televangelists captured the hearts and minds of millions of people and only the human behavior of a few such as infidelity or unacceptable sexual behavior has limited their influence. This political right has made efforts to control appropriate behavior of families. Spokespersons have been leaders in the anti-abortion movement and work continuously to unify the American people to a single set of conservative values. Their power and influence have fluctuated. For example, the shift from a Republican controlled White House to a Democratic one may be a harbinger of a reduced conservative movement and a renewed interest in more liberal religious institutions.

Traditional Protestant religious institutions as well as Catholic and Jewish religious organizations have not experienced growth in numbers or influence in these past decades. However, a small but significant minority of individuals are creating new journeys of the spirit. Using a combination of religious tenets from far eastern religious traditions along with humanistic principles derived from the great philosophers of world societies, another new religious movement is emerging in which the spiritual journey not only encompasses individual transformation but also good community work.

Families today and in the future will be able to make a choice of one of these major religious systems. The basis of such a choice is problematic. The ultimate determinant will be the family's response to the exhortations of ideology, laws and legislation that shape religious behavior, and the inner motivation that guides the individual to behave according to her or his principles regardless of the consequences. A multimodal religious system will exist in the future in American society, providing choices for families without being coerced by an authoritarian religious system.

THE GENDER REVOLUTION

There has been a growing awakening of consciousness in the twentieth century, and a number of revolutions in our ways of thinking and behaving. Many changes in legislation have occurred in meeting the requirements of the revolutionaries. The Blacks in the 1950s, students in

the 1960s, and women in the 1970s engaged in activities pressing for enlightenment in place of the shadows of discrimination, intolerance, and prejudice. They were successful in creating new paradigms on how to feel and think, perceive and evaluate relationships. Although all that they desired to achieve was not obtained, enough occurred to redirect the course of the society from the traditional structures of power and control, and create a sustained driving force to work on the democratization of American society.

The gender revolution took as its prototype the Black and student movements of the previous decades but functioned less in the streets and more in the home. As family ideologies and practices began to change, men and women began to move more towards equitable relationships in the family. The consequences were felt throughout society. As more women entered the workforce they benefited from the efforts of earlier previous leaders of social and political change who had promoted legislation to provide equal opportunities for people of any gender, race, nationality, or creed. The trend is towards greater roles and power for women in American and other complex societies. Even if there is a shift from the current increasing incidence of women entering the workforce to one of election to being a manager of an evolutionary household, my definition of homemaker, the change in relationships within the family will not revert to the old superordinate/subordinate pattern. Equity and sharing will continue to dominate and grow in both prevalence and incidence in the coming years. Equity implies fairness and the portrait of the future of gender relations within the family is one of complementarity, fairness in the allocation of responsibilities and services. Partnership and empowerment of all family members is the predicted model that will influence the structure and processes of other organizations and institutions.

CONCLUSION

These views of the future of families focus on awakening and change; new paradigms and journeys for members of families. The question is whether enough members will take the risk and challenge and move out of encrusted old patterns and encapsulated egos.

Teilhard de Chardin expresses far better than I what is emerging from a deepened consciousness.

> Everywhere on Earth, at this moment in the new spiritual atmosphere created by the idea of evolution, there float, in a state of extreme sensitivity, love of God and faith in the world. The two essential components of the ultrahuman. These two components are everywhere "in the air,"...Sooner or later there will be a chain reaction. (Russell, 1983)

Notes and References

IMMIGRANT FAMILIES IN THE CITY—MARK HUTTER

References

Anderson, Michael. 1971. *Family Structure in Nineteenth Century Lancashire.* Cambridge: Cambridge University Press.

Archdeacon, Thomas. 1983. *Becoming American: An Ethnic History.* New York: The Free Press.

Hareven, Tamara K. 1975. "Family Time and Industrial Time: Family and Work in a Planned Corporation Town, 1900–1924." *Journal of Urban History* 1 (May): 365–389.

Jones, Maldwyn Allen. 1960. *American Immigration.* Chicago, University of Chicago Press.

Metzker, Isaac (ed.) 1971. *A Bintel Brief.* New York: Ballatine Books.

Riis, Jacob A. 1957/1890. *How the Other Half Lives: Studies Among the Tenements of New York.* New York: Hill and Wang.

Seller, Maxine. 1977. *To Seek America: A History of Ethnic Life in the United States.* Englewood, New Jersey: Jerome S. Ozer, Publisher.

Yancey, William L., Eugene P. Ericksen, and Richard N. Juliani. 1976. "Emergent Ethnicity: A Review and Reformulation." *American Sociological Review* 4 (June): 391–402.

Yans-McLaughlin, Virginia. 1971. "Patterns of Work and Family Organization." Pp. 111–126 in *The Family in History: Interdisciplinary Essays,* edited by Theodore K. Rabb and Robert I. Rotberg. New York: Harper Torchbooks.

INTERPRETING THE AFRICAN HERITAGE IN AFRO-AMERICAN FAMILY ORGANIZATION—NIARA SUDARKASA

References

Agbasegbe, B. (1976) "The Role of Wife in the Black Extended Family: Perspectives from a Rural Community in Southern United States," pp. 124–138 in D. McGuigan (ed.) *New Research on Women and Sex Roles.* Ann Arbor: Center for Continuing Education of Women, University of Michigan.

———. (1981) "Some Aspects of Contemporary Rural Afroamerican Family Life in the Sea Islands of Southeastern United States." Presented at the Annual Meeting of the Association of Social and Behavioral Scientists, Atlanta, Georgia, March 1981.

Allen, W. R. (1978) "The search for Applicable Theories of Black Family Life." *Journal of*

Marriage and the Family 40 (February): 117–129.

———. (1979) "Class, Culture, and Family Organization: The Effects of Class and Race on Family Structure in Urban America." *Journal of Comparative Family Studies* 10 (Autumn): 301–313.

Aschenbrenner, J. (1973) "Extended Families Among Black Americans." *Journal of Comparative Family Studies* 4: 257–268.

———. (1975) *Lifelines: Black Families in Chicago.* New York: Holt, Rinehart & Winston.

———. (1978) "Continuities and Variations in Black Family Structure," pp. 181–200 in D. B. Shimkin, E. M. Shimkin, and D. A. Frate (eds.) *The Extended Family in Black Societies.* The Hague: Mouton.

———. and C. H. Carr (1980) "Conjugal Relationships in the Context of the Black Extended Family." *Alternative Lifestyles* 3 (November): 463–484.

Bender, D. R. (1967) "A Refinement of the Concept of Household: Families, Co-residence, and Domestic Functions." *American Anthropologist* 69 (October): 493–504.

Billingsley, A. (1968) *Black Families in White America.* Englewood Cliffs, NJ: Prentice-Hall.

Blassingame, J. W. (1979) *The Slave Community.* New York: Oxford University Press.

Colson, E. (1962) "Family Change in Contemporary Africa." *Annals of the New York Academy of Sciences* 96 (January): 641–652.

DuBois, W. E. B. (1969) *The Negro American Family.* New York: New American Library. (Originally published, 1908).

Elkins, S. (1963) Slavery: A Problem in American Intellectual Life. New York: Grosset and Dunlap. (Originally published, 1959).

English, R. (1974) "Beyond Pathology: Research and Theoretical Perspectives on Black Families," pp. 39–52 in L. E. Gary (ed.) *Social Research and the Black Community: Selected Issues and Priorities.* Washington, DC: Institute for Urban Affairs and Research, Howard University.

Fortes, M. (1949) *The Web of Kinship among the Tallensi.* London: Oxford University Press.

———. (1950) "Kinship and Marriage Among the Ashanti," pp. 252–284 in A. R. Radcliffe-Brown and D. Forde (eds.) *African Systems of Kinship and Marriage.* London: Oxford University Press.

———. (1953) "The Structure of Unilineal Descent Groups." *American Anthropologist* 55 (January–March): 17–41.

Frazier, E. (1966) *The Negro Family in the United States.* Chicago: University of Chicago Press. (Originally published, 1939).

Furstenberg, F., T. Hershbert, and J. Modell (1975) "The Origins of the Female-headed Black Family: The Impact of the Urban Experience." *Journal of Interdisciplinary History* 6 (Autumn): 211–233.

Genovese, E. D. (1974) *Roll Jordan Roll: The World the Slaves Made.* New York: Random House.

Goody, J. (1976) *Production and Reproduction: A Comparative Study of the Domestic Domain.* Cambridge: Cambridge University Press.

Gutman, H. (1976) *The Black Family in Slavery and Freedom: 1750–1925.* New York: Random House.

Herskovits, M. J. (1958) *The Myth of the Negro Past.* Boston: Beacon. (Originally published, 1941).

Johnson, C. S. (1934) *Shadow of the Plantation.* Chicago: University of Chicago Press.

Kerri, J. N. (1979) "Understanding the African Family: Persistence, Continuity, and Change." *Western Journal of Black Studies* 3 (Spring): 14–17.

Landman, R. H. (1978) "Language Policies and Their Implications for Ethnic Relations in the Newly Sovereign States of Sub-Saharan Africa," pp. 69–90 in B. M. duToit (ed.) *Ethnicity in Modern Africa.* Boulder, CO: Westview Press.

Linton, R. (1936) *The Study of Man.* New York: Appleton-Century-Crofts.

Lloyd, P. C. (1968) "Divorce Among the Yoruba." *American Anthropologist* 70 (February): 67–81.

Maquet, J. (1972) *Civilizations of Black Africa.* London: Oxford University Press.

Marshall, G. A. [Niara Sudarkasa] (1968) "Marriage: Comparative Analysis," in *International Encyclopedia of the Social Sciences, Vol. 10.* New York: Macmillan/Free Press.

Murdock, G. P. (1949) *Social Structure.* New York: Macmillan.

Nobles, W. (1974a) "African Root and American Fruit: The Black Family." *Journal of Social and Behavioral Sciences* 20: 52–64.

——. (1974b) "Africanity: Its Role in Black Families." The Black Scholar 9 (June): 10–17.

——. (1978) "Toward an Empirical and Theoretical Framework for Defining Black Families." *Journal of Marriage and the Family* 40 (November): 679–688.

Okediji, P. A. (1975) "A Psychosocial Analysis of the Extended Family: The African Case." *African Urban Notes, Series B,* 1(3): 93–99. (African Studies Center, Michigan State University)

Onwuejeogwu, M. A. (1975) *The Social Anthropology of Africa: An Introduction.* London: Heinemann.

Oppong, C. (1974) *Marriage among a Matrilineal Elite: A Family Study of Ghanaian Senior Civil Servants.* Cambridge: Cambridge University Press.

Owens, L. H. (1976) *This Species of Property: Slave Life and Culture in the Old South.* New York: Oxford University Press.

Perdue, C. L., Jr., T. E. Barden, and R. K. Phillips [eds.] (1980) *Weevils in the Wheat: Interviews with Virginia Ex-Slaves.* Bloomington: Indiana University Press.

Powdermaker, H. (1939) *After Freedom: A Cultural Study in the Deep South.* New York: Viking.

Radcliffe-Brown, A. R. (1950) "Introduction," pp. 1–85 in A. R. Radcliffe-Brown and D. Forde (eds.) *African Systems of Kinship and Marriage.* London: Oxford University Press.

—— and D. Forde [eds.] (1950) *African Systems of Kinship and Marriage.* London: Oxford University Press.

Rivers, W. H. R. (1924) *Social Organization.* New York: Alfred Knopf.

Robertson, C. (1976) "Ga Women and Socioeconomic Change in Accra, Ghana," pp. 111–133 in N. J. Hafkin and E. G. Bay (eds.) *Women in Africa: Studies in Social and Economic Change.* Stanford: Stanford University Press.

Shimkin, D. and V. Uchendu (1978) "Persistence, Borrowing, and Adaptive Changes in Black Kinship Systems: Some Issues and Their Significance," pp. 391–406 in D. Shimkin, E. M. Shimkin, and D. A. Frate (eds.) *The Extended Family in Black Societies.* The Hague: Mouton.

Shimkin, D., E. M. Shimkin, and D. A. Frate [eds.] (1978) *The Extended Family in Black Societies.* The Hague: Mouton.

Shorter, E. (1975) *The Making of the Modern Family.* New York: Basic Books.

Smith, R. T. (1973) "The Matrifocal Family," pp. 121–144 in J. Goody (ed.) *The Character of Kinship.* Cambridge: Cambridge University Press.

Stack, C. (1974) *All Our Kin.* New York: Harper & Row.

Staples, R. (1971) "Toward a Sociology of the Black Family: A Decade of Theory and

Research." *Journal of Marriage and the Family* 33 (February): 19–38.

———. [ed.] (1978) *The Black Family: Essays and Studies.* Belmont, CA: Wadsworth

Stone, L. (1975) "The Rise of the Nuclear Family in Early Modern England: The Patriarchal Stage," pp. 13–57 in C. E. Rosenberg (ed.) *The Family in History.* Philadelphia: University of Pennsylvania Press.

Sudarkasa, N. (1973) Where Women Work: A Study of Yoruba Women in the Marketplace and in the Home. *Anthropological Papers* No. 53. Ann Arbor: Museum of Anthropology, University of Michigan.

———. (1975a) "An Exposition on the Value Premises Underlying Black Family Studies." *Journal of the National Medical Association* 19 (May): 235–239.

———. (1975b) "National Development Planning for the Promotion and Protection of the Family." *Proceedings of the Conference on Social Research and National Development,* E. Akeredolu-Ale, ed. The Nigerian Institute of Social and Economic Research, lbadan, Nigeria.

———. (1976) "Female Employment and Family Organization in West Africa," pp. 48–63 in D. G. McGuigan (ed.) *New Research on Women and Sex Roles.* Ann Arbor: Center for Continuing Education of Women, University of Michigan.

———. (1980) "African and Afro-American Family Structure: A Comparison." *The Black Scholar* 11 (November–December): 37–60.

———. (1981) "Understanding the Dynamics of Consanguinity and Conjugality in Contemporary Black Family Organization." Presented at the Seventh Annual Third World Conference, Chicago, March 1981.

Tilly, L. A. and J. W. Scott (1978) *Women, Work, and Family.* New York: Holt, Rinehart & Winston.

Uchendu, V. (1965) *The Igbo of South-Eastern Nigeria.* New York: Holt, Rinehart & Winston.

Ware, H. (1979) "Polygyny: Women's Views in a Transitional Society, Nigeria 1975." *Journal of Marriage and the Family* 41 (February): 185–195.

Woodson, C. G. (1936) *The African Background Outlined.* Washington, DC: Association for the Study of Negro Life and History.

FAMILY DECLINE IN AMERICA—DAVID POPENOE

Notes

1. Norval Glenn, ed., "The State of the American Family," *Journal of Family Issues* 8 (No. 4, December 1987), Special Issue.

2. Sar A. Levitan and Richard S. Belous, *What's Happening to the American Family?* (Baltimore: Johns Hopkins, 1981), pp. 190, 15.

3. Sar A. Levitan, Richard S. Belous, and Frank Gallo, *What's Happening to the American Family?* (rev. ed.) (Baltimore: Johns Hopkins, 1988), pp. vi, viii.

4. Carl N. Degler, *At Odds: Women and the Family in America from the Revolution to the Present* (Oxford, England: Oxford University Press, 1980); Lawrence Stone, *The Family, Sex, and Marriage in England 1500–1800* (New York: Harper and Row, 1977); Steven Mintz and Susan Kellogg, *Domestic Revolutions: A Social History of the American Family* (New York: Free Press, 1988).

5. Andrew Cherlin and Frank F. Furstenberg, Jr., "The Changing European Family: Lessons for the American Reader," *Journal of Family Issues* 9 (No. 3, 1988), p. 294; John Modell, Frank F. Furstenberg, Jr., and Douglas Strong, "The Timing of Marriage in the Transition to Adulthood: Continuity and Change, 1860–1975," *American Journal of Sociology* 84 (1978), pp. S120–S150.

6. Susan Cotts Watkins, Jane A. Menken, and John Bongaarts, "Demographic Foundations of Family Change," *American Sociological Review* 52 (No. 3, 1987), pp. 346–358.

7. Andrew J. Cherlin, *Marriage, Divorce, Remarriage* (Cambridge, MA: Harvard University Press, 1981).

8. All data are from the U.S. Census Bureau, unless otherwise indicated.

9. Arthur G. Neal, Theodore Groat, and Jerry W. Wicks, "Attitudes about Having Children: A Study of 600 Couples in the Early Years of Marriage," *Journal of Marriage and the Family* 51 (No. 2, 1989), pp. 313–328; Joseph Veroff, Elizabeth Douvan, and Richard A. Kulka, *The Inner American: A Self-Portrait from 1957 to 1976* (New York: Basic Books, 1981); James A. Sweet and Larry L. Bumpass, *American Families and Households* (New York: Russell Sage Foundation, 1987), p. 400.

10. David E. Bloom and James Trussell, "What Are the Determinants of Delayed Childbearing and Permanent Childlessness in the United States?" *Demography* 21 (No. 4, 1984), pp. 591–611; Charles E. Westoff, "Perspective on Nuptiality and Fertility," *Population and Development Review Supplement* (No. 12, 1986), pp. 155–170.

11. John D'Emilio and Estelle B. Freedman, *Intimate Matters: A History of Sexuality in America* (New York: Harper and Row, 1988).

12. From a 1987 study sponsored by the National Academy of Sciences, reported in *The New York Times,* February 27, 1989, p. B11.

13. Daniel Yankelovich, *New Rules: Searching for Self-Fulfillment in a World Turned Upside Down* (New York: Random House, 1981), p. 94.

14. Suzanne M. Bianchi and Daphne Spain, *American Women in Transition* (New York: Russell Sage Foundation, 1986); Victor R. Fuchs, *Women's Quest for Economic Equality* (Cambridge, MA: Harvard University Press, 1988).

15. Data assembled from U.S. Census reports by Maris A. Vinovskis, "The Unraveling of the Family Wage since World War II: Some Demographic, Economic, and Cultural Considerations," in Bryce Christensen, Allan Carlson, Maris Vinovskis, Richard Vedder, and Jean Bethke Elshtain, *The Family Wage: Work, Gender, and Children in the Modern Economy* (Rockford, IL: The Rockford Institute, 1988), pp. 33–58.

16. Lenore J. Weitzman, *The Divorce Revolution* (New York: Free Press, 1985).

17. Paul C. Glick, "Fifty Years of Family Demography; A Record of Social Change," *Journal of Marriage and the Family* 50 (No. 4, 1988), p. 868.

18. Robert Schoen, "The Continuing Retreat from Marriage: Figures from the 1983 U.S. Marital Status Life Tables," *Social Science Research* 71 (No. 2,1987), pp. 108–109; Teresa Castro Martin and Larry L. Bumpass, "Recent Trends in Marital Disruption," *Demography* 26 (No. 1, 1989), pp. 37–51.

19. Sanford M. Dornbusch and Myra H. Strober, *Feminism, Children, and the New Families* (New York: Guilford Press, 1988).

20. Sandra L. Hofferth, "Updating Children's Life Course," *Journal of Marriage and the Family* 47 (No. 1, 1985), pp. 93–115.

21. The 20-year downward spiral of family households came to a (temporary?) halt in the 1986–87 period, when the percentage of family households increased slightly, as documented in Judith Waldrop, "The Fashionable Family," *American Demographics* (March 1988).

22. Susan Cotts Watkins, Jane A. Menken, and John Bongaarts, op. cit., 1987.

23. Eugene Smolensky, Sheldon Danziger, and Peter Gottschalk, "The Declining Significance of Age in the United States: Trends in the Well-being of Children and the Elderly since 1939," in John L. Palmer, Timothy Smeeding, and Barbara Boyle Torrey, eds., *The Vulnerable* (Washington, DC: Urban Institute, 1988), pp. 29–54.

24. Report of House Select Committee on Children, Youth and Families, *The New York Times,* October 2, 1989, p. A12.

25. Kingsley Davis, ed., *Contemporary Marriage: Comparative Perspectives on a Changing Institution* (New York: Russell Sage Foundation, 1985).

26. Mary Ann Glendon, *The Transformation of Family Law* (Chicago: University of Chicago, 1989).

27. Robert N. Bellah, Richard Madsen, William M. Sullivan, Ann Swidler, and Steven M. Tipton, *Habits of the Heart: Individualism and Commitment in American Life* (Berkeley, CA: University of California Press, 1985).

28. Victor Fuchs, *How We Live* (Cambridge, MA: Harvard University Press, 1983).

29. Jean Bethke Elshtain, *Public Man, Private Wonwn: Women in Social and Political Thought* (Princeton, NJ: Princeton University Press, 1981).

30. Francesca M. Cancian, *Love in America: Gender and Self-Development* (Cambridge, England, and New York: Cambridge University Press, 1987).

31. *U.S. Children and Their Families: Current Conditions and Recent Trends, 1989* (Washington, DC: U.S. Government Printing Office). Nicholas Zill and Carolyn C. Rogers, "Recent Trends in the Well-being of Children in the United States and Their Implications for Public Policy," in Andrew Cherlin, ed., *The Changing American Family and Public Policy* (Washington, DC: Urban Institute, 1988), pp. 31–115; Peter Uhlenberg and David Eggebeen, "The Declining Well-being of American Adolescents," *The Public Interest* (No. 82, 1986), pp. 25–38.

32. Samuel H. Preston, "Children and the Elderly: Divergent Paths for America's Dependents," *Demography* 21 (No. 4, 1984), p. 443.

33. Frank F. Furstenberg, Jr., "Good Dads-Bad Dads: Two Faces of Fatherhood," in Andrew Cherlin, ed., *The Changing American Family and Public Policy* (Washington, DC: Urban Institute, 1988), pp. 193–218.

34. Barbara Ehrenreich, *The Hearts of Men: American Dreams and the Flight from Commitment* (New York: Anchor, 1983).

35. E. Mavis Hetherington and Josephine D. Arasteh, eds., *Impact of Divorce, Single Parenting, and Stepparenting on Children* (Hillsdale, NJ: Lawrence Erlbaum Associates, 1988); Sara McLanahan and Karen Booth, "Mother-Only Families: Problems, Prospects, and Politics," *Journal of Marriage and the Family* 51 (No. 3, 1989), pp. 557–580.

36. Urie Bronfenbrenner, *The Ecology of Human Development* (Cambridge, MA: Harvard University Press, 1979).

37. Alan Wolfe, *Whose Keeper? Social Science and Moral Obligation* (Berkeley, CA: University of California Press, 1989).

38. Peter L. Berger and Richard J. Neuhaus, *To Empower People: The Role of Mediating Structures in Public Policy* (Washington, DC: American Enterprise Institute, 1977).

39. Betty Friedan, *The Feminine Mystique* (New York: Laurel, 1983, 1963).

40. Sylvia Ann Hewlett, *A Lesser Life* (New York: William Morrow, 1986).

41. David Popenoe, *Disturbing the Nest: Family Change and Decline in Modern Societies* (New York: Aldine de Gruyter, 1988).

THE FEMALE WORLD OF CARDS AND HOLIDAYS: WOMEN, FAMILIES, AND THE WORK OF KINSHIP— MICAELA di LEONARDO

Notes

1. Acknowledgment and gratitude to Carroll Smith-Rosenberg for my paraphrase of her title, "The Female World of Love and Ritual: Rela-

tions between Women in Nineteenth-Century America," *Signs: Journal of Women in Culture and Society* 1, no. 1 (August 1975): 1–29. [*Signs: Journal of Women in Culture and Society,* 1987, vol. 12, no. 3] © 1987 by The University of Chicago. All rights reserved 0097-9740/87/1203-0003$01.00.

2. Ann Landers letter printed in *Washington Post* (April 15, 1983); Carol Gilligan, *In a Different Voice* (Cambridge, Mass.: Harvard University Press, 1982), 17.

3. Heidi I. Hartmann, "The Family as the Locus of Gender, Class, and Political Struggle: The Example of Housework," *Signs* 6, no. 3 (Spring 1981): 366–94; and Christopher Lasch, *Haven in a Heartless World: The Family Besieged* (New York: Basic Books, 1977).

4. Representative examples of the first trend include Joann Vanek, "Time Spent on Housework," *Scientific American* 231 (November 1974): 116–20; Ruth Schwartz Cowan, "A Case Study of Technological and Social Change: The Washing Machine and the Working Wife," in *Clio's Consciousness Raised,* ed. Mary Hartmann and Lois Banner (New York: Harper & Row, 1974), 245–53; Ann Oakley, *Women's Work: The Housewife, Past and Present* (New York: Vintage, 1974); Hartmann; and Susan Strasser, *Never Done: A History of American Housework* (New York: Pantheon Books, 1982). Key contributions to the second trend include Louise Lamphere, "Strategies, Cooperation and Conflict among Women in Domestic Groups," in *Women, Culture and Society,* ed. Michelle Zimbalist Rosaldo and Louise Lamphere (Stanford, Calif.: Stanford University Press, 1974), 97–112; Mina Davis Caulfield, "Imperialism, the Family and the Cultures of Resistance," *Socialist Revolution* 20 (October 1974): 67–85; Smith-Rosenberg; Sylvia Junko Yanagisako, "Women-centered Kin Networks and Urban Bilateral Kinship," *American Ethnologist* 4, no. 2 (1977): 207–26; Jane

Humphries, "The Working Class Family, Women's Liberation and Class Struggle: The Case of Nineteenth Century British History," *Review of Radical Political Economics* 9 (Fall 1977): 25–41; Blanche Weisen Cook, "Female Support Networks and Political Activism: Lillian Wald, Crystal Eastman, Emma Goldman," in *A Heritage of Her Own,* ed. Nancy F. Cott and Elizabeth H. Pleck (New York: Simon & Schuster, 1979); Temma Kaplan, "Female Consciousness and Collective Action: The Case of Barcelona, 1910–1918," *Signs* 7, no. 3 (Spring 1982): 545–66.

5. On this debate, see Jon Weiner, "Women's History on Trial," *Nation* 241, no. 6 (September 7, 1985): 161, 176, 178–80; Karen J. Winkler, "Two Scholars' Conflict in Sears Sex-Bias Case Sets Off War in Women's History," *Chronicle of Higher Education* (February 5, 1986), 1, 8; Rosalind Rosenberg, "What Harms Women in the Workplace," *New York Times* (February 27, 1986); Alice Kessler-Harris, "Equal Employment Opportunity Commission vs. Sears Roebuck and Company: A Personal Account," *Radical History Review* 35 (April 1986): 57–79.

6. Portions of the following analysis are reported in Micaela di Leonardo, *The Varieties of Ethnic Experience: Kinship, Class and Gender among California Italian-Americans* (Ithaca, N.Y.: Cornell University Press, 1984), chap. 6.

7. Clearly, many women do, in fact, discuss their paid labor with willingness and clarity. The point here is that there are opposing gender tendencies in an identical interview situation, tendencies that are explicable in terms of both the material realities and current cultural constructions of gender.

8. Papanek has rightly focused on women's unacknowledged family status production, but what is conceived of as "family" shifts and varies (Hanna Papanek, "Family Status Production: The 'Work' and 'Non-Work' of Women," *Signs* 4, no. 4 ([Summer 1979]: 775–81).

9. Selma Greenberg, *Right from the Start: A Guide to Nonsexist Child Rearing* (Boston: Houghton Mifflin Co., 1978), 147. Another example of indirect support for kin work's gendered existence is a recent study of university math students, which found that a major reason for women's failure to pursue careers in mathematics was the pressure of family involvement. Compare David Maines et al., *Social Processes of Sex Differentiation in Mathematics* (Washington, D.C.: National Institute of Education, 1981).

10. Larissa Adler Lomnitz and Marisol Pérez Lizaur, "The History of a Mexican Urban Family," *Journal of Family History* 3, no. 4 (1978): 392–409, esp. 398; Matthews Hamabata, *For Love and Power: Family Business in Japan* (Chicago: University of Chicago Press, in press); Sylvia Junko Yanagisako, "Two Processes of Change in Japanese-American Kinship," *Journal of Anthropological Research* 31 (1975): 196–224; Maila Stivens, "Women and Their Kin: Kin, Class and Solidarity in a Middle-Class Suburb of Sydney, Australia," in *Women United, Women Divided*, ed. Patricia Caplan and Janet M. Bujra (Bloomington: Indiana University Press, 1979), 157–84.

11. Carol B. Stack, *All Our Kin: Strategies for Survival in a Black Community* (New York: Harper & Row, 1974). These cultural constructions may, however, vary within ethnic/racial populations as well.

12. Elizabeth Bott, *Family and Social Network*, 2d ed. (New York: Free Press, 1971); Michael Young and Peter Willmott, *Family and Kinship in East London* (London: Routledge & Kegan Paul, 1957); and idem, *Family and Class in a London Suburb* (London: Routledge & Kegan Paul, 1960). Classic studies that presume this class difference are Herbert Gans, *The Urban Villagers: Group and Class in the Life of Italian-Americans* (New York: Free Press, 1962), and Mirra Komarovsky, *Blue-Collar Marriage* (New York: Random House, 1962). A recent example

is Ilene Philipson, "Heterosexual Antagonisms and the Politics of Mothering," *Socialist Review* 12, no. 6 (November–December 1982): 55–77. Edward Shorter, *The Making of the Modern Family* (New York: Basic Books, 1975), epitomizes the pessimism of the "family sentiments" school. See also Mary Lyndon Shanley, "The History of the Family in Modern England: Review Essay," *Signs* 4, no. 4 (Summer 1979): 740–50.

13. Stack, *All Our Kin*, and Brett Williams, "The Trip Takes Us: Chicano Migrants to the Prairie" (Ph. D. diss., University of Illinois at Urbana-Champaign, 1975).

14. David Schneider and Raymond T. Smith, *Class Differences and Sex Roles in American Kinship and Family Structure* (Englewood Cliffs, N.J.: Prentice-Hall, Inc., 1973), esp. 27.

15. See Nelson Graburn, ed., *Readings in Kinship and Social Structure* (New York: Harper & Row, 1971), esp. 3–4.

16. The moral mother/cult of domesticity is analyzed in Barbara Welter, "The Cult of True Womanhood, 1820–1860," *American Quarterly* 18, no. 2 (Summer 1966): 151–74; Nancy Cott, *The Bonds of Womanhood: "Women's Sphere" in New England, 1780–1835* (New Haven, Conn.: Yale University Press, 1977); and Ruth Bloch, "American Feminine Ideals in Transition: The Rise of the Moral Mother, 1785–1815," *Feminist Studies* 4, no. 2 (June 1978): 101–26. The description of the general political-economic shift in the United States is based on Harry Braverman, *Labor and Monopoly Capital: The Degradation of Work in the Twentieth Century* (New York: Monthly Review Press, 1974); Peter Dobkin Hall, "Family Structure and Economic Organization: Massachusetts Merchants, 1700–1850," in *Family and Kin in Urban Communities, 1700–1950*, ed. Tamara K. Hareven (New York: New Viewpoints, 1977), 38–61; Michael Anderson, "Family Household and the Industrial Revolution," in

The American Family in Social-Historical Perspective, ed. Michael Gordon (New York: St. Martin's Press, 1978), 38–50; Tamara K. Hareven, *Amoskeag: Life and Work in an American Factory City* (New York: Pantheon Books, 1978); Richard Edwards, *Constested Terrain: The Transformation of the Workplace in the Twentieth Century* (New York: Basic Books, 1979); Mary Ryan, *The Cradle of the Middle Class: The Family in Oneida County, New York, 1790–1865* (Cambridge: Cambridge University Press, 1981); Alice Kessler-Harris, *Out to Work: A History of Wage-earning Women in the United States* (New York: Oxford University Press, 1982).

17. Ryan, *Cradle of the Middle Class,* 231–32.

18. Sylvia Junko Yanagisako, "Family and Household: The Analysis of Domestic Groups," *Annual Review of Anthropology* 8 (1979): 161–205.

19. See Donald J. Treiman and Heidi I. Hartmann, eds., *Women, Work and Wages: Equal Pay for Jobs of Equal Value* (Washington, D.C.: National Academy Press, 1981).

20. Lamphere (n. 4 above); Jane Fishburne Collier, "Women in Politics," in Rosaldo and Lamphere, eds. (n. 4 above), 89–96.

21. Nancy Folbre and Heidi I. Hartmann, "The Rhetoric of Self-Interest: Selfishness, Altruism, and Gender in Economic Theory," in *The Consequences of Economic Rhetoric,* ed. Arjo Klamer and Donald McCloskey (New York: Cambridge University Press, forthcoming).

MEXICAN AMERICAN WOMEN GRASSROOTS COMMUNITY ACTIVISTS: "MOTHERS OF EAST LOS ANGELES"—MARY PARDO

Notes

On September 15, 1989, another version of this paper was accepted for presentation at the 1990 International Sociological Association meetings to be held in Madrid, Spain, July 9, 1990.

1. See Vicky Randall, *Women and Politics, An International Perspective* (Chicago: University of Chicago Press, 1987), for a review of the central themes and debates in the literature. For two of the few books on Chicanas, work, and family, see Vicki L. Ruiz, *Cannery Women, Cannery Lives, Mexican Women, Unionization, and the California Food Processing Industry, 1930–1950* (Albuquerque: University of New Mexico Press, 1987), and Patricia Zavella, *Women's Work & Chicano Families* (Ithaca, N.Y.: Cornell University Press, 1987).

2. For recent exceptions to this approach, see Anne Witte Garland, *Women Activists: Challenging the Abuse of Power* (New York: The Feminist Press, 1988); Ann Bookman and Sandra Morgan, eds., *Women and the Politics of Empowerment* (Philadelphia: Temple University Press, 1987); Karen Sacks, *Caring by the Hour* (Chicago: University of Illinois Press, 1988). For a sociological analysis of community activism among Afro-American women see Cheryl Townsend Gilkes, "Holding Back the Ocean with a Broom," *The Black Woman* (Beverly Hills, Calif.: Sage Publications, 1980).

3. For two exceptions to this criticism, see Sara Evans, *Born for Liberty, A History of Women in America* (New York: The Free Press, 1989), and Bettina Aptheker, *Tapestries of Life, Women's Work, Women's Consciousness, and the Meaning of Daily Experience* (Amherst: The University of Massachusetts Press, 1989). For a critique, see Maxine Baca Zinn, Lynn Weber Cannon, Elizabeth Higginbotham, and Bonnie Thornton Dill, "The Costs of Exclusionary Practices in Women's Studies," *Signs* 11, no. 2 (Winter 1986).

4. For cases of grassroots activism among women in Latin America, see Sally W. Yudelman, *Hopeful Openings, A Study of Five Women's*

Development Organizations in Latin American and the Caribbean (West Hartford, Conn.: Kumarian Press, 1987). For an excellent case analysis of how informal associations enlarge and empower women's world in Third World countries, see Kathryn S. March and Rachelle L. Taqqu, *Women's Informal Associations in Developing Countries, Catalysts for Change?* (Boulder, Colo.: Westview Press, 1986). Also, see Carmen Feijoó, "Women in Neighbourhoods: From Local Issues to Gender Problems," *Canadian Woman Studies* 6, no. 1 (Fall 1984) for a concise overview of the patterns of activism.

5. The relationship between Catholicism and political activism is varied and not unitary. In some Mexican American communities, grassroots activism relies on parish networks. See Isidro D. Ortiz, "Chicano Urban Politics and the Politics of Reform in the Seventies," *The Western Political Quarterly* 37, no. 4 (December 1984): 565–77. Also, see Joseph D. Sekul, "Communities Organized for Public Service: Citizen Power and Public Power in San Antonio," in *Latinos and the Political System,* edited by F. Chris Garcia (Notre Dame, Ind.: University of Notre Dame Press, 1988). Sekul tells how COPS members challenged prevailing patterns of power by working for the well-being of families and cites four former presidents who were Mexican American women, but he makes no special point of gender.

6. I also interviewed other members of the Coalition Against the Prison and local political office representatives. For a general reference, see James P. Spradley, *The Ethnographic Interview* (New York: Holt, Rinehart and Winston, 1979). For a review essay focused on the relevancy of the method for examining the diversity of women's experiences, see Susan N. G. Geiger, "Women's Life Histories: Method and Content," *Signs* 11, no. 2 (Winter 1982): 334–51.

7. During the last five years, over 300 newspaper articles have appeared on the issue. Frank Villalobos generously shared his extensive newspaper archives with me. See Leo C. Wolinsky, "L.A. Prison Bill 'Locked Up' in New Clash," *Los Angeles Times,* 16 July 1987, sec. 1, p. 3; Rudy Acuña, "The Fate of East L.A.: One Big Jail," *Los Angeles Herald Examiner,* 28 April 1989, A15; Carolina Serna, "Eastside Residents Oppose Prison," *La Gente UCLA Student Newspaper* 17, no. 1 (October 1986): 5; Daniel M. Weintraub, "10,000 Fee Paid to Lawmaker Who Left Sickbed to Cast Vote," *Los Angeles Times,* 13 March 1988, sec. 1, p. 3.

8. Cerrell Associates, Inc., "Political Difficulties Facing Waste-to-Energy Conversion Plant Siting," Report Prepared for California Waste Management Board, State of California (Los Angeles, 1984): 43.

9. Jesus Sanchez, "The Environment: Whose Movement?" *California Tomorrow* 3, nos. 3 & 4 (Fall 1988): 13. Also see Rudy Acuña, *A Community Under Siege* (Los Angeles: Chicano Studies Research Center Publications, UCLA, 1984). The book and its title capture the sentiments and the history of a community that bears an unfair burden of city projects deemed undesirable by all residents.

10. James Vigil, Jr., field representative for Assemblywoman Gloria Molina, 1984–1996, Personal Interview, Whittier, Calif., 27 September 1989. Vigil stated that the Department of Corrections used a threefold strategy: political pressure in the legislature, the promise of jobs for residents, and contracts for local businesses.

11. Edward J. Boyer and Marita Hernandez, "Eastside Seethes over Prison Plan," *Los Angeles Times,* 13 August 1986, sec. 2, p. 1.

12. Martha Molina-Aviles, currently administrative assistant for Assemblywoman Lucille Roybal-Allard, 56th assembly district, and former field representative for Gloria Molina when she held this assembly seat, Personal Interview, Los Angeles, 5 June 1989. Molina-Aviles,

who grew up in East Los Angeles, used her experiences and insights to help forge strong links among the women in MELA, other members of the coalition, and the assembly office.

13. MELA has also opposed the expansion of a county prison literally across the street from William Mead Housing Projects, home to 2,000 Latinos, Asians, and Afro-Americans, and a chemical treatment plant for toxic wastes.

14. The first of its kind in a metropolitan area, it would burn 125,000 pounds per day of hazardous wastes. For an excellent article that links recent struggles against hazardous waste dumps and incinerators in minority communities and features women in MELA, see Dick Russell, "Environmental Racism: Minority Communities and Their Battle against Toxics," *The Amicus Journal* 11, no. 2 (Spring 1989): 22–32.

15. Miguel G. Mendívil, field representative for Assemblywoman Lucille Roybal-Allard, 56th assembly district, Personal Interview, Los Angeles, 25 April 1989.

16. John Garcia and Rudolfo de la Garza, "Mobilizing the Mexican Immigrant: The Role of Mexican American Organizations," *The Western Political Quarterly* 38, no. 4 (December 1985): 551–64.

17. This concept is discussed in relation to Latino communities in David T. Abalos, *Latinos in the U.S., The Sacred and the Political* (Indiana: University of Notre Dame Press, 1986). The notion of transformation of traditional culture in struggles against oppression is certainly not a new one. For a brief essay on a longer work, see Frantz Fanon, "Algeria Unveiled," *The New Left Reader,* edited by Carl Oglesby (New York: Grove Press, Inc, 1969): 161–85.

18. Karen Sacks, *Caring by the Hour.*

19. Juana Gutiérrez, Personal Interview, Boyle Heights, East Los Angeles, 15 January 1988.

20. Erlinda Robles, Personal Interview, Boyle Heights, Los Angeles, 14 September 1989.

21. Mina Davis Caulfield, "Imperialism, the Family, and Cultures of Resistance," *Socialist Revolution* 29 (1974): 67–85.

22. Erlinda Robles, Personal Interview.

23. Ibid.

24. Juana Gutiérrez, Personal Interview.

25. Frank Villalobos, architect and urban planner, Personal Interview, Los Angeles, 2 May 1989.

26. The law student, Veronica Gutiérrez, is the daughter of Juana Gutiérrez, one of the cofounders of MELA. Martín Gutiérrez, one of her sons, was a field representative for Assemblywoman Lucille Roybal-Allard and also central to community mobilization. Ricardo Gutiérrez, Juana's husband, and almost all the other family members are community activists. They are a microcosm of the family networks that strengthened community mobilization and the Coalition Against the Prison. See Raymundo Reynoso, "Juana Beatrice Gutiérrez: La incansable lucha de una activista comunitaria," *La Opinion,* 6 Agosto de 1989, Acceso, p. 1, and Louis Sahagun, "The Mothers of East L.A. Transform Themselves and Their Community," *Los Angeles Times,* 13 August 1989, sec. 2, p. 1.

27. Frank Villalobos, Personal Interview.

28. Father John Moretta, Resurrection Parish, Personal Interview, Boyle Heights, Los Angeles, 24 May 1989.

29. The Plaza de Mayo mothers organized spontaneously to demand the return of their missing children, in open defiance of the Argentine military dictatorship. For a brief overview of the group and its relationship to other women's organizations in Argentina, and a synopsis of the criticism of the mothers that reveals ideological camps, see Gloria Bonder, "Women's Organizations in Argentina's Transition to Democracy," in *Women and Counter Power,* edited by Yolanda Cohen (New York: Black Rose Books, 1989): 65–85. There is no direct relationship between this group and MELA.

30. Aurora Castillo, Personal Interview, Boyle Heights, Los Angeles, 15 January 1988.

31. Aurora Castillo, Personal Interview.

32. Erlinda Robles, Personal Interview.

33. Ibid.

34. Reynoso, "Juana Beatriz Gutiérrez," p. 1.

35. For historical examples, see Chris Marín, "La Asociación Hispano-Americana de Madres Y Esposas: Tucson's Mexican American Women in World War II," *Renato Rosaldo Lecture Series 1: 1983–1984* (Tucson, Ariz.: Mexican American Studies Center, University of Arizona, Tucson, 1985) and Judy Aulette and Trudy Mills, "Something Old, Something New: Auxiliary Work in the 1983–1986 Copper Strike," *Feminist Studies* 14, no. 2 (Summer 1988): 251–69.

36. Mina Davis Caulfield, "Imperialism, the Family and Cultures of Resistance."

37. Aurora Castillo, Personal Interview.

38. As reconstructed by Juana Gutiérrez, Ricardo Gutiérrez, and Aurora Castillo.

39. Aurora Castillo, Personal Interview.

40. Juana Gutiérrez, Personal Interview.

41. Lucy Ramos, Personal Interview, Boyle Heights, Los Angeles, 3 May 1989.

42. Ibid.

43. For an overview of contemporary Third World struggles against environmental degradation, see Alan B. Durning, "Saving the Planet," *The Progressive* 53, no. 4 (April 1989): 35–59.

44. John Logan and Harvey Molotch, *Urban Fortunes* (Berkeley: University of California Press, 1988). Logan and Molotch use the term in reference to a coalition of business people, local politicians, and the media.

45. Mike Davis, "Chinatown, Part Two? The Internationalization of Downtown Los Angeles," *New Left Review*, no. 164 (July/August 1987): 64–86.

46. Paul Ong, *The Widening Divide, Income Inequality and Poverty in Los Angeles* (Los Angeles: The Research Group on the Los Angeles Economy, 1989). This UCLA-based study documents the growing gap between "haves" and "have nots" in the midst of the economic boom in Los Angeles. According to economists, the study mirrors a national trend in which rising employment levels are failing to lift the poor out of poverty or boost the middle class; see Jill Steward, "Two-Tiered Economy Feared as Dead End of Unskilled," *Los Angeles Times*, 25 June 1989, sec. 2, p. 1. At the same time, the California prison population will climb to more than twice its designed capacity by 1995. See Carl Ingram, "New Forecast Sees a Worse Jam in Prisons," *Los Angeles Times*, 27 June 1989, sec. 1, p. 23.

47. The point that urban land use policies are the products of class struggle—both cause and consequence—is made by Don Parson, "The Development of Redevelopment: Public Housing and Urban Renewal in Los Angeles," *International Journal of Urban and Regional Research* 6, no. 4 (December 1982): 392–413. Parson provides an excellent discussion of the working-class struggle for housing in the 1930s, the counterinitiative of urban renewal in the 1950s, and the inner city revolts of the 1960s.

48. Louise Tilly, "Paths of Proletarianization: Organization of Production, Sexual Division of Labor, and Women's Collective Action," *Signs* 7, no. 2 (1981): 400–17; Alice Kessler-Harris, "Women's Social Mission," *Women Have Always Worked* (Old Westbury, N.Y.: The Feminist Press, 1981): 102–35. For a literature review of women's activism during the Progressive Era, see Marilyn Gittell and Teresa Shtob, "Changing Women's Roles in Political Volunteerism and Reform of the City," in *Women and the American City*, edited by Catharine Stimpson et al. (Chicago: University of Chicago Press, 1981): 64–75.

49. Karen Sacks, *Caring by the Hour*, argues that often the significance of women's contributions is not "seen" because they take place in networks.

50. Aurora Castillo, Personal Interview.

HOUSEHOLD STRUCTURE AND FAMILY IDEOLOGIES: THE DYNAMICS OF IMMIGRANT ECONOMIC ADAPTATION AMONG VIETNAMESE REFUGEES—NAZLI KIBRIA

Notes

1. Whereas households are residential units, families may be defined as kinship groups in which the members do not necessarily live together. As in the case of a household in which members do not see themselves as kin, it is possible for the household and the family to be units that are entirely distinct. More commonly however, the household and family are vitally connected. As Rapp (1992:51) observes, "families organize households." That is, notions of family tend to define the membership of households as well as relations between household members.

2. For a review of the literature on family adaptive strategies, see Moen and Wethington 1992.

3. Studies of Vietnamese refugee communities in other parts of the country reveal similar employment patterns (Gold 1992; Rumbaut 1989).

4. The Vietnamese American practice that I observed of bringing diverse resources together extends the concept of income diversification, which has been noted by studies of developing societies to be a common strategy for dealing with risky economic contexts (Agarwal 1992; Perez-Aleman 1992).

5. All names have been changed to maintain anonymity.

References

Agarwal, Bina
1992 "Gender relations and food security: Coping with seasonality, drought and famine in South Asia." In *Unequal Burden: Economic Crises, Persistent Poverty and Women's Work,* eds. Lourdes Beneria and Shelley Feldman, 181–219. Boulder, Colo.: Westview Press.

Aldrich, Howard E., and Roger Waldinger
1990 "Ethnicity and entrepreneurship." *Annual Review of Sociology* 16:111–35.

Angel, Ronald, and Marta Tienda
1982 "Determinants of extended family structure: Cultural pattern or economic need?" *American Journal of Sociology* 87:1360–1383.

Bolles, A. Lynn
1983 "Kitchens hit by priorities: Employed working-class Jamaican women confront the IMF." In *Women, Men and the International Division of Labor,* eds. June Nash and M. Patricia Fernandez-Kelly, 138–60. Albany, NY: State University of New York Press.

Caplan, Nathan, John Whitmore, and Marcella Choy
1989 *The Boat People and Achievement in America: A Study of Family Life, Hard Work and Cultural Values.* Ann Arbor, Mich.: University of Michigan Press.

Caplan, Nathan, Marcella Choy, and John Whitmore
1992 "Indochinese refugee families and academic achievement." *Scientific American* 266:36–42.

Coleman, James
1988 "Social capital in the creation of human capital." *American Journal of Sociology* 94:S95–S120.

di Leonardo, Micaela
1987 "The female world of cards and holidays: Women, families, and the work of kinship." *Signs* 12:440–453.

Dinerman, Ina R.
1978 "Patterns of adaptation among households of U.S.-bound migrants from Michoacan, Mexico." *International Migration Review* 12:485–501.

Ewen, Elizabeth
1985 *Immigrant Women in the Land of Dollars: Life and Culture on the Lower East Side, 1890–1925.* New York: Monthly Review Press.

Gardner, Robert W., Robey Bryant, and Peter Smith
1985 "Asian Americans: Growth, change and diversity." *Population Bulletin* 40.

Geschwender, James A.
1992 "Ethgender, women's waged labor, and economic mobility." *Social Problems* 39:1–16.

Glazer, Nathan, and Daniel P. Moynihan
1963 *Beyond the Melting Pot.* Cambridge, Mass: MIT Press.

Glenn, Evelyn Nakano
1991 "Racial ethnic women's labor: The intersection of race, class and gender oppression." In *Gender, Family and Economy: The Triple Overlap,* ed. Rae Lesser Blumberg, 173–201. Newbury Park, Calif.: Sage Publications.

Gold, Steven J.
1992 *Refugee Communities: A Comparative Field Study.* Beverly Hills, Calif.: Sage Publications.

Gold, Steven J., and Nazli Kibria
1993 "Vietnamese refugees and blocked mobility." *Asian and Pacific Migration Journal* 2:1–30.

Grasmuck, Sherri, and Patricia Pessar
1991 *Between Two Islands: Dominican International Migration.* Berkeley, Calif.: University of California Press.

Hein, Jeremy
1993 *States and International Migrants: The Incorporation of Indochinese Refugees in the United States and France.* Boulder, Colo.: Westview Press.

Hume, Ellen
1985 "Vietnam's legacy: Indochinese refugees prosper in U.S., drawing on survival skills, special values." *Wall Street Journal,* March 21.

Kibria, Nazli
1990 "Power, patriarchy and gender conflict in the Vietnamese immigrant community." *Gender & Society* 4:9–24.
1993 *Family Tightrope: The Changing Lives of Vietnamese Americans.* Princeton, NJ: Princeton University Press.

Lieberson, Stanley
1980 *A Piece of the Pie.* Berkeley, Calif.: University of California Press.

Luong, Hy Van
1984 "'Brother' and 'uncle': An analysis of rules, structural contradictions and meaning in Vietnamese kinship." *American Anthropologist* 86(2):290–313.

Massey, Douglas, R. Alarcon, J. Durand, and H. Gonzalez
1987 *Return to Aztlan.* Berkeley, Calif.: University of California Press.

Min, Pyong Gap
1988 *Ethnic Business Enterprise: Korean Small Business in Atlanta.* Staten Island, NY: Center for Migration Studies.

Moen, Phyllis, and Elaine Wethington
1992 "The concept of family adaptive strategies." *Annual Review of Sociology* 18:233–51.

Morawska, Ewa
1985 *For Bread With Butter.* New York: Cambridge University Press.

Ogbu, John U.
1978 *Minority Education and Caste.* New York: Academic Press.

Pedraza, Silvia
1991 "Women and migration: The social consequences of gender." *Annual Review of Sociology* 17:303–25.

Pedraza-Bailey, Silvia
1985 *Political and Economic Migrants in America: Cubans and Mexicans.* Austin, Texas: University of Texas Press.

Perez, Lisandro
1986 "Immigrant economic adjustment and family organization: The Cuban success story re-examined." *International Migration Review* 20:1, 4–20.

Perez-Aleman, Paola
1992 "Economic crisis and women in Nicaragua." In *Unequal Burden: Economic Crises, Persistent Poverty and Women's Work,* eds. Lourdes Beneria and Shelley Feldman, 239–259. Boulder, Colo.: Westview Press.

Petersen, William
1971 *Japanese Americans.* New York: Random House.

Philadelphia City Planning Commission
1984 Socioeconomic Characteristics for Philadelphia Census Tracts: 1980 and 1970. Technical Information Paper.

Portes, Alejandro, and Robert Bach
1985 *Latin Journey: Cuban and Mexican Immigrants in the U.S.* Berkeley, Calif.: University of California Press.

Portes, Alejandro, and Ruben Rumbaut
1990 *Immigrant America: A Portrait.* Berkeley, Calif.: University of California Press.

Rapp, Rayna
1992 "Family and class in contemporary America." In *Rethinking the Family: Some Feminist Questions,* eds. Barrie Thorne and Marilyn Yalom, 49–70. Boston: Northeastern University Press.

Rumbaut, Ruben G.
1989a "The structure of refuge: Southeast Asian refugees in the U.S., 1975–85.' *International Review of Comparative Public Policy* 1:97–129.
1989b "Portraits, patterns and predictors of the refugee adaptation process: Results and reflections from the IHARP Panel study." In *Refugees as Immigrants,* ed. David Haines, 138–183. New Jersey: Rowman and Allenheld.

Rumbaut, Ruben, and Kenji Ima
Forthcoming *Between Two Worlds: Southeast Asian Youth in America.* Boulder, Colo.: Westview Press.

Seller, Maxine S.
1981 "Community life." In *Immigrant Women,* ed. Maxine Seller, 157–166. Philadelphia, Penn.: Temple University Press.

Sibley Butler, John
1991 *Entrepreneurship and Self-Help Among Black Americans.* Albany, NY: State University of New York Press.

Stack, Carol
1974 *All Our Kin: Strategies for Survival in a Black Community.* New York: Harper and Row.

Steinberg, Stephen
1981 *The Ethnic Myth.* Boston: Beacon Press.

Wood, Charles H.
1981 "Structural changes and household strategies: A conceptual framework for the study of rural migration." *Human Organization* 40: 338–344.

Wolf, Diane L.
1990 "Daughters, decisions and domination: An empirical and conceptual critique of household strategies." *Development and Change* 24:43–74.
1992 *Factory Daughters: Gender, Household Dynamics, and Rural Industrialization in Java.* Berkeley and Los Angeles: University of California Press.

FRATERNITIES AND COLLEGIATE RAPE CULTURE: WHY ARE SOME FRATERNITIES MORE DANGEROUS PLACES FOR WOMEN?—A. AYRES BOSWELL AND JOAN Z. SPADE

References

Barthel, D. 1988. *Putting on appearances: Gender and advertising.* Philadelphia: Temple University Press.

Boeringer, S. B., C. L. Shehan, and R. L. Akers. 1991. Social contexts and social learning in sexual coercion and aggression: Assessing the contribution of fraternity membership. *Family Relations* 40:58–64.

Brownmiller, S. 1975. *Against our will: Men, women and rape.* New York: Simon & Schuster.

Buchwald, E., P. R. Fletcher, and M. Roth, eds. 1993. *Transforming a rape culture.* Minneapolis, MN: Milkweed Editions.

Burke, P., J. E. Stets, and M. A. Pirog-Good. 1989. Gender identity, self-esteem, physical abuse and sexual abuse in dating relationships. In *Violence in dating relationships: Emerging social issues,* edited by M. A. Pirog-Good and J. E. Stets. New York: Praeger.

Gwartney-Gibbs, P., and J. Stockard. 1989. Courtship aggression and mixed-sex peer groups. In *Violence in dating relationships: Emerging social issues,* edited by M. A. Pirog-Good and J. E. Stets. New York: Praeger.

Herman D. 1984. The rape culture. In *Women: A feminist perspective,* edited by J. Freeman. Mountain View, CA: Mayfield.

Holland, D. C., and M. A. Eisenhart. 1990. *Educated in romance: Women, achievement, and college culture.* Chicago: University of Chicago Press.

Horowitz, H. L 1988. *Campus life: Undergraduate cultures from the end of the 18th century to the present.* Chicago: University of Chicago Press.

Hunter, F. 1953. *Community power structure.* Chapel Hill: University of North Carolina Press.

Jenkins, M. J., and F. H. Dambrot 1987. The attribution of date rape: Observer's attitudes and sexual experiences and the dating situation. *Journal of Applied Social Psychology* 17:875–95.

Janis, I. L. 1972. *Victims of groupthink.* Boston: Houghton Mifflin.

Kalof, L., and T. Cargill. 1991. Fraternity and sorority membership and gender dominance attitudes. *Sex Roles* 25:417–23.

Kimmel, M. S. 1993. Clarence, William, Iron Mike, Tailhook, Senator Packwood, Spur Posse. Magic…and us. In *Transforming a rape culture,* edited by E. Buchwald, P. R. Fletcher and M. Roth, Minneapolis, MN: Milkweed Editions.

Koss, M. P., T. E. Dinero, C. A. Seibel, and S. L. Cox. 1988. Stranger and acquaintance rape: Are there differences in the victim's experience? *Psychology of Women Quarterly* 12:1–24.

Koss, M. P., C. A. Gidycz, and N. Wisniewski. 1985. The scope of rape: Incidence and prevalence of sexual aggression and victimization in a national sample of higher education students. *Journal of Consulting and Clinical Psychology* 55:162–70.

LaPlante, M. N., N. McCormick, and G. G. Brannigan. 1980. Living the sexual script: College students' views of influence in sexual encounters, *Journal of Sex Research* 16:338–55.

Lisak, D., and S. Roth. 1988. Motivational factors in nonincarcerated sexually aggressive men. *Journal of Personality and Social Psychology* 55:795–802.

Malamuth N. 1986. Predictors of naturalistic sexual aggression. *Journal of Personality and Social Psychology* 50:953–62.

Martin, P. Y., and R. Hummer. 1989. Fraternities and rape on campus. *Gender & Society* 3:457–73.

Miller, B., and J. C. Marshall. 1987. Coercive sex on the university campus. *Journal of College Student Personnel* 28:38–47.

Moffat, M. 1989. *Coming of age in New Jersey: College life in American culture.* New Brunswick, NJ: Rutgers University Press.

Muehlenhard, C. L., and M. A. Linton. 1987. Date rape and sexual aggression in dating situations: Incidence and risk factors. *Journal of Counseling Psychology* 34:186–96.

O'Sullivan, C. 1993. Fraternities and the rape culture. In *Transforming a rape culture,* edited by E. Buchwald, P. R. Fletcher, and M. Roth. Minneapolis, MN: Milkweed Editions.

Peterson, S. A., and B. Franzese. 1987. Correlates of college men's sexual abuse of women. *Journal of College Student Personnel* 28:223–28.

Sanday, P. R. 1990. *Fraternity gang rape: Sex, brotherhood and privilege on campus.* New York: New York University Press.

West, C., and D. Zimmerman. 1987. Doing gender. *Gender & Society* 1:125–51.

TWO CAN MAKE A REVOLUTION—EGON MAYER

Notes

1. Francesco Alberoni, *Falling in Love* (New York: Random House, 1983), p. 6.

2. Ibid., p. 17.

3. John B. Halsted, *Romanticism: Definition, Explanation, and Evaluation* (Lexington, MA: D.C. Heath and Company, 1965).

4. Edward Shorter, *The Making of the Modern Family* (New York: Basic Books, Inc., 1975); Ellen K. Rothman, *Hands and Hearts: A History of Courtship in America* (New York: Basic Books, Inc., 1984).

5. Morton M. Hunt, *The Natural History of Love* (New York: Alfred A. Knopf, Inc./Minerva Press, 1959, 1967).

6. Ibid., p. 26.

7. Joseph Stein, *Fiddler on the Roof.* Broadway musical.

8. Hunt, *The Natural History of Love,* p. 25.

9. William M. Kephart, *The Family, Society, and the Individual,* 3d Ed. (New York: Houghton Mifflin Company, 1972), p. 137.

10. Shorter, *The Making of the Modern Family,* p. 148.

11. Selma Stern, *Court Jew* (Philadelphia, PA: Jewish Publication Society, 1951).

12. Rothman, *Hands and Hearts,* pp. 28–29.

13. Jan Lewis, *The Pursuit of Happiness: Family and Values in Jefferson's Virginia* (New York: Cambridge University Press, 1983).

14. Shorter, *The Making of the Modern Family,* pp. 121–122.

15. Ibid., p. 148.

16. J. Hector St. John Crevecoeur, *Letters of an American Farmer* (New York: Dolphin Books, n.d.), pp. 49–50.

17. Israel Zangwill, *The Melting Pot* (New York: Macmillan Company, 1908).

18. Arthur Mann, *The One and the Many* (Chicago: Chicago University Press, 1979), p. 100.

19. Ibid., p. 75–76.

20. Ibid., p. 111.

21. Ibid., p. 117.

22. Heinrich Graetz, *History of the Jews* (Philadelphia, PA: The Jewish Publication Society, 1956), v. 5, p. 697.

23. Malcolm H. Stern, "Jewish Marriage and Intermarriage in the Federal Period, 1776–1840," *American Jewish Archives* (November 1967), pp. 142–143.

24. Milton L. Barron, "The Incidence of Jewish Intermarriage in Europe and America," *American Sociological Review* 11:1 (February 1946), pp. 6–13.

25. Moshe Davis, "Mixed Marriage in Western Jewry," *Jewish Journal of Sociology* 10:2 (December 1968) pp. 177–210.

26. Ande Manners, *Poor Cousins* (Greenwich, CT: Fawcett Publications, 1972), p. 25.

27. Arthur Ruppin, *The Jews in the Modern World* (New York: Arno Press, 1973), pp. 318–321.

28. Chaim I. Waxman, *America's Jews in Transition* (Philadelphia, PA: Temple University Press, 1983), pp. 29–31.

29. National Jewish Population Study, "Intermarriage" (New York: Council of Jewish Federations, 1971). Mimeograph.

30. Isaac Metzker, *A Bintle Brief* (New York: Ballantine Books, 1971), pp. 76–77.

31. Ibid., pp. 91–92.

32. Julius Drachsler, *Democracy and Assimilation* (New York: Macmillan Company, 1920), p. 126.

33. Milton M. Gordon, *Assimilation in American Life* (New York: Oxford University Press, 1964), p. 80.

34. Elihu Bergman, "The American Jewish Population Erosion," *Midstream* 23:8 (October 1977).

35. Andrew M. Greeley, *Crisis in the Church* (Chicago: Thomas More Press, 1979), p. 150.

36. Richard D. Alba, "Social Assimilation among American Catholic National Origin Groups." *American Sociological Review* 41:6 (1976), pp. 1030–1046.

37. Konrad Bercovici, *Crimes of Charity* (1917).

38. Michael Novak, *The Rise of the Unmeltable Ethnics* (New York: Macmillan Publishing Company, 1971).

39. Herbert J. Gans, *The Levittowners* (New York: Vintage Books, 1969); Michael Parenti, "Ethnic Politics and the Persistence of Ethnic Identification," *American Political Science Review* 61 (September 1967), pp. 717–726.

40. Bill R. Lindner, *How to Trace Your Family History* (New York: Dodd Mead Company, 1978); Arthur Kurzweil, *From Generation to Generation: How to Trace Your Jewish Genealogy* (New York: Morrow, 1980).

41. United Jewish Appeal, *Book of Songs and Blessings* (New York: United Jewish Appeal, 1980), p. 25.

42. Floyd J. Fowler, *1975 Community Survey: A Study of the Jewish Population of Greater Boston* (Boston: Combined Jewish Philanthropies, 1977); Albert Mayer, *The Jewish Population Study of the Greater Kansas City Area* (Kansas City: Jewish Federation, 1977); Bruce A. Phillips, *Denver Jewish Population Study* (Denver: Allied Jewish Federation, 1982).

43. David M. Eichhorn, *Conversion to Judaism* (New York; Ktav Publishing House, Inc., 1965), p. 213.

44. Slogan from a popular bill board advertisement in the New York area for Levy's Real Jewish Rye Bread.

ONE STYLE OF DOMINICAN BRIDAL SHOWER—ADELE BAHN AND ANGELA JAQUEZ

Notes

1. Arnold van Gennep, *The Rites of Passage* (Chicago: Univ. of Chicago Press, 1960), p. 67.

2. Of the seven showers observed, there was nudity or near-nudity of the bride-to-be in six cases. There was some discrepancy in the reports of the respondents about its occurrence at showers. Some respondents said that it was not typical and, in fact, violated strong norms of personal modesty.

3. The word "conventional" represents what the respondents say is more like an "*American shower*" (emphasis ours).

4. The respondents noted that some girls had attended sex education classes in school in New York City. Some said they had gotten information from friends and had attended other showers. Many made a point of saying that their mothers had told them nothing.

5. For a general discussion, see Manuel de Js. Guerrero, *El Machismo en Republica Dominica* (Santo Domingo, R.D.: Amigo del Hogar, 1975).

6. See Glenn Hendricks, *The Dominican Diaspora* (New York: Teachers College Press, 1974).

7. Comparative family structure, including Latin America, is described in Betty Yorburg, *Sexual Identity: Sex Roles and Social Change*

(New York: John Wiley & Sons, 1974). See also Vivian Mota, "Politics and Feminism in the Dominican Republic: 1931–45 and 1966–74," in June Nash and Helen Icken Safa (eds.), *Sex and Class in Latin America* (Brooklyn: J. F. Bergin, 1980).

8. At the showers, alcoholic beverages are typically served only to the bride-to-be.

THE FEMINIZATION OF LOVE—FRANCESCA M. CANCIAN

Notes

1. The term "feminization" of love is derived from Ann Douglas, *The Feminization of Culture* (New York: Alfred A. Knopf, 1977).

2. The term "androgyny" is problematic. It assumes rather than questions sex-role stereotypes (aggression is masculine, e.g.); it can lead to a utopian view that underestimates the social causes of sexism; and it suggests the complete absence of differences between men and women, which is biologically impossible. Nonetheless, I use the term because it best conveys my meaning: a combination of masculine and feminine styles of love. The negative and positive aspects of the concept "androgyny" are analyzed in a special issue of *Women's Studies* (vol. 2, no. 2[1974]), edited by Cynthia Secor. Also see Sandra Bem, "Gender Schema Theory and Its Implications for Child Development: Raising Gender-aschematic Children in a Gender-schematic Society," *Signs: Journal of Women in Culture and Society* 8, no. 4 (1983): 598–616.

3. The quotations are from a study by Ann Swidler, "Ideologies of Love in Middle Class America" (paper presented at the annual meeting of the Pacific Sociological Association, San Diego, 1982). For useful reviews of the history of love, see Morton Hunt, *The Natural History of Love* (New York: Alfred A. Knopf, 1959); and

Bernard Murstein, *Love, Sex and Marriage through the Ages* (New York: Springer, 1974).

4. See John Bowlby, *Attachment and Loss* (New York: Basic Books, 1969), on mother-infant attachment. The quotation is from Elaine Walster and G. William Walster, *A New Look at Love* (Reading, Mass.: Addison-Wesley Publishing Co., 1978), 9. Conceptions of love and adjustment used by family sociologists are reviewed in Robert Lewis and Graham Spanier, "Theorizing about the Quality and Stability of Marriage," in *Contemporary Theories about the Family,* ed. W. Burr, R. Hill, F. Nye, and I. Reiss (New York: Free Press, 1979), 268–94.

5. Mary Ryan, *Womanhood in America*, 2d ed. (New York: New Viewpoints, 1979), and *The Cradle of the Middle Class: The Family in Oneida County, N.Y, 1790–1865* (New York: Cambridge University Press, 1981); Barbara Ehrenreich and Deirdre English, *For Her Own Good: 150 Years of Experts' Advice to Women* (New York: Anchor Books, 1978); Barbara Welter, "The Cult of True Womanhood: 1820–1860," *American Quarterly* 18, no. 2(1966): 151–74; Carl N. Degler, *At Odds* (New York: Oxford University Press, 1980).

6. Alternative definitions of love are reviewed in Walster and Walster, Clyde Hendrick and Susan Hendrick, *Liking, Loving and Relating* (Belmont, Calif.: Wadsworth Publishing Co., 1983); Ira Reiss, *Family Systems in America,* 3d ed. (New York: Holt, Rinehart & Winston, 1980), 113–41; Margaret Reedy, "Age and Sex Differences in Personal Needs and the Nature of Love" (Ph.D. diss., University of Southern California, 1977).

7. Abraham Maslow, *Motivation and Personality,* 2d ed. (New York: Harper & Row, 1970), 182–83.

8. Zick Rubin's scale is described in his article "Measurement of Romantic Love," *Journal of Personality and Social Psychology* 16, no. 2 (1970): 265–73; Lillian Rubin's book on

marriage is *Intimate Strangers* (New York: Harper & Row, 1983), quote on 90.

9. The emphasis on mutual aid and instrumental love among poor people is described in Lillian Rubin, *Worlds of Pain* (New York: Basic Books, 1976); Rayna Rapp, "Family and Class in Contemporary America," in *Rethinking the Family,* ed. Barrie Thorne (New York: Longman, Inc., 1982), 168–87; S. M. Miller and F. Riessman, "The Working-Class Subculture," in *Blue-Collar World,* ed. A. Shostak and W. Greenberg (Englewood Cliffs, N.J.: Prentice-Hall, Inc., 1964), 24–36.

10. Francesca Cancian, Clynta Jackson, and Ann Wysocki, "A Survey of Close Relationships" (University of California, Irvine, School of Social Sciences, 1982, typescript).

11. Swidler.

12. *Webster's New Collegiate Dictionary* (Springfield, Mass.: G. C. Merriam Co., 1977).

13. Paul Rosencrantz, Helen Bee, Susan Vogel, Inge Broverman, and Donald Broverman, "Sex Role Stereotypes and Self-Concepts in College Students," *Journal of Consulting and Clinical Psychology* 32, no. 3 (1968): 287–95; Paul Rosencrantz, "Rosencrantz Discusses Changes in Stereotypes about Men and Women," *Second Century Radcliffe News* (Cambridge, Mass., June 1982), 5–6.

14. Nancy Chodorow, *The Reproduction of Mothering* (Berkeley: University of California Press, 1978), 169. Dorothy Dinnerstein presents a similar theory in *The Mermaid and the Minotaur: Sexual Arrangements and Human Malaise* (New York: Harper & Row, 1976). Freudian and biological dispositional theories about women's nurturance are surveyed in Jean Stockard and Miriam Johnson, *Sex Roles* (Englewood Cliffs, N.J.: Prentice-Hall, Inc., 1980).

15. Carol Gilligan, *In a Different Voice* (Cambridge, Mass: Harvard University Press, 1982), 32, 159–61; see also L. Rubin, *Intimate Strangers.*

16. Talcott Parsons and Robert F. Bales, *Family, Socialization and Interaction* (Glencoe, Ill., Free Press, 1955). For a critical review of family sociology from a feminist perspective, see Arlene Skolnick, *The Intimate Environment* (Boston: Little, Brown & Co., 1978). Radical feminist theories also support the feminized conception of love, but they have been less influential in social science, see, e.g., Mary Daly, *Gyn/Ecology; The Metaethics of Radical Feminism* (Boston: Beacon Press, 1979).

17. I have drawn most heavily on Ryan, *Womanhood,* (n. 5 above), Ryan, *Cradle* (n. 5 above), Ehrenreich and English (n. 5 above), Welter (n. 5 above).

18. Ryan, *Womanhood,* 24–25.

19. Similar changes occurred when culture and religion were feminized, according to Douglas (n. 1 above). Conceptions of God's love shifted toward an image of a sweet and tender parent, a "submissive, meek and forgiving" Christ (149).

20. On the persistence of women's wage inequality and responsibility for housework, see Stockard and Johnson (n. 14 above).

21. Jean Baker Miller, *Toward a New Psychology of Women* (Boston: Beacon Press, 1976). There are, of course, many exceptions to Miller's generalization, e.g., women who need to be independent or who need an attachment with a woman.

22. In psychology, the work of Carl Jung, David Bakan, and Bem are especially relevant. See Carl Jung, "Anima and Animus," in *Two Essays on Analytical Psychology: Collected Works of C. G. Jung* (New York: Bollinger Foundation, 1953), 7:186–209; David Bakan, *The Duality of Human Existence* (Chicago: Rand McNally & Co., 1966). They are discussed in Bem's paper, "Beyond Androgyny," in *Family in Transition,* 2d ed., ed. A. Skolnick and J. Skolnick (Boston: Little, Brown & Co., 1977), 204–21. Carl Rogers exemplifies the human potential theme of

self-development through the search for whole-ness. See Carl Rogers, *On Becoming a Person* (Boston: Houghton Mifflin Co., 1961).

23. Chodorow (n. 14 above) refers to the effects of the division of labor and to power differences between men and women, and the special effects of women's being the primary parents are widely acknowledged among historians.

24. The data on Yale men are from Mirra Komarovsky, *Dilemma of Masculinity* (New York: W. W. Norton & Co., 1976). Angus Campbell reports that children are closer to their mothers than to their fathers, and daughters feel closer to their parents than do sons, on the basis of large national surveys, in *The Sense of Well-Being in America* (New York: McGraw-Hill Book Co., 1981), 96. However, the tendency of people to criticize their mothers more than their fathers seems to contradict these findings; e.g., see Donald Payne and Paul Mussen, "Parent-Child Relations and Father Identification among Adolescent Boys," *Journal of Abnormal and Social Psychology* 52 (1956): 358–62. Being "closer" to one's mother may refer mostly to spending more time together and knowing more about each other rather than to feeling more comfortable together.

25. Studies of differences in friendship by gender are reviewed in Wenda Dickens and Daniel Perlman, "Friendship over the Life Cycle," in *Personal Relationships,* vol. 2, ed. Steve Duck and Robin Gilmour (London: Academic Press, 1981), 91–122, and Beth Hess, "Friendship and Gender Roles over the Life Course," in *Single Life,* ed. Peter Stein (New York: St. Martin's Press, 1981), 104–15. While almost all studies show that women have more close friends, Lionel Tiger argues that there is a unique bond between male friends in *Men in Groups* (London: Thomas Nelson, 1969).

26. Komarovsky, *Blue-Collar Marriage* (New York: Random House, 1962), 13.

27. Daniel Levinson, *The Seasons of a Man's Life* (New York: Alfred A. Knopf, 1978), 335.

28. The argument about the middle-aged switch was presented in the popular book *Passages,* by Gail Sheehy (New York: E. P. Dutton, 1976), and in more scholarly works, such as Levinson's. These studies are reviewed in Alice Rossi, "Life-Span Theories and Women's Lives," *Signs* 6, no. 1 (1980): 4–32. However, a survey by Claude Fischer and S. Oliker reports an increasing tendency for women to have more close friends than men beginning in middle age, in "Friendship, Gender and the Life Cycle," Working Paper no. 318 (Berkeley: University of California, Berkeley, Institute of Urban and Regional Development, 1980).

29. Studies on gender differences in self-disclosure are reviewed in Letitia Peplau and Steven Gordon, "Women and Men in Love: Sex Differences in Close Relationships," in *Women, Gender and Social Psychology,* ed. V. O'Leary, R. Unger, and B. Wallston (Hillsdale, N.J.: Lawrence Erlbaum Associates, 1985), 257–91. Also see Zick Rubin, Charles Hill, Letitia Peplau, and Christine Dunkel-Schetter, "Self-Disclosure in Dating Couples," *Journal of Marriage and the Family* 42, no. 2 (1980): 305–18.

30. Working-class patterns are described in Komarovsky, *Blue-Collar Marriage.* Middle-class patterns are reported by Lynne Davidson and Lucille Duberman, "Friendship: Communication and Interactional Patterns in Same-Sex Dyads," *Sex Roles* 8, no. 8 (1982): 809–22. Similar findings are reported in Robert Lewis, "Emotional Intimacy among Men," *Journal of Social Issues* 34, no. 1 (1978): 108–21.

31. Rubin et al., "Self-Disclosure."

32. These studies, cited below, are based on the self-reports of men and women college students and may reflect norms more than behavior. The findings are that women feel and express affective and bodily emotional reactions more

often than do men, except for hostile feelings. See also Jon Allen and Dorothy Haccoun, "Sex Differences in Emotionality," *Human Relations* 29, no. 8 (1976): 711–22; and Jack Balswick and Christine Avertt, "Gender, Interpersonal Orientation and Perceived Parental Expressiveness," *Journal of Marriage and the Family* 39, no. 1 (1977): 121–128. Gender differences in interaction styles are analyzed in Nancy Henley, *Body Politics: Power, Sex and Non-verbal Communication* (Englewood Cliffs, N.J.: Prentice-Hall, Inc., 1977). Also see Paula Fishman, "Interaction: The Work Women Do," *Social Problems* 25, no. 4 (1978): 397–406.

33. Gender differences in leisure are described in L. Rubin, *Worlds of Pain* (n. 9 above), 10. Also see Margaret Davis, "Sex Role Ideology as Portrayed in Men's and Women's Magazines" (Stanford University, typescript).

34. Bert Adams, *Kinship in an Urban Setting* (Chicago: Markham Publishing Co., 1968), 169.

35. Marjorie Lowenthal and Clayton Haven, "Interaction and Adaptation: Intimacy as a Critical Variable," *American Sociological Review* 33, no. 4 (1968): 20–30.

36. Joseph Pleck argues that family ties are the primary concern for many men, in *The Myth of Masculinity* (Cambridge, Mass.: MIT Press, 1981).

37. Gender-specific characteristics also are seen in same-sex relationships. See M. Caldwell and Letitia Peplau, "Sex Differences in Same Sex Friendship," *Sex Roles* 8, no. 7 (1982): 721–32; see also Davidson and Duberman (n. 30 above), 809–22. Part of the reason for the differences in friendship may be men's fear of homosexuality and of losing status with other men. An explanatory study found that men were most likely to express feelings of closeness if they were engaged in some activity such as sports that validated their masculinity (Scott Swain, "Male Intimacy in Same-Sex Friendships: The Impact of Gender-validating Activities" [paper presented at annual meeting of the American Sociological Association, August 1984]). For discussions of men's homophobia and fear of losing power, see Robert Brannon, "The Male Sex Role," in *The Forty-nine Percent Majority,* ed. Deborah David and Robert Brannon (Reading, Mass.: Addison-Wesley Publishing Co., 1976), 1–48. I am focusing on heterosexual relations, but similar gender-specific differences may characterize homosexual relations. Some studies find that, compared with homosexual men, lesbians place a higher value on tenderness and verbal self-disclosure and engage in sex less frequently. See e.g., Alan Bell and Martin Weinberg, *Homosexualities* (New York: Simon & Schuster, 1978).

38. Unlike most studies, Reedy (n. 6 above) did not find that women emphasized communication more than men. Her subjects were upper-middle-class couples who seemed to be very much in love.

39. Sara Allison Parelman, "Dimensions of Emotional Intimacy in Marriage" (Ph.D. diss., University of California, Los Angeles, 1980).

40. Both spouses thought their interaction was unpleasant if the other engaged in negative or displeasureable instrumental or affectional actions. Thomas Wills, Robert Weiss, and Gerald Patterson, "A Behavioral Analysis of the Determinants of Marital Satisfaction," *Journal of Consulting and Clinical Psychology* 42, no. 6 (1974): 802–11.

41. L. Rubin, *Worlds of Pain* (n. 9 above), 147.

42. See L. Rubin, *Worlds of Pain;* also see Richard Sennett and Jonathon Cobb, *Hidden Injuries of Class* (New York: Vintage, 1973).

43. For evidence on this point, see Morton Hunt, *Sexual Behavior in the 1970s* (Chicago: Playboy Press, 1974), 231; and Alexander Clark and Paul Wallin, "Women's Sexual Responsiveness and the Duration and Quality of Their Marriage," *American Journal of Sociology* 21, no. 2 (1965): 187–96.

44. Interview by Cynthia Garlich, "Interviews of Married Couples" (University of California, Irvine, School of Social Sciences, 1982).

45. For example, see Catharine MacKinnon, "Feminism, Marxism, Method, and the State: An Agenda for Theory," *Signs* 7, no. 3 (1982): 515–44. For a thoughtful discussion of this issue from a historical perspective, see Linda Gordon and Ellen Dubois, "Seeking Ecstacy on the Battlefield: Danger and Pleasure in Nineteenth Century Feminist Thought," *Feminist Review* 13, no. 1 (1983): 42–54.

46. Reedy (n. 6 above).

47. William Kephart, "Some Correlates of Romantic Love," *Journal of Marriage and the Family* 29, no. 3 (1967): 470–74. See Peplau and Gordon (n. 29 above) for an analysis of research on gender and romanticism.

48. Daniel Yankelovich, *The New Morality* (New York: McGraw-Hill Book Co., 1974), 98.

49. The link between love and power is explored in Francesca Cancian, "Gender Politics; Love and Power in the Private and Public Spheres," in *Gender and the Life Course,* ed. Alice S. Rossi (New York: Aldine Publishing Co., 1984), 253–64.

50. See Jane Flax, "The Family in Contemporary Feminist Thought," in *The Family in Political Thought,* ed. Jean B. Elshtain (Princeton, N.J.: Princeton University Press, 1981), 223–53.

51. Walter Gove, "Sex, Marital Status and Mortality," *American Journal of Sociology* 79, no. 1 (1973): 45–67.

52. This follows from the social exchange theory of power, which argues that person A will have a power advantage over B if A has more alternative sources for the gratifications she or he gets from B than B has for those from A. See Peter Blau, *Exchange and Power in Social Life* (New York: John Wiley & Sons, 1964), 117–18.

53. For a discussion of the devaluation of women's activities, see Michelle Rosaldo,

"Woman, Culture and Society: A Theoretical Overview," in *Woman, Culture and Society,* ed. Michelle Rosaldo and Louise Lamphere (Stanford, Calif.: Stanford University Press, 1973), 17–42.

54. Gilligan (n. 15 above), 12–13.

55. Inge Broverman, Frank Clarkson, Paul Rosenkrantz, and Susan Vogel, "Sex-Role Stereotypes and Clinical Judgments of Mental Health," *Journal of Consulting Psychology* 34, no. 1 (1970): 1–7.

56. Welter (n. 5 above).

57. Levinson (n. 27 above).

58. L. Rubin, *Intimate Strangers* (n. 8 above); Harold Rausch, William Barry, Richard Hertel, and Mary Ann Swain, *Communication, Conflict and Marriage* (San Francisco: Jossey-Bass, Inc., 1974). This conflict is analyzed in Francesca Cancian, "Marital Conflict over Intimacy," in *The Psychosocial Interior of the Family,* 3d ed., ed. Gerald Handel (New York: Aldine Publishing Co., 1985), 277–92.

IS "STRAIGHT" TO "GAY" AS "FAMILY" IS TO "NO FAMILY"?—KATH WESTON

Notes

1. See Godwin (1983) and Hollibaugh (1979).

2. For an analysis that carefully distinguishes among the various senses of reproduction and their equivocal usage in feminist and anthropological theory, see Yanagisako and Collier (1987).

3. On the distinction between family and household, see Rapp (1982) and Yanagisako (1979).

4. On relational definition and the arbitrariness of signs, see Saussure (1959).

5. For Lévi-Strauss (1963b:88), most symbolic contrasts are structured by a mediating

third term. Apparently conflicting elements incorporate a hidden axis of commonality that allows the two to be brought into relationship with one another. Here sexual identity is the hidden term that links "straight" to "gay," while kinship mediates the oppositions further down in the chart. This sort of triadic relation lends dynamism to opposition, facilitating ideological transformations while ensuring a regulated, or structured, relationship between the old and the new.

My overall analysis departs from a Lévi-Straussian structuralism by historically situating these relations, discarding any presumption that they form a closed system, and avoiding the arbitrary isolation of categories for which structuralism has justly been criticized in the past (see Culler 1975; Fowler 1981; Jenkins 1979). The symbolic oppositions examined in this chapter incorporate indigenous categories in all their specificity (e.g., straight versus gay), rather than abstracting to universals of increasing generality and arguably decreasing utility (e.g., nature versus culture). Chronicled here is an ideological transformation faithful to history, process, and the perceptions of the lesbians and gay men who themselves identified each opposition included in the chart. For the deployment of these categories in everyday contexts, read on.

6. Notice how the contrasts in the chart map a relationship of difference (straight/gay) first onto a logical negation (family/no family, or A/NA), and then onto another relation of difference (biological [blood] family/families we choose [create], or A:B). On the generative potential of dichotomies that are constituted as A/B rather than A/NA, see N. Jay (1981:44).

References

Allen, Ronnie. 1987. "Times Have Changed at the *Herald." Gay Community News* (June 28–July 4).

Bourdieu, Pierre. 1977. *Outline of a Theory of Practice.* New York: Cambridge University Press.

Castells, Manuel and Karen Murphy. 1982. "Cultural Identity and Urban Structure: The Spatial Organization of San Francisco's Gay Community." In Norman I. Fainstein and Susan S. Fainstein (eds.), *Urban Policy Under Capitalism,* pp. 237–259. Beverly Hills, Calif.: Sage.

Cook, Blanche Wiesen. 1977. "Female Support Networks and Political Activism: Lillian Wald, Crystal Eastman, Emma Goldman." *Chrysalis* 3:44–61.

Culler, Jonathan. 1975. *Structuralist Poetics: Structuralism, Linguistics and the Study of Literature.* Ithaca, N.Y. : Cornell University Press.

FitzGerald, Frances. 1986. *Cities on a Hill: A Journal Through Contemporary American Cultures.* New York: Simon & Schuster.

Foucault, Michel. 1978. *The History of Sexuality.* Vol. 1. New York: Vintage.

Fowler, Roger. 1981. *Literature as Social Discourse: The Practice of Linguistic Criticism.* Bloomington: University of Indiana Press.

Godwin, Ronald S. 1983. "AIDS: A Moral and Political Timebomb." *Moral Majority Report* (July).

Hocquenghem, Guy. 1978. *Homosexual Desire.* London: Alison & Busby.

Hollibaugh, Amber. 1979. "Sexuality and the State: The Defeat of the Briggs Initiative and Beyond." *Socialist Review* 9(3):55–72.

Jay, Nancy. 1981. "Gender and Dichotomy." *Feminist Studies* 7(1):38–56.

Jenkins, Alan. 1979. *The Social Theory of Claude Levi-Strauss.* New York: St. Martin's Press.

Lazere, Arthur. 1986. "On the Job." *Coming Up!* (June).

Levi-Straus, Claude. 1963. *Totemism.* Boston: Beacon Hill.

Mendenhall, George. 1985. "Mickey Mouse Lawsuit Remains Despite Disney Dancing Decree." *Bay Area Report* (August 22).

Rapp, Rayna. 1982. "Family and Class in Contemporary America: Notes Toward an Understanding of Ideology." In Barrie Thorne with Marilyn Yalom, eds., *Rethinking the Family,* pp. 168–187. New York: Longman.

Saussure, Ferdinand de. 1959. *Course in General Linguistics.* New York: McGraw-Hill.

Silverstein, Charles. 1977. *A Family Matter: A Parents' Guide to Homosexuality.* New York: McGraw-Hill.

Smith, Barbara, ed. 1983. *Home Girls: A Black Feminist Anthology.* New York: Kitchen Table: Women of Color Press.

Watney, Simon. 1987. *Policing Desire: Pornography, AIDS, and the Media.* Minneapolis: University of Minnesota Press.

Yanagisako, Sylvia J. 1985. *Transforming the Past: Tradition and Kinship among Japanese Americans.* Stanford: Stanford University Press.

Yanagisako, Sylvia Junko and Jane Fishburne Collier. 1987. "Toward a Unified Analysis of Gender and Kinship." In Jane Fishburne Collier and Sylvia Junko Yanagisako, eds. *Gender and Kinship: Essays Toward a Unified Analysis,* pp. 14–50. Stanford: Stanford University Press.

KOREAN IMMIGRANT WOMEN'S CHALLENGE TO GENDER INEQUALITY AT HOME: THE INTERPLAY OF ECONOMIC RESOURCES, GENDER, AND FAMILY— IN-SOOK LIM

References

Berheide, Catherine W. 1984. Women's work in the home: Seems like old times. In *Women and the family: Two decades of change,* edited by Beth B. Hess and M. B. Sussman. New York: Haworth.

Berk, Sarah Fenstermaker. 1985. *The gender factory: The apportionment of work in American households.* New York and London: Plenum.

Blood, Robert O., and Donald M. Wolfe. 1960. *Husbands and wives.* New York: Free Press.

Blumberg, Rae Lesser, ed. 1991. *Gender, family, and economy. The triple overlap.* Newbury Park, CA: Sage.

Blumstein. Philip, and Pepper Schwartz. 1983. *American couples.* New York. William Morrow.

Bonacich, Edna, Mokerrom Hossain, and Jae-Hong Park. 1987. Korean immigrant working women in the early 1980s. In *Korean women in transition: At home and abroad,* edited by Eui-Yong Yu and Earl H. Phillips. Los Angeles: California State University Press.

Cho, Hae-Jung. 1988. *Women and men of Korea.* Seoul, Korea: Munhak and Gisung.

Collins, Patricia Hill. 1990. *Black feminist thought.* Boston: Unwin Hyman.

Ferree, Myra Marx. 1979. Employment without liberation: Cuban women in the United States. *Social Science Quarterly* 60:35–50.

Ferree, Myra Marx. 1984. My view from below: Women's employment and gender equality in Working class families. In *Women and the family: Two decades of change,* edited by Beth B. Hess and M. B. Sussman. New York: Haworth.

Ferree, Myra Marx. 1987. The struggles of Superwoman. In *Hidden aspects of women's work,* edited by Christine Bose, Roslyn Feldberg, and Natalie Sokoloff. New York: Praeger.

Gilgun, Jane F., Kerry Daly, and Gerald Handel, eds. 1992. *Qualitative methods in family research.* Newbury Park, CA: Sage.

Glenn, Evelyn Nakano. 1983. Split household, small producer and dual wage earner: An analysis of Chinese-American family strategies. *Journal of Marriage and the Family,* 15:35–46.

Glenn, Evelyn Nakano. 1987. Racial ethnic women's labor: The intersection of race, gender, and class oppression. In *Hidden aspects of women's work,* edited by C. Bose, R. Feldberg, and N. Sokoloff. New York: Praeger.

Haas, Linda. 1987. Wives' orientation toward breadwinning: Sweden and the United States. *Journal of Family Issues* 7:358–8 1.

Hertz, R. 1986. *More equal than others: Men and women in dual-career marriages.* Berkeley: University of California Press.

Hochschild, Arlie, with Anne Machung. 1989. *The second shift.* New York: Avon Books.

Hondagneu-Sotelo, Pierrette. 1992. Overcoming patriarchal constraints: The reconstruction of gender relations among Mexican immigrant women and men. *Gender & Society* 6:393–415.

Hood, Jane C. 1983. *Becoming a two-job family.* New York: Praeger.

Hurh, Won Moo, and Kwang Chung Kim. 1984. *Korean immigrants in America: A structural analysis of ethnic confinement and adhesive adaptation.* Rutherford, NJ: Fairleigh Dickinson University Press.

Kandiyoti, Deniz. 1988. Bargaining with patriarchy. *Gender & Society* 2:274–90.

Kibria, Nazli. 1990. Power, patriarchy, and gender conflict in the Vietnamese immigrant community. *Gender & Society* 4:9–24.

Kim, Ill Soo. 1981. *New urban immigrants: The Korean community in New York.* Princeton, NJ: Princeton University Press.

Komter, Aafe. 1989. Hidden power in marriage. *Gender & Society* 3:187–216.

Korean Survey (Gallup) Polls Ltd. 1987. Life style and value system of housewives in Korea. Seoul, Korea.

Min, Pyong Gap. 1991. Cultural and economic boundaries of Korean ethnicity: A comparative analysis. *Ethnic and Racial Studies* 14:225–41.

Min, Pyong Gap. 1995. Korean Americans. In *Asian American: Contemporary trends and issues,* edited by Pyong Gap Min. Thousand Oaks, CA: Sage.

Pyke, Karen, D. 1994. Women's employment as a gift or burden?: Marital power across marriage, divorce, and remarriage. *Gender & Society* 8:73–91.

Scanzoni, John. 1979. Social process and power in families. In *Contemporary theories about the family,* edited by W. R. Burr, R. Hill, F. I. Nye, and I. L. Reiss. New York: Free Press.

Wallace, Ruth A., and Alison Wolf. 1991. *Contemporary sociological theory: Continuing the classical tradition.* Englewood Cliffs, NJ: Prentice Hall.

Zinn, Maxine Baca. 1990. Family, feminism, and race in America. *Gender & Society* 4:68–82.

Zinn, Maxine Baca, Lyn Weber Cannon, Elizabeth Higginbotham, and Bonnie Thornton Dill. 1986. The costs of exclusionary practices in women's studies. *Signs: Journal of Women in Culture and Society* 11:290–303.

GENDER, CLASS, FAMILY, AND MIGRATION: PUERTO RICAN WOMEN IN CHICAGO— MAURA I. TORO-MORN

References

Acosta-Belen, Edna 1986. *The Puerto Rican woman: Perspectives on culture, history, and society.* New York: Praeger.

Boyd, Monica. 1986. Immigrant women in Canada. In *International Migration: The femal experience,* edited by R. Simon and C. Brettell. Totowa, NJ: Rowman and Allanheld.

Dietz, James L. 1986. *Economic history of Puerto Rico: Institutional change and capitalist development.* Princeton, NJ: Princeton University Press.

Diner, Hasia R. 1983. *Erin's daughters in America: Irish immigrant women in the nineteenth century.* Baltimore: Johns Hopkins University Press.

Ewen, Elizabeth. 1983. *Immigrant women in the land of dollars: Life and culture on the lower east side, 1890–1925.* New York: Monthly Review Press.

Falcon, Luis M. 1990. Migration and development: The case of Puerto Rico. In *Determinants of emigration from Mexico, Central America, and the Caribbean,* edited by S. Diaz-Briquets and S. Weintraub. Boulder, CO: Westview.

Fernandez-Kelly, Maria. 1983. *For we are sold, I and my people: Women and industry in Mexico's frontier.* Albany: State University of New York Press.

Garcia-Castro, Mary. 1985. Women versus life: Colombian women in New York. In *Women and change in Latin America,* edited by J. Nash and H. Safa. South Hadley, MA: Bergin and Garvey.

Glenn, Evelyn N. 1986. *Issei, Nisei, War Bride: Three generations of Japanese women in domestic service.* Philadelphia: Temple University Press.

Glenn, Evelyn N. 1987. Women, labor migration and household work: Japanese American women in the pre-War period. In *Ingredients for women's employment policy,* edited by C. Bose and G. Spitae. Albany: State University of New York Press.

History Task Force. 1979. *Labor migration under capitalism: The Puerto Rican experience.* New York: Monthly Review Press.

Hondagneu-Sotelo, Pierrette. 1992. Overcoming patriarchal constraints: The reconstruction of gender relations among Mexican immigrant women and men. *Gender & Society* 6:393–415.

Juarbe, Ana. 1988. Anaatasia's story: A window into the past, a bridge to the future. *Oral History Review* 16:15–22.

Kibria, N. 1990. Power, patriarchy, and gender conflict in the Vietnamese immigrant community. *Gender & Society* 4:9–24.

Lamphere, Louise. 1987. *From working daughters to working mothers: Immigrant women in a New England industrial community.* Ithaca, NY. Cornell University Press.

Morokvasic, M. 1983. Women in migration: Beyond the reductionist outlook, in *One way ticket: Migration and female labor,* edited by A. Phizacklea. London: Routledge and Kegan Paul.

Pantojas-Garcia, Emilio. 1990. *Development strategies as ideology: Puerto Rico's export-led industrialization experience.* Boulder, CO: Lynne Rienner.

Pedraza, Sylvia. 1991. Women and migration: The social consequences of gender. *Annual Review of Sociology* 17:303–25.

Prieto, Yolanda. 1986. Cuban women and work in the United States: A New Jersey case study. In *International migration: The female experience,* edited by R. Simon and C. Brettell. Totowa, NJ: Rowman and Allanheld.

Rodriguez, Clara. 1989. *Puerto Ricans: Born in the U.S.A.* Boston: Unwin Hyman.

Safa, Helen. 1984. Female employment and the social reproduction of the Puerto Rican working class. *International Migration Review* 18:1168–87.

Sanchez-Ayendez, Melba. 1986. Puerto Rican elderly women: Shared meanings and informal supportive networks. In *All-American women: Lines that divide, ties that bind,* edited by Johnnetta Cole. New York: Free Press.

Sanchez-Korrol, Virginia. 1983. *From colonia to community: The history of Puerto Ricans in New York City, 1917–1948.* Westport, CT: Greenwood.

———. 1986. The forgotten migrant: Educated Puerto Rican women in New York City, 1920–1940. In *The Puerto Rican woman: Perspectives on culture, history and society,* edited by E. Acosta-Belen. New York: Praeger.

Sassen-Koob, S. 1984. Notes on the incorporation of Third World women into wage-labor through immigration and off-shore. *International Migration Review* 18:1144–67.

Simon, Rita, and Caroline Brettell. 1986. *International migration: The female experience.* Totowa, NJ: Rowman and Allanheld.

Simon, Rita, and Margo Corona DeLey. 1986. Undocumented Mexican women: Their work and personal experiences. In *International migration: The female experience,* edited by R. Simon and C. Brettell. Totowa, NJ: Rowman and Allanheld.

Sullivan, Teresa. 1984. The occupational prestige of women immigrants: A comparison of Cubans and Mexicans. *International Migration Review* 18:1045–62.

Tienda, Marta, Leif Jensen, and Robert L. Bach. 1984. Immigration, gender, and the process of occupational change in the United States, 1970–80. International Migration Review 18:1021–43.

Tyree, Andrea, and Katharine Donato. 1986. A demographic overview of the international migration of women. In *International migration: The female experience,* edited by R. Simon and C. Brettell. Totowa, NJ: Rowman and Allanheld.

Weinberg, Sydney Stahl. 1988. *The world of our mothers: The lives of Jewish immigrant women.* New York: Schocken Books.

SHIFTING THE CENTER: RACE, CLASS, AND FEMINIST THEORIZING ABOUT MOTHERHOOD— PATRICIA HILL COLLINS

Notes

1. In this essay, I use the terms "racial ethnic women" and "women of color" interchangeably. Grounded in the experiences of groups who have been the targets of racism, the term "racial ethnic" implies more solidarity with men involved in the struggles against racism. In contrast, the term "women of color" emerges from a feminist background where racial ethnic women committed to feminist struggle aimed to distinguish their history and issues from those of middle-class, white women. Neither term captures the complexity of African-American, Native American, Asian-American and Hispanic women's experiences.

2. Positivist social science exemplifies this type of decontextualization. In order to create scientific descriptions of reality, positivist researchers aim to produce ostensibly objective generalizations. But because researchers have widely differing values, experiences, and emotions, genuine science is thought to be unattainable unless all human characteristics except rationality are eliminated from the research process. By following strict methodological rules, scientists aim to distance themselves from the values, vested interests, and emotions generated by their class, race, sex, or unique situation. By decontextualizing themselves, they allegedly become detached observers and manipulators of nature. Moreover, this researcher decontextualization is paralleled by comparable efforts to re-

move the objects of study from their contexts (Jaggar 1983).

3. Dominant theories are characterized by this decontextualization. Boyd's (1989) helpful survey of literature on the mother-daughter relationship reveals that while much work has been done on motherhood generally, and on the mother-daughter relationship, very little of it tests feminist theories of motherhood. Boyd lists two prevailing theories, psychoanalytic theory and social learning theory, that she claims form the bulk of feminist theorizing. Both of these approaches minimize the importance of race and class in the context of motherhood. Boyd ignores Marxist-feminist theorizing about motherhood, mainly because very little of this work is concerned with the mother-daughter relationship. But Marxist-feminist analyses of motherhood provide another example of how decontextualization frames feminist theories of motherhood. See, for example, Ann Ferguson's *Blood at the Root: Motherhood, Sexuality, and Male Dominance* (1989), an ambitious attempt to develop a universal theory of motherhood that is linked to the social construction of sexuality and male dominance. Ferguson's work stems from a feminist tradition that explores the relationship between motherhood and sexuality by either bemoaning their putative incompatibility or romanticizing maternal sexuality.

4. Psychoanalytic feminist theorizing about motherhood, such as Nancy Chodorow's groundbreaking work, *The Reproduction of Mothering* (1978), exemplifies how decontextualization of race and/or class can weaken what is otherwise strong feminist theorizing. Although I realize that other feminist approaches to motherhood exist, see Eisenstein's (1983) summary for example, I have chosen to stress psychoanalytic feminist theory because the work of Chodorow and others has been highly influential in framing the predominant themes in feminist discourse.

5. The thesis of the atomized individual that underlies Western psychology is rooted in a much larger Western construct concerning the relation of the individual to the community (Hartsock 1983). Theories of motherhood based on the assumption of the atomized human proceed to use this definition of individual as the unit of analysis, and then construct theory from this base. From this grow assumptions based on the premise that the major process to examine is one between freely choosing rational individuals engaging in bargains (Hartsock 1983).

6. The narrative tradition in the writings of women of color addresses this effort to recover the history of mothers. Works from African-American women's autobiographical tradition, such as Ann Moody's *Coming of Age in Mississippi*, Maya Angelou's *I Know Why the Caged Bird Sings*, Linda Brent's *Narrative in the Life of a Slave Girl*, and Marita Golden's *the Heart of a Woman* contain the authentic voices of Black women centered on experiences of motherhood. Works from African-American women's fiction include Sarah Wright's *This Child's Gonna Live*, Alice Walker's *Meridian*, and Toni Morrison's *Sula* and *Beloved*. Asian-American women's fiction, such as Amy Tan's *The Joy Luck Club* and Maxine Kingston's *Woman Warrior*, and autobiographies such as Jean Wakatusi Houston's *Farewell to Manzanar* offer a parallel source of authentic voice. Connie Young Yu (1989) entitles her article on the history of Asian-American women "The World of Our Grandmothers," and proceeds to recreate Asian-American history with her grandmother as a central figure. Cherrie Moraga (1979) writes a letter to her mother as a way of coming to terms with the contradictions of her racial identity as a Chicana. In *Borderlands/La Frontera*, Gloria Anzaldua (1987) weaves autobiography, poetry and philosophy together in her exploration of women and mothering.

7. Notable examples include Lutie Johnson's unsuccessful attempt to rescue her son from the harmful effects of an urban environment in Ann Petry's *The Street;* and Meridian's work on behalf of the children of a small Southern town after she chooses to relinquish her own child, in Alice Walker's *Meridian.*

8. Noticeably absent from feminist theories of motherhood is a comprehensive theory of power and explanation of how power relations shape theories. Firmly rooted in an exchange-based marketplace, with its accompanying assumptions of rational economic decision-making and white, male control of the marketplace, this model of community stresses the rights of individuals, including feminist theorists, to make decisions in their own self-interests, regardless of the impact on larger society. Composed of a collection of unequal individuals who compete for greater shares of money as the medium of exchange, this model community legitimates relations of domination by denying they exist or by treating them as inevitable but unimportant (Hartsock, 1983).

References

Allen, Paula Gunn. 1986. *The Sacred Hoop: Recovering the Feminine in American Indian Traditions.* Boston: Beacon.

Andersen, Margaret. 1988. "Moving Our Minds: Studying Women of Color and Reconstructing Sociology." *Teaching Sociology* 16 (2), pp. 123–132.

Anzaldua, Gloria. 1987. *Borderlands/La Frontera: The New Mestiza.* San Francisco: Spinsters.

Awiakta, Marilou. 1988. "Amazons in Appalchia." In Beth Brant, ed., *A Gathering of Spirit.* Ithaca, NY: Firebrand, pp. 125–130.

Boyd, Carol J. 1989. "Mothers and Daughters: A Discussion of Theory and Research." *Journal of Marriage and the Family* 51, pp. 291–301.

Brant, Beth, ed. 1988. *A Gathering of Spirit: A Collection by North American Indian Women.* Ithaca, NY: Firebrand.

Brown, Elsa Barkley, 1989. "African-American Women's Quilting: A Framework for Conceptualizing and Teaching African-American Women's History." *Signs* 14(4), pp. 921–929.

Chodorow, Nancy. 1978. *The Reproduction of Mothering.* Berkeley, CA: University of California Press.

———, and Susan Contratto. 1982. "The Fantasy of the Perfect Mother." In Barrie Thorne and Marilyn Yalom, eds., *Rethinking the Family: Some Feminist Questions.* New York: Longman, pp. 54–75.

Coleman, Willi. 1987. "Closets and Keepsakes." *Sage: A Scholarly Journal on Black Women* 4 (2), pp. 34–35.

Collins, Patricia Hill. 1990. *Black Feminist Thought: Knowledge, Consciousness and the Politics of Empowerment.* New York: Unwin Hyman//Routledge.

de la Cruz, Jessie. 1980. "Interview." In Studs Terkel, ed., *American Dreams: Lost and Found.* New York: Ballantine.

Davis, Angela Y. 1981. *Women, Race, and Class.* New York: Random House.

Dill, Bonnie Thornton. 1988. "Our Mothers' Grief: Racial Ethnic Women and the Maintenance of Families." *Journal of Family History* 13 (4), pp. 415–431.

Eisenstein, Hester. 1983. *Contemporary Feminist Thought.* Boston: G. K. Hall.

Ferguson, Ann. 1989. *Blood at the Root: Motherhood, Sexuality, and Male Dominance.* New York: Unwin Hyman/Routledge.

Flax, Jane. 1978. "The Conflict between Nurturance and Autonomy in Mother-Daughter Relationships and within Feminism." *Feminist Studies* 4 (2), pp. 171–189.

Glenn, Evelyn Nakano. 1985. "Racial Ethnic Women's Labor: The Intersection of Race,

Gender and Class Oppression." *Review of Radical Political Economics* 17 (3), pp. 86–108.

————. 1986. *Issei, Nisei, War Bride: Three Generations of Japanese American Women in Domestic Service.* Philadelphia: Temple University Press.

Green, Rayna. 1990. "The Pocahontas Perplex: The Image of Indian Women in American Culture." In Ellen Carol Dubois and Vicki Ruiz, eds., *Unequal Sisters.* New York: Routledge, pp. 15–21.

Hartsock, Nancy. 1983. *Money, Sex and Power.* Boston: Northeastern University Press.

Jordan, June. 1985. *On Call.* Boston: South End Press.

LaDuke, Winona. 1988. "They always come back." In Beth Brant, ed., *A Gathering of Spirit.* Ithaca, New York: Firebrand, pp. 62–67.

Lerner, Gerda. 1972. *Black Women in White America.* New York: Pantheon.

Moraga, Cherrie. 1979. "La Guera." In Cherrie Moraga and Gloria Anzaldua, eds., *This Bridge Called My Back: Writings by Radical Women of Color.* Watertown, MA: Persephone Press, pp. 27–34.

Noda, Kesaya E. 1989. "Growing Up Asian in American." In Asian Women United of California, eds., *Making Waves: An Anthology of Writings By and About Asian American Women.* Boston: Beacon, pp. 243–50.

Rich, Adrienne. 1986 [1976]. *Of Women Born: Motherhood as Institution and Experience.* New York: W. W. Norton.

Shanley, Kate. 1988. "Thoughts on Indian Feminism." In Beth Brant, ed., *A Gathering of Spirit.* Ithaca, NY: Firebrand, pp. 213–215.

Smith, Dorothy E. 1990. *The Conceptual Practices of Power: A Feminist Sociology of Knowledge.* Boston: Northeastern University Press.

Spelman, Elizabeth V. 1988. *Inessential Woman: Problems of Exclusion in Feminist Thought.* Boston: Beacon Press.

Tajima, Renee E. 1989. "Lotus Blossoms Don't Bleed: Images of Asian Women." In *Asian Women United of California, eds., Making Waves: An Anthology of Writings by and about Asian American Women.* Boston: Beacon, pp. 308–317.

Terborg-Penn, Rosalyn. 1986. "Black Women in Resistance: A Cross-Cultural Perspective." In Gary Y. Okhiro, ed., *In Resistance: Studies in African, Caribbean and Afro-American History.* Amherst: University of Massachusetts Press, pp. 188–209.

Wright, Sarah. 1986. *This Child's Gonna Live.* Old Westbury, NY: Feminist Press.

Yamoto, Jenny. 1988. "Mixed Bloods, Half Breeds, Mongrels, Hybrids…" In Jo Whitehorse Cochran, Donna Langston and Carolyn Woodward, eds., *Changing Our Power: An Introduction to Women's Studies.* Dubuque, IA: Kendall/Hunt, pp. 22–24.

Yu, Connie Young. 1989. "The World of Our Grandmothers." In Asian Women United of California, eds., *Making Waves: An Anthology of Writings by and about Asian American Women.* Boston: Beacon, pp. 33–41.

BLACK TEENAGE MOTHERS AND THEIR DAUGHTERS: THE IMPACT OF ADOLESCENT CHILDBEARING ON DAUGHTERS' RELATIONS WITH MOTHERS— ELAINE BELL KAPLAN

Notes

1. The mothers of teen mothers (including those who themselves were teenage mothers) will be referred to as adult mothers.

References

Allen, Lind, and Darlene Britt
1984 "Black women in American society." In *Social Psychological Problems of Women,* eds. A. G. Rickel, M. Gerrard, and I. Iscoe, 33–47. New York: Hemisphere.

Apfel, Nancy. H., and Victoria Seitz
1991 "Four models of adolescent mother-grandmother relationships in Black inner-city families." *Family Relations* 40:421–429.

Bell Kaplan, Elaine
Forthcoming *'Not Our Kind of Girl:' Black Teenage Motherhood: Realities Hiding Behind the Myths.* University of California Press, June 1997.

Brewer, Rose
1995 "Gender, poverty, culture, and economy: Theorizing female-led families." In *African American Single Mothers,* ed. Bette J. Dickerson, 164–178. Beverly Hills, Calif.: Sage, Inc.

Burton, Linda M., and Vern L. Bengston
1985 "Black grandmothers." In *Grand Parenthood,* eds. Vern Bengston and J. Roberston, 75–110. Beverly Hills, Calif.: Sage, Inc.

Collins, Patricia H.
1987 "The meaning of motherhood." Sage 2:32–46.
1990 *Black Feminist Thought.* New York: Routledge.

Elliott, Marta, and Lauren J. Krivo
1991 "Structural determinants of homelessness in the United States." *Social Problems* 38:113–131.

Fischer, Lucy R.
1986 *Linked Lives.* New York: Harper & Row.

Furstenberg, Frank, Jr.
1980 "Burdens and benefits." *Journal of Social Issues* 36:64–87.

George, Susan M., and Bette J. Dickerson
1995 "The role of the grandmother in poor single-mother families and households." In *African American Single Mothers,* ed. Bette I. Dickerson, 146–163. Beverly Hills, Calif.: Sage.

Geronimus, Arline T.
1990 "Teenage birth's new conceptions." *Insight* 30:11–13.

Gilligan, Carol
1990 In *Making Connections,* eds. Carol Gilligan, Nona P. Lyons, and Trudy J. Hanmer, 6–29. Cambridge: Harvard University Press.

Goffman, Erving
1963 *Stigma.* Englewood Cliffs, NJ.: Prentice-Hall, Inc.

Hardy, Janet B., and Laurie S. Zabin
1991 *Adolescent Pregnancy in an Urban Environment.* Washington, D.C. The Urban Institute.

Ladner, Joyce, and Ruby M. Gourdine
1984 "Intergenerational teenage motherhood." Sage 1:22–24.

MacLeod Jay
1987 *Ain't No Makin' It.* Boulder, Colo.: Westview Press.

Mayfield, Lorraine P.
1994 "Early parenthood among low-income adolescent girls." In *Black Family, 4th Edition,* ed. Robert Staples, 230–242. Belmont, Calif.: Wadsworth Publishing Co.

McGrory, Mary
1994 "What to do about parents of illegitimate children." *The Washington Post,* February 15:25.

Mills, C. Wright
1956 *The Sociological Imagination.* New York: Oxford University Press.

Moynihan, Daniel P.
1965 *The Negro Family: The Case for National Action.* U.S. Department of Labor: Washington, D.C.

Musick Judith S.

1987 "The high-stakes challenge of programs for adolescent mothers." A report for the Ounce of Prevention Fund, 1–4. Chicago, Ill.: Department of Children and Family Services.

Myers Wright, Lena

1980 *Black Women: Do They Cope Better?* Englewood Cliffs, NJ.: Prentice-Hall.

Oakland City Council Report

1988 "Women and children in Oakland, September, 1988." Unpublished report.

Reinharz, Shulamit

1992 *Feminist Methods in Social Research.* New York: Oxford University Press.

Rich, Sharon

1990 "Daughters' views of their relationships with their mothers." In *Making Connections,* eds. Carol Gilligan, Nona P. Lyons, and Trudy J. Hanmer, 258–273. Cambridge: Harvard University Press

Rogers Earline, and Sally H. Lee

1992 "A comparison of the perceptions of the mother-daughter relationship: Black pregnant and nonpregnant teenagers." *Adolescence* 107:554–564.

Russo, Nancy F.

1976 "The motherhood mandate." *Journal of Social Issues* 32:143–153.

Stack, Carol

1974 *All Our Kin.* New York: Random House.

Staples, Robert

1994 "The family." In *The Black Family,* ed. Robert Staples, 1–3. Belmont, Calif.: Wadworth.

Stokes, Randall, and John P. Hewitt

1976 "Aligning actions." *American Sociological Review* 41:838–849.

Wilson, William J.

1987 *The Truly Disadvantaged.* Chicago: University of Chicago Press.

NONFAMILY LIVING IN CONTEXT: HOUSEHOLDS, THE LIFE COURSE, AND FAMILY VALUES—FRANCES K. GOLDSCHEIDER AND CALVIN GOLDSCHEIDER

Notes

1. Although the possibility exists, and perhaps should be fostered, that young adults could live with their parents in an interdependent relationship of mutual agreement and respect, few we have mentioned this to consider it feasible, either ever or at least until the child is well past the teenage years.

2. The predecessor data set to HSB, NLS72 (the National Longitudinal Study of the High School Class of 1972) obtained *no* information from the parents of students or from the students about their parents' marital statuses until the reinterview of 1986, 14 years after the original interviews and after most studies of the transition to adulthood had moved on to more recent cohorts of young adults.

3. This result may parallel those of fertility expectations, which are much more likely to be accurate when asked of married than of unmarried women (see the studies in Hendershot and Placek 1981).

4. Religiosity may be influenced by nonfamily living as well as influencing it.

5. It was also the case that the measure of parental contributions was obtained several months *after* the measures from which we constructed expectations for nonfamily living, so without parental communication, they had no idea whether such support would be forthcoming.

6. When we refer to a "strong" family structure, we do not mean that this is an unambiguously "good thing." Under many circumstances, strong families can seriously inhibit the independence of some or all of their members. However,

they can also provide the support their members need to achieve many of their personal goals.

7. Like all cross-sectional inferences, of course, this interpretation could be in error if the Cubans who arrived in the United States at an earlier point, that is, whose high school age children have American-born parents, were very different from the more recent streams of Cuban immigration.

8. Islam may be overtaking Judaism as the "third" largest religion in many portions of the country, but the Jews are clearly ahead in terms of current strength of community and political institutions. Moslems and Mormons, another rapidly growing group, appear in our data as part of the residual "other" religion category. Despite their heterogeneity, members of this group tend to have nonfamily living patterns very similar to Protestant fundamentalists.

9. Of course, those who argue this way tend to ignore the ways in which family roles are, in fact, more important for men than for women, such as for their mental and physical health and survival (Kisker and Goldman 1987; Riessman and Gerstel 1985; Kobrin and Hendershot 1977).

References

Alba, Richard. 1990. "Social assimilation among American Catholic national origin groups." *American Sociological Review* 48: 240–247.

Easterlin, Richard, C. Macdonald, D. Macunovich, E. Crimmins, 1992. "Causes of the change in intergenerational living arrangements of elderly widows in the United States." Paper presented at the Conference on Intergenerational Relations, RAND Corporation, Santa Monica, Calif.

Goldscheider, Calvin. 1986. *Jewish Continuity and Change: Emerging Patterns in America.* Bloomington, Indiana University Press.

Goldscheider, Calvin, and W. Mosher. 1988. "Religious affiliation and contraceptive us-age: Changing American patterns, 1955–82." *Studies in Family Planning* 19:48–57.

Goldscheider, Frances, and J. DaVanzo. 1985. "Living arrangements and transition to adulthood." *Demography* 22:545–563.

Goldscheider, Frances, and C. Goldscheider. 1989. "Family structure and conflict: Nest-leaving expectations of young adults and their parents." *Journal of Marriage and the Family* 51:87–97.

Goldscheider, Frances K., and L. Waite. 1991. *New Families, No Families? The Transformation of the American Home.* Berkeley, University of California Press.

Greeley, Andrew, 1989. "Protestant and Catholic: Is the analogical imagination extinct?" *American Sociological Review* 54:485–502.

Hendershot, Gerry, and P. Placek, eds. 1981. *Predicting Fertility: Demographic Studies of Birth Expectations.* Lexington, Mass.: Lexington Books.

Jones, Elise, and C. Westoff. 1979. "The end of 'Catholic' fertility." *Demography* 16:209–217.

Kennedy, Robert. 1972. *The Irish.* Berkeley: University of California Press.

Kisker, Ellen, and N. Goldman. 1987. "Perils of single life and benefits of marriage." *Social Biology* 34:135–140.

Kobrin, Frances E., and C. Goldscheider. 1978, *The Ethnic Factor in Family Structure and Mobility,* Cambridge, Mass.: Ballinger.

Kobrin, Frances E., and G. Hendershot. 1977. "Do family ties reduce mortality? Evidence from the United States, 1966–1968." *Journal of Marriage and the Family* 39:737–745.

Levy, Frank. 1997. *Dollars and Dreams: The Changing American Income Distribution.* New York: Russell Sage Foundation.

Light, Ivan, and E. Bonacich. 1988. *Immigrant Entrepreneurs.* Berkeley: University of California Press.

Riessman, Catherine, and N. Gerstl. 1985. "Marital dissolution and health: Do males or females have greater risk?" *Social Science and Medicine* 20:624–630.

Waldinger, Roger, H. Aldrich, and R. Ward. 1990. *Ethnic Entrepreneurs.* Beverly Hills, Calif.: Sage.

INTIMATE STRANGERS: THE ELDERLY AND HOME-CARE WORKER RELATIONSHIPS— MARK HUTTER

Notes

1. All names have been changed to preserve anonymity.

References

Brody, Elaine M. 1990. *Women in the Middle: Their Parent-Care Years.* New York: Springer.

Brody, Elaine M., S. J. Litvin, C. Hoffman, and M. H. Kleban. 1992. Differential effects of daughters' marital status on their parent care experiences. *The Gerontologist* 32(1): 58–67.

Cherlin, Andrew, and Frank F. Furstenberg, Jr. 1986. *The New American Grandparent: A Place in the Family, A Life Apart.* New York: Basic Books.

Conover, Ted. 1997. "The last best friends money can buy." *The New York Times Magazine.* November 30: 124–130, 132, 144, 147, 148, 150, 152.

Davis, L. L. 1992. "Building a science of caring for caregivers." *Family and Community Health* 15(2): 1–9.

Gans, Herbert. 1962. *The Urban Villagers: Group and Class in the Life of Italian-Americans.* New York: The Free Press.

Gelman, David, with Pamela Abramson, George Raine, Peter McAlvey, and Peter McKillop.

1985. "Who's taking care of our parents?" *Newsweek* (May 6):61–68.

Karner, Tracy X. 1998. "Professional caring: Homecare workers as fictive kin." *Journal of Aging Studies* 12(1): 69–82.

Litvin, Sandra J. 1992. "Status transitions and future outlooks as determinants of conflict: The caregiver's and care receiver's perspective." *The Gerontologist* 32(1): 68–76.

Lofland, Lyn H. 1992. "Love and human connection." Pp. 161–178 in Candace Clark and Howard Robboy (eds.), *Social Interaction: Readings in Sociology* Fourth Edition. New York: St. Martin's Press.

Lopata, Helena Z. 1969. "Loneliness: Forms and Components." *Social Problems* 17:248–261.

Marrone, Robert. 1996. *Death, Mourning, and Caring.* Pacific Grove, CA: Brooks/Cole Publishing.

Newsweek. 1990. "Trading Places." (July 16).

Newsweek. 1997. "Caring from afar." (September 22): 87–88.

Rosow, Irving. 1976. "Status and role change through the life span." In R.H. Binstock and E. Shanas (eds.), *Handbook of Aging and the Social Sciences* (pp. 229–234). New York: Van Nostrand.

Shanas, Ethel. 1980. "Older people and their families: The new pioneers." *Journal of Marriage and the Family.* 42(1): 9–15.

Thorson, James A. 1995. *Aging in a Changing Society.* Belmont, CA: Wadsworth Publishing Company.

THE VICTIMIZED SELF: THE CASE OF BATTERED WOMEN— JOHN M. JOHNSON AND KATHLEEN J. FERRARO

Notes

1. We owe a debt of gratitude to David Altheide, Paul Higgins, Mildred Daley Pagelow, and

Carol A. B. Warren for comments on an earlier draft of this paper.

2. Data for our respective researches have been gained from direct field observations, depth interviewing, various kinds of official documents, and surveys. More details on the data collection and analyses are to be found in Johnson (1975, 1981) and Ferraro (1979a, 1979b, 1981). An important resource for the research was the personal experience of the authors as cofounders and early leaders (1977–79) of an Arizona shelter for battered women.

References

Davidson, Terry. 1978. *Conjugal Crime.* New York: Hawthorn.

Ferraro, Kathleen J. 1979a. "Hard Love: Letting Go of an Abusive Husband." *Frontiers* 4(2):16–18.

———. 1979b. "Physical and Emotional Battering." *California Sociologist* 2(2):134–49.

———. 1981. "Battered Women and the Shelter Movement." Ph.D. dissertation, Department of Sociology, Arizona State University.

———. 1982. "Rationalizing Violence." Unpublished paper.

Gelles, Richard J. 1976. "Abused Wives: Why Do They Stay?" *Journal of Marriage and the Family* 38:659–68.

Hughes, Everett C. 1958. *Men and Their Work.* New York: Free Press.

Johnson, John M. 1975. *Doing Field Research.* New York: Free Press.

———. 1981. "Program Enterprise and Official Cooptation of the Battered Women's Shelter Movement." *American Behavioral Scientist* 24:827–42.

Martin, Del. 1976. *Battered Wives.* San Francisco, CA: Glide.

Pagelow, Mildred Daley. 1981. *Women-Battering.* Beverly Hills, CA: Sage.

Rasmussen, Paul K. and Kathleen J. Ferraro. 1979. "The Divorce Process." *Journal of Alternative Lifestyles* 2:443–60.

Roy, Maria (ed.). 1977. *Battered Women.* New York: Van Nostrand.

Walker, Lenore E. 1979. *The Battered Woman.* New York: Harper and Row.

TEN MYTHS THAT PERPETUATE CORPORAL PUNISHMENT— MURRAY A. STRAUS

Notes

1. The average age is eight because almost no one remembers anything specific about what happened at ages two and three the actual peak years for corporal punishment... Even at age eight, memory for specific details is poor. So the figure of an average of six times is almost certainly much lower than the actual number of times these students were hit when they were eight years old.

2. Charts 22–1 and 22–2 are based on data from Sears, Maccoby, and Levin (1957).

References

Alvy, Kirby T., and Marilyn Marigna. 1987. *Effective Black Parenting.* Studio City, CA: Center For the Improvement of Child Caring.

Bavolek, Stephen J. 1992. *The Nurturing Programs.* City Utah: Family Development Resources.

Calvert, Robert. 1974. "Criminal and Civil Liability in Husband-Wife Assaults." Chapter 9 in *Violence in the Family,* edited by S. K. Steinmetz and M. A. Straus. New York: Harper and Row.

Crozier, Jill and Roger C. Katz. 1979. "Social Learning Treatment of Child Abuse." *Journal of Abnormal Child Psychology.* 10: 213–20.

Day, Dan E. and Mark W. Roberts. 1983. "An analysis of the Physical Punishment Component of a Parent Training Program." *Journal of Abnormal Child Psychology* 11:141–52.

Deley, Warren W. 1988. "Physical Punishment of Children: Sweden and the USA." *Journal of Comparative Family Studies.* 19:419–31.

Dinkmeyer Sr., Don and Gary D. McKay. 1989. *Systematic Training for Effective Parenting.* Circle Pines, MN: American Guidance Service.

Gordon, Thomas. 1975. *Parent Effectiveness Training.* New York: New American Library.

Haeuser, Adrienne A. 1988. *Reducing Violence Towards U.S. Children: Transferring Positive Innovations from Sweden.* Milwaukee WI: Department of Social Welfare, University of Wisconsin, Milwaukee.

Higgins, E. Tory and John A. Bargh. 1987. "Social Cognitions and Social Perception." *Annual Review of Psychology* 38:369–425.

Hirschi, Travis. 1969. *The Causes of Delinquency.* Berkeley and Los Angeles: University of California Press.

Kadushin, Alfred and Judith A. Martin. 1981. *Child Abuse: An Interactional Event.* New York: Columbia University Press.

Larzelere, Robert E. 1986. "Moderate Spanking: Model or Deterrent of Children's Aggression in the Family?" *Journal of Family Violence* 1–27–36.

Larzelere, Robert E. 1994. "Empirically Justified Uses of Spanking: Toward a Discriminating View of Corporal Punishment." *Journal of Psychology and Theology.*

LaVoie, Joseph C. 1974. "Type of Punishment as a Determination of Resistance To Deviation." *Developmental Psychology.* 10: 181–189.

Matteson, Margaret E., Earl S. Pollack, and Joseph W. Cullen. 1987. "What Are the Odds that Smoking Will Kill You?" *American Journal of Public Health* 77:425–31.

Newson, John and Elizabeth Newson. 1963. *Patterns of Infant Care in an Urban Community.* Baltimore: Penguin Books.

Patterson, Gerald R. 1982. "A Social Learning Approach to Family Intervention." *Coercive Family Process.* Eugene, OR: Castalia.

Reed, William H., Edward K. Morris and Jerry A. Martin. 1975. "Effects of Positive and Negative Adult-Child Interactions on Children's Social Preference." *Journal of Experimental Child Psychology* 19:153–164.

Rosemond, John K. 1981. *Parent Power: A Common Sense Approach to Raising Your Children in the '80s.* Charlotte, NC: East Woods Press.

Sears, Robert R., Eleanor C. Maccoby, and Harry Levin. 1957. *Patterns of Child Rearing.* Evanston, IL: Row, Peterson, and Company.

Stern, Daniel. 1977. *The First Relationship: Mother and Infant.* Cambridge, MA: Harvard University Press.

Tannatt, Lupita Montoya and Kirby T. Alvy. 1989. *Los Ninos Bien Educados Program.* Studio City, CA: Center for the Improvement of Child Caring.

Webster-Stratton, Carolyn, Mary Kolpcoff, and Terri Hollinsworth. 1988. "Self-Administered Videotape Therapy for Families with Conduct-Problem Children: Comparison with Two Cost-Effective Treatments and a Control Group." *Journal of Consulting and Clinical Psychology* 56:558–66.

Webster-Stratton, Carolyn. 1990. "Enhancing the Effectiveness of Self-Administered Videotape Parent Training for Families with Conduct-Problem Children." *Journal Abnormal Child Psychology* 18:479–92.

THE SOCIAL SELF AS GENDERED: A MASCULINIST DISCOURSE OF DIVORCE— TERRY ARENDELL

Notes

1. Although still largely untapped in this regard, the paradigm of human behavior offered by the tradition of symbolic interaction offers rich ground for theoretical exploration of gender relations and gender identity, its acquisition and alteration. Perinbanayagam—in his contemporary works which seek to develop "a workable synthesis of various perspectives on language, self, and action" (Perinbanayagam 1985b, p. xv) and which newly "locate a theoretical tradition," that is, symbolic interaction (Davis 1985, p. ix)—briefly acknowledges the engenderment of identity in his broad treatment of human agency:

> "A self then has an identity as well as a disidentity, albeit an implicit one most of the time. The identity is *to begin with* [italics mine] based on gender: boys and girls have to be helped to identify their own categories and identify with them as well" (Perinbanayagam 1985a, pp. 318–319).

The concept of *program,* especially as elaborated by Perinbanayagam (1985) has particular salience for investigation of gender identity.

2. Because these fathers saw themselves as having integrated masculine and feminine traits and behaviors in their adjustments to the postdivorce situation, the term "androgynous" is used to characterize them. According to Lindsay (1990, p. 13), "The concept of *androgyny* refers to the investigation of characteristics defined as feminine with those defined as masculine. A new model emerges which maintains that it is possible, and desirable, for people to express both masculine and feminine qualities since they exist in varying degrees within each of us anyway [Bem, 1974; 1975; Kaplan and Bean, 1976]. Androgyny allows for flexibility in the statuses we possess and gives us greater adaptability to the variety of situations we must confront. Ideally, androgyny eliminates the restrictions imposed by gender roles and increases opportunities to develop to our fullest potential. Although the concept of androgyny has been criticized for its ambiguity and lack of definitional rigor [Trebilcot, 1977; Locksley and Colten, 1979; Morgan, 1982a], it at least provides an alternative to images of men and women based on traditional gender roles." See also Deaux and Kite (1987).

3. That most of the participants readily asserted that the superiority of their perceptions and definitions gave them the prerogative to dismiss the wife's point of view is consistent with various theoretical arguments regarding the effects of stratification and differential socialization on interactions (Chodorow 1978; Harding 1983; and Gilligan 1982). Glenn (1987, p. 356), for example, noted:

> "It can be readily observed in a variety of situations that subordinates (women, servants, racial minorities) must be more sensitive to and responsive to the point of view of superordinates (men, masters, dominant racial groups) than the other way around."

4. Goffman (1975, p. 5), for example, early on observed that "ritually speaking, females are equivalent to subordinate males and both are equivalent to children" in depictions of gender in advertisements. He suggested that relations between men and women are based on the parent–child complex.

5. For a relevant analysis of gender division of labor in families which uses the meso domain or mesostructural approach, see Pestello and Voyandoff (1991). Although not utilized, the

meso domain or mesostructural approach could be applied to the data obtained in this study; see, for example Maines (1979; 1982) and Hall (1987; 1991).

6. The recently implemented New York State Child Support Standards Act of 1989 (referred to usually by the fathers in the study as the new Child Support Guidelines) was held almost unanimously by these fathers to be grossly unjust and biased against non-custodial parents, primarily fathers; the extensive media coverage given to the Support Guidelines had reinforced many men's sense of being victimized by divorce. Moreover, according to the men in the study, the New York State Child Support Standards Act leads fathers to conclude that they should seek sole custody in order to avoid paying the mandated levels of child support.

7. That children are a form of property which belongs to the father who then is granted custody at the time of separation or divorce has a long history: "This was an unequivocal paternal right" (Polikoff 1983). Even though traditional "father right" has undergone considerable challenge and change, contemporary divorce law and procedures tend to reinforce the stance that children are objects over which to be fought.

8. Despite efforts in every state over the course of the last two decades to reform divorce law and to reduce the level of acrimony involved, the adversarial approach to adjudicating matters of child custody, child support and spousal maintenance, and property settlements persists (Weitzman 1985; Emery 1988). Marcus (1989) details the divorce law reforms in New York State specifically.

9. I am using the term *parenting partnership* rather than shared parenting or co-parents because it suggests a greater flexibility than do the other two terms. An array of types of parenting partnerships is available. For example, divorced parents could choose and develop a distant partnership in which the parents have relatively infrequent communication between them. Most probably, such a parenting partnership would be one in which one parent does most of the childcare and childrearing, even if the other sees the children regularly. On the other hand, the partnership could be a tight-knit and even friendly one in which the parents routinely and frequently communicate about a range of issues concerning their children. Most typically, but not exclusively, in this kind of parenting partnership arrangement both parents would be highly involved in the caring and rearing of their children, even to the point of sharing parental responsibilities equally as was the case for several of the participants in the study who had negotiated and developed such postdivorce partnerships with their former wives. Those worked out by the participants in the present study were flexible arrangements and had been privately, not legally, negotiated and worked out. The term is also more appropriate for the postdivorce situation than shared parenting or co-parents because the latter are commonly used in reference to parenting activities done in the context of marriage.

References

Arendell, Terry. 1986. *Mothers and Divorce: Legal, Economic and Social Dilemmas.* Berkeley: University of California Press.

———. 1992. "After Divorce: Investigations into Father Absence." *Gender & Society.* December, forthcoming.

———. Forthcoming. *Fathers and Divorce* (Tentative title). Berkeley: University of California Press.

Bernard, Jessie. 1981. "The Good-Provider Role: Its Rise and Fall." *American Psychologist* 36:1–12.

Berger, Peter and H. Kellner. 1964. "Marriage and the Social Construction of Reality." *Diogenes* 46:1–25.

Blumer, Herbert. 1969. *Symbolic Interactionism: Perspective and Method.* Englewood Cliffs, NJ: Prentice-Hall.

Bordo, Susan. 1990. "Feminism, Postmodernism, and Gender-Scepticism." Pp. 147–159 in *Feminism/Postmodernism,* edited by Linda J. Nicholson. New York: Routledge.

Bourdieu, Pierre. 1987. *Outline of a Theory of Practice.* Cambridge: Cambridge University Press.

Broverman, I., M. Broverman, F. Clarkson, P. Rosenkrantz, and S. Vogel. 1970. "Sex-Role Stereotypes and Clinical Judgments of Mental Health." Journal of Consulting and Clinical Psychology 34:1–7.

Cancian, Francesca. 1987. *Love in America: Gender and Self Development.* New York: Cambridge University Press.

Chodorow, Nancy. 1978. *The Reproduction of Mothering.* Berkeley: University of California.

Clatterbaugh, Kenneth. 1990. *Contempory Perspectives on Masculinity: Men, Women and Politics in Modern Society.* Boulder, CO: Westview Press.

Cohen, Theodore. 1989. "Becoming and Being Husbands and Fathers: Work and Family Conflict for Men." Pp. 220–234 in *Gender in Intimate Relationships: A Microstructural Approach,* edited by Barbara J. Risman and Pepper Schwartz. Belmont, CA: Wadsworth Publishing Company.

Coltrane, Scott. 1989. "Household Labor and the Routine Production of Gender." *Social Problems* 36:473–490.

Cooley, Charles. 1981. "Self as Sentiment and Reflection." Pp. 169–174 in *Social Psychology Through Symbolic Interaction* (2nd edition), edited by Gregory Stone and Harvey Farberman. New York: John Wiley and Sons.

Daniels, Arlene Kaplan. 1987. "Invisible Work." *Social Problems* 34:403–415.

Davis, Fred. 1985. "Foreword." Pp. ix–xi in *Signing Acts: Structure and Meaning in Everyday Life,* by Robert Perinbanayagam. Carbondale: Southern Illinois University Press.

Deaux, Kay and Mary E. Kite. 1987. "Thinking About Gender." Pp. 92–177, in *Thinking About Gender: A Handbook of Social Science Research.* Newbury Park, CA: Sage Publications.

Emery, Robert. 1988. *Marriage, Divorce, and Children's Adjustment.* Newbury Park, CA: Sage Publications.

Family Law of the State of New York. 1990. Flushing, NY: Looseleaf Law Publications.

Flax, Jane. 1989. "Postmodernism and Gender Relations in Feminist Theory. Pp. 51–74 in *Feminist Theory in Practice and Process,* edited by Micheline Maslon, Jean O'Barr, Sarah Westphal-Wihl, and Mary Wyer. Chicago: The University of Chicago Press.

Folberg, Jay and Ann Milne. 1988. *Divorce Mediation: Theory and Practice.* New York: Guilford Press.

Foote, Nelson. 1981. "Identification as the Basis for a Theory of Motivation." Pp. 333–342 in *Social Psychology Through Symbolic Interaction* (2nd edition), edited by Gregory Stone and Harvey Farberman. New York: John Wiley and Sons.

Furstenberg, Frank. 1988. Good Dads-Bad Dads: Two Faces of Fatherhood. Pp. 193–207 in *The Changing American Family and Public Policy,* edited by Andrew Cherlin. Washington, DC: Urban Institute.

Furstenberg, Frank, S. Philip Morgan, and Paul Allison. 1987. "Parental Participation and Children's Well-Being After Marital Dissolution." *American Sociological Review* 52:695–701.

Gilligan, Carol. 1982. *In a Different Voice: Psychological Theory and Women's Develop-*

ment. Cambridge: Harvard University Press.

Glaser, Barney and Anselm Strauss. 1967. *The Discovery of Grounded Theory.* New York: Aldine.

Glenn, Evelyn Nakano. 1987. "Gender and the Family." Pp. 348–380 in *Analyzing Gender,* edited by Beth Hess and Myra Marx Ferre. Beverly Hills: Sage Publications.

Goffman, Erving. 1975. *Gender Advertisements.* New York: Harper and Row.

Hall, Peter. 1987. "Interactionism and the Study of Social Organization." *The Sociological Quarterly* 28:1–22.

———. 1991. "in Search of the Meso Domain: Commentary on the Contributions of Pestello and Voydanoff." *Symbolic Interaction* 14(2):129–134.

Harding, Sandra. 1983. "Why Has the Sex/Gender System Become Visible Only Now?" Pp. 311–324 in *Discovering Reality: Feminist Perspectives on Epistemology, Metaphysics, Methodology, and Philosophy of Science,* edited by Sandra Harding and Merrill Hintikka. Dordrecht, Holland: D. Reidel Publishing.

Hearn, Jeff. 1987. *The Gender of Oppression: Men, Masculinity and the Critique of Marxism.* New York. St. Martin's Press.

Hetherington, Elizabeth, Mavis Cox, and Richard Cox. 1976. "Divorced Fathers." *The Family Coordinator* 25:417–428.

Hochschild, Arlie. R. 1983. *The Managed Heart: Commercialization of Human Feeling.* Berkeley: University of California Press.

Hochschild, Arlie R. with Anne Machung. 1989. *The Second Shift.* New York: Viking Press.

Jaggar, Allison. 1983. Feminist Politics and Human Nature. Totowa, NJ: Rowman and Allenheld.

Kay, Herma Hill. 1990. "Beyond No-Fault: New Directions in Divorce Reform." Pp. 6–36 in *Divorce Reform at the Crossroads,* edited by Stephen D. Sugarman and Herma Hill Kay. New Haven: Yale University Press.

Kimmel, Michael. 1987. "The Contemporary Crisis of Masculinity in Historical Perspective." Pp. 121–154 in *The Making of Masculinities: The New Men's Studies,* edited by Harry Brod. Boston: Allen and Unwin.

LaRossa, Ralph and Maureen Mulligan LaRossa. 1989. "Baby Care: Fathers vs. Mothers." Pp. 138–154 in *Gender in Intimate Relationships: A Microstructural Approach,* edited by Barbara J. Risman and Pepper Schwartz. Belmont, CA: Wadsworth Publishing Company.

Lindsay, Linda. 1990. *Gender Roles: A Sociological Perspective.* New York: Prentice-Hall.

Maines, David. 1979. "Mesostructure and Social Process." *Contemporary Sociology* 8:524–527.

———. 1982. "in Search of Mesostructure: Studies in the Negotiated Order." *Urban Life* 11:267–279.

Marcus, P. 1989. "Locked In and Locked Out: Reflections on the History of Divorce Law Reform in New York State." *Buffalo Law Review* 37:374–395.

Mead, George H. 1934. Mind, Self and Society. Chicago: University of Chicago Press.

Mnookin, Robert and L. Kornhauser. 1979. "Bargaining in the Shadow of the Law." *Yale Law Journal* 88(950):952–958.

Mnookin, Robert, Eleanor E. Maccoby, Catherine R. Albiston, and Charlene E. Depner. 1990. "Private Ordering Revisited: What Custodial Arrangements Are Parents Negotiating?" Pp. 37–74 in *Divorce Reform at the Crossroads,* edited by Stephen D. Sugarman and

Herma Hill Kay. New Haven: Yale University Press.

Pateman, Carol. 1990. *The Disorder of Women: Democracy, Feminism, and Political Theory.* Stanford: Stanford University Press.

Perinbanayagam, Robert. 1985a. "How to Do Self with Things." Pp. 315–340 in *Beyond Goffman,* edited by S. Riggins. Berlin: Mouton-de Gruyter.

———. 1985b. *Signifying Acts: Structure and Meaning in Everyday Life.* Carbondale: Southern Illinois University Press.

Pestello, Frances and Patricia Voyandoff. 1991. "In Search of Mesostructure in the Family: An Interactionist Approach to Division of Labor." *Symbolic Interaction* 14(2):105–128.

Phillips, Roger and Faith Gilroy. 1985. "Sex-Role Stereotypes and Clinical Judgments of Mental Health: The Broverman's Findings Reexamined." *Sex Roles* 12(1–2):179–193.

Pleck, Joseph. 1985. *Working Wives Working Husbands.* Beverly Hills: Sage Publications.

———. 1989. Men's Power with Women, Other Men, and Society: A Men's Movement Analysis. Pp. 21–29 in *Men's Lives,* edited by Michael Kimmel and Michael Messner. New York: Macmillan Press.

Polikoff, Nancy. 1983. "Gender and Child-Custody Determinations: Exploding the Myths." Pp. 183–202 in *Families, Politics, and Public Policy,* edited by Irene Diamond. New York: Longman.

Riessman, Catherine. 1990. *Divorce Talk: Women and Men Make Sense of Personal Relationships.* New Brunswick, NJ: Rutgers University Press.

Risman, Barbara. 1989. "Can Men 'Mother'? Life as a Single Father." Pp. 155–164 in *Gender in Intimate Relationships: A Microstructural Approach,* edited by Barbara J. Risman and Pepper Schwartz. Belmont, CA: Wadsworth Publishing Company.

Risman, Barbara and Pepper Schwartz. 1989. "Being Gendered: A Microstructural View of Intimate Relations." Pp. 1–9 in *Gender in Intimate Relationships: A Microstructural Approach,* edited by Barbara J. Risman and Pepper Schwartz. Belmont, CA: Wadsworth Publishing Company.

Rosenblum, Karen. 1990. "The Conflict Between and Within Genders: An Appraisal of Contemporary Femininity and Masculinity." Pp. 193–202 in *Families in Transition,* edited by Arlene Skolnick and Jerome Skolnick. Glenview, IL: Scott, Foresman, and Company.

Rubin, Gayle. 1975. "The Traffic in Women: Notes on the Political Economy of Sex." In *Toward An Anthropology of Women,* edited by R. Reiter. New York: Monthly Review Press.

Schwenger, Peter. 1989. "The Masculine Mode in Speaking of Gender." Pp. 101–113 in *Speaking of Gender,* edited by Elaine Showalter. New York: Routledge.

Spanier, Graham and Linda Thompson. 1984. *Parting: The Aftermath of Separation and Divorce.* Beverly Hills: Sage Publications.

Stone, Gregory. 1981. "Appearance and the Self: A Slightly Revised Version." Pp. 187–202 in *Social Psychology Through Symbolic Interaction* (2nd edition), edited by Gregory Stone and Harvey Farberman. New York: John Wiley and Sons.

Strauss, Anselm. 1989. *Qualitative Analysis in the Social Sciences.* Cambridge: Cambridge University Press.

Tannen, Deborah. 1990. *You Just Don't Understand: Men and Women in Conversation.* New York: Ballantine Books.

Teachman, Jay. 1991. "Contributions to Children by Divorced Fathers." *Social Problems* 38(3):358–371.

United States Bureau of the Census. 1989. *Statistical Abstracts of the United States, 1988.*

National Data Book and Guide to Sources. Washington, DC: U.S. Government Printing Office.

Vaughan, Diane, 1986. *Uncoupling: Turning Points in Relationships.* New York: Oxford University Press.

Wallerstein, Judith and Sandra Blakeslee. 1989. *Second Chances: Men, Women, and Children a Decade After Divorce.* New York: Ticknor and Fields.

Weitzman, Lenore. 1985. The Divorce Revolution. *The Unexpected Social and Economic Consequences for Women and Children in America.* New York: Free Press.

LIFE-SPAN ADJUSTMENT OF CHILDREN TO THEIR PARENTS' DIVORCE—PAUL R. AMATO

Notes

1. Furstenberg, Jr., F. F. and Cherlin, A. J. *Divided families: What happens to children when parents part.* Cambridge, MA: Harvard University Press, 1991, pp. 1–15; Uhlenberg, P. Death and the family. *Journal of Family History* (1980) 5:313–20.

2. Cherlin, A. *Marriage, divorce, remarriage.* Rev. ed. Cambridge, MA: Harvard University Press, 1992.

3. Bumpass, L. Children and marital disruption: A replication and update. *Demography* (1984) 21:71–82.

4. For examples, see the articles in *The child in his family: The impact of disease and death.* E. J. Anthony, ed. New York: Wiley, 1973.

5. Crook, T., and Eliot, J. Parental death during childhood and adult depression: A critical review of the literature. *Psychological Bulletin* (1980) 87:252–59.

6. The cross-sectional and longitudinal designs are used widely in adjustment research and other developmental research because they are suited for studies in which there are one or more nonmanipulable independent variables. In this instance, the researcher must select subjects who already possess different levels of a particular characteristic. Examples of nonmanipulable independent variables include age, sex, marital status of parents, and socioeconomic status. The use of nonmanipulable independent variables in a study usually precludes the use of true experimental designs which involve the random assignment of subjects to groups. Subjects are randomly assigned to eliminate the influence of extraneous variables. If the influence of extraneous variables has been accomplished in a study and there are significant differences found between groups on a dependent variable, then the researcher may state with confidence that the independent variable caused the results to differ between groups. In studies without random assignment of subjects, including those using cross-sectional and longitudinal designs, statements about cause and effect relationships cannot be made. Researchers are unable to determine which variable caused which or if some other extraneous variable(s) could be responsible for an observed relationship between the variables. It should be noted that this difficulty is inherent in the literature on adjustment to divorce. Although cause and effect relationships may not be known, what is known is that there is a correlation between parental marital status and children's adjustment, and the knowledge that this correlation exists helps to assist the process of policymaking in this area. For a further discussion of the differences between experimental and nonexperimental designs, see Miller, S. A. *Developmental research methods.* Englewood Cliffs, NJ: Prentice-Hall, 1987; Cozby, P. C., Worden, P. E., and Kee, D. W. *Research methods in human development.* Mountain View, CA: Mayfield, 1989.

7. The optimal comparison group would be families that would potentially divorce, but stay

together for the sake of the children. However, this population of families would be very difficult to sample. Another available comparison group would be continuously intact two-parent families. However, this comparison group is not consistently used by researchers. Many classifications in cross-sectional research are based on the current marital status of parents. The intact group is heterogeneous as to marital history, and the divorced group is not similar as to the time of divorce or the age of the children when it took place. Some of the most prominent longitudinal studies have no comparison group of intact families. See, for example, Wallerstein, J. S., and Corbin, S. B. Father-child relationships after divorce: Child support and educational opportunity. *Family Law Quarterly* (1986) 20:109–28; Maccoby, E. E., and Mnookin, R. H. *Dividing the child: Social and legal dilemmas of custody.* Cambridge, MA: Harvard University Press, 1992.

8. For example, a researcher using a cross-sectional design might study four different groups of children, grouped by age (for example, 3, 6, 9, and 12) and parental marital status (married or divorced) to see if children from divorced families exhibit significantly more aggression than children from intact families. If the researcher finds that aggressive behavior is, indeed, significantly more likely in children from divorced families, the researcher cannot determine the direction of the relationship, that is, whether the divorce increased aggression in these children or high levels of aggression in the children caused the divorce. In addition, the researcher is unable to determine if some extraneous variable caused both high aggression and divorce, for example, low socioeconomic status.

For the developmental researcher, there are advantages and disadvantages to using this type of research design. The cross-sectional design is relatively inexpensive and timely, which makes

it a popular choice for many researchers. However, a number of difficulties may threaten the validity and reliability of the results. These difficulties include the following: there is no direct measure of age changes; the issue of individual stability over time cannot be addressed; there is a possibility of selection bias; there may be difficulty establishing measurement equivalence; and there is an inevitable confounding of age and time of birth. Some of these problems are avoidable with adequate planning and control; however, the problem of the confounding of age and time of birth (cohort) is intrinsic in the cross-sectional design, and it is impossible to avoid.

Another design that is available to researchers but is seldom used is called the cross-sectional-sequential design. A cross-sectional-sequential study tests separate cross-sectional samples at two or more times of measurement. In comparison to a standard cross-sectional design, this sequential design has the advantage of at least partly unconfounding age and year of birth (because there are at least two different cohorts for each age tested), and it also provides a comparison of the same age group at different times of testing (called a time-lag comparison). It would be advantageous to use this research design in the future for some types of adjustment research.

9. There are major advantages and disadvantages to this type of design. The advantages include the following: a researcher can observe actual changes occurring in subjects over time; irrelevant sources of variability are not of concern; there are no cohort effects because the same cohort is being studied over time and there is no selection bias. Disadvantages that may influence reliability and validity include the following: an expensive and time-consuming design; subject attrition; selective dropout; possible obsolescence of tests and instruments; a potentially biased sample; measurement of only a single cohort; effects of repeated testing; reac-

tivity; difficulty of establishing equivalent measures; and the inevitable confounding of the age of subjects and the historical time of testing. As with the cross-sectional design, some of these problems are avoidable. However, it is impossible to avoid the confounding of age with time of measurement in the longitudinal approach. This confounding follows from the fact that the age comparisons are all within subject. Therefore, if we want to test subjects of different ages, we must test at different times. For an in-depth discussion of longitudinal designs, see Menard, S. *Longitudinal research.* Series: Quantitative App-lications in the Social Sciences, No. 07-076. Newbury Park, CA: Sage, 1991.

A design that is available to developmental researchers and is more complicated but should assist in disentangling the contributions of age, generation, and time of measurement is called the longitudinal-sequential design. In this design, the samples are selected from different cohorts (that is, years of birth), and they are tested repeatedly across the same time span. This design offers at least three advantages over a standard longitudinal design. The longitudinal comparisons are not limited to a single generation or cohort because samples are drawn from different birth years. In addition, there is a cross-sectional component to the design because different age groups are tested at each time of measurement. Finally, the same age group is represented at different times of measurement. More information is provided than in a standard longitudinal design, and there is greater opportunity to disentangle causative factors. See Baltes, P. B., Reese, H. W., and Nesselroade, J. R. *Life-span developmental psychology: Introduction to research methods.* Monterey, CA: Brooks/Cole, 1977.

10. Wallerstein, J. S. Children of divorce: Preliminary report of a ten-year follow-up of young children. *American Journal of Orthopsychiatry* (1984) 54:444–58; Wallerstein, J. S. Children of divorce: Preliminary report of a ten-year follow-up of older children and adolescents. *Journal of the American Academy of Child Psychiatry* (1985) 24:545–53; Wallerstein, J. S. Women after divorce: Preliminary report from a ten-year follow-up. *American Journal of Orthopsychiatry* (1986) 56:65–77; Wallerstein, J. S. Children of divorce: Report of a ten-year follow-up of early latency-age children. *American Journal of Orthopsychiatry* (1987) 57:199–211; Wallerstein, J. S., and Blakeslee, S. *Second chances: Men, women, and children a decade after divorce.* New York: Ticknor and Fields, 1989; Wallerstein, J. S., and Corbin, S. B. Daughters of divorce: Report from a ten-year follow-up. *American Journal of Orthopsychiatry* (October 1989) 59:593–604; Wallerstein, J. S., and Kelly, J. B. *Surviving the breakup: How children and parents cope with divorce.* New York: Basic Books, 1980.

11. For a discussion of sampling, see Kerlinger, F. N. *Foundations of behavioral research.* New York: Holt, Rinehart and Winston, 1973.

12. It should be noted that there are no perfect random samples on this subject. The national studies select ever-divorced families, who are limited by geography, the choice of schools included (rarely private schools, which is a problem in places where a large segment of children, often those with the best advantages, are not enrolled in public schools), or use the court sampling frame, which offers insufficient address data to draw a comprehensive sample.

13. This type of random selection of samples should not be confused with random assignment of subjects to groups.

14. For a discussion of matching, see note no. 6, Miller.

15. See, for example, Guidubaldi, J., Cleminshaw, H. K., Perry, J. D., and McLoughlin, C. S. The impact of parental divorce on children:

Report of the nationwide NASP study. *School Psychology Review* (1983) 12:300–23; Hetherington, E. M., Cox, M., and Cox, R. Effects of divorce on parents and children. In *Nontraditional families.* M. E. Lamb, ed. Hillsdale, NJ: Lawrence Erlbaum Associates, 1982, pp. 223–88; see note no. 10, Wallerstein and Kelly.

16. See, for example, Baydar, N. Effects of parental separation and reentry into union on the emotional well-being of children. *Journal of Marriage and the Family* (1988) 50:967–81; Enos, D. M., and Handal, P. J. Relation of parental marital status and perceived family conflict to adjustment in white adolescents. *Journal of Consulting and Clinical Psychology* (1986) 54:820–24; Mechanic, D., and Hansell, S. Divorce, family conflict, and adolescents' well-being. *Journal of Health and Social Behavior* (1989) 30:105–16.

17. Amato, P. R., and Ochiltree, G. Child and adolescent competence in intact, one-parent, and stepfamilies. *Journal of Divorce* (1987) 10: 75–96.

18. See Glass, G. V., McGaw, B., and Smith, M. L. An evaluation of meta-analysis. In *Meta-analysis in social research.* Newbury Park, CA: Sage, 1981.

19. The term *meta-analysis* refers to the quantitative combinations of data from independent studies. The procedure is valuable when the result is a descriptive summary of the weight of the available evidence. Summaries are necessary primarily because there are conflicting results in the literature and, at some point, it is valuable to know where the weight of the evidence falls. The primary goals of meta-analysis include determining whether significant effects exist for the topic being reviewed, estimating the magnitude of effects, and relating the existence and magnitude of effects of variations in design and procedure across studies. Proponents of meta-analysis argue that meta-analysis can achieve a greater precision and generalizability of findings than single studies. They then have the potential to provide more definitive evidence for policymaking than can be realized by other means. However, there are logical and methodological difficulties with the technique that need to be understood when interpreting the results of any meta-analysis. First, there is the problem of the selection of studies, that is, how to determine which studies should be included in the meta-analysis. Oakes contends that any rule establishment in this area presents impossible difficulties. A second problem is that, if a researcher includes only published studies in the meta-analysis, there is the danger of overestimating differences between groups. This danger arises because journal articles are not a representative sample of work addressed in any particular research area. Significant research findings are more likely to be published than nonsignificant research findings. To control for this problem, the researcher must trace unpublished research and incorporate it into the analysis. A third problem is that the use of meta-analysis may overinflate differences between groups because a high proportion of reported statistically significant results are spurious. Finally, because of the diversity of the types of samples that are included in the meta-analysis, it is difficult—if not impossible—to know what population the results are applicable to. For more in-depth discussions of the technique, its advantages, and its disadvantages, see note no. 18, Glass, McGaw, and Smith; Oakes, M. The logic and role of meta-analysis in clinical research. *Statistical Methods in Medical Research* (1993) 2:146–60; note no. 6, Miller; Thompson, S. G., and Pocock, S. J. Can meta-analyses be trusted? *The Lancet* (November 2, 1991) 338:1127–30; Wolf, F. M. *Meta-analysis: Quantitative methods for research synthesis.* Series: Quantitative Applications in Social Sciences, No. 07-059. Beverly Hills, CA: Sage, 1986.

20. Amato, P. R., and Keith, B. Parental divorce and the well-being of children: A meta analysis. *Psychological Bulletin* (1991) 100:26–46. Studies were included if they met the following criteria: (1) were published in an academic journal or book, (2) included a sample of children of divorce as well as a sample of children from continuously intact two-parent families, (3) involved quantitative measures of any of the outcomes listed below in note no. 21, and (4) provided sufficient information to calculate an effect size.

21. In the meta-analysis for children, measures of well-being were coded into the following eight categories: academic achievement (standardized achievement tests, grades, teachers' ratings, or intelligence); conduct (misbehavior, aggression, or delinquency); psychological adjustment (depression, anxiety, or happiness); self-concept (self-esteem, perceived competence, or internal locus of control); social adjustment (popularity, loneliness, or cooperativeness); mother-child and father-child relations (affection, help, or quality of interaction), and other.

22. Mean effect sizes ranged from .06 for the "other" category (not significant) to −.23 for conduct (p .001), with an overall effect size of −.17 across all outcomes. Effect sizes reflect the difference between groups in standard deviation units. A negative effect size indicates that children of divorce exhibit lower well-being than do children in intact two-parent families. With the exception of the "other" category, all mean effect sizes were statistically significant (p .001).

23. Amato, P. R., and Keith, B. Parental divorce and adult well-being: A meta-analysis. *Journal of Marriage and the Family* (1991) 53:43–58.

24. In the meta-analysis for adults, outcomes were coded into the following 15 categories: psychological well-being (emotional adjustment, depression, anxiety, life-satisfaction); behavior/conduct (criminal behavior, drug use, alcoholism, suicide, teenage pregnancy, teenage marriage); use of mental health services; self-concept (self-esteem, self-efficacy, sense of power, internal locus of control); social well-being (number of friends, social participation, social support, contact with parents and extended family); marital quality (marital satisfaction, marital disagreements, marital instability); separation or divorce; one-parent family status; quality of relations with one's children; quality of general family relations (over-all ratings of family life); educational attainment (high school graduation; years of education); occupational quality (occupational prestige, job autonomy, job satisfaction); material quality of life (income, assets held, housing quality, welfare dependency, perceived economic strain); physical health (chronic problems, disability), and other.

25. Mean effect sizes ranged from −.02 for relations with children (not significant) to −.36 for becoming a single parent (p .001), with an effect size of −.20 across all outcomes. All mean effect sizes were significant (at least p .01) except for relations with children and self-concept.

26. Kendall-Tackett, K. A., Williams, L. M., and Finkelhor, D. Impact of sexual abuse on children: A review and synthesis of recent empirical studies. *Psychological Bulletin* (1993) 113:164–80. Effect sizes in this meta-analysis ranged from .39 to .66, indicating poorer adjustment for sexually abused children than for nonabused children.

27. Rutter, M. Sex differences in children's responses to family stress. In *The child in his family*. Vol. 1. E. J. Anthony and C. Koupernik, eds. New York: Wiley, 1970.

28. See, for example, Booth, A., Brinkerhoff, D. B., and White, L. K. The impact of parental divorce on courtship. *Journal of Marriage and the Family* (1984) 46:85–94; Smith, T. E. Parental separation and adolescents' academic

self-concepts: An effort to solve the puzzle of separation effects. *Journal of Marriage and the Family* (1990) 52:107–18.

29. Slater, E., Steward, K. J., and Linn, M. W. The effects of family disruption on adolescent males and females. *Adolescence* (1983) 18:931–42.

30. See Peterson, J. L., and Zill, N. Marital disruption, parent-child relationships, and behavior problems in children. *Journal of Marriage and the Family* (1986) 48:295–307; Hetherington, E. M., and Chase-Lansdale, P. L. The impact of divorce on life-span development: Short and long term effects. In *Life-span development and behavior.* P. B. Baltes, D. L. Featherman, and R. M. Lerner, eds. Hillsdale, NJ: Lawrence Erlbaum Associates, 1990.

31. See note no. 7, Wallerstein and Corbin.

32. Hetherington, E. M., Camara, K. A., and Featherman, D. L. Achievement and intellectual functioning of children in one-parent households. In *Achievement and achievement motives.* J. T. Spence, ed. San Francisco: W. H. Freeman, 1983.

33. Del Carmen, R., and Virgo, G. N. Marital disruption and nonresidential parenting: A multicultural perspective. In *Nonresidential parenting: New vistas in family living.* C. Depner and J. Bray, eds. Newbury Park, CA: Sage, 1993, pp. 13–36.

34. See note no. 10, Wallerstein and Kelly.

35. See note no. 10, Wallerstein and Blakeslee.

36. For a summary of these studies, see Amato, P. R. Children's adjustment to divorce: Theories, hypotheses, and empirical support. *Journal of Marriage and the Family* (1993) 55:23–38.

37. See note no. 20, Amato and Keith.

38. Furstenberg, Jr., F. F., and Nord, C. W. Parenting apart: Patterns of child-rearing after marital disruption. *Journal of Marriage and the Family* (1985) 47:893–904; Seltzer, J. A. Relationships between fathers and children who live apart: The father's role after separation. *Journal of Marriage and the Family* (1991) 53:79–101.

39. This trend was confirmed in the meta-analysis by Amato and Keith; see note no. 23. For examples of studies, see Amato P. R. Parental absence during childhood and depression in later life. *Sociological Quarterly* (1991) 32:543–56; Gregory, I. Introspective data following childhood loss of a parent: Delinquency and high school dropout. *Archives of General Psychiatry* (1965) 13:99–109; Saucier, J., and Ambert, A. Parental marital status and adolescents' optimism about their future. *Journal of Youth and Adolescence* (1982) 11:345–53. Our meta-analysis also showed that, although children who experience parental death are worse off than those in intact two-parent families, they have higher levels of well-being than do children of divorce.

40. Cochran, M., Larner, M., Riley, D., et al. *Extending families: The social networks of parents and their children.* Cambridge, MA: Cambridge University Press, 1990; Dornbusch, S., Carlsmith, J. M., Bushwall, S. J., et al. Single parents, extended households, and the control of adolescents. *Child Development* (1985) 56:326–41.

41. Kelly, J. B. Current research on children's postdivorce adjustment: No simple answers. *Family and Conciliation Courts Review* (1993) 31:29–49.

42. Amato, P. R., and Rezac, S. J. Contact with nonresident parents, interparental conflict, and children's behavior. Paper presented at the Annual Meeting of the Midwest Sociological Society. Chicago, IL, 1993; Healy, Jr., J., Malley, J., and Stewart, A. Children and their fathers after parental separation. *American Journal of Orthopsychiatry* (1990) 60:531–43; see note no. 15, Hetherington, Cox, and Cox.

43. See note no. 15, Hetherington, Cox, and Cox. See also Simons, R. L., Beaman, J., Conger, R. D., and Chao, W. Stress, support, and an-

tisocial behavior traits as determinants of emotional well-being and parenting practices among single mothers. *Journal of Marriage and the Family* (1993) 55:385–98.

44. Kline, M., Tschann, J. M., Johnston, J. R., and Wallerstein, J. S. Children's adjustment in joint and sole physical custody families. *Developmental Psychology* (1989) 25:430–38. Guidubaldi, J., and Perry, J. D. Divorce and mental health sequelae for children: A two year follow-up of a nationwide sample. *Journal of the American Academy of Child Psychiatry* (1985) 24:531–37; and Kalter, N., Kloner, A., Schreiser, S., and Olka, K. Predictors of children's postdivorce adjustment. *American Journal of Orthopsychiatry* (1989) 59:605–18.

45. Guidubaldi, J., Cleminshaw, H. K., Perry, J. D., et al. The role of selected family environment factors in children's post-divorce adjustment. *Family Relations* (1986) 35:141–51; see note no. 15, Hetherington, Cox, and Cox. See note no. 10, Wallerstein and Kelly; note no. 44, Kalter, Kloner, Schreiser, and Olka; note no. 30, Peterson and Zill.

46. Of course, it is also likely that well-behaved children allow parents to behave in a positive and competent manner, whereas ill-behaved children stimulate problematic parental behaviors. Undoubtedly, children influence parents just as parents influence children. However, this does not invalidate the notion that divorce-induced stress can interfere with a person's ability to function effectively as a parent and that a parent's failure to function effectively might have negative consequences for children.

47. Emery, R. Interparental conflict and the children of discord and divorce. *Psychological Bulletin* (1982) 92:310–30; Grych, J. H., and Fincham, F. D. Marital conflict and children's adjustment: A cognitive-contextual framework. *Psychological Bulletin* (1990) 108:267–90.

48. See note no. 28, Booth, Brinkerhoff, and White. See note no. 16, Enos and Handal; and Mechanic and Hansell; Long, N., Forehand, R., Fauber, R., and Brody, G. H. Self-perceived and independently observed competence of young adolescents as a function of parental marital conflict and recent divorce. *Journal of Abnormal Child Psychology* (1987) 15:15–27; see note no. 30, Peterson and Zill.

49. Cherlin, A. J., Furstenberg, Jr., F. F., Chase-Lansdale, P. L., et al. Longitudinal studies of effects of divorce on children in Great Britain and the United States. *Science* (1991) 252:1386–89. Similar findings were reported by Block, J. H., Block, J., and Gjerde, P. R. The personality of children prior to divorce. *Child Development* (1986) 57:827–40.

50. Johnston, J. R., Kline, M., and Tschann, J. M. Ongoing postdivorce conflict: Effects on children of joint custody and frequent access. *American Journal of Orthopsychiatry* (1999) 59:576–92; Kurdek, L. A., and Berg, B. Correlates of children's adjustment to their parents' divorces. In *Children and divorce*. L. A. Kurdek, ed. San Francisco: Jossey-Bass, 1983; Shaw, D. S., and Emery, R. E. Parental conflict and other correlates of the adjustment of school-age children whose parents have separated. *Journal of Abnormal Child Psychology* (1987) 15:269–81.

51. It is also probable that children's problems, to a certain extent, exacerbate conflict between parents.

52. Duncan, G. J., and Hoffman, S. D. Economic consequences of marital instability. In *Horizontal equity, uncertainty, and economic well-being*. M. David and T. Smeeding, eds. Chicago: University of Chicago Press, 1985; Weitzman, L. J. *The divorce revolution: The unexpected social and economic consequences for women and children in America*. New York: Free Press, 1985.

53. McLeod, J. D., and Shanahan, M. J. Poverty, parenting, and children's mental health. *American Sociological Review* (1993) 58:351–66.

54. Williams, D. R. Socioeconomic differentials in health: A review and redirection. *Social Psychology Quarterly* (1990) 52:81–99.

55. McLanahan, S., and Booth, K. Mother-only families: Problems, prospects, and politics. *Journal of Marriage and the Family* (1989) 51:557–80.

56. See note no. 15, Guidubaldi, Cleminshaw, Perry, and McLoughlin.

57. McLanahan, S. Family structure and the reproduction of poverty. *American Journal of Sociology* (1985) 90:873–901.

58. For a review of the effects of serial marriages (involving three or more marriages) and divorces on child adjustment, see Brody, G. H., Neubaum, E., and Forehand, R. Serial marriage: A heuristic analysis of an emerging family form. *Psychological Bulletin* (1988) 103:211–22.

59. Hodges, W. F., Tierney, C. W., and Buchsbaum, H. K. The cumulative effect of stress on preschool children of divorced and intact families. *Journal of Marriage and the Family* (1984) 46:611–19; Stolberg, A. L., and Anker, J. M. Cognitive and behavioral changes in children resulting from parental divorce and consequent environmental changes. *Journal of Divorce* (1983) 7:23–37.

60. See note no. 16, Baydar. Hetherington and her colleagues found that the remarriage of the custodial mother was associated with increased problems for girls but decreased problems for boys. Hetherington, E. M., Cox, M., and Cox, R. Long-term effects of divorce and remarriage on the adjustment of children. *Journal of the American Academy of Child Psychiatry* (1985) 24:518–30.

61. Amato, P. R., and Booth, A. The consequences of parental divorce and marital unhappiness for adult well-being. *Social Forces* (1991) 69:895–914.

62. For similar perspectives, see Hetherington, E. M. Coping with family transitions: Winners, losers, and survivors. *Child Development* (1989) 60:1–14; Kurdek, L. A. An integrative perspective on children's divorce adjustment. *American Psychologist* 36:856–66.

63. Glendon, M. A. *The transformation of family law: State, law, and family in the United States and Western Europe.* Chicago: University of Chicago Press, 1989. See note no. 52, Weitzman.

64. See note no. 63, Glendon; Sweet, J. A., and Bumpass, L. L. *American families and households.* New York: Russell Sage Foundation, 1990.

65. See note no. 1, Furstenberg and Cherlin.

66. See note no. 7, Maccoby and Mnookin.

67. Seltzer, J. Legal custody arrangements and children's economic welfare. *American Journal of Sociology* (1991) 96:895–929.

68. Arditti, J. A. Differences between fathers with joint custody and noncustodial fathers. *American Journal of Orthopsychiatry* (1992) 62:186–95; Bowman, M., and Ahrons, C. R. Impact of legal custody status on fathers' parenting postdivorce. *Journal of Marriage and the Family* (1985) 47:481–88; Dudley, J. R. Exploring ways to get divorced fathers to comply willingly with child support agreements. *Journal of Divorce* (1991) 14:121–33; Leupnitz, D. A comparison of maternal, paternal, and joint custody: Understanding the varieties of postdivorce family life. *Journal of Divorce* (1986) 9:1–12.

69. See note no. 68, Arditti; Little, M. A. The impact of the custody plan on the family: A five year follow up. *Family and Conciliation Courts Review* (1992) 30:243–51; Shrier, D. K., Simring, S. K., Shapiro, E. T., and Greif, J. B. Level of satisfaction of fathers and mothers with joint or sole custody arrangements. *Journal of Divorce and Remarriage* (1991) 16:163–69.

70. Buchanan, C. M., Maccoby, E. E., and Dornbusch, S. M. Adolescents and their families after divorce: Three residential arrangements

compared. *Journal of Research on Adolescents* (1992) 2:261–91; Glover, R. J., and Steele, C. Comparing the effects on the child of postdivorce parenting arrangements. *Journal of Divorce* (1989) 12:185–201; Wolchik, S. A., Braver, S. L., and Sandler, I. N. Maternal versus joint custody: Children's postseparation experiences and adjustment. *Journal of Clinical Child Psychology* (1985) 14:5–10.

71. Kline, M., Tschann, J. M., Johnston, J. R., and Wallerstein, J. S. Children's adjustment in joint and sole physical custody families. *Developmental Psychology* (1988) 25:430–38; Leupnitz, D. *Child custody.* Lexington, MA: D. C. Heath, 1982; Pearson, J., and Thoennes, N. Custody after divorce: Demographic and attitudinal patterns. *American Journal of Orthopsychiatry* (1990) 60:233–49.

72. See note no. 68, Arditti; note no. 71, Pearson and Thoennes; Steinman, S. The experience of children in a joint custody arrangement: A report of a study. *American Journal of Orthopsychiatry* (1981) 24:554–62.

73. Nelson, R. Parental hostility, conflict, and communication in joint and sole custody families. *Journal of Divorce* (1989) 13:145–57.

74. Buchanan, C. M., Maccoby, E. E., and Dornbusch, S. M. Caught between parents: Adolescents' experience in divorced homes. *Child Development* (1991) 62:1008–29; Johnston, J. R., Kline, M., and Tschann, J. M. Ongoing postdivorce conflict: Effects on children of joint custody and frequent access. *American Journal of Orthopsychiatry* (1989) 59:576–92.

75. Downey, D., and Powell, B. Do children in single-parent households fare better living with same-sex parents? *Journal of Marriage and the Family* (1993) 55:55–71.

76. U.S. Bureau of the Census. *Child support and alimony: 1987.* Current Population Reports, Series P-23, No. 167. Washington, DC: U.S. Government Printing Office, 1990.

77. Public Law No. 100-485, reprinted in *1988 U.S. Code Cong. & Admin. News,* 102 Stat. 2343.

78. See note no. 52, Duncan and Hoffman.

79. Furstenberg, Jr., F. F., Morgan, S. P., and Allison, P. D. Paternal participation and children's well-being after marital dissolution. *American Sociological Review* (1987) 52:695–701; King, V. Nonresidential father involvement and child well-being: Can dads make a difference? Paper presented at the annual meeting of the Population Association of America. Cincinnati, OH, 1993.

80. For a discussion of child support reform, see Garfinkel, I. *Assuring child support: An extension of Social Security.* New York: Russell Sage Foundation, 1992; Garfinkel, I., and McLanahan, S. S. *Single mothers and their children: A new American dilemma.* Washington, DC: Urban Institute Press, 1986.

81. Seltzer, J. A., and Bianchi, S. M. Children's contact with absent parents. *Journal of Marriage and the Family* (1988) 50:663–77; Seltzer, J., Schaeffer, N. C., and Charng, H. Family ties after divorce: The relationship between visiting and paying child support. *Journal of Marriage and the Family* (1989) 51:1013–32.

82. Britto, K. The Family Support Act of 1988 Welfare Reform (Public Law 100-485). Vol. 2, No. 3. National Conference of State Legislatures. Denver, CO, 1989.

83. Aldous, J. Family policy in the 1980s: Controversy and consensus. *Journal of Marriage and the Family* (1990) 52:1136–51.

84. Grych, J., and Fincham, F. D. Interventions for children of divorce: Toward greater integration of research and action. *Psychological Bulletin* (1992) 111:434–54.

85. Anderson, R. F., Kinney, J., and Gerler, E. R. The effects of divorce groups on children's classroom behavior and attitudes toward divorce. *Elementary School Guidance and Counseling* (1984) 19:70–76; Crosbie-Burnett, M., and Newcomer,

L. L. Group counseling children of divorce: The effects of a multimodel intervention. *Journal of Divorce* (1989) 13:69–78. Pedro-Carroll, J., and Cowan, E. L. The children of divorce intervention program: An investigation of the efficacy of a school based intervention program. *Journal of Consulting and Clinical Psychology* (1985) 53:603–11; Stolberg, A. J., and Garrison, K. M. Evaluating a primary prevention program for children of divorce. *American Journal of Community Psychology* (1985) 13:111–24.

86. Bloom, B. L., Hodges, W. F., and Caldwell, R. A. A preventive program for the newly separated: Initial evaluation. *American Journal of Community Psychology* (1982) 10:251–64; Bloom, B. L., Hodges, W. F., Kern, M. B., and McFaddin, S. C. A preventive intervention program for the newly separated: Final evaluations. *American Journal of Orthopsychiatry* (1985) 55:9–26; Zibbell, R. A. A short-term, small-group education and counseling program for separated and divorced parents in conflict. *Journal of Divorce and Remarriage* (1992) 18:189–203.

87. Wallerstein, J. S. The long-term effects of divorce on children: A review. *Journal of the American Academy of Child Adolescent Psychiatry* (1991) 30:349–60.

STEPFAMILIES IN THE UNITED STATES: A RECONSIDERATION— ANDREW J. CHERLIN AND FRANK F. FURSTENBERG, JR.

Notes

1. Based on 1985 data, Larry L. Bumpass, James Sweet, and Teresa Castro Martin (1990) estimated that 72% of recently separated women would remarry. But remarriage rates have declined further since then. A 1992 Census Bureau report suggests that the true figure may be closer to two thirds; see US Bureau of the Census (1992c). The most recent estimate for men— 78% remarrying within 10 years—is from the 1980 Census data and is probably too high now. See James A. Sweet and Larry L. Bumpass (1987).

2. All of the findings in this paragraph are from Larry Bumpass, James Sweet, and Teresa Castro Martin (1990).

3. We calculated this figure (and the 11.2% figure in the next paragraph) based on information from the June 1990 Census on children living with neither parent, as reported in US Bureau of the Census (1992a); information on the biological versus nonbiological status of parents of children who were living with two parents, in the June 1990 *Current Population Survey* (US Bureau of the Census 1992c); and the distribution of living arrangements of all children, in the March 1992 *Current Population Survey* (US Bureau of the Census 1992b).

4. In 33 of the States, it was legal in 1993 for a stepfather to divorce his wife and marry his wife's daughter. See Margaret Mahoney (1993) and Mary Ann Glendon (1989).

References

Aquilino WS. 1991. Family structure and home leaving: A further specification of the relationship. *J. Marriage Fam.* 53:999–1010

Bachrach C. 1983. Children in families: Characteristics of biological, step-, and adopted children. *J. Marriage Fam.* 45:171–79

Beer WR, ed. 1988. *Relative Strangers: Studies of Stepfamily Processes.* Totowa, NJ: Rowan and Littlefield

Bernstein AC. 1988. Unraveling the tangles: children's understanding of stepfamily kinship. See Beer 1988, pp. 83–111

Bohannan P, ed. 1971. Divorce chains, households of remarriage, and multiple divorcers.

In *Divorce and After,* ed. P Bohannan, pp. 128–39. Garden City NY: Anchor

Booth A, Edwards JN. 1992. Starting over: why remarriages are unstable. *J. Fam. Issues* 13:179–94

Brand E, Clingempeel WG, Bowen-Woodward K. 1988. Family relationships and the children's psychological adjustment in stepmother and stepfather families. See Hetherington & Arasteh 1988, pp. 279–98

Bray JH. 1988. Children's development during early remarriage. See Hetherington & Arasteh, pp. 279–98

Bumpass LL, Sweet JA. 1989. National estimates of cohabitation: Cohort levels and union stability. *Demography* 25:615–25

Bumpass LL, Sweet JA, Martin TC. 1990. Changing pattern of remarriage. *J. Marriage Fam.* 52:747–56

Bumpass LL, Sweet JA, Cherlin AJ. 1991. The role of cohabitation in declining rates of marriage. *J. Marriage Fam.* 53:913–27

Capaldi DM, Patterson GR. 1991. Relation of parental transitions to boy's adjustment problems: 1. A linear hypothesis; 2. Mothers at risk for transitions and unskilled parenting. *Dev. Psychol.* 27:489–504

Cherlin AJ. 1978. Remarriage as an incomplete institution. *Am. J. Sociol.* 84:634–50

Cherlin AJ, Furstenberg FF, Jr. 1992. *The New American Grandparent: A Place in the Family, A Life Apart.* Cambridge, Mass: Harvard Univ. 158pp.

Coleman M, Ganong L. 1990. Remarriage and stepfamily research in the 1980s: Increased interest in an old family form. *J. Marriage Fam.* 52:925–40

Davis K. 1948. *Human Society.* New York: Macmillan

Eisenstadt SN. 1966. *From Generation to Generation.* New York: Free

Fine MA, Fine DR. 1992. Recent changes in laws affecting stepfamilies: suggestions for legal reform. *Fam. Relat.* 13:334–40

Furstenberg FF, Jr. 1979. Recycling the family: Perspectives for researching a neglected family form. *Marriage Fam. Rev.* 2:12–22

Furstenberg FF, Jr. 1981. Remarriage and intergenerational relations. In *Aging: Stability and Change in the Family,* ed. RW Fogel, E Hatfield, SB Kiesler, E Shanas, pp. 115–142. New York: Academic

Furstenberg FF, Jr. 1987. The new extended family: The experience of parents and children after remarriage. In *Remarriage and Stepparenting: Current Research and Theory,* ed. K Pasley, M Ihinger-Tallman, pp. 42–61. New York: Guilford

Furstenberg FF, Jr, Cherlin AJ. 1991. *Divided Families: What Happens to Children When Parents Part.* Cambridge, Mass: Harvard Univ. 85 pp.

Furstenberg FF, Jr, Nord CW. 1985. Parenting apart: Patterns of childrearing after divorce. *J. Marriage Fam.* 47:893–904

Furstenberg FF, Jr, Sherwood KE, Sullivan ML. 1992. *Caring and Paying: What Fathers and Mothers Say about Child Support.* New York: Manpower Demonstration Res.

Furstenberg FF, Jr, Spanier GB. 1984. *Recycling the Family: Remarriage after Divorce.* Newbury Park Calif: Sage

Ganong LH, Coleman M, Mapes D. 1990. A meta-analytic review of family structure stereotypes. *J. Marriage Fam.* 52:287–97

Glendon MA. 1989. *The Transformation of Family Law: State, Law, and Family in the United States and Western Europe.* Chicago: Univ. Chicago.

Goldscheider FK, Goldscheider C. 1993. *Leaving Home Before Marriage: Ethnicity, Familism and Generational Relationships.* Madison: Univ. Wisc.

Granovetter MS. 1973. The strength of weak ties. *Am. J. Sociol.* 78:1360–80

Hetherington EM. 1987. Family relations six years after divorce. In *Remarriage and Stepparenting: Current Research and Theory,* ed. K Pasley, M Inhinger-Tallman, pp. 185–205. New York: Guilford

Hetherington EM, Arasteh JD, eds. 1988. *Impact of Divorce, Single Parenting, and Stepparenting on Children.* Hillsdale NJ: Lawrence Erlbaum

Hetherington EM, Clingempeel WG, eds. 1992. Coping with marital transitions. *Monogr. Soc. Res. Child Dev.* Vol. 57, Nos. 2–3

Hetherington EM, Jodl KM. 1993. Stepfamilies as settings for child development. Presented at the Natl. Symposium on Stepfamilies, State College Penn.

Ihinger-Tallman M, Pasley K. 1987. *Remarriage.* Newbury Park, Calif: Sage

Johnson CL. 1988. *Ex Familia: Grandparents, Parents, and Children Adjust to Divorce.* New Brunswick, NJ: Rutgers Univ. Press

Keshet JK. 1988. The remarried couple: stresses and successes. See Beer 1988, pp. 29–53

Kiernan KE. 1992. The impact of family disruption in childhood on transitions made in young adult life. *Pop. Stud.* 46:213–34

Maccoby EE. 1992. Family structure and children's adjustment: Is quality of parenting the major mediator? In *Coping with Marital Transitions,* ed. EM Hetherington, WG Clingempeel, pp. 230–38. *Monogr. Soc. Res. Dev.* Vol. 57, Nos. 2–3

Mahoney M. 1993. Untitled commentary presented at the National Symposium on Stepfamilies, Penn. State Univ., State College, October 14–15

Marsiglio W. 1992. Stepfathers with minor children living at home: Parenting perceptions and relationship quality. *J. Fam. Issues* 13:195–214

Martin TC, Bumpass LL. 1989. Recent trends in marital disruption. *Demography* 26:37–51

Papernow P. 1988. Stepparent role development: from outsider to intimate. See Beer 1988, pp. 54–82

Parkes CM, Hinde JS, eds. 1982. *The Place of Attachment in Human Behavior.* New York: Basic

Pasley K, Ihinger-Tallman M, eds. 1987. *Remarriage and Stepparenting: Current Research and Theory.* New York: Guilford

Schneider DM. 1980 *American Kinship: A Cultural Account.* Chicago: Univ. Chicago. 2nd ed.

Seltzer JA. 1991. Relationships between fathers and children who live apart: The father's role after separation. *J. Marriage Fam.* 53:79–101

Spanier GB, Furstenberg FF, Jr. 1987. Remarriage and reconstituted families. In *Handbook of Marriage and the Family,* ed. MB Sussman, SK Steinmetz, pp. 419–34. New York: Plenum

Sweet JA, Bumpass LL. 1987. *American Families and Households.* New York: Russell Sage

US Bureau of the Census. 1992a. *Current Population Reports. Series P23–181. Households, Families, and Children: A 30-year Perspective.* Washington, DC: US Govt Printing Off.

US Bureau of the Census. 1992b. *Current Population Reports. Series P20–468. Marital Status and Living Arrangements: March 1992.* Washington, DC: US Govt Printing Off.

US Bureau of the Census. 1992c. *Current Population Reports. Series P23–180. Marriage, Divorce, and Remarriage in the 1990s.* Washington, DC: US Govt Printing Off.

White LK. 1993. *Stepfamilies over the life course: Social support.* Presented at Natl.

Symposium on Stepfamilies. State College Penn.

White LK, Booth A. 1985. The quality and stability of remarriages: The role of stepchildren. *Am. Sociol. Rev.* 50:689–98

Woodhouse B. 1993. Hatching the egg: A child-centered perspective on parents' rights. *Cardozo Law Rev.* 14:1747–865

Wu LL, Martinson BC. 1993. Family structure and the risk of a premarital birth. *Am. Sociol. Rev.* 59:210–32

Zill N. 1988. Behavior, achievement, and health problems among children in stepfamilies: Findings from a national survey of child health. See Hetherington & Arasteh 1988, pp. 325–68

FAMILIES IN TIME TO COME: TAKING A POSITION ON TRENDS AND ISSUES— MARVIN B. SUSSMAN

Reference

Russell, P. 1983. *The Global Brain* (p. 179). Los Angeles, CA: J. P. Tarcher, Inc.